SUMMA THEOLOGIÆ

subsistant DEF 69

Timothy McDermott was born in St Helens, Lancashire, in 1926 and studied science at Liverpool and Cambridge universities. In 1947 he joined the Dominican Order and after studies in philosophy and theology at Oxford taught theology there and at Stellenbosch in South Africa. During this time he collaborated in the sixty-volume translation of the *Summa* published in the 1960s.

In 1970 Professor McDermott returned to the teaching of science and until he retired in 1986 taught and researched the theory of computer languages and artificial intelligence at the universities of London, Cape Town and Tasmania. During the writing of the present volume he was visiting Fellow at St Edmunds College, Cambridge and was until recently a visiting associate professor at the University of Illinois at Urbana-Champaign, USA. He is currently living in South Africa.

St Thomas Aquinas

Summa Theologiæ

A CONCISE TRANSLATION

EDITED BY
Timothy McDermott

Allen, Texas

NIHIL OBSTAT
Anton Cowan, Censor

IMPRIMATUR
Monsignor Ralph Brown, V.G.
Westminister

May 10, 1989

The Nihil Obstat and Imprimatur are official declarations that the material reviewed is free of doctrinal or moral error. No implication is contained therein that those granting the Nihil Obstat and Imprimatur agree with the contents, opinions, or statements expressed.

First published in USA in 1989
by Christian Classics
First published in paperback in 1991
by Christian Classics

Send all inquiries to:

CHRISTIAN CLASSICS
200 East Bethany Drive
Allen, Texas 75002-3804

Telephone: 877-275-4725 / 972-390-6300

Fax: 800-688-8356 / 972-390-6560

Printed in the United States of America

Library of Congress Catalog Card Number:
91 73302

ISBN 0-87061-211-5 (Hardbound)
ISBN 0-87061-210-7 (Softbound)

5 6 7 8 9   06 05 04 03 02

Contents

Editor's note

The Dominican friar St Thomas Aquinas – hereafter called Thomas – started writing this comprehensive theology for his students in 1265, and left it unfinished at his death nine years later. The present translation is an attempt to make this impressive work accessible to twentieth-century reading habits. For this reason it differs in three respects from previous translations: in concision, in trying to avoid technicality, and in format.

The concision has been achieved not by selecting out parts, but by compressing and distilling the whole. My aim was to try and say all that Thomas wanted to say, in his own words, but in a text condensed to about one sixth of its length. Of course, there are omissions: passages discussing the details of Old Testament ritual and law, expositions of ancient biology of the embryo or physiology of the emotions which are now mainly of historical interest; here the editing keeps only enough to give the feel of Thomas's treatment. At the opposite extreme, however, many passages – such as Thomas's proofs for the existence of God, his discussion of the nature of the human soul, his analysis of moral actions, his exposition of the Christian doctrines of the incarnation and redemption, his discussion of transubstantiation – are already so concise in the author's text that the only feasible compression is that achieved by adopting a modern format. But in between these two extremes, my attempt has been to express the whole sense of Thomas's arguments in as few words as possible: those words being Thomas's own, readably but faithfully translated into modern English.

Within certain limits it has seemed possible to be faithful without being over-technical, to avoid technicality of expression without sacrificing the exactness of expression which technical terms help to achieve. It would be unthinkable to translate an Aristotelian like Thomas without use of the technical terms *matter* and *form*; but I see no reason why a translator shouldn't avail himself of modern turns of phrase in which those technical words are still alive in much the Aristotelian sense. So, for example, the translation does not talk, technically, of educing a new form from matter, if it can talk, non-technically, of matter taking on a certain form; or of forms existing in matter, if it can talk of forms under which matter exists. Indeed, it is my opinion that, by translating in this way, one can recover original meanings of terms long encrusted with technical barnacles.

Finally, the format is modern: paragraphed, with paragraphs grouped in titled sections, and sections gathered into chapters. The original work has a format shaped by the conventions of medieval debate: the text divides into hundreds of topics called *questions*, each topic consisting of a sequence of dilemmas called *articles*, each dilemma posed by three short arguments called *objections* against some traditional position called the *sed contra*, and resolved by an argued point of view called the *response* applied to each objection in *answers to the objections*. This is a very powerful format but difficult for the modern reader, and for that reason, and to achieve compression, I have preferred a modern format of paragraphed, continuous text. This text follows exactly the order of the original text; the classical references to major parts of the *Summa* map to this text as follows: Ia pars, pp 1–163; IaIIae, pp 167–324; IIaIIae, pp 325–467; IIIa pars, pp 471–600. Marginal numerals reference the start of each included question and article, the question numerals (in bold type) starting from 1 again on pp 1, 167, 325, and 471. Omission of a marginal numeral indicates omission of a whole article or question; omission of part of an article is regarded as condensation and not specially indicated. Passages in square brackets are editorial insertions of words to which nothing directly corresponds in the original text. Italics are used in several related ways: for emphasis, to indicate a technical term or a word from another language, to distinguish mention of words from use of them, and to indicate quotation of another author. The source of these (possibly condensed) quotations can be found in the index of quotations at the back of the book.

This book is not intended as a commentary, only as a useful translation for first reading. There has been room only for a minimum of editorial comment, first a preface to the work as a whole, and then at the head of each chapter a short introduction highlighting the structure and main ideas of that chapter. I have tried to write these introductions in such a way that they can be read as one continuous summary of Thomas's philosophical and theological positions. Any reader who wants to pursue matters more deeply can go on to the sixty-volume translation made in the 1960s, with its Latin text, notes, appendices and glossaries. Where each of these volumes begins is indicated in the margin of the present text; thus the beginning of volume 50 is indicated by printing in the margin [vol 50].

I would like to thank all those too numerous to mention separately who helped by reading and commenting on sections of the translation while the work was in progress. I owe a special word of gratitude to St Edmunds College, Cambridge, for providing me with several months of hospitality and a visiting fellowship while working on the translation, and to the computer science department of the University of Illinois at Urbana-Champaign for allowing me to use their facilities to produce several updatings of the text. I thank the English Dominican friars, especially those in Cambridge, for their interest and the use of their library; and I owe special gratitude to the translators of the sixty-volume *Summa Theologiæ*. Lastly, I would like to thank my publishers for their help and encouragement, especially Chris Falkus whose enthusiasm saw the book started and Alex Bennion who guided it to completion.

My family exercised an amused patience with a work which took a long time to get finished, so I want to make special mention of them. At an early stage of the translation on my word-processor, my small daughter hid within the text her own name. If, in the process of revision and publication, that name has disappeared from view, let me record it here, dedicating this volume above all to Clare Teresa, her brother and sisters and her mother, in some recompense for all they give to me.

Timothy McDermott, March 7, 1988

Preface

WHAT THE *SUMMA* IS ABOUT

St Thomas and our time. Even the deepest, most universal human questions change their emphasis with time. Questions about God are an example. The Old and New Testaments ask who is God, which of the many gods is the one true God? Influenced by Greek tradition the western church gradually turned to asking what is God, what makes the true God god and not creature? We today are more prone to ask where is God, what (if anything) in our world betrays his presence? But this contemporary emphasis is only the newest facet of an old question, emphasized because previous answers neglected it. To appreciate the question as a whole we need to know not only its modern treatment, but also its history. In that history Thomas Aquinas is one of the giants. He was, of course, a man of his time – legend has it that even as a child he asked his teachers *What is God?* – but he was a great man of his time, responding to questions in ways which carried their development forward, rather than in words and ways of thought already conventional and acceptable. Most of us are already behind our times; but Thomas was a man open to the future, and we are his heirs.

What obscures this, at least for English-speaking people, is the six-teenth-century bifurcation in our culture. Thomas, appropriated by the Catholic and clerical branch of that culture, was for that very reason largely ignored by the Protestant and lay branch; these thinkers saw Thomas and his times as just what they were trying to escape. And many people still see the Middle Ages as a great backwater into which the river of history poured for centuries before finally, in the sixteenth century, making a new start: then only did Western history return to its true source in the pure reason of Greece and Rome and the pure word of the Old and New Testaments, so that religion, government and learning could burst free from the stagnancy of the medieval church. If we have difficulty relating to the products and institutions of medieval culture – admiring the cathedrals but finding them as distant as Stonehenge, taking universities for granted only because we never think of them as medieval inventions, dismissing friars and monks as part of that enclosed clerical culture we have passed by – then Thomas's *Summa Theologiæ*, a cathedral in words from a friar in a medieval university, could appear to us merely a cultural fossil.

The truth is that the seeds of the sixteenth-century Reformation and Renaissance were sown in a more far-reaching renaissance and reform that took place three to four hundred years earlier, when expanding agricultural wealth was spawning vast social and political changes. The population was increasing by leaps and bounds, towns were being founded and expanded, a new urban way of life and thought was developing, an acquisitive and entrepreneurial spirit was starting to treat wealth as capital rather than as a means of power and magnificence, a society of dynastic family and tribal institutions like the splendid abbeys and quasi-sacred regal courts was yielding place to the market-town bishops and their cathedrals, and to institutions such as the universities, governed by guild and corporation. In men's minds the picture of the world as a mirror and sacramental symbol of eternity was beginning to fade before the picture of a world moulded by men and developing towards a temporal future. If the dike broke finally in the 1500s and 1600s, the waters that burst out had been building up since the 1100s and 1200s. The thinkers of that period were admittedly unable to see with historical eyes what was happening, unable to articulate the social, economic and political forces acting on them, but they were moved nevertheless by those forces to see things in new ways, to phrase their questions in a new language and give them new answers, many of these questions and answers being the forebears of our own. Thomas, the greatest of these thinkers, was no exception here: his life reflected the changing current of the medieval times in which it was lived.

Thomas in his time.   Thomas's life started in a world on the wane: born in the castle of Roccasecca, the youngest son of a family of one-time counts of Aquino but now in decline, vassals to the king of Sicily and Holy Roman Emperor, that extraordinary Frederick II who was himself a sort of foretaste of the Renaissance princes to come. From the age of five Thomas was brought up in the Benedictine monastery of Monte Cassino to a life of manual labour, prayer and scriptural reading, and the idea seemed to be that he should stay there for the rest of his life and perhaps become abbot of the place. It was war between Frederick and the Pope that changed all this: the abbey was closed for a time, and the fourteen-year-old was sent to complete his studies at the secular university of Naples, which Frederick had founded for the education of his court functionaries. At that time Naples was the only university to be teaching not merely the Aristotelian logic known already in the previous century, but also the rest of Aristotle's philosophical work only now beginning to infiltrate Christendom's borders by way of Islamic scholars in Spain and at Frederick's Sicilian court. And here, in Naples, in this atmosphere of new thought and a new world dawning, the Benedictine oblate, Thomas, met the newly-founded mendicant and preaching order, the Dominican friars, who only twenty years earlier had been dispersed by their founder throughout the universities of Europe.

If Aristotle represented a new current in secular thinking, the friars were the most radical representatives of the new spirit of reform within the church. In the Benedictine tradition that spirit of reform was represented by the Cistercians, an order founded a century earlier to renew monastic isolation from the world by pursuing a rigorous discipline and eschewing ostentation. Their very success, however, made monastic institutions even more efficient, so that personal abnegation of pomp and circumstance led almost directly to even greater communal wealth and power. The Cistercians were men of the land rather than of the town, rich rather than poor, aristocrats rather than men of the people, representatives of the established order rather than rebels. When called in as missionaries at the beginning of Thomas's century, to counter the enthusiasms and hysteria of wandering lay preachers of conversion, the Cistercians were a dismal failure. Their place was taken by reformers outside the monastic tradition, the friars who based their life on the gospel description of Christ's apostles, *going out two by two to preach in town after town, taking nothing for their journey but a staff: no bread, no wallet, no money in their belts, wearing sandals and only one tunic,* boasting that their cloister was the world. The friars were not monks and prepared themselves for their task of preaching not in the isolation of monastic schools of prayer and spiritual reading, but in the universities of the day where the world's administrators and state functionaries were being educated.

At Naples, then, Thomas was faced with, and made, his choice of worlds. In 1244, at the age of twenty, after a year of struggle with his family and the powers that be, he turned his back on monastic life, and went as a Dominican friar to start his studies in the university of Paris under master Albert the Great, the famous German friar who was just beginning his encyclopedic commentaries on the work of Aristotle. Three years later, when Albert was sent to Cologne to found a study-house, Thomas went with him, and four years later, when the Dominicans needed a new master at Paris, at a time when religious masters

were exceedingly unpopular there and the spread of Aristotelian influence was causing alarm to the church, Albert recommended that Thomas
be groomed for the job. So in 1252 Thomas returned to Paris as bachelor,
and after lecturing for four years on the *Sentences* of Peter Lombard,
the accepted theology textbook of the day, he received his master's
degree and succeeded, at the extraordinarily early age of thirty-two, to
the theology chair Albert had occupied eight years earlier.

So began one of the most packed and prolific philosophical and
theological careers in history. Three years teaching at Paris were followed
by nine years in Italy: six at Orvieto where the papal court was then
situated, two at Rome founding a new study-house, and then a further
year at the papal court, now moved to Viterbo. In 1269 he was called
back to Paris for a further three turbulent years at the university, and
then, given the chance to choose for himself where to set up yet another
Italian study-house, he returned to Naples, the city in which he had
chosen his way of life twenty-eight years before. It was there, late in
1273, that he suddenly stopped all writing and teaching – a stroke? or
an ecstasy? or both? – and by March 1274 he was dead at the age of
forty-nine or fifty. The last seventeen years of his life had been a
Dominican conventual life, but one packed with the teaching of theology
students, public controversy against the anti-religious, the anti-Aris-
totelian and the Arabizing factions of the day, voracious reading of more
and more texts being translated from the Greek (fathers of the church
and Aristotle) and the practically continuous writing of his own vol-
uminous works.

Thomas's writings.   Some of these works are edited versions of
lectures on various topics. From his first Parisian period, for example,
we have the young bachelor's edited commentary on the *Sentences* (his
first comprehensive study of theology, running to over 1,500,000 words);
then the new master's courses on Matthew's gospels and Isaiah's prophecies, his maybe monthly public debates on theological questions of his
own choosing collected in the *Quaestiones Disputatae de Veritate*, and
his twice-yearly public debates on questions thrown at him by his
audience (*Quaestiones Quodlibetales* 7-11). From the period in Orvieto
we have lectures on the book of Job; from Rome public debates collected
in the *de Potentia*, the *de Malo* and the *de Spiritualibus Creaturis*; from
Viterbo lectures on the prophet Jeremiah. On his return to Paris Thomas
lectured on Paul's epistles and the gospel of John, and conducted debates
collected in further series of *Quaestiones Disputatae*. In Naples he appears
to have been lecturing on the Psalms at the time of his disablement.

Accompanying these lectures were works specially written for various purposes. Some of these were polemical contributions to contemporary controversies: a defence of the religious life during his first teaching sojourn at Paris and two more during his second, a criticism of some Greek theologians while at Orvieto, contributions to Parisian pamphleteering among Aristotelian factions about the alleged eternity of the world and the alleged sharing of one mind by all men. Others were commentaries on well-known traditional texts. Already at Paris he commented on theological works by the early Christian philosopher Boethius; at Rome he produced a commentary on the *Divine Names* – a work by some early Syrian monk which enjoyed great authority in the Middle Ages because it attributed itself (falsely) to Denys the Areopagite, a convert of St Paul's. At the same time he was producing, at the Pope's request, a gloss on all four gospels, the so-called *Catena Aurea* or Golden Chain. Down the centuries this has proved to be one of his most popular works, a continuous commentary on the gospel text built out of quotations from twenty-two Latin fathers and fifty-three Greek fathers, some of whom had to be newly translated for the purpose. This work did more than anything else perhaps to open up Latin theology to the Greek tradition, and certainly Thomas's own thinking showed its influence. While he was producing this work Thomas came to know William of Moerbeke, a Dominican translator from the Greek, living at Rome and Viterbo. At that time William was producing new translations of Aristotle's works, and it is surely no coincidence that after completing the *Catena Aurea* and returning to the Aristotelian atmosphere of Paris, Thomas embarked on the most prolific five years of Aristotelian commentary in western history. During his second Parisian stay he produced an astonishing series of line-by-line commentaries on the works of Aristotle: on the *de Anima*, the *de Sensu et Sensato*, the *de Memoria et Reminiscentia*, on the Physics and on the Metaphysics, on the Ethics and the Politics, on the *Perihermeneias* and the Posterior Analytics, and on a spurious work which he recognized as stemming rather from the neo-Platonist Proclus: the *de Causis*. The avalanche continued at Naples with commentaries on the *de Caelo et Mundo*, the *Meteorologica*, the *de Generatione et Corruptione*.

Such an output in barely twenty years is enough to take one's breath away. Yet it still leaves out three of the four comprehensive works on theology which Thomas produced during his lifetime, and of which the *Summa Theologiæ* here translated is one. The first of these comprehensive theologies we have already mentioned, the edited commentary on Peter Lombard's *Sentences* produced when a bachelor at

Paris. Another work, the *Compendium Theologiæ*, is incomplete and has never been satisfactorily dated. Yet a third comprehensive study of theology was begun in his third year as master at Paris: the so-called *Summa contra Gentiles*, an apology for the Christian faith apparently intended for use by Dominican missionaries among the Moslem and Jewish scholars of Spain. This work is of extraordinary philosophical depth and lucidity, and shows the influence of the Islamic tradition of Aristotelian commentary, and especially of the great Moslem philosopher of the tenth century, Avicenna (Ibn Sina). It also sees the development of a mature writing style which was to stand Thomas in good stead for the rest of his life. It was completed at Orvieto in 1264, a highly condensed work of some 350,000 words. In the following year, Thomas moved to Rome and had again to lecture to theological students. At this time, apparently after an aborted attempt to adapt his earlier work on the *Sentences*, he decided to write yet another comprehensive theology from scratch, one which could serve as a new textbook of theology for his students. This is the work concisely translated in this volume, the *Summa Theologiæ*. Thomas was to work on it for the next seven years and leave it unfinished; even so, it comprises, as did his commentary on the *Sentences*, over 1,500,000 words.

Gradually, but only gradually, the *Summa* became the accepted textbook of theology in the Catholic church; it is said to have lain on the altar alongside the scriptures during the Council of Trent, a symbol of orthodoxy to Catholics, of the adulteration of the pure word of God to Protestants. In the years following the Counter-Reformation the spirit of innovation was not greatly in favour in the church, and under the weight of more and more scholarly commentaries the theology of Thomas became more and more a fossilized letter. At the end of the last century an attempt was made to revitalize Thomistic studies, and Pope Leo initiated the great work of producing a critical text of all Thomas's works, beginning with the *Summa*. A hundred years later the job is still unfinished, and the text of the first part of the *Summa* will at some time have to be done again. Since the second Vatican council Thomist dominance in Catholic theology has been in decline, just at the time when secular philosophers are discovering that mental activity did not cease between the death of Aristotle and the birth of Descartes. Perhaps for this very reason there is now new hope for the much healthier study of Thomas for his own sake that certain scholars have pioneered over the last half-century. It is this hope that has led to the present translation, addressed to any reader – professional or amateur, philosophically or theologically inclined – who would like to be able to lift the *Summa* from his shelf as a unity, and leaf through it back and forth following the threads of what must be the most unified comprehensive theology in Christian history.

Nature and mechanism.   Translation cannot, of course, remove all our modern problems with Thomas's way of thinking. Many arise from clashes between his assumptions and our own, the greatest, perhaps, being the clash of our unconscious mechanist assumptions, fostered by centuries of scientific endeavour and technological success, with Aristotle's and Thomas's concept of nature and the natural order. Mechanism colours all our thought about the material world: the explanations we seek are practically always explanations of *how things work*, our assumption being that natural things are machines of some sort, identifiable by their external roles and functions, and implemented by organized coincidences of inner component parts, each of which, in turn, is a mechanism with a function in the larger machine. Always there are wheels within wheels, we think, and what really exists are the simplest and most fundamental of these wheels, whatever our contemporary science deems the most fundamental particles of reality at the moment.

Such presuppositions are bound to clash with the quite different presuppositions that underlie, for example, the five ways of proving there is a God that Thomas sets out in chapter 1 below.* There Thomas maintains that God's existence is not self-evident, and must be made evident from the world we see. This, he thinks, is what men are doing when they worship and convince themselves vaguely and generally that there exists a providence. Such arguments of the common man, Thomas as philosopher must make more articulate and precise. But the world Thomas's common man sees is not the world perceived by the reductive abstractions of science. Thus Thomas does not share our modern relay-race conception of the world process: our concept of causality as a handing-on or propagation of something, say energy, from present states of affairs to future states of affairs; and he is not arguing that such a process must have had a temporal start. Indeed he will maintain (ch 4 p 82) that such relaying can occur without beginning and without ending because its connecting links are coincidences, and the relayers simply temporal tools of whomever (or whatever) has the *idea* of the relay-race

* Readers of the editor's note will already know that the division of the present work into chapters is not Thomas's own, and that Thomas's own divisions are to be found in the marginal references to the text. Nevertheless, it seems easier and more direct in this preface and in the commentary passages at the head of each chapter to talk as though the chapter divisions were original.

in *the first place*. Here we have two departures from the way science looks at things. Firstly, there is the search for a *first place* which is not a temporally first move in the process but rather some sort of extra-temporal base and foundation for every move in the process. And secondly, this first foundation is conceived of as underlying the process in the way an *idea* or purpose underlies the processes that implement such purposes in the world of man. The irony of the clash is that each party thinks of the other party's assumptions as something that it has outgrown. The theoreticians of modern science think of themselves as having rescued human thought from an Aristotelian and medieval anthropomorphism, and having won through to a proper objectivity; Aristotle, followed by Aquinas, thought he had overcome the abstract reductive view of existence found in earlier mathematicizing thinkers, and had won through to appreciation of the concrete variety of what actually exists. For modern science is in essentials a return to a way of thinking found among the earliest Greek philosophers, and a way of thinking which Aristotle and Thomas thought they had outgrown.

> Early philosophers felt their way to the truth slowly step by step. They began somewhat crudely by thinking that only bodies we can sense exist, that the essential substance of such bodies [*what* they really are] is uncaused, and that they change only [*how* they are] in inessentials, being now rarefied, now condensed, separating and combining under the influence of attraction and repulsion, mind and so on. Later thinkers worked out the distinction within essential substance between its matter (uncaused, as they thought) and the forms of substance such matter takes on, and realized that bodies change even the substantial form [of *what* they really are] under the influence of more cosmic causes such as Aristotle's *inclined circle* or Plato's Ideas. So far all thinkers were seeking only particular causes for *what* or *how* particular beings were. But some thinkers eventually considered being as such, and asked why things exist at all. And this meant seeking a universal cause of everything including the basic matter (or potentiality of form) present in all substances. [ch 4 p 84]

Our twentieth-century conceptions would strike Aristotle and Thomas simply as developed versions of a view they think philo-sophically crude: a view which grants objective status to only the lowest level of description of the world (that of physics and chemistry), regarding natural things as more and more complex organizations of coincidences of such simple objects. For Thomas there is not just one level at which things really exist but many: there are organizations of matter which are not mere products of general laws of attraction and repulsion arranging matter, laws isolated in our laboratory experiments, where measuring instruments abstract from all interference, noise, impurities, foreign bodies, extraneous factors. In the real world what to the physicist is the chance interference of a moment, uncaused and unruly (see ch 2 p 56 and ch 6 p 152), can produce novel historically stable entities. Some of these entities – copper sulphate, for example – may behave stably in ways that the laws of physical and chemical combination of their atomic parts can predict. Still, their actual coming to be could not be predicted; only its possibility. Other entities have novel rules of stable behaviour not predictable from a merely general physics or chemistry, and not understandable except within the context of concrete chance world-history. Living organisms are of this sort, dependent on such a web of chance for their coming-to-be that even their possibility – had they not existed – would have evaded prediction. Thomas's criterion of *objective reality* is any and every stability of identity which is in natural favour with its environment and the world at large. Organisms undoubtedly have the inner organization (or composition out of organs) that characterize machines; but they themselves are not organs, as machines are. For their identity is not a matter of having a function or a role in a larger whole, but of being a viable whole themselves, naturally favoured for survival or stable existence. The favoured stability achieved by an organism or like object is what Thomas calls its *form*: a word which inherits from both the Platonic word *idea* and the Aristotelian *morphe*, literally, shape. But these forms are not to be imagined simply as the observed *shapes* of some passively arranged matter, shapes imposed on the matter from some outside source. They are rather stable terminations or completions of processes of genesis, destinations of changes or movements, realizations tended towards or favoured in the historical and concrete world in which alone such tendencies and favours exist. Forms are nature's intentions worked out in history, the natural identities selected for by the environment in the round of life.

Form and matter, agency and purpose.   An important passage for the understanding of *form* in both Thomas and Aristotle occurs in ch 4 p 87 below. Thomas there defends himself against a too Platonic understanding of Aristotelian form. The stable forms matter takes on, he says, are not to be conceived of as themselves existing in the same sense as the formed matter exists; they are not entities lying latent in some way in the matter before the change, or suddenly appearing from the hand of God; they are precisely the forms of what exists, emerging from the jostle of change that permeates what exists under the influence of whatever agent environment favours those forms of matter. For the environment itself consists of stable identities which are already in favour with the environment, and which therefore in their turn act as *causes* of the emergence of new forms of matter, projecting their own favouredness and stability onto their environments by way of characteristic activities producing characteristic *effects*. That matter takes on a certain form is the doing of an agent giving expression in that way to what it favours or tends towards as a goal: this is how Thomas understands the famous Aristotelian doctrine of the *four causes* so-called: form and matter, agent and goal. And this is the concept of agency which underlies Thomas's formulation of his five proofs for God's existence. Every process, every achievement, has two faces, he thinks; as Aristotle says, though the teacher is not the learner, the *teacher teaching* is the same happening as the *learner learning*, and takes place in the learner. Every realization is as much the doing of a doer as it is the being of whatever is being realized, all matter taking on a form is some agent favouring a goal. Aristotle and Thomas conceive causality not as a relay or linkage between two states of affairs – a parent state and a descendent state – one preceding the other in time; but rather as a second complementary analysis of any single state of affairs. Any state of affairs, over and above its analysis as a change in being or as realization of a new form in matter, can be analysed as the doing of an agent pursuing its goal in that matter.

It must be stressed that Thomas's concept of an agent pursuing a goal is not to be confused with the idea of something serving a purpose or fulfilling a function. This latter notion is more applicable to organs than to organisms. When nature favours the existence of an organism it is not because of some purpose that the organism serves, for organisms have no function. Organs do, but not organisms. In his popular classic on evolution, *Chance and Necessity* [1971], Jacques Monod regards both artificial and living objects as purposive or functional – *teleonomic* is his word. But only artificial objects are purposed, made from outside by a mind. Living objects are purposive, but not purposed. So, just as cameras are functional, eyes are functional, but the camera's design comes from a mind outside it, whereas that of the eye comes from within it (or at least from within the animal to which the eye belongs, which has built itself up by what Monod calls *autonomous morphogenesis* which I translate as *self-construction*). What Monod fails to notice is the difference between organs and organisms. After comparing the functionality of cameras and eyes (both organs) he goes on to compare the functionality of cars and horses (where cars are organs but horses not). As the purpose of eyes is making optical images, so the purpose of horses, he says, is speedy movement! But he does not notice that the first function really defines what an eye is for, whereas the second doesn't at all define *what a horse is for*, whatever that might mean. It emerges in another place that Monod himself doesn't actually think horses are *for* speed. He thinks all organisms have the overriding purpose of reproducing themselves. This in itself is a strange function to have: organisms reproduce themselves in order that they should reproduce themselves in order, etc.... We receive the overwhelming sensation that if there is any real function defining an organism then it remains just over an ever-receding horizon. (This is a phenomenon that always seems to occur when you try to capture the identity of an organic whole in terms of function: compare the attempt of Douglas Hofstadter in another classic, *Godel, Escher, Bach*, to talk of the mind's I as an ever-recursive self-reflection of a program in the brain.) The articulation of the function – the work that the organism is *for* – always just eludes you, because an organism is functionless: no function defines it, its identity is an idle and not a working one. The functional organism is chased perpetually through the reproductive history of the species and never reached; in the meantime the actual organisms are enjoying life.

For organisms are not organs. And that is already sufficient to show that they are not machines. You may ask what an eye is for, but may you ask what a cow is for? Or how a cow works? Or speculate on whether one can implement the function of a cow otherwise? Of course, you may treat organisms as if they were machines, and then one might ask in what way you are treating the cow and say that for you it exists only for the purpose of providing morning milk. You may indeed breed the cow for that purpose. And in the course of time you might even devise an alternative implementation of your milk-machine. So you can give organisms external roles in some mechanically organized system, but of themselves (of the identity that belongs to them as existing independently and naturally) they are not organs of a system, parts of a machine, but members of something quite different which we call an ecosystem.

In an ecosystem organisms do play roles, indeed many different roles, no one of which is sufficient to define or identify them. For they are not simply implementations of a function that the ecosystem demands of them. Rather they are historical facts that have just proved to be viable in that ecosystem, or rather in the ecosystem as itself changed by their viability. The root *eco-* comes from the Greek word for a house, and an ecosystem is something habitable like a house. Viable and habitable are complementary terms: to be viable is to be able to live in what is habitable, to be habitable is to be able to be lived in by what is viable. So the sort of reality and identity to be accorded to organisms is neither the soft sort of reality that organs and artificial things like machines have – the identity of serving a certain purpose, nor the sort of reality that ultimate atomic components of things might be deemed to have – the identity of being the only simple, unanalysable and therefore objectively hard things about; but it is the identity of being really viable wholes in a habitable environment, really having and enjoying life at home in a surrounding space suited to them. This enjoying of life is, in a sense, idle enjoyment, the side of natural existence that cannot be simulated by a machine but is nevertheless favoured by the world we live in. A machine that simulates the eye, for example, does not see, it doesn't experience colour. It functions in response to colour, and allows colours to function through it, but it doesn't see colours. You may say that this is a distinction without a difference, that if, in your simulation, you can get machines to work exactly like organisms that can see (though without the actual seeing component), then really you have simulated all the necessary working of sight, and what is left out is only an idle component. Exactly so. When you are trying to grasp how sight works, the actual seeing is an entirely idle component! But no amount of understanding how seeing *works*, is going to reveal to you (or the machine) the idle experience that accompanies it. Nevertheless I value the idle experience as I value my life, and I value the idle aspect of colour revealed to me as contributing enjoyment to my life. But the contribution resists analysis in terms of purpose and function and composition of functions.

So there is a difference between the goal that natural agency pursues, the realization of form in matter that it favours, and the notion of purpose or function as mechanically understood. Because he wished to stress this difference, Aristotle distanced himself from the mathematicians and mechanists that had preceded him, and developed a philosophy of natural form. And on the basis of this philosophy, Thomas was able to articulate the ordinary man's conviction that there exists a God: an entity that has no functional place in workings of the mechanically conceived world, yet is the source and agency of all the idle enjoyment of life and existence in that world.

Agency and existence. Here we must draw attention to a subtle difference in the emphasis of Aristotle and of Thomas, for in this subtle change of emphasis lies Thomas's ability to harmonize the Christian concept of creation and the Greek concept of the natural world. As we have already seen, for Aristotle as well as for Thomas, all realization of form needs its agent, all achievement of natural being is, complementarily, something's doing. But whereas Aristotle emphasizes reality as the end-point of some process of change in which something that was only possible has now become actual (a process of change which is some agent's doing), Thomas thinks even of the state of actual being resulting from such a process as itself a *realization* that must be accompanied by some agency. Aristotle emphasizes that natural things differ from artificial things in having an internal form (self-constructed, as Monod would say), whereas artificial things depend on a form external to them but internal to the artificer that produces them (his artifice, as Aristotle calls it). But Thomas's preferred way of talking is to say that both kinds of things receive their forms from external agents, but a natural thing receives the form by which it itself exists, whereas an artificial thing receives a form under which something else (the material out of which it is made) exists. When Aristotle calls the state of realization *energeia* or actuality, the word stresses that a state that was previously only possible is now actually present; when Thomas calls it *actus*, the word further stresses that the presence of the state is not only the being of some thing but also the action of some other thing, the doing of an agent. All being is doing, and if the doing itself is also an environmentally-favoured realization or achievement of an otherwise merely possible agency, then as realization it too needs a doer: the first agent's doing must itself be the doing of a second agent. And so on. But not *ad infinitum*, because then there would have been no doing and no realization of being in the first place. Rather *and so on* until we come to a doing that does not have to achieve favour from an environment but already and eternally is doing. Every other being, every other doing must be this being's doing, and this is the being that *all men call God*, and that Thomas, as philosopher, attempts to articulate and make precise in his five ways (ch 1 pp 12–14).

The first four of these ways (all with historical antecedents in Plato and Aristotle and the Arab philosopher Ibn Sina) complement exactly the four ways in which, in the disputation *de Potentia* (qu 3 art 7), Thomas sees God at work in every other thing's doing (cf also below ch 6 p 156). For God, he says, not only creates the intrinsic form that enables things to act and then conserves that form in being, but he provides the movement which stirs it into some particular action and then *co*-operates with that action, using it as if it were his tool for achieving its effect. The first four ways attend in turn to these four modes of active presence of God in all doing and change: the first points to the God who stirs up all processes of change, the second to the God who cooperates in all actions, the third to God as the ever-present conserver of form, and the fourth to God as form's origin. And in the fifth way Thomas explicitly argues that all realization of natural form is the act of some agent favouring a goal, and that even where the immediate agent may not be conscious of the goal that it is favouring, a remoter agent (whose doing the immediate agent's doing is) must have deliberately set up the immediate agent's favouring of that goal. No ball scores goals, we might say, without a footballer, thus modernizing the archer-arrow example which is Thomas's stock-in-trade. Note again that Thomas's interest is not, as a modern scientist's would be, in such preceding movements in the footballer, be they in his leg or his brain, as would relay movement to the ball. Whatever the mechanics of such preceding connected movements might be, what interests Thomas is the resultant process in the ball, seen at one and the same time as movement in the ball, as scoring of a goal, as the doing of a footballer. Without doing, no being: this is the premise he applies to the whole world seen as a stable achievement. The being of the world is the doing of some agent (let us call it God), and without that doing (present in and as the world's being, not distantly preceding it) no world would exist.

In a sense, Thomas here only develops the Aristotelian intuition that the teacher teaching is the learner learning, the real identity of the agent's doing and the effect's being. Yet the God that his proofs point to is far different from the God that Aristotle's philosophy envisages. Aristotle's divinity is eternal thought being thought, the love of which, so to speak, makes the world go round. As we shall see, for Thomas that eternal thought is not merely the object of all worldly agents' love, but the source of it. Thomas's God is an agent engaged not merely in eternal thought, but in an eternal doing of the daily being of an external world. As a result Thomas's world and Aristotle's world differ. Aristotle's world circles perpetually through time everlastingly displaying the pattern of nature. But Thomas's world expresses someone's will, and so, at the philosophical level, a question can be raised: has God willed to make an everlasting world of the sort Aristotle envisaged, or has he willed a world that having burst into existence at some particular time, is now engaged in a continuously developing drama with historical vicissitudes, successes and failures, journeying to some unimaginable future dénouement? Thomas takes his answer from scripture. Beyond all philosophy he professes his faith in a God who is the author of a drama. Even this image fails to grasp all that Thomas's God is, though the way it fails is instructive. In some ways the relation of God to the world is like that of Tolstoy to the world of *War and Peace*. But the enormous difference is that Tolstoy's characters cannot communicate with their author. They can talk among themselves of all that real men can talk about, they can even discuss (interminably) the possibility of a God, as we can. But what they can't envisage is the existence of their actual author, Tolstoy. They are so totally his creatures, as we say, that though they exist for him, he doesn't exist for them. Indeed, they do not exist for themselves. They have not got the same kind of existence as Tolstoy and his readers, or any existence which can communicate with the existence of Tolstoy and his readers. But what God's creatures are given is precisely real existence, and though it may not be the same sort of existence as God's it is certainly not merely existence in God. They communicate in existence with their author, they do not live in isolation from him, they can envisage his existence. His existence is related to theirs as the doing of their being is related to their being, yet both he and they exist. It is the meditation of this truth that gives Thomas's philosophy its unique and distinct taste; Thomas is, *par excellence*, the philosopher of creation.

This then is the starting-point for all Thomas's philosophical reflection on God: that the being of the world is the doing of God. On this premise he builds his answers to the questions of his time: *What is God, and man, and the world?* From this premise too we can guess how he might have answered our modern question: *Where is God?* And with it Thomas also illuminates the scriptural answer to the question *Who is God?*

What is God?   The proof that there is a God is only the beginning of what we might call the demonstration of God. We would like to go on to say what kind of god God is. At first sight Thomas's answer to this is pessimistic. Any effect of a cause demonstrates that its cause exists, he says. God's effects then are enough to prove that he exists, but they are not enough to help us comprehend what he is. As Thomas will show, in chapter 1, affirmations saying what God is can't in themselves distinguish him from other things: we can only say, rather emptily, that when God is such-and-such he is more such-and-such than anything else. Thomas believes that we can distinguish God from other things with the help of eliminations (Thomas's version of what the tradition called *negative theology*), but these tell us what God is not rather than declaring what he is. Negations are, so to speak, the shadows cast in our language by the affirmations we would like to make: God's simpleness, for example, his lack of parts, is a shadow thrown onto our expectation of what perfection is – richness of complexity – by God's all-embracing concentration of perfection in one entity, a perfection that sums every variety of created perfection that imitates it. In similar ways, Thomas will show that God is-and-isn't in space: not existing in space as himself located, but present as the active doing of all spatial location and locatedness; and even more mysteriously, that God is-and-isn't in time: not himself measured by time but present in all temporal measuring and measuredness. The principle appealed to throughout is the same principle that led to God's existence in the first place: God exists as the doing of all being, the existence that acts in all existence, an existence in the world's existing but not of it, no thing, but not therefore nothing.

As an example of the sort of thing Thomas thinks we can say about God let us take a closer look at his discussion of God's simpleness, the shadow cast in our language by God's perfection. The discussion falls into two main parts. In the first (ch 1 pp 14–15) Thomas eliminates from God the kinds of complexity or compositeness that accompany matter: divisibility into extended parts, and the distinction within material entities between the entity that takes on a certain form and the form as such. (Thomas is a trusting author assuming an honesty and fairness in his readers which he has sometimes been denied. When we read him saying that material entities differ from their forms we mustn't jump to the conclusion that he thinks forms and entities exist in the same sense. In fact we have already seen that the entity and its form share one existence but in different senses: the entity is what really exists, the form is that in the entity which attracts the world's favour and so gives it its claim to existence.) Now the form of a material organism, its claim to stability, is something that comes and goes with the favour of an agent environment shaping the matter. But might there not exist entities with a claim to stability which is quite impervious to such change? We could call such entities, on analogy with the stabilities of material natural objects, forms, but they would not be forms of matter. Thomas takes it that the proofs of God's existence prove the existence of one such form; whether others exist is a question he holds over until the nature of mind is discussed.

In the first part of his discussion on God's simpleness, then, Thomas shows that God is not a form of matter. In the second part (ch 1 pp 15–

16) he focuses on such compositeness as might still be found even in a form that was not a form of matter: mightn't such a form have properties over and above those that actually defined it? mightn't it share parts of its definition (defining it generically) with other entities while other parts were specific to itself? mightn't the form be such that it could lay claim only to a *share* in existence, so that having this form would be what existing means for this entity but not what existence means in general, for any and every entity? Thomas's discussion tries to show that even this compositeness must be absent from God if he is to be the doing of all being. God exists (as is proved by the existence of his effects) but he does not *share* existence in the way everything else does, he is not a member of the genus *thing* – he is no thing, though not nothing. He is his own existence: not even the existence that other things share, but the doing of that existence.

Because he is the doing of all existence, God must comprehend in himself, Thomas argues, all the various perfections of existent things. Thomas is here appealing to the notion that caused perfection must pre-exist in some way in its cause, a sort of expansion of the argument he has already made that God's existence is shown by the fact that his effects exist. The notion is not derived from thinking of causality as a sort of animal reproduction. Reproduction is relay causality again, and interprets the *pre-* of *pre-exists* in a merely temporal sense. Something more *a priori* is being said. Thomas's frequently quoted adage that *What an agent does reflects what it is* glosses the idea that what an effect is is (at least partly) determined by its agent. A tree, being a naturally stable entity, will have an effect upon its environment and upon what that environment favours. In what ways? In ways appropriate to it as a tree! In the case of trees what the effect is is (at least partly) determined by the *nature* of the agent, what the agent is. But this built-in favour of natural agents for certain effects must eventually rely, so Thomas argues in the fifth of the five ways, on an agent with mind and will, who shapes effects in accordance with his own nature in the sense that he shapes them according to his plans and choices. As Thomas argues later (ch 2 p 44), the perfections of all creatures reflect ways in which God sees and loves the perfection present in himself. And by *perfections* Thomas means the existent and attractive goodnesses of things, the achievements of things which objectively attract desire (or as I have preferred to say, favour), the values that belong to them in themselves. Thomas indeed identifies being good with existing, though when an existing being is called good we say something about it that has not been said by simply calling it existing. To say that something exists is to say what the mind sees in it, its actuality, its first distinctness from what is merely potential, its having that primary stability and identity that comes from having a form, abstracting for the moment from those abilities and dispositions which result from the form and make a thing a good instance of its sort. And upon this abstract view of existence it is possible to build an abstract account of the world in which existence becomes merely the arbitrary actuality of what might have been merely possible, an account in which being is merely being the value of a variable. But in the concrete existence is also being good, the concrete completeness of things which attracts the world's favour and our love. And since love makes an agent out of the thing that loves, that which attracts love attracts more and more existent perfection through that agent. Thomas gives these ideas their first airing in his discussion of perfection and goodness in God, but he will return to them and develop them as mind and love in God and in angels and in men become the successive objects of his study. Mind takes in the forms of things, but love is drawn out to the goals in things and leads to action. God is not simply perfect good himself but the good doer of all other goodness, and in this lies both his uniqueness – his distinctness from all other things – and his community with them.

Knowing and talking about God.   The community of God with the world allows us to know God and talk truth about him; the uniqueness and distinctness of God make such knowledge and talk difficult and problematic. As to knowledge of God, Thomas makes two points worth underlining. He maintains that, in principle, any mind can have God revealed to it, not only mediately through God's effects but directly and immediately. He thinks it would be incoherent to say something had a mind but could not know God. This is because, following Aristotle, he defines mind as a susceptibility to the existence of things just as sight is a susceptibility to the colour of things. And God exists; there is a community of existence between him who is, so to speak, doing exist-ence and all other things whose existence is done-existence. He who is doing existence must exist and exist surpassingly. As we have said, God is the author of existence in a much deeper sense than Tolstoy is the author of *War and Peace*: the characters in Tolstoy's work are not given an existence which brings them into relation with their author, they are not given true existence in their own world. But God's creatures really relate to their author because he makes them really exist. Knowing God in himself is possible to created minds. Nevertheless, and this is the second point to underline, knowing God in himself is not *naturally* possible to created minds. Minds know certain things more naturally than others, knowing those other things by analogy with what are their natural objects of knowledge, with what are their paradigmatic objects. But no such analogy can suffice to give knowledge of God in himself (the doing of all existence) to a mind that takes done-existence as its natural and paradigmatic object, to any mind other than God's own. So God must be known in some other way, not natural; and Thomas envisages a situation in which minds would actually know God not by God acquiring existence-as-known (some conceptual mode of existence) in their knowing, but by the mind acquiring existence-as-knowing (the so-called *light of glory*) in God's own knownness to himself. This is Thomas's way of conceiving the heavenly contemplation of God to which faith in God's grace and revelation will bring us, he believes, in a life to come. But in our life here below, he stresses, faith gives us no vision of God in himself; we see him only through his effects in the way natural to all men, though what those effects are and what they have to say to us about God is made clearer to us by a faithful listening to the word of scripture.

As to the possibility of talking truly about God, Thomas is modest but optimistic: words can say how God is even if they can't show him as he is. For we can find out how to use them to assert truth so that they confine us only as to mode of expression and not as to content. Thomas, as chapter 2 (and indeed the whole of the *Summa*) will show, has no objection to being confined as to mode of expression: to anthropomorphisms, for example. Indeed he would think discontent with that stupid and self-destructive. But he thinks we can use language's capacity to affirm and deny identities to over-rule the very distinctions that formulation in language seems to be presupposing: presupposing, that is to say, not for truth but for representation. He agrees with Aristotle that words signify things by way of our conceptions of them, so that if our conceptions are inadequate the inadequacy is reflected in the words. Now on the whole our conceptions are tailored to the natural material world: language attributes predicates to subjects, for example, because in the paradigm case on which we model every truth we wish to enunciate, natural entities are the subject of natural properties. When we meet something not so structured our language will nevertheless suggest (by its structure) that the thing in question possesses the corresponding paradigmal structure in reality. But nothing can stop us using the wrongly structured language to formulate a direct denial of the structure it itself suggests. In this sense we can learn to use words of God without seeing what they mean. This is a distinction which makes little or no sense for words like *man* or *stone*, where our rules of usage are continuous with our living usage of the things themselves. But we have no such familiarity where God is in question. We know only rules laid down by our need to talk of an author of this world, and those rules turn out always to be at odds with the usual rules of grammar designed for talking about the world itself. So our language can *say* something which it cannot *show*! Thomas's usual example is that of abstract and concrete nouns: is God (if good at all) to be called a good thing or goodness itself? Both and neither is his answer. When we want to deny that God is a mere abstraction then we shall call him a good thing, even though that suggests that he is composite of substance and properties like the things of this world. When we want to deny *that*, then we shall rather call him goodness itself, even though that now suggests that he is abstract. Other examples mentioned by Thomas are our language's requirement of tensed verbs, suggesting that all action and all existence must occur in time; and the way in which language assumes that the relationships of an agent to what it acts upon must always be accompanied by movement (ch 3 pp 77–8 and ch 4 pp 85–6).

But how do we know what we can truly say of God? The principle that guides Thomas is always the same: causality. God is the doer of all perfection, the originating source of all form, so that though those forms cannot apply to him in the way that they do to creatures, nevertheless he who does wisdom must in some sense be wise, and he who does goodness must in some sense be good, and he who does existence must in some sense exist. Not in the same sense but in some analogical sense. The use of the word *analogy* here is itself exploiting a sort of analogy: an analogy of God-talk with our everyday use of words with related meanings, and especially when the relatedness is one of cause to effect. Medicines are called healthy, for example, because they make organisms healthy in a primary sense of the word. Complexions are called healthy because they are symptoms and effects of healthy organisms. Not that saying God is *good* simply says that he is the cause of goodness. Some words said of God do simply express such a relationship of causality, but in the case of the word *good*, although we know and say that God is good because he is the cause of goodness, we nevertheless wish to express what he must be in order to be that cause. This is a difference which Thomas compares (again in a sort of analogy) to the difference between the etymology of a word and its use. (Here I have deliberately talked twice of a *sort* of analogy, because I was referring to a parallel or comparison. Aristotle called such parallels analogies, but did not use the word when discussing cases of related meanings. Thomas in his early works followed a medieval tradition which used the word *analogy* of both parallels and related meanings, but in later works he reserved it for the latter – exactly the opposite of Aristotle's use. His commentators developed a doctrine of analogy which returned to the earlier medieval tradition.) The ability to talk truly about God depends essentially for Thomas on the world being related to God as its agent, its being being his doing: the analogies we use in talking of God are affirmations forced through the teeth of their own modes of representation, guided by the notion of an ultimate cause that is the doing-being of all that we experience as done-being.

God in the image of man: knowing.   However different from Aristotle's the view of God so far developed, it still seems very far from ordinary Christian ideas. But what we have discussed so far is what Thomas has to say in his first chapter below, the one entitled *What God is not*. That chapter is followed by two more, the first developing the notion of God's personal and historical providence as the Old and New Testament conceived of it, and the second developing the peculiarly Christian view that the word of God and the spirit of God are also persons, and that there are three persons in the one God. Thomas's optimism that language can express truths about God is shown to the full in these chapters. In the first he develops a picture of God in terms of the things of which we know men capable, an anthropomorphic picture, if you like. God stands behind the world as an artificer stands behind his handiwork: his knowledge has pre-planned it, his love pre-chosen it, and his power to implement his plans has brought it into being. But these anthropomorphisms are probed and criticized at every turn. What can knowledge be like in God? What sort of will has he? What is God's power?

Chapter 2 is not only the first place in which Thomas treats of God's knowing; it is the first place in which he treats of mind and knowing at all. His intention is to treat there whatever belongs to the perfection of mind and knowing as such, and so of whatever can be attributed, analogically, to the agent of all knowing. At later stages of the *Summa* he will develop what he has said in such a way that he can characterize created minds (ch 4 pp 94ff) and the embodied minds of men (ch 5 pp 108ff). What we shall say here, though directed more immediately to what Thomas says about God, must serve also as preface to the later question of *What is man?*

For Thomas

knowing is not an activity terminating in an external effect; it interiorly perfects the knower in the same way that existing perfects what exists: but whereas existing is actually having one's own form, knowing is actually having the form of what one knows [ch 2 p 39]

Knowing, we might say, is a kind of existing with. In man the forms of what we know, as distinct from our own form, must be acquired (or, as Thomas puts it, received). But not as matter acquires form. Matter acquires form by changing its previous form in order to become something new; it takes on form in the way a potentiality to be formed in a certain way takes on realization. The way forms are acquired by one who knows them is quite different: the knower does not change what he is in order to take on the new form, for it is precisely characteristic of him as able to know that he can take in the new form without taking it on, exist with it rather than under it, acquire it as one realization acquiring another. (Let me note here that in contexts such as these I have made use of a translator's privilege and deliberately translated Thomas's one word *receive* sometimes as *take on* and sometimes as *take in*. It seemed to me the very best way of reminding the reader of the distinction I have just been making, a distinction which is the very foundation of Thomas's philosophy of mind.) In Thomas's view, and in this he follows Aristotle, even the senses as such acquire the forms they take in without taking them on, without receiving them into matter; and this even when the reception is accompanied or preceded by some material change. Seeing colour is not becoming coloured, and feeling hot is not to be identified with becoming hot. The same applies to mind.

Activity is of two sorts: agency that induces external change (cf illuminating) and activity that produces no external effect but simply perfects itself in some way (cf glowing). What both have in common is actualization of the agent (cf being alight). Activities like desiring, perceiving or understanding are not external activities but interior perfections: when we understand our mind is actualized in some way, but not so that it acts on what it understands, and not so that what is understood undergoes change. Rather our mind and what it understands become one thing – we call it the *actually understanding mind* – one single source of the activity of understanding. By *becoming one thing* I mean that what we understand is joined to our mind, either by identity of substance or by some likeness. So mind isn't either active or passive in understanding, except coincidentally as when the union of mind with thing understood presupposes some activity or passivity: the activity, for example, of our *agent mind* bringing to light the species of what is to be understood, and the passivity of our *receptive mind* taking in that understandable species (as a sense-power takes in a perceptible appearance). The activity of understanding is something which follows on such activity or passivity, as an effect follows on its cause. Just as glowing bodies will glow once they are actually alight, so our mind knows anything understandable once that is actually present in it ... [3] Our mind doesn't relate to what it understands as an agent to something that it is acting on, but mind and known object together make up one agent, even if grammatically we use the active and passive voices to express their involvement in that agent's activity ... [8] The operation of understanding doesn't exist *between* the person understanding and what he understands; it issues from both conjoined ... [*de Veritate* 8 6]

So for knowledge it isn't enough for a knower merely to make contact with the thing he knows [as with something external]; that thing must unite with the knower as his form, either in identity of substance or by some likeness ... [*de Veritate* 8 7 [2]]

Even if the senses also take in forms without matter, they are powers that utilize sense-organs, organizations of matter. Such organizations of matter are so balanced and tempered that they can react to a form and take it in *intentionally*, as Thomas says, without having to yield their organization up to that form physically. But, of course, on occasion the loudness of a sound or the brightness of a light does disturb the temper of the organ and then we cannot hear or see: the material taking on of the form interferes with the intentional taking in of that form. It is Thomas's contention (argued in depth later in ch 5 p 109) that mind cannot use any like organization of matter as a mind-organ, partly because minds don't suffer the same danger of succumbing to becoming the objects they know, partly because material organs can only be tempered to react to spatial and physical forms whereas mind is, in Aristotle's phrase, a susceptibility to being in general, and partly because material organs can react only to particular individual instances of forms rather than to their general applicability to all such instances.

Any form taken on by matter becomes the form of some particular individual, but forms taken in by mind are not so particularized. To take a form into mind is to understand it, and since what we chiefly understand is the general, forms are taken into mind in their general applicability to many individuals. So the fact that minds take in forms does not show that they are material, but precisely that they are not. [*de Spiritualibus Creaturis* 1 1]

This then is how Thomas views mind, and it is mind viewed in this way that he attributes to God. But in God the interior activity of knowing does not presuppose, as it does in man, any previous activity or passivity in relation to external things, and God does not have to import the forms he knows from an outside world. There is nothing therefore in God to correspond to the prior experience, imagination and abstraction that a man requires and which Thomas describes below (ch 5 p 131). God's knowledge is the actualization of a presupposed unity with the forms of all things (including himself), but he does not first have to take those forms in. All perfections pre-exist in him as their doer, all articulate form is being articulated by him, his knowing is identically his doing. In fact his knowledge does not even actualize a presupposed unity, but that unity is always actualized: in God, mind (the ability) and what it understands and the form by which it understands and the act of understanding are all identically God's act of existing and God's act of creating. However, the multiplication of human words (and the relations of these words to one another) are all necessary if man is to express to himself the identity in God, for each word in isolation grasps only a part of God's reality.

So God will know himself by being himself, and other things by doing them (though his doing is his being). This is the principle which guides Thomas in his unravelling of the problems of what God knows. By knowing himself as the doing of things God sees what he does, sees it so to speak from its intended-side, from its claim to a share in the world's existence, not from its factual outside, as a man does. We say *sees* because God is present to the presence of things (as we are when seeing), whether that presence has come about factually and contingently as one of the chances of the world-process, or whether it is a necessity of that process. In either case the thing was created by God either as a necessity or as a contingency, and he sees it for what it is. For this reason too he knows individuals and not just classes of individuals: each individual as such is a reflection of God, and not just its nature or its form. God is present too in his doing to future events, to all tensed nows in their nowness. Of course, if he is present to the tensed now which now is, then he must know what we call *the time*, the time that it is now. And in knowing *the time* now, he also knows all other tensed nows as not *the time* now. But then he also knows them as *the time* at the time they were or will be, and all other tensed nows as not *the time* then. Clearly, Thomas's illustration of the man on the hilltop seeing the road of life's journey laid out before him in its sequential happenings only partially resembles the reality of God's eternal relationship to time. It fails to locate the hilltop in a non-spatial and non-temporal relationship to the journeying; in man's meditation on God that location must be done by way of specifying God as the doer of time, and specifying eternity as the mode of duration of that doing.

God in the image of man: loving.   God not only knows, but loves. Forms, we have said, are not just the factual shapes taken on by a passive matter, but they are destinations, completions, realizations of becoming and change. To whatever takes on form the possession of form is a satisfaction, and from that springs a way of talking of natural tendencies as natural desires or loves seeking that satisfaction. Such language is not claiming that natural things have intentional tendencies towards forms, but simply saying that they do *tend* to forms, and that not by chance. Plants, for example, can be said to have a *natural* desire to survive, a desire built into them and derived from the favour of the environment that brought them about in the first place. However, things endowed with awareness and the ability to know, whether that be sensation or mind, things that can take in forms, do have intentional tendencies towards the things from which the forms were taken in, the things those forms are said to re-present. An animal, for example, besides having a natural desire to survive, as plants do, and a natural pleasure in warmth built in to its reflexes, also has an appetite for what it sees as good for its whole self: an appetite by which it judges what its self as a whole should do in reaction. The animal has not only a natural desire but an *animal* desire to survive. Man too has such a natural desire, and such an animal desire, but because he has a mind and a susceptibility to being as such (and not just objects of sense), he has also what Thomas often calls a *rational* desire or will, an appetite for being as such, for letting things be. We should note that the word *will* for Thomas does not first connote a power to dominate things but a *willingness* to be attracted by them. The fundamental activity of will is not making decisions, choosing between things, but the activity of loving, of consent to their creation. Like knowledge this is an interior activity, not an agency acting externally; but whereas knowledge takes in forms from things into ourselves, love inclines our affections from ourselves into things. Anything which knows must love, and anything which knows things as truths (in itself) must also love them as goods (in themselves). God is no exception; though God's love is inclined towards things creatively, by its inclination creating the very goodness to which it inclines, just as his knowledge represents their forms creatively, creating their truth and existence by representing them as truly existent.

Because love is our leaning towards things it is the interior principle that issues in external action, our primary ability to direct and govern our power of external movement. In that guise it does itself appear as *power*, the sense of *will* that seems to be primary in English. But that is never for Thomas the most profound view of will, and he always means by it first and foremost our appetite for goodness and being as such. This is the essence of will, prior to its appearance as will-power; and the spontaneity that characterizes will as freedom from natural or animal determination is prior to the notion of freedom of choice. When Thomas, for example, asks whether God's will is all-powerful that means to him something like: can his love ever be over-powered? Of particular interest then is whether God can will evil. The answer to this problem is briefly sketched when it is first mentioned in chapter 2, and then repeated in greater detail when Thomas discusses evil in the created world (ch 4 pp 91ff) and whether God can be said to cause sin (ch 8 p 261). His answer turns on his concept of evil as a misdirection of being away from fullness of being. Nobody, in fact, can will evil as such, he says, because nobody can love evil as such. That is a contradiction in terms. The possibility only seems a possibility because the word *will* as meaning exercise of power has come loose from the word *love* as meaning leaning towards good. But one can will evil incidentally in the process of willing being that is in some way unfulfilled. God himself does this when he wills pain and suffering – the so-called penal evils, or rather when he does not stop willing what brings pain and suffering in its wake. But the ultimate misdirection of being away from all good he does not and cannot will, since it would be the willing of being away from himself. Man, however, can do this, and such willing the Judaeo-Christian tradition has called *sin*. Notice that sin is in one sense a grand fiction: man acts as though what he was doing was misdirected and withdrawn from God's plan in itself, and indeed this is what he wants to be the case, though it never is so in fact. Man truly sets himself up as a misdirector of being and that is sin, but God in allowing him to do this is not sinning: he neither sins nor wills man to sin, but he does allow the free creature to will what he wills, while himself pursuing the direction of what man does to his own good ends.

So Thomas connects willing with loving. In the second part of the

Summa, starting at chapter 7, he will explain at length how man's love needs strengthening by virtuous dispositions in order to constitute a reliable source of good action. When discussing God he briefly adverts to the scriptural view of God as the primordial pattern and source of all these virtues, of all fulfilment and perfection of human abilities. Human virtue, as Thomas learnt from Aristotle and will himself teach in part 2, is primarily a matter of prudence or discretion – a fulfilment of knowledge in pursuit of good – and justice – a fulfilment of will as a principle of external action. God's prudence is more often called his providence, and it is accompanied by the universal justice of a just judge. This is a justice not merely tempered by mercy but springing from mercy, since it is not a payment of debts exacted from God by creatures, but a willing, loving, merciful creation by God of creatures to whose being he consents and who can be owed things. Sometimes Thomas says that God owes payments of such debts to himself, or that he is a law unto himself, but that precisely means that by God's mercy he has created a world in which we are enabled to claim from him. He owes creatures by reason of his own goodness. He himself is the justice that lays down the standards. Indeed God himself will be the standard that human virtue is to pursue. In the second part of the *Summa* our very existence, our being ourselves, will be seen as a journey towards God's fullness, towards an achievement of God; and God's own life will be the measure of how we are to live.

Providence then is God's prudence, the virtue of knowing how to choose well, how to plan choices according to the possibilities of pursuing some goal. As with God's knowledge and God's love, God's prudence (compounded of both) is creative: that is to say, his plan does not depend on what the possibilities are, but what the possibilities are are themselves part of the plan. The plan is an eternal plan: indeed it is God himself as representation of the world, and it is to be implemented in time with our cooperation. That implementation is the subject of chapter 6; but in chapter 2 it is God as planner that holds the attention. Because the determination of what is possible and what is impossible is itself part of God's plan, events when compared to God as their cause cannot be classified as either chance or determined; that distinction is one which assesses events in relation to their more immediate causes. God has the choice of leaving an event to happen without a created cause (though he is still causing it), or of causing it to be a event determined by the natural processes that he has created (without thereby losing his freedom in respect of it). It is but a step from this notion of providence to that bugbear of Christian theology: predestination. This name has been given in history to that part of the providential plan which relates to the dispatching of men to their eternal target. For Thomas predestination is an eternal reality, not a temporal property of those predestined, and as such it does not *pre*-determine whether that goal will be achieved by chance or by created determinism or by free will. For God can operate something by way of our free will without that will ceasing to be free, just as he can produce natural effects naturally. Notice that predestination is causative of the free acts of those who attain the target, and of the grace by which they are enabled to perform such acts, but that reprobation is an absence of such predestination and not causal of sin. Nor can you split up the free acts of those predestined into what is of God's grace in the act and what is of human freedom, since the free act as such is the effect of grace: to say that God's predestining is consequent upon his foreseeing that someone will make good use of given grace appears to make a cause dependent on its own effects (ch 2 p 58). Not that there is anything against saying that in God's plan something is planned to follow on some previous free act; but that free act is also in the plan. Of course, as Thomas realizes, all this raises the question of why God predestines this one rather than that. The best answer Thomas can give is that God chooses arbitrarily like a bricklayer choosing this brick rather than that when he has more bricks than he needs and there is nothing to choose between the bricks that he has. But, of course, God himself has planned it so that he has more bricks than his wall requires. So we are told that God's gifts are God's gifts, and that to choose sometimes to give and sometimes not to give is neither unjust nor unreasonable. And since man has freely sinned, the fact of penalty and that not giving grace will condemn a man to that penalty is also neither unreasonable nor unjust. These are negative answers designed to show not that God's choice is reasonable in this or that way, but that, in principle, the choice is not unreasonable. If one persists in asking: But why didn't God . . .? Thomas's eventual answer is: I don't know the reason! But he resists the next step of saying: Well then, God behaved badly; because precisely, one doesn't know God's reason.

The picture of God as loving planner of the world must be completed by attributing to him power to implement his plans. Again Thomas is using the way we talk about human planning and government, but trying to ensure that what he says in that language is truly applicable to God. God's power to implement, for example, is not something distinct from and prior to his actual act of implementation, something which has to be realized in doing; rather both his power and his doing are identically his act of existing! But God's power does precede his effects, in the sense that eternity precedes time. We speak of God's power as unlimited, and that gets us into difficulties. We are trying to distinguish (again) divine power from all created power: and since created powers are measured by the limits of what they are capable of, we say that no such limits measure God's power. But then we ask: aren't there limits in some sense to his power? aren't there some things that God cannot do, like squaring a circle? Thomas would prefer to say that such things cannot be done, cannot in fact be, rather than that God cannot do them: they cannot be done in some absolute sense which depends not on limitations of God's power but on the meaning of the word *to be* and on logic. God can do all that can be done. But now our language suggests that this logical definition of possibility in some way predates God. Well, perhaps the answer is that it predates our *expression in language* of God's power. We place impossibilities next to possibilities as two parts of some larger domain: the domain of propositions that syntax allows us to make. In our way of thinking this does precede God's power, though in reality God's power has preceded our mind's way of thinking. In creating the world and our minds God created that distinction between logic and fact that our mind is exploiting.

Where is God?   There is however another problem raised by the concept of God's power. Because God is being pictured in language usually used of men, the concept of a God of power cannot fail to conjure up the picture of a human ruler or a human judge. God rules over and sits in judgment upon, he is an authority, a God from above; and this is a concept unpopular in modern times precisely because we suspect authority and have had too much experience of unjust judges and the dependence of rule upon hidden forms of violence. And this modern suspicion is surely bolstered by the words of the New Testament itself which says that *God sent his only Son into the world not to judge the world, but that the world might be salvaged through him. The son of man came not to be served, but to serve and to give his life as a ransom for many.* Jesus took one of the themes of the Old Testament and made it his primary picture of God; he replaced the picture of God sitting upon a throne of power and judgment with one of God going bail for man, coming down into the dock and taking upon himself man's punishment, allowing himself to be held up to mockery and scorn while the world, in the person of Pilate, usurped the judgment seat. In Jesus God did not sit in judgment on criminals but was crucified between them, sharing their lot *in extremis.* In the New Testament the ruler of the world is not God but Satan, and God manifests his glory by coming as a suffering servant to cast Satan down from heaven, to reject the picture men have of heaven as the source of accusation and hostile judgment. *Now is the judgment of this world*, says Jesus as he approaches Calvary, *now shall the ruler of this world be cast out; and I, when I am lifted up from the earth, will draw all men to myself.* It is the Pharisee of the gospels, the anti-Christ of John's epistle, the continued observers of the Law in Paul, who attempt to keep the picture of God as power going. *But the word of the cross*, writes Paul, *which is folly to those who are perishing, is for those being saved the power of God ... Jews demand a show of power, Greeks seek wise words, but we preach Christ crucified, a stumbling-block to Jews and folly to Gentiles, but to those who are called, be they Jew or Greek, the power of God and the wisdom of God. For God's fool is wiser than men, and God's weakling more powerful than men.* Thomas commenting on this passage in the most powerful days of Christendom, said Paul had been talking of the period before Christendom triumphed, but that now that the victory of Christ has been won, the wisdom of the Greeks (and the power of governments?) has been turned to good use by Christ's church. This is not a sentiment that recommends itself to Christians in the twentieth century. Or so at least, we can hope. We have another answer to the question *Where is God?* Our God shows himself not in the prudence and power of the rulers of this world, but in the powerlessness and foolishness of the poor.

We said earlier that Thomas was a man of his time, but a giant of his time: a man who laid foundations for the questions to come. The question of where God is is an example worth pondering. Our picture of power contains elements which, even on philosophical grounds, as Thomas saw, must disappear from our assertions about God's power. God, for example, does not exist as some powerful manipulator behind the scenes, scanning the choices he could make and playing the master, choosing the actual from the possible and imposing it on his players in the actual world, while he remains in the larger world of the possible. All human power shows itself in the pre-determination of events, but God's home, so to speak, is in the actual events themselves; he dwells in them, be they free or determined in the worldly sense of those words, laying on them no pre-determinations of his own. He is neither a God from above, nor yet a God from below led by the events, but he is a God in the events as we and the world determine them, because he is a God within our and the world's determining of them. The principle that would lead us to such a conclusion is there in Thomas. He perhaps followed his own time, seeing God's agency primarily as the culmination of a hierarchy of worldly agencies and powers intermediately determining worldly effects; nevertheless he shows the way to our time when he attends, within this intermediate determinism, to the immediacy with which God applies worldly causes to worldly effects, and to the immediacy with which he acts in chance events and in men's free acts, using even these as his tools [cf ch 1 p 22].

The fundamental insight as always is that every natural doing and every chance doing in the world, and every free doing of man, is a tool of the doing of God; and it is an insight which permeates the whole of volume 2 of the *Summa*. In that volume he treats extensively one particular way in which, as chapter 6 below argues, God is at work in all the doings of the world. In chapter 5 Thomas introduces man* as the creature who, in the material world, is most to the image of God. The beginning of volume 2 sees that image primarily in the way man, alone among material creatures, can master his own doing: so that his doing, we might say, is a doing-doing and not simply a done-doing, and gives us some image of God's being, which, as we have seen, is a doing-being rather than a done-being. As the chapters of volume 2 unfold we see more and more clearly that the reason for this mastery in man, this power over his own action, is the existence within him of an objective (Thomas says rational) love of what is good as such. Thrown into more modern ways of speech, the idea is something like the following. A baby, we can suppose, starts off as something being *subjected* to a sensed world that bombards it. Gradually, as in other animals, there is decided, in terms of the desires and fears experienced, the structure of importance that the world is going to have for this animal. Part of that structure is species-decided (Thomas's *natural* love), part of it individual-decided (Thomas's *animal* love) and part, in man, objectively-decided (Thomas's *rational* love or will). By *objective* I mean that the animal's desires and fears are themselves externalized in some way as a world to which some other interior is being *subjected*, and then even the natural and animal loves of the individual are assessed for their objective satisfactoriness. This is what defines man (at least as an ideal): that in him there seems to exist a sort of objective dissatisfaction that takes notice of the imperfect ways in which built-in desires and fears achieve their objective, namely, our own good. At that moment of taking notice, we discover a will towards a more integrated, *unanimous* self. In men it is not merely that the organization of an animal self wishes to preserve itself by organizing the environmental world; but that we wish to reorganize our

---

* See ch 11 p 376 for my apology for using the word *man* rather than *human being*.

own selves satisfactorily, according to a sort of intent of a new and better self. If this is a correct interpretation of the chapters Thomas spends on the nature of human action, its goodness and badness in terms of external and interior (or willed) goodness, the development of strengths of self (virtuous dispositions that tend to good action) or weak selves (vicious dispositions that tend to bad), and the ever-present notion of a rule or standard to which the self and its actions must conform, then we can also use it to explain how the doing-being of God is present within this doing-doing of man. For the intent of an objectively-organized self is identically the intent of the universe as I would author it were I its author. And then the intent of the actual author of the universe appears as another which I would like mine to conform to, an intent which in my pursuit of an organized self I will want to be revealed to me and to acknowledge, the intent of the universe that is God's love for the world which I shall want to implement, and so return. The will that I discover within me is already an interior implicit pull of God's intent, calling me to make myself a tool of that intent. Faith, hope and charity (which tradition calls *theological*, or *deiform*, virtues) are our explicit willing acknowledgement of that intent when it is revealed to us, our commitment to the venture of implementing it, and our happy identification with the love revealed in it.

The distinction just made between the implicit pull of God's intent, and our explicit acknowledgement and identification with it, is meant to express the distinction Thomas makes between what is natural to man and what he regards as *supernatural*. In general, Thomas does not mean by the supernatural the miraculous. The miraculous, if it occurs, is something outside the ordinary course of nature; but the supernatural is something which though it exceeds the power of some particular nature considered in itself, does not exceed its power when we consider that nature in its context in Nature as a whole. The tides, for example, are natural phenomena, beyond the capacity of water as such, but natural to water in its context as sea, subject to the pull of sun and moon [cf ch 6 p 157]. So too, for Thomas, creation and the salvation of sinners and faith, hope and charity are beyond the powers of creatures and in that sense supernatural, but within the established order of causes, within Nature in a broad sense. For the human response to God's power in these cases is like the response of the sea to the sun and the moon: man has a *natural capacity for grace, being made in God's image*; and *to be able to have faith or the love of charity is natural to man, though actually having them is a grace reserved to believers* (ch 9 pp 320–1).

When one thing is naturally subordinate to another, its perfection consists not only in what it can do on its own but also in what it derives from the higher nature: thus the sea not only moves downward with water's natural heaviness, but also moves in and out tidally under the influence of the moon. Now the only nature that relates immediately to God is that of reasoning creatures; they grasp the meaning of good and existence in general and so can relate immediately to the source of existence as such. The perfection of such creatures consists therefore not only in what they can do naturally on their own, but also in what they can do by supernaturally sharing God's own goodness. So man's ultimate happiness consists in a sort of supernatural sight of God, which he must learn from God as from a teacher, step by step as is man's natural way. But, as Aristotle says, *learners, if they are to attain full knowledge, must put faith in their teachers.* So to see God man must first believe him, as students believing a teacher. [ch 10 p 331]

It is clear that the relationship between the natural and the supernatural is a good deal more subtle than many of Thomas's successors have taken it to be, and not at all exhausted by the familiar quote that *grace fulfils nature*. The foundations of the relationship are laid in chapter 2 already when providence and predestination are discussed, and we are told that there is no distinguishing within a good human action what is of God's grace and what is of man's freedom (p 58). The basic points are repeated in chapter 6, as we have noted, when Thomas is discussing how God operates in all natures including men's free wills, like Nature operating in a nature. The capital letter there represents God's priority (so that he can be said to operate); yet Nature uses nature as its tool (so that they can be said to cooperate) (pp 155–6). These fundamental categories of operation, cooperation and tool recur again and again throughout the *Summa* and perform the task of bringing the categories of the natural and supernatural together in actuality even if they are distinguishable in theory.

Without God's grace Thomas says we cannot respond to God's intent explicitly, and at the end of the first part of volume 2 (chapter 9 in this translation) he defines grace as the loving favour of God operating and cooperating with man's doing, so that the intent of man and the intent of God become one. For Thomas this is the true place where God's power shows itself, this is *where* God is. Thomas makes here a wholly surprising but satisfying connection: he compares what the Christian tradition says about grace and charity (God's love) with what Aristotle had said about human friendship. God's love, operating within men's, plants in us our faith to acknowledge God's love present in the world; and then, cooperating with men's love, helps us implement God's intent for the universe, however much that may be beyond man's natural powers. When our efforts cannot achieve something on their own but only by cooperating with another who has achievement within his gift, then we can be said to be *earning* or *deserving* the achievement rather than ourselves *effecting* it. So Thomas never tires of quoting Aristotle's dictum that what we can do with the help of a friend we can in some sense do ourselves. This, in the last analysis, is Thomas's reason for maintaining that grace is not simply the external favour in God, but something residing in us and empowering us.

These explanations of chapter 9 are essential to the discussion of the role of Christ in God's world. Already in chapter 3 we have been introduced to the notion of God expressing himself to himself in a Word, a Word in which godhead is as truly present as in he who is saying the Word. And God is also drawn to himself with a Love, which is also God. And at the end of that chapter we are told that this eternal presence of God to himself through a Word of Love is a presence which has come visibly and explicitly into time and into this world, into history: God's primordial grace to the world, so that (by faith, hope and charity) it can become a presence in all human intent.

> Man naturally comes to the unseen by way of the seen; so it was fitting for him to learn of the invisible sending of the persons of God through visible creatures. The Holy Spirit, coming forth as a love, is fittingly the sanctifying gift; and the Son, as source of the Spirit, fittingly the author of sanctification. And so the Son was sent visibly as the author of salvation and the Holy Spirit as its sign. The Son became one in person with the visible creature in which he appeared, so that whatever we say of this creature we can say of the Son. And in order to show himself as author of sanctification, the Son was sent visibly in a rational nature, characterized by mastery over its own actions. But since any creature can symbolize sanctification, the Holy Spirit does not need to become one in person with it, nor does the creature need to last beyond the period of its functioning. [ch 3 pp 80–1]

In chapters 13 to 15 Thomas spells out the detail of this view of Christ. Grace in Christ is the very union of man with God in one person, issuing in the great act and symbol of Calvary. The general remarks made about grace earlier are brought to bear in chapter 14 on the Christian doctrine of Calvary as a gracious act of *redemption*, that is to say, *ransom*.

> Christ's sufferings, considered as something done by God, can be said to *effect* our salvation, but as willed by Christ with his human soul are said to *earn* it; and as something undergone in the flesh are variously said to be the *amends made for us* if thought of as freeing us from liability to punishment, our *ransom* if thought of as freeing us from slavery to sin, and our *sacrificial offering* if thought of as reconciling us to God. [ch 14 p 529]

Thomas is talking of the historical event of Calvary and giving a masterly summary of how Christians have interpreted it through the centuries with analogies from human social life. Fundamentally, the event is seen as a human action (Christ willingly underwent it) performed with the help of God's grace, and acting as a tool of the divine intent for the universe and mankind. That divine intent is revealed in this very action as the salvage of an integrity in man and creation that has been ruined by the omnipresence of sin – action not directed to the objective intent of what is good as such. When theologians talk of the event as *effecting* such salvage, says Thomas, they are thinking of it as a tool of God at work in it; when theologians talk of it as *earning* that salvage, they are thinking of Christ's human will cooperating with God in it. When they talk of it as an amends made, or a ransom paid, or a sacrifice offered, they are looking at the fleshly fact of the event itself, its role in history of turning the process of sin and uncreation round, whether that process be thought of as an incurring of penalties (God's penalties being naturally consequent on sin rather than imposed by special dictate), a being caught in sin's net, or a being separated from God's intent. Of course, if we ask further, *how* exactly such an event could salvage us from the disintegration of the world, under what precise aspect God's power was effective in Calvary, then Thomas's answer is, as St John's was: as love. God's love called to our love in that event and attracted us to respond; there at one and the same time was shown the power and the powerlessness of God, since love cannot force the response it asks for. The power of Calvary cannot be seen in any guarantee Calvary contains that it *must* succeed in drawing all men back to love, but simply in the fact – and seen from the perspective of history, the chance fact – that Calvary *will* succeed in changing history in that way. *And I when I am lifted up will draw all men to myself.* For Calvary – such is the Christian hope and faith – is a new beginning to creation, a new seed which will propagate itself through the calvaries of those who respond, and by so doing call their neighbours to respond in turn, throughout history. This is the response God's love calls for but has not the power to force; nevertheless, when the response comes, God will be at work in the responding just as he was in the calling.

In chapter 15, the part of the *Summa* that Thomas was writing when he finished his course on earth, Thomas explores what might be called the mechanism by which the call of Calvary, and the opportunity to respond to it, is spread through the world: the Christian *sacraments* or sacred ceremonies in which both call and response are acted out and made ever present in their power and powerlessness. Again, what he has to say can only be understood because of the preparation he has given us in earlier chapters. God's intent and love and presence is to permeate our intent in living and does that explicitly when we respond with faith and love and hope (chapter 10), expressing themselves in a life lived for the common good of all (chapter 11). As part of living a life for others (justice) we recognize that we are also living our life for God by symbolic acts of recognition and celebration of God's goodness (religion). Among those acts are counted the sacraments (ch 11 p 409), the great acts of mime and make-believe by which men of all cultures have celebrated God's gifts (the harvests, the seasons, the sun and the moon). As part of the Jewish, and then the Christian, revelation there comes a new explicitness to religion, a new explicitness to sacramental worship, in which we celebrate the gift of God's love and presence and redemption given into all human living and human history on Calvary. See especially the discussion of the Old Law and the New in chapter 9. In the Christian sacraments, and especially in the eucharist, to which all the other sacraments are ordered, we make present to ourselves the presence of God through Calvary; and God uses our celebrations as his tools to introduce himself and his intent into our lives, and continually reinforce that presence.

What then is God? The love revealed on Calvary calling to men. Where then is God? In the acts of love by which men respond to the call, and so keep God's love alive and calling today: actions which are themselves kept alive by God's eternal love. God both operates in our love and is a cooperation with it: the love itself and the acts of mime and make-believe which nourish it. The rule of God is within *us*; whatever sins *we* forgive, they are forgiven in heaven.

Who is God?   So we arrive at the God of the New Testament: the Father who *sent* his Son to save us from sin, to die and rise again and leave his Spirit abroad in the world we inhabit today. In arriving at this God we have perforce left philosophy and the limits of what it can say far behind. We have moved into a different discipline of revealed theology which Thomas calls *sacra doctrina*, literally, holy teaching. In what remains of this preface we shall try to understand how Thomas distinguished holy teaching from philosophy, and what he thought it added to that discipline. This in fact is the subject of his own introduction to the *Summa*, which follows immediately upon this preface; so to talk of it will enable us to move smoothly forward into this impressive work.

Thomas says in his introduction that he intends, in the *Summa*, to hand on holy teaching, and that he will first argue for the existence of such teaching, define its nature and describe its language and style. But some commentators have been left puzzled: for the introduction seems to argue for a divine self-revelation, define a human theological science, and describe the style of the Christian bible. Two clues point to an answer. Firstly, Thomas talks of holy teaching in the past tense: asking not whether we need it but whether we needed it, thus identifying it with something God did in history. And secondly he asks whether the *teaching* was needed over and above man's naturally-developed *learning*. God-given teaching is contrasted with man-acquired learning: what God did filled some gap in human science, and revealed something man couldn't learn.

Contrasting teaching and learning as alternatives is unusual in Thomas. Normally, like Aristotle, he regards *teacher teaching* and *student learning* as simply two aspects of a single activity taking place in the student. Teaching describes it as someone's doing, learning as someone's becoming; development of any human science then is at once teaching and learning. *All learning and teaching,* Aristotle says, *builds on what is already known,* and a science, in particular, articulates the way in which knowledge of some subject depends on a seminal idea or premise defining that subject. This ideal of scientific order is still present in today's physical theorizing about observed experience and experiment. The initial step in a modern physical theory is not so much particular observed phenomena or a particular technique of mathematics or logic, as some way of conceiving the phenomena which makes such a technique applicable to them for the first time. Stephen Toulmin gives the example of geometrical optics and its seminal idea of light as travelling in straight lines: *the notion of a light ray,* he writes, *one might describe as our device for reading the straight lines of our optical diagrams into the phenomena,*

phenomena which we prepare for the interpretation by observing them through the filtering and abstracting medium of measuring instruments. The idea of a light-ray is a sort of premise so representing light that the technique of geometrical diagrams becomes applicable to it for the first time; and from such a premise, often expressed in an image or model, issues that organization of observed and measured data which constitutes a modern scientific theory. Such a science we could say approaches its subject with two concepts: one with which to identify it and one with which to organize predictions about it. The identifying concept locates the subject in our experience enabling us to direct our measuring instruments at it; the organizing concept defines it in the theory, and so interprets and predicts the data those instruments will yield. If we could have a science in which those two concepts were the same, in which the organizing concept was what, in experience, we identified our subject to be, we would have the kind of science that Aristotle (and Thomas) sought: for physics and metaphysics, they thought, rested on ideas of change and being that were embedded in human experience. They sought to conceive light in such a way that it might enter not the world of scientific calculation, but the world of ordinary human experience, to articulate its role in the community of the universe within which man lives and moves and has his being. For Aristotle and Thomas nothing enters into being simply as a phenomenon; to exist is to have a significance in the world, to have point, to act out a role. And their ideal of science was to identify such roles and organize all that could be said about things around those identifying roles. When then Thomas says in the first few words of his *Summa* that his aim is to teach beginners – those who want to learn – how to articulate scientific order – literally, an *order of learning* – within holy teaching, he is saying that he wants to show them how God's act of self-revelation, mediated through the scriptures, can identify God in their lives, and how it can be used to organize all that can be said of God into a science of theology.

There is of course a difficulty: sciences are built on what men can see, on experience and the light of reason, whereas God's teaching is built on the light of revelation – which Thomas believes doesn't offer vision but only hearsay. So it is at this point that Thomas temporarily uses the words *learning* and *teaching* to contrast two types of science: humanly discovered sciences and divinely revealed theology. Both types of science are learnt and taught: humanly discovered sciences, however, are essentially learnt and only incidentally taught, revealed theology essentially taught and only incidentally learnt. The humanly discovered sciences rest on insights natural to men, the authority of which must in time replace the temporarily accepted authority of teachers, so that the erstwhile student becomes the author and source of his own knowledge. Even the learning of men about God, though *learnt by few over long periods and mingled with much error*, is still in principle a *seeing* what is true. The teaching of God, on the other hand, though taking place in men learning (as all teaching takes place in some learning student) derives from insight natural only to God and unavailable to man: God's eternal knowledge of himself. So Thomas draws a bold analogy here to the very example of modern physical science used above by Toulmin: geometrical optics. In that science one idea of light gained by experience identifies light as our subject of study, but another idea borrowed from geometry predicts its properties. The first idea tells us what to look at with our instruments, whilst the second explains the data our instruments will yield. Optics, Thomas says, requires a sort of faith in what only geometry can see. So it is with theology: it must put its faith in God's eternal knowledge, identifying the author of nature discovered in experience with the God who uncovers himself in Christ, and letting God's view of himself illuminate our secular and Christian experience. Of course, there is faith and faith. In a later passage Thomas says that even the devils believe the revelations of God, not out of choice, nor because they see, but with a belief forced from them by the evidence of signs and consequences. The faith optics has in geometry is of that sort too, justified by the accuracy of its predictions, seen to work. But, Thomas will say, faith in God's revelation is of a different sort: a choice made from love, a commitment to a life of friendship with someone we believe will not fail us or himself or the world.

Theology and scripture.   This is where the scriptures come in: they are the record, accepted on faith, of a history in which such friendship was offered, to Israel, in Christ, to the church. If the original obscure oracles of prophets and histories mythically interpreted, the poetic writings and symbolic rituals, the collections of laws and proverbs, the letters and oral reminiscences and meditations of Jesus's followers have during the long centuries of church life been filtered, abstracted and distilled into those systems of articulated propositions called *creeds* – the *articles of faith* which Thomas sees as the seminal premise of theology – still faith is not a mere intellectual assent to propositions but a response to the friendship they articulate and a gift of ourselves to him who has made himself known in the history the scriptures record. The full understanding of Thomas on the relation of the scriptures to faith and theology would require us to refer to several connected passages on later pages: ch 1 p 26 on how we know God, ch 12 pp 444ff on how prophets know him and communicate their knowledge, ch 10 pp 328ff on our faith in what they reveal, and especially on the so-called articles of faith. There are also a few words about teaching in the section dealing with the role of men in the running of the world: ch 6 p 161. All these sections betray a fundamental model of revelation as *teaching*, a model with great strengths but also perhaps the weakness of requiring from faith a greater degree of propositional articulateness and awareness than is perhaps the case. It is one thing to ask of faith that it explicitly recognize the existence of a loving providence in the world, and so distinguish itself from man's natural awareness of God's world; and quite another to think that only those people who can articulate their faith in propositional form are going to be saved. Many men can articulate better in deeds than in words. Thomas perhaps can't help thinking of revelation as teaching in the manner of the medieval schools, with God as the great schoolman expounding truth to his students: Abraham, Moses and the prophets, who, but for the needs of the ordinary people without education, might have written it all down in the analytic language of the great philosophers rather than the metaphor and symbolism of the poets. In this he is in one sense a child of his time, but in another he is in fact dissociating himself from much contemporary barren typology that could read anything into anything.

Thomas considers it not a small part of the theologian's task to demonstrate to men of good will, believers or non-believers, that the scriptural teaching is reasonable, not in the sense of being demonstrable by reason, but in the sense of not obfuscating or contradicting or restricting reason but opening possibilities of deeper and wider truth. A revelation that showed contempt for human reason and freedom could not, in Thomas's view, truly come from the God who created man reasonable and free. God's point-of-view cannot abrogate or replace the view he planted in us by nature but must fulfil it, get the most out of it. Faith, according to Thomas, subordinates our minds not to God's authoritarian will but to his authoritative insight: we believe what he says only because we believe he sees. Faith may not involve any insight into the truths believed, but it involves a love of such insight and a love of truth; and it produces the kind of *feeling* for truth that virtuous dispositions like justness or chasteness give for what is just or what is chaste.

The *Summa* then is written in a different sort of language from the scriptures, the literal language of argument, the analytic and technical language that aiming at clarity in argument necessarily develops. In large part this language is learned from Aristotle and echoes his ideas, but it is employed in the service of other ideas which spring from a tradition nurtured on the metaphor and typology of the scriptures: ideas such as that of man made in God's image to till and keep the garden of creation, or of Christ as priest of a new passover sacrifice. It would, for example, be perfectly possible to treat the *Summa* as though it was simply a sort of Christian supplement to Aristotle: the first part adding to Aristotle's theology of divine thought at the eternal centre of the ever-turning world, the Christian notion of a personal providence, and to Aristotle's psychology of man the Christian concept of bodily resurrection; the second part adding divine friendship and a life to come to Aristotle's ethics. But in this way of looking at the *Summa* the core is Aristotelian and scripture contributes the extras. This is not how the work is really structured. Despite all the difference in style what guides the structure of the *Summa* is the structure of the scriptures themselves and their fundamental theme. That theme might briefly be expressed as one of creation, un-creation and re-creation, or of creation, collapse and salvage, finally leading to the building of a house for all. The Old Testament pursues this theme first of all at the level of the natural order of the cosmos itself: the creation brings habitable land out of the chaotic waters (or a garden out of the desert) and culminates in Adam, the human, the world's husbandman; but Adam's failure to shoulder the task brings collapse and un-creation and return to the waters of the flood; and re-creation becomes a matter of a pact with Noah and his sons. But now the theme returns at the level of the political order of humanity: the ideal unity of nations created by the Semite, Hamite and Japhetite genealogies of Noah's sons collapses when the nations' languages are scattered at Babel, and re-creation depends on Abraham, called away from his own father's house to father a new nation, the house of Israel, by which all the nations will bless themselves. The whole Old Testament now devotes itself to pursuing this theme at its third level: Israel (as Matthew's gospel hints) is created during the generations from Abraham to David, uncreated during the generations from Solomon's building of the temple to the exile in Babylon, but guaranteed a re-creation when a new house will be built for God in their midst. According to the New Testament the whole of this creation (the cosmos centred round humanity centred round Israel centred round the new house of God, Jesus of Nazareth) went through the worst the forces of un-creation could do to it during Jesus's life: but his journey to Jerusalem into the old temple, to exile and to death, emerged to salvage and re-creation at his resurrection, and the spirit of his passing is now alive in the new world of the church. This journey is the backbone of the *Summa*. In part one, after three chapters which, so to speak, explore what came before creation, Thomas examines the seven days of Genesis culminating in the creation of Adamic man to God's image (chapters 4-6). Part two, starting from this notion of man as God's image, explores man's responsibilities and then moves to consider the historical fact of his failure: sin, death and uncreation (chapters 7-8). There follows the scriptural record of the journey of salvage: the giving of the law first and then the new law of grace (chapter 9), the life of the Spirit which is the wind of Christ's passing through death to resurrection (chapters 10-14), and which now blows through the whole world (chapter 15).

Introduction

THE LEARNING OF MEN AND THE TEACHING OF GOD

Introduction

THE LEARNING OF MEN AND THE TEACHING OF GOD

My aim in this book is to introduce beginners to what God taught us [in the scriptures] as concisely and clearly as the subject-matter allows, and in scientific order.

Why we needed to be taught by God.   For our human well-being we needed teaching by God's revelation to supplement learning by our own natural powers of reasoning. God has destined us for a goal beyond the grasp of reason – *No eye has seen what you have prepared for those who love you* – and since we must set ourselves this goal and pursue it we needed teaching about it beforehand. We even needed revealed instruction in things reason can learn about God. If such truths had been left to us to discover they would have been learnt by few over long periods and mingled with much error; yet our whole well-being is centred on God and depends on knowing them. So, in order that more of us might more safely attain him, we needed teaching in which God revealed himself.

This teaching of God is a new science of God.   Theology as God taught it differs in kind from the theology of philosophers. Sciences are differentiated by different ways of knowing things: astronomers prove the earth round with abstract geometrical argument [from the shape of its shadow], physicists prove it from earth's concrete physical properties [: gravity attracts matter into a ball]. So something that is the subject of a naturally learned discipline when known by the light of reason becomes the subject of another science when known by the light of God's revelation. Not all sciences have to be based like arithmetic and geometry on self-evident premises known by the light of natural intelligence; some sciences base themselves on premises known by the light of a higher science e.g. optics on geometrical principles, harmony on arithmetical. The teaching of God is such a science. It is based on premises known by the light of a higher science, namely God's own knowledge of himself shared with the blessed in heaven. These premises are the articles of faith revealed by God and taken on faith in the science God taught us, just as harmony takes on faith premises the arithmetician provides. [Science is concerned with generalizations rather than individual events;] the science God has taught us in scripture concerns itself with the individual lives of people [like Abraham, Isaac and Jacob], but not primarily. It uses such lives as examples of how we should live (as moral science does), and to assert the credentials of the men who handed on to us God's revelation, on which the science taught in scripture is based.

3   The teaching of God is a single unified science. Whatever we know through scripture we know in one and the same way, by divine revelation; and there is one main subject-matter, God, with everything else treated as beginning or ending in God. As revealed by God, matter that would otherwise be the subject of diverse natural sciences, belongs to the one teaching, a sort of imprint of God's own knowledge in which everything

4 is seen at once. For God in knowing himself knows all that he has made, so that his teaching transcends the distinction between pure and applied knowledge. It is chiefly pure, concerned with God more than with human behaviour, which it treats as the means of achieving that perfect

5 knowledge of God which constitutes eternal happiness. Because it pursues this eternal goal, to which all other goals are subordinate, it surpasses all other applied sciences; and it surpasses all other pure sciences because of its transcendent subject-matter and sure conclusions, dependent not on the fallible light of natural reason, but on the infallible light of God's own knowledge. Doubts about the articles of faith [on which this teaching is based] arise not from any uncertainty in their subject-matter but from our feebleness in understanding. And that is why God's teaching sometimes makes use of other sciences, not as superior sources of knowledge, but as subordinate ones with which human reason is more at home and from which it can more easily be

6 led towards what transcends reason. This science shares in the wisdom of God, though it is not the wisdom we call a gift of the Holy Spirit. The gift of wisdom is a sort of judgment by sympathy in divine matters, like the moral judgments to which virtue inclines us; the wisdom of this teaching is a judgment by knowledge, like the moral judgments even non-virtuous moralists can make. It is a wisdom gained by study, though its premises are revealed.

7   The subject-matter of a science is like the defining object of an ability

or disposition, meaning by defining object that precise aspect of objects which makes them objects of that ability. Men and stones, for example, are objects of sight precisely as coloured, so colour is the defining object of sight. Now God's teaching treats everything in terms of God, either as being God himself or as beginning and ending with him. So God is the real subject of this science. Its first premises are the articles of faith, which is about God; and since sciences wholly derive from their first premises, this science inherits faith's subject-matter. However, we cannot argue from a definition of God in this science, because we do not know how to define him. Instead we argue from his effects, be they nature or grace. In certain natural sciences we do the same, proving things about causes not from their definitions but from their effects.

The language and style of God's teaching.   This teaching is like 8 every science in accepting its premises, the articles of faith, without proof and then inferring conclusions from them by argument. (St Paul, for example, assuming Christ's resurrection, argues to ours.) But because there is no higher science than that contained in holy scripture, it must like metaphysics – the highest natural science – defend its own premises against attack; appealing to whatever part of God's revelation its attacker accepts, or, if he is an unbeliever, solving whatever arguments he brings against the faith. The faith rests on the unfailing truth of God so arguments denying it must contain fallacies which can be refuted. The type of argument most characteristic of this teaching is argument from authority, since it rests on revealed premises and must therefore rely on the authority of those through whom the revelation was made. This does not make it a less worthy science; for although quoting human authority is the weakest type of argument, quoting divine authority is the strongest. There is also a place for the authority of reason: the grace of God does not replace nature but fulfils it, and reason serves faith in the same way that our natural inclination of will serves [the supernatural love called] charity. So God's teaching also quotes philosophers' perceptions of the truth, though only as extrinsic probable authorities. Its intrinsic authorities are the scriptures (as certain authorities) and the teachers of the church (as probable, since our faith rests not on any revelations such teachers may have received, but on the revelation made to the apostles and prophets who wrote the canonical scriptures).

   The scriptures also use symbol and imagery. All our knowledge starts 9 in sense-perception, and it is natural for us to arrive at an understanding of immaterial things by way of things we sense. For this reason the scriptures use imagery to present spiritual truths to people otherwise unable to grasp them. Poets use imagery for the sake of representation itself in which men take a natural delight; this teaching uses it as a necessary means towards something else. But what scripture says symbolically in one place it always explains more expressly in another, and the symbols are drawn from humble things so as not to mislead us into taking their application to God literally. Imagery reveals what God is not rather than what he is, and this fits the way we know God in this life.

10   [One feature of scripture's style is unique.] St Gregory says that *scripture transcends all other sciences by the way it uses one and the same discourse to tell history and reveal mystery.* The author of the scriptures is God, who has power to endow with significance not only words but also things themselves. In every science words have meaning; in this science alone what is meant by the words has further meaning. We call the first meaning of the words the *historical* or *literal* meaning; and the further meaning, based on the literal meaning, we call the *spiritual* meaning. The spiritual meaning can itself be multiple: the Old Testament prefigures the New, and the deeds of Christ and what prefigured them symbolize how we ought to behave today and the eternal glory to come. There can also be more than one literal meaning of a scriptural text: for literal meaning is meaning intended by the author, and the author of scripture is God whose mind grasps all things at once. Every spiritual meaning is founded on a literal meaning, and from that alone should we argue, not from allegory. Moreover, anything necessary for faith contained in a spiritual meaning is conveyed clearly and literally in some other place in scripture. We must not forget that the literal meaning of a parable or figure of speech is not the figure of speech itself but what it is used to say. When scripture talks of God's arm it is not literally attributing a bodily limb to God but that which an arm represents: power to act. With this proviso we can say that the literal meaning of scripture is never in error.

The fundamental aim of God's teaching, then, is to make God known, [vol 2] not only in himself but as the beginning and end of all things and of reasoning creatures especially. So we devote

PART ONE of this book to God,

PART TWO to the journey to God of reasoning creatures,

PART THREE to Christ who, as man, is our road to God.

Part I
GOD

Chapter 1

WHAT GOD IS NOT

To start with we ask whether there is a God, and if so, in what way he exists, or rather in what ways he does not.

Introductory comment. Theology, Thomas has said in the introduction, is like geometrical optics in the way it relies on another science for its explanatory concepts. Theology's explanations, he has said, take on faith God's own idea of himself and the world: God and men as friends, wanting to share eternal life together, mutual objects of each other's happiness. But theology must first identify its subject in terms of man's experience. So the *Summa* starts with man's idea of God: God as the author of nature, God as *providence*, the notion of God implicit in man's religious behaviour toward God.

A quotation from an earlier work shows Thomas's approach:

An awareness of God, though neither clear nor specific, exists in practically everyone. Some people think this is because it is self-evident that God exists, just as other premises of reasoning are self-evident. Others, with more truth, think natural use of reason leads men straightaway to some sort of knowledge of God: for when men observe the sure and ordered course that things pursue by nature, most people see that rule cannot exist without a ruler and that somebody must be producing the order they observe. Such thought, however, is not yet specific enough for men to know whether only one such ruler exists. Compare what happens when we observe the movements and actions of human beings, and see that in men there must exist some cause of such behaviour that doesn't exist in other things; we proceed to call it *soul* though as yet we don't know what it is (whether perhaps it is bodily) or how it operates . . .

Philosophic demonstration adds to this first knowledge of God and betters it, by characterizing him more specifically.

Demonstration shows God to be unchangeable, eternal, not bodily, in no way composite, unique, and so on; and by eliminating attributes from him in this way distinguishes him in our minds from other things. For knowledge can be made more specific by negatives or by affirmatives: we can specify man either as the reasoning animal, or as the one creature who is neither unreasoning nor inanimate. There is however this difference: affirmations tell us both what a thing is and how to distinguish it from others, whereas denials distinguish it from others without telling us what the thing itself is. Demonstration makes knowledge of God more specific in this latter way ... [*Summa Contra Gentes 3 38*]

In the present chapter Thomas expands on this quotation. Asking **Is there a God?** he first rejects any self-evidence of God (*pace* Anselm and his ontological argument): God's effects have to make him evident, producing in us that first vague belief in and worship of a providence that Thomas thinks all men display. That providence is what all men call *God* (p 34, cf ch 11 p 305), but it needs further philosophic reflection to make it more specific. On the general subject of how man first knows things vaguely – *someone approaching* – and only later specifically, see ch 5 p 134. In the case of God the specification is done by eliminations. God is non-composite, though that is not to be construed as imperfection, but as a concentration of all perfections in **God's simple perfection. God exists without limit,** uncontained by either space or time, yet present to all space and all time. Such eliminations set God apart from everything else we know, and ensure that he is unique. Faith tells us that with God's help in the life to come **we can know God but not comprehend him;** but the knowledge of God achieved by unaided human reason in this life only *identifies* him (through the relationship of effect to cause that the world bears him) providing us with no seminal *organizing* idea of what God is. Indeed, that is precisely how he is identified: as the cause of which we can form no idea, not even the idea of what the word *cause* means when said of him; for **we can talk about God but not define him.** We can, so to speak, deduce what must be said of him if language is to be language: God is he who has the doing, nay, he who is the Doing, of the world. But we find ourselves unable to *see* what those words say.

The content of this chapter is discussed in more detail in the editor's preface, pp xxix–xxxviii.

Is there a God?

That there is a God needs proof. St John Damascene says *the* 2 1 *awareness that God exists is implanted by nature in everybody.* But not in any clear or specific way. Man is by nature aware of what by nature he desires: a happiness which he will find only in God. But to be aware of a desired happiness is not, simply speaking, to be aware of God; any more than to be aware of someone approaching is to be aware of Peter, even should it be Peter approaching. Many, in fact, believe the ultimate good which will make us happy to be riches, or pleasure, or some such thing. Nor can we say without qualification that the proposition *God exists* is self-evident: for example, that the word *God* means *that than which nothing greater can be meant*, and since a being would not be as great as could be meant if it did not exist, it follows from the meaning of the word *God* that God exists. In the first place, though a proposition is self-evident when the predicate forms part of what the subject means, if there are people to whom the meanings of subject and predicate are not evident, then the proposition, though self-evident in itself, is not so to those people. Now someone hearing the word *God* may very well not understand it to mean *that than which nothing greater can be meant*; indeed, some people have believed God to be a body. And, in the second place, even if the word *God* were generally recognized to have that meaning, nothing thus defined would thereby be granted existence in the world of fact, but merely as thought about. Unless one is given that something in fact exists than which nothing greater can be thought – and this nobody denying God's existence would grant – the conclusion that God in fact exists does not follow. I do in fact hold that the proposition *God exists* is self-evident in itself: for God, we shall argue, is his own existence. But because this is not evident to us the proposition is not self-evident to us. It needs to be made evident by means of things less evident in themselves but more evident to us, namely, God's effects. In the words of St Paul, *we know the hidden things of God by looking at* 2 *the things that he has made.* Besides demonstrations that argue from cause to effect (following the natural order of things themselves and showing *why* things are as they are), there are demonstrations that argue from visible effects to hidden causes (following the order in which we know things and simply showing *how* things are). For any effect of a cause demonstrates that its cause exists: it could not occur unless its cause first existed. In such proofs the central link is not what the cause is (since we cannot even ask what a thing is until we know that it exists) but what the name of the cause is used to mean; and, as we shall see, what the word *God* means derives from his effects. God's effects then are enough to prove that God exists, even if they are not enough to help us comprehend what he is.

3 **There is a God.**   There are five ways of proving there is a God:

> The first and most obvious way is based on change. We see things changing. Now anything changing is being changed by something else. (For things changing are on the way to realization, whereas things causing change are already realized: they are realizing something else's potential, and for that they must themselves be real. The actual heat of a fire causes wood, already able to be hot, to become actually hot, and so causes change in the wood. Now the actually hot cannot at the same time be potentially hot, but only potentially cold. So what changes cannot as such be causing the change, but must be being changed by something else.) This something else, if itself changing, is being changed by yet another thing; and this last by another. Now we must stop somewhere, otherwise there will be no first cause of the change, and, as a result, no subsequent causes. (Only when acted upon by a first cause do intermediate causes produce a change; if a hand does not move the stick, the stick will not move anything else.) We arrive then at some first cause of change not itself being changed by anything, and this is what everybody understands by *God*.

> The second way is based on the very notion of cause. In the observable world causes derive their causality from other causes; we never observe, nor ever could, something causing itself, for this would mean it preceded itself, and this is not possible. But the deriving of causality must stop somewhere; for in the series of causes an earlier member causes an intermediate and the intermediate a last (whether the intermediate be one or many). Now eliminate a cause and you also eliminate its effects: you cannot have a last cause, nor an intermediate one, unless you have a first. Given no stop in the series of causes, no first cause, there will

be no intermediate causes and no last effect; which contradicts observation. So one is forced to suppose some first cause, to which everyone gives the name *God*.

The third way is based on what need not be and on what must be, and runs as follows. Some of the things we come across can be but need not be, for we find them springing up and dying away, thus sometimes in being and sometimes not. Now everything cannot be like this, for a thing that need not be, once was not; and if everything need not be, once upon a time there was nothing. But if that were true there would be nothing even now, because something that does not exist can only be brought into being by something already existing. If nothing was in being nothing could be brought into being, and nothing would be in being now, which contradicts observation. Not everything therefore is the sort of thing that need not be; some things must be, and these may or may not owe this necessity to something else. But just as a series of causes must have a stop, so also a series of things which must be and owe this to other things. One is forced to suppose something which must be, and owes this to nothing outside itself; indeed it itself is the cause that other things must be.

The fourth way is based on the gradation observed in things. Some things are better, truer, more excellent than others. Such comparative terms describe varying degrees of approximation to a superlative; for example, things are hotter and hotter the nearer they approach what is hottest. Something therefore is the truest and best and most excellent of things, and hence the most fully in being; for Aristotle says that the truest things are the things most fully in being. Now *when many things possess some property in common, the one most fully possessing it causes it in the others: fire*, as Aristotle says, *the hottest of all things, causes all other things to be hot*. Something therefore causes in all other things their being, their goodness, and whatever other perfection they have. And this is what we call *God*.

The fifth way is based on the guidedness of nature. Goal-directed behaviour is observed in all bodies obeying natural laws, even when they lack awareness. Their behaviour hardly ever varies and practically always turns out well, showing that they truly tend to goals and do not merely hit them by accident. But nothing lacking awareness can tend to a goal except it be directed by someone with awareness and understanding; the arrow, for example, requires an archer. Everything in nature, therefore, is directed to its goal by someone with understanding, and this we call *God*.

God's simple perfection

3 1 **God is not, like creatures, made up of parts.**   God is spirit, without bodily dimensions. Firstly, no body can cause change without itself being changed. Secondly, things with dimensions are potential of division. But the starting-point for all existence must be wholly real and not potential in any way: though things that get realized begin as potential, preceding them is the source of their realization which must be already real. Thirdly, living bodies are superior to other bodies; and what makes a body living is not the dimensions which make it a body (for then everything with dimensions would be living), but something more excellent like a soul. The most excellent existent of all then cannot be a body. So when the scriptures ascribe dimensions to God they are using spatial extension to symbolize the extent of God's power; just as they ascribe bodily organs to God as metaphors for their functions, and postures like sitting or standing to symbolize authority or strength.

2   God is not matter under a certain form. Firstly, matter is defined by its potentiality to take on forms, while God is wholly realized. Secondly, the primordial source of perfection must be perfect of himself and no mere receiver of perfection; but when matter takes on form it receives its goodness and perfection from that form. Thirdly, things are active in virtue of their form. Since God's activity is underived, he must be essentially form and not part form part matter. Of itself, any form material things assume can be common to many such things; the individualness of the things derives from their matter, which as ultimate assumer of forms cannot be assumed by anything else. But forms not of the sort material things assume must themselves subsist as things, and since they cannot be assumed by anything further are individual of

3 themselves. God is such a form and has no need of matter. Things part matter and part form cannot be identified with their own natures or essences. Essence or nature includes only what defines the species of a thing: *human nature* means what defines man, what makes man man, and that does not include *this* flesh and *these* bones or *this* colour or anything peculiar to *this* man. So a man includes more than his human nature, which is conceived of as his formative part making a man of the

matter that makes him individual. In contrast, the individuality of things not composed of matter and form does not derive from this or that individual matter: the forms of such things are intrinsically individual and stand on their own as things. Such things are identical with their own natures. So God is identical with his godhead and his life and whatever else belongs to his nature. Notice however that we talk about simple things on the model of the composite things from which our knowledge derives. To refer to God as subsistent we use concrete nouns, since the subsistent things with which we are familiar are composite; to express God's simpleness we use abstract nouns. So when we talk of the godhead of God, the diversity implied is to be attributed not to God himself but to our way of conceiving him.

God is not only his own godhead; he is also his own existence. Firstly, 4 properties that do not define a thing derive either from what does define it (when common to a species, like humour in men), or from an outside cause (like heat in water). But existence, if it does not define a thing, cannot derive from what does define it, for that would mean the thing depended on itself for existence. So unless existence defines God he must receive it from outside. Secondly, unless existence defines God he will have a potentially existent nature: for it is existence that realizes forms and natures. (We use the verb *is* to signify both the act of existing, and the mental uniting of predicate to subject which constitutes a proposition. In the first sense we cannot know the existence of God any more than we can define him; but we can say there is a God, framing a proposition about God which we can know to be true by argument from his effects.) God cannot be classified as this or that sort of thing. Firstly, 5 we classify by differentiating some generic notion into species, each species being based on a different way of realizing the potentiality on which the generic notion is based; but no realizing of potentialities occurs in God. Secondly, it is God's nature to exist, so the only genus to which God could belong would be the genus of existent and that is no genus at all; genera are differentiated by factors not already contained within those genera, but no factor could differentiate unless it already existed. Thirdly, things sharing a generic nature differ in existence: horses from men, this man from that man; so that the nature and existence of anything in a genus differ. In particular, God is not a substance; for existing independently does not define a substance (existing determines no genus at all), but being a sort of thing that can exist independently, and God is not a sort of thing. Finally, God has no 6 properties other than his nature. Firstly, because such properties realize potentialities of their possessor. Secondly, because as Boethius says, *though an existent may have other properties as well, existence is simply existence.* Thirdly, properties are always derived, either from outside or from what one is oneself.

7   God then is altogether simple: there is in him no distinction of spatial parts, of form and matter, of nature and individuality, of nature and existence, of genus and difference, of subject and properties. For everything composite is secondary, caused, a realized potentiality. Moreover, no composite and its components can share every predicate in common: no part of a foot is a foot, and though every drop of water is water, the drops are of less volume than the whole. Now things possessing forms may contain elements of otherness, but not forms themselves: white things can have non-white elements, but whiteness can't. God however is form itself, indeed existence itself. Whatever derives from God resembles him, but in the way that an effect resembles its primary cause; and effects are of their nature composite, not being their own existence. In our world perfection is built up of many elements; but divine

8   perfection is simple and single as we shall see. God does not enter into the composition of other things: he is not the soul of the world , nor the form of all things, nor – as David of Dinant most stupidly believed – the ultimate unformed matter of things. Firstly, the cause of a thing cannot also be its form or matter. Secondly, components derive their activity from the composite (hands do not act, but men by using their hands). Thirdly, matter is primary only in the sense in which potentiality precedes realization; and the forms matter takes on are secondary to forms that stand by themselves.

4 1 **Nevertheless God's perfection is all-embracing.**   [In the material world lack of parts implies imperfection and incompleteness:] simply to exist seems the lowest common denominator of all perfections. Yet in fact to exist is the perfection of perfections; everything else is potential when compared to existence, nothing is actual except by existing, and the act of existing is the ultimate actualization of everything, even of forms. Everything else acquires existence, and existence acquires nothing: we talk of *the existence of men* and think of men acquiring existence like a further form, not of existents acquiring humanity. Now God is not the primordial potentiality of things but their active origin, and as such realized and actual. Indeed, as the origin of all activity God is supremely actual, and thus supremely perfect, since perfect means achieved, realized, lacking nothing one's particular mode of perfection

2 requires. Moreover, his perfection is all-embracing: the diverse (and sometimes opposed) perfections of creatures all pre-exist united in God,

without detriment to his simpleness; just as *the divers energies of the things we sense are primordially present in the sun without diversity.* For the perfections of effects pre-exist in their causes, though not always in exactly the same form. In the potentialities of the matter from which they come, effects pre-exist in a less perfectly realized way; in the power of their active causes they pre-exist in a more realized way. In God then, the first active cause of everything, all perfections must pre-exist in the most realized way. Moreover, God is self-subsistent existence and must therefore contain the full perfection of existence. (Because heat is something that hot things only have a part in, they fall short of perfect hotness; if heat could subsist on its own nothing would limit its hotness.) Now all perfections are modes of the one perfection of existing (it is by existing in a certain way that a thing is in its way perfect). So God can lack no perfection that things possess. Not everything that exists need be living or wise (for nothing that has only a part in existence need share every mode of existence); but God's existence is also life and wisdom (for when existence subsists on its own it cannot lack any perfection of existence).

There are as many ways of things resembling one another as there 3 are ways of sharing a form. To be perfectly alike things must share the same species of form to the same degree (like two equally white things); less perfectly alike are things which share the same species of form to different degrees. But things may also be alike by sharing a form not of the same species. For what a thing does reflects what its active self is; and since a thing is active in virtue of its form its effects must bear some likeness to that form. When men reproduce themselves, agent and effect are of one species and their likeness is a specific likeness. But when the agent is outside the species, there is likeness of form but not specific likeness: the things the sun produces bear a certain likeness to the sun [being sources of energy] but they are not of the same species. If the agent were outside even genus, its effects would bear an even remoter resemblance to the agent, presenting only the sort of analogy that holds between all things that have existence in common. And this is how everything that receives existence from God resembles him; precisely as existing it resembles the primary universal source of all existence. Creatures are compared to God not as to a thing of some different genus, but as to something outside of and prior to all genera. They bear God the analogy that God exists by nature and they partake existence. But we would not say that God resembles creatures. *Mutual likeness obtains between things of the same order but not between cause and effect,* as pseudo-

Denys says: a portrait can take after a man but a man does not take after his portrait.

5 1 **What is goodness?** To be good is to be of value, where value is consequent on perfection (since we value what makes for perfection), and perfection is a degree of achieved actuality. Obviously then, being good is really the same thing as existing, since that is how things achieve actuality, but the word *good* expresses the notion of value left unexpressed by the word *existing*. So the words *good* and *existing* are not simply interchangeable. To say a thing exists without further qualification is to call it a substance, pointing out its initial distinctness from mere potentiality. As possessed of further actualization, it can be said to exist in this or that respect: to be white, for example. Being white is not what first removes the thing from mere potentiality; to be white a thing must already exist. *Good* on the other hand expresses the notion of value and perfection, and thus the notion of completeness. To be called *good* without qualification a thing must be completely perfect; when its perfection is not as complete as it should be (even though it has some perfection just by existing) we don't call it *good* without qualification but *good* only in respect of that perfection. To exist without qualification is to achieve an initial actuality, to be good without qualification is to achieve complete actuality. Still, initial existence is a
2 *sort* of goodness, and complete goodness a *sort* of existence. The idea expressed by a word is something conceived in the mind from things and expressed in speech. An idea is more fundamental when it is met with earlier in this process of conception. The first idea met with in mental conception is that of an existent (to be known, Aristotle says, a thing must actually be); which is why the mind's primary and distinctive object is what exists, just as what makes a sound is the primary object of hearing. Existing therefore is a more fundamental idea than being good. But being good, conveying as it does the notion of value, implies being an end or goal, and this is the starting-point of causal action, the cause of causality itself; for no agent acts except for some goal, and no matter would acquire form unless an agent acted on it. So, as causative of action, the goodness of things precedes their existence as goal precedes form. Not only is good, as goal, rested in by what has achieved it, but moved towards by what is still only potential. Existence, in contrast, involves no causal relation at all unless it be that of form, a causality found only in things which have achieved actuality.
3   Inasmuch as they exist, all things are good. Being a substance, or being of such a size or sort, or being anything less general than this,

narrows the idea of existing by mentioning what kind of thing exists. Being good does not narrow existing in this way, but merely expresses a notion of value and perfection associated with the very existence of things whatever kind they be. If mathematical objects existed as such, the existence they had would be good. But they have separate existence only in the mind, which abstracts them from matter and change, and thus from the notion of ends or goals motivating change. Note that it is admissible to conceive something as existing without conceiving it as good, since existing is a more fundamental concept than goodness. In causal action everything starts with the good end which motivates the agent to act, and so to elicit the final form of the effect. In the caused thing we find the opposite order: first, the form itself brings with it existence; next, there is the operative power which brings perfection of existence (for a thing is perfect, Aristotle says, when it can reproduce itself); so that finally, the thing realizes the notion of goodness. It is usual to distinguish three different meanings of good: the *useful*, the *worthy* and the *delightful*. For whatever is of value, and can satisfy desire, is good. That which satisfies as a stage on the way to something else we call *useful*; that which satisfies of itself we call *worthy*, and the satisfaction found in it *delight*. So the primary sense of good is *worthy*, the second *delightful* and the third *useful*.   4   6

God's goodness.   An effect's perfection and form consists in resembling its cause, since what a thing does reflects what it is. So the cause itself is of value and desirable and can be called *good*, what is valued being a share in resembling it. Clearly then, since God is the primary operative cause of everything, goodness and value fittingly belong to him. Of the things that value or desire God, some know him in himself (the privilege of reasoning creatures), others know his goodness as participated somewhere or other (and this is possible even to sense-perception), whilst yet other things lack all knowledge but desire by nature, directed to their goal by some higher being with knowledge. There is a threefold perfection in things: firstly, they are established in existence; secondly, they possess in addition certain properties necessary to perfect their activity; and a third perfection comes when they attain some extrinsic goal. Now this threefold perfection belongs by nature to no caused thing, but only to God, who alone exists by nature, has no added properties (power, wisdom and the like which are additional to other things belonging to him by nature), and is not disposed towards an extrinsic goal but is himself the ultimate goal of all other things. Clearly then only God is perfect and good by nature. The goodness of   6 1   2   3

created things is something added to their nature: either their existence,
4 or some added perfection, or some relatedness to a goal. There is nothing
to stop us naming a thing after something else if the name is a relative
term; as when we name something by the place it is in, or by some
external measure. But opinions have differed concerning non-relative
terms: Plato, for example, believed that the forms of things exist
separately and individual things are named after these separate forms
which they participate in some way. He believed in separate Ideas of
man and horse called Man-as-such and Horse-as-such; and in separate
Ideas of being and unity called Being-as-such and Unity-as-such, by
participating which everything was said to be and to be one. The existent
Good-as-such and Unity-as-such he believed to be the supreme God,
by reference to whom all other things were said to be good by participation. Now although, as Aristotle repeatedly proves, the part of this
opinion which postulates separate, self-subsistent Ideas of natural things
is absurd, nonetheless that there exists some first thing called God who
is good by nature is absolutely true. And because of this we can talk of
all things as being good by divine goodness: the pattern, source and goal
of all goodness. Nevertheless the resemblance to divine goodness which
leads us to call a thing good is something present in the thing itself,
belonging to it as a form and thus naming it. And so there is one
goodness in all things and yet many.

God exists without limit

7 1 **God is not limited in any way.** In one sense form limits matter:
matter before taking on a form is potential of many forms, but afterwards
is determined to the form it assumed. In another sense matter limits
form: a form as such can be common to many things but as acquired
by matter is determinately this thing's form. Now form in limiting
matter perfects it, so matter's lack of limit is an imperfection; whereas
matter does not perfect form but rather restricts its scope, so form's lack
of limit is a perfection. This notion of form is most fully realized in
existence itself, and in God existence is not acquired but is itself
subsistent. God then is unlimited and perfect. Spatial boundaries are
spatial forms, so to speak. So lack of spatial limits is limitlessness of a
material kind and not to be ascribed to God.
2   Nothing else is altogether unlimited; though matter, when determined
by the form of some substance (wood, for example) and limited simply
speaking, is still potential of many accidental forms (shapes, for example)

and in that respect unlimited. And created forms that are not forms of matter but subsist of themselves (which some people believe angels to be) are unlimited inasmuch as they are not contained in and restricted by matter. But since they acquire their existence and are not to be identified with it, their existence must be contained in and restricted by some specifying nature, and so is not altogether unlimited. In fact, God himself, although of unlimited power, can no more make an absolutely unlimited thing than he can make an unmade thing. For to make something the nature of which is simply to exist is a contradiction in terms, since subsistent existence is uncreated existence. The power of understanding is in a sense unlimited because it is not a form of matter. Angels, for example, contain no matter; and in man, the power of understanding belongs to the organizing form of the body but is not itself attributable to any organ of that body.

Two kinds of limitlessness are actually impossible: infinite size and 3 infinite number. Even the spatial objects of mathematics cannot be imagined actually to exist except under some form, for actuality requires form. For spatial objects this form is shape, and since shape must have boundaries, such objects will be limited in size. And in fact geometers do not postulate infinite lines but lines which are potentially as long as required and which they then call infinite. Space divides without limit, for this is a material lack of limit: division proceeds from whole to parts in the direction of matter; but multiplication in size proceeds in the direction of completion and form and so cannot proceed without limit. Changes and time are never actual all at once but part after part, the whole never being wholly actual. But spatial wholes are actual all at once. So material, extensive limitlessness is compatible with temporal wholes but not with spatial wholes: changes and time can be endless but not bodily space. As to unlimited number: certain Arab philosophers 4 held that an unlimited number of things can never be essential to anything, for since there is no traversing the infinite whatever needed it would never come about. They thought however that an unlimited number of things could happen by chance. But this is impossible. Any actual set of objects must be a specific set, and sets are specified by the number of objects they contain. No number however is infinite since numbers are counts built up one at a time; so no set of objects can even happen to be infinite. Number can only be potentially infinite: the more one divides something the greater the number of parts, and just as there is no potential limit to division of a continuum, so there is no potential limit to the growth of number. But potential infinities are actualized not all at once but bit by bit, first some specified number, then more, and so on endlessly. Each specific number can co-exist with more; but no number can co-exist with total lack of limits.

8 1 **So God is present everywhere in everything.** God is present everywhere in everything: not indeed as part of their substance, but in the way agents are present to and in causal contact with what they act upon. Since existence itself is what God is by nature, he it must be who causes existence in creatures. During the whole period of a creature's existence, then, God must be present to it in the way its own existence is. Now existence is more intimately and profoundly interior to things than anything else: everything else is potential compared to existence. So God must exist and exist intimately within everything. However powerful an agent is its action only reaches distant things through intermediaries. The omnipotence of God then is shown not by his distance from things but by the way he acts on them without intermediary, for nothing is distant from God in the sense of not having him within itself. Though the unlikeness of things to God in nature or grace can be called distance.

2   Place itself is a sort of thing, so there are two senses in which God is everywhere in every place. First as making all places what they are (the way he is in anything), and secondly as *filling* every place, not as bodies do by excluding some other body but by giving existence to whatever occupies the place. And wherever God exists he exists wholly. Whole is relative to parts: either components of nature like form and matter and genus and species, or spatial components. Whatever is wholly in a place spatially cannot be outside the place, since its extent is measured by the extent of the place. But a thing's nature is not measured by its place, so that something can by nature be wholly in more than one place: the nature of whiteness is wholly present in every point of a white surface, though its extent is not. Immaterial things have only wholeness of nature; and just as the soul is wholly present throughout the body so

3 God is wholly present everywhere within every thing. Besides existing by his own activity in his effects, God can also exist in minds as the object of their mental activity, as what is known exists in the knower and what is desired in the desirer. In this way God exists in those actually knowing and loving him, or disposed to do so; and since this is God's gracious gift to reasoning creatures we call it existing by *grace* in his chosen friends. The way he exists in everything we call existing in things by *substance, presence* and *power*. A king, for example, exists by power everywhere in his kingdom, by presence everywhere in his field of vision, and by substance wherever he is sitting. But God is by power everywhere, and by presence everywhere (seeing everything), and by

substance everywhere (causing everything's existence). Another unique way in which God exists in a man by being one person with him we will study later.

Only God is everywhere wholly and by nature. To exist everywhere 4 belongs to the universe but with a different part in each place, not wholly. And if all that existed in the whole universe was a single grain of wheat, that grain of wheat would exist everywhere; but only under those circumstances, and not by nature.

God does not alter and is not in time. God, we have said, is 9 1 entirely actual, without any unrealized potentiality; but things only alter if they are somehow potential. God is also entirely without parts; but things only alter if part of them persists and part of them passes away. God is also infinitely perfect embracing within himself the fullness of perfection of all existence; but things only alter by acquiring something they do not already have. God understands and loves himself, and the Platonists would call that movement in God; but we are talking only of movements which alter things from potentiality to realization. Only God 2 is changeless. Every creature alters due both to its own potentiality and another's power. Just as before creatures existed their existence was possible, not because of some created potentiality but simply because of God's power, so, now that they do exist, it is in the creator's power for them not to. So all creatures can be changed by another's power, namely God's. And all in their own ways are also changeable by their own potentiality.

Boethius defined eternity as *the instantaneously whole and complete* 10 1 *possession of endless life.* We derive this idea of eternity by contrasting it with time, which, as Aristotle says, *measures before and after in changes.* An unchanging thing displays no *before and after*, nor does it begin or end. So we call it eternal: meaning that it itself is endless, without beginning or end, and that the eternity which measures it has no before and after but is instantaneously whole. Time is successively actualized, in a present instant which is never complete. So to deny that eternity is time Boethius called it *instantaneously whole*; and then to deny temporal instantaneity he called it *complete.* Just as the notion of time starts from 2 the notion of the present moment as passing, so the notion of eternity starts from the idea of an instant that abides. Eternity principally characterizes God who is utterly unchangeable. Indeed, because he is his own unvarying existence, God and eternity are the same thing. So God is not really measured by eternity; this notion of measurement is only our way of conceiving the matter. Verbs of different tenses are

applied to God not because he varies from past to present to future, but
3 to show that his eternity encompasses every phase of time. Truths exist
in the mind; so necessary truths are eternal only because they exist in
the eternal mind; nothing besides God is eternal.

4   Time differs from eternity not primarily because it begins and ends
(for conceivably the heavens might go round and round for ever), but
because it measures changes whereas eternity is an instantaneous whole
measuring abiding existence. Though what time measures must perhaps
begin and end: even if the heavens revolved for ever, what time would
measure is not the whole duration (since the infinite is unmeasurable),
but each revolution separately from beginning to end. We could also
say that time is potentially divisible into parts that begin and end: days
and years, whereas eternity is not. The present moment persistently
underlies time, altering state continuously; it corresponds to the thing
whose change is being measured, which remains the same in substance
throughout time altering only its position, first here and then there.
Time corresponds to the change, and consists in the passing of the
present moment as it alters state. Eternity however remains unchanged
both in substance and in state, and thus differs from the present of time.

6   Some say there is only one time for all temporal things just as there
is only one number series for all objects we number. But this is not an
adequate explanation: time is not measure abstracted from what it
measures, but a measure in measured change itself; if it were not it
would lack continuity, for the continuity of ten yards of cloth derives
not from the numbering but from the cloth. Others say time is one
because eternity, the source of time, is one; or because matter, the
fundamental subject of change, is one; but neither derivation is adequate,
for things that are one only in source or subject (especially in a remote
source or subject) are not one simply speaking. The true reason there is
only one time is that there exists one simple fundamental process in the
world measuring all other changes. Time not only measures this process
but is also its property; so time is one because this process is one. Other
processes are merely measured by time, so that time is not diversified
by their diversity. For this process to measure others it does not have
to cause them but only to be simpler than them.

11 1 **There is only one God.**   Whatever exists is *ipso facto* individual; to
be one it needs no extra property and calling it one merely denies that
it is divided. Simple things are neither divided nor divisible; composite
things do not exist when their parts are divided. So existence stands or
falls with individuality, and things guard their unity as they do their

existence. But what is simply speaking one can yet in certain respects be many: an individual thing, essentially undivided, can have many non-essential properties; and a single whole, actually undivided, can have potentially many parts.

Only when one is used to count with does it presuppose in what it counts some extra property over and above existence, namely quantity. The one we count with contrasts with the many it counts in the way a 2 unit of measurement contrasts with what it measures; but the individual unity common to everything that exists contrasts with plurality simply by lacking it, as undividedness does division. A plurality is however *a* plurality: though simply speaking many, inasmuch as it exists, it is, incidentally, one. A continuum is homogeneous: its parts share the form of the whole (every bit of water is water); but a plurality is heterogeneous: its parts lack the form of the whole (no part of a house is a house). The parts of a plurality are unities and non-plural, though they compose the plurality not as non-plural but as existing; just as the parts of a house compose the house as material, not as not houses. Whereas we define plurality in terms of unity (many things are divided things to each of which is ascribed unity), we define unity in terms of division. For division precedes unity in our minds even if it doesn't really do so, since we conceive simple things by denying compositeness of them, defining a point, for example, as lacking dimension. Division arises in the mind simply by negating existence. So the first thing we conceive is the existent, then – seeing that this existent is not that existent – we conceive division, thirdly unity, and fourthly plurality.

There is only one God. Firstly, God and his nature are identical: to 3 be God is to be this individual God. In the same way, if to be a man was to be Socrates there would only be one man, just as there was only one Socrates. Moreover, God's perfection is unlimited, so what could differentiate one God from another? Any extra perfection in one would be lacking in the other and that would make him imperfect. And finally, the world is one, and plurality can only produce unity incidentally insofar as it too is somehow one: the primary and non-incidental source of unity in the universe must himself be one. The one we count with measures only material things, not God: like all objects of mathematics, though defined without reference to matter, it can exist only in matter. But the unity of individuality common to everything that exists is a metaphysical property applying both to non-material things and to God. But what in God is a perfection has to be conceived by us, with our way of understanding things, as a lack: that is why we talk of God as lacking a body, lacking limits and lacking division.

We can know God but not comprehend him

[vol 3] 12 1 God is wholly actual; he contains no unrealized potential. So nothing in him poses an obstacle to knowledge. Nevertheless what is in itself knowable may be beyond the understanding of some particular mind, just as the sun is too bright for the eye of a bat; and for this reason some people think created minds can never see God as he really is. This is a mistake. Man's ultimate happiness consists in his highest activity, exercising his mind, and if created minds can't see God then either men will never be happy or their happiness must lie elsewhere than in God. That is not only opposed to our faith but makes no natural sense. It is human nature to wonder at things and seek out their causes, and this natural tendency of reason would remain unfulfilled if we couldn't know the first cause of everything. To know God is not disproportionate to created minds. Though proportion sometimes implies quantitative relationship like double or equals, it can mean any kind of relationship; and in this sense creatures are proportioned to God as effects to their cause and as partial realizations to what is fully actual.

2 **Knowing God in the life to come.**   So how can we see God? First we will need a power of sight, and then the object will have to come into actual sight in some way. Physical things like stones come into sight when a likeness of them (not, of course, their physical substance) enters the eye. Now God is both source of our ability to understand, and also a possible object of that understanding. Since our ability to understand is not God, but created, it must be a shared likeness of his primordial intelligence, a sort of intellectual light deriving from his primordial light. Thus to be able to see God we need to have in ourselves a sort of likeness of him, namely, our power of sight. But no sort of likeness can bring God into actual sight as an object. God's essence is to exist, and since no created form is like that, none can represent him to our minds. Moreover, God transcends definition by realizing in himself to the fullest degree every perfection created minds can express or understand, and no created form could represent that to our minds since they are all determinately this or that perfection. To say that God was actually seen by way of a likeness would be to say that God's substance itself was not seen. God's substance is existence itself. Other intelligible forms of things, which are not their own existence, exist in mind by a sort of mental existence which forms the mind and brings it to actual understanding of those things. But God is in a created mind by his own

substance itself already actually understood, and making our minds actually understand.

Our senses cannot perceive God, for what we sense by bodily organs 3 must also be bodily. God has no body and cannot be sensed or imagined, but only understood. Augustine thought it *probable that when the eyes of the blessed see the new heaven and the new earth, they will see God present everywhere governing things, as we now see the life of the living breathing people around us; for that they are alive is not something we believe, but something we see as soon as we look at them.* But even so, our bodily eyes do not perceive those people's life directly: rather, as soon as our senses perceive the people, some other cognitive power accompanying our senses perceives their life.

To be known a thing must be present in the knower, so how it is 4 known depends on how it can be present, given the ways in which knower and known exist. Bodies, for example, exist individually instantiated in this or that matter; self-subsistent forms like angels exist outside matter with a received existence differing from what they are; only God is his own existence. The human soul exists as a form matter takes on, and so what it knows most naturally are individual bodies. We sense them with our bodily organs in their individuality; and then our understanding, which is not the activity of any bodily organ, takes the natures that exist individually instantiated and considers them *universally* in abstraction from individual matter: something sensation is unable to do. What angels know most naturally are immaterial forms, but these are beyond the reach of our natural understanding in this life when soul and body are united. To know self-subsistent existence is natural only to God and beyond the natural power of any created mind; for no creature can be its own existence. So unless God himself, by his grace, enters a created mind and makes himself intelligible to it, no such mind can ever see God. Eyesight is an entirely bodily ability that can't be raised to an immaterial level; our eyes see only this or that instantiation of a nature without abstracting it. But the mind already transcends the material to some extent by nature, abstracting from concrete individuals and mentally separating out a form from the particular matter that took it on. So the mind can be raised even higher by God's grace to know substances that actually subsist independently of matter, and independently subsisting existence.

When created minds do see God's substance, the very substance of 5 God himself forms their understanding; but then something more than their nature is needed to predispose them to such sublimity: what we call a *light of glory. The brightness of God will illuminate her*, namely, the community of those who see God. This supernatural light likens us to God: *when he shall appear we shall be like him and shall see him just as he is.* The function of this created light is not to make God's substance understandable (that it is of itself), but to strengthen our understanding in the way skills and other dispositions strengthen our ability to do things. It is not a medium through which God is seen, but something enabling us to see him immediately. It is created but not natural, for it could only be natural to a creature that was by nature divine, and that

6   is self-contradictory. This light makes the creature *like God*. The more such light there is in the mind, the more perfectly the mind sees God. And those who have the greater love have the more light. Greater love causes greater desire, and desire is itself in some way a predisposition making man fit to receive what he desires. So those who love more will see God more perfectly and be more blessed.

7   Created minds, however, will always find God incomprehensible. Comprehension is perfect understanding, understanding something to the fullest extent that it is capable of being understood. God's existence is without limits and allows of limitless understanding, and since no created light of glory can be infinite, no created mind whatever can understand God limitlessly. It is not that some part of God remains unseen (God has no parts), but that created minds cannot see him with the perfection God's nature allows. When someone believes a proposition he cannot prove, he may understand every part of it – subject and predicate and that a connection is being made between them – but the whole is still not understood as well as it might have been.

8   Causes contain their effects implicitly, so that in seeing God everything else can be seen as effects precontained in their cause. But only men of sharp intelligence straightaway see all the implications of premises; duller minds must have each conclusion spelled out. No created mind can comprehend God and what his power implies; so by seeing God we do not see everything he does or can do. Our natural desire to know everything that can perfect our understanding (the natures of all things and the laws that govern their behaviour) will be satisfied when we see God. But to know every single thought and deed of every particular individual adds no perfection to our minds; we have no natural desire to know that, nor the things God might bring about but doesn't. God is the fount and source of all being and all truth, and just to see him so satisfies our natural desire for knowledge that we require nothing more

10 for happiness. We can't understand more than one thing at a time, because we understand by way of mental representations, and a single mind can no more be formed by many representations at once than a

single body can have many shapes. We can think many things at once only if we think them through one representation. Thus parts of a whole, if they each have their own representation, must be thought one after another; but if all are represented in the one representation of the whole they can be thought together. So the things we see when seeing God are not seen one after the other through many representations, but all at once in the one substance of God.

Knowing God in this life.   In this life our souls exist in their bodies, 11 so what we naturally know are bodies and anything that can be known by way of bodies. In this life we cannot know God in himself. But even in this life we see and judge everything in God, if that means by way of God's light; for even the natural light of reason is a share in God's light. In the same way we see and judge all visible things in the light of the sun, but without seeing the sun's substance itself. Our natural knowledge 12 starts from sense-perception and reaches only as far as things so perceived can lead us, which is not far enough to see God in himself. For the things we sense, though effects of God, are not effects fully expressing his power. But because they do depend on him as their cause, they can lead us to know that he exists, and reveal to us whatever is true of him as first cause of all such things, surpassingly different from all of them. By 13 God's grace we can know him better than by natural reason alone, which depends on images drawn from the world of the senses and on the natural light of our intelligence abstracting understandable concepts from these images. God's gracious revelation helps in both respects: the light of grace strengthens our natural light of intelligence, and on occasion God also forms interior images for prophets to see, and external sounds and bodily creatures as at Christ's baptism, all more expressive of divine things than anything we can perceive naturally. So although in this life revelation cannot show us what God is in himself, but joins us to him as unknown, nevertheless it helps us know him better, showing us more and greater works of his, and teaching things like his being three persons, which natural reason could never have known. Faith then gives us a sort of knowledge, for when we believe, our minds assent to something knowable; but not to something *we* see but to something he whom we believe sees. Faith falls short of understanding, for a mind that understands assents to what it itself sees in the light of the first premises of understanding.

We can talk about God but not define him

13 1 Aristotle says *words express thoughts and thoughts represent things*. So words refer mediately to things by way of our conceptions: we talk about things in the way we know them. Now in this life we know God only through creatures: as their non-creaturely transcendent cause. So our words for God do not express him as he is in himself. (In this they differ from words like *man* which express what a man is in himself; for we define the meaning of *man* by declaring what makes man man.) Our words for God then, express him in ways more appropriate to the material creatures we naturally know. In such creatures a subsistent whole comes to exist when matter takes on a certain form. The form is not itself subsistent, but determines the way the composite whole subsists. To express the subsistent composites we use concrete terms, but to express what determines the ways in which they subsist we use abstract terms: whiteness, for example, names what makes things white. Now God is both non-composite *and* subsistent: so we must use abstract terms to express his lack of composition [*He is goodness itself*] and concrete terms to express his subsistence and wholeness [*He is a good God*]. Neither way of talking fully measures up to his way of existing; but in this life we do not know him as he is in himself. In the same way, we use tensed verbs and participles to talk of God's eternity (which includes all time); for we can understand and express the simpleness of eternity only in terms of time's multiplicity [*He is, he was, and he always will be*].

2 **Can words express what God is?** Do our words say anything of what God is? Negative and relative terms clearly do not; they say what God is not, and how he relates to other things (or better, how other things relate to him). Opinions have differed about non-relative and affirmative terms like *good* and *wise* and the like. Moses Maimonides said these were negations masquerading as affirmations, and others said they were disguised predications of a causal relation to creatures: *God is good* meant *God causes goodness in creatures*. Neither view is acceptable. In the first place, neither view explains why certain words are not used of God: we don't say *God is a body* even though he causes bodies, and though it might be a way of denying that he is merely unformed matter. Secondly, on these views *goodness* would apply first and foremost to creatures and only secondarily to God. And thirdly, people who speak of a living God want to say more than that he causes life and differs from non-living bodies.

In our view then such words do say something of what God is, though inadequately, because we can only talk of God as we know him, and we know him only through creatures, which represent him inadequately. All creatures resemble and represent God, for all creaturely perfections pre-exist in God in one all-embracing perfection; but they resemble him not as things of one kind resemble each other, but as effects partially resemble a cause of a higher kind yet fall short of reproducing its form (as earthly sources of energy, for example, resemble the sun). So *God is good* means neither *God causes goodness* nor *God is not bad* but *What in creatures we call goodness pre-exists in a higher way in God.* God is not good because he causes goodness; rather because he is good goodness flows out into things. As Augustine says, *because* he *is good,* we *exist.*

So in using such words of God we must distinguish what they 3 express – goodness, life and the like – from their manner of expressing it. What they express belongs properly, and indeed primarily, to God and only secondarily to creatures. But their manner of expressing it is appropriate only to creatures and inappropriate to God. When a creaturely mode of existence is included in what the word means, as materiality is included in the meaning of *rock*, the word can apply to God only metaphorically, but when the mode is not included in what a word means but affects only its manner of meaning it (as with words like *existent* and *good* and *living*), then the word can apply to God literally.

[God is one in all respects; nevertheless we say many different things 4 about him.] That causes no difficulty where negations and relations are concerned: these differ according to the things we want to deny of him or relate to him. But how do non-relative affirmations – all of which say something (if imperfectly) of what God is – differ in meaning? Words mean what we conceive the things they signify to be. Now we know God only by way of creatures, through concepts corresponding to the many and various creaturely perfections that pre-exist unified in him. So the words we use of God all express (imperfectly) one and the same thing in God, but do so by way of many different conceptions in us, and so are not synonymous. Words that express the same thing under different aspects have different meanings simply speaking, since words can express things only as we conceive them. This is why such words 5 are not used univocally, [i.e. in exactly the same sense,] of God and of creatures. *Wise* used of a man expresses his wisdom as distinct from his substance, powers, existence and so on; the word, so to speak, delimits that perfection. But when we use it of God we don't want to express anything distinct from his substance, powers and existence: what that word expresses in God must not be confined by that expression of it but must surpass it. Now such words are not pure equivocation either, for then all talk about God would be invalidated by logical fallacy. Such words apply to God and creatures neither univocally nor equivocally but by what I call analogy (or proportion). This is the way a word like *healthy* applies to organisms (in a primary sense) and to diets (as causing health) or complexions (as displaying it). Whatever we say of God and of creatures we say in virtue of the relation creatures bear to God as to the source and cause in which all their creaturely perfections pre-exist in a more excellent way. In language, the equivocal presupposes the univocal. But in causation the univocal presupposes the non-univocal. Non-univocal causes cause entire species, in the way the sun helps generate the whole human race. Univocal causes cause individuals of the species [in the way men reproduce men]. Causes of individuals presuppose causes of the species, which are not univocal yet not wholly equivocal either, since they are expressing themselves in their effects. We could call them analogical. In language too all univocal terms presuppose the non-univocal analogical use of the term *being*.

6   When words are used analogically, one use is primary and helps define the others. It is because organisms can be called healthy in the first place that the word can be used secondarily of diets and complexions with reference to that first use. Words used metaphorically of God apply primarily to creatures and only secondarily to God, and this would be the case with non-metaphorical words too if they simply expressed God's causality. But, as we have seen, calling God good or wise doesn't simply mean that he causes wisdom or goodness in creatures, but that he himself possesses these perfections in a more excellent way. As expressing these perfections the words apply first to God and then to creatures (since the perfections derive from God); but because we know creatures first, our words were first devised to describe creatures and so have a manner of expression appropriate only to creatures.

7 **Words expressing God as related to the world.**   Some words imply a relationship to creatures and apply to God from a certain point in time, not eternally. For every relationship involves two related terms. Sometimes relationships are not real in either term, but arise from the way we think of the terms: we think identity, for example, by thinking one thing twice over and relating it to itself; and occasionally we relate what exists to what does not exist, or generate purely logical relations like that of genus to species. Sometimes relationships are real in both terms: grounded in the quantity of both, in the case of relationships like

big/small or double/half, or in their activity and passivity, in the case
of causal relationships like mover/moved and father/son. Sometimes
relationships are real in only one of the terms, with the other merely
thought of as related [reciprocally] to that one; and this happens whenever the two terms exist at different levels. Thus seeing and understanding really relates us to things, but being seen and understood by
us is not something real in the things; and similarly a pillar to the right
of us does not itself have a left and a right. Now God exists at an entirely
different level from creatures, and he is thought of as related to them,
only because they are really related to him. As a consequence, words
implying such relationships can apply to God from a certain point in
time, not because of change in God but because of change in the
creatures; just as I might say a pillar started to be on my right not
because the pillar moved but because I did.

Calling God *Lord* directly relates him to creatures and indirectly says
something of what God is, since lordship presupposes power and God
is power. Calling God *Saviour* or *Creator* directly expresses something
of what God is (for he is his own actions) and indirectly relates him to
creatures. Both sorts of word apply to God from a certain point in time
inasmuch as they relate him, directly or indirectly, to creatures; but
they also apply to him eternally inasmuch as they express, directly or
indirectly, something of what God is. [According to Jeremiah God
always loved us], for knowing and willing are actions within their agent
and so exist eternally in God. But actions like creation and salvation we
conceive of as proceeding from God into their external effects, and so
causing relationships which apply to God from a certain point in time.
God is truly *Lord* because a real relationship of subjection to God
exists in his creatures. Whether the two terms of a relationship exist
simultaneously depends not on the level of the things related but on
whether the relations as such entail each other (like double/half and
father/child do). Thus, though what we know can pre-exist our knowing
it (since potentiality does not entail its actualization), nevertheless its
being known by us and our knowing it exist simultaneously. So,
although God pre-exists all creatures, he was not *Lord* until such time
as there were creatures subject to him; being lord and being subject
entail one another and must exist simultaneously.

Names for God.   St John Damascene variously derives the Greek 8
word for God – *theos* – from Greek words for running, burning and
gazing at, all of them activities. Nevertheless the word expresses not
what God does but what God is. For what names derive from and what

they are adopted to express is not always the same thing: sometimes we learn a thing's nature from its behaviour, and name it after a particular property or behaviour that it exhibits. Only immediately perceptible things like heat and cold and whiteness are not named after other things. Now God we know only by his actions and effects, so our names for him derive from such activities. In particular, the name *God* derives from his activity of universal foresight or *providence*. But it has been generally adopted to express the being whose nature it is to exercise such universal foresight for things. When a thing's behaviour leads us to understand how it should be defined, then our name for it (even if derived from its behaviour) expresses what it is by definition, what makes it what it is. But from God's effects we do not understand how to define him, but only that he causes, differs from and surpasses his creatures. Only in this sense does the word *God* express what God is: something existing over everything, the source of everything, and set apart from everything.

9   Forms instantiated in individuals are always in principle (and often in practice) common to many such individuals, and named by common nouns. For we understand such natures by abstracting them from their instantiations, so that whether they are instantiated once or many times makes no difference to what is understood. Individuals however are distinct from each other, with names proper to them in principle and shared only metaphorically, as when we call a brave man an Achilles. This would also be the case with forms not instantiated in individuals but subsisting as individuals themselves, were we to understand them and name them in the way they actually exist. But since we understand simple things only on the model of things composed of form and matter, we represent them as subsistent by using concrete nouns for them just as we would for composite things.

The word *God* then is a common noun expressing a nature restricted in fact to one individual but thought by us as though it was in principle common to many; like the word *sun*. Though sometimes we also use the word metaphorically for those who partially resemble God: *I say you shall be gods*. If however there was a name which referred to God not as having such and such a nature but as being this individual, it would not apply to others in principle: and such perhaps is the Hebrew name *YHWH*. Words like *good* and *wise* derive from perfections creatures receive from God and are adopted to express not God's nature but the perfections common to God and to creatures; the word *God* however derives from an activity peculiar to God which we constantly experience, and the word has been adopted to express his nature.

Both the believer denying and the pagan asserting an idol to be God 10
are using the word to mean the true God; for if they meant false god
then what the pagan said would be true! God revealed his name to 11
Moses as *He who is*. And this is a most appropriate name inasmuch as
it derives not from any particular form but from existence itself, and in
its manner of expression does not as other names do delimit God's
substance, and represents God's existence in the present tense as *knowing
neither past nor future*. But as regards what they express, the name *God*
which signifies him as having the divine nature, and the name *YHWH*,
which signifies him (if we may so put it) as an individual, are more
appropriate names. *Goodness* is the fundamental name of God as cause
but not simply speaking, for causing presupposes existence.

We can make affirmative statements about God. In every true affirmat- 12
ive statement subject and predicate signify under different aspects what
is in some way identical: either the subject refers to an individual under
one form and the predicate expresses some other form that individual
assumes; or, in propositions of identity, the mind introduces a diversity
of subject and predicate, and then, by means of the affirmation itself,
re-asserts the thing's identity. Now God, altogether one and simple in
himself, is known to us by way of many different concepts, all of which
correspond, as we know, to one and the same simple thing. In talk about
God we represent this conceptual plurality by the plurality of subject
and predicate, and God's real unity by connecting subject and predicate
in one affirmative statement. To understand things in ways otherwise
than they exist is an error only if the way in which we know them is
attributed to the things themselves. But our minds understand material
things immaterially, without thinking them immaterial; and simple
things on the model of composite ones without thinking them composite.
So the fact that our statements about God involve composition does not
make them false.

Chapter 2

GOD'S LIFE

[vol 4] We turn now from what God is to what he does: his interior activity of knowing and willing, and his power to produce external effects.

Introductory comment. Thomas's first chapter has already taken a decisive step beyond the Aristotelian concept of the divine, though not altogether beyond what Thomas thinks man could have learnt by exercise of his reason. For Aristotle the divine was the fulfilment of all being, an eternally happy life of (impersonal?) intelligence beyond all the motions and alterations which are aroused in other beings by the tug of attraction for a divine life they can never wholly emulate. Thomas's God is not simply a centre of attraction for the universe but its agent, the doing of all being. That this is a step beyond Aristotle is something Aristotle would have disputed, and it must wait for discussion till creation is discussed in chapter 4. For in making the step Thomas is guided by the concept of God developed in another tradition, developed in the history of Israel and recorded in scripture: a God who in his knowledge and in his love has created a creation, which he knows and loves and plans and cares for in the tiniest detail. It is to God in his personal providence that Thomas now turns.

In so doing he is putting into practice the mixture of serene acceptance and close criticism of human ways of talking about God that he has shown at the end of the last chapter. Man thinks of God in the way he thinks about other things – as endowed with a nature, showing itself in abilities and dispositions, which he exercises from time to time – and in so doing can speak truth about God through a sort of analogy. For all the perfections of life that other beings exercise through their possession of natures and abilities and dispositions, are concentrated in God into a simple perfection of active existing. Thomas serenely accepts the inadequate composite ways of expression as part of his human status, confident that what is expressed, if one remains critically alert, can nevertheless be the simple truth. So he talks in this chapter as though we are moving on from considering God's substance to consider his activities (knowing and loving and external agency); and as though his activities exercised many different abilities (mind and will and power to move); and as though these abilities were endowed with good dispositions (prudence – i.e. providence, justice and mercy) as in man. These distinctions are all part of the scaffolding and structure of the language he is using to talk about God, but he will remind us constantly that in God substance and ability and disposition and activity, interior or external, are all identically one simple act of existing that we cannot get our language round, except inadequately in these many partial ways, discussing first whether **God knows** and what he knows, then whether **God loves** and is just and merciful as the bible says, whether **God plans** with prudence the whole of history, profane and sacred, and whether **God acts** in creation as well as enjoying the kind of life that Aristotle had already described – **God's happy state**.

This chapter affirms that God is a living God, using a positive analogy from the living things known to us in this world. At p 49 (cf ch 5 p 119) Thomas will articulate what is often called the *ladder of life*, the different levels of ability in natural creatures to originate their own movements, starting from the most primitive forms of plant-life and reaching up to man. At each level of self-movement the concept of self is further developed, firstly as some sort of origin of external movement, and then of levels of interior life (sensation and imagination and their accompanying appetites) reaching a summit in the creatures we call persons: individuals who can reason and understand, love and choose and so exercise a special independence and freedom of action (ch 3 p 68). It is to this summit of life as we perceive it in the world that God is now compared, though God, as doer of all existence, must possess these perfections of existence – knowing and loving, living and originating movement in others – in a doing-mode that will transcend all created modes of such activities.

The contents of this chapter are discussed in more detail in the editor's preface, pp xxxvii–xlv.

I.   God knows

14 1 God is his own knowing.   God is aware; he knows things. To be aware is not only to be what you yourself are, but to take in what other things are too. Plants, for example, lack awareness and are restricted in nature by the limitations of matter: their matter takes on a single form and that makes them what they are. But things with awareness are open in nature, and to that extent free from the limitations of matter. The sense-organs of animals take in sensible qualities of material things without the matter of those organs taking on those qualities itself; and our mind uses no material organ at all, and is in a sense everything, as Aristotle says. So God, as the being most distant from matter, is also the most perfectly aware and knowing. Although we use the same words to signify God's perfections as we do to signify perfections of creatures, the words signify the perfections in imperfect ways appropriate only to creatures. Our words signify awareness as though it were a quality of things, whereas in God it is his very substance; and knowledge names a disposition not always being exercised in man, whereas in God it is pure activity.

2   External activity is defined by referring to some object of the activity outside the agent, namely, its effect; but interior activity is defined by an object of the activity within the agent, the object's very existence within the agent being the activity. As Aristotle says, the activity of sensing is an actualizing of what was there to be sensed; and the act of understanding is an actualizing of what was there to be understood. For we actually sense or understand something when our ability to sense or understand is activated by the form of what it senses or understands. Our senses (or understanding) and what we sense (or understand) differ only as different potentials of one and the same activity. But in God there is no potentiality: all is pure activity. In him then there can be no difference of understanding and what is understood: his understanding is never without its activating form, as ours sometimes is, and that activating form is his very understanding. God is himself known to himself. Our mind is a potential to take in forms that give it understanding; just as matter is a potential to take on forms that give it existence. We cannot actually understand anything until activated by the form of what we understand; but then, in understanding the thing, we understand our own understanding of it, and in knowing the act of understanding, know our power of understanding. God however is the pure activity of knowing (just as he is the pure act of existing), and so
3   understands himself through himself. God's perfect actuality in existing,

free from all matter and potentiality, makes him completely knowable
and completely knowing. So he knows himself as well as he can be
known, he perfectly comprehends himself.

Knowing is not an activity terminating in an external effect; it
interiorly perfects the knower in the same way existing perfects what
exists: existing is actually having one's own form, knowing is actually
having the form of what one knows. But God has no form other than
his very act of existing, so knows himself by his very substance. In God
intellect, and what it understands, and the form by which it understands,
and the very act of understanding, are all one and the same.

God knows everything that exists or that can exist. *Everything
is exposed and open to his eyes. Nothing is hidden from his sight.* Everything
pre-exists in God as an effect in its first cause; and since in God
existence and knowledge are identical, everything is in God's knowledge,
and there moreover in the mode of God's existence, namely, as
knowable. God sees himself in his own substance; and other things he
sees not in their substance but in his, as in a mirror. Now the perfection
of creatures comprises not only what they all have in common, namely
existence, but also what distinguishes them, for example, life, understanding and the like. So all this pre-exists in God. To know himself
perfectly then, God must know every way in which things can participate
his perfection; and to know the nature of existence perfectly he must
know all the forms it can take. So God knows each thing's special nature
in its distinctness from others. The eye cannot know the stone as it
exists in the eye, but through the image of the stone in the eye knows
the stone as it exists outside the eye. And though the mind can know
the stone as it exists in the mind, it also knows it as it exists in nature.
The more perfectly a thing exists in the knower, the more perfectly the
thing itself is known. God knows things as they exist in himself, but
because they are in him he also knows them in their own nature,
and all the more perfectly because of the more perfect way they
exist in him. We know discursively, one thing after another and sometimes one thing because of another as when conclusions are derived
from premises. But everything existing because of God he sees at one
glance in himself, as we see conclusions in premises at the end of their
derivation.

The form which makes a thing what it is, also inclines it to do what
it does. But since forms in the mind represent both what is and is not
the case, they can form our actions only as inclined this way or that by
desire of our will. Since knowing and existing are the same thing in

God, we can say that it is God's knowledge that causes all things (given the conjunction of his will). Our knowledge derives from things, but things, in their turn, derive from God's knowledge; so the things which prescribe standards for our knowledge have standards prescribed to them by his, just as an actual building mediates the knowledge of its designer to the knowledge of someone who studies it once it is built.

9 Things not actually existing may yet exist in God's power, or in that of his creatures, as something they could do or have done to them, or could think or imagine or express in some way. So because God knows everything he can do and everything that creatures can do or think or say, he can have knowledge of what does not exist. Things that do not exist nor ever have existed nor ever will exist, God is said simply to know; but things that did once exist or will exist, he is said to see. For we see what exists in front of us; and God's knowing is his existing, eternally present to the whole of time, and present to anything existing

10 at any time as to something existing in front of him. Evil exists where good is lacking; so God, in knowing every good thing, must also know evil, just as in seeing light we also see darkness. To know a thing by way of something else is an imperfect way of knowing it if the thing can be known in itself. But evil cannot be known in itself, since it is nothing but lack of good; it can only be defined or known by way of good.

11 **God knows individuals.** Part of our perfection is knowing individuals. Now the separate perfections of creatures are one and the same perfection in God; so though we know the general and the immaterial in one way and the particular and material in another, God knows both in one single act of understanding. To explain how this can be so some people say God knows the particular by way of its more general causes, in the way astronomers know of future eclipses. But this is not enough: general causes cause only forms and properties, which however much they are combined never yield the particular until taken on by some particular matter. To know Socrates is white and the son of Sophroniskos and whatever else of this sort can be said of him, is not to know the individual Socrates himself. By this method God would never know individuals in their particularity. We must rather say that God's knowledge has the same extension as his causality. Now he causes not only the forms that things have in common, but also the matter by which they are particular; so in knowing himself as the cause of things God knows things both in general and particular, as an architect would know his buildings if he designed their materials as well as their forms. Our minds abstract forms of individual things from what particularizes them,

so cannot know the individual through those forms. But the form through which God knows things is his own substance, immaterial not by abstraction but by nature, and causing everything, general and particular, in things. God knows, and even sees, an infinite number of 12 things: for he sees every thought and feeling of men for ever. We by sense-perception know only single individuals through particular images; and though mentally we can know through one general likeness a whole species consisting of infinitely many individuals, we do not know them in their distinctness one from another. But God's substance is an adequate likeness of everything that is and that can be, both in general and particular, and so he knows an infinite number of things in their distinctness and particularity. To know infinity in the manner it exists would be to know it bit by bit; which would be never to know it, for whatever amount was perceived more would remain to be perceived. But God knows infinity not by enumerating it bit by bit, but simultaneously with no before or after. And so the infinite is said to be finite to God's knowledge; because contained by it, not bridged by it. As Aristotle says, nothing – finite or infinite – can bridge the infinite, because bridging involves crossing bit by bit.

God knows the future.   God knows future events still undetermined. 13 When we think of such events actually happening we think of them as present, not future; already determined, not things that could still go either way; so knowable with certainty, as when Socrates is seen to be sitting. But when we think of such events foreshadowed in their causes we think of them as future and as yet undetermined (since their causes will sometimes fail to produce them); so knowable only conjecturally through their causes and not with certainty. Now God knows such events not only in their causes but also as actual happenings. Though they happen one after another, God's knowledge of them happening is not itself successive (like ours), but instantaneously whole. His knowledge, like his existence, is measured by eternity, which in one and the same instant encompasses all time; so his gaze is eternally focused on everything in time as on something present and known to him with certainty, even though it is future and undetermined in relation to its cause. Effects can fail because their immediate causes fail, even when their more remote causes do not; grass fails to grow because some immediate cause fails, even though the sun goes on rising and setting. In the same way, though God's knowledge is infallible and the cause of everything, what he knows may still be a fallible event because of immediate causes. But what about the statement: *if God already knows* *something will happen, then it* will *happen?* If this statement is true, and if its antecedent condition (God's eternal knowledge of the event) is determined, then it would seem that the consequent (the event's happening) must be determined. To escape this conclusion some argue that the antecedent condition is not determined, because though eternal and signified as past, its truth relates to the future. But this wouldn't remove its necessity: whether the future is determined or not, what is already related to that future is already determined. Others say the antecedent combines the necessity of God's knowing with the non-necessity of the happening, and that such a combination of necessity and non-necessity is itself non-necessary. But this won't do either: for the non-necessity qualifies the verb in the object clause, not that in the main clause. Just as it can be true that I say something false, so it can be a necessity that someone knows a non-necessity. Others concede the necessity of the antecedent, but say the consequent fails to be necessary because the antecedent (God's knowledge) is only a remote cause of the consequent (the happening), which can fail because of some more immediate cause. But if you say this then you are saying the whole conditional statement is false, like the statement *if the sun rises and sets the grass will grow*. The true solution to the problem is this: when an antecedent contains something referring to an act of mind, the consequent must be understood not as it exists in itself but as it exists in that act of mind; in this case the event must be understood as it is known by God, that is, as a present event. And as such it is indeed necessary, because as Aristotle says, what exists, when it exists, must exist. What happens in time is also known by us in time, moment by moment, but by God in an eternal moment, above time. We, unlike God, know undetermined future events as such, and so cannot have certain knowledge of them; just as travellers on a road cannot see people coming after them, though someone with a bird's eye view of the road can see every traveller. What *we* are certain of must already be determined in itself, whereas what God is certain of need not be determined absolutely in its own proper causes, but only as object of God's knowledge. So when it is said that *what God knows exists of necessity*, we must distinguish two interpretations: the first says that the things God knows are necessary things (attaching necessity to the things referred to in the proposition), and that is false; the second says the proposition *if God knows something it exists* is necessary (attaching the necessity to the connection the proposition expresses), and that is true. It has been objected that this distinction only applies when we refer to things by way of forms they can exist without: *that white be black* is impossible as a proposition; that a white *thing* be black is possible, but only for things that don't have to be white. But, the objection proceeds, everything that exists has to be known by God. This objection would hold if being known determined a thing intrinsically, but in fact it refers to an act of the knower; so though a thing cannot exist without *reply to objc⊗* being known by God, nevertheless it can have attributes that don't belong to it as known; just as stones can be material in themselves though not in the mind.

God knows propositions. Because God knows everything creatures 14 are capable of, he knows all possible propositions. But just as he knows material things immaterially, and composite things simply, so he knows propositions not by making or breaking connections in his mind, but *God knows* by simple knowledge of what they express. The forms in our mind do *propositions* not represent everything at once; in knowing what man is we do not know everything else about him but must build our knowledge of him bit by bit, making connections by framing propositions. But God in knowing himself knows what things are and everything else about them. To make a propositional connection is to say that something exists in some way; and so God, whose substance is existence, is a likeness of anything that can be said in a proposition. But can God's knowledge 15 change then? Did he once know that Christ was going to be born, and now know that he is not going to be born? [Abelard's] answer was that *Christ will be born*, *Christ is being born*, and *Christ has been born* are all the same proposition; but this is a mistake. Differences in syntax make different propositions. Moreover, it would mean that a proposition once true is always true, whereas Aristotle says that the proposition *Socrates is sitting down* changes from true to false when Socrates stands up. I would prefer to deny, as regards propositions, that what God knew he still knows. But that doesn't mean God's knowledge has changed. He eternally knows some things to exist at one time and not at another, and some propositions to be true at one time and false at another.

Our knowledge may be labelled theoretic not practical on three counts: 16 *3 marks of* because①it is not about anything we can make (but about God, for *theoretic* example, or the laws of nature); or because②it considers something we *knowledge* can make (for example, a house) in a theoretic way, analysing it and defining it, rather than considering how to make it; or because③we consider how to make it not actually in order to make it, but in order to know the truth. God's knowledge of himself is altogether theoretic (he cannot be made); but all other things he knows in both a theoretic and a practical way; and whatever he actually makes he knows with practical purpose. Though God cannot do evil, it is nevertheless a matter for his practical knowledge just as good is, inasmuch as he permits or prevents it and makes it serve his purposes. In the same way, illness is matter for a doctor's practical knowledge since he must cure it. So God's theoretic knowledge of himself includes theoretic and practical knowledge of everything else.

15 1 **God's ideas.** By *Ideas* [the Platonic tradition] means independently existing forms of things. Forms of things can exist outside them either as patterns for them to conform to, or as means of knowing them. Whatever doesn't come about by chance must have been aimed at by an agent possessing a model of its form: either by nature (as when a man begets a man or fire fire) or as an idea in the agent's mind (as when a man builds a house). The world is a product not of chance but of God's mind, and the model of its form in God's mind we call an *Idea*. God's substance is cause and model of everything except himself; and

2 so is the Idea of everything except himself. In any production the ultimate end in view is the province of the principal agent: so the order of the whole universe is directly intended by God and not the chance result of a chain of agents. But no architect can plan a house without having an idea of each separate part of it; so in God's mind everything must have its own special idea. This doesn't make God composite; for these ideas are not forms in his mind by which his mind is made actually knowing rather than not knowing; but they are in the mind as objects of knowledge, known and used as a pattern in making. The special nature of each creature is its own way of conforming to God's nature. So when God knows his nature as conformable to in such and such a way by creatures of such and such a sort, he is knowing his nature as the concept and Idea special to those creatures. God in one act of knowing knows many things and knows that he knows them, which is

3 to have in his mind their many Ideas as many known objects. As patterns for making those things he has made at some time or another, Ideas belong to God's practical knowledge; as concepts for knowing things, even things he has never made, Ideas belong to his theoretic knowledge. Evils do not have Ideas in either way, for God knows evil only by way of good. Plato is said to have thought matter uncreated; it had no Idea but was joint cause of things with Ideas. *We* say God created matter already formed, so that it has an Idea, but not one distinct from the Ideas of the things of which it is a part. Matter can neither exist nor be known in itself. Plato said the only Idea of individuals was the Idea of their species, since nature's only aim in producing individuals is preservation of the species. But as we shall see later God's providence

cares not only for species but also for individuals.

Truth and knowledge. *Truth and falsehood*, Aristotle says, *are in the* 16 1
mind, not in things. Desire goes out to things and desirability or goodness
primarily characterizes things, though as a consequence the desire of
good may itself be called good. Knowledge however takes things in, and
truth, which knowledge pursues, primarily characterizes minds, though
as a consequence things may be called true in relation to minds. Things
essentially relate to the mind on which they depend for existence; they
relate non-essentially to minds which only know them. Thus man-made
things are called true in relation to human minds (a house when it
conforms to its architect's idea, a statement when it expresses true
knowledge); whilst natural things are called true in relation to God's
Ideas of them. Truth then is primarily defined as a quality of mind:
truth reveals and makes clear what is; but secondarily as a quality of
things relating them to the mind that originates them: *each thing's truth
is its possession of the being established for it.* The usual definition: *truth
is a correspondence of thing and mind,* can be interpreted either way.

A thing, to be true, must have the form appropriate to its nature. So 2
a mind truly knows when it possesses the form appropriate to knowing,
or in other words, is conformed to what it knows; and we define truth
accordingly as a conformity of mind and thing. Knowing truth is
knowing that conformity. Truth therefore cannot be perceived by the
senses: we see by way of some image corresponding to the thing we see,
but we do not *see* that correspondence itself. Our mind however can
know its own conformity to the thing it knows, for we not only conceive
what things are, but also judge them actually to be such as we have
conceived them to be, and so for the first time know and speak truth.
This we do by *connecting and disconnecting*: in our propositions forms
signified by predicates are applied to or removed from things referred
to by subjects. So the senses and the mind when conceiving a thing's
nature can know truly, but do not know or say truth; and the same
applies to verbal expressions – however complex – that lack sentence-
structure. Truth can be a quality of the senses and of the mind conceiving
natures as it can of any other thing; but it is not present in them as an
object of knowledge. Yet this is the primary meaning of truth: it is truth
as known that perfects the mind. In the proper meaning of the word
truth is found only in a mind making connections and disconnections.

To be is to be knowable; so just as being good is really the same thing 3
as existing, though the word *good* expresses a notion of value left
unexpressed by the word *existing*, so being true and existing are the

same thing, but the word *true* expresses a relation to the mind. Things and thoughts exist and things and thoughts are true; but existence applies primarily to things, and truth primarily to thoughts, because of the difference in notion. The truth that the non-existent does not exist is based not on any real existence or knowability of the non-existent, but on the knowability and mental existence lent it by a construction of our minds. Truth accompanies the knowing of what exists; the notion of existence does not presuppose the notion of truth, but the notion of

4 truth presupposes the notion of existence. Truth however follows more closely on existence than goodness does; anything that exists in any way is immediately true, whereas only what exists in some perfect way is of value and therefore good. The mind understands the will, and the will wants the mind to understand; so truth is a particular instance of good, which the will seeks in general; and good is a particular instance of truth, which the mind seeks in general. The first idea we conceive is that of an existent, then that we understand what exists (and so we conceive truth), and then that we value it (and so we conceive goodness).

5 God is his own act of existence, and not only conforms with but is identified with his own act of understanding: the cause and measure of all other existence and understanding. So not only is truth to be found

6 in God, but God is the source and highest form of truth. When words are used analogically, one use is primary and enters into the definition of the others. Only organisms possess health, but diets are called healthy as causing health and complexions as displaying it. If by truths we mean objects of knowledge, then there are many created truths even in one mind, but all reflect the one divine truth. If by truths we mean true things, then all things are true to one divine truth to which they conform

7 by their many separate existences. Statements in words are called true not because the words know the truth, but because the mind that frames them does. So if no mind was eternal no truth would be either. The idea of a circle, and the equality $2 + 3 = 5$, possess eternal truth only in God's mind. General ideas are said to apply always and everywhere because they abstract from the here and now; but actually to exist eternally they need an eternal mind. It was true from eternity that things now existing were going to exist, only inasmuch as they pre-existed in an eternal cause, namely God. Since our minds are not eternal the truth of any statements we make is not eternal either, but had a beginning sometime. And before such truths existed there was not even the truth that such truths did not exist, except in God's mind, whose truth is eternal. But now it is true to say such truths did not then exist: but true only with its truth in our mind now, not with any truth that existed

then. For truths about something non-existent are based not on any
real existence of the non-existent but on a mental existence lent it by
a construction of our minds. It is true now that such truths did not exist
only because *we* conceive a non-existence preceding their existence.
Truths in our minds can alter either because things remain the same 8
while our opinions change, or because things change while our opinion
remains the same. But truth in God's mind is unalterable. *Socrates is*
sitting is truly an assertion that Socrates is sitting whether Socrates is
sitting or not; but it asserts it truly only when Socrates is sitting.
Socrates' seatedness varies before, during and after his sitting; and so
the truth caused by his sitting alters, as indicated by our saying *Socrates*
will sit, *Socrates is sitting*, *Socrates was sitting*. At any one time one or
other of these propositions is true, but that doesn't imply the existence
of one single unalterable truth.

The possibility of falsehood. Simply speaking, man-made things 17 1
are false or faulty when they lack the form they were meant to have.
The things God makes cannot be essentially faulty in this way, for
everything happens as he means it to happen, with the possible exception
of the faults creatures with free will commit when they depart from his
idea of them. Such things can only be called false non-essentially in
relation to our minds: when they are not as they are said to be, or appear
to be. Truth itself cannot be perceived by the senses, but the senses 2
perceive truly when they perceive things as they are and falsely when
they perceive them otherwise. When we see a man, for example, what
we see directly is colour (which as such defines sight), and what we see
indirectly is shape and size (which as such affect all the senses), and
neither directly nor indirectly as such but incidentally we see his
humanity, because this coloured object happens to be a man. Senses
misrepresent what they directly perceive rarely, and only because of
some chance disorder in the sense-organ: the sick tongue finds sweet
things bitter. But even healthy sense-organs can make mistakes about
what they perceive indirectly. Senses have the sensations they say they
have; but sometimes those sensations do not correspond to the thing as
it is. So our senses can mistake things, but not sensations. Imagination
can be false since it represents even absent things, and by taking the
imaginary for the real we can deceive ourselves. To exist is actually to 3
have one's own form, and to know is actually to have the form of what
one knows. Things cannot fail to be what their form makes them though
they can lack incidentals: a man is a man, even if he has lost a foot.
Similarly we cannot fail to know the thing whose form is making us

know, even if we get incidentals wrong. Thus sight can't mistake what directly defines it – colour – but only what it sees indirectly or incidentally; and simply speaking the mind can't make false concepts but only false connections and disconnections, attributing to the things it conceives something inappropriate or incompatible. (Though the mind differs from the senses in being able not only to know falsely but also to know falsehood). By making false connections however the mind can be said in a qualified sense to make false concepts: either by falsely applying a concept to things to which it does not apply, or by connecting unconnectable concepts in a pseudo-definition. As colour is the defining object of sight, so *what a thing is* is the defining object of understanding; and we properly understand something only when we can demonstrate its truth by referring it back to some definition of what a thing is. It is in that sense that Augustine said we can't understand falsehood; he did not mean that our minds can't make mistakes. Self-evident principles are those known as soon as their terms are known, since they are propositions in which the predicate forms part of the subject's definition; so we cannot be wrong about them just as we cannot define things

4   falsely. Falsehood is not merely a negation or lack of truth, but its contrary. A negation posits nothing and designates no subject (all sorts of things cannot see); a lack posits nothing but designates a subject (only things that should see can be called blind); but a contrary posits some opposed thing in the designated subject. Now just as truth posits a perception that corresponds to things, so falsehood posits a perception that does not. Truth and goodness are universal notions applicable to everything that exists; so just as every lack requires an existent subject, so every evil a good subject, and every falsehood a true subject; but this is not the truth to which it is contrary.

18 1   **God lives.** The most obviously alive things are animals, and these are said to start living when they first make their own movements, and to lose their lives when they stop moving themselves and can only be moved by others. So what defines life is self-movement: movement either in the strict sense of change (acquiring perfection) or in the wider sense of being active (enjoying the perfection acquired). The natural state of heavy and light bodies is to be at rest in the place natural to them; they move only when away from such a place. But the living movement of plants and other living things is not movement to or from a natural state; it *is* their natural state, and to lose it is to lose their

2   natural state. Often we name things after some external behaviour they exhibit, since that is how we come to know them. Thus properly

speaking *to live* means not to move oneself but to be a substance naturally capable of self-movement or self-activation, *living* is having such a nature, and *life* is the abstract word for this just as *movement* is the abstract word for moving. But *life* is sometimes used less properly to mean life's activities. On earth we distinguish four classes of living things; things which can feed, and so grow and reproduce; things like oysters which can feel as well but cannot move about; things like quadrupeds and birds and other developed animals which can move around; and finally men who can understand. For some activities men have not only natural abilities, but additional competences and skills making the activities second nature and satisfying. Activities in which a man finds satisfaction, for which he has a bent, on which he spends his time and to which he devotes his life, are also called by a kind of analogy a life: we talk of a life of pleasure or a life of virtue, of living a contemplative or an active life, and of an eternal life of knowing God.

God is supremely alive, for he most perfectly acts of himself without being moved by others. In actions we distinguish three factors: first, the goal which motivates the agent; second, the chief agent acting in virtue of his own form; and sometimes thirdly, some instrument which acts not in virtue of its own form but in virtue of the chief agent and merely carries out his action. Now certain living organisms move themselves only to the carrying out of actions, the form and goal of such actions being determined by their natures; such are the plants, growing according to a form laid down by nature. Other organisms move themselves by themselves acquiring the forms in virtue of which they move: such are the animals, moving according to forms which are not laid down by nature but perceived by the senses. Of these some like oysters hardly move more than plants, expanding and contracting in response to touch, whereas others move themselves about in space, responding not only to contact but to things perceived at a distance. However none decide the goals of their actions, and the responses they make to the forms they perceive are laid down by nature. So there are yet higher animals who move themselves by deciding their own goals; and that requires reason and intelligence to know how goals and means relate, and how to adapt one to the other. In us intelligence moves itself to some things but other things are laid down for it by nature: basic premises of thought which it cannot deny, and an ultimate goal which it cannot help willing. Only he whose nature is not laid down by another, but is his very act of understanding, possesses life to the utmost degree, and that is God. Earth's living things die, so need reproduction to preserve the species and food to preserve the individual. All such living things are bodies organized for growth, but this is not required in God.

God loves

God's will.   To exist is actually to possess our own natural form; to know actually to possess the form of what we know. When things haven't got their natural form and perfections they seek them and do not rest till they have them; and in things lacking awareness we call this tendency towards their natural good their natural desire. In the same way things with understanding have a natural tendency to seek whatever they understand as good, not resting till they possess it; and this tendency we call will. So anything that has understanding has will, just as anything that has sense-perception has animal desire. We call will a desire or an appetite, though it doesn't only desire what it doesn't have but also loves and takes delight in what it does have. And this is how will exists in God, who eternally possesses the good which delights his will, since it is nothing other than his substance.

A natural thing has a natural tendency not only to seek its own good, not resting until it possesses it, but also to make it as available as possible to others: the fulfilment of every active thing is to express itself in act. This too we find in things with will: as far as they can they communicate what good they possess to others. God wills himself to exist, and also other things with himself as their goal, for it befits God's goodness to offer other things a share in it. Nothing but his own goodness causes God to will other things, and he wills many such things in the one simple, single act of willing his own goodness.

God cannot but will his own goodness, just as we cannot but will happiness, and just as all our faculties cannot but respond to their defining objects: sight, for example, to colour. But in willing goals we don't have to will everything ordered to those goals, but only things without which the goal cannot be achieved. Now God's goodness is perfect whether other things exist or not, so he is not obliged to will them. But if he wills them, then on that supposition he cannot unwill them, because his will is changeless; just as, if Socrates is sitting then he cannot be standing, though he does not have to sit. The fact that God wills what he wills eternally doesn't mean he has to will it. That God doesn't have to will created things is not a weakness in his will; rather, God's goodness is perfect without them, so there is no must in them. The existence of things as known is an existence in the knower; but their existence as willed is the existence they have in themselves.

Now things [pre-]exist in God's mind with [his] necessary existence; but in themselves don't have to exist. So God has to know what he knows, but doesn't have to will what he wills.

The cause of things is God's will, not any necessity of his nature. 4
Anything that acts by nature has to have its goal, and its way to that goal, laid down for it by a higher intelligence: an archer must decide the arrow's target and flight. Moreover, natural causes have limited natures and limited effects; but God's nature is unlimited, embracing every perfection of existence, and can issue in defined effects only by the definition of his intelligence and will. Finally, effects issue from causes according to their mode of pre-existence in the cause, which in God is their existence in his mind; and it is will that moves us to implement what we have in mind. Even in us mind plans, will commands and our ability to act implements one and the same effect; and in God all these are one.

When our mind moves from knowing a premise to knowing a con- 5
clusion we can say knowing the one caused us to know the other. But when in one mental act we see premise implying conclusion, there are not two knowledges one causing the other, but one act of seeing the premise as cause of the conclusion. So also with willing, where goals relate to subgoals as premises to conclusions. When goal and subgoals are willed in separate acts, willing the goal causes willing of the subgoals; but when both are willed in one and the same act, then there is no causality of acts of will, though the subgoals are willed in order to attain the goal. Now God understands everything in the one act of understanding himself; and wills everything he wills in the one act of willing his own goodness. So there is nothing causing his act of will: he wills x to cause y, but x does not cause him to will y. God wills a world order in which created effects have their determinate created causes. Whatever effect of his presupposes another depends on that other effect as well as on God's will; but some primary effects depend only on his will. God willed men's hands as tools at the service of their minds, and their minds in order that they might be men, and men to enjoy him and to make the universe complete, and that for no further created end. That depends only on God's will, but everything else on the order of causes he has established.

Our God is in the heavens; he does whatever he pleases. A thing can lack 6
a particular form – not be human or not be alive – but nothing can lack the universal form – not exist. And what is true of form is also true of agency. Things can happen outside the control of particular causes, but not outside the control of that most general cause to which all particular

causes are subject. For what hinders one particular cause's effect is intervention by another one, and that intervention is itself controlled by the most general cause. Since God's will is the universal cause of all things, it is always effective; when something appears to escape his control in one way it is subjected to him in another: those who by sinning escape his will as much as they are able, are subjected to it once more when in justice they are punished. But doesn't Paul say that *God desires all men to be saved and come to the knowledge of the truth*; yet it doesn't happen! John Damascene understood these words to refer to an initial will of God rather than to his final will, a distinction applicable only to what God wills, not to his act of willing in which there is no before and after. Something judged good or bad in isolation, may in context turn out to be the opposite: a just judge who initially wills all men to live may yet finally will a murderer to hang. God's initial will is every man's salvation, but his justice may finally require some man's damnation. But notice that our initial will is not simply speaking our will, but only in some qualified sense. Willing a thing is willing it as it exists in itself in all its particularity; we will simply speaking what we will in its particular context, what we will finally. Simply speaking, the just judge willed the murderer to hang; only in a qualified sense, considering him as everyman, would he have had him live. So this is a *would that* – a wish – rather than a will. Clearly then whatever is simply speaking God's will happens, even if contrary to an initial will.

7   *God is not a son of man that he should repent.* It is one thing to change purpose; quite another to purpose change. With unchanged purpose we can will that one thing happen now and its opposite later; to change purpose would be to start willing what previously we had not, and that presupposes either a change in how we are (so that something new starts being good for us) or a change of mind about what we think good for us. What God is and what he knows cannot change, so his will must remain unchanged too.

8   Some things God wills happen deterministically and some not. We cannot attribute this to fallible intermediate causes; for this would imply that secondary causes can render God's will ineffective, and assumes that the distinction of fallibility and infallibility in causes is not God's doing in the first place. Rather God wills some things to happen deterministically and some not, so that the world may have its own natural order. To some effects he assigns infallible causes so that they always happen; to others fallible causes so that sometimes they don't. So what God wills to happen doesn't happen non-deterministically

because fallible causes intervene; God wills them to be subject to those fallible causes so that they may happen non-deterministically.

Nothing can ever tend to evil as such, be the tendency natural, animal or, like the will, intelligent. Evil is the opposite of good, and good is by definition what we tend towards. But tendencies can lead to evil indirectly: lions kill deer for food, not for killing's sake; and lust is after pleasure, not the disorder of sin as such. Because the indirect evil is a lack of some good, it won't be willed even indirectly unless the good which accompanies the evil is desired more than the good which is lacking. Now God wills some goods more than others, but none more than his own goodness. So he cannot in any way will wrongdoing, which deprives actions of orderedness to God's goodness; but he can will natural defects and penalties indirectly by willing the goods of natural order and justice which lead to such evils. Some think that God wills evils to happen because of the good that follows. This is a mistake. Good follows from evil indirectly despite the intentions of the evildoer. That evils happen is not directly good but only indirectly, and cannot be willed directly by God. God is neither willing evils to happen, nor [ineffectively] willing them not to happen: he wills not to stop evils happening, and this is to will good. [9]

Certain things, like happiness, we will of necessity by a natural instinct; but in regard to everything else we have free choice. So too God must will his own goodness, but in regard to everything else can freely choose. [10]

God is love. *God is love.* The primary activation of any tendency whatever, will included, is love. Attraction to good is by nature prior to repulsion from evil: displeasure presupposes pleasure, and hatred love. And attraction to good in general precedes attraction to some special aspect of good: love of good – present or absent – precedes pleasure in its presence, or desire of it in its absence. So every activation of a tendency has love at its root: nobody desires or enjoys what he doesn't love; nobody hates or is displeased by things unless they oppose his love. So whoever, like God, has a will must also love. Our wills move our bodies by way of our animal desires. Animal desires are always accompanied by bodily changes – especially round the heart, the centre of animal movement – and are consequently called *passions*; whereas similar movements in the will we call *acts*. Love then in God is not a passion but an act. Some passions, moreover, imply lack of fulfilment: desire implies absence of good, sadness presence of evil. So God is said to desire or to feel sad or angry only metaphorically, by an analogy [20] drawn from the effects of such passions. But God can properly be said to love and feel pleasure, though as acts, not as passions. The act of loving has two objects: the good you want for somebody, and the person you want it for. For true love wills good to someone. If the someone is yourself, then love seeks a unity with the good you want; if it is someone else, then love creates a community with him, for you treat him as yourself, willing *his* unity with the good as you would your own. God's love too seeks unity (though God is already one in substance with the good he loves, his own goodness), and community, since he wills good to others.

2   *You love everything that exists and loathe none of the things you have made.* Everything that exists is, as such, good, and has God as its cause. Clearly then God loves all things, willing them every good they possess; yet not as we do. Our love doesn't cause a thing's goodness; rather the thing's goodness, real or imagined, evokes our love, and enlists our help in preserving and furthering that goodness. But God's love evokes and creates the goodness in things. The lover in loving the good of the beloved and planning and working for it as though the beloved was himself, is transported out of himself into the beloved; and we must dare to say with pseudo-Denys that in the abundance of his loving kindness and providence for everything that exists, God too is ecstatic with love. Friends must be rational creatures, able to return our love and share our life, and able to be well and happy or the reverse, so that one can properly will their good. Properly speaking, God loves non-rational creatures not as friends but as things wanted for rational creatures and himself. God is not in need of them, but he wills them for the sake of his goodness and our benefit. For you can want for others as well as for yourself. God loves sinners as beings he has created, but he hates their sinning, which is a way of not being and is not God's doing.

3   God loves everything with the same simple uniform act of will; but just as we love those persons more to whom we will greater good, even when we will it with no greater intensity, so too with God. God's love causes the goodness in things, and one thing would not be better than another unless God loved it more.

21 1   **God is just and merciful.**   *The Lord is just and loves justice.* There are two kinds of justice. One deals with give-and-take transactions like buying and selling, and is called by Aristotle commutative justice. There is none of this in God: *Who has given him a gift that might be repaid?* The other deals with distribution of a community's goods to its members in proportion to their worth, and is called distributive justice. Good

order in a family or community is a sign that such justice exists in the community authority; and the good order of the natural and moral world is a sign that it exists in God. Some moral virtues deal with emotions: moderation or restraint with desires, courage with fears, mildness with anger; such virtues are ascribed to God only metaphorically since God does not possess emotions. Other moral virtues deal with deeds such as giving and spending: justice, generosity, munificence; and these because they perfect our willing can be ascribed to God. Will seeks what the mind presents as good, so God can only will what his wisdom, as a sort of just law, decrees to be right. Everything he does he does justly, just as we do when we act according to law; though in our case the law comes from a superior authority, while God is a law unto himself. God renders what is due both to himself and to created things. God's due is that his wisdom and will should be fulfilled and his goodness revealed; and a creature's due is that it should be given what its nature and constitution require. This last due follows from the first, and in rendering it God is not paying creatures a debt, for everything draws on him and he on nothing. And so God's justice is sometimes called doing what befits goodness, and sometimes requiting deserts.

The Lord is gracious and merciful. In us mercy starts as a feeling of compassion for another's plight (as if it were our own), and goes on to do something to relieve it. God is not affected by feelings of sadness, but as source of all goods he is above all a reliever of need. So he is good in giving perfections, just in distributing them in balanced ways, generous in giving from goodness rather than for advantage, merciful in relieving need with those gifts. If to someone owed one pound you give two out of your own pocket you are not doing something unjust, but something generous and merciful. The same is true if you remit a debt or pardon an offence; forgiving is a form of giving. Mercy does not oppose justice, but fills it out. God's justice is based on his mercy, for nothing is due to any creature except because of something it already is or will be because of God's goodness. Mercy starts all God's works and grows in all that follows, God always giving beyond the measure of a creature's due.

God plans

God is prudent or provident. *It is your providence, O Father, that steers all things.* The proper function of the virtue of prudence, according to Aristotle, is to plan for goals: one's own life, and the matters of any family, city or state for which one is responsible. God is prudent or provident in this last way: nothing needs planning in God himself, the ultimate goal of all, but his planning of the universe is called his providence. This planning or providence is eternal, though its implementation and management takes place in time. Providence is an act of mind but one which presupposes willing of a goal, for no one decides how to achieve a goal unless they want it. So too in man the virtue of prudence presupposes other moral virtues disposing us to desire what is good.

2   Some thinkers deny providence altogether saying chance rules the world; others think God looks after everlasting things like species but not after perishable individuals, with the possible exception of men. God however looks after all creatures in general and in particular. Action is an adapting of things to a goal; and if anything an agent does turns out to be badly adapted to that agent's goal, this must be due to interference by another cause outside the agent's control. But God is the first cause of everything that exists, in general and in all particulars, perishable or imperishable; so nothing that exists can escape his planning for a goal, his providence. Those who say God does not care for the perishable world argue, it seems, from the existence there of chance events and evils. But events are called chance because they escape a particular causal ordering; God's universal ordering they cannot escape, and in relation to that they are planned and provided for. A master may send two servants unbeknownst to each other to the same place, planning them to meet, but as far as they are concerned the meeting happens by chance. In the same way defects and death are against the natures of particular things but part of the universal plan of nature: what is death and loss to one thing is birth and gain to another and to the universe as a whole. God, as the universal planner of all that exists, permits particular defects so as not to hinder the perfect goodness of the universe. Those who say that because nature is deterministic it is not subject to providence, are misled by the fact that human planning cannot change nature but only make use of it. But God is the author of nature and its determinism. Cicero thought what men decided was not planned by God, and the Preacher wrote that *God made man in the beginning and then left him in the hands of his own counsel.* But God is the cause of our very acts of free choice, and man's prudence is contained within God's providence as a particular cause subject to a universal one. When St Paul asks whether *God is concerned for oxen,* he is not doubting God's providence for lesser animals, but arguing a special providence for men who, because they are masters of their own actions, are thought worthy of punishment and reward.

God does not use intermediaries to plan anything but attends to everything himself in the smallest detail. He implements his plan and manages the world through intermediaries, not because he lacks power in himself, but because in his abundant goodness he wants to share the dignity of cause with creatures. That God has planned everything does not make it happen necessarily. Rather he plans infallible causes for events that must occur, and fallible causes for events that may or may not. *Must be* and *may not be* are modes of being as such, and thus subject to God's universal providence and plan for the whole of existence though to no lesser prudence.

Predestination.   The goal God plans for us is an eternal life of seeing God, beyond our natural powers to achieve. Things that cannot reach a goal under their own power have to be consigned there; an archer must dispatch the arrow to its target. The creatures capable of eternal life are all intelligent creatures, who can be brought there by God's dispatching, so to speak; and the plan for this dispatching pre-exists in God, his providence for part of his world. We call it predestination, since *destination* names the goal of consignment or dispatching. It is better for us not to know whether we are predestined, lest the non-predestined despair and the predestined become careless. Predestination itself is not a property of those predestined but something in God: the plan in his mind destining some to eternal life. But the implementation of this plan, the calling and glorifying of men, is an activity of God that takes place in those he has predestined. *Those he predestined he also called, and those he called he also glorified.*

It is also part of God's providence that he permits some not to reach the goal of eternal life; and this is called reprobation or rejection. Neither predestination nor reprobation are simply God's foreknowledge but parts of his plan: predestination includes his will to confer grace and glory, and reprobation includes his consent to wrongdoing and to the infliction of the penalty of damnation for that wrongdoing. Predestination causes the future glory and the present grace of those predestined; but reprobation does not cause present wrongdoing, though it causes God to leave the sinner to himself, and causes his future eternal punishment. Wrongdoing is the free act of someone rejected and deserted by grace. For reprobation by God does not diminish the powers of the person rejected. He is still capable, absolutely speaking, of acquiring grace, though to say both that this will happen and that he is reprobate would be a contradiction in terms. In the same way, predestination does not take away free will, though to say a person is predestined entails saying he will be saved. The reprobate-as-such cannot acquire grace, but of his own free will he lands himself in this or that sin and that can rightly be called his fault.

*problem is /
clash between
'cannot' & 'free will'*

4   By its very meaning predestination implies love and choice. Love because God is willing the good of eternal life to those he predestines; choice because he wills them to be singled out in this way. *We* single out who we will love because of some goodness they already have; but *he*, in loving someone, causes the goodness which singles them out. Clearly then in him choice presupposes love, and predestination choice. God shares his goodness with all things unreservedly, but this or that good he chooses to give to some and not to others.

5   *He saved us, not because of any good deeds we ourselves had done, but because of his own mercy.* God's acts of will are not caused – he does not will this because he wills that – but what he wills has its reasons – he wills this to happen for the sake of that. No one then is mad enough to say that a man's deserts cause God's [eternal] act of predestining him; but we might ask whether God pre-ordained himself to grant the result of predestination to people because of their deserts. Origen believed so, and talked of deserts inherited from some previous life; though St Paul had ruled this out when he wrote, *Before they were born or had done anything either good or bad – so not because of their works but because of his call – Rebecca was told: The elder will serve the younger.* Pelagians believe the deserts of this life cause predestination's effects to follow, saying God finishes the work we start. But again St Paul has written *We are not sufficient to think our own thoughts as our own*; and what is there earlier than thought? So others say that the deserts that follow on predestination's effects are the reason for it, meaning that God gives grace to a man, and has pre-ordained himself to give it, because he foresees this man will use it well. But this opinion seems to make a distinction between an effect of grace and an effect of free will as if the same effect didn't proceed from both together. For whatever in our actions causes predestination cannot also be predestination's effect. There is however no such distinction between what is of free will and what is of predestination, no more than the effects of an intermediate cause can be distinguished from the effects of a primary cause: God's providence produces its effects through the actions of intermediate causes.

Our opinion is that the effects of predestination may be considered separately or as a whole. Separately considered, there is nothing to stop one effect being the cause and reason for another: later effects being goals of earlier ones, and earlier effects disposing the recipient for later ones. Thus we may say that God pre-ordains himself to give glory where it is deserved, and pre-ordains himself to give grace so that it can be deserved. Considering the effects of predestination as a whole, however, they cannot in any way be caused by us. Whatever in man prepares him for eternal life is already an effect of predestination; even the very first preparation for grace needs God's help: *Turn us back to yourself, Lord, that we may turn back.* The reason for the effects of predestination taken as a whole is God's goodness, the final goal and first agent of everything.

God wills to manifest his goodness in man both as mercy sparing those he predestines, and as justice punishing those he rejects. And this is the reason why he chooses some and rejects others, according to St Paul. But as to why he chooses just these and rejects just those, one can give no reason but God's will. Why is some matter created as fire and other as earth? For the sake of natural variety. But why this matter as fire and that as earth? Because God willed it that way. Just as the builder's will decides what stone goes here and what there in a wall; the art of building requiring only some here and some there. That equals should be treated unequally is not unjust of God, since the effects of predestination are not owed to man but are gifts of God's grace. Favours and free gifts a person can give as he pleases, here or there, more or less, without prejudice to justice, as long as no one is deprived of his due. As the householder in the parable says: *Take what belongs to you and go. Am I not allowed to do what I choose with what belongs to me?*

God knows how many individual perishable things he has created, though he has not predefined how many cattle and how many flies as such, but provides whatever number is necessary to preserve the species. But the number of the predestined he not only knows but predefines, since they are chief parts of his creation. And the number of the reprobate depends on the number of the elect. As to what the actual number is, God alone knows. The eternal happiness of seeing God is not something natural to us, and especially not after inherited sin has deprived our nature of its original grace; so those who achieve it will be in a minority. All the greater then is God's mercy which brings some to a goal which most will fall short of in the common course and expectation of nature.

The prayers of holy men cannot cause God to predestine someone, but in God's providence they can be intermediate causes of the effects of predestination. Just as God provides natural causes for natural effects, so he provides whatever promotes a man's salvation, be it his own prayers or those of others or their good deeds. *For we are fellow-workers with God.* His own power is sufficient, but he uses intermediate causes so as to maintain order and beauty in things and to share with creatures the dignity of being causes.

God acts

25 1 **God's power.** We distinguish active power, the ability to act upon another, from passive potentiality, the ability to be acted upon by another. Active power is not contrasted with actuality but depends on it; things act only if actualized. But passive potentiality contrasts with actuality; things are acted upon only in the respects in which they are not yet actualized but potential. God then cannot have potentialities but must have active power. In God power and action are the same and both are his substance and existence. In creatures power is power of action and effect; in God it is power of effect only, since God's action is his very substance. Unless we say the distinction arises from our way of understanding God: since God's substance foreshadows in a non-composite way every different created perfection, we think of him as action and as power, just as we think of him as nature and as someone with a nature. Power is the ability to execute what will commands and mind plans; but in God the three are identical.

2 The more perfectly we possess the form by which we are active, the more power to act we have. God acts by his own unlimited substance and so his power is unlimited. When cause and effect are of the same species, the power of the cause is measured by its effect; but God is not in the same class as anything else, even generically. His power is always greater than any effect, is infinite even if no effect of his can be infinite, but is not for that reason pointless, since his power does not exist for the sake of effects, but effects rather exist for his sake.

3 God is said to be all-powerful in the sense that he can do whatever can be done. But if *can be done* means *can be done by creatures* this definition is insufficient, and if it means *can be done by God* then it is circular. So it must mean what is absolutely possible: such that subject and predicate are compatible. Reflect that every agent expresses itself in its actions; and so to every active power there corresponds a possible object, something able to receive the actuality on which the power depends: the power to heat acts on things that it is possible to heat. Now the actuality on which God's power is based is unlimited existence, not confined to any kind of being but foreshadowing every existent perfection. So what is absolutely possible, and measures all-power-fulness, is whatever is compatible with existence. But nothing is incompatible with existence except non-existence. So the only things escaping

God's all-powerfulness and absolutely impossible are things involving simultaneous existence and non-existence. It would be better to say such things cannot be done than that God cannot do them. Ability to sin is ability to fail in an action, and that is incompatible with all-powerfulness. God's omnipotence is shown above all in his forgiveness and mercy, and in the completely undeserved first creation of all good things. That the past should not have happened is absolutely impossible, and contains a contradiction; but that the dead should rise again does not, so, though it is impossible to any natural power, God is able to do it. When a goal and the means to it are commensurate, there will be a definite wise way of doing things; but God's goodness is a goal immeasurably exceeding created things, so that God's wisdom is not tied to one course of events and no other. Simply speaking then God has the power to do things differently from the way he does them. Power implements what will commands and knowledge plans. So anything he can implement as such, and that means anything non-contradictory, lies in his absolute power; and anything which implements the just commands of his will is said to lie in his ordered power. It is in his absolute power to do other things than he has foreseen and pre-ordained himself to do; but it cannot actually happen. For his deeds are subject to his foreknowledge and pre-ordination; whereas his power of action is of his nature. The reason God actually does something is that he wills to do it; the reason he *can* do it is not because he wills to, but because such is his nature.

God's happy state

Happiness is the perfection of intelligent natures, and consists in the exercise of intelligence, which takes in everything. So God is happiness itself. According to our ways of thinking, we must think God's happy state as presupposed to the act of will which reposes in it; so we identify it with an act of mind. The object of this act is always God, and in this sense everyone's happiness is God. But the act is God only in God; in those called to share his happiness it is a created act in them. Whatever we desire in any happiness whatsoever, true or imagined, exists in a transcendent way in God's happiness. The happiness of the contemplative life is there in the constant and assured contemplation of himself and of everything else; the happiness of the active life in the management of the whole universe; and earthly happiness (which

Boethius says consists of pleasure, riches, power, status and fame) in the joy he has in himself and others, in his assured possession of everything that riches could promise, in his all-powerfulness and rulership of all and in the praise of all creation.

Chapter 3

FATHER, SON AND HOLY SPIRIT

Introductory comment. In this chapter Thomas takes his final step towards the God that the Bible reveals. The last chapter developed the picture of God as a personal providence with loving plans for his creation: the God of mercy and justice, love and compassion revealed in the pages of the Old Testament. In this chapter we are introduced to the God of the New Testament, who calls creation to share the fellowship of his own life, Father, Son and Holy Spirit, through sharing in the life, death and resurrection of Jesus of Nazareth.

The Old Testament, as we saw in the preface (p lvii), pictures God as creatively building in history a house for all to inhabit: a universe built round humanity as cornerstone, with humanity in turn built around the house of Israel, a nation centred on God's house, which in Moses' time was a tent and which Solomon replaced with a magnificent temple. The Old Testament record of the vicissitudes of this creative plan ends with it still unimplemented. The New Testament sees itself as implementing the Old, by undoing the identification of God's house with Solomon's temple and identifying it with Jesus of Nazareth. His life ended with a journey into conflict with the temple which resulted in the temple's destruction and with Jesus raised up as the new cornerstone of creation, breathing forth from his cross the creator Spirit of the new Israel (as Matthew sees it), of a new mankind (as Luke sees it), and of a new universe (as Paul and the book of Revelation see it). In all these ways of presenting Jesus' role he occupies a place already defined by the Old Testament pattern of creation which he is fulfilling, the place of the old temple. But in the writings of St John there is a radically new twist: the whole pattern is turned inside out and rather than Christ being the final step of created history we have history portrayed as a created extension of the life of Christ, thought of as the beginning of all history! Jesus is identified with the creative command that set history and creation in motion: *Let there be light!* In Jesus this *old commandment which we have had from the beginning* is newly present and active among us, *for in him the darkness is passing away and the real light has already begun to shine.* That is the command which John calls *the word of life* and *the word that was in the beginning with God* and *the word that was God* for *God is light.* In Jesus *that word was made flesh and set up its tent among us. Before Abraham was, I am. I came forth from God.* And at the end of Jesus' life, as John tells, he returned to the Father on the cross, breathing forth and *handing on* his Spirit. The doctrine of the Trinity formulates this revelation made in the life of Christ, made indeed particularly in the moment of the death of Christ, the moment of new creation. The doctrine of the Trinity teaches that before creation took on its revealed pattern, that pattern was already the pattern of God's life; and this chapter, in which Thomas treats that doctrine, is the central chapter of the *Summa*, the view of God on which is based the whole of Christian theology.

It is not a doctrine Thomas thinks men can prove. He asks rather **how we can conceive of distinct persons in God** and, following Augustine, tries to illustrate the life of God with a fragile analogy drawn from the interior life of men. But only revelation can decide whether such an analogy holds between God's knowing and loving and man's (where interior words or concepts and interior loves for things might be thought to be rather imperfect stand-ins for the things themselves). The basis of the doctrine – *the facts* – remains what God has said in scripture about Jesus Christ: the Creator Word of the Genesis story and the giver of the Holy Spirit of God alive in the great works of revealed history. Thomas is simply trying to find some way of making sense of this, some way of continuing the thinking about God in the previous chapters so that it will fit *the facts*.

The discussion in the middle of the chapter parallels the last part of chapter 1 (p 30). There we considered the language and names we use for God; here Thomas considers the names used for **the three persons of God** – Father, Son, Word, Image, Holy Spirit, Love, Gift – and **the grammar of the Trinity**, the way language about the Trinity must keep its content from being misled by the mode of expression in which it has to be framed.

The end of the chapter makes the link between the pattern of created history and the pattern of God's life. Revealed history is **the sending of the persons of God**: the historical *coming forth* of the Word and the Spirit into the visible world of creation, and the *putting on* of those sendings by individual men's faith and love. Those sendings into the hearts of men and into history as such, are outer created *incarnations*, so to speak, of the inner eternal issuings which those divine persons are. Revealed history, summed up in the moment on Calvary, is in a sense God's published autobiography in our language, which he wants to write intimately in our hearts; and theology is an attempt to read that autobiography and comment on it.

How we can conceive of distinct persons in God

Coming forth in God. *I came forth from God.* Arius interpreted Jesus' *I came forth* to mean *came forth as an effect from a cause*, saying that the Son issued from the Father as his first creation, and the Holy Spirit from Father and Son as the creation of them both. But neither Son nor Holy Spirit would then be true God. Sabellius interpreted *came forth* to mean *came forth as a cause expressing itself in an effect*, saying that the Father himself is Son as taking flesh and Holy Spirit as giving life and holiness. Both opinions identify the coming forth with the kind of external activity one finds in bodily creatures, rather than with an interior activity like knowing which stays within the knower. For in any act of understanding there issues within the one who does the understanding a conception of what he understands, derived from what he knows about it. This conception is a sort of word we think, which we express in the word we speak. So the coming forth within God in which Christians believe should rather be interpreted on this analogy of a word said by a mind within itself. Whatever is emitted externally is distinct from its source, but the more perfectly something is emitted interiorly, the more united it is with its source. Better understanding implies more intimate identification with what is conceived (in the act of knowing, knower and known become one); so since God's understanding is perfect, his word must be perfectly one with its source. We call the emitting of this word in God *begetting* or *birth*. An animal is born when it issues from a living being with which it is one, and starts to exist as a living being reproducing the same species. Nothing in God starts to exist; but God's word does issue from a being with which it is one, by a living activity of reproduction (since the mind conceives a likeness of what it knows) to exist in the same nature (since in God understanding and existence are identical). So this emitting is in God

[vol 6] 27 1

2

Handwritten marginalia: Jn 8:42 · "coming forth from God" · modalism - Jesus' just "made" of God - not really distinct · God "understanding" · inner + outer words · vs "coming forth w/in God - God understand. of itself's word · "begetting"

Son

imply to object

how / Son "re-ceiver Xistno"

Spirit
knowing —
willing (love)

spirit

"breathing out"

relatedness -

a begetting and the word emitted is a Son. Even in human minds we talk of conception, since the word in our mind reproduces the thing we know; but only in God do we find identity of nature. Not all receiving presupposes a receiving subject: otherwise how could we say we receive all that we are from God? What is born in God is not a subject receiving existence from his begetter, for in God existence is itself subsistent; but he is said to receive existence because he is divine existence as coming forth from another. God's existence contains in its own perfection both emitted word and emitter, as it contains everything else belonging to its perfection.

3   [*The Spirit of truth who comes forth from the Father.*] The conception of a mental word or idea brings what is known and expressed in the word into the knower. Similarly in the activity of our wills the issuing of a love in us brings what is loved into the lover. So not only is there emitting of a word in God but also issuing of a love. Mind and will are identical in God, but their difference in notion requires a relatedness between an issuing of a word and an issuing of a love; for will loves only what mind conceives. So, just as there is relatedness of word to source in God even though mind and its word are one and the same substance, so, though mind and will are the same in God, a relatedness distinguishes

4 the coming forth of his word from that of his love. The will acts not by taking in a likeness of what it wills, but by inclining towards the thing willed itself. What issues in willing therefore is not a likeness but more an impulse and urge towards something; and what issues in the way of love in God is not a begotten son, but rather a spirit. This word [the Latin for *breath* or *wind*] names some urge or impulse of life, such as a lover feels when impelled or moved to do something. Likeness arouses a love, but that love is not itself a likeness. Creatures pass on their natures only by begetting, so there is no special name available to us to characterize this second way of communicating God's nature. We call it *breathing out*.

28 1 **Relatedness within God.**   Relationships of fatherhood and sonship really exist in God. It is peculiar to relatedness that thought can ascribe it without falsehood to things in which it does not really exist; other categories of attribute like quantities and qualities are defined as modifications of their subjects, but relatedness is defined only as a reference to something else. Sometimes this reference arises from a connection things themselves have by nature, but sometimes only from a link made in our minds. Since the coming forth of word and spirit in God are within God's substance, the relationships that arise must really exist in

his nature. Creatures issue externally from God, and God stands outside the whole order of creation. Because he creates by an act of mind and free will he is not related to creatures by any necessity of his nature; though creatures are by their natures dependent on God. So no real relatedness to creatures exists in God, though a real relatedness to God exists in creatures. But with what issues within God's nature, the story is different. Again, relationships which hold between things only as objects of thought are merely logical; but the relatedness of a word conceived by mind to the mind conceiving it is real: the mind is real and the word is its real product, as really related to the mind as the physical products of bodies are related to bodies. So fatherhood and sonship in God are real relationships.

The attributes of a thing that differ from its substance fall into 2 categories, all having the same general way of existing, but each having its own defined nature. The general way they exist is in a subject but not as a subject. And, except for the category of relatedness, their definitions refer to this subject: quantities are measures of it, qualities its dispositions, and so on. But the definition of relatedness refers not to the subject in which it exists, but to something outside. Even created relationships, then, as relating, stand beside their subjects, affecting them but not intrinsically, facing towards something else; though, as existing, they depend upon the existence of their subject.

Now what in creatures differs from their substance, exists as substance when transferred to God. Viewed as existent, then, a relatedness really existing in God exists as God's substance, altogether identical with him. But viewed precisely as relating it relates not to God's substance but to the opposite term of the relationship. In other words such a relationship is really the same thing as God's substance, but when we understand it as a relationship we understand something left unexpressed in the word substance, namely, the reference to an opposite term. When we name creatures by relationships we leave unexpressed some reality they have over and above those relationships; but in God there is no other reality, only the one reality not totally expressed by the relational name.

The very idea of relatedness involves over-againstness, one to other, 3 and thus distinctness. So real relationships in God imply real distinctness in him; not of distinct absolute realities for he is one undivided substance, but of distinct terms of the relationships. As Aristotle says, the same change is both active doing and passive undergoing, though doing is not the same thing as undergoing. Doing describes the change as coming from something; undergoing describes it as occurring to something. In the same way although fatherhood and sonship are both identical with God's substance, their own proper meanings oppose them as distinct

4 relationships. *The same road leads from Athens to Thebes and from Thebes to Athens* but the directions are different. It would be wrong to identify fatherhood with sonship; though we could identify both of them with some non-relative reality lying between them, were there such a thing.

Aristotle says relatedness is either quantitative or based on doing and being done. In God there is no quantity, and the relatedness of God based on his external creative activity does not really exist in him. So we are left with relatedness based on those activities in which something issues interiorly. These are two: the mind's activity in which a word is emitted, and the will's in which a love is breathed out. Each of these sets up two relationships: the relatedness of what issues from its source, and the relatedness of the source itself. In God understanding and what it understands, will and what it wills, are identical; so there is no real relatedness between any of these terms. But there is a real relatedness to a word, which is not what is understood but what the mind conceives or expresses of the thing being understood.

29 1 **The meaning of** *person.* Boethius defines a person as *an individual substance of a rational nature.* In every category of being we find general sorts and particular instances of those sorts: but whereas instances of sorts of substances exist independently and are individual in themselves, other attributes are instantiated by belonging to this or that individual substance. So individuality belongs specially to substances, and even more specially to reasoning substances, who have independence in action. Activity is a characteristic of individuals; but reasoning individuals are not just in activity like other things but determine this activity for themselves. This is emphasized by giving such individuals a special name: persons. The soul [like the body] is a *part* of man's nature, and even when it exists separately from the body it is still by nature the body's complement. It can no more be called an individual substance than can our hand or any other part of us; and so by neither

2 name nor nature is it a person. Aristotle distinguished two meanings of the word *substance.* Firstly, the *what a thing is,* as given by its definition [and contrasted as a category of being with the *where it is, how it is, how much it is,* etc]. This he called in Greek *ousia,* which translates into Latin as *essentia* [, and into English as *isness*]. Secondly, *substance* means an individual subject subsisting in this category of substance, [the thing whose *what* we are giving]. *Subject* is the general name for anything that

can be described in this way; but as existing independently and not
within something else it is said to be *subsistent*, as instantiating a nature
it is called a *natural thing*, and as subject to properties a *substance*. What
all these names signify generally, the name *person* signifies in the special
case of rational substances. Where we talk of three persons in God, the
Greeks talk of three hypostases. A straight rendering of that would be
three substances; but since this could also mean *three essences*, we avoid
that error by rendering it as *three subsistents*. The essence of something
is given by its definition and includes whatever makes it to be of such
and such a species; hypostasis and person add to that whatever makes
it this individual.

   Person names the most perfect things in all nature, subsistent beings
with a rational nature. God's nature embraces every perfection; so God
too is called a person, but in a much higher way than creatures. The
word is not used of God in scripture; but it expresses what scripture
says in many places: that God is the peak of independent and intelligent
existence. If we are to limit ourselves to scriptural words then we will
have to speak of God only in Hebrew and Greek! Men have to find new
words to express their old faith because they have to reply to new
heresies. God has a rational nature, in the sense not of discursive
reasoning but of intellect; he is individual in the sense of unshared; and
a substance in the sense of self-existent.

   But it is one thing to ask what *person* means in general and another
to ask what *person* means used of God. In any kind of nature *person*
means what is distinct in that nature. In human nature, for instance, it
signifies *this* flesh and *these* bones and *this* soul, which make a man *this*
man; though these are not part of what *person* means, they are part
of what *human person* means. What are distinct in God however are
relationships of origin. These relationships are identical with God's
substance, so they subsist: just as godhead is God, so fatherhood is God
the Father, a divine person. *Divine person*, therefore, means relationship
as subsistent substance – a hypostasis – subsisting in God's nature, and
as such identical with that nature. So we can say that the word *person*
signifies a relationship directly and the nature indirectly: the relationship
being signified not as a relationship but as a hypostasis. But we can also
say that the word *person* signifies the nature directly and the relationship
indirectly: the nature now being signified as identical with a subsistent
hypostasis, distinct because of its relationship indirectly signified. Before
heresy misrepresented things, the meaning of the word *person* was
overlooked and it was used like any other non-relative term; but its
adoption by councils to stand for relationships wasn't just arbitrary; it

fitted the word's meaning. [For if *person* could mean only God's nature, then talking of three persons would have fanned heresy, not silenced it.]

30   Abstract number, and consequent notions of more or less, exist separate from things only in our minds; in creatures one is less than two and two less than three, but the Father contains as much as the whole three-in-one of the Trinity. In God the three is not counted by the ones.

2

3   Number that counts quantity arises from division of a continuum, exists only in material things, and can be applied to God only metaphorically; oneness and manyness in immaterial things arise from formal difference, add nothing positive to the things, but simply deny existence of any such difference within each thing. Calling God's substance one means that it is undivided; calling a particular person of God one means that that person is undivided; and calling the persons of God many means that each of them is undivided, for the many is what is made up of ones.

4   So *person* is a shared common name. But it is not the name of some reality shared in common, like *godhead* is; if that were true the three would be one person. Nor is it the name of a logical notion like the words *genus* and *species* are: persons are real things. Rather, just as among human beings, it is a name conceptually common in the way terms of indeterminate individuality are. A specific or generic name like *man* or *animal* names an actual nature things share; the names *genus* and *species* name only the ways in which we conceive such sharing; a term of indeterminate individuality is a phrase such as *a man*, which signifies some undetermined individual instance of an actual nature, subsisting of itself and distinct from others; the name *Socrates* names *this* individual determinate and distinct in *this* flesh and *this* bone. The name *person* is like the phrase *a man* but signifies an individual not as individuating his nature but as subsisting in it distinctly. And this is something conceptually common to all the persons in God.

31 2   Heresies are the result of bad formulations, says St Jerome; so we must talk of the Trinity with caution and restraint, trying to tread a middle way between Arius' three substances and Sabellius' one person. To avoid Arianism we call the persons *distinct*, but not *different* or *diverse* (which would imply distinction of form), nor *separate* or *divided* (which would imply parts of a whole), nor *unequal* or *unlike* or *foreign*. To avoid Sabellianism we do not call any person the *singular* or *unique* God, and do not say that God is *combined* or *solitary*. If you are asked who a man is you answer with the name of the individual subject, Socrates; if you are asked what he is you say an intelligent animal. Since the distinctions in God are of persons, not of natures, we can say the Father is another

who from the Son but not another *what*; and you can say God is one *what* but not one *who*.

Natural reason cannot discover the Trinity of persons in God; it learns about God from his causing of creatures, and knows only what characterizes him as the source of everything that exists. This was the starting-point we adopted earlier when discussing God. But the power to create is shared by the whole Trinity; so though natural reason can learn things about God's nature and unity it knows nothing about the distinction of God's persons. Trying to prove the Trinity by reason would injure the faith by denying the surpassing dignity of its subject-matter, and making it a laughing-stock to unbelievers, who would think our belief relied on such unconvincing arguments. The only way of proving matters of faith is to quote authorities to those who accept them; to those who don't, we must be content to show that what the faith teaches is not impossible. What then of St Augustine's explanation of the Trinity, which appeals to the way a word and a love issue in us, and which we ourselves used above? Sometimes opinions are grounded in conclusive proof; sometimes all we can show is that adopting a particular hypothesis will explain the known facts, though other positions may do so too. The reasons we gave for the unity of God are of the first sort; but the reasons we gave for the Trinity show only that if God is a Trinity everything fits. An analogy from our minds cannot conclusively prove anything about God, since mind does not mean exactly the same thing in God and in us. But we had to know about the Trinity, primarily so that we might be clear about the salvation of mankind, which was accomplished by the Son made flesh in the giving of the Spirit.

We use words of God in ways designed for material things: using concrete names to express subsistence and wholeness, and abstract names to express non-compositeness. So just as we use both *God* and *godhead* to name God's substance, so we use both *Father* and *fatherhood* to name that divine person. Firstly, this enables us to answer questions like *What makes God one?* (his godhead) and *What makes the persons three?* (their constitutive notions, like fatherhood and sonship). And secondly, it enables us to distinguish in the one person of the Father relatedness to two others, the Son and the Spirit. The Son and Spirit do not share one relationship to the Father (for if they did they would not be distinct persons), so we have to conceive two reciprocal abstract relationships (or notions) in the one person of the Father. Such notions are real in God but are thought of and named not *as* real but as ways of knowing the persons. Thus the Father is known to us by his *unbegottenness*, as himself issuing from no other source, and by his *fatherhood*, as source of the Son, and by his *shared relation to the Spirit*, as source of the Spirit. The Son is known by his *sonship*, as issuing from the Father, and by his *shared relation to the Spirit*, as source of the Spirit. And the Spirit is known by his *procession*, as issuing from the other two persons. So here are five notions, four of them (not *unbegottenness*) relationships, and four of them uniquely identifying persons (not the *shared relation to the Spirit*). Three of them – fatherhood, sonship and procession – are constitutive of the persons. Substance and person in God are signified as really in God, so God is one and God is three; but the notions are signified as ways in which we know the

4 persons, so God is not five. The primary truths revealed by God are direct matters of faith, and obstinately to deny them leads to heresy: for example, that God is three in one, and that the Son of God became flesh. Other things are indirectly matters of faith, in the sense that unless they are true something contrary to faith will follow. To deny such things before the connection with faith has been settled is not heresy, especially if not done obstinately; but once the connection has become clear, and especially after a church decision on the matter, denial would involve heresy. The five notions above are an example of such indirect matters of faith.

The three persons

[vol 7] 33 1 **Father.** A *beginning* is simply a starting-point, so names the Father. But *cause* is a narrower term implying diversity of substances with one depending on the other; and there is disparity of perfection or power between any kind of cause and its effects. *Beginning* can be used where no such disparity exists but only sequential order, as when we call a point the beginning of a line.

2 St Paul says *I bend my knee to the Father of my Lord Jesus Christ, from whom all fatherhood in heaven and on earth is named.* A begetter always begets his like; that begetter and begotten are one in substance in God, but in creatures one in species only, shows that begetting and

3 fatherhood belong first to God, and only secondly to creatures. Fullness of fatherhood and sonship is found in God the Father and God the Son, since they are one in nature and glory. Creatures are sons of God only to certain degrees of likeness: sub-rational creatures show only traces of likeness – he is *Father of the rain* – but rational creatures are all made in God's image, and some of these are called adopted sons by a likeness of grace – *the Spirit bears witness to our spirit that we are God's sons, and*

as sons, also heirs – while others, by a likeness of glory, have already inherited – *we hope for the glory of God's sons.* The coming forth of creatures outside God is grounded in the coming forth of a person within God; for just as a craftsman first conceives an idea in his mind and then produces articles modelled on the idea, so the Son issues from the Father before creatures do, and creatures are called *sons* because they share in the likeness of Son and Father, *predestined to be made conformable to the image of his Son.*

Son, Word and Image. A *word* is most commonly an external voicing (rehearsed in imagination) which *says* something the mind is conceiving. A voicing which does not say anything is not a word. So the first and root sense of *word* is the mind's inner concept, the second the voicing that expresses this, and the third the imagined rehearsal of the voicing. A fourth but figurative meaning of *word* is the matter referred to or enjoined by somebody's words. In God *word* has its root sense: as Augustine writes *Whoever can grasp the nature of a word, not simply before it has been sounded, but even before its sound has been put together in imagination, can glimpse some likeness of that Word of whom it was said: In the beginning was the Word.* Now it belongs to the meaning of concept that it issues from something else, namely the knowing of the one who conceives it; so *word*, said of God, signifies something issuing from another, and names not God's substance as such but exclusively a person distinct on the basis of origin.

Word is the only term related to knowledge that names a person, since it alone names something as issuing from another. The mind itself, when active according to the form of something it knows, is something self-contained; and so also the act of knowing, which is related to the active mind as existence is to what actually exists, since knowing is not an external but an interior activity of the mind. *Knowing* implies a relatedness of knower to known but no notion of origin: in us it implies taking in the form of what we know so as to make the mind actively knowing; in God it implies complete identity of knower and known in every respect. But *saying* primarily implies a relatedness to a conceived word – since to say is to utter a word – and then relates us by way of the word to what is known and revealed in the word uttered. So only the person in God who utters the Word *says* it; but all know and are known and are *said* by way of the Word. [Only one person in God is *said* in the way words are said; but all are *said* in the way things are said in words.]

The person who issues as word in God's knowing is called the Son, 2 and the way in which he issues is called begetting. In us knowing and existing are different things, and what exists in our mind is not part of us by nature; but in God to exist and to know are one and the same, and God's word is not something added to his substance or an effect of his, but exists in him by nature, and is therefore subsistent, as everything in God's nature is.

3   God knows himself; he knows and also makes creatures. God's Word expresses what is in God the Father; God's Word expresses and also produces what exists in creatures. *He spoke and they were made.* Personal names involve a side-reference to a nature, since a person is an individual substance of a rational nature. So although the names of the persons in God signify their personal relationships and not their relatedness to creatures, nevertheless there is a side-reference to nature and hence to creatures. Because the Son is begotten God he is also unbegotten Creator.

35 1   An image not only resembles its original in species or in something characteristic of its species (shape, for example, in bodily things), but it also originates from it. Now in God any name implying origin and 2 coming forth is a personal name. In the Greek church the Holy Spirit is often called the image of Father and Son; but the Latin church follows the scriptures in calling only the Son *the Image of the invisible God, the firstborn of creatures.* Though the Holy Spirit, like the Son, comes forth with the Father's nature and in the Father's likeness, he is called neither *begotten* nor *Image*; and this is because the Son comes forth as a word, and a word is by definition like in kind to its source. But to be like in kind to its source is not part of the meaning of a love, even if it does characterize the Holy Spirit inasmuch as he is God's love. A king's image can be found in his son who shares his species, and on his coin, a thing of a different nature. The Son is God's image in the first way, man in the second. To mark this imperfection Genesis says man is made *to God's image* implying that the process is not complete.

36 1   **Holy Spirit, Love and Gift.**   There is no proper name for the coming forth of a love in God, nor for the relationships and person involved. Usage has adopted the notions of *procession* and *breathing out* to express the relationships, and scripture uses *Holy Spirit* for the name of the person. The word *spirit* suggests an urge or impulse towards something – *spiritus* means breath or wind – and it is characteristic of a love to urge and impel the lover's will towards what he loves. And the word *holy* 2 describes things devoted to God. Persons in God are not distinguished by any nature (for they are three in one nature), but only by reciprocally

opposed relationships: fatherhood and sonship are so opposed and constitute two persons, but the one Father can have two relationships (to the Son and to the Holy Spirit) which are not so opposed. The only relationships reciprocally opposed in God are relationships of origin: *rel of Son to Spirit* origin to what originates, and what originates to origin. So for Son and Holy Spirit to be distinct, either the Son must issue from the Spirit, which no one maintains, or the Spirit must issue from the Son, which is the faith we confess. This fits with the modes in which each of them comes forth, for love comes forth from word: we love only things which our minds have grasped by conceiving them. When someone knows 37 1 something there arises a kind of mental conception of the known thing within the knower which is called a *word*. In a similar way, when someone loves something there arises a love of it, what I might call an imprint of the loved thing in the affection of the lover, making the loved thing present in the lover as the known thing is in the knower. In regard to mind we have words available to describe both the relationship of knower to known (*knowing*) and the process of mental conception (*saying a word*). But in regard to will, we have only a word to describe the relationship of the lover to what he loves (*loving*), and none to describe the relationships between the affective imprint arising in the lover and its source. So the poverty of our language forces us to overload the word *love*, just as though we were to call the Word conceived knowledge or begotten wisdom. So if love names the relation of the lover to what he loves, love is something belonging to God's nature like knowledge and knowing. But if love names what comes forth in love then love is a personal name; and if loving means breathing out such a love it characterizes a mode of coming forth like saying and begetting do. When interpreted in this way, to love is to breathe out a love, just as to say is to produce a word, and to bloom is to produce a flower. And as the tree blooms in its flowers, so the Father says himself and his creatures in his Word or Son, and Father and Son love both themselves and us in the Holy Spirit, the love coming forth in them. The Father loves not only the Son but himself and us in the Holy Spirit, because the Holy Spirit comes forth as a love of the primal goodness with which God loves himself and all his creatures.

A *gift* is both the donor's to give and the recipient's when given. By 38 1 origin the Son belongs to the Father; and as a possession that we can freely use or enjoy as we wish, a person in God can belong by gift from ? above to intelligent creatures united to God. Other creatures can be acted upon by the persons in God, but only intelligent creatures can reach the state in which, by sharing in God's word and the love issuing from him, they are free to know God truly and love him rightly. So a divine person can be a gift. If the gift belongs to its donor by origin, as Son belongs to Father and the Holy Spirit to both of them, then the

2 gift is personally distinct from the giver, and *gift* is a personal name. It is indeed the proper name of the Holy Spirit. For gifts are freely given without thought of repayment out of love; it is because we will good to someone that we give him gifts, our love of him being our first gift. Since the Holy Spirit comes forth as a love, he comes forth as a first Gift. As Augustine says: *through the Gift that is the Holy Spirit their many individual gifts are distributed to the members of Christ's body.* The Son, because he issues as a Word, which by definition must resemble its source, has Image as his proper name; even though the Holy Spirit is also like the Father. In the same way, the Holy Spirit, because he issues from the Father as a love, has Gift as a proper name, even though the Son is also given. For the giving of the Son itself issues out of the Father's love: *God so loved the world as to give his only begotten son.*

The grammar of the Trinity

39 1 Person means a relationship subsisting in God's nature. Such a relationship differs from God's substance only conceptually; but it is really opposed to and therefore really distinct from the relationship reciprocal to it. And this is why God, though one substance, is three persons. Created subjects cannot be distinguished by relationships but only by substance, for relationships in creatures are not subsistent. But in God they are, and when they are opposed to one another can

3 distinguish subjects. Different languages have their different idioms. Because of the three persons in God, Greek talks of three hypostases, and Hebrew uses the plural form *Elohim*. But lest it be thought that godhead is being multiplied, we Latins do not talk of three substances

7 or Gods. Attributes of God's nature are better known to reason than the characteristics of the persons, for we can argue to them from creatures. The use of such attributes [common to all three persons] as though they were proper to a particular person is called *appropriation* of the attributes, and happens either because of some likeness (as mental attributes are appropriated to the Son who comes forth as a mental word), or because of some unlikeness (as Augustine says we appropriate power to the Father to avoid the suspicion that he is old and infirm like human fathers).

40 1   Because God is not composed of matter and form abstract and concrete are identified in him: God is his godhead. And because he is

not composed of substance and non-essential properties everything in him is substance: God's wisdom and power are God. Personal characteristics too are identified with persons as abstract with concrete: fatherhood is the Father, sonship is the Son and procession is the Holy Spirit. But non-personal characteristics are also identifiable with the persons, since everything in God is his substance. So the shared breathing out of the Spirit is identified with Father and Son, not as though it was a single subsistent person, but as a characteristic identified with the one substance of the two persons. Origination is thought of as an 2 act: e.g. fathering, relationship as a form: e.g. fatherhood; and since relationships follow on acts, certain authors say that the relationships merely *reveal* distinctions that are *constituted* by origination. But origination is thought of as extrinsic to the persons, a way from one to the other, whereas what distinguishes them must be thought of as intrinsic; and since it cannot be their common substance it must be their relationships. So though the persons are distinct both by relationship and origin, it is better to say that they are distinguished primarily by relationship. *Father* names the person himself, since it signifies the relationship that constitutes him distinct; *begetter* and *begotten* name only characteristic modes of origination, not constitutive of the persons. A relationship qualifying a subject presupposes its distinctness, but a subsistent relationship constitutes the distinctness. Whatever is related has to do with something other, and that *other* is its correlative, simultaneous not prior to it by nature. The characteristics of originated persons pre- 4 suppose their being originated, and the non-constitutive relationships of originating persons presuppose their act of originating (the shared relationship of Father and Son to Holy Spirit presupposes the shared breathing out of the Spirit); but where the relationship is constitutive, as with fatherhood, the relationship – as relationship – presupposes the act of originating (relationships presuppose actions), yet at the same time the act presupposes the relationship – as constitutive of the person (actions presuppose agents).

Since origination can be properly described only by actions, we have 41 1 to attribute to the persons of God characteristic actions; just as to describe the origination of creatures from God we must attribute actions to his substance. These personally characteristic actions are really identical with their relationships, and differ only in the way they are thought. Our first experience of one thing originating from another is movement; movement takes a thing away from the state it was in of itself, and so clearly needs a cause. And so *action* was first used to mean origination of movement: movement as it exists in the thing being moved by an

external cause was called passive movement or *passion*, and the originating of the movement, beginning from the agent and ending in the
moving thing, was called *action*. Take away the movement (for in God
there is no movement) and the *action* that produces a person can be
nothing more than the relationship involved in originating as such: the
relationship of a beginning to the person issuing from that beginning.
But the language in which we have to talk of these things is the one we
learned from the world of sense-experience, in which action and passion
imply movement and differ from the relationships consequent on that
movement. So, although actions and relationships are identical in God,
they differ in the way we think them. Passion then is only ascribed to
God in a grammatical sense, in the way we think the *being begotten* of
the Son.

2   Willing is sometimes a source of action – as when craftsmen will their
work – and sometimes merely accompanies – as I am a man willingly.
In this second sense the Father begets the Son willingly just as he is
God willingly. But in the first sense, though God the Father brought
forth creatures by his will, *if anyone says that the Son was made by God's
will as if a creature, let him be anathema*. Natural causes always act in
the same way, whilst will does not; what things do reflect what they are,
and whereas things have only one nature, we, by mind, take in the forms
of other things, and, by will, can act according to any of these many
forms: what the will does reflects not what the agent is but what he
plans and wills his effect to be. So will produces effects that can be
otherwise; nature things that must be the way they are. But the will also
has a nature, and certain things are willed naturally: in man's case
happiness, in God's case himself. And since the Holy Spirit issues as a
love within God's love of himself, he issues by nature, even if within
the will. And in the same way God knows himself naturally, and the
conception of God's word is by nature. An extrinsic necessity is forced
on us by an external agent or by some *sine qua non* of an external goal.
Since God serves no goal and cannot be forced, begetting in God is not
a necessity in this sense. But an intrinsic necessity is something that
cannot not be, and in this sense God is necessary and the Father's
begetting of his Son.

3   The difference between begetting a son and making things, is that
making uses external material whilst a man begets a son from himself.
Now, where craftsmen make from materials, God makes from nothing
(not meaning that he uses nothingness as a material to make being from,
but that he makes the whole of what he makes without need of material
at all). If the Son issued from the Father as emerging from nothing he

would be related not as a Son to the Father but as an artefact to its maker. To be a true son, God's Son must be begotten of the Father's substance; but not in the same way as human sons, where part of the human father's substance enters into the substance of his son. God's substance cannot be divided, and God the Father begets his Son by bestowing his whole substance upon him, the only distinction preserved being that of who originated whom.

That a source precedes in time what derives from it may be due to the type of agent and the type of action involved. Voluntary agents can choose to have it so: just as they can choose what to do, so they can choose when. Natural causes may need to mature before they can act, like men before they can father children; but even if they could act immediately they existed, still the successiveness of the action itself could delay the existence of the effect. Now the Father begets his Son by nature, not by will; but with a nature perfect from all eternity; and his begetting is not successive because it is not a material change. So the Son has existed simultaneously with the Father from all eternity; and the Holy Spirit likewise is co-eternal with them both.

The sending of the persons of God

Things sent have senders and destinations: they issue from a sender by command or advice – or by origination, like a tree sending out shoots – and come to exist in a new place or in an old place in a new way. The persons of God then can be sent, by originating from someone and coming to be somewhere in a new way. Thus the scriptures tell us the Son was sent into the world by the Father – even though *he was in the world* already – because he started to exist there in the flesh. We have different ways of describing the origination of persons in God: *proceeding* and *issuing* make reference only to the source; *begetting* and *breathing out* refer also to the eternal term of the action; *sending* and *giving* imply a destination in time, for to be newly somewhere or to be possessed by some creature is a temporal event. So the persons of God are sent or given in history; they are begotten or breathed out from all eternity; and they proceed or issue in both senses. The Son, for example, comes forth as God from all eternity and in history is sent both to be a man visibly and to dwell in men invisibly. The sending of the persons of God to exist somewhere in a new way, or the giving of them into a creature's possession, can only happen by grace making us holy. God's general way of existing in things is by substance, presence and power, in the way agents exist in their effects by sharing perfection with them.

But over and above this there is a special way God can exist in intelligent beings, as someone known and loved. Creatures by knowing and loving God attain him in himself, so that God is not only said to exist in them but to dwell in them as in a temple. This new way in which the persons of God can exist in rational creatures depends on grace making them holy; and thus only by way of such grace can a person of God be sent or come forth in time. In the same way things are possessed only when they can be used and enjoyed at will, and to have the ability to enjoy a divine person requires grace to make us holy. In the very gift of that grace the Holy Spirit is possessed and dwells in man; and so is himself given and sent. For the gift of grace making us holy empowers us not only to use that created gift freely, but to enjoy the person of God, who through that gift is himself invisibly sent and given. The grace prepares us to possess the person, so that we can say the Holy Spirit is given in the gift of grace, and the grace is itself given by the Holy Spirit: *the love of God is poured forth in our hearts by the Holy Spirit.*

4   The Son and the Holy Spirit can be sent, but not the Father, because he does not originate from another; nevertheless he, with Son and Holy
5 Spirit, causes grace and through grace dwells in us. Through grace, as St John says, the whole Trinity dwells in man: *we will come to him and make our abode with him.* Grace makes the soul like to God; and the persons of God are sent to dwell in souls who by some gift of grace have been made like to those persons. The Holy Spirit is a love, and so by the gift of love the soul is likened to the Holy Spirit, and in that gift the Holy Spirit is sent. The Son is the Word; not just any word but a word breathing out a love. So the Son is not sent in every gift perfecting the mind, but only through the sort of instruction of mind that bursts forth in loving affection. We distinguish the sending of Son and Holy Spirit according to their origin (as we distinguish being begotten from being breathed out), and although both sendings share grace as a root effect, nevertheless we can distinguish them in two effects of grace: enlightenment of mind and enkindling of affections.

7   Man naturally comes to the unseen by way of the seen; so it was fitting for him to learn of the invisible sending of the persons of God through visible creatures. The Holy Spirit, coming forth as a love, is fittingly the sanctifying gift; and the Son, as source of the Spirit, fittingly the author of sanctification. And so the Son was sent visibly as the author of salvation and the Holy Spirit as its sign. The Son became one in person with the visible creature in which he appeared, so that whatever we say of this creature we can say of the Son. To show himself as author of sanctification, the Son was sent visibly in a rational nature,

characterized by mastery over its own actions. But any creature can symbolize sanctification: the Holy Spirit does not need to become one in person with it, nor does the creature need to last beyond the period of its functioning. The invisible sending need not always be made visible by external signs; but *to each is given the manifestation of the Spirit for* 1 Co 12:7 *the common good* of the church, in order to strengthen and spread faith. Since this began in Christ and the apostles, the Holy Spirit was sent specially upon Christ and the apostles and certain early saints who were in a sense the church's foundation: ① at Christ's baptism in the form of a dove (a fertility symbol which marked out Christ as the giver of the grace of spiritual rebirth); ② the transfiguration in the form of a bright cloud (a symbol of overflowing instruction); ③ to the apostles in the form of a mighty wind (symbolizing their power to administer the sacraments) and tongues of fire (symbolizing their office of teaching). But the sending of the Holy Spirit to the Old Testament patriarchs was not made visibly, and had to wait on the full visible sending of the Son, when the Spirit made known the Son as the Son does the Father.

If sending means originating the person sent then the Son is sent only 8 by the Father, and the Holy Spirit by Father and Son. But if sending means causing the effect in which the sending happens, then the whole Trinity sends each person sent.

Chapter 4

CREATION

Introductory comment. The God who has been revealed in the last three chapters of the *Summa* is the God who revealed himself in the history of creation as recorded in the Old and New Testaments. In this chapter Thomas takes his first step in the *Summa*'s account of that history – a treatment of the first chapter of Genesis. In the Genesis story the first emphasis falls on God's unparalleled creative power to do something without precedent (the Hebrew meaning of the verb translated *create*): *The whole world began as pure invention of God ... He spoke the word and it was invented.* The first section below – **God as creator** – assesses the difference this makes to the Greek view of the world: God is the world's active source, not merely its exemplar or goal to be imitated, as Aristotle had argued. Beyond the unmoved mover, the ultimate environment in the physical world whose favour decides the forms that matter will take on, there must be a source of the very existence of those forms and that matter and indeed of the Aristotelian unmoved mover. It is the world's very being that is God's doing, God's making, without the use of tools or intermediary agents, made out of nothing, not from some presupposed material, or as some sort of emanation of God's substance. The section identifies and defines the absolute distinction between God – existence subsistent – and the things which exist by his fiat: the Being that does being, and the being that is thus done.

The second emphasis of the Genesis story falls on the order in nature that God created, the world as inhabitable blessing for its inhabitants: light from darkness, land from the floodwaters, the beginning of providence. So the remaining sections of this *Summa* chapter are devoted to the good **order and variety of creation**. This variety is not to be construed as a falling-away from the sheer existence of God into levels of non-existence, but as God's art expressing in the *this is not that* distinctions of finite things the

single simple concentrated perfection of his own existence, and
calling into existence creaturely artists to cooperate with him in
his creation. *God saw his creation, and it was very good.*

It comes as a surprise when the first great distinction within
what God has created is said to be the distinction of **good and bad**
in creation. But it is a fundamental and immediate consequence of
composition in creation that creatures may suffer a loss of their
integrity or be parts detachable from the whole. So primary is this
distinction of good and evil, that it has often been used to model the
distinction between the Creator and his world, and even thought to
exist as a struggle within the Creator himself. By ranking it as a
created distinction, but the first, Thomas is at once repudiating
and yet acknowledging the force of the Manichean heresy he had
to meet in his own times and which he found *more mistaken than
even pagans are* [ch 10 p 340].

The other great created distinction, according to Thomas, is
that between **spirit and matter**. Spirit, here given its Greek sense
of mind and seen as immaterial over against matter, is identified
with the biblical category of *angels*. Whatever may be thought of
this identification, the important point again is that the distinction
is a created one, that cannot adequately model the distinction of
the Creator from his world. God is no more captured by this idea
of *spirit* than he is by the biblical concept of *angel*. To Thomas's
anti-emanationism and anti-Manicheanism is added an anti-
gnosticism (in modern terms, an anti-born-again position, since
born-again religion worships spirit as something over against the
material world, rather than as God's love acting through it). At its
end, the chapter considers the Genesis account of material creation,
preparing the way for the creature with whom God will identify
in history, in preference to the angels: man in whom spirit and
matter are at one.

God as creator

God as source of the world.   A perfection many things share must [vol 8] 44 1
derive from an agent which is that perfection subsistent. Now God is
subsistent existence and the only such being there is (just as whiteness,
if it subsisted of itself instead of being received into many white subjects,
would be the only whiteness). So all the other things that share existence
in diverse degrees, must derive it from the one first being that exists to

the full. Dependence on an agent, though not part of a caused being's definition, is a necessary property of anything that only shares existence: such beings can no more exist without being caused than men can be men without having a sense of the comic. But since being caused is not essential to being as such, there exists an uncaused being. Even necessary effects require agents: *effects would not exist if their cause didn't* is a true conditional that applies even in cases where its antecedent and consequent do not. Even the objects of mathematics are caused, though mathematics abstracts from this.

2   Early philosophers felt their way to the truth slowly step by step. They began somewhat crudely by thinking that only bodies we can sense exist, that the essential substance of such bodies [*what* they are] is uncaused, and that they change only [*how* they are] in inessentials, rarefying and condensing, separating and combining under the influence of attraction, repulsion, mind and so on. Later they worked out the distinction within essential substance between its matter (uncaused, as they thought) and the form of substance taken on by such matter, and realized that bodies change even the substantial form [of what they are] under the influence of more cosmic causes such as Aristotle's *inclined circle* or Plato's Ideas. So far they were seeking only particular causes for what (or how) particular beings were. But some thinkers eventually considered being as such, and asked why things exist at all. And this meant seeking a universal cause of everything including the basic matter (or potentiality of form) in all substances. [Science] deals only with the particular changes and transformations that matter undergoes, taking its existence for granted; but when we talk of the derivation of things from their universal source of existence, this includes deriving their matter, for the passive basis of things is reasonably to be derived from their primary active source. Not that matter is produced unformed. What are produced are actually formed existent things which are not purely actual but also potential; but their potentiality is caused by whatever causes their existence as such.

3   God is also the prototype of everything. Just as craftsmen shape their material after some pattern they have in sight or mind, so God's wisdom which shapes the whole order and diversity of the universe has patterns of everything in mind, which we have called Ideas. These Ideas are many only in their relation to things and are not really distinct from God's substance, diversely reflected in those things. God then is the prototype of all things, though special groups of things may also have their own created prototypes.

4   Actions always seek goals (otherwise only by chance would actions

have determinate effects): and what the agent seeks to induce is also what the recipient seeks to receive. Now some agents are not pure agents: they act only because acted upon, and in order to get something for themselves. But the first agent is pure agent acting not to get something but to communicate his own perfection and goodness; and all his creatures in seeking their own perfection seek to reflect the perfection and goodness of God. So God's goodness is the goal of everything. In reproduction the form reproduced is the goal only inasmuch as it is a likeness of the reproducer's form which he is seeking to communicate. Otherwise what is reproduced would be of more value than the reproducer, since goals are more valuable than means to goals. Whatever good anything wants, be it in a rational, animal or natural and unconscious way, God is the ultimate goal sought, for nothing is good or desirable except by having some likeness to God.

So the one God is the agent, prototype, and goal of all things, and the source of their matter: all different ways in which our minds conceive him, and some of them presupposed to others.

Creation is God's way of causing.   Nothing existent can be pre- 45 1
supposed to the issuing of everything existent from its first source. Just as man begets man from what is not yet man, so creation – our name for the issuing of all existence – must proceed from what is not existent at all, from nothing. *From nothing* can mean either *after nothing* (that is, following on nothing), or *not from something* (that is, not out of any presupposed material).

Crafts presuppose materials provided by nature; natural causes pre- 2
suppose matter which they form and transform; but if God presupposed anything in this way he would not be the universal cause of all existence; so he must bring things into existence from nothing. We think of creation as a change, even though it isn't. In a change something begins in one state and ends up in another; but in creation there is nothing to begin with and the whole substance of a thing is produced, though we imagine the thing as first non-existent then existent. A change relates in one way to the agent causing it (it is that agent's action), and in another way to the subject undergoing it (it is that thing's subjection to the agent). If we think away the change, only the diverse relationships in creator and created remain. Nevertheless, we talk of creation in the way we think of it, as a change and as a making out of nothing. But making and being made are more appropriate terms than changing and being changed, since what they directly signify is the relatedness of cause to effect and effect to cause, with change implied only on the side.

3 The createdness of creatures is simply their relatedness to their Creator as source of their being; and the active creating of them is God's action, identical with his substance and conceptually related to creatures. Creatures are really related to God but God is only conceptually related to creatures. Since createdness is something real in creatures, it is itself something created. But that doesn't mean created by another creation (and so on *ad infinitum*); for relatedness refers of itself and doesn't need another relatedness to relate it. When we think creation as a change, we think the creature as its end-result; but since in truth creation is a relatedness of the creature, it presupposes the existence of the creature, just as all properties do. Though this relatedness has a certain priority inasmuch as it relates the creature to its source. Nor does this force us to say creatures are being created throughout their existence, since creation names the relatedness to the Creator at its first appearance.

4 Only what exists can properly be called created. Forms and properties exist not as existent things but as ways in which such things exist: whiteness exists when something is white. Which is why Aristotle says properties belong in existence rather than exist. So forms and properties are not created so much as co-created; and what are properly created are subsistent things. We say existence is the first thing created, not meaning that existence is itself a created thing, but that existence is what makes things objects of creation. For it is as existing at all that things are called created, not as being this or that existent. We use the same turn of speech when we say colour is the first thing we see, although properly speaking we only see coloured things.

5 The most widespread of all effects is existence itself; so it must be the effect proper to the first and most wide-ranging of causes, namely God. In other words, creation is an action peculiar to God himself. Now sometimes things can share in an activity peculiar to something else, not by their own power but by acting as a tool of the other's power. But this only happens when the tool has something of its own to contribute, preparing the main effect; the tool would otherwise be useless, and specific jobs would not require specific tools. Thus a saw by cutting wood, its own speciality, shapes a bench, the carpenter's speciality. But God's proper effect in creating is what every other effect presupposes, namely existence itself. Nothing can act as a tool and contribute to that effect, for creation presupposes nothing that the operation of a tool could prepare. So it is altogether impossible for creatures to create, either by their own power or as tools and intermediaries.

6 Since what things do reflect what they are, God creates inasmuch as he exists; and his existence is his substance, common to all three

persons. Creating then is not peculiar to any one person, though the different ways in which the persons originate link them differently to creation. Just as a craftsman's work proceeds from an idea conceived in his mind and from a love which bends his will to that work, so God the Father produces creatures through his Word, the Son, and his Love, the Holy Spirit. God's substance is common to all three persons, but according to a certain precedence, received by the Son from the Father, and by the Holy Spirit from them both; and so also with the power of creating. So in the creeds the Father is called *Creator* as not receiving his creative power from any other person; but we say *all things were made through the Son* as through an intermediary having creative power from another, an origin originated; and we confess the Holy Spirit to be *Lord and Lifegiver* to everything created by Father and by Son.

Effects represent their cause: either by imaging and reproducing the 7 form of the cause, or as traces of the cause, which do not reproduce the form of the cause but only signify its causal presence, in the way smoke signifies fire and tracks show that someone has passed that way but don't give us a picture of him. Creatures endowed with mind and will can image the Trinity by conceiving an idea [of God] from which a love bursts forth. But all creatures bear traces of the Trinity deriving from the persons as effects from a cause: for every creature subsists in itself, has its own specific form, and relates to others. As created substance it signifies its causal origin, and so is a trace of the Father, who is the origin without origin; as having a specific form it is a trace of the Word, since works of craft derive their form from their craftsman's conception; and as related to others each creature is a trace of the Holy Spirit, God's Love, since its relation to others derives from its creator's will.

Where do forms come from? Some said they could not arise from 8 natural causes, and must already exist hidden in some way in matter, confusing potential with actual existence: matter is potential of forms but that is not a pre-existence of the form in any normal sense. Others said an immaterial agent must contribute or cause the forms by a sort of creation; so that creation must accompany every operation of nature. This is a misunderstanding of forms, thinking of natural forms of bodies as themselves subsistent rather than as ways in which things exist. The truth is that forms do not come into being; what comes into being is the composite, formed out of matter, and that comes to be by natural causes. Creation is not mingled with the operations of nature, but presupposed to such operations; forms are not created but co-created. The active properties of natural causes act as tools of the forms that determine what kind of substances those causes are. So operations of nature not only propagate those properties but also reproduce those forms.

46 1 **Did the world begin?**   It cannot be proved that the created world existed for ever. The fact that even before it existed such a world *could* exist, does not mean that something potentially the world existed, but only that God's power of creation existed, or simply that an existent world is not a contradiction in terms. Even imperishable things, which cannot now not be, have had that property only from the moment they were constituted imperishable, and before that did not exist. Before the world existed there wasn't even a vacuum; for a vacuum is not a simple absence of something but a space capable of housing bodies in which no bodies exist; and before the world existed there was no place and no space. Particular causes presuppose time just as they presuppose matter, and we can rightly think of them as acting after a time without having acted earlier; but we mustn't think of the universal cause of all things, time included, as acting at some moment but not earlier, as if time pre-existed his action. Rather he freely decided to give a time-span to what he made, to show his creative power: for a world that had a beginning more clearly points to its cause than one that has existed for ever. God exists *before* the world in eternity, not in time. Unless we think of some imaginary everlasting time which does not really exist; just as we sometimes say there is nothing outside the universe, where the word *outside* signifies some imaginary space added on to the dimensions of the universe. Effects proceed from natural causes according to the natural form of these causes, but from causes with wills according to forms preconceived by those causes. So although God was from all eternity the sufficient cause of the world, no world had to come into being except the one conceived by him, namely one that exists after not having existed and thus most clearly points to its author. The eternity of God's activity (identical with his substance) doesn't mean his effects must be eternal, but they must be as God wills them to be: existing after not having existed.

2   But neither can it be proved that the world began. For when and where a thing exists is abstracted from in its definition: and proofs rest on definitions. So there is no proving that men and skies and rocks did not always exist. Nor can we search God's will, except as regards things he cannot but will, and creatures are not of that sort. But God can reveal his will to man and be believed. That the world began is therefore an object of faith, not of proof or science. And it is as well to remember this so that one does not try to prove what cannot be proved and give non-believers grounds for mockery, and for thinking the reasons we give

are our reasons for believing. Those who think the world always existed could agree that God made it out of nothing; agreeing that it was not made from anything, but not that it was made after nothing, as *we* understand the word *creation*. However far back in the past we go, from that day to this is a finite time and can be traversed. [To argue that if the world always existed an infinite number of past days would have had to be traversed to get to today] tries to talk as though there actually were two points in time with an infinite number of days between. Causes essential to an effect cannot be multiplied infinitely; the stick moving the stone, the hand the stick, and so on for ever. But an incidental infinity of causes is not thought impossible, if they all fill one place in the causal hierarchy; a workman could go on for ever changing hammers when they break, since it is incidental to the causality of the hammer that another preceded it. And this is the case with procreation: it is incidental to a man procreating that he was procreated, because he procreates as a man, not as a son of a man; and all men procreating fill the same place in the causal hierarchy, so that procreation could last for ever. But this would not be so if the dependence were through this man to chemical elements to the sun and so on for ever.

When we say *God created heaven and earth in the beginning* of time, 3 we mean that earth and sky were created together with time, not that the action of creation was itself in time.

The variety and order of creation

Matter does not require any distinction between things; on the 47 1 contrary, matter as such is formless and adaptable to any form. Nor is such distinction due to secondary agents, as though the variety of things in the universe resulted from coincidence of causes, which is to say from chance, and was not planned by one first cause. God planned to create many distinct things, in order to share with them and reproduce in them his goodness. Because no one creature could do this, he produced many diverse creatures, so that what was lacking in one expression of his goodness could be made up by another; for the goodness which God has whole and together, creatures share in many different ways. And the whole universe shares and expresses that goodness better than any individual creature.

In order to rule out the idea that the distinctions of things arose from 2 two competing sources, one good and one evil, Origen suggested that God created only reasoning creatures, all equal, in the beginning, and that inequality arose from their free choice when some turned in varying degrees to God, and some turned in varying degrees away. Those who turned to God were promoted to the various ranks of angels according to their deserts, and those who turned away were confined in different bodies according to their degree of fault. Were this true the bodily universe would have been created not to share God's goodness but to punish sin, which contradicts Genesis: *God saw all the things that he had made and they were very good.*

God's wisdom is the cause of the distinctions and the inequality of things. Species are distinguished by form, individuals by matter. The second distinctness serves the first: one imperishable individual would be enough to preserve its species; but many individuals are needed to preserve a species if things are to be born and die. But distinctness of form always requires inequality, for *forms are like numbers, varying by adding or subtracting one.* Species in nature are arranged in steps: compounds above elements, plants above minerals, animals above plants, men above other animals; and under each of these headings one species above another. Only when granting rewards, is inequality deserved as Origen thought; inequality of parts in something we make does not depend on their deserts or their material, but on what the completion of the whole requires. Roof and foundations don't differ because their materials are different; but to complete the different parts of his house the builder looks about for diverse materials, and makes such if he can.

2a   [A group of moorish thinkers denied all created activity, saying it was not fire which heated things but God acting in the fire. If this were so there would be no point in attributing to things any active powers or qualities or forms. So we say that the very inequality of things established by God's wisdom means that one thing must act on another, for to be higher in the scale of being a thing must be actual in some respect in which lower things are potential, and it is in the nature of actual things to act on what is potential. Though God is the first pattern of all creatures, creatures can be secondary patterns for each other. God is the ultimate goal of all creatures, but creatures can also serve each other: so matter serves form, elements compounds, plants animals and animals man. The order of the world consists in creatures acting on, patterning themselves on and serving one another.][1]

3   All things deriving from God are ordered to one another and to him.

[1] The preceding paragraph is found in only one manuscript of the *Summa* and has generally been omitted by editors. But it makes a point referred to later by the author, and seems interesting in its own right.

And that is what makes the unity of the world. Material plurality cannot *unity of / world-* be a goal, for it has no determinate limit and what is without end cannot be an end. To say two worlds are better than one would make a goal of plurality; so that however many worlds God made one more would have been better.

Good and bad

To know what badness is you must understand good. Whatever is of 48 1 value is good, and that includes all natural existence and perfections. Badness then cannot be a particular sort of existence or form or nature; it cannot be anything but absence of good. *The basic contrariety*, says Aristotle, *is having versus not having*; good and bad don't describe sorts of things, but a division according to which every form is a good and every lack as such bad. Good and bad define sorts of things only in moral matters where actions are defined by reference to their willed goal. Even there absence of a right goal does not define a moral act unless it accompanies a wrong goal; just as natural things can only lack the form of one substance by possessing the form of another. So the morally bad is a good lacking some other good; the intemperate man does not aim at unreason but at sensuous pleasure unreasonably. So the bad as such does not define anything, but only as accompanying a good. Does evil have effects? In the sense that forms have effects – whiteness, for example, makes something white – bad destroys good simply by being a lack of it. But in the sense that agents have effects and goals the effect of motivating agents, bad does not have effects as such, that is as a lack, but only as accompanying a good; for agency results from form, and only perfections can be goals.

The completeness of the universe requires perishable as well as 2 imperishable things; and thus things which can sometimes go bad. Bad is as real as decay, since decay is itself bad. But there are two senses in which things can be said to exist: firstly, the sense in which all ten basic *bad does not exist* categories of real thing – substance, quantity, quality, and so on – exist: *as / things in / 10* and in this sense no lack or bad exists. Secondly, the sense in which *categories do* what makes some proposition true exists, the sense in which we use the verb *to be* to unite subject to predicate, and ask whether something or *but it does in the* other *is* so. And in this sense we say blindness and other like lacks exist, *sense of subject n* and in this sense bad exists. By not making this distinction people have *predicate of. pro-* been led from saying that certain things are bad or that bad exists in *position –* things to the belief that bad itself is a sort of thing. The universe as a *has produced /* whole is better and more complete for including some things which can, *linguistic illusion (Witt.*

genstein) that "bad" exists

and unless God prevents it do, fall short of goodness. Pseudo-Denys tells us that providence does not abrogate nature, but fulfils it, and it is natural that what can fall short sometimes will. And Augustine writes that God is powerful enough to bring good from bad. If God did not permit bad, many goods would disappear: fire cannot exist without consuming air nor lions survive without killing asses; nor could we praise the righting of wrongs or the endurance of suffering if wickedness did not exist.

3   Mere absence of good is not bad; otherwise the non-existence of anything would be bad, and whatever was without some good quality: man, for example, would be bad because he is not as swift as a goat or as strong as a lion. It is the deprivation of good which is bad: blindness, for example, which is lack of sight. Deprivation occurs only in subjects capable of possessing an absent form; and all such capability is good, being ordered towards good. So bad only ever occurs in good subjects, subjects possessing some other good than the good to which the bad is
4   opposed: what is blind can't see but it is still an animal. There is the ①good which bad opposes and wholly eliminates (as darkness eliminates light), ②the good which is its subject and which it neither eliminates nor diminishes (the nature of the air which was light and is now dark), and ③the good which is the subject's readiness to receive the eliminated perfection, and which is diminished by an increase in contrary dispositions. This readiness can occasionally be diminished endlessly, but it can never be completely eliminated since it is rooted in the substance of the subject. Thus you may interpose opaque screens between the sun and the atmosphere endlessly without taking away the transparency to light that air has by nature; and you may heap sin upon sin endlessly, interposing obstacles between God and yourself that will weaken your readiness to accept his grace, but you can't eliminate entirely a readiness for grace that you have by nature.

5   The first actualization of anything is the form which constitutes it one thing; the second is its activity. A thing may go bad by losing its form or some part required for wholeness (going blind or losing a limb), or by not acting as it should, either omitting to act or acting in an undue manner. Reasoning creatures with wills can be bad in special ways. In them loss of form or wholeness can be characterized as inflicted (which means unwillingly undergone), whilst willingly not acting as one should can be characterized as fault. Where will is concerned then badness may
6   be distinguished as either inflicted or a fault. Faults are greater evils than inflicted evils, even than inflicted loss of grace and eternal life. Firstly, because faults, not afflictions, make people bad. A good man

simply speaking is one who acts and uses his gifts well, all of which he
does by his will. Now faults are misdirected acts of will, whereas
afflictions merely deprive us of things our will can make use of; so faults
are greater evils than afflictions. Secondly, God causes afflictions but
not faults. For afflictions deprive us of creaturely goods, whereas faults
directly oppose the uncreated goodness, conflicting with the fulfilment of God's own will and that love which loves his goodness in
itself and not simply its likeness in creatures. So faults are worse than
afflictions.

If something lacks a disposition it ought by nature to have, some
cause must be responsible, and that cause must exist, and as such be
good. So evil is caused by good. And indeed we have already seen that
evil can only exist in a good subject (its material cause). Evil has no
formal cause (since it is not form but lack of form) and no goal or final
cause (since it is lack of due order to a goal). But it has, not intrinsically
but incidentally, an agent cause. Bad actions, for example, result from
defective ability of the agent or its tool: babies cannot walk because they
lack power to move their limbs, the disabled because they lack the limbs
to move. Bad effects however can result either from defects of the agent
or its material, or sometimes – when the effect is not specific to the
agent – from the very ability of the agent. For when the form an agent
aims at involves necessarily loss of another form (as fire consumes air),
then the very strength of the fire causes the bad loss of air. Only
incidentally, however, for the intended effect is the production of fire,
to which the loss of air is incidental. Defects in the specific effects of
agents (fire failing to heat) reduce to defective agent ability or defective
material, and such deficiencies are incidental to the active goodness of
the agent. So what is bad is always caused, incidentally, by good. The
cause of moral evil is deficient in a different way from the cause of
natural evil. A natural cause reproduces itself in its effect unless impeded
by some external factor, and this vulnerability to external factors is
itself a defect; so naturally bad effects can only arise from some deficiency
already present in the agent or the material. But a morally defective
action arises from a will defective in that act, because not in that act
subjecting itself to its own rule. This defect is not itself a fault; but fault
results from acting while in this defective state.

Badness of action always results from defectiveness in the agent, and
since God has no defects, bad actions cannot be traced back to God as
cause. But badness of form in things can be traced back to God, in both
the natural and the moral world. For any agent which produces a form
from which privation and decay follow causes that decay. Now Go in

creating aims at the good order of the universe, and that involves things that can decay and sometimes will; so God as a consequence of causing the world order incidentally causes decay. The course of justice is also part of this world order and requires punishment of sinners. So God is the author of inflicted evils, but not, for the reasons given above, of faults.

3   Nothing can be essentially or completely evil, for if all good was eliminated in something there would be no subject left to be evil. Nor can there be intrinsic sources of evil. Those who believe in two sources of things, one good and one evil, think there must be particular contrary causes for particular contrary effects, and forget there must be a universal cause of everything. Seeing fire burn down the poor man's house they call fire evil by nature, forgetting that it cannot be judged in relation to one particular event but only in its place in the whole ordered scheme of things. [Some say evil must have an intrinsic cause, for if it was only caused incidentally it would happen infrequently.] But evil is infrequent. Things that decay, and thus are subject to natural evils, are a very small part of the universe. And in each species defects are the exception. Only among men does it seem that most are bad following their senses rather than their reason, even though what is good for man is what reason judges good, not what his bodily senses prefer.

Spirit and matter

[vol 9] 50 1 **The world of pure spirits.**   All creatures are patterned after God himself. Now effects most resemble their cause when they resemble its very way of causing, which in God's case is by intelligence and will; so without created intelligences the universe would be incomplete. Since bodies and bodily powers cannot exercise intelligence (being limited to the here and now), a complete universe must contain creatures without bodies. The ancient philosophers, who saw no difference between intelligence and sensation, thought nothing existed but bodies they could sense and imagine; but the fact that intelligence is a higher power than sensation suggests that there exist things without bodies that only intelligence can grasp. Such intelligences are not like us, at times actually knowing and at times merely retaining the power to do so; they actually know all the time.

2   Everything acts in accordance with the kind of substance it is. Now intelligence is a wholly immaterial activity; since the object which defines its special character is a form that must be abstracted from any particular instantiation in matter if the mind is to grasp it. So substances to be

intelligent must be wholly immaterial. We define a thing's species – its special level of being – by differentiating a more generic notion. In the material world this differentiation of a genus reflects matter being determined to a special level of being by a form. But in the immaterial world no such determination of one constituent by another occurs, and each thing simply exists at its own determinate level of being. Genus and difference, therefore, do not reflect two distinct constituents in an immaterial thing, but the thing itself thought first indeterminately (generically) and then determinately (differentiated into species). Form received into matter constitutes it into some species of thing. But it is not received into mind in that way. Forms received into mind exist there as forms, in the way the mind knows them. Some compositeness of potentiality and actualization does exist in angels however. For reflect that material things are composite in two ways. Form unites with matter to constitute some substance, but the substance so constituted is not its own existence; rather it is related to that existence as a potentiality to what actualizes it. So where there is no matter, but a form subsists on its own, this relation of form to existence as potentiality to actualization remains. Only in God does existence itself exist.

Since the incorruptible heavenly bodies are immeasurably larger than 3 our little globe of bodies that change and perish, it is reasonable to presume that immaterial substances too will immeasurably outnumber material ones. Members of species agree in form but are materially 4 *angels* distinct. Since angels are not composed of matter and form, there cannot be more than one angel in any species. A thing perishes when its matter 5 loses that form; because angels are forms subsisting independently their substance is imperishable. [Gregory says *all things would come to nothing without the Almighty's sustaining hand,*] but this does not mean that angels in themselves are perishable, but that their existence is caused in them by God. We do not call things perishable because God by withdrawing his sustaining power could bring them to nothing, but because within themselves they contain the seeds of decay: competing elements or some other liability to change.

No <u>intelligence as such needs a body</u>. The reason man's soul needs a 51 1 body is because it is only potentially intelligent, not knowing everything innately but needing to acquire knowledge through bodily experience of the sensible world. But whatever sort of thing has imperfect instances must also have perfect ones; so there must exist perfect instances of *arg. for angels* intelligence, not needing to acquire knowledge from the sensible world, and so not having bodies. These we call angels.

When bodies are in place their dimensions arc contained in those of 52 1

the place. But angels exist anywhere their powers are applied. So they are not measured by places or positioned in them or contained by them. Rather they can hold and contain places and their contents, just as soul
2 holds body together rather than body soul. Bodies are contained in places, sharing their dimensions; angels, though not contained, apply themselves to defined places, here rather than there; but God is neither
53 3 contained in nor at a particular place but everywhere. For angels to change place takes time: continuous time for continuous movements, discontinuous for discontinuous movements. But not the time that measures the rotation of the heavens and all the bodily changes that result from it, since angels' movements don't result from it. In discontinuous movement, the angel is now here now there with no time-interval between.

54 1 **Knowledge among spirits.** Only God is pure actuality, identical with his own existence and activity. If angels were their own activity of understanding there wouldn't be different levels of understanding among them: for that is caused by unequal sharing of what it is to understand. External activities really go out from agents to the subjects they act on; but though we talk of interior activities [like sensation, understanding and willing] as though they went out from agent to object this is not really so. Such activities in reality result from a union of object with agent. When the object to be understood has become one with the mind there results an effect different from either, namely the act of understanding.

interior activities

2   Clearly, external activity cannot be identified with an agent's existence: such activity flows out from the agent whereas existence is something intrinsic. And interior activity as such has no limits: in principle we can understand or will anything, and we need particular objects to specify the activity. Existence however is always of one particular genus and species in creatures; only God's existence is unlimited and all-embracing. In God alone then can existing be identified with under-
3 standing and willing. It is not any creature's nature simply to exist, but its nature is a potentiality actualized by existence. Active powers however are actualized by activity; and since no creature's activity can be identified with its existence, no creature's nature can be identified with its active powers. [It is not only a material thing that can have properties other than its substance.] Pure forms which are not their own existence, but are potential of existence, can have such properties; and especially properties that are common to a species. Properties restricted to individuals and not common to a whole species result from the matter

by which the form is individualized.

Human minds are both active and receptive in relation to imagination: 4 our agent mind illuminates our images so that they can affect our receptive mind, just as light activates colours to affect our sight. We have receptive minds because we are able to know before we actually do; we have a capacity for knowledge which is actualized when we acquire knowledge, and further actualized when we actively attend to what we have acquired, and this capacity we call our *receptive mind*. We *receptive mind* DEF have agent minds because we know the natures of material things which exist outside the mind in ways only potentially immaterial and intelligible; we must have some power of making them actually intelligible, and this power we call our *agent mind*. None of this applies to *agent mind DEF* angels whose knowledge is always actualized, and of actually intelligible objects.

Whatever makes the mind actively knowing is a form of the mind, 55 1 just as every agent's activity is the result of some form. But only God knows everything by his own nature; angels cannot know everything by nature and their minds need further forms to complete their knowledge. Aristotle says the activity of sensing actualizes what is there to be sensed; but he does not mean that the sense-faculty itself is a representation of what it senses; but rather that the faculty and the sense-representation are joined like potentiality and actualization to make one thing. And when the activity of understanding is said to actualize the thing to be understood, we don't mean that the mind's substance itself represents what is understood, but that the mind is formed by such a representation. The forms by which angels know are not drawn from things but are 2 innate. Human souls have intellectual capacities not innately fulfilled, but only gradually in time by forms drawn from things. But the higher spiritual substances called angels have intellectual capacities innately fulfilled by forms accompanying their natures, by which they can know all that it is natural for them to know.

Interior activities presuppose a union of agent and object: actual 56 1 sensation presupposes union of the object to be sensed with the sense-power. The object united with the power plays the same role in interior activity as the form activating the agent plays in external activity: fire heats because hot, the eye sees the object whose form is present in it. If an object's form is able to be present in a knower, he has the ability to know that object; but he will not actually know it until the form becomes actually present in him. But if an object's form is always actually present in him he does not first need to be conformed to the object before knowing it. Clearly then being affected by an object is not part of knowing as such, and only potential knowers need it. Moreover, it makes no difference whether an activating form exists in an agent or is itself the agent: heat would be no less hot if it could exist on its own than when existing in fire. In the same way in the world of understanding if some form to be understood could exist on its own, it would understand itself. And that is the way an angel understands itself, by the very form 2 which is its substance. Each angel is imprinted by the creative Word of God with the forms of all things, spiritual and corporeal. With this difference: he receives his own form both as a nature to subsist in and a form to know himself by, but the forms of other things only as forms 3 to know them by. Things can be known by existing in the knower (as light would be if it existed visibly in an eye), and this is how angels know themselves; or by being imaged in the knower (as stones are seen by likenesses generated in the eye); or by their images being imaged (as when we see things in mirrors). To know God's substance is to know God in the first way: a knowledge which creatures cannot acquire by their own natural powers. To know *the invisible things of God through the things he has made* as we do in the present life, is to know him in the third way – *in a mirror*. The way angels naturally know God is halfway between these two, and like the second way, for they know themselves as images of God and mirrors reflecting him.

58 1   Human minds are potentially knowledgeable before they acquire knowledge and then potentially knowing when not attending to the knowledge they have acquired. Angels are never potentially knowledgeable about what they know by nature, but only about what God reveals to them. On the other hand, they can be potentially knowing about their natural knowledge (by not attending to it), but never about what they see in the Word of God, at which they are always gazing, for the vision of the Word is their happiness, and happiness is an activity not just an acquisition.

3   Man's is a lower form of mind which to achieve complete knowledge of truth must engage in a discursive process, moving from one known thing to another. If men were able in the very knowing of premises to see all the implied consequences, there would be no need of this process; and this is what happens in angels. That is why we call them intelligences, for intelligence is our name for grasping first principles. But the human soul we call rational, because it acquires knowledge of truth through processes of reasoning; and this happens because our light of intelligence 4 is dim. And just as the mind in reasoning relates conclusions to premises, so the mind when forming propositions relates predicates to subjects. It would never need reasoning if it could see a conclusion's truth just by

seeing a premise, and it would never need propositions if it could know everything attributable or non-attributable to a subject just by knowing its definition. In both cases it is the dimness of our light of intelligence which prevents us seeing everything implicit in some initial grasp. But the light of intelligence is at full strength in angels, and they need neither reasoning nor propositions, though understanding both: for they understand the composite and the changing and the material, in a simple unchanging immaterial way.

Love and will among spirits.   Because everything derives from 59 1 God's will everything has its own kind of tendency to good. Plants and non-living things have only natural tendencies, unconsciously and by nature adhering to what is good for them. Animals have sense-stimulated appetite, not knowing the meaning of good as such, but attracted to particular goods sensed as sweet or white or the like. Some creatures however embrace good with a will, knowing, as only minds can, what good means. And this is the best way of tending to good: not unconsciously as if aimed at it only by someone else, nor pursuing only this or that good suggested by the senses, but seeking good as such and in general. Since angels have minds to know the meaning of good in general, clearly they have wills. A thing's nature is its intrinsic constitution, and 2 whatever reaches out beyond that thing is additional to its nature. Now the will is attracted by whatever is good. So will and nature are distinct unless every good willed belongs by nature to the one willing it; this happens only in God, who wills things outside himself by willing them to share his good. Will also differs from mind in both men and angels, because knowing takes in the known, while willing goes out in some way to what is willed. Now it is one thing to take in what lies outside, and another to tend towards it. So mind and will differ in creatures, though not in God who contains in himself all being and all good. What distinguishes powers is not a material but a formal difference between their objects: a difference in the meaning of object. Every good thing is a true thing and vice versa (which is why the mind can understand good and the will desire truth), but the difference in meaning between truth and good suffices to distinguish two faculties: mind and will.

Some things don't decide on action but are made to act by others, as 3 arrows are shot at targets by archers. Other things such as the lower animals, do in a way decide on action, but not freely: sheep flee the wolf because they judge it dangerous, but the judgment is not free but imposed on them by nature. To act from a free judgment one must have a mind to know what good means in general and decide that this, not that, is good. So wherever there is mind there is free will.

60 1   All natures bring with them natural tendencies or appetites or loves. Wherever there is the nature of mind there is natural tendency in the will; wherever sense-awareness, a natural tendency in the sense-stimulated appetite; and where there is no awareness there is an orientation of nature itself to things. So in the angel then there is a natural willing love. Such natural love is never wrong, since it is a tendency imposed by the author of nature.

2   Men know certain premises by nature, and from these come to know certain conclusions, not by nature but by teaching or discovery. Since goals are like premises of willing, men will their ultimate goal of happiness by nature, and then in pursuit of that goal will whatever else they will. The love of the goal willed by nature we call *natural love*, and the derived love of things for the sake of that goal we call *loving from choice*. There is however a difference between mind and will. Knowing takes in what it knows, and it is an imperfection of mind in man that he does not take in by nature from the start all that can be known but must expand his knowledge from certain starting-points. Love on the other hand goes out to things, some of which are good and desirable in themselves, and others good and desirable in relation to other things. So it is no imperfection of will if one thing is desired naturally as a goal, and another thing from choice as leading to the goal. Because angels are by nature perfect in mind, they always know naturally and do not need to reason, but they love both naturally and from choice.

3   We distinguish *friendship*, with which we love any independently existing thing to whom we will good, from *desire* with which we love any goods we want for him. To love knowledge, for example, is not to will good to knowledge but to want to possess it. Now everything seeks by nature to get what is good for it: clearly this is so in creatures without awareness, and in the same way both angels and men naturally seek their own fulfilment. By nature then angels and men love themselves [with friendship], having a natural desire for their own good; and when they 4 choose their own good they love themselves also from choice. And in loving themselves they love whatever is united to them: if united in nature with a natural love, else with love of a different kind. Angels therefore love one another with a natural love, since they share a nature in common; and according to whether they have other things in common or not they love in some other way.

5   By nature parts of the body will risk themselves in order to defend the whole: without thinking, the hand wards off the blow that will harm the whole body. And in society virtue imitates nature, so that the good

citizen risks death for the common good; if he were part of society by
nature it would be a natural tendency. Now by nature every creature by
being himself belongs to God; so the natural love of angels and men is
first and foremost for God and then for themselves. If it were not so,
their natural love would be perverse and would have to be destroyed
rather than fulfilled by the love of charity. One naturally loves oneself
more than something else of equal rank because one is more united to
oneself, but if the other thing is the entire ground of one's own existence
and goodness then by nature one loves it more than oneself: by nature
parts love the whole more than themselves, and individuals the good of
the species more than their individual good. God however is not only
the good of a species but good as such and for all; and so by nature
everything loves God in its own way more than itself. Since God is
everything's good and naturally loved by all, no one can see him for
what he is and not love him. But when we do not so see him and know
him only through some effect or other which displeases us, we may hate
God in that respect; though even then as the good of all we still by
nature love him more than ourselves.

The creation of the angels.   Angels are part of the universe; they do   61 3
not constitute a world on their own, but form one world with the
physical universe. So it seems unlikely that God whose *work is perfect*
would create angels on their own before the rest of creation, though this
is the universal view of the fathers of the Greek church.

There is a twofold happiness or fulfilment of creatures with minds: a   62 1   *twofold*
happiness which they can achieve by their own natural powers (which,   *happiness*
in man's case, Aristotle identified with the fullest contemplation possible
in this life of the highest object of human knowledge, God); and a
happiness which we look forward to in a future life of seeing God as he
is, and which transcends the nature of any created mind. Angels were
created happy in the first sense, for what men acquire in stages by
processes of learning angels were perfect enough to possess from the
start. But the ultimate happiness which transcends nature they could
not possess at creation, for it is the end of nature not its beginning.

Our will tends by nature towards what is natural to us, but it needs   2
help from some higher source than nature to pursue what transcends
nature. Since the ultimate happiness of seeing God as he is transcends
the nature of any created mind, without activation by God – which we   *grace is*
call the help of grace – no created will can act to acquire that happiness.   *needed for*
Angels have a natural love for God as source of their natural being, but   *2nd, higher*
this does not suffice to turn them to God as someone whose sight will   *happiness*

make them happy, which is what we are now discussing. To turn to
God in the fulfilled love of happy possession needs what we may call
fulfilling grace; to turn towards him and deserve such fulfilment needs
what we may call *grace-as-disposition*, disposing us to act deservingly; but
to turn towards him to receive grace-as-disposition does not presuppose a
previous disposition (and so on *ad infinitum*), though it needs God to
turn us, as we read in Lamentations: *Turn us back to yourself, Lord, and
we will be turned.*

3   Probably the angels were created in a graced state. The tendencies
that accompany a form must be such as suit the subject's nature: in the
case of an intelligent being they must freely tend towards what he wills.
So grace inclines but does not compel; one can refuse to use it and sin.
Since heaven is the goal for natures aided by grace, it would not be
appropriate to create angels already there; but grace is the source rather
than the goal of an angel's activity, and could appropriately be given it

4   at creation. Perfect happiness belongs by nature to God alone, for whom
existing and being happy are the same thing. But for creatures being
happy is not theirs by nature but the ultimate goal of their activity.
When a goal is not beyond an agent's powers his activity effects the goal,
as doctoring effects health; but when the goal exceeds the agent's power
and must be looked for as another's gift, then activity can only deserve
the goal. And so it is with ultimate happiness: it is beyond the natural

5   powers of angel and man and can only be deserved. It can however be
deserved by a single action, not only by angels but also by men, for any
action motivated by charity deserves happiness.

8   An angel seeing God relates to him as anyone not seeing him relates
to the common notion of good. Just as no one can will or do anything
without adhering to good, and cannot willingly turn away from good as
such, so no angel in heaven can will or do anything without adhering to
God, and cannot sin. To be able to draw more than one conclusion from
given premises shows power of mind; but to draw a conclusion not
warranted by the premises is a fault. In the same way to be able to
choose more than one course of action leading to a goal is a fulfilment
of freedom; but to choose a course departing from the goal and to sin
is a defect of freedom. There is a greater freedom of choice in angels

63 1 that cannot sin, than in us who can. A sin is something not done rightly
as it should have been done, whether the sin transgresses rules of nature,
art or morals. Only if the rule of action were the agent's power itself
could an action never be wrong; and only God's will is its own rule of
action, not having to conform to any higher goal. So only God's will
can do no wrong; all created wills of their very natures can sin. Choices

can be sinful in two ways: either by choosing what is bad, or by choosing in an unruly way what is in itself good. (The first sort) of sin always involves ignorance or error, otherwise one could not choose bad as good. An adulterer, for example, even if in general he judges truly what is right and wrong, makes an error in this particular case, choosing the pleasure of his unruly action as something good to have just at this moment, under the influence of passion or a bad habit. (The second sort) of sin involves no ignorance but merely inattention to things one should attend to. And this is the only way angels could have sinned, turning by choice to their own good, without attending to the rule of God's will.

The seven days of material creation.   *And God said: Let there be* [vol 10] 67 1
light. Just as *seeing* initially meant eyesight but was extended by usage to all the senses (*see how hot it is*, we say) and even to the mind, so *light* started by meaning what makes things visible to the eyes and has now been extended to mean whatever makes things known. Light can't be 2 a body [consisting of matter with dimensions]. In the first place, no two bodies could occupy the same place [as light and air do]. And secondly, bodies take time to move whereas the propagation of light is instantaneous; as soon as the sun rises in the east the whole dome of the sky from east to west is illuminated. Thirdly, if light was a body its matter would have to assume some other form during darkness: but what form? And where would all the matter needed for generating a sky full of light come from each day? And is it sensible to posit such a large body decomposing just because the sun disappears? If you say the light doesn't decompose but gets carried round with the sun, then what about covering a candle and darkening a whole house? It doesn't seem the light contracts to pack round the candle, for things get no lighter there than they were before. The whole idea offends not only against reason but against our light not ·body sense-experience, so light can't be a body.

Genesis distinguishes three regions of formlessness: *darkness* above 69 1 in the heavens, *the deep* between, a disordered immensity of waters, and an earth *without form* below, covered over with the waters. On the first day the heavens above were given form, and because the rotation of the heavens generates time night and day were distinguished. On the second day the air and waters between were distinguished and put in order by the creation of the sky. And on the third day the earth below was formed, emerging from the waters. The earth was doubly formless, *without form* 2 *and void*, covered with water and empty of plantlife; but on the third day the waters were withdrawn and the earth as a result brought forth vegetation. Just as days one, two and three saw the distinction and 70 1 forming of the heavens, the waters and the earth, so days four, five and six saw the adornment of the heavens with the lamps of sun, moon and stars, of the waters and air with fish and birds, and of the earth with animals [and men].

73 1   To arrive at final happiness our first need is nature and our second grace. Fullness of happiness is reserved till the end of the world, but pre-exists in its causes: in nature at creation, and in grace when the Word became flesh in Christ, for *grace and truth came through Jesus Christ*. So the seventh day of creation completed nature, the coming of Christ completed grace, and the end of the world will complete glory.

3 The *good* that God sees on each day of creation is nature's first seeds; the *blessing* of the seventh day is the propagation of nature.

Chapter 5

MAN'S PLACE IN CREATION

Introductory comment. In the last few chapters we have watched Thomas marrying Aristotle – the learning of men – to the Christian scriptures – the teaching of God. So far it has been a marriage between Aristotle's metaphysics and the Christian belief in a creator God, who is the doing of all being. At the end of the last chapter, when Thomas was examining the account in Genesis of the creation of the material universe (in greater detail than we have been able to reproduce), we glimpsed Aristotle's physics and biology. Now it is the turn of Aristotle's theory of man, his psychology so-called: the culminating point of his biology, man as mind in matter. Thomas relates this to the culmination of the Genesis account of creation, the figure of Adam (the Hebrew word for *human being*): made in the image of the God who has the doing of all being, and put in charge of the garden of God's material creation to till it and to keep it.

The chapter falls into two parts: in the first, Thomas re-examines the learning of men about man: human nature, human abilities, human knowledge; in the second he comments on the teaching of God about Adam. In talking about human abilities Thomas writes

> Only God is his own activity and his own ability to act. To have soul is to be alive (the actualization achieved in us by being born); but if it were also to be engaged in activity then we would be in non-stop activity all our life long. Our first actualization, life, is capable of further actualization, activity, but this belongs not to soul's substance but to its potential, not to what it is but to what it can do. [p 118]

is/do

We must beware of the wrong resonances in this word *soul*. In Latin *anima* means *that which animates*, so that a more modern rendering might well be *life*. And indeed, in Aristotle's and Thomas's philosophy, all living things have soul. Moreover, life or soul

anima –
that weh
animates

is not conceived as another thing inside a living thing, but as the form of being under which matter exists in a living thing. In living things matter exists in the form of *organized body*, structured by way of different organs into a cooperative unity that in some special way (not shared by chemical compounds) acts as a self. There are different levels of acting as a living self, all dependent in some way on the degree of organization of the body. Plants grow and reproduce themselves, animals have the further relative independence of motion and perception of their environment, man seems to be capable of a yet deeper selfhood, but that too is a way of being alive in an organized body born with a certain form. Thomas's task is to articulate the form life takes in man (man's nature), and then to go on to the further actualizations which this first actualization makes possible: the potentialities of human life (man's abilities) and their exercise (man's activities).

However, there is a profound difficulty about **human nature**, and the difficulty has introduced into the meaning of *soul* those other resonances of which we should beware. In the previous chapter Thomas has spoken of one of the great divisions which cuts across creation: that between spirit and matter. Spirit, he has claimed, is immaterial because it can take *in* the forms of other things, can have them in mind without taking them *on* in the way matter must do (cf preface p xxxviii). This clear division makes it profoundly difficult to articulate the nature of man, for here is something that is both spirit and matter -- **embodied spirit** – and so has often been thought of as really two things in temporary (and perhaps unfortunate) co-habitation: an exiled spirit (called the soul) and its prison-house (the body). Around this primary difficulty cluster others raised by many unsuccessful attempts to cope with the first: the Platonic doctrine of the immortality of the human soul, the medieval Arabic teaching that all men partake of one communal mind, the soul-language of Christian writers equating the soul with the person as the object of God's love and attention. Thomas refuses such language: the person is the I who walks and talks, who sees and hears and understands, the composite of body and soul. And he asserts this strongly in the language of Aristotle: the soul is a part of me in the sense that anything's form is a part of it; the soul is to the body as form to matter under that form. The soul is an actualization of potentialities of matter that organizes matter into a body. But Thomas does believe that in man there are spiritual potentialities of mind and love to which his organized body contributes not the tools they need for their operation (as it contributes to reproduction the reproductive organs, or to perception the sense-organs), but the world they need as object of their operation: the world which the growth and movement and perception and memory and imagination of man's animal body has revealed in its complex richness and *within* which man is existent, the organically experienced world of which mind can now take in the truth and to which the will can respond with love, the animally acquired world which Thomas in his discussions simply calls our *phantasms*, the world of our sense-imagery. This is the fundamental insight of the section, but its defence takes all Thomas's subtlety.

After discussing man's nature Thomas turns to consider his **human abilities – bodily and spiritual**: his bodily functions, then his abilities to take in the world, from his sense-perceptions to his mind, and in parallel to that his abilities to respond to the world, from his sense-urges to his free will. In other places Thomas frequently compares the inner relationships that must hold between these abilities if man is to preserve his integrity, with the external relationships Genesis conceived Adam to have with other living creatures living a vegetable or an animal life. The subject will recur in the parts of the *Summa* which deal with man's moral control over his spiritual and bodily abilities. For a corollary of man's complex nature is that human being is, so to speak, a task for man, a task which lies at the heart of the task of creation. This is why the *Summa*, when it turns in part two to discuss the return of God's creation to its maker, actually concentrates on the return of man to his maker: the theological study of man comprises not simply his biology and his psychology, but ethics.

This is also why Thomas, when he comes to discuss the activation and exercise of these human abilities, concentrates exclusively on **how man knows**. The question of how he loves is deferred to part two of the *Summa*, where it will occupy centre stage for six chapters. In this chapter he concentrates on how objects of the body, so to speak, become objects of the mind: how through a cooperation of sense-faculties and mental abilities we know material things and through them whatever else we know; how we abstract, how we know the general and the particular, the simple and the composite. At the end of the section he asks whether the mind can turn away from the world presented to it through the body to know spirits directly, or our own mind. Not naturally, is the answer; naturally we only know spirits through their agency, if any, in the material world; and that goes for our own spiritual potentialities too, known only as that which is actively knowing the material world. If the soul after death and before the resurrection of its body is to know at all it must be by a divine intervention: God must speak concepts, so to speak, into the separated soul; and even then it will not be I, the person, who knows, but only my soul, a part of me! I, the person, am dead.

The chapter ends with a return to **the Genesis of man** in the scriptures, concerned with man in history: what could have been and what is. Adam in Paradise is the prototype of humanity as God intended it, set in the garden of creation to till it and to keep it, for in Genesis Paradise is not simply a paradisal state without pain or death, but a task. Adam is created in the image of God's uncreated love, called to be the husbandman of creation, joining God in the task of bringing creation to a successful fulfilment. In Thomas the task is seen more narrowly in terms of an integrity within man that Adam enjoyed and lost, and which now needs to be cultivated in the sweat of brow of this world. But Thomas is also conscious of Adam as microcosmos, so that the order man has to bring into his own bodily and moral life, stands as symbol for an order that has to be brought into society and the physical environment (cf pp 146–7 below).

Human nature – embodied spirit

[vol 11] **What is man?** We turn now to man, a creature who is neither pure spirit nor pure body, but has a nature compounded of both. The theologian considers man's nature primarily from the point of view of his soul. And if we want to know what sort of thing soul is we must start from how we use the word *anima* [which *soul* translates]. *Animate* means living and *inanimate* non-living, so *soul* means that which first animates or makes alive the living things with which we are familiar. Life mostly shows itself in the two activities of awareness and movement, and though these activities have particular sources (the eye for sight, for instance), those sources are organs or instruments of a first source of life. That first source cannot itself be a part of the body: bodily parts are not alive, or sources of life like the heart, simply by being bodily, but by being bodies of such-and-such a sort (otherwise all bodies would be alive and sources of life). Now what *makes* the body actually of such-

and-such a sort we call its soul, its first source of life: not itself body but an actuation of body (just as the heat of hot bodies is not itself body, but an energy of bodies).

The human soul, however, because it is a source of mental activity, must itself subsist, even though it is not a body. For the mind understands all physical things. But if what knows has the nature of some particular thing it knows, that nature hinders it from knowing anything else (everything tastes sour to a soured tongue); mind, then, cannot have any determinate physical nature. And for the same reason it can't use a bodily organ with a determinate physical nature: for coloured glass colours what is seen through it just as much as colour in the eye itself. Mind then has an activity of its own in which the body has no part. Now to act on its own, it must exist on its own; since the way a thing acts depends on the way in which it exists. So the human soul or mind, though non-bodily must be self-subsistent. Sometimes anything that subsists is called an individual thing, at other times only what is whole according to the nature of some species. The first use of individual excludes things that exist only as properties and forms of something subsistent; the second use excludes component parts as well. A hand is individual in the first sense, not the second; and the human soul too, though subsistent, because it is only part of man, is individual only in the first sense. Only the whole composed of body and soul is an individual in the second sense. If a thing is properly to subsist on its own it must neither exist in nor be a component part of something else: we don't talk of eyes and hands subsisting or acting on their own. What we talk loosely of parts doing, is really done by the whole acting through the parts. Thus, men see with their eyes and feel with their hands (in a stronger sense though than hot things heat with their heat, for properly speaking heat does not *do* any heating). Saying souls understand is like saying eyes see, and what we mean is that men understand with their souls.

Mind needs body not as an organ or instrument of its activity but to present it with objects, for images are to mind as colour to eyes. Needing body in this way doesn't make minds non-subsistent, any more than sensation's need of external sense-objects makes animals non-subsistent. Animal souls however, because they do not act on their own – sensation being an activity of body and soul – do not exist on their own. Physical changes accompany the action of sense-objects on the senses, and too intense an object can injure the sense. But this doesn't happen to the mind; rather understanding what is most intelligible helps with understanding what is less. What tires our bodies is not understanding

[margin notes, handwritten:]
soul actuates body, making it of such a sort

2 human soul subsists since it knows every object, mind can't have a determinate physical nature – nor does it use a bodily organ of determinate physical nature – it has activity of its own + ... ? exists on its own

3 i.e. animal souls don't exist on their own –

as such, but the use of our senses to supply the mind with images. Man then is not soul alone. Sensing is one of man's activities, though not peculiar to him, and this shows that individual men are not simply souls, but composed of body and soul. This particular man comprises this soul in this flesh and these bones, and man as such comprises soul and flesh and bones, for whatever is essential to every member of a species is essential to the species. Not everything individual is an individual substance or person: for that its nature must be complete; my soul is only a part of my nature, and no more a person than my hands or my feet are.

5   **Man's soul is immortal.**   To know things is to take in their form; and since our minds know things precisely as instantiations of natures – stones *qua* stones – they must take in the form of stone as such, as form. Now the way a thing is taken in depends on what takes it in; so the receptive mind itself must be form as such, not matter under some form. If minds were matter under some form, then the forms they take in would be individualized; and minds would know only particular things, as the senses do which receive forms into material organs. For matter individualizes form. Minds then, because they know forms as such, are not themselves composed of matter and form. The way mind takes in forms is quite different from the way matter takes them on, and this shows in the forms received; for matter individualizes any form it takes on, but the mind takes in the pure form as such.

6   The human soul, then, as source of our intelligence, cannot decompose. Because it is self-subsistent, it doesn't perish with the body as the souls of other animals do; but neither can it decompose itself. For forms are precisely what make things actual and give them existence. Material things come to be precisely by being formed, and perish when they lose their form. But subsistent forms cannot lose themselves. Even if souls *were* composed of matter and form, as some people think, they still couldn't decompose. For things decompose only when their forms are displaced by incompatible forms; the stars of heaven whose matter is not subject to such forms never decompose. Minds too do not take on forms; they take them in by knowing them. But *knowing* a form is compatible with knowing the forms that are incompatible with it; indeed knowing a thing entails knowing its contrary. So there is no way in which minds can decompose. An indication of this is the special way in which we manifest the general natural desire for survival. In things which possess awareness this desire reflects that awareness: now, whereas the senses are aware only of here-and-now existence, minds grasp

existence as such, whenever and wherever, and as a result things with minds naturally desire to live for ever. But a drive of nature can't be *[handwritten: ?]* pointless, so no substance with mind can decompose. The soul can cease to exist, but that means only that the creator can stop holding it in being; it doesn't imply a tendency in the created soul itself to decompose. Soul's substance doesn't contain body, but must of its nature be joined *[handwritten: 7]* to body; for properly speaking, it is not soul that has a specific nature, but the thing body and soul compose. The soul needs a body even to exercise its own activity, and this very fact shows that souls are lesser minds than angels, who exist without bodies.

Embodied mind.   Mind is the form of man's body. Active things 76 1 *[handwritten: mind DEF !]* must have forms by which they act; only healthy bodies heal themselves, and only instructed minds know. Activity depends on actuality, and what makes things actual makes them active. Now the soul is what makes our body live; so the soul is the primary source of all those activities that differentiate levels of life: growth, sensation, movement, understanding. So, whether we call our primary source of understanding *[handwritten: mind and soul]* mind or soul, it is the form of our body. This is Aristotle's proof in his *[handwritten: = equivalent ?]* book *On the Soul*; and to deny it one would have to find some other way in which each man's activity of understanding is his own (as we experience it to be). Aristotle says actions can be ascribed to things in three ways: *with intrinsic appropriateness to them as a whole (as healing to doctors), or to a part of them (as seeing to men because they have eyes), or entirely coincidentally (as building to white men, since their whiteness is irrelevant to their building).* Clearly I don't understand coincidentally: I understand as a man and I am a man by nature. So either I understand as a whole (which is Plato's position identifying man with his mind) or I understand with a part of myself. Now Plato's position is untenable, because I experience myself both understanding and sensing, and, since I cannot sense without a body, my body must be part of me. So the mind with which I understand, must also be part of me, united in some way to my body.

Ibn Roschd, in his commentary on Aristotle's *On the Soul*, maintained *[handwritten: error #1]* that mind and body were united through the forms of mind's objects. These he said had two subjects: the receptive mind and the images present in our bodily senses; so that they served to link the receptive mind to the body of this or that man. But such linking would not be enough to make the mind's activity my activity. The analogy with the senses that Aristotle uses to explain mind shows us why. Mind, he says, is related to images as sight is to colours; as sight conforms to colours, so the receptive mind conforms itself to our images. But clearly the fact that the colours to which our sight conforms are in a wall doesn't mean that the wall sees, but only that it is seen. So the fact that the receptive mind conforms to my images doesn't mean that I understand, but only that I and my images are understood.

nicer
of a photograph
error #2

So other thinkers have argued that mind is united to body by acting on it, and that this unites mind and body enough for understanding to be ascribable to the composite whole. But this fails on many counts. First, the only way my mind acts on my body is by arousing its desire, and that presupposes understanding. So I don't understand because I am acted on by mind, but on the contrary I am acted on by mind because I understand. Secondly, I am an individual with a single nature composed of matter and form, and if the mind is not that form then it must act from outside my nature, on the whole of me. But understanding is an activity that remains interior to its agent, not crossing over into other things in the way that, say, heating does. So I can't be said to understand because I am acted on by mind. Thirdly, the only sort of thing to which you can ascribe an action acting on it is a tool, like the carpenter's saw. So understanding ascribed to me because I am acted on by mind must belong to me as a tool; and that contradicts Aristotle's statement that understanding uses no bodily organ. Fourthly, though the action of a part can be ascribed to the whole, it can't be ascribed to another part, except coincidentally: men see with their eyes but their hands don't. So if I and some mind together made up some whole, the actions of the mind couldn't be ascribed to me. And if I were the whole, composed of mind and the rest of me, with the mind united to my other parts only by acting on them, then I would have no unity strictly speaking and therefore no existence simply speaking, since things exist in the way they are one. So we are left with only one way in which we can ascribe understanding to a man: Aristotle's way, in which the mind is man's form.

The same conclusion emerges if we ask what constitutes humankind a species. The natures of things are known from their activities, and the activity marking human animals out from all other animals is understanding (which is why Aristotle locates man's final happiness in this activity). So what decides man's species must be what makes him understand; and since what decides a thing's species is the form that makes the thing what it is, this in man must be mind. Note then that successive levels of form master physical matter more and more, displaying behaviour and abilities less and less confined by matter. Chemical compounds behave in ways irreducible to the behaviour of their elements; and the abilities of higher forms transcend those of elemental matter even further: plant forms more than metal forms and animal forms more than plant forms. Of all these the human form is the highest, with abilities so transcending physical matter that it possesses an activity and ability which physical matter in no way shares: the power of mind.

Aristotle calls the human soul the highest form in nature, and thinks natural philosophy should culminate in its study. He says it is *separate, yet in matter, since men and the sun generate men from matter*: separate, because mind is not the power of a bodily organ in the way sight is the power of our eyes; in matter, because it is the form of our body and the term of human reproduction. The existence the soul itself has it shares with the physical matter it forms, so that the existence of the composite whole is the existence of the soul itself. This does not happen with other forms because they are not self-subsistent. And this is why when the body decays the human soul continues to exist of itself whereas other forms don't. But to be united with a body is as natural to the soul as floating upward is to lightweight things. Held down, light things remain light, with an affinity and inclination to float upward. So too the human soul, existing away from its body, has a natural affinity and inclination to be one with it again.

Each man has his own individual mind.   It is quite impossible for 2 all men to share one mind. If Plato is right and a man is his mind, then, if we shared one mind, you and I would be one man with different accessories, like a man now in a shirt and now in a coat; which is quite ridiculous. And if Aristotle is right and the mind is an ability of soul and soul is man's form: then a number of individuals could no more share a single form than they can share a single existence, since it is form that gives existence. And so also with every other model of a single mind united with one man here and another man there. For however mind is united to this or that man, the rest of him will obviously be mind's tool, since his animal powers all obey mind and minister to it. Now clearly one agent using two tools does two actions while remaining one agent: a man using both hands is a single toucher even if he touches twice. And many agents using one tool do one action, while remaining many: many people pulling on one rope are many pullers giving a single pull. A single agent using a single tool does a single action: a workman using a hammer is one hammerer doing one hammering. So if you and I had two minds but shared one eye we would be two seers with but a single seeing; but if we shared one mind, then whatever number of other things we had as tools of mind, you and I would never be anything but one knower. Add the fact that mind in knowing uses no other tool than the mind itself, and it will follow that a shared mind would do only one action: that is, that all men would be one knower engaged in one act of knowing per known object. Some have thought they could differentiate my knowing from yours by the different images in our heads, for my image of a stone is not yours, and these different images received into the one receptive mind could produce different actions, just as different images of things in one eye produce different acts of seeing. But what the mind receives into itself are not images themselves, but forms abstracted from the images to make them ready for understanding. From different images of one sort of thing, a single mind would abstract a single understandable form, just as a man abstracts from his many images of stones one understandable definition of a stone through which his mind can know the nature of all stones in one act, despite the diversity of his images. So if all men had one mind, the different images in you and me could not, as Ibn Roschd imagined, differentiate my knowing from yours. It goes against all reason, then, to maintain that all men share one mind.

That minds and ideas exist individually does not prevent them knowing generalities, as existing materially would. The multitude of things that share one nature are distinguished by material features peculiar to them as individuals; and if the likenesses by which these things were known were also material, embedded in matter, then they would reflect the general nature under these many distinguishing features, and fail to yield knowledge of the nature in its generality. But a likeness that has been abstracted from its embodiments in particular matter will reflect the nature without these many distinguishing features, and give general knowledge. So generality of knowledge says nothing about whether minds are one or many: even if we all shared one mind it would still be an individual one, and the likenesses by which it knew things in general would be individuals. Multiplying minds doesn't multiply what mind knows, for as Aristotle says it is not the stone that is in our mind but its likeness. Yet it is the stone that we know, not its likeness (unless we are reflecting on our own knowing), for otherwise we would know not things but ideas. So just as many eyes with many images see the same colour, so many minds know the same known thing. The only difference, in Aristotle's opinion, is that whereas we sense things in their particularity just as they exist outside, we know the natures of extra-mental things not in their extra-mental mode of existing, but in general, abstracted from any particularizing features.

Each man has a single soul.   If Plato is right and souls are not the 3
forms bodies have but agents acting on them, one and the same body
could well be acted on by several souls, especially if they acted on
different parts of it. But if souls are forms of bodies then it doesn't seem
possible for several essentially different souls to unite with one body.
Firstly, an animal with more than one soul wouldn't be one animal in
any straightforward sense of the word *one*. For oneness is an accompaniment of existence; and what makes a thing one strictly speaking is the
single form making it what it is. Whatever is designated by two or more
forms – a *white man*, for example – is not one thing, simply speaking.
Secondly, predicates arising from different forms connect coincidentally
(*per accidens*) if independent of one another (*what's white is sweet*), or
with that type of intrinsic appropriateness (*per se type 2*) in which the
subject helps define the predicate (*surfaces are coloured*, since colour
presupposes surface). So, if we were animals by one form and men by
another, *what's man is animal* would be coincidentally true if the two
forms were independent, else intrinsically appropriate *type 2* if animality
presupposed humanity. Now clearly neither alternative is true: men are
animals *per se*, not coincidentally, but humanity presupposes animality
and not vice versa. Now animal can be predicated *per se* of man in this
way (*per se type 1*) only if the same form makes us both men and animals.
Thirdly, the fact that the soul's activities when intense interfere with
one another shows they must have the same source: one and the same
soul in man is the source of his sense life and mental life and vegetative
life. Aristotle compares the sequence of grades of life with that of
geometrical shapes, each shape overlaying and extending the one before.
Just as the area of a pentagon hasn't two shapes – pentagon and
quadrilateral – but the quadrilateral area is included in the pentagonal,
so one and the same soul is the basis of our mental activity and includes
in its potential the sense-potential and metabolic potential of animal and
plant souls. To begin with, the embryo has only animal soul, but this is
later displaced by a more perfect soul with both mind and senses. [When
we distinguish what is generically common from what differentiates a
species of that genus] we are abstracting in thought things that are in
reality one. The potential of the human soul includes and extends that
of the animal soul, so we abstractly conceive the potential of sense-
activity separately as something incomplete and material and generically
common to men and animals, and the potential of mind as something
added in man to complete and differentiate and give specific form to
him.

    If the human soul or form supervened on a body already existing as a 4 substance under some other form, then the human form wouldn't give man his existence as a substance: indeed, man wouldn't exist strictly speaking but merely be one of the ways something else existed. The mind then is the only form in man under which he exists as a substance; including in its potential the potentials of the animal soul, the vegetative soul and all the more elementary forms. The human soul in man, the animal soul in animals, the vegetative soul in plants – in general the higher forms of higher substances – all effect what elementary forms effect in lower things. Aristotle defined soul as *that which actuates an organized physical body with the potential of life, a potential not existing apart from the soul.* Clearly he is including soul in what it actuates, as one might say heat actuates hot bodies and light actuates things that shine, not meaning things that are already shining without the light but the things light makes shine. When Aristotle says soul actuates the body he describes, he means that it is soul which makes it a physical body and organizes it and gives it the potential of life. This first actuation he calls potential in relation to a second possible actuation, namely activity; and *apart from the soul* no such potential would exist. Once the soul is united to the body as form by its very existence, it goes on to move the body to activity. Through this power of movement the soul is the activating part of man, and the already animated body the activated part. Ibn Sina thought elements maintained their own substantial forms intact in compounds, the compound merely averaging out their conflicting properties. But this is impossible, for the different forms would have to exist in different parts of the matter, and so there would be no true fusion of elements, but only juxtaposition of minute particles that the senses could not discriminate. Ibn Roschd thought elements had forms halfway between accidental and substantial forms, and that they varied in intensity, becoming less intense in compounds and striking a sort of equilibrium from which a single form emerged. But this is even more inconceivable: a thing either is substantial or it isn't, substantial forms can't vary in intensity, and there is no halfway house between substances and concomitant accidents. So we prefer Aristotle's position: the forms of elements don't actually exist in compounds but only virtually, by way of their peculiar behavioural properties, which persist less intensely in the compound; and these properties dispose the matter to become the new compound substance, be it animal or mineral.

5 **The human body.** Matter exists for the sake of its forms, not the forms for the sake of their matter, so we explain the sort of body a man has by looking at what his soul needs. Now the human soul is the lowest

grade of mind in nature's hierarchy, since its knowledge of truth is not inborn (like angels) but gathered from sense-experience of things spatially outside it. As such, it needs a body suited to sensing. Now the basis of all sensation is touch and an organ of touch must balance the opposing qualities of hot and cold and moist and dry in order to sense them all acutely. So men's bodies are made more sensitive to touch than animals' in this way, and intelligent men's even more than others: *tender flesh goes with a quick mind*, says Aristotle. But why not join an imperishable soul to an imperishable body? It is no use answering that originally Adam's body was imperishable, because that was not by nature but by a grace of God; otherwise Adam's sin would have left him immortal. Rather we must admit that, whereas some characteristics of its matter suit a form, others are just unavoidable consequences. Carpenters make saws of iron for cutting hard things, but as a result the teeth will blunt and rust in time. In the same way the mind needs a body of balanced composition, but that means it will one day die. If you say God could have avoided this remember what Augustine says: the way things are in nature depends more on what nature needs than on what God can do. Anyway God does provide grace to heal death; and mind's grasp of generalities sets no limit to what man himself can do; so although nature can't endow him with the fixed instinctive responses, defence mechanisms and protective covering which it gives to other animals of limited awareness and powers, still it gives him reason and hands – those tools of tools – with which to make his own tools to suit every sort of purpose.

Since bodily matter is dimensioned, the mind can think of it first as dimensioned, then as divided, then as diversified according to its grade of form. But really one form gives matter all these attributes, even if the mind distinguishes them. You can divide a whole into quantitative parts, or into the parts of its definition, or into various things it has the ability to do. When a homogeneous whole is divided quantitatively, its form is also coincidentally divided (whiteness with the white surface); but the same is not true of heterogeneous wholes. So to the question whether whiteness exists whole in every part of a white surface or only in the whole, we would have to make a distinction: the quantitative wholeness (which whiteness possesses only coincidentally) is not whole in every part, and no part of the white surface is as able to affect our sight as the whole; but the definition of whiteness is realized in every part. To a similar question about the soul, however, we can dismiss quantitative division, and say simply that whereas the whole essence of the soul is realized in every part of the body, not the whole of what it can do: for only the eye sees and only the ear hears. Note too that, since the soul requires a heterogeneous body, it relates principally and immediately to the whole body as to its appropriate matter, and only secondarily to parts of the body according to their place in the whole. Some powers of the soul, like intellect and will, belong to its transcendence of the capacity of the whole body, and are not located in any part of it, but other powers are shared with the body and are located, not everywhere the soul is, but in the parts of the body appropriate to their activity.

Human abilities – bodily and spiritual

77 1. Abilities belong to the same category of being as do the ways of actually existing they make possible; our abilities to act can no more constitute our substance than can the activities themselves. Only God is his own activity, and so only God is his own ability to act. To have soul is to be alive (the actualization achieved in us by being born); but if it were also to be engaged in activity then we would be in non-stop activity all our life long. Our first actualization, life, is capable of further actualization, activity, but this belongs not to soul's substance but to its potential, not to what it is but to what it can do. So we distinguish a soul's powers and abilities from its substance; for no actuality precisely as such is potential. If *accident* or *concomitant* means what can exist only in a pre-existent subject then the soul's abilities, not being its substance, must be its concomitants: there is no halfway house between needing or not needing a subject. But if *concomitant* means a property not necessitated by the nature of a thing, then there is a halfway house between substance and concomitants: namely those properties which derive necessarily from a thing's nature. In this sense the soul's abilities are neither its substance nor its concomitants but its natural properties.

3. Abilities are potentials for activity, and we differentiate them as we do activities according to different ways in which things can be objects of activity. The object of a receptive power's activity is whatever initially stimulates it (colour in the case of sight); the object of an agent power's activity is its final goal (adult size in the case of our power of growth). So what begins and what ends an activity can decide its type. Not that every difference in object defines a new type of ability, but only differences relevant to the object as object. Thus, the objects of sense are qualities that affect us, and any relevant differences in such qualities (colour, sound, etc) differentiate types of sense (sight, hearing, etc); but differences in objects irrelevant to their colour (musician, grammarian, big, small, man, stone) don't differentiate types of sight. Abilities, though

they pre-exist their activities, are defined in terms of them, just as *abilities & do-* agencies are defined by their goals. Though the objects of an activity *find in terms of* are external to it, the activity begins and ends with them and is internally *activities –* adapted to them. Our soul's many abilities derive from it in an order. 4 Certain abilities are of their nature subordinate to others: vegetative *hierarchical order* powers to sense-powers, and sense-powers to the mind which controls *of soul's abilities* and directs them; though we develop such powers in the reverse order.

Abilities like mind and will, which exercise no bodily organ, are 5 properties of soul; but sense-powers and vegetative powers do exercise bodily organs and are properties of the composite of body and soul, but are called powers of soul because it is through soul that the composite possesses them. A subject which previously existed only potentially 6 acquires actual existence when it acquires its substantial form; a supervening concomitant or accidental form, on the other hand, acquires actual existence from its subject, which already existed actually even if it only potentially possessed this supervening form. Subjects as potential take on such supervening forms, but as actual they themselves produce them. I am thinking of supervening forms characteristic of their subjects: non-characteristic forms are produced in their subjects by external agents, but characteristic forms or properties derive from the subject's own actuality, not by a subject acting to modify itself in some way, but by its actuality overflowing naturally into that property, as light naturally overflows into colour. So the soul's abilities, whether they be properties of the soul itself or the body-soul composite, derive from their subject's actuality and thus from the soul, the source of that actuality.

Bodily life.   We distinguish three sorts of soul, four levels of life, and 78 1 five types of ability in souls: vegetative, sense, appetitive, locomotive and mental. Sorts of soul we distinguish by the degree to which their activity transcends that of physical nature. The rational soul's activity so far transcends the physical that it is not the activity of any bodily organ; the sense-soul's activities are activities of bodily organs consequent on physical changes of the organs, but are not themselves physical changes; whereas vegetative activities such as digestion proceed in bodily organs by the instrumentality of physical changes, and transcend physical action only by being internally, not externally, caused (a characteristic of all living activities). Types of ability we distinguish by their objects. The only object of the vegetative powers is the body in which they reside, so they differ in type from abilities which relate to any object that can be sensed (sense abilities) or that can exist (mental abilities). Relating us to such external objects we have abilities that unite objects to us by taking in their forms (the senses less generally, the mind for all objects whatever), and abilities that incline and draw us towards objects (appetites, the objects of which are initial goals to be aimed at, and locomotive abilities, the objects of which are terms of the movements which achieve our aims). The levels of life are plants (with only vegetative abilities), immobile animals such as shellfish (adding sense), the higher animals (adding locomotion), and men (adding mind). Appetitive abilities add no new level to life, since *anything with sense-power has appetite*. Anything at all has its natural tendency (its *natural desire*); and any ability tends naturally towards its object in this way. But there is a special tendency consequent on awareness, called *animal desire*, which requires a special ability over and above awareness's natural tendencies. For desire seeks the thing itself, not just that likeness of things in us that makes us aware of them. An animal's sight will tend naturally towards what is visible to fulfil its function of seeing; but the animal itself seeks the actual thing it sees, with an animal desire, not just for seeing but for other purposes. If all we needed things for was perception,

2 we wouldn't need this special ability called appetite. By vegetative powers we mean the abilities to reproduce and bring living bodies into existence, to grow to a proper size, and to digest food so as to maintain that existence and size. The last two abilities affect the actual body they reside in, but the reproductive ability acts to produce other bodies, and so approaches the dignity of sense-powers. Digesting food serves growth; both serve reproduction. Such powers are often called natural powers, because their effects – existence, size and self-preservation – are similar to effects in [inanimate] nature, though more perfectly achieved; and because they act by means of natural [physico-chemical] forces.

3 **Our senses.**   Nature doesn't give us sense-powers to fit our sense-organs, but organs to fit our powers. Every sense-power is an ability to receive a particular stimulus from external objects, and what differentiates our sense-powers are different types of stimuli. But being physically affected by this stimulus [e.g. heated by heat] is not enough for the sensing of it [otherwise everything heated would feel heat]; the stimulus must be received intentionally, in the way eyes receive colour without becoming coloured. Sight – the least physical of the senses – is the only entirely intentional sense; in hearing and smell the objects sensed undergo physical change (for sounds are movements of the air, and smells arise when things are heated), and in taste and touch the sensing organs undergo change as well. Size and shape haven't got a particular sense to themselves: they are objects common to the senses

(all attributes of extension) affecting a sense not immediately but by way of the quality that stimulates that particular sense (extension being the immediate subject of such qualities: surface, for example, of colour). Size and shape are however genuinely sensed, not merely known because of what is sensed [as the meanings of spoken words are]; for size and shape modify the sense-stimulus itself. Higher animals must be aware **4** of something not only when it is present to their senses but also in its absence, so that they can be prompted to seek it. So they not only need to receive, but also to retain, impressions of sense-objects presently affecting them. The senses reside in material organs, and since matter must be moist to receive impressions but dry to retain them, the ability to receive sense impressions differs from the ability to retain them. In addition, animals need to be attracted and repelled not only by what pleases or displeases their senses but by what is useful or harmful in other ways: the straws birds collect must look good for nest-building. So animals must be able to perceive a significance in things that is not merely an externally perceptible quality. In addition to their particular senses (and the common root of those senses) for receiving sense impressions and their imagination for storing them, animals must therefore have an instinctive judgment for certain further significances of things, and a memory for storing those (for what is memorable to animals is what is harmful or agreeable, and pastness itself is important to them in this way). Judgment of this sort in men includes an element of calculation, working out particular significances as reason does general ones; and memory in man doesn't just have immediate recall of things past, but by a quasi-logical process of recollection searches out past memories guided by their particular significances. Particular senses discern the particular sense-stimuli proper to them, but to distinguish white from sweet we need some common root sensitivity in which all sense-perceptions meet, and where we can perceive perception itself and become aware that we see. When a particular sense is aware of the quality that is affecting it we see, but when affections of sense affect some common root sensitivity we see that we see.

Mental ability.   Aristotle says *mind is a sort of susceptibility*. In the **79 2** strict sense of the word, we are susceptible to unnatural and uncongenial things like sickness or sadness; less strictly, to any alteration in which something is lost, be it congenial or not; and most broadly of all, to any sort of fulfilling alteration, even if nothing is lost. It is in this last sense that man's mind is a susceptibility to being in general. God's mind is his very substance in which all being pre-exists originally and virtually as in its first cause. So God's mind is not potential or receptive of being in general but its active creator. Created minds, on the other hand, because their being is not infinite, are only potential of being in general, and actualized by the things they understand. Angels' minds are so actualized from the first moment of their creation, but the human mind, being the lowest and furthest away from God's perfect mind, starts as a sheer potential of understanding – *a blank page on which nothing is written* – and only later acquires actual understanding. This is why human understanding is a susceptibility in the third sense above, and why we call it a *receptive mind*.

tabula rasa

3   But Aristotle also says that *in the mind, just as in the rest of nature, besides what is receptive of existence there is what makes things exist.* According to Plato the forms physical matter takes on exist on their own account outside matter as actual objects of understanding called *Ideas*. Physical matter and mind are both *formed* by *participating* these Ideas: matter into particular things with their own specific and generic natures, and mind into knowledge of such species and genera. But according to Aristotle the forms of physical things exist only in matter and not as actually understandable. Since we can only understand what is actually understandable (just as we can only sense what is actually there to be sensed), our minds need to make things actually understandable by abstracting their forms from their material conditions. Our ability to do this we call our *agent mind*. Things outside us are already actually able to be sensed, so our senses need only to be receptive; but the mind must be part active, part receptive, for nothing material is actually understandable, and an immaterial receptive mind would be no use to us without an agent mind to make material things actually under-

Plato – participation

agent mind – abstracts forms from material conditions

4   standable by abstraction. Each of us has such an agent mind, for we are aware of ourselves abstracting. It doesn't activate our receptive mind as if it were itself an object of knowledge (if it did, its universality would give us all knowledge at a stroke). Rather it produces the objects that do activate our mind, given the help of imagination and the senses and practice in understanding (for understanding one thing leads to understanding others: we pass from terms to propositions, and from premises to conclusions).

6   If memory means only our ability to retain knowledge then mind is itself memory; but if we define it as knowing the pastness of what is past then it must be a sense-power able to grasp the particular: for the past as past is some particular then. Pastness can qualify both what we know and our act of knowing it. The two go together in sensation, where we sense what is presently affecting our senses; so that animals simul-

memory – is "knowing" pastness of / past'

taneously remember past sensing and the sensed past. But to the mind the pastness of what we understand is irrelevant; we understand human nature as such, common to past, present and future men. Yet our acts of understanding are particulars occurring now, tomorrow or yesterday, just like acts of sensing. They, like the mind itself, are immaterial particulars, so the mind knows them in the same way it knows itself. In a sense then the mind too remembers the past by knowing its own past acts, though it cannot understand the material particular there-then-ness of the past. Sometimes the mind is merely capable of knowing something, sometimes it is actually attending to something it knows, and sometimes it is in a knowledgeable state or disposition halfway between potentiality and act, in which it possesses knowledge but is not actually attending to it.

Reasoning relates to understanding as journeying to rest. Journeys 8 start and end in states of rest, and human reasoning journeys from what it immediately understands (its first premises) along the road of investigation and discovery, later returning along the road of judgment to analyse its findings and test them against those first premises. Even in nature one and the same tendency moves things to places and then keeps them at rest there. All the more then is it one and the same ability that we exercise when reasoning and understanding. Some philosophers 10 make a fourfold division of mind: as agent, as receptive, as disposed and as fulfilled. Of these the agent mind and the receptive mind are distinct abilities (an ability to do always differs from an ability to be). But the other two are states of the receptive mind, which is sometimes only capable of knowing (receptive), sometimes actually knowledgeable (disposed to know), and sometimes actually attending to what it knows (fulfilled). We don't have one mind for planning action and one for 11 pursuing truth. It is irrelevant to understanding as such whether we make practical use of what we understand or merely attend to its truth. *Practical understanding differs from theorizing only in intention.* The practical mind only plans what we do, it doesn't actually do it; and planning is a kind of understanding. Being good and being true imply one another: we value truth as a good, we perceive goodness as a truth about things. We can desire to know what is true, and know how to do what is good. In pursuit of truth we reason to what is true from 12 theoretical premises, in planning action we reason to what to do from practical premises. Understanding these premises needs no other ability than mind; but it is a special competence or disposition of that ability. In the case of practical principles we call it *synteresis* [or moral sense], and talk of it as *prompting to good and crying out against evil*, since first principles initiate all our investigations and judge all our findings. 13 Conscience on the other hand is neither ability nor disposition, strictly speaking, but the activity of consciously applying our knowledge to what we do: witnessing to what we do and don't do, legislating about what we should and shouldn't do, and defending or accusing us when we have or haven't done well. We are not always engaged in such activities, but our disposition to engage in them, and especially our competence of first principles called *synteresis*, is always there, so sometimes this moral sense itself gets called our conscience.

80 1 **Urges, inclinations and desires.**   Forms are accompanied by tendencies: matter under the form of fire, for example, tends to rise skyward and to propagate itself. Things lacking awareness have just the natural form that constitutes them the unique things they are and the natural tendencies accompanying such a form are called natural inclinations or desires. But things with awareness are so constituted by their natural forms that they can take in the forms of other things: the senses taking in all forms perceptible to sense and the mind all forms that can be understood, so that through mind and the senses the human soul is in a fashion everything, and bears a resemblance to God *in whom everything pre-exists*. Because they possess forms in this more perfect way, creatures with awareness possess a more perfect sort of inclination or tendency directed to things they are aware of, and not merely to things they incline to naturally. This more perfect inclination is the soul's ability to desire. We are aware of things as perceptible or understandable, but we desire them as congenial or good. Since there are different ways in which things can be objects of our activities, they require different abilities in the soul. Each ability is a sort of form or nature with a natural tendency towards its own natural object. But over and above all this is the animal desire that follows on awareness, tending not to what suits this or that 2 ability (to sights or sounds), but to what suits the whole animal. Our abilities to desire are abilities to respond to perceived stimuli. To respond to sense-perceptible stimuli we need sense-appetite, and to respond to stimuli which we mentally perceive we need a mental appetite. It is precisely because things stimulate our desires through our perceptions of them that different types of perception differentiate desirability as such. Mental appetite can be stimulated by individual things existing outside the mind, but this happens by way of some general stimulus they instantiate, such as being good. As Aristotle remarks, *we can hate the whole genus of robbers*. Moreover, with our mental appetite we can desire immaterial things like knowledge and virtue, which the senses

cannot perceive. Both mind and sense, however, command the same motor abilities: the higher appetite by way of the lower, in the way general principles affect us by way of their particular applications.

Sense-appetite.   Sense-appetite takes two different forms: one pleasure-seeking or *affective* and the other *aggressive*. The former drives animals to pursue what pleases their senses and avoid what hurts them, the latter drives them to resist whatever threatens pleasure or introduces danger, to confront difficulties and to overcome obstacles. These two drives cannot be reduced to one; for sometimes animals put up with pain (against their pleasure-seeking instincts) in order to fight obstacles (in accordance with their aggressive instincts). Nevertheless all aggressive emotions begin and end in pleasure-seeking: discomfort breeds anger and this, if it cures the situation, restores contentment. What animals fight about is their pleasures: food and sex. Reason can control such emotion. In other animals emotions follow *instinctive judgment* (sheep fear wolves because they instinctively judge them to be hostile); but in man, a sort of *calculation* replaces instinctive judgment, making particular associations and connections. These particular connections are subject to the influence and control of general connections; we argue to particular conclusions from general premises. So reason can command the appetites of sense, both affective and aggressive, and control feeling. Arguing from general premises to particular conclusions is the work of reason rather than of simple understanding, so it is better to talk of us controlling our affections and our aggression by reasoning than by understanding. And we experience this in ourselves: we appeal to general considerations in order to calm or to incite our anger and our fears. The motor activities consequent on feeling are also under the control of our wills. Other animals react straightaway to feelings of pleasure or aggression (when sheep are afraid of wolves they run away immediately) for no higher appetite opposes them; but human beings do not react immediately but wait for will's command, since our lower appetites need our higher appetite's consent. Aristotle says *our soul rules our physical body like a tyrant ruling slaves*: its commands are irresistible, and every member of the body subject to will reacts immediately in the way the soul desires it to. But *our mind rules our appetites like a president ruling free men*: our sense-appetites have a domain of their own in which they can oppose reason's decisions. Appetite responds not only to instinctive judgment (in other animals) and calculation guided by general reasoning (in man), but also to sensation and imagination. We experience conflict between our feelings of pleasure or aggression and our reason when we sense or imagine pleasurable things that reason forbids or painful things it commands. Such conflict is still compatible with obedience. Our external senses require stimulus from external objects the presence of which reason cannot totally control. But our interior powers of knowledge and desire don't need external objects, and are subject to reason, which can excite or temper feeling and conjure up images.

82 1   **Will.**   What can't be otherwise is necessary. The necessity may be absolute, a necessity of intrinsic nature: either of matter (things composed of opposing elements must decompose) or of form (the three angles of a triangle must equal two right angles). Or the necessity may be need, imposed extrinsically by goals which can't otherwise be achieved or achieved properly (food is needed for survival, a horse for a journey). Or the necessity may be coercion, imposed extrinsically by an agent which won't allow one to act otherwise. Coercion is altogether incompatible with will: our will inclines us to things, and movement in accord with such inclinations is called voluntary, just as movement in accord with natural inclination is called natural; but movement that goes against inclination is called forced or coerced. So movements can no more be both coerced and voluntary than they can be both forced and natural. Need, however, is compatible with will, when there is only one way of achieving a goal: if we will a voyage we must needs will a ship. And necessity of nature is also compatible with will: indeed just as mind must by nature assent to the first principles of thought, so will must by nature consent to our ultimate goal of happiness (goals playing the same role in activity as premises do in thought). For everything must have a basic invariant nature underlying and presupposed to everything else. We can control our behaviour by choosing this or that means to our ends, but our desire for our ultimate end is not something in our control.

2   However not everything we will has to be willed[, just as not everything we think has to be thought]. The mind doesn't have to think thoughts that have no necessary connection with first principles (merely factual propositions, for instance, that can be denied without falsifying such principles); but it has to give assent to necessary propositions (demonstrable conclusions, for example, that cannot be denied without falsifying first principles), once their necessary connection with first principles has been demonstrated. And so it is with the will. The will doesn't have to want limited goods that have no necessary connection with happiness and that a person can be happy without; but other things do have a necessary connection with happiness, joining men to God, in whom alone true happiness is to be found. Before we see God and are

sure of this necessary connection, our will doesn't have to want either God or the things of God; but when we see him as he is, our wills won't be able to help wanting him, just as now we can't help wanting to be happy.

Mind and will.   To will a desirable good we must know the way in which it is good and desirable, something more abstractly simple and more excellent than the actual object willed. [So in the abstract the mind is the more excellent faculty.] Understanding, however, takes things in and is concerned with their truth in the mind, whereas willing tends towards the goodness of things in themselves; so when things exist more excellently in themselves than in the mind, willing them is preferable to knowing them (loving God to knowing him); but when they exist more excellently in the mind, knowing them is preferable to loving them. Our mind sees the good in things and this motivates our will (as goals motivate agents); but it is our will, as agent of our overall goal, which impels our mind and all our other powers to pursue their own particular goals. For what motivates a power is a particular goal suited to it: colour attracts sight and truth attracts the mind; but what attracts will is every good and goal as such. So the will is the overall motive power behind all human activity, save only those vegetative activities that are involuntary and natural. Mind and will can be regarded either as particular abilities with their own distinct activities, or as concerned with all-embracing objects: the mind as an awareness open to all that exists and is true, and the will as attracted towards everything good. If we consider the mind as all-embracing and the will as a special ability, then the mind includes the will and the act and object of willing as special instances of mind's object: existent true things. But if we consider the will as all-embracing and the mind as something special, then the will includes the mind and its act of understanding and its object (truth) as special goods. The actions and objects of mind and will mutually include each other: the mind understands the will's willing, the will wills the mind's understanding, good is something true and understandable, truth is something good and desirable. The mutual inclusion is not circular, but is grounded in mind to begin with. For every movement of will presupposes an act of knowledge, but not every act of knowledge presupposes our will; ultimately our planning and understanding issue from the mind of God, as even Aristotle says in his Eudemian Ethics.

5 **Emotion and will.**   Sense-appetite is not concerned with all good in general because sensation cannot perceive generalities, and that is why the sense-appetite has two parts concerned with particular kinds of good: the affective part concerned with what pleases the senses and is naturally congenial, and the aggressive concerned with repelling and attacking dangers. Will, however, is concerned with good in general, whatever its form, and does not divide into these two parts. Ordinarily by *love* and *desire* we mean the emotions and excited feelings that characterize sense-appetite; but we can also mean simple attraction without emotion or excitement, and then we can use the words of acts of will, such as characterize even angels and God.

[margin: love as act of will]

83 1 **Free will.**   *God made man in the beginning, and left him free to make his own decisions.* Men make free decisions; otherwise advice and encouragement, directives and prohibitions, rewards and penalties would all be pointless. Things without awareness – stones and suchlike – act without judging; dumb animals judge instinctively, but not freely: sheep decide by nature, not by argument, to run away from the wolf; but men make up their own minds: in place of a natural repertoire of particular instincts they have a general capacity to reason, and since particular matters like what to do in this or that situation are not subject to conclusive argument men are not determined to any one course. Because they reason they are free to make their own decisions. Freedom is self-determination, but being a cause of action doesn't imply being its ultimate cause, even when the action is our own. God is the ultimate cause of all causes, natural and voluntary, working in each in a way appropriate to it. That God is at work in them doesn't prevent natural causes acting naturally or voluntary causes acting voluntarily; rather it enables them so to act. Jeremiah says *man's course is not in his control,* but he means that man can't always put his choices into effect, that he can be obstructed, like it or not. But the choices themselves are ours, given God's help. [Aristotle says *the goals we pursue are determined by the sort of persons we are.*] If he means the sort of persons we are by nature, then we all by nature have minds which desire happiness naturally and not freely, and our own natural bodily constitutions and temperaments which, unlike our non-bodily minds, are determined by physical causes and dispose us to choose this goal rather than that (though since our lower appetites are subject to reason this leaves our freedom intact). If however Aristotle means the sort of person we develop into, then all of us have dispositions and emotions which dispose us one way rather than another, though these again are subject to reason, and in any case we

chose to acquire them. Freedom is a fundamental capability of the soul, 2
not just a disposition. A disposition to freedom couldn't be natural like
our disposition to know the first premises of all reasoning, for what we
are disposed to naturally we can't control, so that our freedom itself
would be unfree. But neither could freedom be an acquired disposition,
since we are free by nature. Moreover, dispositions incline us to do
things well or badly whereas what we do freely can be done either way.
So freedom is an ability, not a disposition. Man *lost by sin* not this
natural freedom from compulsion, but his freedom from guilt and
unhappiness. Freedom is properly an ability to choose, and involves 3
both the mind deciding what is preferable, and the will accepting this
decision. But what we choose is what best serves our goal, what is
usefully good, and since goods and goals are objects of desire, choice
must fundamentally be a sort of desire and freedom an ability to
desire. Indeed freedom is nothing other than the will itself. Just as 4
we distinguish understanding (assenting to something in itself) from
reasoning (deriving one thing from another), so we distinguish willing
(consenting to something for its own sake) from choice (desiring something for the sake of something else). For means are to goals as conclusions are to premises. Now we have already pointed out that
understanding and reasoning are two actions of one power, related as
resting in a place and moving from one place to another. In the same
way, willing and choosing are actions of the same power: the ability to
will and the ability to choose are one and the same ability.

How man knows

Knowing material things.   The earliest philosophers thought the [vol 12] 84
world contained only material things, continually changing, about which
nothing could be known with certainty: as Heraclitus put it, *you can't
step in the same river twice.* So Plato, to account for what we do know
with certainty, said that each particular thing we sense we classify as a
man or a horse or whatever because of a share it has in some Form or Idea
that exists independently of matter and change. Scientific definitions and
proofs and other products of intellectual activity relate to these Forms
and not to the material things we sense. But this is a mistake: firstly, it
rules out natural science, which deduces truths about matter and change
by appealing to material causes of change; and secondly, it seems
ludicrous to interpose between ourselves and the obvious objects of our
enquiries other objects so essentially different that knowing them can't

help us judge the objects we sense. Plato was apparently misled by the opinion that *like knows like* into thinking that since knowing is characterized by generality, necessity and invariance, what is known must exist in immaterial and unchanging ways outside the mind. But this is unnecessary. Even the qualities we sense exist in different ways in different objects (more or less intensely or with different associated qualities), and exist differently again in the senses themselves (where the colour of the gold exists without the gold itself). In the mind too then forms of bodies that are material and changeable can be received in a way appropriate to the recipient: immaterially and unchangeably. Changes presuppose something that doesn't change: qualitative change presupposes a persistent substance, and change of substance some identity of the underlying matter. Moreover, changing things are subject to invariant relations: though Socrates is not always seated, still it is invariably true that when seated he isn't walking about. So an unchanging science of changing things is quite possible.

2   Philosophers before Plato all held that *like knows like*; and recognizing that what we know is material they thought what knows must share the nature of some material element, like fire. But how would it be enough to have the nature of an element? We would have to share the nature of every compound too, bones and flesh and every sort of thing. Moreover if we understand fire by being like fire, why doesn't fire outside the mind understand itself? The truth is that material things are present in the mind not materially but immaterially: when we know a thing it remains other than us, [we don't become it,] whereas when matter takes on some form a new individual results. Clearly then, being aware is exactly the opposite of being material. Things that take on forms only through their matter, like plants, are not aware at all; whereas minds which take in likenesses of things' forms abstracted from matter and from all the particularities that go with it, know things better than the senses which take in forms without matter but particularized by it. The only person who knows everything by his own nature is God, who contains everything immaterially by nature (since his effects pre-exist in his power). [Men do not know things by nature.] They come to know things that previously they were only able to know: in the case of sensation the change is brought about by objects acting on the senses, in the case of mind by study or research. For the mind is not born possessed of the likenesses by which we sense and understand, but must acquire them [:as Aristotle says, it starts life *as a clean slate*]. Plato had believed the mind was filled with such likenesses by nature and that union with the body prevented it considering them. But it is surely

[marginal annotations:]
reply to Plato —
error of maxim
"like knows like"

an unchanging
science of
changing things is
possible

objd to pre-So-
cratics

tabula rasa?

impossible for minds so to forget what they possess by nature as not to know they know; and especially if what is supposed to obstruct this natural activity is an equally natural union with the body. In any case, men born blind know nothing of colour, so they aren't born with the likenesses of all things in their mind.

Our dependence on our senses.   Democritus and other early phil- 6 osophers confused mind with the senses, and thought we know by means of images that sensed objects transmit and impress on our senses. Plato on the other hand thought mind was an immaterial power using no bodily organ but knowing by participating Forms that exist abstractly; and he also thought (and Augustine echoes this opinion) that external objects don't act on our senses as such, but that the soul forms our sense-images when objects act on our sense-organs. Aristotle trod a middle path: he agreed with Plato that mind differs from the senses, but maintained that sensation is an activity in our body caused by external bodies impressing themselves on our senses (acting on them rather than transmitting something to them, as Democritus had said). Body however has no share in the mind's activity, which must be caused by something higher than impressions made on us by bodies: not impressions from higher things such as Plato posited, but a higher agency in the mind itself (our *agent mind*) making sense-images actually understandable by abstracting ideas from them. Sense provides the images, but they are not enough to affect the receptive mind; they provide only the material for knowledge which must be made actually understandable by the agent mind. The mind itself then makes no use of a bodily organ, but in this 7 life it exists in a body acted on by things, and actually to understand those things it must have recourse to our sense-images of them: not only to learn about the things in the first place but also to make use of what it learns. Organic disorders that affect imagination (as in delirium) or memory (as in paralysis) prevent us actually understanding things we have already learnt. Moreover, we know by experience that when we try to understand something we imagine examples in which we can inspect, so to speak, what we want to understand; and when helping others we proffer examples to stimulate their imaginations and thus their understanding. Now why is this? Because every ability to know has an object that specially suits it. The minds of angels, being quite separate from bodies, know firstly other such separate substances and through them material substances. But human minds, existing in bodies, know first the natures of material things, and by knowing the natures of what they see derive some knowledge of what they cannot see. Now

natures must be known (marginal note) by definition such natures belong in individual bodies: a stone must be
known by their (marginal note) a *this stone* and a horse must be a *this horse*. We haven't full and true
inherence in particular (marginal note) knowledge of what it is to be a stone (or any other material thing) unless
bodies (marginal note) we know it in particular stones, in stones we sense and imagine. So in
order actually to understand the things we are suited to understand we
must have recourse to how we imagine them, to see how general natures
exist in particular instances. A knowledgeable man has a likeness of
what he knows stored in his receptive mind even when not actually
attending to it. But when he actually attends he applies this stored
knowledge to the thing of which it is a likeness, namely the nature as it
exists in particulars. Even immaterial things which can't be imagined
are known by way of analogies with material things which can; so to
8 know them we must have recourse to images of material things. Aristotle
says that just as practical knowledge aims at doing things, natural science
aims at understanding what we sense. A smith can't make proper
judgments about knives unless he knows what they are supposed to do,
and a natural scientist can't make proper judgments about natural objects
unless he can sense them. We know nothing in this life except by way
of the natural things we sense, so, if our senses are out of commission,
we can't judge anything properly. In sleep we are more or less gassed.
When we eat and drink well a lot of gas is formed, and both senses and
dreaming (marginal note) imagination cease to function. In fever there is less gas but we have
disordered and distorted dream-images. As sleep wears off, especially in
sober and strongly imaginative men, these dreams are better ordered;
and sometimes even the inner root of our senses starts to operate and
while still asleep we perceive that we dream. The more the senses and
imagination are released the more the mind's judgment is freed, but
never altogether. When we awake we always find flaws in reasoning done
while asleep.

85 1 **Abstraction of ideas.**   What we know depends on the level at which
we know. Sense-powers are functions animating bodily organs and know
forms as they exist in bodily matter, instantiated and particularized.
Angels' minds exist without bodies and know forms existing out of
matter, and material things as reflected in such forms (in God or the
angels themselves). In between, the human mind, which though not a
function animating a bodily organ is nevertheless an ability of a soul
animating a body, knows forms which exist only instantiated in bodily
matter, but knows them in abstraction from any particular instance
sensed or imagined. Our minds understand material things by abstracting ideas of them from their images, and then use such knowledge to

acquire knowledge of immaterial things. Plato overlooked the way mind is joined to body in man and thought its immateriality enabled it to know not by abstracting ideas, but by participating in Ideas already existing abstractly and apart. Abstracting *A* from *B* can mean denying *A*'s connection with *B*, or simply thinking *A* without thinking *B*. Abstracting what in reality is connected generates falsehood if done the first way, but not if done the second. To say, for example, that an apple's colour exists somewhere else than in the apple would be a lie, but to think the colour without thinking the apple, and to express it in words, involves no lie; for apples don't enter our definition of colour and colour can be understood without understanding anything about apples. In the same way we can think what defines a material thing, stone, man or horse, without thinking of any additional individual peculiarities it may have; and this is precisely what we do when we abstract the general nature of what we understand from any particular way in which we imagine it. Understanding things otherwise than the way they exist is false understanding if *otherwise* describes the way we understand them to exist in themselves, but not if it describes the way they exist in our understanding. A man would falsely abstract the form of stone from matter if he denied its connection with matter, as Plato did; but there is nothing false about what a man understands existing immaterially in his mind, though materially in the thing understood. To understand natural things is not, as some have thought, to abstract their forms wholly from matter; for matter is part of the definition of natural things. We must rather distinguish matter in general (flesh and bones, say) from particular designated matter (this flesh and these bones), allowing that mind abstracts the species of natural things from any particular matter we perceive but not from perceptible matter in general. The nature of man, for example, cannot be mentally abstracted from flesh and bones in general, though it can be abstracted from this flesh and these bones, which belong only to this individual and not to the definition of his species. Objects of mathematics, however, abstract from perceived matter both in particular and in general; though from thought matter only in particular and not in general. By perceived matter I mean matter as underlying perceptible qualities (hot, cold, hard, soft, etc), and by thought matter I mean substance as underlying quantity. Clearly a substance must have quantity before it can have perceptible qualities. So numeric and dimensive quantity and boundary shape can be thought without thinking perceptible qualities, and thus be abstracted from all perceived matter. But they cannot be thought without thinking underlying substance, and so cannot be abstracted from thought matter in general. Nevertheless, because they can be thought apart from this or that substance they can be abstracted from particular thought matter. There are even things we can abstract from thought matter in general: things like being and oneness and potentiality and realization; for these can exist without any matter at all as immaterial substances prove. Plato overlooked these two ways of abstracting, and thought that everything mind abstracts really has an abstract existence. [Aristotle said that images are to mind as colours to sight.] However, colours exist in particular bodily matter in the same way as eyesight exists and can therefore affect our sight. But sense images represent particulars and exist in bodily organs, and since that is not the way our receptive mind exists, they can't of themselves affect our mind. The agent mind must itself turn to those images, and produce by its own power in the receptive mind a representation as to species of whatever the images represent as individual. This we call abstracting the species from the sense-images. What we don't mean is that numerically one and the same form moves from image to receptive mind, in the way a body moves from place to place. The agent mind by its very union with the body's senses lights up the imagination and prepares it for abstraction ; and then it goes on to do the abstracting, producing from representations of particular instances of things in the imagination a representation of the species of the things in the receptive mind. Our mind both abstracts the species *from* images when it attends to the general natures of things, and understands the species *in* the images when it has recourse to the images in order to understand the things whose species it has abstracted.

2 **The general and the particular.**   [What we see is not the images in our eyes, but the things they image.] In the same way, what we know is not the abstracted species in our mind. If we did, all science would be about ideas, not about real things outside the mind; and (as some ancient philosophers wrongly thought) all appearances would be true. Rather the abstracted species is the means by which we know what we know. Just as the form that makes a natural thing externally active reproduces itself in an effect (heat producing heat), so the form that makes a thing interiorly active represents its object. By the image in the eye we see the thing it represents; and by the abstracted species imaging things in the mind we understand the things it images. Though, because our minds are self-reflective, we can also reflect on our own understanding and understand, in a secondary sense, the abstract species by which we understand. [If we ask *But where is what we actually understand, since, as actually understood, it must be immaterial and so cannot exist*

outside the mind?,] we will have to distinguish what is understood from our actual understanding of it, just as we must distinguish what is conceived in an abstract general concept from the abstract generality of the conception. The nature that is being understood or abstracted or thought with generality exists only in particular things; but the understanding or abstracting or generality of it exists in the mind. We see the same thing in sense-perception. Sight perceives the colour of an apple but not its scent. Where then is the colour that is seen without the scent? In the apple, clearly. Though that it is seen without the scent belongs to it only in relation to sight, where colour can be imaged without scent. In the same way, the human nature we understand exists only in this or that man, but that this nature is perceived apart from its particular instantiations, that it is abstracted and clothed in generality, belongs to it only as perceived by mind, where the species of man is represented without any particularities of instantiation. [But, since Aristotle said, *words express mental concepts*, are abstract ideas what we talk and think about?] Mental activity combines two activities which in the senses are distinct: external perception in which we are simply affected by what we sense, and interior imagination in which we create images of things that are not and perhaps never have been present. The receptive mind is affected by an abstracted species, but when so affected it formulates definitions and propositional connections, which we express in words. Words express not the abstracted species themselves but judgments formulated by the mind about external things.

What do we know first, the particular or the general? Well, our mind's knowledge arises out of sense-perception, and so, in this sense, knowledge of the particular (sense-knowledge) precedes knowledge of the general (mental knowledge). But since our mind is not born with actual knowledge but acquires it, to arrive at complete, distinct, determinate knowledge it must go through a stage in which its knowledge is incomplete, indistinct and confused, knowing wholes without properly and precisely knowing their parts. We know animals, for example, indistinctly when we know them in general simply as animals; but we know them distinctly when we know rational and non-rational animals, men and lions. So our minds know animal first and man later, and similarly with whatever is more and less general. Sense-knowledge is ordered in the same way for the same reason: something approaching is first seen as a body, then as an animal, then as a man, and finally as Plato or Socrates; and *children begin by calling all men Daddy*, distinguishing men from non-men before they distinguish this man from that. The generality attaching to a nature – its relatedness to many

particular instances – results from abstraction, so in this sense a generalized nature presupposes its instances, and does not, as Plato thought,
precede them. But the nature existing in the instances can be thought
of in two ways. In the genetic process the more general precedes the
less (foetuses are animal before they are human), but in nature's purposes
the perfectly actual precedes the imperfect and potential (nature, in
producing the animal foetus, is aiming at producing a man). So our
minds know animals in general before distinguishing men and horses;
yet know man in general before distinguishing in him animality and
rationality. Thus when defining A in terms of B we presuppose knowledge of B as such (otherwise the definition would give no information);
but we know A before we know that B contributes to defining it: we
know men in a confused sort of way before we know how to define them.

   In what sense has the general a causative role? The generalized nature
which results from abstraction does in a sense cause knowledge; but –
pace Plato – not every cause of knowledge is a cause of existence (for
causes can be known by effects and substances by their properties); and
in any case, as Aristotle said, generalized natures in this sense are neither
causes nor substances. Instances, however, of generic or specific natures
existing in particular things are in a sense formal causes of those
particulars: matter makes the particulars particular and form determines
their species. However, the generic nature of something is material to
its specific nature, being based on what is more material in the thing:
we are animals because we have senses, men because we have minds. So
neither the particular nor the genus, but the species, is the final cause
ultimately aimed at by nature; the goal of reproduction is the form, and
matter serves that goal. None of these ways of seeing the general nature
as causative, however, implies that it is less known to us: sometimes
effects reveal causes but sometimes causes reveal effects.

5 **The simple and the composite.**   In order to understand, human
minds make and unmake connections. They acquire knowledge, and so
bear a certain resemblance to things which get born and grow to
completion by stages. For we don't grasp a thing completely from the
start, but our first grasp of what it is opens it to understanding, and
from that we come to understand the properties and relationships that
are peculiar (or maybe coincidental) to what it is. To do this we make
and unmake connections between what we grasp, and reason from one
connection to another. The minds of God and angels, however, resemble
things perfect from the outset, and in their first grasp of what a thing
is they know everything that we find out by making connections and

reasoning. Though the mind abstracts from sense-images, it cannot actually understand what it abstracts without turning again to sense-images; and this introduces tense into the connections mind makes or unmakes. Two sorts of combination in material things correspond (with differences) to our mental making and unmaking of connections. To matter combining with form correspond all mental connections attributing a general nature to some instance of it (for generic natures are based on what is general but material, differentiated into species by what is formal; whilst particulars derive from this or that particular matter). And to the combination of something's substance with its supervening properties correspond mental connections attributing properties to subjects. But there are differences between mental connections and combinations in things. The elements that combine in a thing differ from each other, but mental connections express the identity of what they connect. Thus we do not say *Man is whiteness*, but *Man is white*, for it is the same subject that is both man and white. Similarly with form and matter: one and the same thing is animal (possessing a sense nature), rational (possessing a mental nature), man (possessing both), and Socrates (combining all this with some particular matter); and we make mental connections attributing one to the other based on this identity. A sense can make a mistake about its own particular stimulus (sight 6 about colour, for instance) only indirectly, because of some deficiency in its organ. But it can err about stimuli not peculiar to that sense – misjudging shape and size – and especially about what it senses only indirectly – as when it mistakes gall for honey because it is the same colour. The reason is obvious: the object peculiar to an ability defines it; it cannot err about that and still be the same ability. Now understanding is defined as understanding what a thing is, so it cannot as such err about that. But it can make mistakes when connecting up and reasoning about anything else relating to that thing. It will not err about those propositions which we understand immediately we know what they are about (the first premises of science), or about conclusions derived with certainty from such premises. However, the mind can, indirectly, err about what a composite thing is: not because of some deficiency in an organ (since mind is not a function of an organ), but because defining such a thing presupposes making connections, and a definition can either get applied to the wrong thing (circle to triangle) or itself include impossible combinations (*winged rational animal*). Non-composite things cannot be defined erroneously, though we can fail altogether to understand them.

In our present life what we first understand are the natures of material 8 things as we abstract them from sense-images. Thinking about this will tell us whether we understand the simple before the composite or vice versa. In one sense, extended wholes are non–composite, actually ①undivided though divisible, and are understood as such before we have any understanding of their parts; we know things indistinctly before we know them distinctly. In another sense, every specific nature (humanity, ②for example) is understood as an indivisible whole before we analyse it into its defining elements, and begin to make and unmake connections with affirmations and denials; for specific natures are the very first things we understand. Finally, there are altogether simple elements, like points ③in a line or the units of counting, which we only know after divisibility, as lacking it: thus we define a point as that which has no parts, and unity as indivisibility. To be indivisible in this way is opposed to being bodily, and bodies are what we primarily understand. It would be Platonist to think that what we primarily understand are separately existing simples. In the process of acquiring scientific knowledge, we don't always argue from principles and elements, since our knowledge of such intelligible principles sometimes comes through their sensible effects. But when a science is complete all such effects are explained in terms of their causes.

86 1 **What don't we know?**   This or that matter gives material things their particularity; but since we understand such things by abstracting their general nature from such matter, our mind has no direct knowledge of material objects in their particularity. Indirectly by a sort of reflection it does know particulars, for we can actually understand by way of abstracted species only by turning back to view them in sense-images. This is how our minds formulate propositions such as *Socrates is a man*, and choose particular actions as conclusions of a reasoning process premised by general practical principles but mediated by particular 2 sense-perceptions. Our mind is proportioned to knowing material things, so infinity applies to it in the way it applies to material things, not actually but potentially: our mind can understand one thing after another without ever exhausting its capacity to understand more. We cannot however actually consider an infinite number of things: for what we consider together must have a single form, which infinity can't have, since it is never whole (however much you take of infinity, as Aristotle said, there is always something over). Nor could we be potentially knowledgeable about an infinite number of things without previously having actually considered them. Infinity in material things is matter undetermined by form, and unformed infinity is as such unknowable; but God's infinity is form unlimited by matter, and as such knowable,

though not by us in the present life where we are naturally adapted to know material things and God only in his effects. There may be infinite species of numbers and geometrical figures, but our mind naturally knows them by abstraction from sense-images; so someone who has not imagined them cannot know them except generically, as implicit in some general rule, indistinctly and potentially. Nothing is so unnecessary 3 that no necessity at all attaches to it: even if it is not necessary for Socrates to be running, it is nevertheless necessary that when he runs he moves. Non-necessity in things is due to their matter; necessity is a consequence of form. Now matter particularizes, whereas generality follows on the mind's abstraction of form from particularizing matter: the mind as such knows the general directly, whereas the senses (and the mind indirectly) know particulars. So what may or may not be so is known directly by the senses and indirectly by the mind; whilst any general necessity attaching to it is known by mind. All science then is concerned with what can be known generally and necessarily, either about things that must exist (in some sciences) or about things that need not exist (in others). Future things are in time and particular, so 4 mind can know them only by a sort of reflection on sense; though they may instantiate general notions that mind can itself grasp and prove scientifically. Only God knows the future as it will be in itself, for it presents itself to his eternal gaze together with the whole course of time. We know the future only as foreshadowed in present causes: with scientific certainty if these causes totally determine it (as when we predict eclipses), but otherwise with varying degrees of probability depending on how inclined the causes are to those effects.

Knowing ourselves. The human mind is only potentially a mind, 87 1 holding the same place in the world of understanding as matter holds in the world of sense (which is why we call mind receptive). Of itself then it is able to understand, but not able to be understood until actualized. In our present life our mind turns naturally to the material things we sense, and only understands itself when brought to act by species abstracted from things sensed. This abstraction is caused by the light of the agent mind, the source of the actual intelligibility of everything we understand and hence of the receptive mind itself. So our mind knows itself not by its own substance but by its activity: each man through his experience of his own acts of understanding perceives himself to possess a mind (for that there is required only the mind's presence to itself), and through consideration of those acts he can come to a general understanding of the mind's nature (but that requires

3 diligent and subtle investigation). For God understanding himself and understanding his act of understanding is the same thing. For angels they differ but happen together; for in understanding itself an angel realizes itself, and any act of understanding a thing must understand what realizes it. But the human mind primarily understands not itself but external material things; secondarily its own act of understanding such things; and finally itself, the power of understanding realized in that act. The act of human understanding does not perfect and realize the material thing it understands: so the act by which we understand a stone is not the same act as that which understands us understanding the stone, and so on. But there is nothing awkward about the mind being potentially subject to an infinite regress. What activates the external senses is an external object operating on a material organ. Since nothing material can operate on itself, external sense activity is not perceptible to the external sense itself, but only to a central common sensitivity. Our minds however are not activated by material operation

4 on an organ, and can perceive their own activity. A thing's tendencies are of the sort the thing itself is: natural tendencies exist in natural things by nature, the desires sensation arouses are themselves sensibly perceptible to the desirer, and a person's acts of will (tendencies consequent on his understanding) exist understandably *in his mind* as in their origin and subject. But that means they can be understood by his mind: he can both perceive that he wills, and understand what willing is. Mind and will are different powers, but they are powers of one subject, the soul, deriving one from the other in a certain sense, so that whatever is

88 2 in will is also in mind. Created immaterial things have quite a different nature from material things (the potentiality they have is not a material potentiality [to decompose]); they are nevertheless logically categorizable as substances, since they are something other than their own existence. God however is neither naturally nor logically similar to material things; so that images drawn from material things, though they give us positive but non-specific knowledge of angels, give us no such knowledge of God.

89 1 **The soul after death.**   It is hard to see how, out of its body, the soul could know anything. In the body, experience shows that we understand only by turning to sense-images. Now if that was unnatural for the soul, resulting only from being tied to a body (as Platonists think), then obviously, once the hindrance of body went, the soul would act naturally again and understand things in a simple angelic way without recourse to sense-images. But that would mean the union of soul and body had

served the body but not the soul, and form serving matter rather than vice
versa is nonsensical. However, if it is natural to the soul to understand by
turning to sense-images, then death won't change the soul's nature, and
after death, when the soul has no sense-images to turn to, it presumably
won't understand anything naturally. This difficulty disappears if we
remember that activity realizes a thing's being, so that the way something
exists determines the way it acts. The soul doesn't change its nature
but it exists in two ways, one natural (united to a body) and one
unnatural (separated from its body); just as heavy bodies, without
changing their nature, can exist grounded (their natural place) or
suspended. When naturally united to its body the soul understands in
a natural way through recourse to sense-images, but when unnaturally
separated from its body it understands without sense-images, in a way
unnatural to it though natural to angels. The soul is united to a body
in order that it can exist and operate naturally, understanding with the
help of sense-images; but it can exist separately and understand in a
different way. In this separate state the soul doesn't understand by way
of innate ideas (for at birth the mind is a clean slate), nor by way of
ideas it abstracts at that time (for it no longer possesses the senses and
imagination by means of which it can make such abstractions), nor by
ideas previously abstracted and stored (for then infants could understand
nothing after death); but by ideas deriving from God's mind, in the way
angels understand. As soon as it stops turning to the body, the soul
turns to this higher source. Such knowledge is not for that reason graced,
but still natural, God being the author of both nature and grace. In its
separate state the soul is immediately intelligible to itself, not merely
reflectively known as that which is understanding the ideas it is abstracting from sense-images. God, as we saw, knows all things in general and
in particular, since he knows himself as causing everything in general
and in particular; and immaterial things share this knowledge through
ideas which are likenesses of God. But separated souls know in this way
only the particular things to which they are already bound by some
previous knowledge or affection or natural relationship or divine ordering: for what we receive we receive in ways appropriate to what we
already are. We acquire knowledge in this life through acts of understanding in which our minds are turned towards sense-images; our
minds acquire the facility to attend to abstracted ideas, and our imaginations and memories the aptitude to provide abstractable images. So the
knowledge we acquire, like the acts which acquire it, resides primarily
and formally in the mind, but materially and dispositively in our sensitive
powers. These dispositions to knowledge disappear when the body dies,

8 but the knowledge in the mind remains. The souls of the dead are barred from converse with the living, and Gregory the Great and Augustine agree that they know nothing of what goes on among us. As to the souls in heaven, Augustine thinks it unlikely they know about us, since after his mother died she no longer visited and consoled him as she had before, and her happier state of life would surely not have made her less kind. But Gregory's opinion that those who see God know all that passes here below seems more probable. But because they are perfectly attuned to God's just will they remain content and do not intervene in our lives unless God plans it so.

The Genesis of man   *cf PL*

[vol 13] 90 1 *God formed man from the slime of the earth and breathed into his face*
2 *the breath of life, and man became a living soul.*   Only what possesses existence and is subject of its own existence – substance – properly exists; all supervening properties exist not as themselves possessing existence but as forms under which a substance exists. Whiteness's existence is really the existence of something as white. This is true of all non-subsistent forms; so, properly speaking, it is not such forms but the things of which they are forms that come into existence. The soul however is a subsistent form and can properly be said both to exist and to come into existence. But since it does not come from pre-existent
3 matter (only bodies do that), it must come by a new creation. Only God can create. All secondary agents presuppose material provided by a primary agent, which they then transform. Since the human soul does not come into existence by transformation of pre-existent matter, it
4 must be produced by God's immediate creation. The soul however is only part of man, and naturally perfect only when united to its body, so it was fittingly created in its body, not before it. If it was a natural species of thing the soul would be a sort of angel; but by nature it is the
91 2 form of a body, the formal element in an animal. Forms in matter are caused by forms in matter, when composite material things generate one another. The only immaterial thing that can produce something material without needing previous material is God; he alone can create new matter. So Adam's body was formed by God immediately, there being no preceding human body that could generate a body of like species to
3 itself. Because the senses are mainly concentrated in the face, other animals have faces close to the ground to look for food and provender; but men have raised faces so that their senses, especially the finest and

most discriminating sense of sight, may experience sense-objects in
every direction of heaven and earth. Man's upright carriage also releases
his hands for various useful purposes. And since he does not have to
use his mouth for gathering food, it is not oblong and hard as in other
animals but adapted for speech, the special work of reason. So man's
upright carriage is not like that of the plants, for they have their roots
(which are their mouths) in the earth.

It is not good for man to be alone; let us make him a help that is like 92 1
himself.   The help God makes for man is not for any sort of work (for
there other men would be more help than a woman) but for producing
children. In plants, which have no nobler function in life than propagation, the active and passive abilities to propagate are joined at all
times. In the higher animals however there is more to life than that, so
the active male and passive female partners mate only at certain times,
constituting the sort of unity a plant is always. Aristotle called the female
a male manqué. The particular nature of the active male seed intends to
produce a perfect likeness of itself, and when females are conceived this
is due to weak seed, or unsuitable material, or external influences like
the dampness of the south wind. But this is because nature as a whole
intends women; and in this sense they are not manqué but intended by
God, the author of nature as a whole. The type of subordination in
which servants are managed in their master's interests came in after sin;
but the subordination seen in households or cities, where management
is for the benefit of the subordinates themselves, would have obtained
even without sin. And such is the natural inequality and subordination
of women to men, who are by nature more reasonable and discerning.
[Some say God should not have produced Eve to be an occasion of sin
for Adam, but] if God removed from the world everything which man
has made an excuse for sin, the world would be a poor place. What is
a general good must not be sacrificed because of some particular abuse,
especially since God is powerful enough to turn any evil to good account.
Forming Eve from Adam's rib signified companionship, not domination 3
(so not from his head) nor yet subjection (so not from his feet); and it
also symbolized the establishment of the church by the sacraments
of blood and water flowing from the side of Christ sleeping on the
cross.

Let us make man after our own image and likeness.   An image not only 93 1
resembles, it expresses: however like each other two eggs may be, one
does not express the other and is not its image. But the resemblance

man bears God derives from God as from an original, so scripture describes man as made to God's image; where the preposition *to* signifies approach to something at a distance, the original in this case being

2 infinitely distant from the image. An image must also resemble its original in species, or in some attribute like shape peculiar to that species, where likeness in species means likeness down to the last thing differentiating the species. Things in general resemble God in existing, some things also in being alive, and some finally in intellectual discernment: the closest likeness to God in creation. Properly speaking

4 then, only creatures with intellect are made to God's image. And the point at which such creatures most closely resemble God is when they imitate his self-understanding and love. So there are three levels to the imaging of God by man: the very nature of mind gives to all men a natural aptitude for understanding and loving God; grace adds to some men an actual if imperfect understanding and love of God; and the glory of heaven brings this to perfection. The principal constituent of God's image in man, mind, is found in both male and female human beings; which is why Genesis says *To God's image he created him (namely, mankind); male and female he created them.* A secondary image of God as beginning and end of creation is however to be found only in male man, the beginning and end of woman: and this is what made St Paul say that *the man is the image and glory of God, and the woman the glory of man, for Adam was not from Eve but Eve from Adam, and Adam was not for Eve, but Eve for Adam.*

5 That man is made in the image of God's nature implies that all three
6 persons of God are represented in him. In other creatures, and in other parts of man than his mind, there is not the same image or likeness in species to God, but only the sort of trace that all causes leave even in effects unlike in species. Thus we talk of tracks left by animals as traces, fires leave traces of themselves in ashes, and armies traces in the ravaged countryside. An image of the uncreated Trinity can be found in creatures with reason, who utter a word in their minds, and in whose wills a love issues, so representing God in species. In other creatures there is no such word-source or word or love; but [in the three goods of being in condition, form and order, Augustine finds in everything God makes] a trace of the fact that source, word and love exist in its maker. For a creature's shaping and conditioning indicate that it *comes from* somewhere; its specific form indicates its maker's *word* as a house's shape indicates its architect's idea; and its functional order indicates its maker's

7 *love* as a house's uses indicate what its architect willed. A first image of the Trinity in our minds is found in our activities of thinking out and

formulating an inner word from the information we have, and then
bursting out from this in a love. But since such activities exist implicitly
in their sources [memory, understanding and will], a secondary image
of the Trinity exists in our powers and dispositions to act. The kind of 8
word and love we have in our heart varies according to what it is we are
conceiving and loving: stone or horse. So God's image is to be found in
the conceiving of a word that expresses what we know of God and a
love flowing from that; in other words, in the soul attending directly to
God. Though the mind can also attend indirectly to God (as to an object
seen in a mirror) when, as Augustine says, it remembers and understands
and loves itself, and perceives there a trinity: not God indeed, but an
image of God; and then moves through that to God.

God made man right.   No one can wilfully turn away from happiness, for 94 1
man wants happiness by nature. So no one seeing God for what he is
can wilfully turn his back on God. Plainly then, since Adam sinned, he
had not seen God for what he is. The disembodied state of the soul after 2
death differs from its present embodied state in being unnatural; but
Adam's state of innocence and man's state after sin differ as integrated
and disintegrated states of a soul which has preserved its natural way of
existence unimpaired. In the state of innocence, just as now, man's soul
was adapted to controlling and perfecting and giving life to his body,
but in so fully integrated a way that his body was completely at the service
of his soul without hindrance. And since the way of understanding
appropriate to a soul that must control and perfect the body's animal
life is by recourse to sense-experience, this was also Adam's way of
understanding. The things that were made in the beginning were made 3
not only to be themselves but to start other things existing, and that is
why they were produced in a state of perfection. Adam was created
mature in body, capable of immediate procreation, and mature in soul,
capable of immediate education and instruction of others. So he knew
all that men normally have to learn, everything implicit in the first self-
evident premises, all natural knowledge: *he gave all animals their names.*
And since controlling his own and other people's lives also involved
knowing life as destined to a goal beyond nature, Adam needed to know
the supernatural things required to direct life in that state of innocence,
just as nowadays we need the faith. But Adam did not know other things
not naturally knowable but not required for directing life: such as men's
thoughts, or the indeterminate future, or details like the number of
pebbles in some river.

The integrated state of Adam in which his reason was submissive to 95 1

God, his lower powers to his reason, and his body to his soul, seems to imply that he possessed God's grace from the start; for this is an integration not written into man's nature, otherwise it would have remained after sin. The primary submissiveness of Adam's reason to God must have been more than natural, and therefore due to a gift of grace; for effects cannot be more potent than their cause. In us feeling is partly but not wholly subject to reason: sometimes our feelings pre-empt and hamper reasoned assessment, whilst at other times they presuppose it. In the state of innocence the lower appetites were completely subject to reason, and all feelings presupposed reasoned assessment. Virtues are what dispose our reason towards God and our lower powers towards the standards set by reason; so the very rightness of man's first state required him to possess all virtue. Some virtues, like charity and justice, contain no implication of imperfection, and others, like faith and hope, imply imperfections which were compatible with Adam's state (not yet seeing God and not in full enjoyment of him); so these existed in Adam without qualification, both the dispositions and the acts that proceed from them. But virtues like repentance and compassion that imply imperfections incompatible with Adam's state could only exist inactively, as dispositions to act when required, in the way Aristotle says shame exists in an earnest man.

96 1 *Let him rule the fishes of the sea and the birds of the sky and the beasts of the earth.* In nature the less perfect serve the more perfect: plants feed on the earth, animals on plants, and men on both plants and animals. Moreover, the instincts of animals to behave in certain particular ways is a sort of sharing in man's universal practical sense which can reason out all behaviour. So the subordination of animals to man is natural. To think wild and aggressive animals were originally peaceable, not only to men but also to other animals, is quite irrational. How could man by sinning change the nature of animals from vegetarian to carnivorous? Hostility between animals is natural, but it no more made them insubordinate to man then than it makes them insubordinate to God and his providence now. Man would have been an instrument of that providence then, just as he is now with domesticated animals, giving his tame hawks hens to eat. Instinctively geese follow a leader and bees obey a queen: all animals share by nature in the practical sense we have by reason. And at that time all animals would have obeyed man of their own accord, 2 as the ones he has domesticated do today. Man was master of other things to the measure that he was master of himself. He shares reason with the angels, sense-powers with other animals, natural vital powers

with plants, and the body itself with all non-living things. Reason is master, not subject (so man never had mastery over angels); feelings of aggression and desire man masters to some extent by reason's command (and so in the state of innocence he could command animals); but his own body and vital forces man masters not by command but by use (and so in the state of innocence he could not command plants and non-living things to change their behaviour, but would have had no trouble using their behaviour for his purposes). Of course, disparities existed 3 in that first state: disparities first of all in sex and age, but also in moral and intellectual proficiency (men being free to work to different extents at doing and willing and knowing things), and again in physical strength (since this is influenced by food and climate and the stars one is born under). But none of this would have implied natural defect or sin. Free 4 men exist for their own ends, as Aristotle says; whereas slaves serve others. Such slavery can't exist without suffering: everyone values his own good, and does not willingly cede it exclusively to another. But men can be subordinate to one another and yet remain free, if the good being served is their own or a common good. Such subordination would have existed in the state of innocence, since man is by nature a social animal, and people living a social life need some single authority to look to their common good. If some men are more knowledgeable and just than others the right thing is to use that to the others' benefit.

Death entered the world through sin.   Before sin then, man must have 97 1 been immortal. Not because he was immaterial like angels, or made of a kind of matter that cannot lose its form like the stars of heaven, nor because of some inherent disposition preserving him from his natural mortality like the glorified in heaven, but because God gave his soul supernatural ability to preserve his body from decay as long as it itself remained submissive to God. In the state of innocence man preserved 2 his body from external injury by his own wits, helped by God's providence which so cared for him that nothing dangerous took him by surprise. As Augustine says *Adam was provided with food against hunger,* 4 *with drink against thirst, and with the tree of life against the ravages of old age.* But the tree of life couldn't be the sole source of immortality. For one thing the tree of life couldn't give the soul its ability to preserve the body from injury; and for another, the potency of any material thing is finite and the effects of the tree of life would wear off in time, after which man would either move on to a life in the spirit or need another dose.

98 1 *Increase and multiply and fill the earth.* Unless there had been reproduction in the state of innocence to propagate the human race, man would have urgently needed to sin, seeing it would have brought such good. For among corruptible things, in which only the species lasts for ever, nature's main aim is the good of the species and its reproduction. Only among incorruptible substances is nature interested in individuals. So man needed to reproduce for the sake of his perishable body; though as regards his imperishable soul man needed nature (or better the author of nature, who alone creates human souls) to be interested in a multitude of individuals for their own sakes. So in the state of innocence reproduction was needed not for conservation of the species but for multiplication of individuals. In the present state of things, when owners multiply, property must be divided up, since, as Aristotle says, common property breeds discord. But in the state of innocence men's wills would have been well enough disposed for them to use their common property in a manner suited to each without danger of discord; as we indeed often see good men doing nowadays.

2   Some early theologians seeing intercourse besmirched by lust in our present state, thought reproduction would have happened without intercourse in the state of innocence. But this is unreasonable. It is in man's nature, like that of other animals, both before and after sin, to reproduce by intercourse, and nature has provided him with the organs needed for the purpose. In our present state the natural mating of male and female is somewhat disfigured by unbalanced desire, but this would not have happened in the state of innocence where the lower powers obeyed reason. Because animals lack reason, people sometimes say that men become like animals during intercourse, when reason is unable to balance the pleasure and heat of desire. But in the state of innocence nothing would have escaped reason in that way. Yet the pleasure would not have been any less; in fact it would have been greater given the greater purity of nature and sensitivity of body men then had. Rule by reason requires not that the pleasure should be less, but that the desire for it should be within reasonable bounds. Men who eat moderately can take as much pleasure in their food as gluttons do, but their desire doesn't wallow in the pleasure. In the state of innocence there would have been no great esteem for sexual abstinence, which we esteem nowadays not because it reduces fruitfulness but because it tempers lust.

99 1   Things beyond nature only faith can teach, and for faith we need authority. So, without God's authority, we can only assert what is in the nature of things. Now scripture tells us God created man right, so that his limbs, for example, would obey his properly ordered will. But

a properly ordered will tends only to the behaviour appropriate to one's age. So newly-born infants would only have had power to move their limbs appropriately to their age, sucking the breast and so on. Weakness 2 of seed or unsuitable material are not the only causes of females being conceived, but also external circumstances such as the direction of the wind or an idea in the mind. And this would have been particularly likely in the state of innocence, when the body was more subordinate to the mind, so that the sex of the child could have been decided by the parent. The integrated state in which man was created was a state of 100 1 our nature, not deriving from the natural constitution of man, but from a gift of God given to human nature as a whole. We know this because its opposite, inherited sin, attaches to nature as a whole and passes from parent to child. When authority is silent we can only believe what 101 1 accords with nature. Now men naturally learn by sense-experience, so those born in a state of innocence would also have acquired their knowledge over a period of time by discovery and instruction, though without the difficulties we have. And, as infants, they would no more have had mature use of their reason than they had of their bodily limbs.

People who locate Paradise at the equator do so because they think 102 2 the evenness of day and night produces a temperate climate there, never too cold and never too hot. Aristotle however expressly says that the region is so hot that it is uninhabitable; and this seems more likely, seeing that even countries where the sun never passes directly overhead have excessively hot climates from mere proximity to the sun. In any case we believe Paradise to be situated in the most temperate locality, whether that be on the equator or elsewhere.

Chapter 6

RUNNING THE WORLD

Introductory comment. The position of this chapter in the structure of the *Summa* is significantly ambiguous. God in himself, the coming forth of creatures (especially man) from God, and their return: these were to be the three components of that structure (Introduction p 5). In the first three chapters of his first part Thomas has talked of God in himself, and in the next two of the creation of creatures, and especially of man; from the start of the second part onwards (chapter 7) he will be talking of the return of man and creation to God. But in between there occurs this chapter 6, and significantly it belongs to both parts. For it is in fact about how the return to God of creatures, the world-process, is itself something issuing from God. We are, so to speak, at the turning-point of the *Summa*'s structure.

The first part of the chapter is about **God's role** in the process, the way in which its running issues from him. The word *running* translates *gubernatio* which gave us the English word *government* and literally means the steering of a ship. It is the word translated *guidedness* in the fifth way of proving God's existence from his effects in this world. But what we read is not a mere repetition of the subject of chapter 4: God as creator. Thomas uses the word *creation* to represent that mode of agency of the world that is God's uniquely, shared with no intermediaries and presupposing no material; the running of the world, in contrast, is God's in the first place, but he has planned it to be done through his creatures: they are to share agency of the world with God, as *secondary* causes. The function of this chapter is to introduce the notion of creaturely cooperation with God in his running of the world: in maintaining it in existence and running order, and in the achievement of its ends. It is of course possible for God to bypass secondary causes and do miracles, but Thomas regards God as doing a greater thing when he works within the natural order (operating within and cooperating with the natures he has created), and within our very wills (operating within and cooperating with their voluntary willing).

The second part of the chapter turns to consider **the role of creatures** in the world-process. The creatures' cooperation is discussed in the same order in which their creation was discussed in chapters 4 and 5: first, the angels and devils; then, material causes; and finally, men. I have retained only a few points from these discussions, for their subject is what one might call the mechanism of the world-process, and in that perhaps the medievals have least to offer us. We learn that **angels** can communicate with each other and have been used by God to communicate revelation to men (the word *angel* means *messenger*) and give men the benefit of their prudence (the *guardian angel*). **Devils** in contrast are the tempters *par excellence*, though Thomas points out that men on their own are also quite capable in this role. The discussion of **material causes** offers some insights into the medieval view of the physical world: the lowest causes in the hierarchy are the *active qualities* of the *elements*, the highest the *heavenly bodies*, the stars. The discussion of the stars (echoed later in ch 11 p 412) has an importance greater than may at first appear. By way of its discussion (and rejection) of astrology it tackles the questions of chance and determinism (pp 159–61 below). The stars can't directly affect human voluntary action and are not the arbiters of our fate: astrology is false. The stars do not even reign supreme in the material world, for there are always chance events which escape them: determinism is also false. Fundamentally chances are coincidences, not *naturally* unified events, and so have no *naturally* unified cause; coincidences can only be unified in a mind. Chance then escapes the natural causality of the stars. It does not escape God's causality; but God's causality, as we have seen in chapter 2 (pp 56–7), does not make things happen necessarily. If Thomas had been writing his *Summa* today this is the point at which he would have had to come to terms with modern pictures of the world-process, and tell us how he would view the reduction of all activity to physico-chemical interactions, and how reconcile the chance and necessity of evolution with God's causality. Finally, **men** have a part to play with God in the running of the world. The rest of the *Summa* will have much to say on how that part has been played out in history. In this chapter we restrict ourselves to (three ways) in which men affect the world: they teach, some of them (mainly old women) appear to cast spells but perhaps don't, and they reproduce themselves by producing the embryo to which God adds a human soul. It is perhaps noteworthy that teaching and reproduction are not examples of man's expansive exploitation of the world's resources, but of a tradition moving steadily on from generation to generation.

God's role

[vol 14] 103 1   Some early philosophers said everything happened by chance, but the reliable and regular pattern of nature shows that someone is running or managing the world. Indeed God's goodness requires that whatever he brings into existence he should also guide to its goal, and that is what running something means. Rational creatures tend or act towards goals under their own agency, knowing what goals are and what it is to serve goals. Other things tend or act towards goals under the agency and direction of others, like arrows aimed by archers. The arrow's alignment on a target shows someone aimed it in that direction; and in the same way, the regular course of mindless nature plainly reveals that the world is guided by some plan. Even what is by nature stable needs a guiding hand to preserve it from dissolving into the nothingness from which it came. The fixed nature of a creature that determines how it behaves is imposed on it by God directing it to a goal, just as determinate movement towards a target is imposed on an arrow by its archer. But the determination a creature receives from God constitutes its nature, whereas what man artificially imposes on a natural thing is a coercion.

2   A goal peculiar to one thing is good in some particular way; but the goal of the universe must be altogether good. But whatever is altogether good must be good essentially and as such, goodness itself. Goods within the universe only share goodness; so the goal of the whole universe must be some good outside it. For we achieve goals not only by acquiring intrinsic forms (like health or knowledge), but also by making or acquiring extrinsic things (building a house or buying a field), or even by representing them (making a statue of Hercules). So the goal towards which all things are guided can be something outside the universe to be possessed and represented, which everything strives to share in and imitate as far as possible. The intrinsic good of cosmic order is certainly a goal of the universe, but one that is ordered ultimately to a further extrinsic good, as order in an army serves its commander's purpose.

3   Management or government is guidance of the governed towards some good end, and involves unity; for no existence is possible without unity. Any government of a group aims at unity and peace, and since a number

of people can't unify and pacify a group unless they themselves are first united, it seems that the best government will come from one person rather than from many. God's management of the world does many things. There is one actual goal: the imitation of the highest good. But there are two general means by which God achieves that: he holds things in existence, maintaining the good in creation that imitates God's own goodness; and he stimulates and directs creatures to pursue good and so imitate God's causality. And these general activities involve countless particular ones. The very occurrence of chance in the world shows it to be governed. For unless some higher aim governed changes in this world (especially in mindless things), nothing could be unintentional, which is what chance means. Different sorts of things are governed differently by the one divine governing plan: those that act autonomously by nature and are masters of their own acts are governed not only by God working within them but also by commands and prohibitions, rewards and punishments making the good attractive and the bad repugnant. God does not govern creatures that lack reason in this way, for they are acted on rather than themselves acting. Reasoning creatures govern themselves by mind and will, both of which need God's mind and will to rule and complete them.

Management involves making a plan – providence – and implementing it. The planning of the world is done immediately by God, the implementation by means of others. For the best plan is the one which takes into account the particular circumstances in which actions take place, and God's plan must therefore extend down to the minutest details. But the best implementation is the one offering the greatest fulfilment to the things being governed, sharing with them not only goodness but the causing of goodness; a good teacher doesn't only teach his students but makes them too into teachers.

If things escape a particular cause it is because some other cause intervenes, in subordination to a more general cause. Now God is a principal cause: not just in one class of causes but universally over everything that exists. Nothing can escape his rule; and whatever seems to do so viewed from one particular angle is found to fall under it in some other way. What is called bad escapes some particular orderedness to good, but if it escaped God's management entirely it would not exist at all. And though chance events escape the influence of particular causes, in relation to God's universal plan nothing happens by chance. The very fact that something escapes an immediate cause is itself planned and implemented by God. So things can resist a particular cause that is implementing God's government, but they cannot resist God's government in general. Nothing can seek evil as such, and all seeking, natural or voluntary, is a thing's own initiative implementing God's ordering. Even sinners are intent on some good, and thus not totally resistant to the pattern of God's government; but because their actions conflict with the particular good their nature or status in life requires, they incur God's just punishment.

104 1 **Holding everything in existence.** Some agents cause the occurrence of an effect without directly causing its existence: thus builders bring houses into existence, but into an existence which depends on the structure of the house, maintained in it by the natural strength of the materials used. Builders use wood and stone and cement to take on and maintain the structure of a house, in the same way that chefs employ fire's natural energy to cook food. So the existence of a house depends on the nature of its materials, its occurrence on the work of the builder. In this respect things in nature resemble artefacts: agents that do not cause the form of an effect as such do not cause its existence under that form, but only its occurrence. Clearly nothing of the same species as an effect can cause the effect's form as such (for then it would be causing its own form which is identical in definition); what it causes is acquisition of the form, its occurrence in this or that matter. This is how men beget men and fire kindles fire. But when an effect is not of the same species as its agent (earthly effects of heavenly bodies, for example) the agent can cause the effect's form as such and its existence, not merely its acquisition by matter and its occurrence. Now just as effects don't occur in the absence of the agent of their occurrence, so effects don't exist in the absence of the agent of their existence. Hot water will stay hot even after the fire has gone out, but air doesn't stay illuminated for a single moment after the sun stops shining; it is in the nature of the sun to give light, but the air shares the light without sharing that nature. Now the whole of creation relates to God as air to the sun: God alone exists by nature – existing is what he is – whereas creatures only share in existence – existing is not what they are. Hence, as Augustine says, *If, at any time, the ruling power of God were to desert what he created, his creation would immediately lose its form, and all nature would collapse.* Whatever actually possesses form exists, given the influence of God; just as air that possesses transparency is lit up, given the influence of the sun. The possibility of spirits and heavenly bodies not existing resides not in their form or matter, but in God, who can withhold his influence. For God can no more confer on a creature continued existence without activity on his part, than he can confer on it uncausedness. The

activity by which God maintains things is no new activity, but the continued act of giving them existence, an act which is not a process in time. Just as light in the air is maintained by the continued shining of the sun. Now one thing can maintain another in existence in two ways: 2 indirectly, as a side effect of impeding its destruction; or directly, of its very nature, by being an agent on which it depends for its existence. In both these ways some created things maintain others in existence. For though God created everything without intermediaries, creation established an order among things by which some depend on others to maintain their existence, given a principal dependence for maintenance on God himself. No creature can cause another to acquire a new form or disposition, except by inducing change in some presupposed subject; but once the form or disposition has been introduced it can be maintained without further change of the effect. Before things existed God had the 3 power not to give them existence, and thus not to make them. So, in the same way, after they have been made, he has the power to cut off the inflow of existence, so that they cease existing; that is, he has the power to annihilate them. But there is no point in him doing it. For his 4 goodness and power are shown better by eternally maintaining both spirits and matter in existence.

Directing the world to its goal. *God is at work in us, in our willing* 105 3 *and our achieving.* Two kinds of agent act on the will, as on the mind: the object of the will's activity (the good willed) and the creator of the very ability to will. Any good can act as an object on the will, but only God can do so with complete effectiveness; the will is receptive to all good, just as the mind is receptive to all of existence, but created goods are particular and only God contains all good. For the same reason only God can give us the ability to will; for in willing we incline to good in general, and that is an inclination proper to the source of all movement towards good, whose goal is the goal of all goals. In human affairs too it is the head of a community who directs it towards the general good. In both ways then movement of our will belongs properly to God, but particularly in the second way, because there it is inclined interiorly. When one thing is moved by another in a way opposed to its own inclination it is said to be coerced, but not when it is moved by the giver of its own inclination. God moves our will but he does not coerce it. We are moved voluntarily when we move ourselves from within; but since that interior ability to move ourselves comes from outside, moving ourselves is not always opposed to being moved by another.

Lord, thou hast wrought all our works in us. God is at work in all 5 creaturely activity, but not on his own without intermediaries, as if creatures were powerless to do anything themselves: as if fire didn't make things hot, but only God acting in the fire. That would deprive creation of all causal order and derogate the creator's power; for part of any agent's power is its ability to pass on power to act to its effects. What would be the point of giving things powers they would never use? Or indeed of them existing at all, since activity is what things exist for? So we must understand God to act in things in such a way that the things act themselves. To explain this, recall that there are four kinds of cause. *Matter* does not initiate actions but is a subject receptive of their effects; but *goal*, *agent* and *form* combine to cause actions, goals moving agents, and agents applying forms and acting in accord with their own forms. A craftsman, for example, prompted to act by the goal of making a box or a bed, brings his saw into action, using its sharpness to cut with. In these three ways God acts in every activity. Firstly, as goal: every activity pursues some real or apparent good, and since things cannot be or seem good except by bearing some resemblance to God as highest good, God himself is causally present in the goal of every activity. In a similar way, in any hierarchy of agents the first agent, in virtue of which the others are active, moves the others to act; so secondly, all agents act in virtue of God, causing in them their actions. Thirdly, God not only moves things to act by applying their forms and powers to an action (as a craftsman might cut with a saw he hasn't himself made), but he is also the one creating and maintaining the forms of those created agents. Forms are within things, and all the more interior, the more basic and general the form; and God is the proper cause of existence in general, the most interior thing of all; so God's activity is deep within everything. Even nature's activities are to be attributed to God working within nature: *You clothed me with skin and flesh, you structured me of bone and sinew.* God therefore gives form to things, maintains them in existence, applies them to their actions, and is the goal of all activity.

6 **Miracles.** Every cause radiates order in its effects, with the orders of minor causes comprehended in the order of major ones. Thus a father's ordered family forms part of an ordered city, and that forms part of an ordered realm. Now God cannot act against the order he radiates himself, for that would conflict with his own foresight, will and goodness; but if he wants to he can override secondary orders, bypassing their causes so that he himself produces their normal effects or effects beyond their power. When an agent that is not the cause of some thing's natural

movement moves it, he acts against its nature (as when men lift heavy weights against gravity); but when an agent is the cause of a thing's natural movement, then he does not act against its nature even when he is not acting through its nature. Thus, even though water's natural flow is downwards, tides are not against nature, since they are caused by the heavenly bodies from which earthly bodies derive their natural tendencies in the first place. So, as Augustine says, *whatever the author of nature does is natural.* The moral order is centred on the first cause himself, the measure of all justice; so God never acts against that order. The things God does when he bypasses the causes we know about we call miracles. Creation, however, and the salvation of sinners, though only God can accomplish them, shouldn't properly be called miracles; for they aren't meant to be accomplished by other causes. They don't depart from the natural order, since they were never within nature's powers.

The role of creatures

Angels. We can have something in mind in three ways: we can know 107 1 it habitually (or have it in memory, as Augustine would say), be actually thinking about it, or be projecting the idea. The transition from habitual knowledge to actual consideration is under will's control, a habitual disposition being *something we make use of as and when we want.* And again it is the will that projects our ideas, to get them put into effect or to make them known. Actual thinking about what is stored habitually in our mind we sometimes call talking to ourselves (our thoughts being like inner words). So, since an angel simply by willing to make a thought known to another can make it known to him, we can call that talking to him; for saying something is nothing more than making known what one thinks. A man's inner thoughts are doubly barricaded off from others: by his own will to keep the thought in rather than make it public (and only God can see through that barricade), and by his body's opaqueness which requires him to use outwardly perceptible signs. As Gregory says, *we stand behind the wall of our body, sheltered from strangers' eyes in the hidden recesses of our mind; and when we wish to, we step forth through the gateway of language to show ourselves as we are within.* But angels have only the first barricade, and as soon as one of them wants to make known his thoughts they are made known.

Two things are needed for faith. Firstly, our mind must be disposed [vol 15] III 1 to obey our will's attraction to God's truth, for mind assents to truths of faith not out of rational conviction but because will tells it to. Such

a disposition of mind is a gift from God alone. But secondly, what a believer is to believe must be preached to him. And though men can do this (*faith coming by hearing* as St Paul says), it was first done by angels
113 1 revealing God's mysteries to men. *He has given his angels charge of you*
2 *to guard you in all your ways.* Two things are needed for doing good. Firstly, we must be attracted to the good by basic virtuous dispositions; and secondly, our reason must be competent to discover suitable ways of achieving the good to which virtue attracts us (a competence Aristotle calls *prudence*). In the first regard God is man's guardian, acting without intermediary, and instilling into him grace and virtue. In the second regard, God is man's universal teacher and guardian, but his teaching
4 to men is mediated by angels. Jerome says *every soul has its angel appointed to guard it.* Because our present life is a sort of road home along which many dangers, internal and external, lie in wait, an angel guard is appointed for each man as long as he is a wayfarer. But when he reaches the end of the road he will no longer have a guardian angel, but either an angel who shares with him the kingdom or a demon punishing him in hell.

114 2 **Devils.**   To ''tempt'' means properly to test or to try out, and the immediate goal of testing is knowledge. Such knowledge may be sought with the good purpose of promoting the one tested, or with the bad purpose of deceiving and ruining him; though men sometimes try each other out just for curiosity's sake (and when they try God out in this way, as though unsure of his power, they sin). The devil tests in order to harm people and throw them into sin: indeed this sort of tempting is regarded as his special job, and when a man does it he is regarded as an agent of the devil. God however tests so that others may know. The world and the flesh are sometimes called instruments of temptation, because the way a person reacts to fleshly desires and worldly fortune reveal what sort of person he is, and the devil uses these in his tempting.
3 Causes can be direct or indirect. Indirect causes dispose to an effect (dry the wood that later burns); and in this sense the devil has caused all our sins, because by instigating Adam's sin he brought about proneness to sin in the whole human race. But direct causes actually produce their effects, and in this sense the devil doesn't cause every sin, since some are committed not at the devil's instigation but from free choice and weakness of the flesh. As Origen says, even without the devil men would have the urge for food and sex, urges which give rise to many disorders unless reason controls them, especially now our natures are injured. Whether we keep such desires in order is up to our free will, and there

is no need to blame everything on the devil's prompting.

Material things. Being active is making something actual in some   115 1
way and is an inseparable consequence of being actual oneself; which is
the reason agents reproduce themselves. If an agent's form were not
limited to a particular volume of matter it would be unrestrictedly and
generally active; restricted to this or that matter it is active only in a
limited and particular way. Thus, if fire existed separately from matter,
as Platonists imagine, it would in a sense activate all fires. But particular
instances of fire in this or that particular body of matter activate only
particular instances of fire, this one activating that one through bodily
contact. This is the way bodies react with one another, acting in the
respects in which they are actual and being acted on in the respects in
which they are potential. Bodies are active not only in the modification
of existing substances but in the formation of new ones. For though an
active quality like heat is itself only a modification of a body, that body
uses the activity of such a quality as an instrument or tool in the
formation of new bodies (as, for example, when we use our natural
bodily heat to turn our food into flesh). Heat by its own power can
propagate itself as a modification; for it can act outside its own subject
even if it can't exist outside it (unless of course you imagine that one
and the same instance of a modification migrates from agent to recipient
in the way Democritus thought of activity, as migration of atoms). The   3
only sources of activity to be found in earthly bodies are the active
qualities of their elements, hot and cold and the like. And if earthly
substances were differentiated merely by such qualities (sometimes
rarefied, sometimes concentrated, as the very early physicists held), then
those qualities would suffice for all earthly activity without postulating
any higher source. But rightly seen, such qualities provide only the
material conditions for the formation of natural substances, and what is
merely material cannot act alone without a higher source of activity.
This Aristotle finds in the coming and going of the heavenly bodies that
cause the [seasonal] variations in the formation and decomposition of
bodies on earth. Whatever is responsible on earth for the propagation
of species acts as a tool of heavenly bodies: *men and the sun propagate
man.*

Fate. The direct influence of heavenly bodies is on bodies as such,   4 *influ. of
heavenly bodies*
but they also incidentally affect those powers of the soul exercised by
bodily organs (since a disorder in the organ will impede the exercise of
the power). If mind and will were powers of that sort, then the heavenly

add by instinct

bodies could influence our human actions and choices; like all other animals man would act by natural instinct (since what is done under influence of the heavenly bodies is done naturally) and like all other natural things his actions would be determined and not free. But this is clearly not so, and is at variance with all human social converse. Nevertheless the heavenly bodies exert influence on our minds and wills indirectly, by influencing what comes to them through our lower powers. Our minds, however, differently from our wills. For our mind depends absolutely on what it receives from the senses, and disorders of imagination and memory and instinctive judgment needs must disturb the mind. Our wills however have no need to follow lesser inclinations: though feelings of aggression and desire influence the will, the will is still free to accept or repel them. So the influence of the heavenly bodies on our lower powers touches our will, the immediate cause of our human

6   actions, less than it does our mind. Our wills then can obstruct the influence of the heavenly bodies on ourselves and on anything within our power. But nature is not free to accept or repel their influence, which is why some think everything in nature happens of necessity, making the assumptions that everything has a cause, and that if a cause is given its effect must follow. But Aristotle has refuted both these assumptions. Firstly, some causes bring about their effects often but not always. This, however, is because other causes impede them, so one might argue that the impeding occurs necessarily. Secondly then we have to point out that only what exists as really one thing has a cause as such. That a thing is white has a cause, and that it is musical, but that it is both white and musical has no cause as such, since that is not really one single way of existing. Now clearly concurrence of an impeding cause with a cause that usually brings about an effect can happen by accident, and as such have no cause at all. A meteor falling to earth has its heavenly cause, and so may the existence of combustible material at a certain place on the earth's surface; but that the one falls on the other and causes a fire is an accident without heavenly cause. So not all effects of heavenly bodies happen of necessity.

1161   Sometimes what happens by chance or luck as far as minor causes are concerned, is the very thing intended by some higher cause. Like the meeting of two servants, each sent by their master to the same place unbeknownst to each other; as far as they are concerned the meeting is unintended and chance, but not so to the master who planned it. Now those who do not want to refer chance events in this world to any higher cause deny all fate and providence whilst others see the higher cause in the heavenly bodies and equate fate with the disposition of the stars under which someone was born or conceived. This doesn't hold water for two reasons. Firstly, because human actions are influenced by heavenly bodies only incidentally and indirectly, as we said, whereas fate is held to be a direct cause of what it decrees. Secondly, no natural cause can intend what is only one by accident: no heavenly body can have as its natural effect that somebody digging a grave finds a treasure. What happens by accident in this world, in nature or in human affairs, must rather be referred to God's plan. For only minds can invest what happens by accident with unity, either just by formulating the proposition that the gravedigger finds a treasure, or by implementing that proposition: persuading an ignorant peasant to dig a grave where we know treasure is hidden. So there is no reason why the chance accidents of this world cannot be referred to a higher mind, especially if it is the mind of God who alone can act on our wills and thus on human actions. And then the fact that everything happening in the world is as it were decreed in God's plan could be called *fate* [the Latin word for *decreed*]. The doctors of the church, however, prefer not to use that word, because it has been twisted to mean the disposition of the stars. Augustine, for example, tells the people who attribute human affairs to fate, meaning God's power and will, to hold on to their opinion but correct their language. God's ordering of things is called his providential plan, when considered 2 as pre-existing in God, and fate when considered in the causes God uses to implement it. In respect of such causes fate is fallible, but as 3 deriving from God's plan it has a certain necessity: a necessity which is hypothetical and not absolute, the necessity that if God foresees this will be, then it will be. But anything God does without intermediary, 4 like creating things and bringing spirits to glory, is not subject to fate because not subject to secondary causes.

Men.   There exists in every man a beginning of knowledge in the light 117 1 of his agent mind. By that light he knows by nature from the start certain general premises of all knowledge; and these he applies to his particular sense-memories and experiences so that, by proceeding from the known to the unknown, he can discover for himself things of which he was ignorant. Teachers too build on what their students know, for as Aristotle says, *All teaching, all learning derives from what is already known.* There are two ways in which a master leads his students from known to unknown. He provides tools which the students can use themselves: suggested conclusions, examples, likenesses, exceptions. And he helps develop the student's mind, not by interior illumination as angels do, but by taking the students through proofs from premises to conclusions which they had not enough logical competence to deduce for themselves. In this way the provider of the proof actually causes knowledge in his listener, for as Aristotle says, *proofs are arguments that* ⟨ *bring knowledge.*

proofs - Aris.

3   Ibn Sina attributed bewitchment to a tendency for bodily matter to obey spirits even more than natural forces. He thought strongly imaginative people could cast spells over matter with their *evil eye*. But we have shown that matter is at the beck and call of God alone, not spirits. And so it would be better to say that strong imagination – and especially the strong stirrings of wickedness which mostly affect old women – produce changes in the subtle spirits of the bewitcher's own body, which then radiate out through the eyes in poisonous looks to infect the surrounding air and, in particular, the tender bodies of children.

*ouch - / evil
eye - he is .
Italian*

118 1   There is no soul or part of a soul in semen, only an active movement from the soul of the progenitor directed towards the soul of the progeny; just as there is no form of the bed to be made in the saw but only movement towards such a form. In higher animals propagated by intercourse, the male semen is the active element and the female provides the material of the foetus. From the start this has dormant in it, so to speak, a vegetable form, which awakens when it starts to assimilate nourishment. This matter is gradually transformed by the male seed into animal form. That animal form is not already in the parent's semen, since then parent and child would have the same form, and we would have not so much propagation as nourishment and growth. Rather the semen produces the animal form in some principal part of the foetus, and then the foetus completes itself by nourishment and growth. Meanwhile the semen and its active power dissolve away, since it is only a tool of the progenitor and stops acting when its effect has been produced.

reproduct.

2   Some say the embryo lives not with its own soul but with that of its mother, or is made active by the power of the semen. But you can't be alive from outside; so the soul must already exist in the embryo, first as able to nourish itself, then as able to sense, and finally as able to understand. Yet others say that man has three superimposed souls: the first vegetative one, then a sensitive soul, then one with mind; and others that the first vegetative soul itself is gradually transformed into a sensitive soul by the active power of the semen, and then into an intelligent soul by the external enlightenment of God. But souls differ one from another in kind, not merely in degree; and you cannot gradually change one into another as you alter qualities. When a new soul comes along, combining the previous soul's powers with further ones, the previous soul must be

displaced. And so at the end of the process of human generation, God
creates an intelligent soul with nutritive and sensitive powers, replacing   *see 115*
the previous souls. If you say that unless the agent that generates the
body also gives it its form, form and body will not make one thing, then
I reply that the argument only holds for unrelated agents. When the
agents are in a hierarchy the lower ones may dispose the matter and the
higher one introduce the form. The whole of bodily nature is God's
instrument, so there is no reason why a bodily power can't form man's
body and his intelligent soul be created in him by God alone.

Part II
JOURNEYING TO GOD

Chapter 7

HUMAN LIFE AS A JOURNEY TO GOD

So far we have discussed God and the world he created by his will and [vol 16] power. Since man is made in God's image, he too originates his own works, using his own free will and power to act. So now we turn to consider human life, its ultimate goal, and how men achieve or fail to achieve it.

Introductory comment. In the first part of his *Summa* Thomas has discussed God as he who is the Doing of the universe. One creature in the universe, Adam (man), was made to God's image, destined to be God's cooperator in the fulfilment of creation, set in the garden of the universe to till it and to keep it. For Thomas this is because man by nature can grasp the meaning of goodness, and so be attracted to goodness as such. Other creatures have by nature particular goals to which they are directed, particular things which fulfil them and which their natures seek; but only man has the ability to assess whether what first attracts him is an authentic goal and will bring true fulfilment, to compare apparent goodness with an understanding of the meaning of goodness and be drawn only to a goodness that realizes his understanding, to regulate his activity by *right reason.*

The notion of goodness employed here can be illustrated from earlier passages of the *Summa*:

Being good, conveying as it does the notion of value, implies being an end or goal, and this is the starting-point of causal action, the cause of causality itself; for no agent acts except for some goal, and no matter would acquire form unless an agent acted on it ... In causal action everything starts with the good end which motivates the agent to act, and so to elicit the final form of the effect. In the caused thing we find the opposite order: first, the form itself brings with it existence; next, there is the operative power which brings perfection of existence (for

[handwritten margin notes:]
among / creatures,
only man
understands
goodness + is attracted
to it

good as value
is end/goal —
this is / cause
of all

in / caused thing, /
opposite order :
1. form (existence)
2. operative power
(perfab of existence)
3. goodness of / / ing

a thing is perfect, Aristotle says, when it can reproduce itself); so that finally, the thing realizes the notion of goodness. It is usual to distinguish three different meanings of good: the *useful*, the *worthy* and the *delightful*. For whatever is of value, and can satisfy desire, is good. That which satisfies as a stage on the way to something else we call *useful*; that which satisfies of itself we call *worthy*, and the satisfaction found in it *delight*. So the primary sense of good is *worthy*, the second *delightful* and the third *useful*. [ch 1 pp 18–19]

The opposite order of things in causal action and in the caused thing, Thomas more often calls the opposite order of *intention* and *implementation*. What moves the agent to implement this form in this matter, is the goal of this form in this matter: the form is the implemented goal, the goal is the intended form; the form is the goal brought to existence, the goal is the form in its projected goodness. In artificial things and organs (where form is function) goodness is usefulness, but in natural organisms goodness is the fulfilment of their own being, of worth in its own right, a good and happy life bringing delight to those who apprehend it. But in all there is a sense in which *my end is in my beginning*, fulfilment is a kind of return to the form which started one's existence. Hidden in this phrase is Thomas's conception of what *should* be. The fulfilment of man's life as gardener of things is to bring them to fulfilment, to *do things well*, and, in so doing, do his own thing well, return to his own nature which is the ability to discern goodness and to pursue it. For being a man is a task; as G. K. Chesterton wrote somewhere we slap men on the back and exhort them to be men, we do not slap crocodiles on the back and exhort them to be crocodiles.

In the chapter that follows then Thomas starts by asking whether **human life has a goal**. We soon discover that he envisages the life of man not merely as a journey back to man's form or nature in the sense we have just been describing, but as a journey back to the agent that intended that form, to the God who created man's nature. This is the step taken by *the teaching of God* that goes beyond what we could learn from *the learning of men*. Throughout the early part of the *Summa* we have been used to expanding the learning of men (mainly Aristotle's physics, psychology and metaphysics) with what the scriptures have taught us about God and his creation, but without the realization that the expansion will eventually involve us in a different conception of what man's journey in life is about. In the very first words of the *Summa* however this was made clear: the reason we needed teaching by God over and above the learning of men was because

> God has destined us for a goal beyond the grasp of reason –
> *No eye has seen what you have prepared for those who love you* –
> and since we must set ourselves this goal and pursue it [being men], we needed teaching about it beforehand. [p 1]

What the scriptures teach is that man failed the gardening task and ruined God's creation, but that God graciously came, as a friend and cooperator, to help him salvage and re-create. In choosing that way to help man with his original goal God gave man's life a new goal, that of fellowship with God himself as friend. The journey of life is no longer simply a journey to fulfilment of man's nature, for that journey has been taken up into a journey into the presence of God himself, into the good life and happy state which God himself is (cf ch 2 pp 61–2). This is Thomas's preferred way of describing the relationship between what later commentators called man's natural and supernatural ends. He does not talk, as they do, of man first knowing God as author of nature, and then as author of supernature. Rather he consistently talks of God, known to man's learning as *the author of nature*, becoming through God's teaching the *object of his happiness*. The word translated *happiness* (or by some authors *bliss*) has more the sense of *happy state* or *blessed state*, meaning a state which has blessedly happened or turned out well, a state of goodhap rather than mishap. It corresponds to the Aristotelian word *eudaimonia*, which some modern scholars translate as *flourishing*. When Thomas uses happiness as a name for God himself he is thinking of God as fulfilled life; and this explains why he talks of happiness as being *accompanied* by delight, rather than as consisting in it.

The goal of human life is one that men must set themselves and pursue by **acting voluntarily**. There is a difficulty in translating the words *voluntary* and *will*. In Latin these are immediately related words: *will* is *voluntas* and the basic meaning of *voluntary* action is action that has *voluntas* in it. Moreover, the basic conception of will is not one of a power exercised freely and autonomously on things, but of the ability to be drawn by the objective goodness of things as such, within and beyond any particular

like a compass - it pts toward / north (= good)

attractions to particular goods that may be built in to us in our bodily nature. There is therefore a conception of freedom involved in the notion of will, a freedom from determination by any particular good, though at the same time, of course, there is a determination towards goodness as such. Thomas examines closely the ways in which other kinds of determination can threaten voluntariness in action: the mind's withdrawal by ignorance or inattention, the effects of emotions like fear and desire, external forces, the power of God. His conclusion is that in most cases what affects the will in this way has been voluntarily consented to. Nevertheless the will's freedom from determination is not thought of in quite the modern way. The will has a nature determined by the general rather than by the particular. As a result, when faced by a good that is all-inclusive and that cannot but be seen to be all-inclusive – as God face to face in heaven – the will will have to embrace it: naturally and voluntarily but not freely. But short of this situation, the determination of what particular good to pursue, and how to do that in the particular circumstances – what form should and can be introduced into the material of the immediately possible – is something the will must provide for itself. Agency in man, then, starts in the will's auto-determination which can be thought, analogically, as an interior activity of planning presupposed to the external action. Thomas must work out the psychology of this first (since this was something he deferred from chapter 5 in the first part); how do reason and will and external powers all cooperate in action? He does this in a section examining various activities of willing: willing, enjoying and intending goals, choosing, accepting and employing means, and submitting external action to the interior control of reason. With that done Thomas turns to the morality of such action, or as he prefers to say, the goodness or badness of such actions. For though there is a special kind of goodness that applies to human actions because of the presence of will in them, and for which we can use the term *moral goodness,* we cannot divorce that goodness from the ordinary goodness and badness of actions, which is related to their fulfilment or not of their own function and form, just like the goodness and badness of things. So that is Thomas's approach: from the goodness and badness of things, he draws conclusions about the goodness and badness of actions (they depend on fulfilling their defining object in the same way that the goodness of things depends on their fulfilling their form or function); and from his general conclusions

"freedom" is absence of determined by particular good and instead by goodness as such

in heaven + / presence of God, I will acts naturally & voluntarily, but not freely.

agency in man

activities of willing

their goodness / badness

about the goodness or badness of actions he draws specific conclusions about the goodness or badness of acts of willing (they
depend on their goal because that is their defining object); and
from the combination of external action and interior action of will
in properly human activity he draws conclusions about the moral
or human goodness of moral or human deeds. And he ends by
relating his findings to various words of moral approbation: how
do good and bad relate to right and wrong, faulty and sinless,
praiseworthy and blameworthy, deserving and undeserving?

Both the psychology and morality of voluntary action has been
discussed in the context of the interior will on the one hand and
external action in the world on the other. But the two are mediated
by animal feeling or emotions, and in the final part of the chapter
Thomas turns to the psychology and morality of feeling. It is
feeling or emotion that immediately moves our bodily powers to
external action, since emotion is the basic animal response to the
stimulus of the external world: affective responses by which
animals are impressed and drawn to and enjoy the good and
flee evil, and aggressive responses to the world's resistance and
difficulty, be it obstacles to enjoying good or fleeing evil. But in
man will can move the emotions: the determination of what good
to pursue influences our affective feelings, and the determination
of what must be regarded as possible influences our aggression.
The emotions become tools of moral action to be incorporated into
the earlier discussion. The effect of this will be seen in the next
chapter when we discuss moral virtue: the dispositions of reason,
will and emotions necessary for man if he is to live a good life.

Human life has a goal

We start by examining this notion of an *ultimate goal*, and then discuss
the happy state which is said to constitute it.

Acting for goals.   Much of what men do they do without deliberation,
even without thinking, absent-mindedly shifting their feet or stroking
their chins. But the only properly human actions are those that mark a
man out as a man, differing from creatures that lack reason in being
master of what he does. A man's human actions are those lying under
his control and proceeding from deliberate will. But the sort of action
proceeding from a particular power [from sight, say, or hearing] is

determined by how objects present themselves to that power [as coloured, say, or making a sound]. So, since objects present themselves to the will as good to pursue i.e. as goals, properly human action is action that pursues goals. The implementation of the goal terminates the action, but the agent's (intention) of the goal is the action's source and cause. Even the ultimate goal of human life, if itself a human action, is action for a goal; for to be properly human it must be willed, and willed action is either some action done at the will's command, like walking or speaking, or it is the very act of willing itself. Now since goals are the objects of will as colours are the objects of sight, then just as seeing is not the primary thing we see but has its own seen object, so willing is not the primary goal we pursue. Man's ultimate goal, then, if it is a human action, is action done at the will's command. And that being so, at least the willing of it is done for a goal. So whatever a man does he does for a goal, even the doing of his ultimate goal.

2   [We are not saying that only reasoning creatures pursue goals. All nature does so.] No agent acts unless aimed at a goal. An agent not aimed at its effect will not do one thing rather than another. And anything aimed at is to that extent a goal. However, in reasoning creatures the aiming is by reasoned inclination of the will, whilst in non-reasoning creatures it is a built-in tendency, an inclination of nature. Reasoning creatures are masters of what they do and move themselves to goals. In contrast, creatures that lack reason tend to goals by nature as if moved by another, not understanding what a goal is, and unable to adapt things to goals, but only able to be so adapted by something else. The whole of non-reasoning nature acts like a tool of God. So the peculiarity of reasoning creatures is not that they pursue goals, but that they do so as though directing themselves there; whereas non-reasoning creatures are directed by another to goals of which they themselves, unless they are animals, are quite unaware. The will responds to good in general, to whatever can be a goal of action. Creatures that lack understanding or awareness of the general cannot will. They act out of a natural or sense-stimulated want of some particular kind of good. Obviously, particular causes depend on general ones, and creatures lacking reason must be aimed at their particular goals by a rational will which goes out to good in general: God's will.

3   The goal of an action decides what kind of an action it is, worthy of praise or of blame. Any process can be regarded as a productive activity, categorized by the kind of agent originating it, or as a transformation undergone, categorized by the kind of thing it ends up producing. Thus warming is defined as the activity of one thing's warmth producing

warmth in another. Now human actions can be defined in both these *in human acts,* ways, since in them man himself acts upon himself; and looked at either *man acts on* way the goal of the action decides what kind of action it is. Human *himself* actions originate from the will, and the will starts from a goal, so human action is originated by its goal. And the end-result of a human action is what the will intended to be its goal. So the goal of a human action decides the kind of human action it is; and this means the kind of moral action it is, for *mores are human ways of acting*, as Ambrose says, and *human act is* moral action is only another name for human action. The fact that a *moral act* single human action can have more than one goal does not affect the matter. A single action done on a single occasion is devoted to one immediate goal which categorizes it, though the immediate goal may be a subgoal of further goals. And though it is true that one and the same physical kind of act, like killing, can on different occasions be willed for different reasons (now as a just execution, now with murderous intent), these killings are then different sorts of action morally speaking, one virtuous and the other vicious. What categorizes processes is the result they lead to of their nature, not what happens on this or that occasion; so the moral goal is incidental to the physical nature of the act, and its physical result incidental to its moral category.

The notion of an ultimate goal.   Among all the goals of human *4 ultimate* actions one is ultimate. You can't have endless ends. If the ordering of *goal* things one to another forms part of their definition and there is no first in order, there will be no others. [A proof without premises proves nothing.] Now goals are ordered one to another, both in the intending of them and in their execution, so in both cases there must be a first in order. The first goal intended makes all the subgoals attractive, and without it nothing attracts. The first means executed makes possible the execution of the others, and without it nothing gets done. The first thing intended is the ultimate goal, the first thing executed the immediate means; and we can't go on endlessly in either direction. Without an ultimate goal nothing would attract us, we could neither finish anything nor get any satisfaction from our actions. Without an immediate means, we could not start anything but would endlessly try to decide how. Of course, if things are ordered to one another extrinsically the ordering can be endless; [numbers can be thought up endlessly precisely because adding one to a number is extrinsic to it]. And in this way the will can endlessly reecho its own action: I can will something and will my willing of it indefinitely. But this multiplication of acts of will is quite extrinsic to the way my goals are ordered.

5 ⫶ A man cannot identify his ultimate goal with more than one thing at a time; for anything so identified will dominate his whole desire, and rule his whole life, and *no man can serve two masters.* Everything is drawn to what best fulfils it, and as ultimate goal we pursue what so fulfils our desire as to leave nothing else to be desired. Moreover, just as the first premises of our knowledge are innately known, so must the primary thing willed be innately desired. Now innate tendencies are determinate, fixed in one direction. So at any one time what is pursued as ultimate goal must be one. Finally, since human actions are categorized by their goals, and all human actions are generically one, they must have one ultimate goal. And just as human nature has one ultimate goal, so each

6 individual sets his will on a single ultimate goal. Everything else we will is willed for this ultimate goal; even play, which we distinguish from work because it serves no extrinsic goal, but which nevertheless delights, relaxes and fulfils the player. Of course, we need not always be thinking of our ultimate goal; but its influence pervades everything we will; just as when we walk along a road we don't think at every step of that step's

7 ultimate destination. So all men agree in pursuing an ultimate goal and seeking their own fulfilment, but they disagree as to where this fulfilment can be found; just as all men like their food tasty, yet disagree as to which food is tastiest. We judge tastiest what most appeals to a cultivated taste, and we should judge our best fulfilment to lie in that which men of ordered affections pursue as ultimate goal. Sinners turn away from the true ultimate goal, but not from an ultimate goal as such, since this is what they seek falsely in other things. And men embrace different ways of life according to the different things in which they seek their ultimate goal.

8   All other creatures share man's ultimate goal, for God is the ultimate goal of all. But men and other creatures differ in the way they achieve him. Men attain their goal by coming to know God and love him; other creatures are incapable of this, but attain their goal by existing and being alive and aware, and so imitating God. We call man's way of attaining his goal being happy.

2 1 **God is our ultimate goal.** Natural wealth, like food and drink, clothing and transport, housing and the like, doesn't suffice to make us happy. Such things are only means of supporting human life: man is wealth's goal rather than wealth man's. And conventional valuables, like money, are even less our ultimate goal, needed only to buy the natural

2 valuables life needs. Honours witness to attainments men already possess. As such they may accompany happiness, but are not the first

cause of it. They are given instead of virtue's reward by people who have nothing better to give: virtue's true reward is happiness itself. Fame is recognition and praise. Man's well-being does not depend on 3 human fame; rather fame recognizes some degree of well-being already there, and this in turn depends on God's recognition and praise. Power 4 can be used well or ill; so happiness is associated with the virtuous use of power rather than with power itself. In general our happiness does not reside in such external goods; for they are found both in good men and in bad; they do not include many things needed for man's well-being, like wisdom and health; they do not preclude misfortune; and whereas happiness must respond to the intrinsic needs of our nature, such goods are largely a matter of external good luck.

External goods are at the service of man's bodily needs; but not even 5 bodily health and well-being suffice for man's happiness. Man is not the supreme good, and his fulfilment lies outside himself; so the ultimate goal of his reason and will cannot be his own continued existence. And even if it were, his body is at the service of his soul providing the material it organizes, and the organs it acts by. Bodily pleasures are 6 not the only, or even the strongest joys. And joy as such is only an accompaniment, though a necessary one, of a happy state. [True, joy is desired for its own sake and not because of something else, if *because* refers to purpose; for joy is but fulfilment of desire for something, and is desired with the same desire as the desired object. But if *because* refers to the shape, or better, the shaper of our desire, then desire is because of something else, namely the object which arouses desire and gives shape to it.] What is enjoyed is the presence of something good and agreeable: actual, expected or at least remembered; and it is in this agreeable good itself, according to its degree of perfection, that partial or total happiness is found. But bodily pleasure cannot claim even this connection with true happiness; for it is the necessary accompaniment of something present and agreeable to the bodily senses, and nothing bodily is sufficient for man's happiness.

What we seek as our goal then is an object to make us happy; happiness 7 characterizes achievement of the goal, and as such is a state of soul, though the object which causes this happy state is something outside the soul. In one sense, man in loving happiness is not loving anything more than himself. Happiness is what we love most if love means desire; but friends are loved rather as persons for whom things are desired, and it is in this way that man loves himself. So love has two different meanings here. Later, when we discuss charity, we shall ask whether man loves someone more than himself with the love of friendship. For

the present we say that what makes us happy is something outside the
8 soul; indeed something outside creation. For our human inclination, our
will, responds to whatever is good as such, just as our understanding
responds to whatever is true as such. So no particular good can satisfy
our will, but only God who realizes every goodness that creatures realize
in their own particular ways. Even the common good of the created
universe of which man is a part, is not man's ultimate goal, for it too
has as its ultimate goal God. Of course, there cannot exist in man, as
an intrinsic and inherent part of his being, any goodness that is not
created and finite; and even the share of goodness possessed by the
entire universe is finite and bounded; but the good a man can entertain
as object [of his knowledge and love] is infinite and uncreated.

3 1 **Happiness is seeing God.**   Happiness is another name for God. God
is happy by nature; he does not attain happiness or receive it from
another. But men become happy by receiving a share in God's happiness,
2 something God creates in them. And this created happiness is a life of
human activity in which their human powers are ultimately fulfilled: for
the goal of anything is fulfilment in activity. True, to exist is already to
live, but to exist is not yet to be happy, except in God's case. When
we speak of leading a life of action or contemplation or pleasure, we
mean by life an exercise of our existent powers in some form of fulfilling
activity; and this is also the way in which our ultimate goal is said to be
eternal life. Now *this is eternal life: to know you, the only true god.* There
are two sorts of activity: one is exercised outside the doer, like cutting
down and burning, and realizes and fulfils the thing it is done to rather
than its doer; so happiness cannot be that sort of activity. The other
sort of activity, like sensing and understanding and willing, is exercised
within the doer and fulfils and realizes him; and such activity can be
happiness. God's happiness is God: for him his very existence is an
activity by which he is fulfilled from within and not from without; but
man's ultimate fulfilment comes by cleaving to God. In our present life
we cannot do this by a single continuous activity but only by many
interrupted acts; God however has promised us perfect happiness in
heaven, and in that happy state man's spirit will be joined to God in
one unbroken everlasting activity. The more we approach such unbroken
activity in this life the more we can call ourselves happy, and so a life
of action, occupied with many things, offers less happiness than a life
of contemplation, engaged in the one activity of gazing at truth. And if
at times a man is not actually so engaged, nevertheless because he is
ever open and ready and turns his very breaks in contemplation, due to

sleep or natural business, to its service, his contemplation seems as if it
were unbroken.

Happiness, because it cleaves to the uncreated good who cannot be 3
seen or touched, is not activity of our senses. But sense-activity, since
it is a pre-condition of understanding, is also a pre-condition of whatever
partial happiness we can achieve in our present life. In the perfect
happiness we hope for in heaven after the resurrection, happiness will
redound from our soul into our body and fulfil our bodily senses; so
that sense-activity will follow from happiness, even though the activity
by which we cleave to God will not require it as a pre-condition. The 4
activity of happiness is an exercise of understanding, not of willing. For
willing a goal is not the same as achieving it: the will can desire absent
goals just as much as it can enjoy achieved ones. Something else than
an act of will is needed to make the goal present. This is obvious in the
case of tangible goals – if money could be got by willing, the needy man
would straightway have as much as he wanted – and it is also true of
spiritual goals. From the start the will wants to achieve it; but to be
achieved it must become present to us in an act of understanding,
after which the will can rest and rejoice in the goal already achieved.
Happiness, then – *joy in the truth*, as Augustine calls it – is essentially
an activity of our understanding, with consequent joy of will. Put another
way, willing is not the primary thing we will, just as seeing is not the
primary thing we see but has its own seen object; and so the very fact
that happiness is the will's primary object guarantees that it is not the
will's own activity. Goals are first apprehended as such by the mind,
not the will; but tending to the goal starts in the will; and that is why
the final consequence of achieving the goal, namely our pleasure and
enjoyment, is attributed to the will. So although love outranks knowledge
en route to the goal, love presupposes knowledge on arrival.

Man's highest activity engages his highest power with its highest 5
object. Man's intelligence is his highest power, and its highest object the
good that is God, an object of contemplative not practical intelligence. So
happiness is above all the activity of contemplating the things of God.
The practical mind pursues knowledge not for its own but for action's
sake, and actions in turn pursue goals. So practical knowledge and the
life of action with which it is concerned cannot be our ultimate goal.
Nevertheless, though the complete happiness to which we look forward
in the life to come is entirely a life of contemplation, and the incomplete
happiness we can have here is first and foremost contemplation, this
latter happiness consists secondarily in knowing how to order our actions
and our passions in practice. Contemplation of God is not achieved by 6

(margin note: contemplat is not achieved by way of speculative sciences)

way of the speculative sciences. The first premises of speculative science are based on sense-experience, and so all speculative science is restricted to truth derivable from experience of the sensible world. But the ultimate happiness which is to fulfil man cannot be knowledge of the sensible world. Nothing can be fulfilled by what is inferior to it unless that too shares in something higher, and then what is derivative must be traced back to what is original. Man must find his final fulfilment in knowledge of something higher than his own mind. Speculative science 7 is but an anticipation of true and complete happiness. The complete happiness of man then lies in what will essentially fulfil his mind; and the complete fulfilment of any power comes from achieving something which fully realizes the nature of its object. Now the proper object of mind is truth, and God alone is essentially true (things are true in the same way in which they exist); so it is contemplation of God, [the source 8 of all being and light], that makes us completely happy. To know something with the mind is to understand what it is; so the mind is fulfilled to the degree to which it knows what things are. If from the understanding of some effect we deduce only that it has a cause without understanding exactly what that cause is, then we are left with a natural desire to know more. We call it wonder and it drives us to investigate until we are satisfied with our understanding of what that cause is. For complete happiness then the mind wants to know the nature of the first cause of everything. Happiness is the cleaving to God as the mind's all-fulfilling object.

(margin note: delight DEF)

4 1 **What happiness brings with it.**   Delight is satisfied desire which has achieved the good thing it wanted. So since happiness is achievement 2 of our highest good it must bring with it delight. The delight however

(margin note: it is secondary to achieving happiness)

is secondary to the achievement. What satisfies the will is the goodness of what was wanted: the goodness of an activity if activity was what was wanted. But if the will seeks satisfaction in an activity it is because that activity itself is desirable; the primary thing desired is the satisfying activity, not the satisfaction itself. The senses cannot perceive goodness as such but only particular pleasurable good things, so animals, responding to sense stimuli, do pursue their activities for the sake of pleasure. But the mind perceives the goodness [of an activity] as such, from the achievement of which pleasure follows. So the mind aims at the good

(margin note: mind aims at goodness as such, not at pleasure)

3 rather than at the pleasure. The joy of seeing God does not count for more than the seeing itself, even if, as St Paul says, charity counts for more than faith. Charity does not seek what it loves for the delight that follows achievement: charity's goal is not delight, but rather the vision

that first makes its goal present. Man is disposed to any understandable 3
goal partly by his mind's initial knowledge of the goal, and partly –
through his will – by the love which first inclines him to it, and by hope
based on how he is placed in relation to what he loves. If what we love
is already present, or if it is not present but utterly beyond our reach
we do not seek it; only if it is possible to reach but out of immediate
reach does the lover hope for it and start to seek it. To these three
dispositions in man then correspond three descriptions of happiness:
vision describes it as perfect knowledge of the goal, *comprehension* or
grasp as the making present of the goal that was hoped for, and *delight*
as satisfaction of the love. If grasp implies containment, then no finite
mind can grasp the infinite God; but if it says no more than the catching
hold of an object within reach, it names precisely the activity of vision,
adding only the idea that vision makes the goal present.

Right willing must precede and accompany happiness. For we will 4
rightly when we are properly adapted to our ultimate goal; and just as
material that is to be shaped must be properly prepared, so nothing can
achieve a goal to which it has not been properly adapted. Nobody then
can achieve happiness unless he wills rightly. [We must will rightly to
achieve happiness just as an arrow must fly straight if it is to hit its
target.] Willing rightly is also an accompaniment of the final happiness
of seeing God, who is goodness itself; for the will of a soul seeing God
must needs love whatever he loves in harmony with the God he sees,
just as the will of someone who does not see God must needs love
whatever he loves in harmony with what he understands goodness to
be. And willing in harmony with God's goodness is willing rightly.

We need our bodies for the partial happiness we achieve in this life, 5
and which consists in the theoretical and practical exercise of our minds,
for such exercise is impossible without bodily imagination. But the
perfect happiness of seeing God face to face, because it transcends all
images, does not depend on our bodies and can be enjoyed by the
disembodied soul. However, being strictly essential to something is only
one way of contributing to its perfection; another is by enhancing the
way something exists, as good looks enhance a body, and quick wits a
mind. So even though our body does not contribute to our perfect
happiness in the first way, it does in the second. For the more perfect
the natural condition of the soul, the more perfectly it can enjoy its
characteristic activity in which its happiness lies. Happiness perfects the
mind – the function of our soul in which it transcends our body's
instrumentality – but it does not perfect the soul as source of the
organization of the body. A disembodied soul is complete enough in

nature to be happy, even though it has lost its natural function of organizing the body. After the dissolution of the body, the existence of the body-soul unity that was the man continues as the existence of his soul; for in any composite of matter and form, the matter, the form and the composite share one and the same existence. And in the case of the soul that existence is a subsistent existence. So, parted from its body, the soul is fully existent, and therefore fully active, though it does not possess the full specific nature of a man. Augustine says that disembodied souls cannot see the eternal God perfectly because they have *a natural yearning for their bodies which distracts them from full immersion in the vision of God*; and he is referring to the desire to enjoy God in such a way that the joy overflows as fully as possible into our bodies. For although the disembodied soul's desire for an object is wholly satisfied in God (for it now possesses what fulfils it), nevertheless it does not possess its object in every way that it could wish; and so when it regains

6 its body its happiness will grow in breadth, though not in depth. The happiness of this life clearly requires a well body, for it consists in the full exercise of our powers, and ill-health will certainly curtail that. But certain people say that no particular disposition of body is required for perfect happiness; indeed that the soul needs to be entirely separated from its body. But this can't be true: it is natural for the soul to be united to its body, so how can fulfilment of soul exclude this natural fulfilment? So we maintain that for our happiness to be complete in every way it presupposes and results in complete well-being of our bodies.

7   The partial happiness of this life does not consist in having external goods, but requires them as tools to serve that exercise of man's powers and skills and virtues in which this life's happiness does consist. But they are not needed for that perfect happiness in which the soul is either

8 without its body or united to one no longer animal but spiritual. The happy man in this life needs friends, not for their external usefulness, since his happiness is from within, nor for pleasure, since his perfect pleasure comes from the activity of virtue, but as contributing to that activity itself. He does good to them, he delights in seeing them do good, and in turn they help him and do good to him. For we need the help of friends in leading the lives of action and of contemplation. And though the companionship of friends is not strictly necessary even in this way to the perfect happiness of our heavenly home, where a man is completely and wholly fulfilled in God, yet the companionship of friends enhances that happiness. Were there but one single soul enjoying God, without any fellowman to love, that soul would be happy. But since there are

fellowmen, our full love of God spills over on to them, so that friendship always accompanies our perfect happiness.

[handwritten margin note: friends arent nesary to prfact hapins - but la accompany it -]

Happiness is possible.   We can be partially happy in this life but not completely and truly. For there are many ills that cannot be avoided in this life: ignorance of mind, unbalanced attachments, all sorts of bodily pains. And we also naturally desire the good things we have to last whereas in this life they pass away. Indeed life itself passes away, though by nature we desire it and wish it to last and shrink from death. Complete and satisfying happiness would satisfy all desires and banish all evils and be incapable of passing away. Man's natural resources then are enough to gain for him virtue and the partial happiness that follows virtue in this life; but not man's nor any creature's natural resources are enough to gain for him ultimate happiness. Yet just as nature provides for man's needs, though denying him the weapons and covering natural to other animals, by giving him reason and his hands to make such things for himself, so too nature provides for man's needs, though denying him the resources to win happiness for himself – an impossibility – by giving him free will to turn to God who can make him happy. As Aristotle puts it, *what our friends enable us to do we have in some sort power to do.* And a nature that can thus achieve utmost perfection, even though needing external help to do it, is of a nobler constitution than a nature that can only achieve some lesser good, even though without external help. The reasoning creature that with God's help achieves happiness is nobler than the creature lacking reason that is not capable of happiness but by its natural powers achieves some lesser perfection. God alone is happy of his very nature; he alone does not come to happiness by way of some prior activity. It is fitting then that men reach happiness by way of many acts which we call merits. As Aristotle says, virtuous acts earn happiness as reward. It is not that God's power needs to be supplemented by this human activity, but that this is the fitting way of doing things. Everyone must want to be happy in general, since that is no more than to want one's wants satisfied, and this everyone must want. But not everyone knows in what special state of activity that happiness is to be found, and so in that respect not everyone wants it. Happiness then, regarded in general as our final and complete fulfilment, draws our wills naturally and necessarily; but in its specific aspect: as this or that special activity of this or that power directed at this or that object, it does not draw our wills with necessity.

Acting voluntarily

qab
f—

morals

properly human
act, viz, voluntary
61

slf-movement

[vol 17] To become happy we must act, so now we ask which of our actions advance happiness and which block the road. This is the subject of morals which, like every other practical science, starts with preliminary generalities [cf chapters 7-9], and then applies itself to the world of the particular in which all actions take place [cf chapters 10-12]. We begin then with a general discussion of action at its most peculiarly human: namely, voluntary action.

To some movements and activities, like bricks falling, there is a proneness within what moves or acts; other movements, like bricks rising, are externally forced. And some things moved from within move themselves and some not. For movements and activities have goals; and only when both the movement and its goal-directedness derive from within – because of some internal awareness of the goal – do we say that the thing is moving itself; if the movement comes from within but something else causes the goal-directedness we would say the thing is moved by the something else aware of the goal. Self-movement we call (voluntary) or wanted; and since it is chiefly men who know what they want and move themselves towards it, voluntariness chiefly characterizes human activity. But the self that does the moving is not necessarily the primary source of the movement. If the wanting as such depends primarily on an inner ability to know and want, that ability itself may yet be affected and motivated externally in other ways: by a new object presented to the senses directly stimulating our desires, for example, or by a physical change in our body occasioning an emotional change in our psyche. In addition, God can move us to action; and not only by the two means we have just mentioned, but also by directly influencing our will; for he is the first author of will as he is of nature, and wields these inner sources of action as his tools, moving will voluntarily and nature naturally.

men
vs
animals

2   Reasoning creatures are perfectly aware of goals: aware of what is in fact their goal, but also aware of the notion of goal as such and the way their activity is adapted to it; whereas other animals are aware only of what their goal is by sense-perception and instinctive judgment. So men's actions are in the fullest sense voluntary: they deliberate about the goal of which they are aware, and about what will lead to it, and are able to pursue it or not; whereas animals' activity is wanted or voluntary in a lesser sense: once they are aware of the goal, they pursue it without

3   premeditation. A steersman may be responsible for a wreck either by directly steering the ship onto the rocks or by not steering when he

could and should do. And similarly if we do not will and act when we can and should do we can be held responsible for not willing and acting. So inaction too can be voluntary: external inaction when one wills not to act, or internal when one doesn't even will. *Not willing to* sometimes means *willing not to* and in that sense what you don't will to do is involuntary; but if taken simply as denying any act of will, the absence of willing may itself be voluntary, i.e. wanted. And just as not willing or not acting at the right time can be voluntary, so also not becoming aware of what is to be done.

By willed acts we can mean either acts like walking or talking, executed by some other power under the will's control or command; or the acts of will that issue from the will itself. Force can obstruct willed actions of the first type [and so cause involuntary action], but it cannot affect the will's own acts since force is external and willing internal. A brick can be forced upward, but not naturally; and a man can be forced to act, but not voluntarily. God has power to move the human will, but not by force; for then there would be no willing involved and the movement would not be in the will but against it. Not all movement due to external agents is forced but only movement contrary to the inner disposition of what they act on; otherwise all basic physical and chemical behaviour would be unnatural and forced, whereas it accords with intrinsic natural properties. And in the same way, when the will is moved by an object of its own desiring it is not forced but acts voluntarily. Behaviour can be natural because something acts that way by nature, or because nature predisposes it to be acted on that way by some external agent. And in the same way, behaviour can be actively voluntary, when we want to do something, and passively voluntary, when we want something done to us. So activity from outside which is acceptable is, strictly speaking, neither forced nor involuntary; even though the one acted on doesn't contribute action of his own he nevertheless contributes the will to be acted on. Some movements of animals are forced in relation to the natural bent of their bodies or their limbs, but natural to them as animals, since animals naturally follow wants.

What is done out of fear, though unwanted in itself, is in the event wanted in order to avoid worse evils. So, since actions are always individual here-and-now actions, what is done out of fear is simply speaking voluntary; and only in a certain respect – namely, when looked at in abstraction from the individual event – unwanted or involuntary. For not only goals willed for their own sake are wanted and voluntary, but also whatever we will for the sake of those goals. Desire however makes acts voluntary rather than involuntary. When we act from fear

4 will directs
    acts prior to act –
    or acts issue
    from will –
    / former can be
    externally forced,
    not / latter
    hnc, God can
    move / will but
    only by grace?
    see 186

5

6 acts from
    fear – do still
    voluntary

7 vs
    acts from
    desire

we have a certain unwillingness to do what we do, but not when we act
from desire. The lustful man goes against previous resolves but not
against what he wants here and now, whereas a frightened man goes
against what even here and now he wants, abstractly considered. When
people are literally mad with desire their actions are mindless and thus
neither wanted nor unwanted; but when desire takes away not their
mind but only their here-and-now consideration of what to do, then this
itself is voluntary, since their will has power to resist such passion.

8 Ignorance can accompany, follow or precede acts of will. It is said to
accompany those acts which would be done even in its absence, so it
does not cause such acts to be unwanted and involuntary, but merely
prevents them being actually wanted. Ignorance follows will when we
directly will it, either because passion or habitual disposition stops us
attending to what we could and should attend to, or because negligence
prevents us acquiring knowledge we should have. Such ignorance cannot
cause involuntariness simply speaking, but only in the possible respect
that it precedes some other willed act which would not knowingly have
been done. Ignorance precedes will when it is not voluntary in the above
sense yet causes one to will something one would otherwise not have
willed, as for example, ignorance of some circumstance of the act
which one had no obligation to be aware of. Such ignorance makes the
succeeding act involuntary simply speaking.

7 1 Circumstances are external conditions of an act which affect it in
2 some way as human action. Moral theologians must take them into
account, since they affect the adaptedness of the action to its goal, its
goodness or badness, and – because ignorance of a circumstance can
make an act involuntary – its merit or demerit. Actions possess goodness
as serving a goal, and so their goodness has a relational character which
can be changed by something outside them, just as characterizations like
small or great can. Totally coincidental connections are irrelevant to a
scientific treatment because of their uncertainty and indeterminacy.
Circumstances, however, comprise only those external conditions of
3 actions that are pertinent and relevant to a moral treatment. Cicero's
jingle enumerates seven categories of circumstance: *who, what and where,
what were the means, why, how and at what time*; and Aristotle further
adds *what about*. Some affect the act itself (*where, when* and *how*), some
its effect (*what*), and some its causes: its goal (*why*), object (*what about*),
agent (*who*) or tools (*what means*). Some causal conditions define the
nature of an action, but only external yet relevant conditions count as
circumstances. For example, that a stolen object is another's defines the
act as stealing, but that it is big or small is counted a circumstance. And

similarly the circumstance *why* refers to possible ulterior motives.

Willing, enjoying and intending goals.   We now consider various different ways of characterizing voluntary actions: firstly, as actions of the will itself (willing, enjoying and intending goals; choosing, accepting and employing means), and secondly, as actions of other powers controlled by will.

Our will is both attracted to what seems good and repelled by what 8 1 seems bad; but we specially use *willing* to name the act of desiring good (the act of shrinking from evil we could perhaps call *won'ting*). Moreover, 2 our will is attracted both to goals and to what serves those goals; but the most basic act of willing is the desiring of what is in itself desirable, namely, goals; we desire what serves a goal not for its own sake but for the sake of the goal, and so what we will in it is in fact the goal. In the strict sense of the word then we will goals, (just as what we understand are premises, and conclusions only when seen as enshrining those premises). Clearly we desire the goal in the means with one and the 3 same act of willing as we desire the means; though there may have preceded pure desire of the goal. Interrupting execution of an action can leave us with the means accomplished but no goal; interrupting willing can leave us with a willed goal but no means.

Our psychological powers can act or not act, and, if they act, do one 9 1 thing or another. So we can ask the cause of the exercise or performance of an act (what moved its subject into action?), and the cause that determined the type of act performed (what gave the act its object?). Moving a subject into action requires an agent attracted by a goal, and since what attracts is goodness as such (by definition the province of the will) it is our will that brings our other powers into action: we use our powers as and when we will. But the type of action is determined by conformation to some object, and since conformation to being and truth as such is by definition the province of the mind, it is the mind that determines the will by presenting to it its object. Theoretical grasp of truth without grasp of its practical goodness or desirability will not move us, any more than merely imagining objects without judging them helpful or harmful stimulates animal emotions. Will moves mind to perform, since the truth mind seeks is one good among others and an instance of what will seeks: goodness as such; but mind determines what it is we will, since we know the good we will as one truth among others, an instance of what mind grasps: truth as such. Because what seems 2 good to us must seem congenial, and that depends on *our* constitution as well as that of the object presented, it is obvious that emotions can

so affect our composure that things appear congenial which would not otherwise do so. In this way emotions can affect the will through its
3 object. Besides moving other powers, the will can also move itself to perform; for by willing a goal it moves itself to will what serves that goal. So the will is formed by the mind presenting its object, but moved
4 to perform by itself pursuing its goal. Things in the external world can obviously be objects for the will and influence it that way; but can anything external move the will to perform? Well, when the will moves itself to perform it starts by willing a goal, and then by a process of deliberation, brings itself to will what serves the goal. But what brought it to will the goal in the first place? Itself perhaps by deliberation based on some earlier willing, and so on. But, as Aristotle points out, the process must start somewhere with an original willing caused from outside, just as natural movement depends eventually on someone setting
6 nature in motion. Things in nature can be set in motion by other things than God, the author of nature, but only God can cause them to move naturally; and in the same way men can be set in motion by other things than God, the author of their wills, but only God can set them in voluntary movement. God moves our wills towards goodness as such, the all-inclusive object of the will; and without this all-inclusive movement by the mover of all things men couldn't will anything. But man uses his own mind to determine whether to will this or that genuine or seeming good; though as we shall see later God sometimes moves some people by his grace to will some particular good.
10 i What belongs intrinsically to a thing as such we call *natural*. If anything is to have properties at all it must first have nature in this sense: thus, understanding presupposes premises which are naturally understood, and willing something willed by nature. For the will (like any power) tends naturally to the object defining it, namely goodness as such, and to that ultimate goal desired in all desiring (in the way first premises are understood in all understanding), and in general to all particular goods natural to the person willing: to knowledge of the truth, to existence, to life. The will, as mistress of its own actions, works in a way which transcends the way nature works, following one determined pattern. Nevertheless, what acts by will first exists by nature, and the will's way of seeking must in some way reflect and incorporate nature's. Every nature is determinate, fixed on one thing, but in the case of immaterial powers the oneness is a oneness of generality: the will, for example, responds to all good as such, and the mind to whatever is true
2 or exists. No object can oblige us to exercise our wills, for, whatever it is, we can omit to think about it, and so omit to will it. But if it is

presented to the will and is good in every way from every point of view, *something good in*
then, if the will wills at all, it is obliged to accept that thing and refuse *every way we*
its opposite. We are obliged to will happiness in this way [and whatever *can't help willing,*
is essential for happiness, like existence and life]. But all other particular *eg, happiness —*
goods, since they cannot contain every good there is, can be regarded
as not good in some respect, and for that reason can be either refused *but any particular*
or accepted. Emotions move the will by predisposing us to judge objects 3 *good can be*
congenial or not. If passion is so great that a man loses all reason, then *refused*
he becomes like the other animals, deprived of all will; but if something
of reason and will remains then passion can always be resisted. The will
cannot always stop desire arising, but it can always refuse to consent to
it. God irresistibly moves causes to effects in ways suited to the nature 4
of the cause; so he moves wills freely. For the will to move necessarily *God moves*
would rather be to resist God's will. The supposition that God is moving *wills freely*
the will to such-and-such an object necessarily entails that the will is
tending to that object; but the tendency is not in itself necessary.

Seeing God is as such an activity of mind, but as the goal of our 11 1
desires it is an object towards which the will moves the mind, and which
the will enjoys when the mind has achieved it. So *enjoying* is an act, 2 *enjoying*
not of the achieving power, but of the power of desire directing the
achievement. In things that lack awareness we find power to achieve
goals but no power to direct the achievement, since this belongs to a
higher power which directs all nature in the way desire directs the
actions of things with awareness. Clearly then only things with awareness
enjoy the goals they achieve. And of these only creatures with reason
are fully aware of their goals as such, knowing their function as goals;
other animals are aware only of the particular things which are their
goals, to which their appetites direct them unfreely by natural instinct.
So reasoning creatures enjoy in a full sense, animals in a lesser way, and
other creatures not at all. The ultimate goal of all life's activity is 3
enjoyable in the fullest sense; whatever exerts a temporary attraction is
enjoyable in a restricted sense; and what is not attractive in itself but
only serves some other goal (like a nauseous medicine) is not in any
sense enjoyable. There is already joy in intending a goal, but not the 4
full joy of really achieving it. Joy in other things differs in kind from *on being on/way to*
joy in God. But joy in moving to God is of the same kind as joy in *God is already joy —*
achieving him, different only in degree.

To intend something is to tend towards it: either actively (the primary 12 1 *intending*
sense), or passively under the influence of some active tendency. Since
all our powers tend to their goal under the influence of the will, *intending*
is primarily an act of will. Reason makes a plan, and will tends to a goal

according to the plan. So intending is willing that presupposes a reasoned plan for reaching the goal. Simple attraction to a goal, without further qualification, we call willing; resting in a goal reached we call enjoyment; but in order to intend a goal we must will it as the terminus of some

2 action directed at reaching it. Going from A to B by way of C, B is our final destination, C an intermediate one. So we can intend goals that are not yet our ultimate goal. To be enjoyed a goal must be an ultimate goal that we can rest in, but any goal that we can move towards can be

3 intended. Clearly we can intend many subordinated goals – final and intermediate – at one and the same time; and since we can prefer one course of action to another because it serves more than one purpose, we can also intend many unsubordinated goals at once. Things which are in reality many can be unified by reason into one terminus of intention.

4 When we will something as means to a goal, one and the same act of will tends towards goal and means together, the goal making the means attractive; just as we see light and colours together, with light making the colours visible. It is one and the same act of will that wills means as a way to a goal (and in that respect is called *choice*), and wills the goal

5 as reachable by the means (and in that respect is called *intention*). Nature intends goals passively, under the active influence of God; and this is the way animals intend goals by natural instinct. But reason intends goals actively.

13 1 **Choosing, accepting and employing means.** Aristotle calls choosing *desirous reasoning or reasoned desiring*; and [Nemesius] says choosing *is neither simply wanting nor simply deliberating but both together*. Clearly acts of will presuppose acts of reason, since we can only desire what we are aware of; so when the will tends to something seen as good because in reason's plan it serves a goal, the act is essentially one of willing, but shaped by reason. *Choosing* then is essentially an act of will, incomplete until the soul actually tends towards the good chosen. Aristotle calls the conclusion of practical argument a choice, only because the decision of reason with which the argument concludes issues in a choice.

2 At first sight it seems obvious that animals choose. Bees, spiders and dogs behave in marvellously clever ways: a hound tracking a stag casts about at a crossing and, not picking up the scent on the first or second path, confidently follows the third without further checking, as though concluding by argument that his quarry must have taken the only path left. Nevertheless, I maintain that to choose is to prefer one of several courses, and where only one course is open choice has no place. Animal appetite differs from will precisely because it tends by nature to this or

that particular good, whilst will by nature tends to good in general, remaining indeterminate as regards particular goods. Only the will can choose, in the proper sense of the term. However, everything made by reason displays reason's design, even if it doesn't reason itself: clockwork and other man-made machinery, for example. Now all nature displays God's art in the way artificial objects do man's; and when animals behave cleverly it is because they are following out superlatively designed processes by natural instinct. But they are not themselves reasoning or choosing, as we see from the fact that all members of the same species behave in the same way. In theoretical science there is nothing to stop 3 conclusions of one argument or science acting as premises of another argument or science (though the first premises of all argument are indemonstrable). And in the same way the goal of one action can be a means to another, and so be subject to choice; but not the ultimate goal of all life. (There is only one ultimate goal,) so where goals are many we can choose between them with some further goal in view.   ?

Goals and what serve goals are either actions, or things made, used or (in the case of goals) enjoyed by men's actions. In this sense choosing is always concerned with actions, and therefore with what is possible. Nobody can achieve (or even intend) a goal by means which are impossible. Willing connects our thinking with our external activity: mind presents will with an object and the will causes external action. So willing moves outward into things, beginning from mental grasp of good as such, and ending by engaging in activities directed at things. What fulfils will then is something good for me to do, in other words, something possible. Fulfilled willing can only will what is good and possible for the one willing; the impossible can only be an object of unfulfilled willing (or wishing), something one would will if it were possible. Now choosing is an àct of will already resolved on what is to be done, so we can only choose what is possible. Though, just as we can will what mistakenly seems good, so we can choose what mistakenly seems possible. A man can will or not will, act or not act; and he can also will 6 and do this or that. For not to will and not to act can seem good to reason; and any particular good can seem good enough or not good enough to choose. Only happiness itself cannot but seem good and so must be willed. Choice, however, is concerned not with the goal of happiness, but with particular means that can realize such a goal; so it is always free and never necessary. Conclusions follow necessarily from a premise, only when the premise is incompatible with their falsity. In the same way, willing a goal necessitates choosing particular means only when those means are or appear such that without them the goal is unachievable. Reasoning about what to do concerns things that may or may not happen: it is not concerned to reach decisions deriving necessarily from categorically necessary premises, but ones based on conditional necessities like *if he runs he won't stay still*. Faced with two things presented as equally attractive, there is nothing to stop us attending to some feature which makes one more attractive, and thus turning our will to one rather than the other.

solves Buridans ass—

14 1   Choosing presupposes reason deciding what to do. Such decision-making is beset with doubt and uncertainty, because changing circumstances make every action a different individual case, so decision-making in turn presupposes a reasoned investigation we call *deliberating*. Choosing is willing according to a plan derived from reasoning, and deliberating is reasoning about material and motive derived from willing. Aristotle called choice *desirous reasoning* to emphasize this mutual influence; and in the same way John Damascene calls deliberation *investigative*

deliberating

DEF

2   *desire*. Goals relate to actions like premises to conclusions; and just as in inquiries we presuppose our premises and investigate conclusions, so too we deliberate not about our goals but about means. The goal presumed by one investigation, however, may have been a means inves-

3   tigated in another. Inquiry and investigation usually concern themselves with the many circumstances attendant on particular contingent cases. We want to know such things not for their own sake (they are small matters compared to necessary and universal truths), but so that we can

4   decide what to do in the circumstances. Though sometimes there is no doubt, since some kinds of behaviour are governed by fixed rules, and

5   sometimes it doesn't much matter what you do. The method deliberation uses is not synthesis (building up something from its elements) but analysis (uncovering the elements out of which something is composed). We start with the first thing we intend, the goal, which will be the last thing we implement, and analyse it to find what we can start to do here and now to realize it. When pursuing a goal we ask if actions are possible only when they suit our purposes; our first question is *do they further the goal?* and only then *are they practicable?* Deliberation has a definite

6   *the goal?* and only then *are they practicable?* Deliberation has a definite starting-point: the goal envisaged and the given facts, be they matters of sense-perception (*this is bread, that iron*) or derived knowledge (*adultery is divinely forbidden, a man needs food to live*). Deliberation has also a definite terminus: something we can start to do here and now. But if an endless number of things crop up for investigation, there is nothing to stop deliberation being potentially endless. Individual and contingent events may be of uncertain nature, but they have the certainty of being here when they are here, which is enough for present action.

deliberation cld be endless, but usually ends where we find smthg we can do —

Actually applying our desire to something is a sort of experience of it as pleasing; and so we call it *accepting* or *consenting*, from *con-sentire*, to feel with. The will consents but the mind assents, though we often use the words interchangeably. Though sticks may touch stones, only people – with the power of moving sticks – can employ them to touch stones; and though animals can desire things (instinctively), they cannot move or apply or employ their own desires, and so cannot give consent to them properly speaking. But we do things in a certain sequence: first we become aware of a goal and then desire it, next we deliberate on the means and then desire them. We desire our ultimate goal by nature, not so much consenting to it as simply willing it; but anything subordinate to that goal is as such matter for deliberation, and so for consent, which applies our desire to what we have by deliberation decided on. Choosing adds some comparison with what is not preferred; so even after consent we still have to choose one from the many things which please us. When only one thing pleases consent is in fact choice, though calling it consent says only that the thing pleases, whereas calling it choice adds that we prefer that thing to the things that don't please.

Using or *employing* things means applying them to action. External things we apply through the instrumentality of our own intrinsic powers and dispositions and bodily organs, and those we apply at will. So will moving and reason planning employ our executive powers as tools by which to use things. Use applies our powers to acting, consent applies our appetites to desiring; but only because we possess reason do we know how to relate and so apply things to one another. Animals instinctively move their limbs to do things, but without being aware of the limb as related to what they do; so strictly speaking they don't *use* their limbs. Whatever is used or applied serves a goal; its ability to serve that goal is often called its usefulness, or even its use. Our willed desire for a goal already disposes us to it (which is why whatever is disposed to a goal by nature can be said to desire it naturally); but desire tries to perfect its relationship into real achievement of the goal. As to something that serves a goal, choosing disposes our will to it, whilst use already begins the second relationship, employing our executive powers towards achieving it. But since acts of will reflect upon themselves we find consenting and choosing and using in every act of will. The will consents to choose and to consent, and uses itself when choosing and consenting.

Actions controlled by reason. Our actions are controlled by reason acting in virtue of some previous act of will (compare the way will chooses and uses in virtue of some previous act of reason). For control is exercised by issuing orders, and order is reason's prerogative. Sometimes reason simply indicates the required order: *This is what you ought to do*; sometimes it also initiates the motion by commanding: *Do this*. Initiating motion must however derive from a previous act of will, the first source of movement in all our actions. The root *subject* of freedom is will, but the root *cause* reason: will is free to move in more than one direction only because reason can have more than one conception of

3 what is good. Giving a command precedes the obeying of it in principle, and also usually in time. Obeying coincides with the act of will called use: you don't *use* a stick until you do something with it. So, after reason's decision concludes deliberation, will chooses; after that, reason gives a command to whoever has to do what is chosen (maybe the person choosing); and then the will of that person begins to use his powers to

4 execute the command. The way something exists determines the way in which it is one: all substances are simply speaking one and any compositeness is secondary. And what is true of naturally existing substances (like men composed of body and soul) is true also of human acts, in which the actions of lower powers are like material activated by an act of a higher power, in the way an agent activates the tools he uses. So the act of commanding and the act commanded are one and the same composite human act. For, as Aristotle says, what is done to a patient *is* the agent's doing.

5   Just as reason can judge it good that something should be willed, so it can command the willing of it. The power that obeys the command doesn't have to be the power that understands it. Bodily organs are only tools of the whole body's action, and the soul's powers too operate on behalf of the whole, the mind doing the understanding for all our powers and the will willing for all. Indeed, it is the man himself that understands and wills and commands himself to will. Though the primordial act of will comes, as we said, not from reason's command but from the instinct

6 of nature or a higher cause. Because reason is self-reflective it can command the doing of its own acts, and sometimes even the nature of those acts. Perception of truth, and assent to what we know by nature, are not under our control; but we can command our assent or dissent or suspension of judgment in matters where our minds are not adequately

7 convinced. Our emotions depend partly on our bodily state (and that escapes reason's control), but partly also on imagination which reason can influence, though occasionally some image or perception has a sudden emotional effect which reason hasn't foreseen. As Aristotle says, reason controls passions *not like a slavemaster but like a ruler of free men*.

8 Reason controls in the way perception controls, so it can control our

animal and human desires, but not our natural tendencies like nutrition and reproduction. What we praise as virtue and blame as vice are not the physiological actions of digestion and gestation, but the desires that serve them: the pursuit of the pleasures of food and sex in the right or wrong proportions. Any movement of the body resulting from our sensitive powers is subject to reason's control, but movements of nature are not. The source of all bodily activity is the heart's movement, so this exists in us by nature as a necessary consequence of life and can't be controlled by reason. Augustine thought our lack of control over our genital motions was a punishment for sin. But as we shall see, what Adam's sin did was to remove a supernatural gift God had given, leaving human nature to itself; so we still need some reason in nature why genital motions are particularly recalcitrant. Aristotle says they are involuntary in the same way as heart movements: heart and genitals are both principles of life, and therefore independent sources of our animality with their own proper natural motions, since the principles of things are always natural.

What makes action good or bad?   Actions are like things: that they [vol 18] 18 1 exist is good as far as it goes, but when they don't exist as fully as they should that is bad. To be fully realized actions, like things, must first 2 be what by definition they should be: things must be rightly formed and actions must have a right object. For the basic moral evil is activity exercised on the wrong object (taking something not your own, for example), just as the basic natural evil is misbegotten form. However good the external object of activity may be in itself, it may not be the right object for this or that action. So an action's goodness or badness is first decided by its object. Now this is not a case of effect causing cause. For one thing, human action is caused by desire, and that is an effect of objects rather than their cause. And even when actions do cause their objects, the goodness of the action's effect is not an agent of the goodness of the action, but actions are called good because they are such as to cause a good effect, the balance between the action and its effect being its goodness.

To be fully realized things must have properties over and above what 3 defines them, and actions too, to be accounted good, must occur in the right circumstances. Circumstances lie outside the specific nature of an action and belong to it like non-defining properties do to things, contributing to its moral goodness in the same way that non-essential properties contribute to natural goodness. Finally, just as certain things 4 depend for existence on outside causes, so human actions can depend for goodness on external goals; for activity must contain a right balance to its goal, even though its goal lies outside it.

4 elements contri- Four elements therefore contribute to a good action: first, its generic
bute to · act's existence as activity at all: secondly, definition by an appropriate object;
goodness thirdly, the circumstances surrounding the act; and fourthly, its relation to a goal. Actions are good in the straightforward sense of the word only when all these elements are present: as pseudo-Denys says, *any defect will make a thing bad; to be good a thing must be wholly good.*

5   Good human actions differ in kind from bad ones. For objects may differ and differentiate activity in relation to one source of activity even when they don't in relation to another: colour and sound distinguish two kinds of sense-perception but not two kinds of mind. Now human actions are good when they accord with reason and bad when they don't (for reason makes man human), and the difference of object which makes actions good or bad is directly related to reason, namely, whether the object suits or not. So goodness or badness of object must define specifically different kinds of reasoned or human or moral activity. Even in nature natural goodness or badness can diversify species, for a dead body is not the same species as a live one. And this is the way goodness and badness in relation to reason diversify species of moral action. Morally bad actions don't lack objects; they have objects lacking reasonable suitability. Thus, in relation to reason, married and adulterous sexual intercourse are two different kinds of act and have different kinds of effect, one earning commendation and the other blame; but in relation

6   to our reproductive powers they are one in species and effect. The goodness or badness of actions derived from their goals also diversifies their moral species. Voluntary action is made up of the external activity
voluntary the will is controlling (defined by the object of that activity), and an
act – 2 parts interior act of will controlling it (defined by the will's object, namely the goal of the activity). This act of will enters into the definition of the external activity, since only when the body is acting as will's tool is its activity morally significant. Human activity therefore is defined formally by its goal and materially by its external object. As Aristotle puts it, *stealing to pay for adultery makes you even more an adulterer than a thief.* Even if the goal is incidental to the external activity as such, it is not incidental to the interior act of will controlling and shaping the external

7   activity. If the object of an external activity is not intrinsically related to its goal (stealing in order to give alms), then the action belongs morally to two disparate species; otherwise (fighting to achieve victory) one species must be subsumed under the other. Which under which becomes clear if we notice that more ultimate goals engage agents of wider scope,

and such agents lay down more general definitions of what gets done. So goals are what define actions most generally, and further specification is due to objects intrinsically related to those goals; for will, with the goal as its object, is general mover of all those powers with particular objects of activity. The goal is the last thing implemented but it is the first thing mentally intended, and moral acts are defined relative to mind.

Some actions then are by definition good (like almsgiving, their object 8 accords with reason); some are by definition bad (like stealing, their object offends reason); whilst others are by definition neutral (like strawpicking, their object does neither). Every object and every goal is naturally good, but this doesn't ensure moral goodness or badness with respect to reason, just as man himself is neither virtuous nor vicious by nature. Actions which are by definition neutral are turned into good or 9 bad actions in individual cases by attendant circumstances, by the intended goal if by nothing else. For it is the function of reason to direct, and any action that proceeded from reason without a due goal would be *ipso facto* bad. Only absent-minded action like stroking one's chin or shifting one's feet can be neutral in the individual case, because not moral at all. What we mean by an action neutral by definition is an action capable of being either good or bad, not an action obliged to be neither: indeed there is no object of our activity that cannot be directed to good or bad by some goal or circumstance. Individual actions may be neither good nor bad in some restricted sense of those words: neither profitable nor harmful to others, for example. But we are here speaking of good and bad in the most general sense of being in harmony or in discord with right reason. Natural things are produced once for all with 10 a defined nature which underlies all supervening modifications. But reason can and must re-examine its products, and what was first treated as a circumstance attendant on the defining object of an action may be reassessed as itself defining the object. The place and time at which you steal are usually circumstances, but if they involve some special contravention of right reason (e.g. stealing in church) then the very definition of the action may be affected and stealing become sacrilege. Circumstance as such cannot affect an action's definition, but circumstance can change into an essential condition of the object defining the action. Some circumstances affect the goodness or badness of actions 11 only when another circumstance has defined their kind: thus taking more or less of something affects the goodness or badness of taking only when the thing is someone else's. Stealing more and stealing less differ in degree of badness, even if not in kind.

19 1 **Good and bad willing.** Good and bad are the primary differentiations of willing just as true and false are of believing; so acts of good will and ill will are different in species, distinguished by their objects, one willing good and the other evil. It is not the willed object's natural goodness that causes the will's moral goodness: the will's object is what reason presents to it as good to will, and as planned by reason it is already a

2 moral object and can cause moral goodness of will. In their first source things must be present simply and essentially. So since good or ill will is the root source of good or bad action, goodness of will must depend on the single essential determiner of goodness in an act, namely its object, and abstract from incidental determiners such as circumstances. Since the object of will is the goal, goodness of object and goodness of goal do not differ for willing as they would for other actions; and there are no other circumstances which could make a good will bad, for if you say someone is willing something good when he shouldn't, either the *when* is part of what he is willing (and then it isn't something good that he is willing), or it is meant to qualify the willing itself (and then there is no such thing as a wrong time for good will).

3 We can perceive particular good things with our senses but not goodness as such; only our minds can grasp that. Yet it is goodness as such that draws the will. So goodness of will in depending on its object depends on mind. Good as good, as attracting, appeals to our will rather than our mind, but only because it first appeals to our mind as true. The will can only be drawn to what reason perceives to be good. Reasoning, to be right about means, depends on our willing the right goal; but willing the right goal depends in turn on perceiving it rightly with our minds. So willing motivates reasoning in one way, and reasoning

4 willing in another (by presenting it with its object). Man's reason can lay down standards by which the goodness of men's wills must be measured, because it is itself a reflection of God's reason, the eternal law. So good will is measured even more by the eternal law than by human reason, and when human reason fails we should fall back on eternal reason. As existing in God's mind, the eternal law is unknown to us; we are aware of it partly because natural reason directly reflects

5 it and partly through additional revelation. But now the question arises: what if reason gets the eternal law wrong? Will our will act badly if it disregards it? Are we bound by a mistaken conscience? Some people say: yes, if conscience is commanding or forbidding something neutral; but no, if it is commanding a bad thing or forbidding a good one. But this is incoherent. What must bind in the neutral case cannot be the true nature of the object (which is neutral), so it must be how reason

presents it; but reason not only presents neutral actions as good or bad, but bad actions (like sex outside marriage) as good, and good actions (like believing in Christ) as bad. So if reason presents an action as bad then willing it will be bad, not because it is bad in itself but because it is presented by reason as bad. We must therefore say quite simply that the will is bound to follow reason, right or wrong. For reason presents its judgment as true and as issuing from God, the author of all truth. Of course, if a man is aware that his reason is commanding something contrary to God's law, then he is not obliged to follow it; but in such a case his reason is not entirely mistaken. So can a mistaken conscience 6 excuse us? Mistakes made willingly, whether directly willed or arising from neglect of what one ought to know, cannot excuse any resulting act of will. But mistakes that arise without negligence from ignorance of some circumstance can make resulting acts of will involuntary and thus excuse them. *Any defect will make a thing bad*, says pseudo-Denys, *to be good a thing must be wholly good*. So willing can be bad either because the thing willed is by nature bad, or because the mind presents it as bad; to will well the thing we will must both be and be seen to be good. But if obeying and disobeying a mistaken conscience are both bad, it seems that men with mistaken consciences are caught in a trap and cannot avoid sin. It is true that if the mistake proceeds from inexcusable ignorance, then the will is obliged to be bad. But there is no trap here, for the ignorance is voluntary and can be undone.

What of the relationship of means to ends? When we will an action 7 because we intend a certain goal, the action's orderedness to that goal contributes to its goodness or badness. If the intention that causes this willing is itself bad, then the willing can't be good: willing almsgiving out of vainglory is willing something good in itself for a bad reason, and as so willed almsgiving is bad and the willing of it bad. But an intention that supervenes after one started willing won't corrupt the willing up to that point, but only from then on. So whether we will bad for good reasons or good for bad reasons the resultant willing will be bad. A good will must will good for good reasons, good for the sake of good. And 8 just as bad actions can be willed with good intentions, so actions can get worse even as intentions get better: how good an action is cannot simply be judged by how good is its intention. For one thing, both in acts of willing and in external activity the actual action willed may not match up to the good goal intended. In external activity, moreover, there can arise obstacles which we are powerless to remove. Nevertheless, since intention provides the reason for willing, a measure of good in the intention does flow over into the willing: the will is willing a great end even if the means taken are not worthy of that end. And we may make similar points about the intensity with which we will actions and intend their goals. Both the interior and exterior parts of an action may be less intensely willed than the goal is – we often have a stronger desire to be well than to take the medicine required – but the intensity of our intention will flow over into the willing. Since a bad intention alone is enough to spoil our willing, the worse the intention the worse the willing; but you can't use the same argument where goodness is concerned.

11   To have a good will man must have as his ultimate goal the ultimate
12 good that God wills. But our minds can often regard one and the same action as good for one reason and bad for another; and one person may want it because of the good while another doesn't because of the bad. A judge, serving the good of the community, may sentence to death a criminal, whose wife and children oppose the sentence as a natural evil for their family. Now God, as the maker and manager of the whole universe, wills what he sees to be good for the whole of that community, namely, his own goodness; whereas creatures grasp only the particular goods appropriate to their own natures. So it can happen that a good will can want something, for a particular reason, that God does not want on universal grounds; or that different men can will opposite things for different reasons and yet all have good wills. But a man willing a particular good does not will it rightly unless he intends to will in it the common good as goal, so that the particular matter is willed as a reflection of the common good that is God. His human will, even if it wills something that God does not will, by conforming to its ultimate goal in the form of its willing in this way, conforms to God's willing of the common good, and sometimes even to the willing of it from charity – the mode in which God wills it. Moreover, by willing the particular good he wills he is conforming to God as active in him, willing him to have the natural inclinations and particular awareness that have guided his willing; even if he does not will what God wills, he wills, as people say, what God wills him to will. For what God wills in particular cases we do not know, and are therefore not bound to will, but we know that he wills good in general, and so by willing what is presented to us as good we are conforming to God's will in the form of our willing. When in glory we come to know God's assessment of each thing we will, we shall conform the matter of our willing to his will as well. But remember, even God does not will damnation for damnation's sake, or death for death's, but only because he wills justice; and it is enough that men too will the preservation of God's justice and the natural order. Conforming to God's reasons for his willing is more truly willing what God wills

than conforming to the particular things he wills, since will intends goals more than means.

Good and bad deeds. Whether what we do externally is good or bad is partly decided by its goal (and so derives from our inner act of willing that goal), and partly by its own right matter and circumstances (determined by our reason rather than our will). So the goodness of a deed in reason's plan precedes our good willing of it, though the actually executed deed derives its goodness from the will executing it. The external deed's goodness is like a form derived from the will as from its cause, but residing in the deed itself as in its proper matter. That the will intends a good end is not enough to make the external deed good; if either the goal intended or the action willed is bad that is enough to make the external deed bad. A man sins not only by willing bad ends but by willing bad actions. The sources of our inner act of willing are our inner powers (mind and will); and of our external deed our body's motive powers. But from a moral point of view the two together constitute a single action that may have more than one reason for being good or bad. Sometimes the only reason for goodness in an external deed is its goal (swallowing unpleasant medicine, for example), and then the same goodness or badness is present immediately in the willing and mediately in the deed. But the matter and circumstances of an external deed may also have a goodness of their own (the medicine may be pleasant), and then the separate goodnesses flow over into one another. The communication of a quality from one member of a species to another involves reduplication of the quality, but when a quality is communicated by analogy all we have is a multiplication of relationships to one and the same instance of the quality: the health resides in the healthy organism and is analogically attributed to the healthy diet that produced it and the healthy complexion that indicates it. And this is the way goodness is communicated between the inner act of willing and the outer deed itself: not by reduplication but by a coordination. If the deed itself added no goodness or badness to the willing of it what would be the point of actually doing or not doing it? Of course, the goodness a deed derives from the willing of its goal cannot add to the goodness of that willing (unless the willing somehow multiplies its own goodness in doing the deed: either by repeating or prolonging itself until the deed is done, or by gaining intensity from the pleasurableness of the deed). But a deed's own goodness of matter and circumstances constitute a goal or terminus of willing which must be achieved if the act of will is to be completely good; unless inability to complete the deed is involuntary. The results of action, if foreseen, affect its goodness or badness: not to refrain from deeds with known bad consequences shows bad will. When results are unforeseen, the deed's goodness will depend on whether such results are usual and natural – proneness to produce good results makes a deed a better act in general. If the results are unusual and coincidental they offer no ground for any judgment.

21 1 **Some terminology.**   *Good* and *bad* are wider terms than *right* and *wrong*. Any lack of good is bad, but only falling short of a goal is wrong, lacking rule. Rule in nature is a thing's natural tendency to a goal, and only those actions go right which accord with the tendency; deviation from this straight path we call a *fault*. In willed activity the immediate rule is reason and above that the eternal law. So an act on line for its goal according to reason and the eternal law is right, while an act which
2 goes awry is wrong and called a *sin*. In their turn, the terms *right* and *wrong* are wider than *praiseworthy* and *blameworthy*; for the latter impute to an agent responsibility for his acts, presuming them voluntary. In the arts reason aims at some particular artistic goal of its own creation, but in moral activity at a goal common to all human living. The artist can sin either as an artist, when he fails his own artistic intentions (and then he is blamed as a bad artist), or he can fail as a man when what he intends fails to accord with the common goal of human life (and then he is blamed as a bad man). The only moral sin is that of failing to aim
3 at the goal of human living, and moral blame is of a man as man. To call an act *deserving* or *undeserving* brings in the notion of just deserts rendered to people for profiting or hurting others. When you help or harm an individual both he and the society to which he belongs owe you deserts; when you help or harm society as such society and all its members owe deserts; and when you help or harm yourself the society
4 you belong to owes them. And if you do something that cannot be related to God as ultimate goal you do him dishonour and deserve redress from him. In any case, as ruler and manager of the whole universe, he has to judge the deserts of every human action. Not everything in man is subordinate to the political community, so not every deed is subject to its judgments; but everything a man has or can have is ordered to God and all human actions merit God's reward or punishment.

Feeling

Let us turn now from specifically human action to the sort of activity [vol 19]
men and animals share: namely, emotional reactions or passions.

Passion is broadly used to mean *being acted on*, the opposite of action. 22 1
It can name any acquiring of a state, even if the recipient loses nothing
by it (though perhaps *realization* would be a better name here). But
strictly speaking *passion* is the exchanging of one state for another
(especially when the exchange is for the worse, since passion implies
being under some external agent's sway, and this is most apparent
when least congenial). In the sense of realization even sensation and
understanding are passions in the soul, since we acquire them. But
exchange of state is a characteristic of bodily changes, so that passions,
in the strict sense, characterize not the soul or psyche as such, but the
whole animal, body and soul. Moreover, things sway us through our 2
appetites rather than our perceptions; for we perceive things as they are
represented to us, truly or falsely, but we are affected by them as they
exist in themselves, good or bad. So the passions or emotions are
appetites not perceptions. True, appetite is usually thought of as more
active than perception, because it motivates our external activity; but
this is precisely because appetite is more possible to and affected by the
externally existent objects of our activities. Such objects affect our
bodily organs not only physically, but also intentionally, as when our
eye receives the impression of colour without itself becoming coloured.
Intentional affection is essential to sense-perception, whereas physical
affection is incidental to perception (eyes get strained by concentrating,
for example, or blinded by the light) but essential to emotion: being
angry, by definition, involves the blood boiling. Of course, we also talk 3
of God and spirits and our own wills loving and enjoying and so on, but
that is only metaphorical description of acts of will that have the same
effect as emotions but lack the element of passion.

Affections like feeling joyful or sad, loving or hating, are reactions 23 1
to what we perceive as straightforwardly good or bad, agreeable or
disagreeable, pleasurable or painful. Sometimes however taking pleasure
in something or avoiding pain from it is not within our immediate power
and requires effort. To deal with such difficulties we are endowed with
emotions that respond to challenges, like boldness, feeling afraid, hoping
and other so-called aggressive emotions. The function of aggressive
emotions is to facilitate affection, so every aggressive emotion ends up
in affective emotion. Antithetic changes or movements sometimes lead 2
to antithetic states, and sometimes, if there is only one state in question,

move to and from that state. Changes of quality like getting whiter or blacker are antithetic in the first way; changes of substance like birth and death are antithetic in the second. Since our affections respond to what we perceive as straightforwardly good or bad, and since good as such cannot repel and bad as such cannot attract, our affections tend either towards good (loving, desiring or enjoying it) or away from bad (hating it, rejecting it or feeling sad at it). Antithetic affections thus react to antithetic objects, good and bad. But aggressive emotions react to what is arduously and difficultly pleasurable or painful, and we get both types of antithesis: hoping, attracted to the difficult because of its goodness, is opposed to despairing, which shuns good because of its difficulty, and feeling afraid, which shuns bad as such, is opposed to boldness, which confronts it as a (hard) way of avoiding greater evil; yet hoping and feeling afraid are also opposed because they are responses

3 to antithetic objects, good and bad. Anger is the only emotion without an opposed emotion. It is provoked by evils already harming us but hard to repel. Such evils we either yield to sadly (an affective emotion) or are impelled to confront angrily. No emotion impels us to avoid the evil, since what is already present is unavoidable: and there is no aggressive emotion tending towards already present good, since such good presents no challenge and is simply affectively enjoyed. The only thing opposed to being angry is its absence, calming down.

4 When a physical agent attracts or repels an object to a place, we can distinguish three effects: first of all the object acquires an inclination or bias towards that place, then (if it is not already there) it is moved there, and (when it is there) it is brought to rest. In emotions, good attracts and bad repels. So good starts by provoking an inclination or bias or affinity to itself, called loving (and opposed to hating); then if not yet possessed the good provokes a movement towards getting it, called desiring (opposed to aversion or disgust); and when it is finally achieved it provokes a repose of desire, called feeling pleased or enjoying (opposed to pain or feeling sad). Our aggressive emotions presuppose the same affective bias or inclination towards seeking good and avoiding evil; but goods not yet acquired provoke hope or despair and evils not yet upon us provoke fear or boldness. Good acquired provokes no aggressive emotion because it offers no challenge; but evil when present provokes anger. So we see that there are three lots of affections: loving and hating, desiring and aversion, feeling pleased and feeling sad; and three lots of aggressive emotions: hoping and despairing, feeling afraid and feeling bold, and feeling angry (which has no antithesis).

24 1 Our animal emotions are more closely allied to mind and will than

our bodily movements, yet such movements when voluntary are morally good or bad. *A fortiori* then emotions must be accounted morally good or bad when they obey or are permitted by our wills. The Stoics thought all emotion evil, the Peripatetics held that in moderation it was good; but the difference was largely one of vocabulary. The Stoics applied the term *will* to all reasonable appetites and *emotion* only to appetites beyond the bounds of reason; whereas the Peripatetics called all animal appetites emotion, saying the reasonable ones were good and the others evil. Passion makes us prone to sin only when it is unreasonable; reasonable emotion is virtuous. No one questions the fact that to be morally good we must be in reasonable control of our bodily movements. Since the emotions listen to reason, to be morally good we must also control them. Just as it is better not simply to will good but also to do it externally, so it is morally better to seek good not merely with a will but also with emotion. When emotions precede the reasoned judgment on which the moral worth of our actions depends, they cloud the judgment and lessen the worth of the actions: deeds of charity done merely from [an emotion of] pity are less praiseworthy than those done from choice. But emotion can also follow judgment: either as overflow from the higher to the lower parts of the soul so that its presence indicates greater intensity of will and thus greater moral worth; or because emotion is a deliberately chosen means to readier action, so that emotion enhances the goodness of the deed. Emotions can be morally classified, just like external activity, into good ones whose object is in tune with reason – e.g. shame, which is fear of what is degrading – and bad ones with objects at odds with reason – e.g. envy, which is feeling sad at someone good. Even animals whose appetites don't obey reason, have a natural instinctive judgment in tune with God's reason, and so a sort of analogy to moral good.

Among affective emotions some, like desiring, are akin to movement and some, like feeling pleased or sad, are akin to being at rest. But all aggressive emotions are akin to movement, since you can't rest when in difficulties. Joy, the affective emotion at rest in good, terminates aggressive movement; whereas feeling sad, the affective emotion at rest in evil, lies halfway between two aggressive emotions: feeling afraid and feeling angry. But, because the feeling of anger, when it has avenged the evil, leads to feeling pleased, all aggressive emotions finally come to rest in affective emotions. Aggressive emotions arise from those affective emotions that are akin to movement, adding something related to the object's difficulty. Hoping adds to desiring a certain buoyancy of spirit in pursuit of what is good but arduous; and feeling afraid adds to

aversion or disgust depression in the face of difficult evil. So all aggressive
2 emotion begins and ends in affective emotion. Every disaffection for evil
presupposes by definition an opposed affection for good: we spurn evil
because we want good. And among the affections for good, loving, which
finds the good agreeable and inclines us to it, precedes desiring, which
actually seeks the good; and desiring precedes being pleased which rests
in the good when achieved. But since we intend things in the reverse
order to that in which they get implemented it is pleasure anticipated
that arouses in us desire and love. (Desire) culminates in pleasure when
lover and beloved are really united, but it arises out of a prior affective
3 unity: the inclination and affinity which is loving itself. Some emotions
spring solely from affective inclination or affinity for something aimed
at (like loving or hating), and others from real presence of something
good or bad (like feeling sad or pleased). Present good arouses no
aggressive emotion, but present evil arouses anger; and because affinity
with a goal precedes achievement of it feeling angry is always the last
aggressive emotion to arise. Among the other aggressive emotions,
those responding to good (like hoping and despairing) precede those
responding to evil (like boldness and feeling afraid): boldness follows
on hope of victory and feeling afraid on despair of it. Anger however
follows on boldness for nobody feels angry or thirsts for revenge unless
he feels bold enough to avenge himself. So if we want to order emotions
in the order of their occurrence: first come loving and hating, then desire
and aversion, then hoping and despairing, then feeling afraid and feeling
bold, then feeling angry, and finally feeling pleased and feeling sad, the
culmination of all the emotions. Emotions first and foremost seek good,
and only consequently shun evil. We order them as we would nature's
intentions rather than nature's processes, which, if they get rid of
contrary states first, do so because of some previously intended goal.
4 Pleasure and sadness are primary emotions because all other emotions
come to rest in them. But feeling afraid and hoping are primary because
they are our culminating movements towards good and evil: loving
arouses desire and culminates in hoping, hating arouses aversion and
culminates in feeling afraid. Despair moves away from good and boldness
moves towards evil, so neither of these emotions can be primary.

26 1 **Loving and hating.**   Natural things tend naturally to goals perceived
not by themselves but by someone else [namely, God]. In addition, we
animals tend by animal appetite or emotion to goals we perceive with
our own senses, tendencies which dumb animals are not free to resist,
but which in man are to some extent under reason's control. Finally,

as reasoning creatures we can also choose to tend of our own free will to goals presented to us by reason. All these tendencies are at root forms of *loving*: in nature natural affinity, in the emotions or will a sort of attachment to the good in question as agreeable. The emotion of love is an affective emotion, directly reacting to goodness, rather than an aggressive one, reacting to challenge. Not only our so-called natural abilities to grow and propagate exemplify natural love, but every faculty of our soul, every part of our body, and every created thing. Everything has a built-in affinity for what accords with its nature. By *passion* we mean some result of being acted on: either a form induced by the agent (like weight) or a movement consequent on the form (like falling to the ground). Whatever we desire acts on us in this way, first arousing an emotional attachment to itself and making itself agreeable, and then drawing us to seek it. The first change the object produces in our appetite is a feeling of its agreeableness: we call this *love* (weight can be thought of as a sort of natural love); then *desire* moves us to seek the object and *pleasure* comes to rest in it. Clearly then, as a change induced in us by an agent, love is a passion: the affective emotion strictly so, the will to love by stretching of the term. Love unites by making what is loved as agreeable to the lover as if it were himself or part of himself. Though love is not itself a movement of the appetite towards an object, it is a change the appetite undergoes rendering an object agreeable. Favour is a freely chosen and willing love, open only to reasoning creatures; and charity – literally, *holding dear* – is a perfect form of love in which what is loved is highly prized. *To love*, as Aristotle says, *is to want someone's good*; so its object is twofold: the good we want, loved with a love of desire, and the someone we want it for (ourselves or someone else), loved with a love of friendship. And just as what exist in the primary sense are subjects of existence, and properties exist only in a secondary sense, as modes in which subjects exist; so too what we love in the primary sense is the someone whose good we will, and only in a secondary sense do we love the good so willed. Friendship based on convenience or pleasure is friendship inasmuch as we want our friend's good; but because this is subordinated to our own profit or pleasure such friendship is subordinated to love of desire and falls short of true friendship.

What causes love, since it is a passion, is its object; and since it is a sort of affinity or agreement with the object, what causes love is the goodness or agreeableness of that object. Evil can only be loved because it seems good, because being partially good it is perceived as wholly so. And the beautiful is a form of the good: if something is agreeable in general we call it good, and if the perception of it is agreeable we call it

2 beautiful. But goodness must be known before it can become the object of love, so knowledge itself can be said to cause love. Knowing is an activity of reason, which abstracts from things and then makes connections between them, needing to know each part and property and power of things if it is to know them perfectly. But loving is an appetite for things as they stand, and to love perfectly we need only love them as they are perceived to exist in themselves. So it can happen that something is more loved than known; we see it often with learning, and the same is true of God. Knowledge is the cause even of the loving all things do by nature; not their knowledge though, but that of the author

3 of nature. *Every living creature loves its like*, says Ecclesiasticus. Actual likenesses – oneness in form – causes love of friendship and goodwill, in which our affections are drawn to others as one with ourselves, so that we want their good as though it was our own. The sort of likeness that holds between a tendency and what it tends towards, or a capability and what it is capable of, causes love of desire and friendships of convenience and pleasure; for any potential has an urge to realize itself and – given awareness – enjoy the realization. But in love of desire we are really loving ourselves, wanting for ourselves the desired good. And since we all love ourselves, with whom we are one in substance, more than others with whom we can only be one in form, if another's likeness to ourselves turned out to hinder our achievement of some good, he would become hateful to us. Which is why, as Aristotle says, *potters always squabble with one another*, competing for business. Oneness of form must be interpreted *mutatis mutandis* as when a gifted singer loves

4 a talented writer. All other emotions imply movement towards or rest in their objects, and presuppose the affinity or attachment to the object that we call loving. So none of them can be the cause of love in general. But in a particular instance love can be caused by some other emotion: pleasure, desire, or hope (because it arouses pleasure and intensifies desire). However, all these presuppose some love already: only someone who already loves and desires money will come to love a benefactor.

28 1   Unity causes love: unity in substance love of oneself, and unity of likeness love of others. Love is also itself a sort of unity, an attachment of heart which imitates unity of substance, relating the lover to a loved friend as to another self, and to what is loved with desire as to something belonging to him. And finally, love causes lovers to seek some appropriate real unity: being together, talking together, doing things together. In knowledge we identify with a representation of what we know, but in love we identify with the thing itself that we love: so love effects a greater

2 unity than knowledge. St John says, *He that dwells in charity dwells in*

God and God in him. The beloved is constantly present in the lover's thoughts, and the lover tries to think himself into the beloved's very soul, in the way St Paul says the Holy Spirit, God's love, *searches even the depths of God*. Moreover, the beloved is present in the lover's affections, by an intimately rooted *heartfelt* attachment and agreeableness. In love of desire the lover is not content with an external relation to what he desires, but wants to enter fully into possession and enjoyment of it; whilst in love of friendship the lover identifies with his friend, regarding his fortunes and his very will as his own. Add to this that friendship is reciprocal. Loving takes us out of ourselves. It disposes 3 us to intense pre-occupation of thought with the beloved, and that abstracts us from other things; as love of desire it directs us towards things we do not yet have (though only for ourselves) and as love of friendship it desires things for people outside us. The lover wants his friend's good, and works for it, though not more than for his own. We do not love friends more than ourselves. Love also causes jealousy. We 4 show antipathy to anything that hinders the achievement and peaceful enjoyment of what we desire (husbands jealously guard their wives); and we are jealous also on our friends' behalf, repelling what people say or do against them. Love of something that cannot be shared or simultaneously possessed causes envy; but nobody envies another his knowledge, since this can be shared, though perhaps people can envy eminent learning. People are better off for loving what suits them, worse 5 off and harmed by loving what doesn't. Here we are thinking formally of love as appetite; materially love involves physiological changes and excessive love could have harmful bodily effects. Formally speaking, love melts the heart (making it malleable and readily able to let a loved object in), and brings pleasure when its object is present and listlessness otherwise, or fever to possess it. To each of these formal effects there correspond physiological changes in our bodily organs. All action 6 pursues goals which must be desired and loved; so whatever anything does is done out of love, be it intellectual, rational, animal or natural [of kinds of love]. And since all the other emotions [even hatred] spring from love, love is also the cause of every action springing from emotion.

Just as everything is naturally in harmony (or in love) with what 29 1 agrees with it, and out of harmony with (dislikes) what threatens to destroy it; so animals and reasoning creatures love or feel harmony with what their senses and reason perceive as agreeable, and dislike or feel discord with what is perceived as threatening and harmful. Existence as such is agreeable rather than threatening, since everything agrees in existing; but the existence of one particular thing may threaten another,

and one and the same thing may be lovable to one thing – by nature
agreeable to it or perceived as good – and hateful to another – by nature
2 threatening or perceived as evil. To be a threat to something is precisely
to destroy or hinder what is agreeable to it; so all hatred of threatening
4 things arises out of love of agreeable ones. *No one*, as St Paul says, *ever
hated his own flesh*: no one wills or does evil to themselves unless it seems
good. Even suicides see death as a good end to wretchedness and grief.
5 Nor can one dislike existence and truth in general, for one can dislike
only what is discordant, and all things agree in existing and being true.
But some particular truth may threaten what one loves and so be disliked;
either we wish it was not true, or want not to know it. Or we may dislike
6 someone who knows our secrets. Aristotle says that *we get angry with
individuals but dislike in general*. Here we must distinguish between
occurring generally, and generality as such. Neither sense-perception
nor sense-appetites can react to the general as such, since what is general
is precisely abstracted from what we sense: matter in its particularity.
Nevertheless our sense-powers relate to things generally: the object of
sight is colour in general (though not colour as general) since colour is
visible *qua* colour, not *qua* this or that colour. And in the same way
sheep don't like wolves in general, since it is not only certain wolves
that threaten them but the whole class of wolves. Contrast anger which
is always directed against some particular harmful action. The senses
perceive something which is open to abstractive generalization, but they
don't perceive its generality. So we cannot dislike what everything
has in common, but we can dislike something common to many but
threatening us.

30 1 **Desiring.**   Every vital ability *wants* what is good for it with a *want*
built in to it by nature, and not consequent on any perception. But
animals have special abilities to want things with an animal want that
follows on a perception; and if it is wanted precisely as pleasurable to
2 the senses the want is the affective emotion we specially call *desire*. A
goal moves us in different ways according to whether it is present or
absent: present it brings us to rest, absent it attracts us to move. So a
pleasurable object by attuning our appetite to itself makes us love, by
attracting us to its absent self makes us desire, and by bringing us to
rest in its presence gives us pleasure. So it is the absent pleasurable and
not just the pleasurable as such that defines desire, just as it is the past
object of sense-perception that defines memory. Sense-perception is
concerned with the particular, and so its different emotions and abilities
3 can be defined by such particular conditions. There are what Aristotle

calls common necessary desires, natural to all animals including man and directed at things pleasurable and agreeable to our animal nature, such as food and drink. And there are distinctive acquired desires found *only man can* only in man, directed at good and agreeable things men have thought *acquire desires* up, over and above what nature requires. This distinction doesn't just distinguish the matters we desire, but by way of that distinguishes formal types of desire: natural desire for what we straightforwardly perceive as attractive, and non-natural desires for what reasoning makes attractive. Physical desires are limited: they desire what nature needs, 4 and nature has determinate goals. Nobody desires here and now an infinite amount of food and drink; though desire can succeed desire endlessly, and we will never stop needing and wanting food, since bodily *non-natural* goods do not last. But non-natural desires are altogether limitless, for *desires is* reason can think things up without end: a man's desire for riches can *limitless* be endless. Though even this must be conceived finitely. No one can take in the infinite as such since, as Aristotle says, the infinite is that of which however much you take something always remains. But the power of reason is limitless, in the sense that it can go on endlessly considering things (elaborating the number series for example), and grasps general concepts which are applicable to an infinite number of individuals.

Feeling pleased or sad.   Aristotle defines pleasure as *the movement* [vol 20] 31 1 *arising in the soul when we perceive ourselves wholly present in a state agreeable to our nature.* Arriving at such a state may take time, but having arrived there is a wholly present state, which inanimate things cannot perceive but which animals do and, because they do, take pleasure in. External movement of an animal towards its goal comes to an end when the goal is achieved, but the felt movement of desire for the unachieved goal is replaced by a felt movement of pleasure in its achievement. Pleasure is in one way a rest for the appetite, because the goal's presence satisfies it; but that satisfaction is itself a movement of the appetite by that goal. Time measures what occurs consecutively; so strictly speaking 2 what takes time are consecutive processes like moving, being at rest, talking and so on. Other things only occupy time incidentally, not by themselves being consecutive processes, but by being subject to them. Being human, for example, is not itself a consecutive process but the terminus of such a process, namely, human reproduction; yet because it is subject to processes of change it occupies time. In the same way being pleased does not itself take time, since it accompanies achievement of a goal, the termination of a process; but if the goal is itself subject to processes of change pleasure will occupy time incidentally. For as

Aristotle says some movements are activations of what is still incomplete and potential, and these are the consecutive processes that take time. But other movements are activations of what is already complete and actual: movements such as understanding, sensing and willing, and feeling pleasure; so these are not consecutive processes taking time.

3 Joy is pleasure in achieving non-natural desires; so in non-human
4 animals we do not talk of joy but only pleasure. Mental perceptions arouse our sense-appetites when brought to bear on particulars, and can arouse a pleasure that affects us bodily; but they can also cause joy which
5 consists in simple movement of will, the mind's appetite. Some living activities like understanding, sensing and willing don't act on or perfect things outside, but realize and perfect those who engage in them. Activities like sensation are good for their agents and perceived as such, so such activities, and not just their objects, arouse pleasure. Clearly there is more of this sort of pleasure in understanding than in sensation: understanding both knows better and is also better known, since the mind is better able to reflect on its activity than the senses are. We prize our minds more, and would rather give up sight than sanity. Again, we get more pleasure from union with the spiritual objects we understand than from the bodily objects we sense: the objects themselves are to be prized more, the ability to understand is a nobler ability, and the union achieved is more intimate, more complete and more lasting. Nevertheless, pleasure in bodily things is more intense: we are more aware of what can be sensed than of what can only be understood, our bodies are also affected, and there is a contrast with painful feelings which doesn't happen with pleasures of understanding. Spiritual pleasures moreover presuppose virtue, so most people fail to experience them and fall back on bodily pleasure. Bodily pleasures are pleasures of sense ruled and controlled by reason; spiritual pleasures belong to the reason
6 which does the ruling and so are sober and moderate of themselves. The pleasure that men take in the senses as sources of knowledge is at its greatest in the sense of sight; the pleasure that all animals take in the senses as tools of survival is at its greatest in the sense of touch, for touch informs us about the elemental qualities that go to make us up: hot and cold, wet and dry. As Aristotle says, *Hounds take pleasure not in scenting hares but in eating them.* The end of physical love is pleasure and especially the pleasure of touch; but it begins with seeing something whose appearance attracts us to love and desire that pleasure.

32 1 The primary source of pleasure is, as Aristotle says, unhindered and congenial activity. No object of activity gives pleasure unless we become joined to it in some way: either just by knowing it, or by possessing it

in some other way and knowing that we do. But possessing is using or having the use of, and requires activity; so all pleasure has its source in activity. Activity gives pleasure inasmuch as it is congenial and suited to the agent; though because man's powers are limited, activity must be kept within limits if it is not to cease being pleasurable and become wearisome. That is why leisure and recreation give pleasure. Change 2 too gives pleasure: partly because we are changeable and what suits us now won't suit us later, and partly because without change particular sources of pleasure might outlast the limited tolerance of our nature. Moreover, we never know things instantaneously, but must move from one aspect to another to get a grasp of the whole. To someone of unchangeable nature and unlimited tolerance, able to grasp instantaneously the whole of what gave pleasure, change would not be pleasurable in the same way. Our greatest pleasure arises when we perceive 3 what is pleasurable to be actually and sensibly present; a lesser pleasure comes from hope, which perceives something pleasurable and can rely on being able to make it present in the future; and the least pleasure is that of memory, in which all that remains is perception of what was pleasurable in the past. Other people's activity can also give us pleasure: 5 actions done for our good, or recognizing our worth, or benefiting our friends and harming our enemies. We get pleasure too from doing good 6 to others, either because they are our friends and it is as though we did good to ourselves, or because the hope of reward pleases us and we enjoy having the capacity and inclination and motive to do good. Actions against others also give us pleasure. Winning is naturally pleasurable because it makes us feel superior; so competitions and competitive games – if we have a hope of winning – always give pleasure. Rebuking people is pleasurable: it makes us feel wise and sometimes it actually profits them. And angry men find revenge sweet. But whereas doing good to others is pleasurable as such, doing them evil can only be pleasurable when it is seen as doing good to oneself.

Physical pleasure can hinder reason by distracting our attention, 33 3 undermining our practical judgment in particular situations (though not our general theoretical judgment about triangles and suchlike), or by causing physiological upsets like getting drunk that fetter reason. But 34 1 no one can live entirely without sensual and physical pleasure. Even people [like the Stoics] who teach that every pleasure is bad will be found enjoying some, and then other people will be all the more inclined to pleasure because of their example, ignoring their teaching. For where human activity and emotions are concerned experience and example carry more weight than words. The truth is that just as some actions are good and some bad, so desiring to act well is good, and desiring to act badly is bad. And since the pleasure accompanying action is even more closely tied to it than the desire preceding it, taking pleasure in acting well is good, and taking pleasure in acting badly is bad. Pleasure in the exercise of reason neither hinders reason nor undermines practical judgment, but physical pleasures may do so by attracting us to something at odds with reason or by paralysing reason's exercise. Pleasure in the marriage act, for example, though it accords with reason nevertheless hinders its exercise, because of the accompanying physiological changes. This doesn't make that pleasure morally bad, any more than being asleep is morally bad: reason requires us to interrupt reasoning from time to time. But one should note that this paralysis of reason, though neither seriously nor trivially wrong morally, has resulted from a moral wrong,

2 Adam's sin, for before that time it did not happen. If the Stoics held all pleasure bad, the Epicureans in contrast held them to be all good of their nature. But this is also a mistake. Reason defines virtue and usefulness, so those things must be good. But our appetites decide what is pleasurable and sometimes at odds with reason. So things can be pleasurable without being morally good, good as reason defines it. Just as not everything desired is intrinsically and truly good, so not every

4 pleasure. Whether our willing be good or bad is judged principally by the goal in which it finds rest and pleasure. People are therefore judged to be good or evil chiefly in terms of what their wills find pleasurable: virtuous people are those who enjoy doing good and bad people those who enjoy acting badly. Sense-pleasures however are no standard of moral good and evil: food delights the senses of good and evil people alike. But a good man's will enjoys them only when they are reasonable, whilst the evil man's will doesn't care about that. Good actions, however, can't be perfectly good unless completed by pleasure in the good done.

35 2   Joy and sadness are words which describe pleasure and pain based on interior perception – understanding or imagination. So we can feel sad about things past, present and future, whereas only something present to our bodily senses can make us feel pain. Objects of touch are painful because besides being felt as discordant they are also physically damaging. The objects of other senses though felt as discordant can only damage us as objects of touch. So other senses cause sadness but not

4 pain, unless pain is to name the whole genus of the unpleasant. Generically pleasure and sadness are opposites, one attracted to its object and the other repelled (attraction and repulsion being appetite's antitheses, as affirmation and negation are reason's). Pleasure and sadness about the same object are opposite in species; and about disparate objects are

disparate (like sadness about a friend's death and pleasure in contemplation); but if their objects are opposed then pleasure and sadness agree in species (like enjoying good and sorrowing over evil). It is not perception that causes sadness but the thing perceived, and that thing is perceived all the more perfectly the more abstract and non-physical the mode of perception. Consequently, interior sadness is the greater, caused by clearer perception of the evil.

If perception of a lack was itself a lack of perception there would be 36 1 no point in asking whether sadness resulted more from absent good than from present evil, for there would be no difference. But perception of lack is something present in the mind. So, since sadness is a sort of repulsion and pleasure a sort of attraction, we shall say that pleasure is primarily response to a good achieved, and sadness response to an evil that has come upon one.

We have many abilities all rooted in a single nature, and when we 37 1 turn all our attention to one we have nothing left for the others. Now physical pain more than anything absorbs our attention, and by our nature we devote ourselves to repelling it. Learning and study also require great attention; so that intense pain inhibits learning, and while it lasts, if intense enough, even inhibits attention to what we already know. We often describe effects of emotion with metaphors drawn from 2 the effects of physical changes: love warms the heart, pleasure enlarges it, sadness weighs it down so that it is held back from freely enjoying what it desires. If an evil is strong enough to banish all hope of escaping it, we feel paralysed, unable to make further interior or sometimes even external movement. We do the things that cause us sorrow less willingly 3 and therefore less vigorously. Sorrow is opposed to life not simply when 4 excessive like other emotions, but of its own nature. For life streams out from the heart to the other organs; the emotions of attraction help this motion along (though they can injure it by excess), but emotions of repulsion are a sort of drawing back and so by their very nature injure the movement of life. Fear and despair are such emotions, and especially sorrow which is depressed by a present evil sufficient it feels to outweigh the future. Sorrow sometimes even deprives us of all reason, landing us in melancholy and madness.

Any rest of body relieves fatigue, no matter what tired us, and any 38 1 sort of pleasure relieves sorrow, no matter what its cause. Tears also are a natural relief from sorrow: firstly, because hurt pent up inside draws attention to itself and hurts more, whereas hurt poured out disperses the attention abroad, so to speak, and lessens our interior pain. And secondly, activities appropriate to one's current state are always pleasurable; and weeping and howling are appropriate to people in pain and sorrow. Effects are agreeable to their causes and give them pleasure; so sadness's very effects relieve sadness, just as joy's effects (laughter, for example) by nature intensify joy, even if when carried to excess they sometimes by accident lessen it. Someone who sees others saddened when he is sad feels they are helping to carry his load, and it seems lighter; but even better, he sees that they love him, and that gives

4 pleasure. *The more you know the more it hurts*, says Ecclesiastes, either because discovering truth is a hard business and never completely successful, or because we discover things we would rather not. But knowing as such is pleasurable and the pleasure spills over from the higher parts of the soul to the lower, relieving even sensible pain.

5 Sleeping and taking a bath and whatever else restores the movement of life in the body also oppose and mitigate sadness, for getting the body into good condition benefits the heart, the beginning and end of all movements in the body.

39 1   Sadness as such is an evil, which hinders rest in what is good. But given that there is something sad and painful present, feeling sad is a good thing; the only alternatives would be insensitivity or welcoming the evil, both of them bad attitudes. By avoiding evil we avoid sadness's cause, but we must be able to recognize and reject evil. The capacity to feel physical pain and shrink from it is a mark of a good constitution;

2 and where interior sadness is concerned, recognizing evil attests reason's good judgment and rejecting it attests our habitual goodness of will. Some things like sin happen with God's permission but are not willed by God; so our will is not at odds with God's when it opposes sin (our own or another's). God however wills the afflictions that happen; nevertheless men of right will don't need to will those afflictions in themselves, as long as they don't rebel against the justice of God's

3 arrangements in general. Sorrow at present evil has no useful purpose as such (for present evil can't be not present); its use lies rather in provoking us to resist and repel evils that ought to be repelled, such as

4 sins or situations offering opportunity for sin. Pain and sadness are not the greatest evil; worse is judging evil to be good and not rejecting it. There is, in fact, in pain and sadness some good, the removal of which would make things worse. There isn't in the same way evil in pleasure, the removal of which would make things better; and that is why there can be a pleasure which is man's greatest good.

Feeling hopeful or despairing. What we hope for has four dis- [vol 21] 40 1
tinguishing characteristics: it is good (not bad, like what we fear), future
(not present, like what we take pleasure in), challenging and hard to
achieve (for hope is an aggressive emotion, not simply an affection
for a future good, like desire), nevertheless able to be achieved (not
unachievable, like what we despair of). That objects of appetite should
be able to be achieved is not altogether irrelevant to them as objects of
appetite, for appetite is the start of movement, and one doesn't move
towards the impossible. So hope is movement of our appetite towards 2
what we perceive as a good difficult, but possible, to achieve in the
future. What makes things possible is power, either our own or someone
else's. We hope in both cases, but in the latter we also expect, looking
not only to the good we hope to achieve but also to the agency by which
we hope to achieve it. When we desire something and think it achievable
we confidently believe we shall achieve it; so the resultant movement of
appetite which we call hope, is often called confidence after the mental
state which precedes it and which is better known to us. What makes 3
things objects of hope is not possibility as a mode which qualifies the
way predicates are true of their subjects, but possibility as being within
someone's capacity. When a challenging and difficult good is considered 4
achievable it attracts us and our appetite approaches it hopefully; but a
good considered unachievable repels us, and the appetite turns away in
despair. So despair is the antithesis of hope as repulsion is of attraction.
Fear is also an antithesis of hope, but as evil is of good. Despair and
hope both presuppose desire, because unless we desire something we
can neither hope for it nor despair of it. You can cause hope by making 5
something achievable or by causing it to be thought achievable. Riches,
courage and experience all make us more capable and give us hope;
instruction, persuasion and (again) experience can change our assessment of our capabilities (generating hope or, sometimes, the reverse).
Inexperience can also generate hope, in the same way that experience
can kill it: young people hope easily because they are intent on the 6
future, high-spirited and prepared for challenge, and because they are
inexperienced enough to think everything possible. Drunkenness too
can raise the spirits and make one inconsiderate of dangers. Sometimes 7
it is not we ourselves who have the capacity to make something possible
but someone helps us. So hope has two objects: what we hope for (and
here love breeds hope) and what makes it possible (and here hope breeds
love). Being loved by someone generates hope in him, and then hope in
him brings us to return his love. Perception of difficulty alerts us and 8
perception of achievability quickens our efforts; so hope inspires us to

apply ourselves to action and to enjoy it. Sometimes however despair of escape makes us fight even more fiercely, in the hope of avenging our own death.

41 1 Feeling afraid or feeling bold.   Passion in the broadest sense means being acted on, and in this sense even sensation and understanding are passions. More strictly passions are appetites, and especially appetites working through bodily organs and accompanied by bodily changes. Most strictly of all, passions involve change for the worse. Feeling afraid is a passion in this strictest sense, second only to sadness and grief: we grieve at evils already present, and are afraid of what is yet to come. Though the future can't be perceived by the senses, perception of what is present arouses in all animals by a sort of natural instinct hope of
2 future good and fear of future evil. Hope is attracted to challenging
3 goods which seem achievable in the future; fear shrinks from evil difficult to resist. Some movements to which nature inclines us are completed without awareness: growing, for instance. Others, grounded in natural inclination, need awareness to complete them, like understanding, sensation, memory and the emotions. Fear (like love and desire and pleasure) is sometimes natural in this latter sense, sometimes not. Feeling afraid of what might damage or destroy us is natural, feeling dismay at what disappoints desire but leaves nature unharmed is not. Fear however is not a word like love, hate, desire and hope, all of which can describe tendencies natural in the first sense, and present in creatures devoid of awareness; for the emotions they describe do not essentially involve awareness (as we have seen joy and sadness do), or run counter to natural inclination (as despair does in failing to pursue good and fear in failing to confront evil because of the difficulties).

42 1   Just as hope centres itself not only on what we hope for but also on whatever helps its achievement, so we are afraid not only of the evil we want to avoid but also of the power that can inflict it: be it God or the
2 power of men, especially when it is destructive or unjust. As Aristotle says, for a man to fear evil it must neither be too far nor too close. A man must have some hope of escape. So natural evils are feared only
3 when they are seen as imminent but escapable. What is completely within our power and control does not frighten us; only what lies outside us. So strictly speaking we cannot fear our own moral faults, which are
4 voluntary, but only external inducements to sin. Shame, for example, is a sort of fear, but not for the actual act of sinning so much as for the consequent external disgrace and ignominy.

44 1   When an animal is hurt nature hoards vital spirits within it to help resist the source of harm. And because this sudden increase in spirits needs to be released, as Aristotle says, hurt animals can hardly stop themselves crying out. But the spirits of people who are afraid do not rise to their lips, but sink down from the heart producing silent trembling. At the prospect of death nature itself shrinks, and withdraws the body's vital heat so that we grow pale; but shame fears what offends not nature but our own desires, so it is our soul that shrinks, so to speak, letting vital heat flow into our empty body so that we blush. The withdrawal 3 of heat from the body's surface raises the internal heat of the body, especially in the lower digestive tract. The body's moisture is absorbed, we feel thirst, and sometimes we empty our bladder. And because heat has left them our hearts flutter, our voices, lower lip and jaw tremble and our teeth chatter, our hands shake and our knees knock. By affecting 4 our limbs and organs in this way fear interferes with our body's ability to act; but in moderation fear makes our soul more attentive and careful about what it is doing. If extreme however it can disturb our reason.

Boldness is fear's antithesis: where fear shrinks from future danger 45 1 lest we lose the battle, boldness confronts it in order to win. Aggressive emotions display two types of antithesis: fear is opposed to hope as evil to good, and opposed to boldness (with despair opposing hope) as retreat to attack. Feeling safe is simply lack of fear, but feeling bold is its antithesis. Hope pursues the [challenging] goods that despair shrinks 2 from, and boldness confronts the evils fear shrinks from. So boldness presupposes a hope of overcoming the evil, just as despair presupposes fear of losing good. Despair presupposes intense fear, boldness intense hope. But the boldness lies in confronting the evil, the hope in wanting to overcome it; so boldness is not a species of hope but one of its effects.

Feeling angry.   Though it is a distinct species of emotion, anger is 46 1 also something common to more than one emotion; not however a generic notion they all exemplify nor yet a cause they all have in common (the common root of all emotion is love), but an effect they all conspire to produce – for anger arises only when endurance of sorrow is combined with the desire and hope of avenging it. Understanding that some human 2 being is white is a more complex kind of understanding than simply grasping the meaning of each of the terms (humanity and whiteness) separately. We can distinguish in the same way simpler appetites such as desire and hope, pleasure and pain, concerned with good or evil as such, from more complex ones concerned with some good or evil happening to something. Love and hatred are sometimes complex in this way: we can love someone (as good) by willing good to him, or hate someone (as bad) by willing him evil. Anger is always complex in this way, and tends moreover to good and evil simultaneously: for it loves and desires avenging as a good to be enjoyed, requiring satisfaction from

3 an opponent or assailant that it confronts as evil. Both the good desired and the evil confronted present challenge and difficulty; so anger is an

4 aggressive emotion. Anger also involves reason [to recognize the injury done] and to recognize what will count as satisfaction for it, but that doesn't mean anger automatically submits to reason; it needs to be controlled by will. As Aristotle says, those who are so drunk they cannot reason don't get angry; the flare-ups come from those who are slightly

5 drunk, who can reason a little but not enough. Desire's objects (food and sex, especially) are more natural than anger's (satisfaction); and desire also accords more with our animal nature, which is seeking to survive. Anger is more a human phenomenon, since there is more of reason in it. As regards individuals, irascible temperaments are quicker

6 to anger than sensual dispositions are to desire. Hatred wills evil as such to its enemy, but anger wills an evil seen as just satisfaction (which could even be a virtuously just thing to do, if moderated by reason). So anger is not as serious as hatred. Anger incorporates measure into the evil it wills and so is more inclined to mercy than hatred, whose willing of evil knows no bounds. Though since anger is more impetuous it can in fact show less mercy; but then it will also pass more quickly, since it is aroused by a particular injury, whereas hatred is aroused by a disposition

7 to regard someone as an enemy. Animals also feel anger, but because of some natural instinct consequent on sense-perception, rather than because of reasoning. When we are angry with inanimate and non-reasoning objects we too feel that sort of anger; for anger based on reasoning can be angry only with those with whom one can be just or unjust. And so not with oneself, properly speaking.

47 2   The cause of anger is always some slight, regarded as unjust. We are especially outraged when we believe the injury to have been deliberate and done out of contempt; but if the injury was done in ignorance or

48 1 from passion we are more inclined to be forgiving. Anger is aroused by painful injury to which satisfaction offers a remedy. Before satisfaction is obtained we hope for it and dwell on the thought of it, and that already arouses pleasure, but not the perfect pleasure in satisfaction achieved,

2 which banishes the pain and quietens the anger. The physical changes that accompany an emotion are suited to that emotion. In the case of anger the heart is greatly upset, and that shows in our external behaviour: *the body trembles, the tongue stammers, the face and eyes blaze; familiar acquaintances pass unrecognized; the lips make sounds but we have no idea*

what we are saying. Angry men betray themselves not knowingly, but 3 because they can't hide things. Their reasoning is not free to know what should be concealed and how to go about it. Sensual desire is deceptive and insidious, since usually the pleasures craved have a certain shamefulness and softness about them that men want to hide; but satisfaction is manly, and men want to display it.

Chapter 8

LIVING WELL AND LIVING BADLY

Introductory comment. In this chapter Thomas considers the inner strength man needs for the journey of life he has just been discussing: for doing things well, for being a man, for becoming friends with God. Things that behave in fixed and predetermined patterns require no additional conditioning to behave well: they are born, so to speak, disposed and prepared for life by nature, mediated through their parents. But men, able to behave in more than one way, setting their own goals and choosing their own means of attaining them, need their bare ability to behave to be conditioned by **dispositions** strengthening them to behave well, need additional *virtue*. Such virtues strengthen man's adherence to his goal of a good life, disposing his desires to *regulation* by his reason which must determine in the light of his goal what in present circumstances is a good thing to do: a reason which must be strengthened in its turn for that regulating task by virtues of prudence and wisdom. What man has by nature is an inclination to goodness in general, but the best ways in which that can be realized among the particular goods of this life, man has to learn by practice. This practice is a self-parenting aided by the community in which we live, a way of naturalizing good choices so that we produce in ourselves those *second natures* of good choice which Thomas here calls dispositions or virtues.

We can of course naturalize bad choices instead, and these *second natures* are the vices. We judge the naturalizations good or bad by judging whether they help or hinder the practice of our natural inclination to goodness as such. **Virtue** is a disposition which strengthens our nature by inclining it to good use, by definition it is a disposition that cannot itself be misused. Here Thomas makes a distinction between dispositions which are virtues only in a qualified sense of the word: the virtues of logicality, for example, of knowledgeableness of various sorts, of artistry. These are virtues which dispose us to doing something well by its own rules, by the

dispositions/virtue

virtues dispose desire to
regulation by reason

+ reason must be
strengthened for its task of
regulating (prudence, wisdom)

focus on choices - good
or bad, he help or
hinder our practice of
our natural inclination
to goodness as such

virtues let help us
attain telos in
practice

rules of what fulfils the form of what we are doing, but they are not moral virtues and therefore not virtues in an unqualified sense. Virtues in an unqualified sense perfect not simply what is done but the human doing of it, ensuring that it was done according to the proper rules of choosing and deliberating and preserving a right respect for goodness as such. These are the moral virtues that put the balance of prudence into our reason, the balance of justice towards others into our will, and the balance of courage and moderation into our own interior emotional readiness to act. Because these virtues perfect not only what is done, but the human doing of it, they stand or fall together, are *connected* as Thomas puts it. They are all parts contributing to one integrity, the submission of a man's life to reason.

But this is only the first journey of life, the return of a man to his initial form, the fulfilment of his nature. God has invited us, as we saw in the last chapter, to a further journey, which will take us back to the agent of our form, our creator; we are invited to a life of friendship with our creator and an eternal life of happiness with him in the future. But this too requires dispositions, dispositions which now reach beyond our nature to the one who gave it, which naturalize in us (as a sort of second nature) his nature and life. The basic disposition here Thomas always calls grace-as-disposition and chapter 9 will examine it in more detail. That disposition upgrades our nature, so to speak, into a nature which shares a life with God, and so it is accompanied by corresponding upgradings of the abilities of our old nature – our mind and will – to share in the mind and will of God: the deiform (in Latin, theological) virtues of faith, hope and love. These virtues are virtues in quite a new mode, strengths in a different but analogical sense to our moral strengths; they join God and ourselves in friendship, they are our adhesion to our new nature as friends of God. But then, to accord our moral action to this new nature, as it was accorded by practice-acquired virtues to our old nature, there are what Thomas calls the God-infused or God-instilled moral virtues. All these virtues are, in their turn *connected*, they stand or fall together, all given with the grace of God's friendship, not acquired by practice: connected in the love of charity, as Thomas puts it. Acquired moral virtue is the virtue of reason realized in our living; grace and the deiform and instilled virtues are the virtue of God's friendship realized throughout our life.

virtue is · form of being - so is vice

Virtue however is a form of being: it disposes us to do well but is not itself the doing of good deeds. And vice is also a form of being: not a bad deed but a disposition to do them. However, one cannot help feeling the change in Thomas's treatment when he turns from considering virtue to considering vice: the treatment of virtue is a treatment of what man could and should *be*, but the treatment of vice actually becomes a treatment of sin and vice, of the bad things man actually *does*. In the discussion of virtues the focus of the analysis lies on discerning the *nature* of virtues (and vices), their kinds and their relationships. In the discussion of sin the emphasis lies on what *happens* when you do wrong (or do well), the disastrous or beneficial effects of such acts, the penalties and the rewards. This doubleness of focus is apparent in the *Summa* from this point onwards. The remainder of the chapter, together with chapter 9 on *Law and Grace* and the whole of part three on *Christ the road to God*, is dominated by the historical focus: what happened in Adam, in Israel, in Christ's life, and how does it affect our journey to God himself. The chapters after chapter 9 which deal with the deiform and moral virtues are exercises in analysis of actions and dispositions to action, their definitions and relationships.

but treatment of vice focuses on sin, bad deeds

old focus - from here on

historical focus vs analytic focus

The discussion of why men sin moves from one focus to the other. At first it is the internal factors involved in sinning that are discussed: bad disposition of will, failure of the faculties which present good to the will for its choice – ignorance in the mind, passion in the emotions. But then we move to discuss external causes of particular actions. Though God doesn't cause sin as such, without his creative power no man could perform any action, sinful action included. God then causes the action which is sinful but not the sinfulness of the action: God doesn't cause the defect in the will but his power enables us to use our will in that defective state, he leaves his causality in operation so to speak (for his own goals) even when the sinner's goal is out of order. The devil does not have any such power; he cannot operate within our wills, only entice them from the outside by manipulating the way we apprehend the world.

even in sin, God continues to operate in our wills

These considerations lead us to our second focus on sin. We return to the scriptural story of creation, uncreation and re-creation referred to in chapter 5 when the Genesis story of man's creation as gardener was told, and the state of integrity which God originally intended for man was described as *an integrated state of*

Adam in which his reason was submissive to God, his lower powers to his reason, and his body to his soul [pp 145–6]. Now we are told that this state of integrity was a quasi-natural accompaniment, so to speak, of human nature in the beginning, designed to be passed on to Adam's progeny as his nature was passed on, by the normal processes of reproduction. But Adam, in the garden, replaced his responsibility towards nature and God with a will to dominate and to master creation. For that he reaped a penalty: by failing his task of tilling and keeping all the trees of the garden, he lost the integrity accompanying his nature. As a result all Adam's sons inherit human nature in a natural state, not with its quasi-natural, original state of integrity. So far, as Thomas points out, this says only that Adam's progeny inherited a penalty for sin, not that the sin itself was inherited. The tradition however says that Adam's progeny not only suffered from the sin, but shared in its guilt! How is this possible? Thomas first makes the difficulty as clear as he can: there seems to be a logical contradiction between saying that something came about through inheritance (that is to say through the natural process of being born and coming into being) and saying that the recipient was *guilty* of it (that is to say had a will involved in the process). In his answer Thomas decides that in fact inheritance cannot be reconciled with *individual* responsibility, and that individually Adam's progeny are not guilty of any inherited sin; it can only be reconciled with a solidary responsibility dependent on a conception of men as all having one will in certain respects. The one will which Thomas identifies is the will of Adam reproducing a faulty nature, a will which runs through reproduced humanity, Thomas believes, like the will of a murderer runs through his whole body. So that the hand of the murderer justly dies along with his head and his heart, not because the hand itself willed the murder, but because the hand was a tool one-with-the-head, one-with-the-will in the willing doing of it. In the same way, Thomas seems to regard our very being in the world without the intended integrity of our nature as a way of being a tool of Adam's sin.

Nowadays, the doctrine of inherited or *original* sin is in disarray because the notion of a solidary will of mankind is in disarray. The biology which underlay Thomas's explanation (the will of Adam carried on through the male active partner in reproduction from generation to generation, and therefore exempting only he who was born without a male father) can no longer support it. What is required of theology today is that it should understand why the doctrine of inherited sin is there in the tradition: as complement of the notion that the only escape from the uncreation the world has suffered at man's hands comes through a single man untainted by responsibility for it, the single salvager of creation and head of a new mankind on his cross. It is the uniqueness of *his* innocence which leads to the doctrine of failed innocence of the whole of mankind without him, and to the doctrine that the only possible return to innocence lies in the whole of mankind uniting with him as head and will. It is my opinion that the core of the doctrine of original sin actually says something about how man is related to Calvary: by his very nature and birth into the world, it says, man is cast with a world that gave rise to Calvary and which Christ's resurrection has left behind, the world which St Paul says is decomposing around us. Only by some grace of love and faith can we reject the cast of that world, and join the company of the man (and God) who by undergoing Calvary accepted his own rejection, rose to a new life and started a new creation. By nature and task, man has a responsibility to be a united Adam, a mankind with one will of cooperation in creation, tilling and keeping the garden: it is that responsibility of unity that mankind has failed in its history of power politics, so that now it has lost all possibility of unity unless the only one who exercises authority through powerlessness and humility and love comes as a grace to take on the leadership of mankind.

Dispositions = habitus

[vol 22] 49 1 **What is a disposition?**   Dispositions, according to Aristotle, are *lasting qualities* or *conditions of things, good or bad, absolute or relative*: 2 health, for example. Technically, a quality is some way in which a substance exists. Matter exists under the form now of this substance, now of that; what differentiates this substance from that can be called its essential quality, and any supervening determinations of the way it exists its non-essential qualities. Such supervening determinations may relate the subject to its own essential nature [*type 1 qualities*], or to the activities [*type 2*] or passivities [*type 3*] that result from the form and matter making up its nature; or they may determine the subject in a quantitative way [*type 4*]. Since quantity as such need be neither good nor bad, nor changeable, it is irrelevant to a type 4 quality as such

[shape, etc] whether it suits or doesn't suit, or is transient or lasting. But type 2 and type 3 qualities enable things to act or be acted on [hard, soft, hot, cold, etc], so they can relevantly be described as susceptible or resistant to change; but not as good or bad, since these words describe something in relation to a goal, and change as such is never a goal. Type 1 qualities, however – those called dispositions and conditions – relate back to a thing's own nature, the goal for which it exists and comes to be; so such qualities are relevantly described as good when they suit the nature of the thing and bad when they don't, and also as susceptible or insusceptible to change, since natures are the goals of change. Shapes and the qualities that enable things to be acted on, when regarded as suitable or unsuitable, are being thought of as conditions or dispositions of a thing in relation to its nature: as part of its beauty or healthiness.

Dispositions enable us to act as and when we want. The goal for which 3 things come to be, their nature, is itself related to further goals: activity and whatever activity can achieve. So dispositions, because they relate directly to a thing's nature, relate also indirectly to its activity as goal of that nature, or as leading to its goal. And if the nature itself consists in a relation to action, then the disposition will relate to action directly. This is the case with dispositions of faculties, since faculties are simply abilities to act.

Dispositions are needed only if

- the subject to be disposed differs from the form or activity to which it is to be disposed, this form or activity realizing some potentiality of the subject;

- there is more than one way of realizing that potentiality;

- realization requires many factors which can combine in various ways to dispose the subject well or ill to the form or activity in question.

What a thing is is completely determined by its form and needs no further disposition; though the subject needed disposing to that form. But forms are further related to activity, as to a goal or means to a goal. When a form is determined to a single determinate activity it requires no further conditioning; but a form like the soul that can act in more than one way needs conditioning to activities by dispositions. So our natural powers [of growth, etc] act without need of disposition, since their nature already determines them to one way of performing. But when one and the same power can ⟨perform well or badly⟩ it needs dispositions to condition it to act well. *ye to suit its nature or not*

50 1 What sort of things need dispositions?   Bodies need no direct dispositions to activity: the activities of bodies in general are already fully determined by their physico–chemical properties, while the activities of living bodies are more properly activities of whatever soul enlivens them, so that what are primarily needed are dispositions of soul and only secondarily conditioning of the body to play its part in such activities easily. As regards dispositions to a form or nature, the body is disposed to the soul by conditions like health and beauty, but these are not dispositions in the full sense, since they depend on naturally transient causes. They can be lasting relative to more unstable conditions, and last as long as their subject lasts; but only qualities of soul are lasting, absolutely speaking, since only the soul is itself lasting.

2   The soul needs no disposition to adapt it to human nature since it is itself the form that makes us human; though in order that it may *share*, as St Peter puts it, *in the nature of God*, its natural substance must be further disposed by a disposition we call *grace*. But because of its many and various activities, the soul above all needs dispositions to activity, disposing its faculties or abilities to act. The supervening properties of a thing belong to it in a certain order; it must be understood to have one property, e.g. surface area, before it can have another, e.g. colour. And in the same way the soul must be presupposed to have faculties

3   before it can have dispositions of those faculties. Our natural powers, however, do not need dispositions; nor do our sense-powers need to be disposed to their natural instinctive activities, but only to respond well or badly to reasoned control of their exercise. Even dumb animals can be trained to respond to human reason and act this way or that, and so they must have dispositions of a sort; but not such as they can ⟨use or not use⟩ at will, which is part of the strict notion of *disposition*. In the area of cognition, sense-perception influences understanding, whereas in the area of appetite ⟨it is appetite aroused by understanding that influences appetite aroused by sense.⟩ So our powers of sense-appetite ⟨are more subject to dispositions than our powers of sense-perception. Reason does influence our *inner* powers of sense-perception, and there are ⟨dispositions that improve our memories and sense-judgments⟩ and imaginations, but our *outer* senses do as their nature dictates and are not subject to dispositions. In this they are like the limbs of our body, which are not themselves subject to dispositions, though there are

dispositions of the powers that control their movements.

According to Aristotle, the sciences, wisdom and our natural insight into first premises are all dispositions of mind. Dispositions are required in anything capable of realization in different ways, and this is above all true of our receptive mind. Just as physical matter is a capacity to take on the kinds of form we sense, so a receptive mind is a capacity to take in the kinds of form we understand; and so it can be subject to dispositions – qualities halfway between mere capacity and fully realized activity. *Justice*, on the other hand, according to Aristotle, *is a disposition to will and do the just thing.* Will, being an ability of reasoning creatures, can act in more than one way, and so needs to be disposed to act in good ways. Indeed the very notion of disposition seems to relate primarily to will, since it is what enables us to act at will. Whereas mind reflects its objects, will (like all powers of appetite) inclines towards its objects. Towards objects to which it is inclined enough by nature it needs no further supervening inclination; but since the goal of human life requires us to incline our will towards specific goals to which we are not determinately inclined by the will's natural capacity for many ways of acting, supervening dispositions are needed to incline will and our other appetitive powers. The will inclines naturally towards whatever reason declares good; but since many different things are good in this way, the will needs dispositions to incline it to more ready pursuit of determinate goods proposed by reason.

The human mind is the least powerful of minds, a mere ability to take in any form that can be understood; just as physical matter can take on any form that can be sensed. Angelic minds, however, are not mere abilities, but are informed with actual understanding by nature. An angel has actual understanding of everything like to itself: itself to begin with, and others to the degree it resembles them. But this only finitely realizes its ability to know, so angels too must be further disposed by mental likenesses to a proper understanding of things. Angels however have no bodies, so don't need disposing to their own natures.

How do dispositions arise? Some things are natural to whole 51 1 species, as laughter is to human beings, some only to certain individuals, as health. Moreover, what is natural may result wholly from nature, or from nature cooperating with an external agent (e.g. medicine). The disposition of the human body to its human form or soul is natural in all four of these ways. But the dispositions of our faculties to activity – though they can (if they dispose the soul) be natural to the whole species and (if they dispose the body) be natural to individuals only – never wholly result from nature (as they do in angels endowed with innate mental representations), but need something more than nature to complete them. In the whole human species, for example, there is an inchoate natural disposition to know truth, called the *understanding of first principles*: given the knowledge of whole and part, nature disposes us to know immediately that a whole is greater than any of its parts. But the knowledge of whole and part has to be abstracted from sense-images derived from sense-perception. There are also inchoate dispositions natural to particular individuals, which depend on the condition of the individual's sense organs, and allow one individual to understand better than another. With regard to the desiring of good the situation is not quite the same. Here the human species needs no inchoate natural disposition, since the faculty of appetite is of its own nature an inclination to its appropriate object; but it does need particular *premises of virtue* such as principles of common rights. Again, certain inchoate dispositions to virtues like chastity or mildness are natural to particular individuals because of particular bodily constitutions. The example of angels illustrates why even [natural] abilities sometimes need completion by further [natural] dispositions. Things are known by likenesses reflecting them in the mind; and for angels to know everything through their own knowing ability would mean that the ability itself would have to be a likeness of everything. Since only God can be this, angels' natural abilities to know must be supplemented by some natural sharing in God's wisdom.

2   Were an agent only active in its activity, that activity would generate no dispositions in the agent; but certain agents (men, for example) are also passive to their activities. When we are actively exercising our ability to desire, that ability is itself being acted on by our perception of objects; and when we actively reason to conclusions, our ability to know is being influenced by our knowledge of some self-evident premise. Repeated activity develops dispositions in abilities that are, so to speak, passively active: our ability to desire develops moral virtues under the influence of reason, our mind develops sciences under the influence of first premises. Reason, however, cannot totally master our ability to desire by a single action; for in such an action it judges only what is desirable for some particular reason in some particular circumstances; whereas a disposition to virtue must so master our ability to desire that it tends in practically all circumstances and as if naturally to a single goal. But when we turn to our cognitive abilities, our receptive mind can be lastingly convinced of the truth of a conclusion by a single application of a self-evident premise, though not if the premise is merely

probable. So though the disposition called belief requires repeated arguments, a single act of reasoning can produce the disposition we call scientific knowledge. Repeated action is also necessary to imprint something firmly on lesser cognitive faculties like the memory. As for bodily dispositions, they can occasionally be produced instantaneously by a single powerful action: health, for example, by a potent drug.

Some dispositions are instilled into men by God: firstly, those grace-given virtues that dispose men to a goal of perfect happiness beyond their natural human powers, and of which God is the only possible source. But secondly also, God displays his power by instilling dispositions which a man would naturally, though less perfectly, acquire by study and habit, like the apostles' knowledge of scripture and languages. Repeated action deriving from such instilled dispositions will strengthen those dispositions but not cause new acquired dispositions, just as medicine taken by a healthy man won't give him a second healthiness.

More sometimes means bigger, sometimes better, as Augustine said. 52 1 Forms can be more or less perfect: sometimes by being more or less what they are, sometimes by being more or less present in their subjects. Difference of degree generates difference of kind only when there are hard and fast distinctions or discontinuities between the degrees; for *kinds are like numbers*, as Aristotle says: add or take away and you get a different kind. As regards a form itself then: if what decides its kind is internal to it then it cannot vary in degree without varying its kind [whiteness can't be more or less whiteness]; but if its kind is externally decided, it can vary in degree and yet retain its kind by retaining its relation to the hard and fast outside criterion (as movements to one destination can vary in intensity). As regards the presence of a form in a subject: this can vary in degree unless the form determines the subject's kind (as is the case with substances), or involves discontinuity by definition (as with numbers or geometrical figures). [Things can be more or less white.] Now dispositions and conditions are specified by reference to something else than themselves; so they can vary in degree within themselves (knowledge can be more or less extensive), and also in their degree of presence in their subject (equally extensive knowledge can be better rooted in one whom nature or habit has made more apt for it). For dispositions and conditions neither decide their subject's kind, nor involve discontinuity by definition. So knowledge can increase by 2 increments – a geometer's disposition to know geometry grows every time he proves a fresh conclusion – or it can increase in intensity – in the swiftness and sureness with which the geometer can make use of one and the same conclusion. Notice that a man who has a disposition 3 is free not to exercise it, and can even act contrary to it, or act less strongly than his disposition enables him to. Actions of strength equal to or greater than a disposition tend to strengthen it; acting less strongly will tend to weaken it.

53 1   A form may be destroyed directly by its opposite, or indirectly by destroying its subject. A disposition like knowledge can't be indirectly destroyed by destroying its primary subject, since minds as such are indestructible, but it can be indirectly destroyed by destroying its secondary subjects, our powers of sense-perception. Can it be directly destroyed? The mental likenesses of things received into our mind have no opposites as such; nor has the agent mind that produces them. So a disposition caused in our receptive mind by direct action of our agent mind (such as knowledge of the first premises of all theoretical and practical science) is totally indestructible by any forgetfulness or error. But a disposition caused in our receptive mind by reasoned argument (such as a science) can be displaced by acceptance of false premises or invalid arguments. As regards virtues: prudence disposes our reason and the above account holds, but the moral virtues dispose our will and appetites to follow reason, and can be destroyed by contrary judgments based on ignorance or passion or deliberate bad choice. Bodily changes cannot radically destroy knowledge but only stop its exercise; but change

3 of mind can destroy it radically, and virtue as well. Failure to exercise dispositions will also weaken or destroy them, since now there is nothing to counteract causes tending to break them down. If you don't use virtue to bring order into your feelings and actions, many disordered feelings and actions will arise from sense-appetites and external pressures, and virtue will weaken and die. And similarly if you don't use your mental dispositions, irrelevant and misleading images spring to mind which, if not cut down and kept in check, will weaken your skill in making right judgments. Time can't affect the mind in itself, but it affects the ability of the senses both to desire and to perceive. *In time*, as Aristotle says, *we lose our memories.*

54 1   Varieties of disposition.   A variety of dispositions can adapt a thing to its nature, because of its many parts: the human body can be healthy in its humours, strong in bone and muscle, beautiful in feature and limb. Similarly passive abilities acted on by more than one object can have more than one disposition disposing them to actions of more than one kind. Generic differences of object will define different abilities, but specific differences of object will define the different actions abilities enable, and thus possible different dispositions. A body can't have more

than one shape at once, because shape, so to speak, finishes a body off; but it is actions and not dispositions that *finish off* our ability to act. So no ability will enable us to do more than one thing at once: our mind can't think two thoughts at the same time, but it can be disposed to know more than one thing.

Dispositions sometimes differ in kind because the agents producing 2 them differ, and sometimes because they dispose towards different natures or to activities specified by different objects. But the objects must differ not simply materially, but formally: in the way they are objects. Astronomers connect earth and roundness by a mathematical link – the shape of eclipses – whilst natural philosophers make the link by arguing from the way heavy things are drawn in to a centre. These different links are like different agents producing different sciences, and in the same way different goals generate different virtues, just as different objects arouse different acts of will. Dispositions may suit nature or 3 conflict with it, and this differentiates them as good or bad in kind. They may also dispose us to act according to different natures, humanly, for example, or divinely. But though some dispositions are good and some bad, all deal with good and bad objects. Nor are dispositions distinguished by what is good or bad in the broadest sense of those terms, as coterminous with existing or lacking existence; but by what is good or evil in relation to some particular nature. More than one good disposition can relate to the same object by according with different natures; and more than one bad by conflicting with nature in different ways.

Virtue

What is virtue?   The word *virtue* [literally, *strength* or *force*] names [vol 23] 55 1 a certain fullness of ability, measured by a perfect fitness to act. Natural agencies possess such fitness for specific actions by nature, and are sometimes themselves called *forces* or *virtues*. But our peculiarly human ability to act according to reason is non-specific, and needs further specification by dispositions fitting us for specific acts. Human strength and virtue lies in such dispositions. *The strength or virtue of a power*, said Aristotle, *is the utmost it can do*, e.g. lift a hundred pounds. Here the word *strength* or *virtue* has been shifted from naming a disposition to naming its object or act. Compare the way *faith* means sometimes what we believe, sometimes the act of believing, and sometimes the disposition to believe; or Augustine's descriptions of virtue as *the good use of our freedom to choose* and *an orderedness of love*.

2   Ability can mean either the ability of some material to *be* something, its potential to be formed; or the ability of something already formed to *do* something, its power. Now the body of a man is material, formed and made human by his soul. His abilities of body, or of body and soul together, are shared with other animals; and it is the abilities of his soul as such which are peculiarly human, and subject to human virtue. Human virtue then is not a disposition to be but a disposition to do. Because virtue is a sort of fitness, one can compare it to health and beauty as Cicero did, fitness of soul to fitnesses of body. But this fitness of soul is an ordering and disposing of its abilities to cooperate in

3   external activity, in doing things. A thing's strength is measured by the utmost of which it is capable; so, because all evil is a falling short and a weakness, virtue must be, as Aristotle said, a disposition *rendering its possessor and his activity good.*

4   We are now ready to comment the traditional definition of virtues as *good qualities of soul disposing us to live rightly, which we cannot misuse, and which God works in us without our help.* This definition collects together the material subject to which virtue gives a form, the kind of form it gives that material, the purpose it serves and its agent cause. The form is defined generically as a *quality* (though disposition would be more precise) and more specifically as a *good quality.* The subject formed is the *soul.* (The subject with which virtue is concerned is not mentioned, for that is its object and defines it as a particular type of virtue.) The purpose is always good action. So to distinguish virtues from vices – which always dispose to bad action – the definition says they *dispose us to live rightly;* and to distinguish them from dispositions which incline us either to good or to evil, it says they *cannot be misused.* As to agency we are given the cause of instilled virtue, namely God. But if this phrase is left out, the rest of the definition would apply generally to all virtue, acquired or instilled. Whiteness is not itself white; but goodness is itself good, since just to exist is a good. So, though forms and qualities do not possess existence in the sense substances do, but exist only as ways in which substances exist, virtues are called good because they make men good; and not merely good by existing, but good by according with reason. The rightness of justice is concerned specifically with lawful rights and duties in the common use of external goods; but there is a general meaning of right living common to all virtues: namely, pursuing due goals and letting the law of God rule our wills. Instilled virtue *God works in us without our help* (though not without our consent); but our own work God works in us with our help, since he is at work within every will and every nature.

Activities which differ generically in their object define different abilities, and activities which differ in species define different dispositions. So different abilities require different dispositions. Dispositions in one ability can however be regarded as effects (or conditions) of dispositions in another, if the second ability controls (or is controlled by) the first. Thus moral virtues, which dispose our appetites to act in accordance with reason, presuppose knowledge; and prudence, which disposes reason to issue good commands, presupposes some initial rightness of will.

Virtues then are dispositions to act well. Now some dispositions enable us to do a thing correctly without determining how that ability should be used. Knowledge is an example, and arts like the art of grammar which grammarians may if they like misuse. But some dispositions enable us not only to do a thing correctly but to use that ability rightly: e.g. justice not only makes us ready in will to do the just thing, but helps us to a just doing of it. Such dispositions incline us to act well and be good in the straightforward sense of those words, and can be called virtues without qualification. But the first type of disposition makes us act well only in the sense of providing the facility for us to do so, and makes us good only in a qualified sense: a good grammarian or a good carpenter. For this reason knowledge and arts or crafts are often distinguished from virtues, though sometimes they receive that name. Clearly virtues in this qualified sense dispose our minds to engage in practical or even purely speculative thought, without relation to willing anything. But unqualified virtues dispose our will or our other powers precisely as controlled by our will. For all our reasoning powers are controlled by will, and any actual doing of good depends on good will. So there are dispositions of mind as controlled by will that are unqualified virtues: faith disposing our speculative mind to assent under the will's influence (for we choose what we put our faith in), and prudence disposing our practical mind. For by prudence I mean a disposition of reason to plan, judge and command right action. It presupposes that a man is well disposed to his goals – the premises of his action – by a right will, and disposes his mind to follow such a will when reasoning about practical matters. Compare the way science in a man's receptive mind presupposes a natural disposition to the premises of thought in his agent mind, and disposes the mind to follow this natural light when reasoning theoretically.

Our aggressive and affective urges are subject to virtue not precisely as sense-urges, but as powers amenable to reason. For if actions proceeding from one power under the control of another are to be perfect, then both powers must be well disposed to the action. In the case of a power that acts because it is acted on, this means conforming to the power that acts on it; so the virtues disposing our powers of aggressive and affective emotion dispose them to conform to reason. Moral virtue is primarily a disposition to choose well, which involves intending a goal (the role of the moral virtue) and picking out the means (the role of prudence). When the emotions are in question, the intending of the goal needs a disposition to good in our aggressive and affective urges. So the moral virtues concerned with emotion must dispose those urges, while 5 prudence disposes our reason. The training of memory and the other powers of sense is not so much a disposition as an accompaniment of mental dispositions; and certainly not a virtue, since virtues reside in our abilities to bring actions to completion, and knowledge of truth is achieved in mind or reason and only prepared for in sense-perception. Will, the urge of reason, moves our sense-urges to act, the action being achieved in the sense-powers; so those powers must be subject to virtue. But our powers of sense-perception rather move our mind, since images affect the mind like colour affects sight; so the act of knowing is achieved 6 in the mind, and cognitive virtues must rather be there. Will, by definition, is an inclination to follow what reason proposes as good and 7 proportioned to the person willing, and no virtue is required for the will to follow that. Only if the good proposed escapes this proportion to us, either because like God's good it transcends the limits of human nature as such, or because like our fellowman's good it transcends the individual, does the will require disposing to it by virtue. So there are virtues disposing the will towards love of God and fellowman: charity, justice and the like. And there are virtues like moderation and courage which temper the emotions to serve the good of the willer himself, to which his will is inclined by nature.

57 1 **Mental virtues – speculative and practical.** Speculative dispositions of mind can be called virtues in the sense that they help us think truly, but not in the sense that they help us make good use of our thinking. The virtues which do this are dispositions of will like charity 2 and justice. Some truths are self-evident and serve as immediately understood premises of further understanding; to the perception of such truths we are disposed by an insight into first principles that we have naturally, whilst other truths are made evident because reasoning from such premises concludes to them. The whole of human knowledge ultimately concludes to the first causes of everything that can be known, and the disposition to know such ultimate causes and thus be able to

pass ultimate judgments on everything we call wisdom; but dispositions to conclude to truths in this or that area of reality we call sciences. There are many sciences dealing with different areas of reality, but only one wisdom. Structurally wisdom is itself a science, drawing conclusions from premises; but what is peculiar to wisdom is its power to judge about everything, including its own premises. So it is a more perfect virtue than science. Insight into principles, the sciences and wisdom are not independent and equal virtues, so to speak, but parts making an ordered contribution to a virtual whole: just as the powers of reason and sense and the vegetative powers do in man. The sciences presuppose insight into first principles, and both are subordinate to wisdom as judge. Belief and surmise, which can be either true or false, are not mental virtues at all.

Arts and crafts are practical dispositions of mind, disposing us to 3 make things as reason thinks right, the aim being to make a work of art good in itself, but not to make the human willing of it good. So art shares with speculative dispositions of mind a concern with how things are in themselves, independently of the way we want them. Both sorts of disposition enable us to do a good piece of work, but not to make good use of it: for this we need virtues to perfect the way we want. Good use will presuppose art; but the craftsman's will to make things with fidelity is an effect of justice. Even speculative thinking makes things: it constructs well-formed statements and arguments, and makes correct measurements. So it requires dispositions which have been called liberal arts, in contrast with our bodily crafts which might be called service arts.

Prudence disposes us not only to do a good piece of work, but to 4 make good use of it: it relates to wanting and presupposes right wanting. Whereas arts and crafts dispose us to make things as reason thinks right, prudence disposes us to do things rightly. Making is acting on some external matter (building, cutting, etc), whereas doing (in this context) is an activation of the agent (seeing, willing, etc). So arts and crafts relate to external production, but prudence relates to man's using of his own powers and dispositions, and disposes him to plan and decide well. In doing goals have the role premises have in thinking; so prudence requires men to be well-disposed to goals, to want rightly. In other words, it presupposes moral virtue, which art does not. Notice that craftsmen who break the rules of their craft deliberately are more esteemed than those who do so unwittingly; whereas in matters of prudence doing something bad deliberately is worse than doing it unwittingly. Both crafts and prudence differ from speculative thought in dealing with contingent reality; but crafts and speculative thought differ from prudence in the way they are virtues. You can talk of generals or pilots as prudent, if they plan well in military or nautical matters; but they aren't prudent without qualification, as is the man who plans living well.

5   Living well is not only doing good things but doing them well, choosing them in a right way and not simply acting on impulse or emotion. Right choosing involves having a right goal and suitably acting to achieve that goal. The dispositions to right goals are the moral virtues in the appetites; the disposition to act suitably to achieve the goal must dispose reason to plan and decide well, and that is the virtue of prudence. Doing something good on another's advice rather than one's own judgment is not yet perfect activity of one's own reasoning and desiring. One does the good but not altogether well, as living well requires. Thinking speculatively seeks the true match of mind to things, which only happens perfectly with necessary truths. But thinking practically seeks the true match to right appetite, and that can only happen in such non-necessary matters as we have power to influence: our own inner activities or external work. So the only virtues concerned with contingent matters are dispositions of practical thought: art for making, prudence for doing.

6 In the case of doing, man's practical reasoning makes plans and decisions just as his speculative reasoning explores and arrives at conclusions, but then goes on to issue commands to do things, and that is its special role. If men made good decisions and then didn't implement them properly, reason's work would be incomplete.

58 1 **Moral virtues.**   *Mores* are customs or the *second natures* that customs breed; and in the latter sense we call certain virtues moral. Moral virtues strengthen our inclinations or appetites, the motive powers of our 2 actions. All such powers of action are amenable to reason, some obeying without demur as do healthy members of the body. And if all our powers obeyed reason in this way we would need virtue only to strengthen reason itself. This is what Socrates believed, equating virtue with prudence and evildoing with ignorance. But our appetites do not always obey reason wihout demur; sometimes our emotions and appetitive dispositions hamper reason's application in particular cases. What Socrates said is thus only half true: men don't do evil knowingly, but only because their reason is misled in the particular act of choice. So for men to behave well not only must their reasons be strengthened by mental virtues, but their appetites too by moral virtues. Appetites are able to cause *human* behaviour only by sharing in reason, and moral virtues are precisely

human virtues because they accord with reason. Moral virtue then is a disposition to choose a balanced course of action such as a prudent man's reason would decide is right. The rightness of reason is prudence, not moral virtue, but it is communicated to moral virtue by prudence inasmuch as prudence directs the moral virtues. Prudence is a mental virtue, but because it is concerned with regulating behaviour by reason, it has the same matter as the moral virtues. Discipline and self-control strengthen the mind to resist being misled by disorderly emotions; but they are not virtues. For mental virtue presupposes right appetites for goals as premises of its practical reasoning; and these are missing in a merely disciplined man. His emotions are precisely not well disposed *in themselves*, so however well disposed his reason is it cannot produce a perfected act, and the disposition in reason is no virtue.

Moral virtues are dispositions to make good choices. Good choices require our appetites to be disposed to a goal in accordance with reason, and right choice of means to that goal, planned, decided and commanded by prudent reason. So moral virtue cannot exist without prudence and understanding. Natural tendencies require no choices or reasoning, but the inclinations of moral virtues involve choice and presuppose a reason strengthened by mental virtue. Natural inclinations to the goals of the virtues are only the beginning of virtue, not its achieved fullness. And the stronger such inclinations the more perilous they are unless controlled by reason making right choices of means to the desired goals. A blind horse does itself more harm the faster it gallops. So although Socrates is wrong to equate moral virtue with right reasoning, virtue is not (as Plato thought) merely inclination in accord with right reasoning, but inclination and right reasoning in cooperation, as Aristotle said. Reasoning about particular matters needs both general and particular premises. The former are guaranteed by natural insight into first principles (e.g. that evil is not to be done) or by practical science; but since in particular cases emotions can obscure the application of these general premises, we need dispositions that will stick to particular premises of action (namely goals) and make right judgments about these goals by second nature. This is what moral virtues do, so prudence needs moral virtues. Art doesn't require such strengthening of appetite, since art's principles are not judged differently by reason because of momentary appetite, as moral premises and goals of action can be.

Virtues are not emotions. Emotions are movements of appetite, virtues dispositions of appetite towards movement. Moreover emotions can be good or bad, reasonable or unreasonable; whereas virtues dispose us only to good. Emotions arise in the appetite and are brought into conformity with reason; virtues are effects of reason achieving themselves in reasonable movement of the appetites. Balanced emotions are virtue's

3 effect, not its substance. The Stoics said that wise men felt no sorrow for no evil could befall them: the only evil they recognized was lack of virtue. But that is unreasonable: man is body and soul and whatever keeps his body alive is good for a man, even if, because it can be misused, it is not his greatest good. And in any case, even virtuous men cannot live without any faults, past if not present; and do well to be sad not only at their own but at others' sins. So sadness is compatible with virtue (just as other balanced emotions are); indeed it is a virtue to be sad about what there is to be sad about, and such sadness has a function in avoiding evil. Virtues arouse delight and quell sadness about what accords with virtue, but arouse sadness about what is at odds with virtue.

4 It is the job of reason to put order into the emotions we feel as well as into the activities we will; so some virtues are concerned with emotions and some with activity.

60 1 **The variety of moral virtues.** There are different kinds of virtue depending on how the objects of our appetites need the control of reason.

2 Certain actions are good or bad in themselves, irrespective of the emotions we deploy in doing them, because they are measured relative to other people. Activities like buying and selling raise the question of what is due to others, and require a virtue of their own (justice) to control this. The measure of good and bad in other activities however relates to the doer, and depends on whether his emotional attitude to the activities is good or bad; so here virtue is chiefly concerned with

3 controlling the emotions (as in moderation and courage). All moral virtues concerned with activity as such can be grouped generally under justice, concerned with whatever can be owed to others. But there are many different sorts of debt: to equals, superiors, inferiors, and owed by contract, by promise or in gratitude. So diverse virtues exist: religion for repaying God, loyalty to family and country, gratitude to benefactors, and so on. One of these special virtues is justice in the strict sense, concerned with debts strictly repayable by a measure of equivalence. There is also a justice that aims at the common good, different from the justice that safeguards individuals' private goods. This communal justice embraces everything under its command, since all virtuous behaviour must serve the general good. So virtues commanded by such communal or legal justice are themselves justice, differing from legal justice only because of the two aspects under which they can be considered: either as operating in areas of their own, or as obeying the commands of justice.

Nor is there only one moral virtue concerned with emotions: since 4
our capacity for aggressive emotion differs from our capacity for affection. Not that every emotion has its own virtue. Antithetic emotions
pertain to one and the same virtue which sets up a balance between them.
Moreover, different emotions are sometimes sequentially ordered to the
same goals: among the affections, for example, love, desire and pleasure
all pursue good, and hatred, disgust and sadness all avoid evil. The
aggressive emotions are also grouped: boldness and fear face great
dangers, hope and despair challenging goods, and anger any harmful
opposition. So we have different virtues: moderation controls all affections, courage controls fear and boldness, enterprise hope and despair,
and mildness anger. Relation to reason differentiates virtue, whereas 5
relation to appetite differentiates emotion. The goods men love, desire
and delight in can be perceived either by the senses or only by the mind,
and can be good for man in himself (body or soul) or in relation to
others. All these differences may cause different virtues. Thus goods
delighting the touch and necessary for the survival of both individuals
and the species (food and sex) require the virtue of moderation. The
pleasures of the other senses are not so violent and present less difficulty
to reason, so do not require virtue in the same way (for virtue is
like craft, as Aristotle says, designed to deal with difficulties). Goods
perceptible only to reason and good for man in himself – money for his
bodily needs, and honours for his soul – divide (as goods of touch do
not) into those that merely attract affection and those that challenge our
aggressive emotions. Money requires both generosity to moderate our
affection for it, and munificence to deal with challenging projects; and
honours require reasonable ambition and enterprise. Goods that relate
to others don't generate challenge in this way, but some virtues are
required for achievements of serious goals (friendliness and sincerity in
both word and deed); and others are for fun and pleasure only (being
good company). Add justice, concerned with activity as such, and we
have eleven virtues distinguished.

Four of these are regarded as [hinge or] cardinal virtues, introducing 6 1 2
reason into our behaviour: prudence by perfecting reason itself, justice
by introducing reason into the willing of our activity as such; moderation
by introducing restraint into our affections, courage by supporting our
aggressive emotions. All other virtues are ordered among themselves
and reduce to these main ones by faculty and object. Many writers treat 3
the four cardinal virtues simply as general groups of virtues: grouping
all virtues of reason under prudence, all virtues concerned with external
dealings under justice, all restraint of affection under moderation and

all support of aggressive emotion under courage. But notice that the principal role of practical reason is commanding action rather than planning or deciding on it; that the principal activity in which rights and dues are found is exchange and distribution of goods according to exact equivalence; that restraint of disordered affections is particularly difficult where pleasures of touch are concerned; and that facing up to fear is particularly needed when in danger of death. So one can regard as cardinal those special virtues which deal with these primary subject-matters: prudence being the virtue of command, justice of equivalent dues, moderation of restraint in touch and courage of facing up to death.

4 Yet another point of view thinks of justice, courage and moderation as general conditions of all virtue whatsoever, since as dispositions all virtues must be resistant to change (*courageous*), and, as virtues, must pursue what is right (*just*), and be measured by reason (*moderate*). 5 Another name for these virtues is the political or social virtues: they govern our natural human life, and we are by nature social or political animals.

62 1   Beyond the human happiness attainable by and proportionate to man's nature, there lies another attainable only by God's power and by sharing God's nature. To achieve this more than natural happiness we need God to give us the kind of start towards it, that our nature gives us towards human happiness. This start we call the theological or deiform virtues, directed to God, instilled by God, and revealed by God in the scriptures. They dispose us to a nature shared with God. Reason and will relate us naturally to God as beginning and end of our nature, but not to him as the object of a happiness out of proportion to our 2 natures. The object of these virtues then is God himself as exceeding 3 all natural knowledge. And to relate us to God in this way we need a virtue to strengthen our minds with truths that God alone sees, but we take on faith. And our wills must move to him as to a goal we can hope to achieve, and cleave to him in that conformity we call love. Faith and hope are words implying imperfection, since faith believes what it does not see, and hope moves towards something it does not possess. So faith and hope in what we could humanly see and possess would fall short of virtue. But having faith and hope in something beyond our human 4 power exceeds all human virtue. As activities faith precedes hope and hope charity; though as dispositions they are all instilled together. For we can only pursue what we perceive, and only come to love people we trust. But charity is more perfect than faith and hope which, without charity, are not perfect. So charity is the mother and root of all virtue. What we hope for must first be loved; but the source from which we

hope for it comes to be loved only later; and then this later love strengthens the former hope.

The beginnings of all virtue other than deiform virtue are native to 63 1 human beings; inasmuch as man's mind naturally knows certain premises of science and behaviour, and his will naturally inclines to what his mind judges good. Moreover, individuals have bodies naturally disposed or indisposed to certain virtues, since our bodily condition affects our sensory organs and our sensing affects our mental powers. Fully achieved virtue, however, is not innate. Nature's ways of doing things are fixed and determined, whereas virtues must react with flexibility to different matters and according to circumstances. Virtues incline us to what is 2 good for us, and if the standard of good is human judgment then virtue can be caused in us by human acts proceeding from reason; but if the standard is God's law then they can only be caused by an activity of God within us. Such divinely instilled virtue cannot co-exist with mortal or fatal sin (for reasons given later), but humanly acquired virtues can. For such virtues are dispositions which we can exercise or not at will; and you can't destroy an acquired disposition with a single opposed act – you have to build up an opposed disposition to do that. The human activity by which we cause virtue in ourselves depends in its turn on beginnings of virtue present in us by nature. Natural insight into the premises of sciences provides the power to generate knowledge of their conclusions, and the natural rightness of reason provides the power for the moral virtues' rightness of appetite derived from it. But to start us 3 to our supernatural goal we receive from God not natural beginnings but theological virtues; and just as the natural beginnings of human virtue are filled out with acquired moral and mental virtues, so too God instils in us dispositions filling out the deiform virtues. The deiform virtues are sufficient to begin our relationship to a supernatural goal, since they link us immediately to God himself; but then the soul must be perfected by other instilled virtues which relate to all other things as ordered to God. The standards set by human reason and divine law are 4 different, e.g. in moderation of pleasure in food. Human reason commands us not to harm our health or hinder our reasoning powers; whereas divine law requires us to *chasten our body and make it our servant*, by abstaining from food and drink. Instilled moral virtue aims at making us good *fellow-citizens with the saints and members of God's household*; whereas the acquired moral virtues aim at good human order. If God was merely causing miraculously the same virtues we usually have to acquire, we would not distinguish a special group of instilled virtues.

64 1   Evil results from over-doing or under-doing the measure good matches up to. The match lies in the middle, between over-doing and under-doing, so moral virtue aims at striking a balance or mean. This is a relative matter. Though the virtue of munificence deals with sums which are large in absolute terms, they must be moderate or balanced in relation to the circumstances, being what reason considers right for the place, the time and the purpose. And though virginity abstains from all sex, and poverty rejects all possessions, such abstinence must exist in balance with God's law and the needs of everlasting life. Otherwise

2   it would be illicit, superstitious and vainglorious. The virtuous balance is a balance of reason. But in justice's case it is also an objective balance between things. For justice is concerned with dealings in external goods, and requires us to give people what we owe them, neither more nor less. The other moral virtues concern our own inner emotions where there is no objective mean (people differ in emotional temperament), and

3   reason must take into account who we are and how emotional. Mental virtues also observe a balance inasmuch as they observe a measure or standard. The standard in theoretical matters is absolute truth, in practical matters true conformity to right will. Now absolute truth is itself subject to a standard: things themselves; so when theorizing our mind must achieve a balance with things, saying that what is so is so, and what is not is not. (Over-doing would be falsely affirming something, under-doing falsely denying.) But when our mind is busy controlling our behaviour, the truth of the mind (measured by reality) acts as a standard for our appetites; and balance, present in prudence as setting standards, is present in the moral virtues as submission to them. For

4   deiform virtues the standard is God himself: his truth sets the standard for our faith, his goodness for our love, and his almighty power and loving-kindness for our hope. Such a standard is way beyond our powers; never can we love God as much as he deserves or believe and hope in him as much as we ought. So here there is no question of striking a mean, but of reaching for a summit. However, another standard on our side does measure deiform virtue. Though we can't reach to God as much as his condition allows, we must reach to him by believing in him, hoping in him and loving him to the measure of our condition. This secondary standard sets up a mean between extremes. From our side hope is a mean between the extremes of presuming from God more than we need or despairing of receiving even what we do need; but on God's side there are no limits since his goodness is infinite. And in the same way faith strikes a mean between opposing heresies from our side, though on his we cannot believe in him too much.

Our initial inclinations to act in accordance with the various virtues 65 1
come from nature or habit and are all unconnected and independent:
our natural temperament and customs may incline us to generosity
without necessarily inclining us to chastity. But achieved moral virtues,
the dispositions to do good deeds well, are all connected and mutually
dependent. For we can't possess moral virtue without being prudent:
since moral virtues are dispositions to make right choices, and that
requires us not only to aim at the right goal, but get the means to that
goal correct by prudent planning, decisions and commands. Prudence,
in return, requires the moral virtues: correct reasoning about the means
to be chosen must start from the goal to be achieved, and to that we are
rightly disposed by moral virtues. A man practised in restraining his
anger but not his pleasure possesses a disposition indeed but not a virtue,
since prudence is lacking in him where pleasure is concerned. Though
sometimes it is only the opportunity that is missing: a man practised in
generosity with small gifts and expenditures, may quickly acquire a
munificent disposition if he comes into money (we can be said to possess
what we can easily acquire). Mental virtues like arts and sciences are
independent, because they deal with disparate fields; but moral virtues
deal with emotions and activity which are all parts of the one subject-
matter of prudence. Not only that, but moral virtues provide prudence
with its goals or premises. Now reason can be right in one subject area
yet wrong in another (as happens in the arts and sciences), but would
be defective if it were wrong about even a single premise.

The moral virtues that dispose us to act well in relation to naturally 2
attainable goals can be acquired by human activity without need of
charity (and are by many pagans). But the moral virtues that dispose us
to act well in relation to our ultimate and supernatural goal cannot be
so acquired and must be instilled by God; such virtues are inseparable
from charity. Prudence's own right reasoning depends much more on
being well adapted to our ultimate goal by charity, than to other goals
by the moral virtues. So instilled prudence needs charity, and so in
consequence do all the moral virtues that depend on prudence. These
instilled virtues are the only ones that are virtues without qualification,
aiming at a goal ultimate without qualification. Others are virtues in a
qualified sense only, aiming at goals ultimate in a certain field. In the 3
world of nature God organizes animal bodies to fit their form of life; in the
same way in the world of grace he instils together with charity, which
aims us at our ultimate goal, all the moral virtues required to live towards
that goal. Not everyone who does the just thing has the achieved virtue 4
of justice, but only those who do it well, choosing what to do prudently.

In the same way not everyone who willingly believes has perfect faith, but only the person who wills with the love of charity; and not everyone who hopes for happiness from God has perfect hope, but only the person who actually deserves to receive it through his love of charity. Instilled moral virtues depend on instilled prudence, which can only exist if charity relates it to its ultimate goal; but faith and hope relate to God of themselves without prudence or charity, though without charity they

5 are not virtues. Charity, on the other hand, cannot exist without faith and hope. For charity is not just any love of God but friendship with him, and that implies mutual love and sharing. This companionship of men with God is a familiar intercourse with him starting through grace in the present life and achieved in glory in the life to come; as we believe and hope. Just as one can't be friends with a man without believing or hoping oneself able to be his companion in such familiar intercourse, so too with God: charity needs faith and hope to exist at all. Charity loves God as object of that eternal happiness in which we believe and for which we hope; so though it is the root of faith and hope as virtues, it nevertheless presupposes their particular functions. And though Christ possessed neither faith nor hope (because of the imperfections of those dispositions), nevertheless instead of believing he saw, and instead of hoping he possessed, so that he most perfectly loved with charity.

66 1 **Ranking the virtues.** Virtues are greater the nearer they approach the root of virtue in reason. Prudence perfects reason itself and is the source of goodness in the other moral virtues; justice, perfecting the will, is to be preferred to courage, perfecting our capacity for aggressive emotion, and courage to moderation, perfecting our affective powers. One and the same virtue can grow, but not extensively like arts and sciences can, for moral virtue extends to all its matter at once. Rather, because of degrees of practice or temperament or perspicacity or grace, a virtue can be more or less perfectly possessed, and strike its balance

2 more or less precisely. Virtues, however, grow all together, proportionately like a man's fingers, sharing the one growth of prudence which makes virtue virtue. But because the inclinations which are the material for virtue are not necessarily equal, and vary with temperament, practice and grace, one saint is praised for one virtue, another for another.

3 The mental virtues strengthening reason can be valued as more general than the moral virtues perfecting our inclinations to good; but since moral virtues are of more value in action, and virtue is defined in relation to action this gives moral virtues the better claim to be called

virtues. Especially compared with speculative virtues which serve no other purpose than themselves, being a beginning of our final happiness of contemplating truth. Moral virtues are the virtues which make a man good without qualification because they enable him to act well. Prudence is not confined to choosing means by which moral virtues can pursue their goals, but also helps determine those goals. For the goal of a moral virtue is to strike the mean in any matter appropriate to it, a mean determined by prudent right reason. Justice, as a virtue of will concerned 4 with relating to others as well as to oneself, is the paramount moral virtue; and among the virtues controlling the emotions, courage, concerned with life and death, is prized above moderation, concerned with whatever immediately ministers to life. Whereas prudence is concerned with the 5 means to happiness, wisdom relates to God himself, the object of happiness, though only imperfectly in this life. Nevertheless, uncertain knowledge of higher things is preferable to more certain knowledge of lesser things, and wisdom, meagre and imperfect as it is, is prized above all other knowledge. Knowing what is meant by existence and non-existence, wholes and parts, and all other terms employed in the first premises of knowledge, is the job of wisdom, since existence is peculiarly God's effect. So although wisdom, like other sciences, depends on insight into first principles, it nevertheless assesses those principles and argues about them with opponents. It is thus the highest of intellectual virtues. All three deiform virtues have God as their object, but charity brings 6 us closest to him. Faith does not see him, hope does not possess him, but love unites us to him affectively in the way the beloved exists in the lover: *he who dwells in charity dwells in God and God in him.* Loving something draws us into its way of existing, whereas knowing it brings it into ours; so since God exists more perfectly in himself than he does in us, loving him (with charity) is better than knowing him (with faith); but because the material with which prudence and moral virtues are concerned exists at a lower level than ourselves, the mental virtue of prudence is to be preferred to the moral virtues. Hope presupposes a love of what one is hoping for, but only a love of desire which loves oneself rather than others; charity implies love of friendship, and hope leads towards such love.

In the life to come there will be no food or sex to take pleasure in, 67 1 *life to come* no death to fear or face boldly, no worldly goods to distribute or exchange: the material of all the moral virtues will disappear. But the formal element that makes virtue virtue will remain: reason will be altogether right and appetites altogether reasonable about the things which constitute the life to come. After the resurrection of our bodies *after resurrection*

we will again have bodily organs with non-rational powers, and because they will be perfectly amenable to reason, there will be courage strengthening our capacity for aggressive emotion and moderation our capacity for affection. But before resurrection those capacities and virtues will not exist as such; only the root or seeds of them in the soul, together
2 with justice in the will. Some say our receptive mind holds likenesses of what it knows only when it is actually thinking about them, and that the only lasting likenesses we have are sense-images and memories stored in the brain and lost when we die. But this doesn't make sense, since if
× likenesses come to exist in the mind they must exist their changelessly in the mode in which the mind itself exists. In this life we require sense-images as backing for these mental likenesses. But, as with the moral virtues, the material of the mental virtues will disappear in the life to come, though what is formal (in this case, the mental likenesses) will remain; souls separately existing will know without the backing of sense-

life to come

3 images, actually thinking but in some different way. Faith and hope will disappear in the life to come. Sometimes lack of a perfection is part of a thing's definition: horses lack reason by definition, and a horse endowed with reason wouldn't be a horse. Sometimes however imperfection doesn't define you, though it is connected with you as an individual for some reason: thus you may lack the use of reason because you're asleep or drunk, and in that case you can regain it without ceasing to be a man. Now imperfection is clearly part of faith's definition – *the substance of what we hope for, the evidence of what we cannot see* – since knowledge that can't see is imperfect. So were faith to gain vision it would cease to be faith. Perhaps faith could remain alongside vision? It is indeed possible for one and the same person to know by the same means two different objects, one perfect and the other imperfect; or to know the same object by two different means, one perfect and the other imperfect; or for two different persons to know the same object by the same means, one perfectly and the other imperfectly. But if faith and vision co-existed, one and the same person would be knowing the same object by the same means perfectly and imperfectly at the same time. Faith's object is more to be prized than science's, since it is the first Truth himself; but science's manner of knowing truth is more perfect, and
4 compatible with vision whereas faith's is not. Change too implies imperfection in its subject by definition, since it is a realizing of something still potential. When the potentiality is fully realized the change stops; things don't go on getting white once they have achieved whiteness. Now hope implies change and movement towards what is not yet possessed; and when it is possessed and God is enjoyed, hope will no

longer be possible. The souls of the saints desire glory for their bodies but they don't strictly speaking hope for it, whether hope means the deiform virtue (which has God for its object rather than a created good) or has its more usual meaning (when its object must challenge us, rather than be a good whose cause is already present and unable to be frustrated). There is however this difference between faith and hope: 5 faith and vision are both knowledge of a sort, but hope and enjoyment differ like movement and rest. Charity is love and so includes no imperfection in its definition: it relates to objects possessed or not possessed, seen or unseen. Charity is not done away with in the perfection of glory but remains the same charity it was before.

The gifts of the Holy Spirit.   To distinguish the gifts of the Holy [vol 24] 68 1 Spirit from virtues remember that scripture calls them *spirits* rather than gifts: *There shall rest upon him the spirit of wisdom and understanding, of counsel and might, of knowledge and reverence for the Lord; and he will find pleasure in fearing the Lord.* So these gifts are inspired by God from without, not moved by reason from within. Now whatever is moved must be disposed to that movement if it is to be moved well. Human virtues are enough to dispose us to do well whatever reason moves us to do, but we need higher dispositions to respond well to the movement of God. These dispositions have become known as gifts, not only because God instils them, but also because they dispose us to receive God's inspiration readily. And this explains why some people say the gifts perfect us for acts higher than acts of virtue. Whenever the prompting 2 of reason needs supplementing by the prompting of the Holy Spirit, we shall need such gifts. Now God strengthens our reason in two ways: naturally in accordance with the natural light of reason, and super-naturally through the deiform virtues. The first strength we possess fully, but the second, to love and know God, only imperfectly. Now a nature or form or virtue possessed perfectly we can exercise by ourselves (given God's interior working in all will and nature); but one possessed imperfectly we need help in exercising. So reason cannot move us to the ultimate supernatural goal to which the deiform virtues imperfectly dispose us, unless the Holy Spirit also moves and prompts us. To reach that goal we need gifts of the Holy Spirit, to relate us to the Holy Spirit 3 in the same way moral virtues relate our appetitive powers to reason. In other words we need dispositions, strengthening us readily to obey the Holy Spirit. Tools that do not cooperate with their agent but are passive in his hands need no such dispositions, but the Holy Spirit moves men in such a way that they themselves act freely and so have need of such

4 dispositions. All men's faculties need God's prompting: to perceive well our speculative reason needs *understanding* and our practical reason *counsel*; to judge rightly our speculative reason needs *wisdom* and our practical reason *knowledge*; whilst our appetitive powers must be strengthened by *reverence* where others are concerned, and as regards ourselves by *might* against dread of danger and *fear* against inordinate longing for pleasure. Tools must first be joined to their users in some way, and the spirit of man is joined to the Holy Spirit by faith, hope and charity: these virtues are the root from which all the gifts derive. Love, hope and delight, as emotions of attraction to good, have names that can be used for the deiform virtues that join us to God. But fear is rather an emotion of repulsion from evil, implying not so much a joining to God as a withdrawal from things (out of reverence for God); so it names not a deiform virtue but a gift that withdraws us from evil more perfectly than moral virtues can.

5 The Holy Spirit dwells in us through charity, as prudence resides in our reason. And just as all moral virtues are connected to one another through sharing the one prudence, so all the gifts of the Holy Spirit are connected with one another through charity: whoever has charity has these gifts, and no gift is possible without charity.

8 The deiform virtues join the soul to God, the mental virtues perfect reason itself, the moral virtues strengthen our powers of appetite to follow the promptings of reason, the gifts of the Holy Spirit strengthen all the powers of the soul to follow God's promptings. So just as mental virtues are prized above moral virtues, so deiform virtues are prized above the gifts of the Holy Spirit and provide the standard for them. But the gifts are prized above all other mental and moral virtues since they strengthen the soul's powers to be moved by the Holy Spirit, whereas other virtues strengthen reason, or other powers in relation to reason.

69 1 **The gospel blessings.** We say a goal is within our grasp when it is close enough for us to have sure hope of attaining it. What brings us close to the blessing of eternal happiness is exercise of the virtues and especially the gifts. So the blessings pronounced by Christ in the gospels and called *beatitudes* are not dispositions distinct from the virtues and gifts, but actions exercising them.

2 Certain actions are proposed in these blessings as deserving happiness and disposing us to possess it, either inchoately or perfectly; and what is presented as reward for those actions is either the perfect happiness of the life to come, or some inchoate beginning of it found in perfect men here and now. Thus the *kingdom of heaven* can be taken to mean the start of the reign of the Spirit in

wise men, the *possession of the land* to mean the heart's repose in desire of a sure and everlasting inheritance, and so on. All of which will be perfectly realized in our heavenly home. A life devoted to pleasure is a 3 false happiness which hinders the true happiness of the life to come; but the happiness of a life active in doing good prepares for true happiness, and the happiness of a contemplative life is already true happiness beginning. So the first blessings dissuade us from a life devoted to pleasure. *Blessed are the poor in spirit* dissuades us from seeking an abundance of external goods; *blessed are the meek* dissuades from aggressive emotions; and *blessed are those who mourn* from affective emotions. The life of doing good is chiefly one of paying dues and spontaneous giving to our fellowmen: hence *blessed are those who hunger and thirst after justice* and *blessed are the merciful*. The contemplative life does not so much deserve blessing as constitute it, but those effects of the active life which dispose us to contemplation, both in ourselves and in relation to our fellowmen, are mentioned: *blessed are the clean of heart* and *blessed are the peacemakers*.

Sin and vice

What is sin?   Virtue is a disposition befitting one's nature, a goodness [vol 25] 71 1 directed towards good deeds. So three things oppose virtue: sins (or misdeeds), evil (the opposite of goodness), and vice (disposition unbefitting to one's nature). Whatever accords with reason is humanly good, 2 whatever goes against reason humanly bad. Human virtue that makes men and their deeds good befits human nature by befitting reason, whilst vice goes against man's nature by going against reason. Man's nature is twofold: he lives by his reason and he lives by his senses. It is through sensing that he learns to reason, but many men never mature beyond the level of sense. Vice and sin result from our following of sense-nature against our rational nature. And going against human rational nature is going against eternal law. Since we call dispositions good (or bad) 3 because they lead to good (or bad) actions, the goodness or badness of actions counts for more than that of dispositions. That dispositions are more lasting is irrelevant, and due to the fact that we cannot be active all the time and that our actions consist in passing changes. Dispositions are agencies of action, actions goals of dispositions, and it is goals that determine goodness or badness. What things do by nature they do 4 necessarily, and movements against nature can occur only because of some externally applied force. But what we do from a disposition of soul is not done necessarily, but as and when we want to make use of our disposition. So men can be virtuous yet not use their virtue and even go against it and sin. However, mortal or fatal sin goes against charity, which is the root of all instilled virtue as such; so one fatal sin can extinguish charity and all instilled virtue as such. (I say *as such* to cover the case of faith and hope which remain as dispositions after a fatal sin, though they have lost their quality of virtue). But venial [literally, excusable] sins do not go against charity so cannot extinguish it or other virtues. And no single act of sin can destroy acquired virtues.

5   *Whoever doesn't do the good he knows he should is guilty of sin.* If we include in the notion of sins of omission simply what makes them sins, then sometimes they involve an interior act (wanting not to go to church) and sometimes no act at all (when it came time to go we didn't think either of going or not going). But if we include in our notion of omission also the causes and occasion of that omission then omissions always involve some act. For unless the cause of an omission was beyond our control (in which case there was no sin), the cause was voluntary and so involved at least some interior act of will. Sometimes such an act is an essential part of the sin of omission bearing directly on the omission (wanting to avoid the fag of going); but at other times it is incidental to it bearing directly on something else which stopped us doing what we should have been doing (we wanted to rest rather, or chose to stay up late the night before). Since we should judge by essentials, not incidentals, it will be more accurate to say that sins of omission involve no action; otherwise contingent circumstances will always have to be an essential part of sins. *Any defect will make a thing bad; to be good a thing must be wholly good.* So we can sin either by doing what we shouldn't or by not doing what we should; but our only deserving actions are those in which we willingly do what we should. To deserve we must act but to sin we needn't. Not only things we actively will are called voluntary, but anything the occurrence or non-occurrence of which is within our control. So since willing or not willing is within our control, not willing something can be called voluntary. A sin of omission violates a command to do something positive, and such commands, though in perpetual force, don't oblige perpetual action. By omitting to act we sin only during the time we were commanded to act.

6   Augustine defined sin as *any word, deed or desire against eternal law.* Sin is a bad human act, where human means voluntary: either an act of exercising the will itself (willing, choosing) or an act commanded by will (external words or deeds). The badness comes from falling short of some standard; and will's standards are two: the immediate standard of human reason itself and the ultimate standard of eternal law, God's

reason. So St Augustine's definition includes both the material element in sin (what makes it a human act) – *any word, deed or desire* – and the formal element (what makes it bad) – *against eternal law*. The point is often made that not all sins are bad because forbidden, some are forbidden because they are bad.. This makes sense if forbidden means forbidden by enacted law. But in terms of what is naturally right (which is first laid down in eternal law, but secondarily by the natural judgments of human reason) every sin is bad because forbidden. Its very disorderedness is a contravention of the law in us by nature. Theologians define sin as primarily offending against God; moral philosophers define it as going against reason.

Classification of sins.   Of the two elements constituting a sin, the voluntary act is directly intended by the sinner (this act in this matter), but its disorderedness (its departure from God's law) is intended only indirectly. For as Denys says *no one intends evil as such*. Sins then are classified according to the voluntary act involved and the object aimed at, rather than by their disorderedness. The goal of an action is its primary source of goodness, the object of the act of will involved. So to classify sins by objects or by goals amounts to the same. Different kinds of causes distinguish different kinds of things in different kinds of ways. Things differ in substance because of different matter or form, the matter determining their generic class, the form defining them more precisely. Movements and actions however differ because of different agents and goals. Agency in the natural world has fixed ways of acting, so that actions in nature can be distinguished not only by their objects – that is their goals or where they end up – but also by the agents from which they start out. But the agency of voluntary actions such as sins has no fixed way of acting, and different kinds of sin can arise from the same agency: fear of humiliation can cause a man to steal or to kill or to desert his post; and all these can also arise from love. So you can't distinguish sins simply by the agency that causes them, but must consider their goals, the object of will. The agency of voluntary actions, because it has no fixed way of acting, must, if it is to cause a human act, be further determined by intending some specific goal. The goal determines both the act's existence and its kind. Of course, the object of any external activity is the matter with which it is concerned, but this features as goal in relation to the interior act of will, and classifies the action.

St Isidore distinguished sins *against oneself, against God and against one's fellowmen*. Sin is disorder, and there are three orders that men

72 1

3

should safeguard: firstly, our deeds and feelings should observe the rule of our reason; secondly, we should observe the rule of God's law; and thirdly, because we are *political and social animals*, we should live in order with our fellowmen. God's order includes reason's order but also adds things beyond reason, e.g. matters of faith; so sin in these latter matters we call sin against God. Reason's order includes the social order but also adds things pertaining only to ourselves, e.g. the exclusion of gluttony; so sin in these matters is sin against ourselves, whilst sin in social matters like theft and murder is sin against our fellowmen. These distinctions are distinctions of object, and therefore classify types of sin opposed to specific types of virtue: the theological virtues which order us to God, moderation and courage which order us in ourselves, and justice which orders us to our fellowmen.

In contrast, the difference between non-fatal and fatal sin (venial and mortal), like all other differences relating to penalty, doesn't divide sin into types of sin. For penalty is clearly not part of what the sinner intends, but attaches only subsequently to the sin by just judgment from outside. So differences of penalty may attach to different types of sin, but do not define them. In fact, the difference of non-fatal and fatal attaches to a difference in the disorder which constitutes sinfulness. Some disorders like death destroy order at source and are thus irreparable, whilst others like sickness are reparable because they leave the source of order untouched. If a sin so disorders our life as to turn it away from its ultimate goal in God, to whom we are joined by charity, then the sin is fatal or mortal; in its nature it is irreparable and brings with it an eternal penalty. But if the disorder stops short of such turning away, the sin is non-fatal or venial, reparable in its nature and undeserving of eternal penalty. So the ways fatal and venial sin turn us away from God differ immeasurably, even if what they turn us towards, the object that determines the type of the sin, may happen to be the same: e.g. first promptings towards the fatal sin of adultery may be non-fatal, whilst idle words, which are usually non-fatal, may on occasion be fatal.

8   A sin's type is determined, not by the element of disorder in the action but by the element of order in it: not by its departure from the rule of reason and God's law (for that is not what the sinner is primarily intending), but by its orderedness to the object at which the sinner is aiming. Distinct types of sin result from the distinct objects that attract us. Clearly what leads us to sin by over-doing is opposed to what leads us to sin by under-doing: we are led to immoderation by love of bodily pleasures, to frigidity by dislike of them; such sins therefore differ in

type, and indeed are opposed. The aim of every virtue is the rule of 73 1
reason, and so all virtues are connected by sharing prudence, which is
right reasoning about what to do. Sins however aim not at departing
from reason but at the desirable goods peculiar to each type of sin; and
these differ, are unconnected and often opposed. One sinful action (even
if fatal) cannot destroy an acquired disposition to virtue. Only if the
action was repeated often enough to generate the opposed disposition
would the virtue be destroyed; and at that moment prudence also would
be lost, every other virtue would lose that sharing in prudence which
makes it an achieved virtue, and only the initial inclination to virtuous
acts would remain. Now this doesn't imply that the sinner would incur
every vice and sin. For one thing many vices oppose each virtue, and
for another, sins also oppose the initial inclinations to virtuous acts yet
these remain. The love of God gathers our dispersed affections into one,
so that the virtues caused by that love are all connected. But love of self
disperses the affections, since man in loving himself desires many and
various temporal goods, so that sins and vices are all disconnected.

Complete lack – death, for example – doesn't have degrees, since 2
there is nothing left to have degrees of. But half-presence, half-absence –
sickness, for example – does. Now vices and sins half-lack good in this
way: the measure of reason has not been entirely destroyed, for as
Aristotle says, *evil if total would destroy itself*: there would be no act or
affection of the agent left to be a sin. Gravity of sin is measured precisely
by the degree to which it departs from rightness of reason. The sin is 3
graver the more the disorder approaches the source of reasonableness in
the act, the higher the goal departed from. Since external things are
ordered to men, and men to God, sins concerned with man's existence
(like murder) are graver than those concerned with external goods (like
theft); but even graver are sins committed against God immediately (like
unbelief and blasphemy). Other things being equal, sins of the spirit are 5
graver than sins of the flesh. The spirit turns us to (and away from)
God, whereas fleshly appetites mainly turn us towards bodily goods. So
sins of the flesh are characterized more by attraction and addiction,
whereas sins of the spirit are characterized more by the turning away
which constitutes fault. Moreover, sins of the flesh offend against our
own bodies, which in charity are to be loved less than our fellowmen
and God, against whom sins of the spirit offend. And thirdly, the more
a man is driven to a sin the less of a sin it is, and we are much more
strongly urged towards sins of the flesh. The reason adultery is graver
than theft is because it is not merely a sin of lust but also itself a sin of
injustice, a type of greed; and a man's wife is dearer to him than his

possessions. Again, if *lust delights the devil*, as Augustine says, it is because it is so addictive: *the desire for pleasure is insatiable*. And if *not containing our lust is more shameful than not containing our anger*, as Aristotle says, that is because lust is further away from reason, and something we share even with brute animals.

6   The immediate cause of sin is the sinner's (will) to sin, and the greater that is the greater the sin. Other causes of sin are mediate, inclining the will towards sin. Some cooperate with the will's own nature, as goals do; so there too the worse the goal intended the worse the sin. But some causes act against the nature of the will, which should move itself freely and reasonably to act. Thus ignorance weakens will's reasonableness, and weakness, force and fear weaken its freedom. Such causes lessen the sin by lessening its voluntariness, and so much so that if the act is altogether involuntary it is no sin at all. If desire is taken to include will itself, then the greater the desire the greater the sin; but if desire means the affective emotions, then the greater the desire before reason judges and will moves the less the sin, but the greater the desire afterwards the greater the sin. There are three ways in which circumstances make a sin

7   worse. Sometimes the circumstance changes the sin's type: sex outside marriage becomes injustice if one of the participants is married to someone else. Sometimes the circumstance doesn't change the sin's type but adds a further reason for its sinfulness: doing something at the wrong time, for example. And sometimes the circumstance makes worse a sinfulness derived from some other circumstance; the more one takes

8   the greater the sin if what one takes is another's. Some harm sins do can be foreseen and intended, and then the more harm the worse the sin, since the harm is a direct object of the sinner. But some harm is foreseen but not intended, and then it only indirectly increases the gravity of the sin, measuring the extent to which the sinner wills the sin, and is not prepared to avoid what in other circumstances he would. Some harm is neither foreseen nor intended: if, nevertheless, it is an essential consequence of the sin it will make the sin worse, but if it is a chance consequence it will not worsen the sin directly (though if the action is illegal the sinner will be held negligent and liable for any unintended damages). Harm the sinner does to himself is judged differently, as serving him right: it never worsens the sin, but if it springs from the nature of the sin then the worse the sin the worse will be the penalty, whether the harm was foreseen or intended or not. It is not the harm as such that makes the sin worse, but the increase of disorder in the sin. Some say that seducing others to sin sexually and lose the life of grace is worse than murder. But murderers directly intend the harm they do

to their fellowmen, whereas a seducer intends not harm but pleasure. Moreover, murder is a sufficient cause of physical death; but no one can be a sufficient cause of someone else's spiritual death, since that depends on a sinner's own will.

The main goals of human activity are God, oneself and one's fellowmen; and sins against our fellowmen are worse the closer those people are to God (by virtue or office) or to oneself (by kinship or friendship), and the more people are affected (as when one offends a head of state). Doing harm to oneself by damaging goods over which one has right of control is less of a sin than doing the same harm to others. But if one has no right over the goods, as is the case with goods given us by nature or by grace, then it is worse to harm oneself: suicide is worse than murder. The more excellent a man is, the more he is to be blamed for deliberate sin; for he is more able to resist, has more to be thankful for, has a special duty to avoid particular sins (judges are there to guard justice and priests to guard chastity), and gives greater scandal.

Why we sin.   Sins are actions. Some actions like cutting or burning are done outside the agent; as Aristotle says, the agent of a change does what he does in what he acts on. But some actions, like desiring and knowing and all moral acts of virtue and sins, are done not outside but within the agent. Since what defines acts as moral is their voluntariness, our will is their proper agency to which they are attributed. But because voluntary acts include not only acts of exercise of the will itself but all acts done under will's control, sin can be attributed not only to the will, but also to every agent power the will can arouse or repress, though not to the parts of the body as such. For parts of the body don't start actions but are merely tools and slaves of the soul's desires, whereas our inner ability to desire is not a slave but a free man in relation to reason, acting as well as being acted on. In any case, the actions of outer limbs take place not in them but in external matter: the murderous death-blow, for example. Our sensuality has been permanently damaged. Throughout life it possesses an inflammability resulting from inherited sin; even when the stain of that sin is removed its effects remain. This inflammability doesn't prevent a man's reason and will repressing each disordered sensual movement of which he becomes aware, by thinking of something else, for example. But while he is doing that another disordered movement can arise: while he is turning his mind from pleasures of the flesh to intellectual matters, for example, there can arise an unpremeditated movement of vanity. So a man can't prevent all such movements; but to be counted a voluntary sin, it is enough that such a movement could have been separately repressed. However, because what a man does without deliberation is not done by him in the full sense of the word, and is not a human action, movements of sensuality that

4 forestall reason are non-fatal sins, unfulfilled sins so to speak. Sensuality can contribute to fatal sin, but what makes the sin fatal is not that contribution, but the contribution reason makes in ordering it to a goal. Fatal sins then are attributed to reason, not to sensuality; just as acts of moral virtue in our emotional faculties have to be accompanied by acts

6 of prudent direction by reason. Just as sins of external action are attributed to reason, so we can attribute to reason those sins in which reason fails to govern our inner feelings, either by commanding an illicit emotion or delaying to put it down. That is why we attribute to reason the sin of dallying with pleasure. It is not taking time that makes dallying a sin of reason, but reason's failure to dismiss the emotion promptly.

8 When we think about sexual sin, we may take pleasure in the thinking as such, or in the sex we are thinking about. Now the thinking as such is not a fatal sin: if it is idle thinking it may be a non-fatal sin, but if it is useful for preaching or discussing morals or some such purpose then it is not sin at all. And the same is true of any pleasure in or consent to the thinking. But if we are taking pleasure in the sexual sin we are thinking about, then our desire is being drawn towards that sexual act; and deliberately choosing such inclination to a fatal sin is already fatal itself.

75 1 Sins are disordered actions. As actions they have causes like any other actions, but as disordered they have the sort of cause absences and lacks have. Now absence of its cause will directly cause absence of an effect; but also, if presence of x inhibits presence of y, then the cause of x will indirectly cause absence of y. Sin however is not a simple absence, but absence of something that should be present; so it needs an indirect inhibiting cause, namely, the direct cause of the act as such. By aiming at some temporal good in a way that lacks direction by rule of reason and divine law, our will causes the act of the sin directly and the disorder of it indirectly, the act's disorder stemming from the will's lack of direction. Whoever defines a cause as something from which some effect necessarily follows, must be thinking of sufficient and unhindered causes. For the effects of even sufficient causes sometimes do not follow, because of other overriding causes (otherwise everything would happen necessarily). And so it is with sins: they have causes, but not causes from which effects follow necessarily. The will, unregulated by right reason or divine law, causes the sin; but the absence of regulation in the will is

not itself evil – not sin, nor even evil derived from sin – but becomes evil only when it proceeds to action. So the cause of the sin with which we started is not itself evil but a good in which another good is absent. A sin has two inner causes: its immediate cause is reason and will, but **2** beyond that there lies imagination and sense-appetite. The cause of sin is an apparent good which, however, lacks the good it should have according to the rule of reason and divine law. The apparent good is presented by imagination to the sense-appetite; the absence of proper rule is attributed to reason (which should have considered it); and the final voluntariness of the act of sin comes from the will. The act of will, given things as we have described them, is already a sort of sin. The power of the will is always there as a potential cause of sin. But it only comes into act by way of preceding movements in the sense-appetite and then reason. Only when something is presented to the sense-appetite as desirable by the senses, and the sense-appetite is attracted to it, and the reason meanwhile stops regulating the process as it should, does the will produce a sinful action.

If external causes of sin exist they will have to act through our sense- **3** appetites or reasons, or immediately on our wills. Now only God can act within the will and he cannot cause sin. Nor in matters of behaviour can reason be compelled to follow external persuasion or sense-appetite to pursue things externally presented; and in any case the sense-appetite cannot compel either reason or will. So although these can all be causes of sin they are not enough of themselves to bring it about; the will is the only sufficient cause of that. Sins can cause sin according to four **4** different types of causality. One sin can be indirect *agent* of another by removing a hindrance to it (by losing us grace or charity or shame or some other thing that restrained us from the other sin); but also direct agent by disposing us to re-commit the same sort of sin more easily. One sin can be another sin's *matter*: greed can provoke strife; or its *goal*: sexual sin can have its eye on theft, and then, because in moral matters goals act like forms, what is materially an act of sex would take on the *form* of theft.

Sinning from ignorance.   Reason governs human activity through **76** its knowledge of both general and particular truths. When we work out how to act we use a sort of syllogism that concludes to a judgment or choice or action. Since every action is something particular, the con- clusion of such a syllogism is a particular proposition, so can only be inferred from a general premise by way of some other particular proposition. Thus we reject this particular act of parricide, because in general we know killing one's father is wrong, and in particular know this man is our father. Two types of ignorance therefore cause us to sin: not knowing that a certain general principle is a rule of reason, and not knowing that a particular circumstance holds. Clearly however ignorance only causes sin if knowing what we did not know would have stopped us sinning. If our will was so disposed that we would have killed the man even if we had known he was our father, then ignorance of the fact didn't cause our sin but merely accompanied it. As Aristotle says, we 2 were acting in ignorance but not through ignorance. Ignorance is more than not knowing; it is not knowing what we could, and in some cases should have known. All men, for example, have the common obligation to know the truths of faith and the universal precepts of law, and individuals ought to know the duties of their own state and job. But some things we are capable of knowing we are not obliged to know, like the theorems of geometry and chance events (except in special cases). When due to negligence, not knowing what one should is a sin, but if there was no way we could have known, the ignorance is not negligent but *unconquerable.* Unconquerable ignorance is never sinful; but conquerable ignorance of things we should have known is. Repentance will not remove ignorance, of course, but it will remove any negligence that 3 made it sinful. If knowing what we didn't know wouldn't have stopped us sinning, then our ignorance didn't make us act involuntarily and doesn't excuse us from sin. And the same is true of ignorance which only accompanies or results from sin. Even ignorance that causes sin may only partially excuse from it. Sometimes the ignorance itself is only partial: the sinner is ignorant of a circumstance that would have kept him from sinning, but knows enough to realize that he is sinning (he strikes a man, for example, under the mistaken impression the man won't strike back). At other times the ignorance itself is voluntary, directly willed or a result of negligence in matters one could and should have known. Only when ignorance is entirely involuntary, either because unconquerable or because it concerns something we are not obliged to 4 know, does it totally excuse us from sin. Only ignorance which causes sin without totally excusing it can lessen it. Ignorance which is directly voluntary would seem rather to intensify the sinfulness; but when indirect (resulting from laziness or too much drink taken) it reduces both the voluntariness and the sin. Thus it is graver to commit murder [when sober than when drunk; because, even if drunkenness is a second sin, it is less grave than murder committed sober would have been.

Sinning from emotion.   Emotions sway our wills only indirectly. 77 1
Firstly, they distract by their intensity, for the more intensely one and
the same soul engages in one activity the less intensely it can engage in
others. And secondly, emotions arouse vehement and disordered images
and judgments in our senses that hinder the reasoned judgment on
which will depends. A man finds it as difficult to escape such images
when in a passion, as the tongue does to taste properly when sick.
Socrates was of the opinion that emotion could never prevail against 2
knowledge; and he was in a sense right, because no one would ever will
evil unless his reason was in some state of error or ignorance. Yet
experience also shows that many do what they know they shouldn't, so
Socrates wasn't altogether correct. For one thing someone who knows
in general that sex outside marriage is wrong, may not recognize a
particular act to be such. And for another, a man may not actually attend
to what he knows, be it general or particular, either because he doesn't
want to, or because of some hindrance of business or sickness; and this
is the way emotion hinders us from attending to what we in general
know. It distracts us, or inclines us to a truth opposed to what we know,
or so affects the body that we are temporarily or permanently deprived
of reason (too much love or anger can drive people mad). Although
knowledge of general truths is more certain, knowledge of particulars is
more important in action; so it is no wonder that passion can get the
upper hand of general knowledge when a man is not thinking about the
particular. It can easily happen that despite being disposed to know the
truth of an affirmative proposition in general, we actually falsely believe
the negative in particular; for actions directly oppose actions not dispositions. Emotion hinders us from bringing the general knowledge we
have to bear on our problem, and suggests to us some other general
premise. Aristotle says the pleasure-lover has four propositions in his
syllogism, two of them general: one is reason's premise that such and
such sex acts are wrong, and the other passion's premise that all pleasure
is to be pursued. Passion stops reason applying the first premise, and
while the passion lasts we apply only the second. Just as drunks enunciate
deep truths but do not understand them, so people under the influence
of emotion may say they shouldn't do something while inside believing
they should.

We call souls weak for the same reason we do bodies: because some 3 *weak souls*
disorder of their parts hinders their proper functioning. Sins begin in
acts of will, which bodily weakness can't hinder but emotion can. So
sins of weakness stem from weakness of soul rather than body, even if
we call it *weakness of the flesh* because our emotional faculties operate

4 through bodily organs. Every sin arises from disordered desire for some
6 temporal good and that arises from disordered love of self. Emotions
that precede free choice influence the will, and lessen the voluntariness
and gravity of resulting sins. But emotions that follow on free choice
and result from intense movement of will increase a sin's gravity, or
7 rather indicate greater willingness to sin. Sometimes emotions are strong
enough to drown reason; men have been driven mad by love or anger.
If such emotions were voluntary to begin with, all the behaviour that
results will be voluntary at source and therefore sinful, just as is the case
with drunkenness. But if the emotion was natural rather than voluntary,
then the behaviour that results is altogether involuntary and sinless.
Sometimes however emotions don't totally interfere with our reasoning,
and reason is able to the get rid of the emotion by diverting our thoughts,
or at least stop it acting, since we can't move our limbs without reason's
8 consent. Inclinations of soul away from one's ultimate goal are always
totally sinful, unless they are instantaneous responses occurring before
reason is able to deliberate about them. But acting from passion is not
such a reflex response and allows time for deliberation. So sins like
adultery and murder are fatally sinful. There are three senses in which
a sin can be called excusable: because some excusing cause like weakness
or ignorance lessens the sin's gravity; because some event of forgiveness
can excuse the sin; or because the sin is of a venial or excusable type,
like idle words. Sins excusable in this last sense are non-fatal, as opposed
to fatal sins.

78 1 **Sinning from bad will.** So sinful human behaviour can result from
mental ignorance or from sensual emotion; or sometimes from disorder
in the will itself, which loves some lesser good too much, and is willing
to suffer loss of spiritual goods in order to retain hold of a temporal
good like riches or pleasure. Whoever does this knowingly wills spiritual
evil, and we say he sins purposely *with bad will*. All sin involves
ignorance. But when we simply do not know that what we do is bad
then we are said to sin from ignorance; if we know it but ignore it here
and now we sin from emotion or weakness; if we know it here and now
but ignore the fact that the good in what we pursue cannot outweigh
the badness of our act, we sin from bad will. We never intend evil for
its own sake but we can intend it as a means of avoiding some other evil
or pursuing some other good. One would prefer the good without the
evil, but given the choice of one or the other we prefer to sin and offend
God rather than be deprived of our pleasure. Sinning from bad will can
be understood either as sinning from vice, from some disposition to act

badly; or as sinning from an act of choice or some preceding sin. In neither of these last cases do we make an act the cause of itself: either an inner act is causing an outer one, or one sin is causing another (though not endlessly, for there is always some first sin uncaused by a previous one). That to which we are disposed by vice or virtue is agreeable to us 2 in itself and congenial, repetition having made it second nature. In vice's case, what is congenial is incompatible with spiritual good, but we choose the spiritual evil rather than do without what is congenial. And this is sinning from bad will. We sin from bad will only when our will of itself 3 chooses evil: either because it is disposed to do so (by a vice acquired through repeated acts which have become second nature, or by some bodily weakness), or because our normal inhibitions to sin (e.g. the fear of hell or the hope of heaven) have been removed by presumption or despair. Sinning from bad will is worse than sinning from emotion since 4 it is more intrinsic to the will, a more lasting source of sin, and involves being badly disposed towards our ultimate goal. Dispositions incline the will from within, so to speak.

Does God cause sin? *God hates nothing he has made.* God cannot 79 1 directly cause sin (either his own or another's) since sin is lack of order to God as goal, and God draws everything to himself as ultimate goal. Nor can God cause sins indirectly: if it happens that he does not give some people the help they need to avoid sin, this must be wisely and justly done, for he is wisdom and justice itself. He can no more be said to cause sins than a pilot can be said to cause the wreck of a ship by not steering it (unless he could and should have been steering). When St Paul says that God *has given them over to corrupted minds, so that they do the things that they should not do,* his very way of speaking implies that they had the corrupted minds already and that God did not interfere with their inclinations. An effect can be traced back through intermediate causes to a first cause only if the intermediary causes are enabled to act by that first cause, but not if the intermediate causes are acting on their own. So sins, freely willed against God's command, cannot be traced back to God as cause. Because sinful actions exist and are actions, they 2 derive from God: all that exists, whatever its manner of existing, derives from the first existent; and all actions are caused by things that actually exist *qua* actually existent, and that actualness is derived from him who is actual by nature. Sin however names these existent actions *qua* defective, with a defect moreover that arises from a created cause – free will – precisely rejecting its orderedness to its first cause, God. That defect can no more be traced back to God than the limp due to a deformity in our legs can be traced back to our power to move our legs, even though no limping movement would exist without that power. God causes the sinful action but he does not cause the sin, for he is not the cause that the action is sinful. Man, on the other hand, causes not only the action but also its defectiveness, for he does not subject himself to God as he ought (even though that is not his primary intention in the sin).

3   God so causes the action that he in no sense causes the accompanying defect; and that is why he is not the cause of the sin. God does however freely choose to withhold the light of his grace from those in whom he finds an obstacle; so that the cause of absence of grace is not only the man who puts up the obstacle, but also God himself. And in this sense one can say that God causes men's blindness and dullness of hearing

4   and hardness of heart. Sin however has two outcomes: one is damnation which it brings on itself; but the other is healing, attached to it in the plan of a merciful God who allows some to fall into sin in order that they may recognize it, be humbled and turn back to him. So the natural outcome of spiritual blindness is damnation (and that is listed as an effect of divine disapproval); but by God's mercy a temporary blindness can bring healing and eventual health of the blinded: not of all the blinded but of those who are predestined, for whom *everything works to their good*. So blindness brings damnation to some and healing to others. That God so orders things that blindness leads some to health is his mercy; that it leads others to damnation is his justice; that he has mercy on some but not all is not partiality or discrimination in God.

80 1   **Does the devil cause sin?**   The only things that can cause sin directly are things that can influence the will: the object that is seen as desirable, and whatever gives will its own inner inclination to will. This inclination comes either from God (who cannot cause sin) or the will itself. But three things are involved in any object influencing the will: the object, appealing to man's will through his external senses, the one who presents the object, and the one who persuades us of the object's goodness (and that could be the devil or some other man). However, none of these three can cause sin directly: for the only object that can compel the will is our ultimate goal, and the devil can cause sin only by persuasion and the presentation of desirable objects. So, though God is the ultimate cause of all our inward movements, that a man's will takes a bad decision comes directly from that will itself, and indirectly from the devil through

2   persuasion and presentation of desirable objects. The devil can cause anything that can be caused by moving bodies around in space, God

permitting. Some such movements stimulate our imaginations, for *during sleep*, Aristotle says, *the blood carries stored sense-impressions to some centre of perception, and it seems to us as though we are sensing external objects.* And by affecting our hearts and bodily humours, our emotions can be similarly aroused. In this way the devil can lead us into sin from within. The devil can even compel man, God permitting, to perform actions 3 which of their nature would be sinful, but even then he can't compel man to sin. Man's only defence is his reason and this can be totally overwhelmed by images and emotions, as we see in cases of demonic possession; but when reason is fettered in this way nothing a man does can be reckoned as sin. Indirectly the devil is the cause of all our sins, 4 since it was he who led the first man into sin, and as a result of that sin human nature is so weakened that we are all prone to sin. But he is not a direct cause, persuading to each and every sin, as Origen showed when he said that *even if there were no devil, men would still desire food and sex and the like, and whether those desires were controlled by reason or not would be up to our free will.*

Can sin be inherited? Men can externally entice other men to sin [vol 26] as the devil does; but there has also been a special human way in which man has caused sin in others, and that is by inheritance. St Paul says 81 1 *Sin came into the world through one man.* He doesn't only mean that Adam gave us an example of sin, for this is attributed rather to the devil: *Death came into the world through the devil's envy.* Rather he means that sin was inherited from Adam as our first parent. This is a matter of Catholic faith, and it is the reason why even newly-born babies are brought to be baptized as if to be washed clean from some infection of guilt. To deny this was Pelagius' heresy, which Augustine exposed in a great many works. But the attempt to explain how the sin of a first parent could be inherited by his progeny has led different theologians down different paths. Some, realizing that only the reasoning soul sins, thought the reasoning soul must be genetically transmitted in the semen, and the infection inherited in this way from soul to soul. Others saw the mistake in this, but tried to show that even if the soul can't be transmitted from parent to children, guilt can, in the way bodily defects are. But all such attempts are bound to fail, for even if some defects of our body, and consequently of our soul, are congenital, nevertheless there seems to be a contradiction between the very notions of inheriting a defect and being guilty of it, since guilt requires voluntariness. Even if the soul itself were passed on genetically, since the infection of a child's soul is not willed by the child, it cannot be guilty or deserve punishment. As

Aristotle says, *we don't blame people for being born blind; we pity them.* So we have to approach the question in quite another way, and say that all men born from Adam can be thought of as one man sharing one nature derived from him, in much the same way that in political matters all the members of a community are thought of as limbs or members of one body, and the community as a whole as one person. Now the actions of bodily members like the hand are voluntary, not with any will in the hand, but with the will of the soul which first set that hand in motion. We wouldn't reckon murder committed with the hand to be the hand's sin if we could think of the hand in itself out of the context of the body; we talk of it in that way only when we think of the hand as part of a whole man moved to sin by the source of such movements in men. In the same way, the disorder inherited from Adam by any particular man is not voluntary with that man's will, but voluntary only with Adam's will which activates all those born from him by the movement of reproduction, just as the will of a man activates all his limbs. This is why the sin deriving from our first parent is called *original* (meaning *by origin or inheritance*), whereas the sins deriving from a man's will to members of his body are called *actual* (sins of action). And just as a sin of action is a *sin of the man*, but not a sin of the limb committing it (except insofar as the limb belongs to the man as a whole); so too inherited or original sin is a *sin of human nature*, not a sin of this or that person (except insofar as that person is receiving his nature from our first parent). *We were by nature inheritors of God's wrath.*

What is genetically transmitted in the semen is human nature and, together with that nature, its sickness. The newborn child shares in the guilt of the first parent inasmuch as his nature is brought into being by a reproductive movement from that parent. Guilt does not exist in the semen, but human nature is there as in a cause, and with the nature comes guilt. You cannot blame the person born as an individual for what he inherits, but as deriving from a certain source he incurs blame from it in the way someone bears a family disgrace because of the fault of some forebear.

2. The sins of our more immediate parents, however, and all later sins of our first parent are not inherited. Children do not inherit from parents what belongs to those parents as individuals, their personal actions and qualities; men skilled in grammar by their own efforts don't pass grammar on in the genes. What parents pass on to their children, barring failures of nature, is the nature of their species: things with eyes produce things with eyes. Vigorous natures can reproduce individual features of their natural disposition like speed or cleverness, but never what is

purely personal. But just as to persons certain things belong in their own right and other things by grace, so too to nature. Certain things result from its own constitutive elements; but the original integrated state of man was a gift of grace bestowed on the whole of human nature in and through its first parent, and then lost by Adam through his first sin. That integrated state would have been inherited from Adam by his progeny together with their human nature; now what is inherited is the opposing disorder. But any other sins of action of Adam or any others of our parents damage not nature as nature, but only nature as it exists in that particular person by affecting his inclinations to action. So others' sins are not inherited. The first sin damaged human nature with damage attaching to it as nature, other sins with damage attaching to it in a particular person.

Death has spread to the whole human race inasmuch as all have sinned. 3
Catholic faith holds firmly that all men deriving from Adam, Christ alone excepted, contracted inherited sin from him; otherwise not everyone would need Christ's redemption and that is erroneous. A reason for this is suggested by our comparison of the way inherited guilt is passed on to Adam's progeny from his sin with the way sins of action are passed on to members of our body moved by our will. Clearly sins of action can be passed on to members of the body under the will's control. Inherited guilt too passes on to all who are brought into existence by Adam's reproductivity. Baptism removes the liability of inherited sin to punishment, and gives the soul spiritual graces. But there remains an effect of inherited sin called inflammability, a disorder of the lower parts of the soul and the body, those parts involved in human reproduction. So even baptized people pass on inherited sin, for they reproduce not the new life of baptism but the old life still retained from primal sin. As Adam transmits his sin to all who are bodily reproduced by him, so Christ transmits his grace to all who are spiritually reproduced by him through faith and baptism; and this not only removes the guilt of Adam from us but also all our own actual sins and leads us to glory.

Only those who are descended from Adam by being brought into 4
existence by the active power of reproduction inherited from him will contract inherited sin from him. Someone fashioned from human flesh by divine power – a power clearly not inherited from Adam – would not contract inherited sin; any more than a hand not moved by a man's will but by some external force would contract the man's sin. A person formed in this way from human flesh would have existed in Adam according to their bodily material, but [would not have been a product of his active reproduction]. Natural science teaches us that the father is 5

the active partner in reproduction and that the mother's part is to provide the material. So inherited sin is contracted through the father and not the mother. If Eve had sinned without Adam their children would not have inherited sin. Nor would they have inherited death and the other natural ills that flesh is heir to. For immortality and freedom from suffering were not properties attaching to material flesh as such in the paradisal state, but were part of the original integrated state in which, as long as the soul remained subject to God, the body remained subject to the soul.

82 1   Inherited sin is a disordered disposition that has resulted from dissolution of the harmony of our original integrated state, just as sickness results from dissolving the harmony of health. It is a lack of that integrated state which shows itself in a disordered condition of the soul's parts. Sins of action are disordered actions; but inherited sin is a certain disordered condition of nature itself, carrying guilt only as deriving from our first parent. Such a disordered condition of nature is a disposition, whereas the disordered condition of sinful actions is not. So as a result of inherited sin there is an inclination in us to disordered action, not directly, as there would be from a personal vice, but indirectly, inasmuch as inherited sin has taken away the original integrated state that would have prevented disordered movement. In the same way bodily sickness indirectly inclines us to disordered bodily movement. Inherited sin is neither an instilled nor an acquired disposition but one born in us by

2 way of a damaged inheritance. In any one person there is only one inherited sin, and in the whole human race it has a single origin and a

3 single definition. The right order of our first state derived from the subjection to God of man's will and all his other parts through his will. What defines inherited sin is the loss of the original subjection of will to God, and every other disorder of the powers of man's soul is, so to speak, matter that is now formed by that loss. Such disorder chiefly consists in disordered turning to temporal goods, and is commonly called concupiscence. So we talk of inherited sin as materially concupiscence but

4 formally the loss of right order. The libido which Augustine said transmitted inherited sin to the child cannot be the actual pleasure of the sex-act, for the sin would still be transmitted even if by God's power we felt no disordered pleasure in the act of reproduction. Rather libido is a habitual state in which our sense-appetites are not subject to reason as they were in the original integrated state of man.

83 1   The inherited sin of all men has its first agent cause in Adam *in whom all sinned*; the instrumental mechanism of this causality is the semen's active capacity for reproducing human nature accompanied by the sin.

So the sin is to be attributed not to our flesh but to our soul. We can see why if we remember that inherited sin passes into Adam's progeny from his will by way of the act of reproduction, just as sins of action pass into other parts of a sinner from his will. Whatever so passes to a part of man capable of cooperating in the fault (as a subject of the fault or as an instrument of it) will share the guilt of the fault, e.g. the will to gluttony passes into the desire of our sense-appetites and into the actual eating movements of hand and mouth, which play an instrumental part in the sin since they act under will's control. But the further effects in the digestive and other internal organs which are not under will's control do not share in the guilt. In a similar way then, since our soul but not our flesh is capable of guilt, whatever damage is wrought in our soul by inherited sin shares in its guilt, but what is wrought in our flesh has only the character of penalty. So our capacity for inherited sin is located in our soul. The general good is to be preferred to the good of individuals. So God in his wisdom does not set aside the general order of things in which souls activate bodies in order to avoid the individual infection of this soul; especially since it is the nature of the soul only to come into existence in a body. It is better for it to exist naturally but infected, than not to exist at all, especially as it can escape damnation by means of grace. Our potential for a sin resides primarily in that part of the soul principally motivated to that sin. For example, if a sin arises from sensual pleasure, the object of sense-appetite as such, then our sense-appetite is by definition our potential for that sin. Clearly inherited sin is caused by reproduction. So the part of the soul which is the primary object of reproduction is our primary potential for that sin. Now the soul is the object of reproduction as form of the body, and that it is of its own substance. So our soul's very substance is our primary potential for inherited sin. Our own wills operate on our powers not on our substance, but the will of our first parent operates by way of reproduction primarily on our substance. The original integrated state of man was also at root a state of our substance, a gift given by God to human nature which is a matter of substance before it is a matter of powers. Powers belong rather to persons since they enable personal actions, and are rather potentials for sins of action, our personal sins. But inherited sin also inclines us to actions, and in that regard affects our powers, and above all the will which is what primarily inclines us to sin. Diseases liable to be passed on to others are called infectious. Now inherited sin is passed on by reproduction, so the powers involved in reproduction are said to carry a special infection: they are our reproductive organs, our capacity for affective feelings and our sense of touch.

84 1 **Sin's effects.** St Paul says *covetousness is the root of all evils*. He has been talking of *those who want to get rich and by so doing fall into temptation and the devil's traps*. So clearly he means by covetousness the disordered love of riches. Riches give men the power to commit all kinds of sin, for as Ecclesiastes says: *all things obey money*. So covetousness is the root of all sins in the sense that it nourishes them all. In moral matters we consider what is commonly rather than always the case, since the will doesn't act of necessity. So avarice is commonly, but not always,

2 at the root of all evils. Ecclesiasticus says *All sins start with pride*. Clearly the writer is talking of unbalanced love of one's own importance, since he adds that *God has overturned the thrones of proud princes* and devotes practically the whole chapter to this theme. Voluntary actions are structured differently in intention and in implementation. Intention starts from a goal, and since the goal of acquiring earthly goods is the attainment of distinction and importance, from this point of view pride, or wanting to be important, is the starting-point of all sins. But to implement sin we start from what provides the opportunity to fulfil sinful desires, and that is riches. So the root of all sins is avarice, as we said. In willing his own importance a man is loving himself, so it matters

3 little whether we say pride or self-love starts all sins. Any vice from which other vices arise is called a leading (or capital) vice, especially if it acts as a goal for other vices and thus defines their viciousness in some way. So a leading vice is not simply one with effects that belong to other vices, but one that directs and so to speak leads other sins. Not only the ultimate sources of all vices (like avarice, their root, and pride, their starting-point) are leading vices, but also all those vices which more

4 immediately are sources of more sins than one. Gregory the Great lists seven such leading vices: vanity, envy, anger, avarice, apathy, gluttony and lust. Sins sometimes act as goals for other sins because the particular sinner is disposed to make one particular sin his goal and commonly commits other sins in pursuit of that one. No rules govern such cases since the varieties of particular dispositions is limitless. But goals also relate naturally to one another, which means certain vices commonly lead to others; and here we can discover rules. Three sorts of things are good for man: what is good for his soul, and has a desirability that only reason uncovers (the importance, reputation and prestige sought in a disordered way by vanity); what is good for his body's survival whether individually (the food and drink sought disorderedly by gluttony) or for the species (the sex-act sought disorderedly by lust); and finally, external goods or riches (sought disorderedly by avarice). In addition, certain goods are neglected because of some incidental evil: either goods for

oneself (apathy neglects our own spiritual good because of the bodily effort involved), or goods for our fellowmen (neglected out of envy when they hinder one's own importance, or out of the vengefulness of anger).

There is a threefold good in human nature: first, the constitutive elements of human nature itself and everything that must accompany them (such as our powers of soul); second, our natural inclination to virtue; and thirdly, the integrated state originally bestowed on all human nature in Adam. The first good sin can neither destroy nor diminish; the latter Adam's sin entirely removed. But the middle good – the natural inclination to virtue – is lessened by every sin we commit, since all human actions set up a bias towards similar actions in the future, and strengthening an inclination to sin weakens the contrary inclination to virtue. One might think, however, that no state of a subject, such as a sin, can act on that subject: to be acted on the subject would have to be potential to that state, whereas the subject actually exists in the state already. But in the first place states don't act on their subjects like agent causes, but like forms: in the sense whiteness acts when we say whiteness makes things white. In this sense there is nothing to stop sin lessening the good in our nature by itself being the lessening: a disordered action. But there is also the disorder that results in the agent, because in such actions one thing acts on another: the things we sense affect our sense-appetites, and these influence our reason and our will, and disorder follows: it is not the state of sin that acts on us, but its object acts on our capacities, and one capacity on another, bringing us into disorder. The natural good we weaken by sin is the natural inclination to virtue that we possess because we are by nature rational. Sin can never totally take our reason from us (if it did we should no longer be capable of sin). And since our inclination to virtue is rooted in our rational nature, sin can't weaken the root of such inclination. But sin can hinder achievement of the goal of those inclinations. And this it can go on doing, without ever totally eradicating the inclination itself. Even in the damned the natural inclination to virtue persists as remorse of conscience. It is no longer effective because in God's justice it lacks grace. The damned are like blind men who have the sort of nature which involves being able to see, but cannot actually see because the causes which should have formed the required organ were lacking.

In the original integrated state of man reason controlled our lower powers perfectly and God perfected the reason subordinated to him. This state was lost to us by Adam's sin, and the resulting lack of order among the powers of our soul that incline us to virtue we call a *wounding* of nature. Ignorance is a wound in reason's response to truth, wickedness in will's response to good; weakness wounds the response of our aggressive emotions to challenge and difficulty, and disordered desire our affections' reasonable and balanced response to pleasure. All sins inflict these four wounds blunting reason's practical sense, hardening the will against good, increasing the difficulty of acting well and inflaming desire.

5 Because death and the other defects due to sin are not intended by the sinner, sin doesn't cause them directly, though it does so incidentally by removing what prevented those defects. Thus, Adam's sin caused death and our other natural defects by depriving us of that original integrated state in which not only our lower powers were under reason's control, but our whole body was preserved from defects by the soul. Such defects then are penalties of inherited sin. They were not intended by the sinner but in God's justice were a deserved punishment. He who takes away the guilt of inherited and actual sins through baptism and penitence, removes also these defects of the body; but only at the time divine wisdom deems right: *he will bring to life your dying bodies by his Spirit which dwells in you.* For to come to the deathless and unsuffering glory which Christ already enjoys and has acquired for us, we must first become conformed to his sufferings. So for a time the ability to suffer must remain in our bodies, so that we can deserve in conformity with Christ his unsuffering glory. Sinful actions can cause bodily defects: e.g. too much food can weaken and kill people; but the effect of them as sins is to deprive us of grace, the function of which is to put right the activity of the soul rather than to hold bodily defects in check as the original integrated state of man did. So actual sin doesn't cause bodily defects in the same way as inherited sin did.

6   The particular nature of each thing aims and acts to conserve its own particular self in being, and death and destruction are against nature in this sense. But nature in general is a power of some universal cause of nature – some heavenly body, perhaps, or some higher substance (God has been called *the nature making nature*) – and the aim of such a power is the good and the survival of the universe itself, which requires a cycle of generation and destruction in things. In this sense of nature, then, death and other defects are natural; not that any form by which things exist and pursue completeness inclines towards death, but matter, distributed in a balanced way among such forms by the universal agent, does. Forms aim at existing for ever if they can, but no form of anything that can be destroyed can actually achieve such everlasting existence; always excepting the rational soul of man, which is not altogether subject to its bodily matter but has a separate activity not shared with matter.

Indestructibility is therefore more natural to man (because of his form) than it is to other destructible things. But his matter too is constituted of opposed elements and so inclines towards decomposition of the whole man. So man is naturally destructible according to the nature of his materiality, left to itself, but not according to the nature of his form. The human body is and is not in balance with its own form. It is of a balanced constitution chosen by nature as the most suitable material for our organs of touch and other powers of sense and movement. But the conditions of matter make it destructible, and that is not something nature would choose if it could avoid it. God, to whom all nature is subject, supplied for nature's defects at man's creation with the gift of a certain indestructibility in the original integrated state of man. And that is why it is said that *God did not make death*, and that death is a penalty for sin.

Sin is a sticking to something against the light of reason and divine law. [vol 27] 86 1 The tarnished brightness resulting from such contact is metaphorically described as a stain of soul. As long as the sinner stays away from the 2 light, the stain of sin persists, but when he returns by grace to the light of reason and God the stain disappears. Merely stopping the act of sin by which man moved away from the light of reason and divine law is not enough to bring him back where he was before; there must be some movement of will in the opposite direction to that of the sin.

[margin note: merely stopping sin is not enough]
[margin note: there must be movement of will toward good]

Sin's punishment. Order that is disturbed must be restored by him 87 1 who imposed the order in the first place. This restoration of order is the penalty for the disturbance. Man's will and nature is subject to three orders: the order of his own reason, that of external government (be it spiritual or temporal, political or domestic), and the universal order of God's rule. Sin disturbs all three orders, by acting against reason, human law, and divine law; so incurs penalties from the sinner himself (his remorse of conscience), from men and from God. By definition sinning issues from the will and one is guilty of it and responsible for it, whereas penalty by definition runs counter to the will. So sinning as such cannot be its own penalty. Indirectly however it can. Sin deprives us of the help of God's grace which would otherwise restrain causes of sin like the emotions and the devil's temptations; and just as lack of grace is a penalty from God so too indirectly any sin that follows. In this sense sin is a punishment for previous sin. But there are also two senses in which a sin can be its own indirect penalty as well. For the action in the sin may affect us of its own physical nature – be it an inner state like jealousy or anger, or an external action accompanied by exhausting

[margin note: indirectly, sin is its own penalty –]
[margin note: sin deprives us of help of God's grace – does no more reason is less able to do its work? so]
[margin note: grace + reason (acquire virtue) a blessed? sw 257]

effort or harm – and may also have harmful consequences.

3   Sometimes when order is subverted the very root of order is irreparably damaged and destroyed, but sometimes, because the root persists, the damage can be repaired. If a sin damages the order of our will to God at its root – the unity with our ultimate goal set up by the love of charity – then the disorder has no power to repair itself, even though God's power can repair it. So all sins that turn us away from God by destroying the love of charity are intrinsically liable to an eternal penalty. No judicial sentence is ever required to match duration of the penalty to duration of the crime. Adultery and murder may be committed in a moment, but their penalty can justly last longer than that. The death penalty, for instance, is measured not by the time it takes to implement, but rather by the everlasting time that it removes us from the society of the living, thus in its way mirroring the eternity of God's punishment. As St Gregory says, *what is just is that someone who sinned in his own kind of eternity against God should be punished in God's kind of eternity*; for by settling on sin as his ultimate goal, the sinner was willing

4   eternity to it himself. It would be inconsistent with divine justice to annihilate the sinner, for that would offend against his liability to everlasting punishment. The guilt has no power to repair itself and would last for ever, and that is why it is liable to an eternal penalty.

5   Some sins however do not turn us away from our ultimate goal, but offend by willing something which has been subordinated to that goal,

6   but willing it not enough or too much. A man's sinful actions make him liable to punishment as someone who has violated God's just order, and can only be reintegrated into it by some recompensing penalty that will restore the balance of justice. So even though the sinful action and the injury it has done may have passed, there remains this debt of punishment. Again the stain of sin cannot be wiped away from a man unless he willingly accepts God's just order, by spontaneously taking on himself some penalty in recompense for his past sin, or by patiently bearing a penalty God imposes, thus giving it the character of reconciliation. Penalties that reconcile, though in the abstract they run counter to our wills, are in the concrete, as reconciliation, willed. So even after the stain of guilt has been taken away, there can remain liability not to penalty simply speaking but to reconciliation. When the stain has gone the wound in the will has been healed; but other powers wounded by the sin still need curative penalties, and there is still the need to re-establish

7   the balance of justice and undo the scandal given to others. Sometimes someone who did not commit the sin may lovingly undergo another's reconciling penalty, e.g. pay his debts. But in the ordinary sense penalties

are imposed for one's own sins of action and for inherited sin (inasmuch as the abandonment of our human nature to itself, stripped of its original integrated state and burdened with all the defects that accompany this stripping, was a penalty for inherited sin). Sometimes however men willingly suffer minor impoverishments so as to gain a major enrichment, *of fasting* and then the sufferings are medicinal rather than punitive. As such no particular sin is their cause, unless one says that the very need for medicine is due to our damaged nature and so is a penalty for inherited sin.

Fatal sin.   Sins metaphorically described as *fatal* or *mortal* are opposed 88 1 to *venial* or *excusable* sins. Disorders in means to goals can be repaired by reconsidering the goal, just as errors in conclusions can be put right by recourse to the premises. But a disordered ultimate goal has nothing more ultimate to repair it, and is like an erroneous premise. So sins with a disordered goal are labelled *fatal*, as being irreparable; while sins which *see 250* simply get the means to the goals wrong are reparable and labelled *excusable*, since a sin is excused when its liability to punishment is lifted. So fatal and non-fatal sins are opposed as intrinsically reparable or irreparable (abstracting from God's power which can cure any evil of body or soul). These are not two different versions of one general notion of sin, for one is called sin only derivatively by an analogy with the other. Excusable sin is not fully a sin, but only bears a relation to fatal sin. It is not *against* the law, because somebody sinning excusably neither does what is legally forbidden nor omits to do what is legally commanded; rather he acts independently of the law by not observing the reasonable way of doing things that the law intended. If men are disposed to refer themselves and all that belongs to them to God, that is enough to save them from sinning fatally whenever some action of theirs is not actually referred to God's glory. Non-fatal sin does not exclude such habitual disposition of human actions to God's glory, but only some action's actual referral; such an action does not drive out the love of charity disposing us to God. When we sin excusably we don't set up an earthly good as fulfilment and goal for ourselves, but simply make use of that good without actually referring it to God, though he remains the goal we are disposed to. Temporal goods are opposed to eternal goods only if chosen as goals or destinations; as means to a goal they don't oppose them.

    We might call sins excusable because they can be excused; in this *2 senses of* sense Ambrose says repentance excuses every sin (and such excuse *"excusable"* follows the sin). Or we can call sins excusable because something in them partially or totally allows them to be excused: partially as when they are committed out of ignorance or weakness (and such excuse lies in a sin's cause), and wholly when they do not disrupt our relationship to our ultimate goal and so deserve only temporal and not eternal punishment. We are discussing sins excusable in this latter sense. The first two meanings of excusable can apply to any type of sin; the third applies only to certain types, where a sin's type is determined by its immediate object (so now the excuse lies in the sin's nature, and we distinguish it from sins fatal by nature). Whenever the will sets itself an objective opposed to the love of charity that relates us to our ultimate goal (be it opposed to the love of God – like blasphemy and perjury – or to the love of our fellowmen – like murder and adultery) then the sin is fatal by nature. But when the immediate object of our will, though disordered, is not opposed to love of God and fellowmen – as in frivolous chatter or immoderate laughter – such sins are non-fatal by nature. Sometimes it can happen that a sin non-fatal by nature because of its immediate objective is made fatal by the sinner choosing it as his ultimate goal or using it as a means to something fatal by nature, e.g. frivolous chatter with a view to adultery. And the reverse can happen: a sinner can introduce excusability into a sin fatal by nature, if it is not fully his own action because indeliberate, e.g. the doubts about faith that take one by surprise.

3 Sinful actions can directly predispose us to other sins of the same kind. But sins non-fatal by nature cannot in this way predispose us to sins fatal by nature, though they can lead to sins that the sinner can make fatal; for the more disposed he is to sin non-fatally the more his desire to sin grows, and eventually he may choose what he has become habituated to as his goal in life. Actions non-fatally sinful in nature can dispose us indirectly to actions fatally sinful by nature, by sapping our resistance to disorder as such, and thus to choosing what is fatally sinful by nature.

4 But a non-fatal sin can't suddenly turn fatal. If the will changes there is a discontinuity of moral acts even if the physical action be continuous. Sins non-fatal by nature can however be fatal on occasion, because made a goal or a means to some other fatal sin; and many non-fatal sins together, though they cannot coalesce into a fatal

5 sin, can nevertheless dispose us to fatal sin. Circumstances cannot make a non-fatal sin fatal while they remain circumstances, but only if they are absorbed into the immediate objective of an action and change its moral type. Protracted and repeated sinning is not as such a circumstance that can change an action's moral type, though it can lead indirectly to disobedience or contempt and that will change the type. Drunkenness however is a different case, because it is a fatal sin by nature. Unnecess-

[margin note:] relat of fatal to non fatal sin –

arily and solely for love of liquor to render ourselves incapable of using *drunkenness* our reasons (that by which we direct ourselves to God and avoid all sorts of sin) is an action expressly opposed to virtue. Drunkenness is only non-fatal because of ignorance and weakness, but ignorance can't excuse frequent drunkenness; the drunk is now choosing to drink too much and returning his sin to its true fatal nature. A non-fatal sin like 6 frivolous chatter can become fatal if we add to it disorder fatal by nature, directing it to illicit sex, for instance; but a fatal sin can't become non-fatal by adding to it some non-fatal disorder: illicit sex isn't less of a sin when indulged in for the sake of frivolous conversation! But something which would of its nature be a fatal sin can be excused by the subtraction of something: when it occurs without deliberation, for example, and takes one by surprise.

That men can pursue what serves a goal in a disordered way while 89 3 still pursuing the goal in an ordered way happens because our ordering of means to end is not now infallible, as it would have been in the original state of integrated nature, when our lower nature was firmly subordinated to our higher nature because our higher nature was subordinated to God. In that state of integration there could be no disorder at all unless it started with an insubordination of man to God, and that would have been a fatal sin. So men in the state of integration could not sin non-fatally without first sinning fatally. By the age that someone 6 starts to use his reason he cannot be totally excused from responsibility for either non-fatal or fatal sin. At that point in his life the first thing that faces him is deliberation about himself. If he at that moment directs himself towards a rightful goal, God's grace pardons his inherited sin; but if he does not use the degree of discernment of which he is capable at that age, he will sin fatally by failing to do what in him lies. From that moment until all his sins are pardoned by grace, he cannot be in a state of non-fatal sin without also being in a state of fatal sin. For the first thing that faces someone arriving at an age of discernment is to think about himself as a goal of other things (since goals are always the first things intended). This is the time laid down for obeying God's positive command to *Turn to me and I will turn to you.*

Chapter 9

LAW AND GRACE

[vol 28] Two agencies outside ourselves influence our behaviour: the devil tempting us to do evil [see ch 6 p 158 and ch 8 pp 262–3 above], and God stimulating us to do good, teaching us by *law* and aiding us by *grace*.

Introductory comment. This chapter is described by Thomas as a discussion of the outside influences on human action, as distinguished from the inside principles that dispositions and virtues and vices are. But the only outside influence that he considers of importance is God, who is, so to speak, both outside and inside. And so the chapter turns into a discussion of what we might call God's interventions in the natural history of human action. Thus, although law is a natural phenomenon among human societies and in men's hearts even – and that is how it is first discussed below – God also promulgated special laws for the human society of Israel that he created: and so we discuss Old Testament law as in a special sense God's law. That law was a tool of the Old Testament plan described above (in the preface p lvii and the introductory comment on ch 3 p 63): to build the unity of mankind (betrayed by Adam as we saw at the end of the last chapter) around the house of Israel worshipping God in the house of the Lord. But this plan too fell short of what was required, according to Christian belief, and the Old Testament law from outside has now been superseded by a New Testament law from inside, the grace of God at work in our hearts through the coming of a new house of God, Jesus of Nazareth, and the new worship that he inaugurated.

The chapter starts then with a treatment of **law in general**. Man by nature lives life in common: the good life is not simply individuals planning their own behaviour by their own prudence for their own goals, but by a communal prudence planning co-operative behaviour toward a common goal. Part of the function of the virtue of justice is precisely to strengthen individuals to pursue a communally good life. Justice enables individuals to submit themselves to regulation by a communal prudence (or providence) existing outside them and influencing them only in the ways free will can be externally influenced: by presentation of objects to their minds and wills as good and desirable, by inducing bodily and emotional changes designed to stimulate such desire. Laws are the dictates of such a communal prudence or providence: regulations serving the community goal devised by communal reason (the collective reason of the people, or the authority representing that reason). To apply such regulations to the behaviour of individually free community members requires promulgation and coercive power in the authority, and wills strengthened by the virtue of justice in the community.

But now Thomas takes a bolder theological step. Law, he says, is a name of God like wisdom and goodness, which we first meet in a human context, but which can then be applied literally and non-metaphorically (though by analogy) to God himself. God himself is an *eternal Law*, the eternal plan of the universe's communal reason or prudence or providence by which God directs the universe towards himself as its communal goal. (Compare ch 2 pp 55ff and the whole of chapter 6). And if God is, identically, law, so too are we in a sense, by way of a natural disposition to mirror the eternal law of God in our own reasons. We have *law in us by nature* (I avoid the misleading translation: natural law), making self-evident the first general precepts of all self-regulation and all enacted law, which Thomas summarizes as *Pursue good and avoid evil*. By considering what man's nature involves, we can derive from these primary precepts many secondary consequential precepts of the law that is in us by nature, and these are frequently explicitated in *enacted law* (e.g. *Thou shalt not kill*); and from the general pattern of doing things laid down in the law we have in us by nature, authorities can specify how we do that in this community or at this stage of history – specifications deriving their force of law not directly from the patterns of law in us by nature, but from the persuasive authority of the particular community acting in keeping with those patterns. Specifications not in keeping with the patterns do not have the character and force of law, but are bad law, indeed forms of lawlessness.

Though most enacted law is *human law*, two historical examples are here called God's law (perhaps we could call them God's human law). For God has created his own community in this world with its own enacted laws. Firstly, he adopted the people of the

[handwritten margin notes: "Law is name of God –"; "✗ we have law in us by nature (the term 'natural law' is misleading)"]

Jews as a community in which to realize God's kingdom, with a law (the *Old Law*) that clearly explicitated the secondary moral consequences of the law in man by nature (through the ten commandments and other biblical moral teaching), and also specified the general pattern of natural respect for God and for fellowmen: by means of special ceremonial injunctions of Jewish worship, and special judicial injunctions governing behaviour towards fellow-Jews and strangers, specifications designed to mark out the Jewish people as in some way chosen by God.

In the Old Law, Thomas thinks, God did the most that could be done in the way of enacted law to help man to a life of perfect justice; but for two reasons it failed to achieve that state of justice, failed (in Thomas's interpretation of a Pauline word) to *justify*. Firstly it had to rely on man possessing a natural justice strengthening his will to accept the law, but in fact he was without such justice, due to sin inherited from Adam (see the previous chapter). Secondly, what the community required for glorious community with God was a justice beyond nature, a justice of the Spirit which was only to be given through Christ. In fact, the Old Law was never intended by God to be perfect; it was intended to prefigure a *New Law* to be promulgated in men's hearts and accepted not by fear of coercion but by love poured forth in our hearts by the Spirit of God himself. The Old Law was the shadow of the New Law thrown back into the past, and the justice it adumbrated was the justice God's gracious gift of Christ would bring. The treatise on law thus leads up, through this notion of a New Law implanted in men's hearts, to what Thomas will next discuss: God's justifying grace.

The meaning of the word **grace** is primarily *favour*: but it is used especially of that act of favour by which God finally salvages his creation from man's mismanagement and salvages it through men, the act of favour by which he, so to speak, accepts man's disintegration and bad will on Calvary and puts a reverse human will into the event, a suffering in redeeming love of the event and of all uncreation. The word *redeem* is a traditional one, the Latin word for *pay back*, and derives its force partly from the notion of ransoming prisoners, and more fundamentally from the Old Testament notion of the *goel*, the kinsman who pays back injury to a victim, originally by vengeance and later by vindication in a court of law. The traditional theological adaptation of this notion to the salvage of creation on Calvary, is that man needed to *pay*

Old Law

New Law

grace

"redeem"

ransom or *make amends* and only God had the wherewithal; so God *gave* the ransom – gave it, not just lent it, by becoming man himself and suffering the penalty. The origins and the uses of the notions of amends and paying back and ransom are not altogether consistent, as we can see.

It is noteworthy that Thomas, while not departing from the above vocabulary, uses it fairly sparingly, and prefers to talk of grace and of Calvary in terms more related to love, and more faithful to the ancient notion of God as man's *goel*. God in his favour and grace comes to man in his trouble as to a kinsman, and adopts him into his family – and the adoption is a real birth into a share in the nature of God, so that grace names not only an act of God but a new disposition in man. What he comes to do is make amends, in the sense of repairing the fracture in creation and the fracture in men themselves in a way only he could do it: by letting his own self, his power of creation be abused by the power of men and of uncreation, letting the forces of uncreation do their worst, suffering their most powerful weapon, death, and in that moment of powerlessness letting the true power of God show. The true power of God is the power of love and the remaking of creation is through the drawing-power of that love, a power which does not display itself in laying down any law or necessity on men, but in the gamble of provoking loving response. For God is lord of chance as we have seen (cf ch 2 p 56 and ch 6 pp 160–1), and on Calvary he showed that he can create a world which will infallibly be fulfilled through the free actions of men.

At the end of the chapter there occurs a distinction between two so-called effects of grace: it works in us to justify or vindicate or redeem, and it works with us to reward our cooperation. For grace is a gift to our cooperation so to speak, giving us back the power of bringing about with God's help a new creation, a power which shares his power of love, his power of powerlessness provoking loving response. That is the real meaning of *merit*: earning or deserving our reward. Meriting names a way of effectively bringing about a result which depends on the power of someone else: the way of bringing something about by cooperating with that person's grace and love.

Law

90 1 What is law? Law is a standard of measurement for behaviour, fostering certain actions and deterring from others. Now setting a standard for human behaviour is what reason is doing when it plans action in pursuit of a goal. So law is reason's doing. Law exists derivatively in the behaviour it regulates, but properly speaking in the reason that does the regulating. It is not however an act of reasoning, but the product of such an act. In the pursuit of truth reason elaborates definitions, then statements, then arguments or proofs; when planning action it elaborates propositions that relate to behaviour as premises of arguments do to conclusions. Such general premises explicitly or implicitly brought to bear on behaviour are what we call law. So we can only accept the saying that *the ruler's will is law*, on the proviso that the ruler's will is ruled by reason; otherwise a ruler's will is more like lawlessness.

2   Law is primarily a product of reason planning action to serve our ultimate goal of human happiness, and properly of happiness in common, for every human individual is part of some completely self-contained community. So a command to do a particular deed is a law in the true sense only when it promotes the general good; where general good means not some generic goodness exemplified in all individual goods, but some single common goal that all serve. Just as when pursuing truth no conclusion stands to reason unless it can be analysed into self-evident first premises, so when planning action no command stands to reason unless it serves our ultimate goal, the general good: only then does it have the force of law.

3   Planning for the general good belongs to the people as a whole or to someone representing them, since those pursuing the goal must do the planning for it. *The aim of legislation,* according to Aristotle, *is the fostering of virtue.* A private person can admonish, but if his admonitions are not heeded then he has no power of enforcement to foster virtue effectively. Because the people and the public authorities do have such power and can inflict penalties, legislation is reserved to them. The good of individuals is not an ultimate goal, but serves the general good; and the good of families serves the good of the self-contained political community. The head of a family can issue commands and orders but not laws in the true sense.

4   Standards of measurement are imposed by applying them to what they measure. So if law is to have binding force it must be applied to those subject to it by some promulgation that brings it to their notice.

There are thus four elements in the definition of law: law is an
ordinance of reason, for the general good, made by whoever has care of
the community, and promulgated. (The law that is in us by nature is
promulgated by God implanting it in our minds as something we know
by nature.)

Types of law.   The plan by which God, as ruler of the universe, 91 1
governs all things, is a law in the true sense. And since it is not a
plan conceived in time we call it the eternal law. It is promulgated
through God's eternal Word, though creatures hear its promulgation
in time. The goal of a law is the goal it actively imposes on those
subject to it; whether the act of making a law serves a goal depends
on whether the lawmaker does. When God governs he is his own goal,
and his own law, so that the eternal law serves no other purpose than
itself.

Everything God plans obeys the standards of his eternal law, and 2
bears the imprint of that law in the form of a natural tendency to pursue
whatever behaviour and goals are appropriate to it. Reasoning creatures
follow God's plan in a more profound way, themselves sharing the
planning, making plans both for themselves and for others; so they share
in the eternal reasoning itself that is imprinting them with their natural
tendencies to appropriate behaviour and goals. This distinctive sharing
in the eternal law we call the natural law, the law we have in us by
nature. For the light of natural reason by which we tell good from evil
(the law that is in us by nature) is itself an imprint of God's light in us.
All our reasoning and willing starts from what we are by nature:
reasoning starts from premises known by nature and willing a course of
action starts from our natural tendency to an ultimate goal. In the same
way any planning of action for a goal must start from the law we have
in us by nature. Even creatures without reason share eternal reason in
their own way; but because reasoning creatures do it with understanding
their sharing in the eternal law is itself law in the true sense, whereas
that of other creatures is law only metaphorically.

Reason when pursuing truth starts from premises which cannot be 3
proved but are known by nature, and draws conclusions that belong to
the various different sciences: these we do not know by nature but work
out by reason. In the same way [when planning action] man's reason
starts from injunctions of law he has by nature as if from general
premises that need no proof, and arrives at more particular arrangements
which, provided they fulfil the other defining conditions of law previously mentioned, are called human laws. Reason in pursuit of truth

shares God's wisdom by knowing certain general premises, but not by knowing every particular truth that God knows. And similarly when planning action man's reason shares God's eternal law by nature, knowing some general principles but not the detailed plans which the eternal law lays down for each single thing. So human reason must go on to enact particular laws. Since whatever we do is particular and might be done otherwise, human laws can't have the same unfailing validity as the proved conclusions of science which express general truths that must be so.

4   The planning of human life required, over and above the law we have by nature and the human laws we make, law made by God. For men are destined for an eternal happiness which lies beyond their natural powers of achievement, and so they needed God to give them laws that could help them plan for that goal. Moreover, men's judgments differ, especially in matters of detail that can be implemented in more than one way, so that if men were to know without doubt what to do and not to do when human laws conflicted, they needed God to give them an infallible law to guide them. Again, though men can only judge overt behaviour, not that which is inwardly hidden, perfect virtue requires regulation of both types of behaviour. Since the law of men is not enough to check and guide what goes on within us, we needed a law of God as well. And finally, as Augustine says, human law can't afford to punish or forbid all wrongdoing: it can only do so by also forbidding a great deal of good and hindering much that serves the general good of human social intercourse. So we needed in addition a law of God that could leave no wrongdoing unforbidden and unpunished.

5   The law of God divides into the Old Law and the New Law, less and more fully developed versions of the same thing, like child and grown-up. St Paul indeed compares Old Law status to being in school, and New Law status to having left school behind. Thus the Old Law directly aimed at an earthly and material general good, whereas the New Law aims at a good that is heavenly and spiritual. Again, the New Law fulfils the Old Law by governing man's inner heart and soul: *the Old Law checks the hand, the New Law the heart.* Thirdly, the Old Law fostered keeping of its commandments by fear of penalties, but the New Law pours love into our hearts by Christ's grace, prefigured in the Old Law but given only in the New. And so Augustine says *there is only a small difference between the law and the gospel:* **timor** *and* **amor** *[fear and love].* The saving of men could only come through Christ, and the law by which all men were to be fully saved could only be given after Christ's coming; before that what was needed was a law which prepared the

people from whom Christ would be born to accept him, and which contained certain rudiments of saving justice.

St Paul talks of *another law in my body fighting against the law in my* 6 *mind*. This sensual tendency (called *inflammability*) is certainly a law in other animals because it is a direct imprint in them of [the eternal] law. But in us it is not so much a law as a departure from the law that is imprinted in our reasons. However, since it was by God's just act that we lost our former integrated state in which reason was in full command, the fact that we now suffer the sway of sensual impulses is a penalty deriving from God's law. Inflammability then is not properly a law, because it inclines us to evil, but rather a just consequence of God's law.

The effect of law. The virtue of subordinates lies in being good 92 1 subordinates of the controlling authority: thus our affections and aggressive feelings are virtuous when well in reason's control. Now all law aims to control those subordinate to it, so it is in the nature of law to foster virtue in its subjects. And if the lawmaker intends what is truly, as God judges it, to the general good, the law will foster truly good men; but if he aims at his own profit and pleasure and opposes God's justice then the law will foster not truly good men but only good citizens of that state. Men good in that sense could actually be thoroughly wicked, as good robbers are. So how far the law makes men good depends on how far the human behaviour it is designed to foster is virtuous behaviour. Every man is part of some political community, and to be good he must act in keeping with the general good. Wholes too must be composed of well-adjusted parts, so the general good of the community depends on the virtue of its citizens, or at least of its leaders (with the others virtuous enough to obey their leaders' commands). Tyrannical law, being unreasonable, is not truly law but a breakdown of law. The only character of law it does have is to be a decree of a presiding authority enforcing obedience on his subjects, aiming therefore to make them good citizens of such a regime even if not good in the true sense.

Laws command, forbid, allow and punish, says Gratian. Laws, like 2 statements, are pronouncements of reason, but statements describe whereas laws prescribe, guiding human behaviour. Behaviour which is by definition good and virtuous the law commands, that which is by definition bad and vicious it forbids, and behaviour by definition indifferent or of little account it allows; and because it persuades men to obey through fear of penalties law also punishes. Anyone can reward but only administrators of a law have authority to impose penalties. So punishing is listed as an effect of law but not rewarding. Someone who gets used to avoiding evil and doing good from fear of penalties may in time come to do these things by choice because he enjoys it. So even by punishing law can foster goodness in men.

[margin note: punishment may lead men to virtue]

93 1 **The eternal law.**   Just as craftsmen must have in mind plans of what they are making – blueprints – so those who govern must have in mind plans of what those subject to their government ought to do – laws. God's wisdom, thought of as the plan by which he created everything, is a blueprint or model; thought of as the plan by which he directs everything to its goal, it is a law. The eternal law is indeed nothing else than God's wise plan for directing every movement and action in creation. Law directs things to one common good, and however diverse the things so directed, as coordinated to one common good they are 2 unified. So the eternal law is one law, one single universal plan. No one but God and those blessed with the vision of God can know the eternal law in itself. But all knowledge of truth is a light radiating from the eternal law, and everyone knows some truth, if only the general principles of the law that we have in us by nature. Those who know more than others know the eternal law better. *We can know the hidden things of God by looking at the things that he has made*, but no one fully comprehends the eternal law, because its effects do not fully reveal it.

[margin note: law as a plan of act]

3   When agents are ordered the agency of the secondary agents derives from that of the primary agent: without it they could not act. Now the eternal law is the plan of government adopted by the supreme authority in the world, so all other plans of government that subordinate authorities adopt must derive from it. In other words all laws that proceed from right reason derive from the eternal law. The inflammability of our sensual nature is called *a law in our body* because of its nature as a penalty imposed by God's justice, and as such it obviously derives from the eternal law. But by inclining us to wrongdoing it runs counter to God's law and is not law at all. Human law is law when it accords with right reason, and as such it obviously derives from the eternal law. But when it deviates from reason it is lawless, and is more a kind of violence. Even lawless law however can bear a certain likeness to law inasmuch as it proceeds from lawful authority; and so in that sense it derives from the eternal law, for *all authority is from the Lord God*. Certain things human law allows not because it approves them but because it is powerless to control them; and that law should not intervene where it is powerless is itself derived from the eternal law. But it is a different

matter entirely when human law approves what the eternal law disapproves.

Everything created, whether it could have been otherwise or had to 4 be as it is, is subject to the eternal law; only God himself is exempt since he is the law. As to God's will, if by that we mean the will itself, identical with God, then it is not subject to the eternal law but is itself the law; but if we mean by God's will what God wills for creation, then that is subject to the law as to God's wise plan. It is in this latter sense that we call God's will reasonable; in the former sense we should rather say his will is reason itself. Even things that have to be as they are, are nevertheless caused, and have their impossibility to be otherwise imposed on them. Far from needing no compulsion to be as they are, they are subject to the most effective compulsion of all.

Law governs the behaviour of those things subject to the lawmaker 5 (nobody, properly speaking, imposes law on his own behaviour). However, when we make use of things subject to us but lacking reason, what gets done counts as our behaviour, the user's not the things', for such things are more acted on than acting. So man can't impose law on non-reasoning things, however subject they are to him. But on reasoning creatures subject to him he can impose law, imprinting on their minds rules of action in the form of the commands he utters. And just as man by utterance imprints inner principles of behaviour on men subject to him, so God imprints principles of behaviour appropriate to them on all natural things, and in so doing commands all nature. So that every movement in nature is subject to God's eternal law. But non-reasoning creatures, though subject to eternal law by being set in motion by divine planning, do not understand divine commands as rational creatures do. The imprinting of intrinsic principles of action on natural things is to them what promulgation of a law is to men. Creatures lacking reason neither share man's plans nor obey them; but they share God's plan by obeying it, since the plan of God is more powerful than those of men. Just as our limbs move according to our plan without sharing (that is, grasping) the plan, so creatures lacking reason are set in motion by God without thereby possessing reason.

We, as reasoning creatures, are subject to eternal law in both ways: 6 in common with creatures lacking reason we have a natural tendency to do what the law commands (for *we are born to virtue*, as Aristotle says); but what is peculiar to us is that we are aware of the law. In evil men both ways of being subject to eternal law are decayed as it were: the natural tendency to virtue spoilt by vice, and the natural knowledge of what is good darkened by passion and habitual wrongdoing. Good men share the eternal law more perfectly in both ways: to their natural knowledge of what is good is added faith and wisdom, and to their natural tendency to do good is added the interior stimulus of grace and virtue. So good men are perfectly subject to the eternal law, always acting in accordance with it; whereas bad men are imperfectly subject to it in the way they act, knowing and tending to good imperfectly. But what is lacking in the way they act is recompensed by the way they are acted on, for when they fail to obey the law that is in them by nature they suffer its decrees. *If you are led by the Spirit of God*, says St Paul, *you are not under the law*. Spiritual men fulfil the law voluntarily with the love of charity poured into their hearts by the Holy Spirit, and so are not *under* the law as under a burden of obligation they are unwilling to bear. Or we could say that since the Spirit of God himself is not *under* the law, neither are deeds which are more his than men's: *where the Spirit of the Lord is, there is freedom*. The eternal law decrees who deserve happiness or misery and thus who will remain happy or miserable; so both the blessed and the damned are subject to it.

94 1 **The law we have in us by nature.**   The law we have in us by nature is the sort of product of reason propositions are. Now we do not identify dispositions with what they produce: our grammatical competence is not itself a grammatically correct sentence. So the law in us by nature is not itself a disposition in the proper sense of the word. Sometimes however we talk of what we are disposed to as though it was itself the disposition: we talk of what we hold to by faith as the faith. In the same way we can talk of the injunctions of the law in us by nature (to which our mind is always disposed but not always attending) as though they were the disposition. In the pursuit of truth the same is true of the premises we accept without proof: they are what we are disposed to rather than themselves a disposition. We can all have such a disposition and yet on occasion be hindered from using it: men can't attend to what they know when sleeping, and children cannot use their dispositions to first premises and to the law in them by nature at all, because they aren't old enough.

2   The injunctions of the law in us by nature are to reason planning action what the first premises of the sciences are to reason pursuing truth: the self-evident starting-points. Man grasps things in a certain order: in the grasp of anything is included a grasp of *being*, so that the first starting-point of thought, accepted without proof, presupposed to everything else, is that you can't simultaneously affirm and deny, being excludes not being. And just as this grasp of being underlies a grasp of

anything at all, so a grasp of *good* underlies all grasp by reason planning action, for action is goal-seeking, and to be a goal is to be good. Since good is grasped as always desirable, the first premise in reason's planning of action is that good is to be done and pursued and evil avoided. And on this are based all the other injunctions of the law in us by nature, which command us to do whatever reason, when planning action, naturally grasps to be good for man, whatever man naturally seeks as a goal. That includes, firstly, whatever accords with the natural tendency every substance has to try and preserve its natural being: so the law in us by nature commands whatever conserves human life and opposes death. Secondly, man naturally seeks whatever accords with his generic animal nature, whatever *nature teaches all animals*: mating between the sexes, and bringing up one's young. And thirdly, man naturally seeks whatever accords with the rational nature that distinguishes him as human: to know the truth about God, for example, and to live a social life; so the law in us by nature commands whatever is relevant to such inclinations, like avoiding ignorance and not offending those we live with. What makes man human is his rational soul, so all men tend by nature to act reasonably, which is to act virtuously. That does not mean that the law which is in us by nature prescribes every specific act of every virtue that can be defined; rather it prescribes the acts to which nature immediately inclines us, but not those that only reasoned investigation can show help us live well. All wrongdoing is unreasonable and thus against nature, if we mean the nature man has as man; but some wrongdoing is specially called unnatural because it goes against even animal nature: homosexual acts, for example, which run counter to the natural mode of intercourse between male and female.

Isidore says *all peoples agree about what is by nature right*. Now reason when pursuing truth chiefly concerns itself with what must always be so, and the truth of its particular conclusions is as free from exceptions as the truth of its general premises. But reason when planning action concerns itself with things that might possibly be otherwise, the field in which men can act; and so, even if its general starting-points allow of no exceptions, the more we get down to particulars the more exceptions occur. In the sciences then both premises and conclusions are as true for you as for me, though not everyone knows them; not everyone knows the angles of a triangle add up to two right angles, yet it is true for everyone. But in practical matters though the general starting-points are as true and right for you as for me, particular courses of action are not; and even when they are, not everyone knows it. Usually deposits ought to be refunded, but cases occur when it would be dangerous and therefore unreasonable to do so: when, for example, what is refunded would be used against one's country. And the more detail we add, saying perhaps that we should return deposits only with such and such provisos and in such and such a manner, the more opportunity we give for exceptional cases where refunding (or not refunding) will be wrong. So particular recommendations occasionally fail. They fail to be right because of other intervening factors, just as in the physical world natural processes occasionally fail when other factors interfere. Or they fail to be recognized as right, due to reason being distorted by passions or bad customs or temperaments: Julius Caesar reported for example that German tribes in the old days didn't think robbery wrong, though it is expressly against the law that is in us by nature.

cf Kant on lying

5   The law of God and the laws of men have *added* many things helpful for human living to the law we have in us by nature. But can they ever subtract from it, so that something which once was law by nature ceases to be so? The first premises of the law that is in us by nature are altogether unalterable. And secondary injunctions (which can be regarded as close consequences of these first premises though less general) must remain right in the majority of cases, though exceptionally because of intervening factors they may change in some particular. Because innocent and guilty alike all die by nature as God's penalty for inherited sin, it is not unjust for God to command the death of any man, innocent or guilty, [as he did Isaac's death]. And since adultery is intercourse with a wife assigned by God's law to someone else, to go in to any woman by divine command [as Hosea did] is neither adultery nor unmarried sex. The same applies to theft, for the things God commands one to take [e.g. the goods of the Egyptians taken by the Israelites] are taken with the consent of their owner, the master of the universe. Whatever God commands in the world of human affairs is just, just as whatever he does in the physical world is in some sense natural. Things can be by nature right either because nature inclines us towards them (e.g. not doing harm to others), or because nature does not incline us to the contrary (going naked, since clothes are products of artifice not of nature). *Common ownership and universal freedom are by nature right* in this latter sense, because private property and slavery are not arrangements of nature but human contrivances for the good running of society. So even here the law in us by nature has been altered only
6   in the sense of being added to. The most general premises of the law we have by nature are known to all and there is no way in which they can be altogether effaced from men's hearts; but passion can stop reason applying general premises in a particular case. And secondary more

particular injunctions (close consequences so to say of the primary premises) can be effaced by mistaken arguments or by perverse customs and habits.

Human law.   Men have a natural bent to virtue, but complete or 95 1 perfect virtue needs moral training. Compare the way man has to manufacture necessities of life like food and clothing: nature starts him off with a mind and hands, but doesn't provide a completed product as it does for other animals. Man however finds moral training hard work on his own. For those blessed by God with good natural temperaments and customs, parental training by admonition is enough; but those who are rebellious and prone to vice and unresponsive to words have to be kept from evil by force or fear, so that others at least are left in peace, and they themselves gradually start doing from choice what earlier they did from fear and so grow virtuous. Now training that operates through fear of penalties is the kind of training law imposes. So men's peace and virtue required human laws: as Aristotle noted, *man when perfectly virtuous is the best of animals, but without law and justice he is the worst*, since he, by reason, can devise weapons to satisfy his lusts and savagery, which other animals cannot. Aristotle thought it *better to regulate issues by law than to leave them for judges to decide*. It is easier to find the few wise men needed to frame good laws than the many needed to judge every case aright. Laws can also be formulated at leisure from accumulated experience, whereas particular cases have to be judged under pressure as they crop up. And finally lawmakers making general judgments for the future are likely to be less prejudiced than those sitting in judgment over immediate issues. The *living justice* needed in a good judge is rare and fragile, so it became necessary wherever possible to decide judgments by law in advance, leaving very little to men's choice; though certain particular issues like what in fact happened can't be covered by law and must be left to judges to decide.

Reason's ultimate standard is the law we have in us by nature, and 2 law framed by men is law only to the extent it derives from that law. If it runs counter in any way to the law in us by nature, it is no longer law but breakdown of law. Some human laws however develop the law in us by nature in the way conclusions develop premises in scientific proofs (you mustn't kill people because you mustn't do them harm); whilst others develop it in the way that craftsmen, by adopting particular specifications, develop some general design (attaching some particular penalty to a crime, for example). Laws of the first type, though humanly enacted, draw some of their force from the law we have in us by nature, but the force of the second type of law comes entirely from human enactment. When Aristotle described *legal rights* as *rights that did not exist until a law was enacted*, he was talking of enactments which specify some general pattern of the law in us by nature. The general premises of law in us by nature cannot be applied in every case in the same way because of the variety of human affairs. And this is the reason enacted laws differ from people to people. Enactments that specify the general patterns contained in the law we have in us by nature depend *not so much on reasoned proof as on the opinion of experienced, senior and prudent people that has to be accepted without proof.*

3   According to Isidore positive or enacted law should be *worthy, fair, possible according to nature and the custom of the land, suited to the place and time, needed, useful, clear (so it can't trap people in its obscurity), serving no private interest but framed for the general good of all citizens.*

4   Classification of human law depends on how we characterize it. As development of the law we have in us by nature, human law divides into the laws of particular states (specifying the general provisions of the law we have in us by nature in ways suited to particular political communities) and the law common to all peoples (the so-called *ius gentium*, which develops the law we have by nature as conclusions develop premises, and governs things like buying and selling and other such necessities of the social life that is natural to man). As serving the general good, human law divides into laws special to each group working for the good of all – priests praying for the people, rulers governing them, soldiers defending them. As instituted by community authority, human law divides according to different types of constitution and regime – monarchies ruled by one person, aristocracies ruled by the virtuous, oligarchies ruled by the rich and powerful, democracies ruled by the people, and tyrannies which are so corrupt as not to be ruled by law at all. The best regime is one blended of these with laws *sanctioned both by men of birth and the people.* As controlling human behaviour, human law divides according to domains of behaviour, laws about adultery, murder and so on.

96 1   **How flexible is human law?**   The law intends the general good, and to measure up to that it must take account of many things relevant to different people engaged in different activities at different periods of time. Standards of measurement are used to bring many different things under one concept; it would be pointless to have different standards for every different thing to be measured, and laws that applied to only one single case would be useless. So control of individual actions is left to

prudent decisions of the individuals involved, while law governs things in general. *You mustn't want the same degree of certainty about everything*, says Aristotle. Physical events and human actions don't have to happen the way they do, so one can know only what usually happens and probably will again.

Standards must be applicable to what they measure. Laws must fit 2 the human condition and be *possible according to nature and the customs of the land*. Now the non-virtuous cannot do the same things as the virtuous, nor children the same as grown-ups. Since then the majority of men to whom human laws apply are not very virtuous, human law *nicely realistic* forbids only the more serious wrongdoing, chiefly what would harm others and must be kept in check if human society is to be preserved. Human law aims at human virtue, but step by step, not all at once; to insist on a degree of perfection that most people cannot manage would only cause them to break out in worse wrongdoing. *Blow your nose too hard and it bleeds. Pour new wine into old wineskins and the skins will burst and the wine pour out.* So *civil laws let many things pass unpunished which God's plan must put right*. Since the immediate objective of any virtue 3 can serve either the individual's private good or the general good of all (you can act courageously to defend the state or your own friend), there is no virtuous action that cannot be commanded by law. Nevertheless human law doesn't command every virtuous action, but only those which serve the general good directly, or – by contributing to civic discipline – indirectly serve the general good of preserving peace and justice. Virtuous actions here mean the kind of actions virtuous people do (some of which the law commands); actions done in the kind of way ? *contra Kant?* virtuous people do them, from a virtuous disposition, have a quality of action which the law cannot command but at which it aims.

Humanly enacted laws can be just or unjust. To be just they must 4 ① serve the general good, must ② not exceed the lawmaker's authority, and must ③ fairly apportion the burdens of the general good amongst all members of the community. Such just laws oblige us in conscience, since they derive from the eternal law. Laws however can be unjust: by serving not the general good but some lawmaker's own greed or vanity, or by exceeding his authority, or by unfairly apportioning the burdens the general good imposes. Such laws are not so much laws as forms of violence, and do not oblige our consciences except perhaps to avoid scandal and disorder, on which account men must sometimes forego their rights. Laws can also be unjust by running counter to God's good, *laws counter to* promoting idolatry say; and nobody is allowed to obey such laws: *we* *God's good* *must obey God rather than men.* *must not be obeyed*

5   Everyone owing allegiance to an authority is subject to the laws of that authority as to a standard by which their actions must be regulated. But some people may not owe allegiance to that authority at all (as for example citizens of another country) and others may be dispensed in some particulars by a yet higher authority. Wicked men are subject to the law by suffering its coercive power; but the virtuous and just obey law with a good will and not because forced to do so. The law of the Spirit is a higher law than that of men and those led by it are exempt from human law in anything contrary to the Spirit's leading; though obedience to human law is one of the things to which the Spirit leads us. Heads of state are exempt from the coercive power of their own laws since people cannot coerce themselves, and there is nobody else who can pass sentence on them if they act illegally. But they must subject themselves to the control of the law voluntarily. Our Lord reproaches those who don't practise what they preach; who *lay heavy loads on other men's shoulders without themselves lifting a finger to help.* In God's judgment then heads of state are not exempt from the control of law, but must voluntarily obey it without coercion. There is a sense, however, in which heads of state are above the law: given good reason they can change the law or dispense from its observance at such and

6   such a time or place. It is by serving men's general welfare that law gets its force and character of law, so when it fails to do so it has no binding force. Now often we find laws the observance of which advances the general welfare on most occasions but is highly harmful to it on some. The lawmaker cannot foresee every single case: and in framing the law to fit most cases he has the general good in view. So if a case crops up in which the general good would be harmed by observing the law, the law must not be observed. All the same if observing the letter of the law holds no immediate danger, it is not for anyone to interpret the law and decide what will best serve the state: it is the rulers who have authority to dispense the law in such a case. Only when the danger is urgent and allows no time for recourse to such higher authority does necessity itself, which knows no law, dispense us.

97 1   Step by step development seems in the nature of human reason: in the sciences later thinkers have developed what earlier thinkers left incomplete, and in practical matters the first constitutions of human communities didn't foresee everything and had to be altered by later generations to remove their defects. Laws may also have to alter because of changed conditions in the society they regulate. Augustine gives the example of a once well-ordered republic that in the course of time sold the popular vote to scoundrels and criminals, so that the authority to

[margin note: heads of state may dispns from law for good reason]

elect was forfeited and reverted to a few just men. But altering laws as 2
such is bad for a community, since custom helps greatly in observance
of law, breaches of common custom seeming much more serious than
perhaps they arc. So changing laws weakens their coercive power and
should only be done if there is an obvious compensating advantage to
the general good: some important gain from the new statute or the
avoidance of some harmful injustice arising out of the customary law.
The success of what craftsmen make depends solely on its design, so
when someone thinks up a better idea the earlier model is changed; but
the greatest power of law comes from custom, so it mustn't be so easily
altered. All law originates from the reason and will of a lawmaker, but 3
men can make known their will by deeds as well as by words, for
whatever they do they presumably think good to do. So if expressing
what we want and mean in words can alter and expound laws, then laws
can also be altered and expounded by repeated behaviour setting up
customs which acquire the force of law: for what we do over and over
again is surely done deliberately. Custom then has the force of law, can   *custom*
abolish law, and is law's interpreter. The law that is in us by nature and
God's law both proceed from God's will, so cannot be changed by
customs proceeding from man's will. But when human law fails to meet
a case, men may act outside the law without doing wrong, and if changed
conditions cause such cases to multiply then the custom will show the
law up as no longer serviceable. Should the reason for the law still hold,   *by reason*
however, law must prevail over custom, until it loses what is an essential   *improper custom*
condition of law: being possible according to the custom of the land. In
a free country where people make their own laws popular consensus in
a course of action expressed by a custom counts for more than the
authority of the head of state, who only has power to make laws in so
far as he represents the people. So although no individual member of a
community can make a law the whole people can. Even where the people
are not free to make or abolish their own laws, a prevailing custom will
still gain the force of law, because the very fact that it has been introduced
seems to show it has the authorities' tacit approval.

Dispensing means measured apportioning out of something common. 4 *dispensing –*
The head of a family is said to dispense the duties and necessities of   *DEF*
their common life to each family member; and the same happens in any
group. Now it can happen that an injunction usually of benefit to all can
be disadvantageous to this or that person on this or that occasion,
hindering something better or leading to some evil. It would be dangerous to let an unauthorized person decide this, except in evident cases
of emergency. So whoever has authority to rule also has authority to

dispense from the human laws he has enacted, and to allow certain people in certain cases where the law fails not to observe it. The general injunctions of law that are in us by nature never fail and cannot therefore be dispensed. But injunctions derived as consequences of these can sometimes be dispensed by men, e.g. not refunding a loan to a traitor. God's law relates to individual men as public law does to private people; and so, just as nobody except the public authority or his delegate can dispense from public law, so nobody but God or his special delegate can dispense from the law of God.

[vol 29] 98 1 **The Old Law.**   St Paul says *the law itself is holy and the commandment is holy, right and good.* There can indeed be no doubt that the Old Law was good, since it was reasonable. But to be perfect what serves a goal must be able to achieve that goal itself. The goal of human law is a state's this-worldly tranquillity, and that can be achieved by forbidding any external behaviour disruptive of the peace. But the goal of God's law is to lead us to eternal happiness, and any wrongdoing, internal or external, will hinder that. So though forbidding wrongdoing and assigning penalties is perfectly adequate as human law, it is not enough for God's law, which must fully equip man to share eternal happiness. That needs the grace of the Holy Spirit, pouring love into our hearts, by which the law is perfectly fulfilled. For the grace of God is eternal life. Now grace is something only Christ can confer, not the Old Law; *the law was given through Moses, grace and truth through Jesus Christ.* So the Old Law was good, but it was not perfect: *for the Law of Moses could not make anything perfect.*

Indeed St Paul says the law killed – not as an agent of death, but as giving death an opportunity. Being imperfect the law gave no grace to help man do what it commanded and avoid what it forbade. The opportunity for death however was not so much given by the law as taken by men. *Sin found its chance,* says St Paul, *and by means of the commandment deceived me and killed me.* So when he also says, *law was introduced so that wrongdoing increased,* the words *so that* express consequence rather than purpose: men took the opportunity offered by the law to do graver wrong: graver because now forbidden by law and so done with greater desire, since we lust all the more after what is forbidden to us. It is a mark of good law that nature and custom find it possible: St Peter calls the Old Law *a yoke which neither we nor our fathers were able to bear* because its yoke was unbearable without the help of a grace which the law did not give.

2   The Old Law was given us by the good God and Father of our Lord

Jesus Christ, to direct us towards Christ, by witnessing to him -- *Moses wrote of me*, says Jesus -- and by preparing us for him, withdrawing us from idolatry into worship of the one God who was to save the whole human race through Christ -- *Before faith came the law kept us all locked up until this faith should be revealed.* Clearly whoever has to ensure something achieves its goal must dispose it to its goal, either by himself or by subordinates. The law which was to bring men to Christ could not have been a product of the devil, since Christ himself was to cast out the devil; *and if Satan casts out Satan his kingdom is divided.* Rather, the same God that was to save men through Christ's grace also gave them the law. But commands given to children must be suited perfectly to the child's condition rather than be perfect in some abstract sense; and that is how the commands of the law were: *the law was our tutor in Christ.* When the time came for its fulfilment by grace the Old Law was supplanted; not because it was evil, but because it was too weak and useless for the new time: *Now that faith has come we are no longer under a tutor.* The Old Law could not save men on its own, but God did not fail men: together with the law he gave the saving help of faith in a go-between to come: faith in Christ saved our forefathers just as it saves us.

St Paul says the law was given by angels. And indeed in any ordered 3 exercise of craft or power, though the main act which completes the work is reserved to the person in charge, everything preparatory is delegated to assistants. So though it was appropriate for the perfected law of the New Covenant to be given directly by God himself made man, the Old Law was given to men by God's assistants, his angels. In the New Testament *God spoke to us in his Son*, in the Old Testament by angels. God instituted the law by his own authority but promulgated it through angels. And it was bestowed together with other special 4 advantages on the people of the Jews, because of the promise made to their forefathers that Christ should be born from them. This promise was made to Abraham not because Abraham earned it but because God freely chose him. And if you press the question as to why he chose this people rather than any other for Christ to be born from, then Augustine's answer will have to do: *why he attracts this one rather than that don't try to decide -- you will only make mistakes.* Christ was destined in the future to save every nation, but still he had to be born from one. So, although 5 certain injunctions of the Old Law proclaimed the law which is in us by nature and as such had to be observed by all -- not as Old Law but as law of our nature, certain other injunctions of the Old Law were peculiar to it and obliged only the people of the Jews: designed to give that people a special holiness out of reverence for Christ who was to be born from them. The special worthiness of the Jewish people as opposed to others lay in their consecration to the worship of God: the same sort of worthiness attaches today to the clerical state as distinct from that of the laity, and to the religious state as distinct from that of the non-religious. Non-Jews could however be admitted to the observances of the law, since they could be saved more perfectly and safely in that way than by simply following the law that was in them by nature. Just as today laity become clerics and non-religious religious, though they could be saved without doing so.

6   It wouldn't have been suitable to give the Old Law immediately after Adam sinned. At that time men still trusted their own reasons and didn't recognize any need of law: what the law that is in us by nature told them had not yet become obscured by customs of wrongdoing. Moreover, law is for peoples. In Abraham's time God gave rules for conducting a household, but only when Abraham's descendants multiplied and became a people freed from slavery was it time to give them a law; for *slaves*, as Aristotle says, *are excluded from the political community*, to which laws are appropriate. For the same reason the law was given to the whole people marked by circumcision, the sign of the promise made to Abraham and believed by him. It was not given solely to the household of David from which Christ would be born.

99 1 **Subdivisions of the Old Law.**   The Old Law is one law with one goal, but issues different commands to cover the different steps to be taken towards that goal. *The goal of the law is the love of charity*, for all law aims at friendship of men with each other and with God. So the whole law is *summed up* in the one commandment: *You shall love your fellowman as yourself*; that is the goal of all other commands, for loving one's fellowmen for God's sake includes loving God, so that this single commandment embraces the two mentioned by our Lord *to which all the law and the prophets reduce*. St Matthew's *Do to men everything you would wish them to do to you* is a sort of explicitation of *Love your fellowman as yourself*.

[margin note: / Golden Rule]

2   Just as human law aims primarily at friendship between men, so God's law aims primarily at friendship of man for God. But love is based on likeness, and to love God, who is most good, man must become good himself. So the Old Law had to contain moral injunctions commanding virtuous behaviour. God's law presupposes the law that is in us by nature just as grace presupposes nature. Human reason couldn't go universally wrong about the most general injunctions of law in us by

[margin note: moral injuncds]

nature, but customs of wrongdoing obscured them in particular cases, and many people's reasons so mistook the moral injunctions derived from those general principles that they judged things licit which were intrinsically evil. So the authority of God's law was needed to help man overcome both of these deficiencies.

Since man is related to God not only by inner acts of believing and 3 hoping and loving, but also by external actions in which he confesses himself God's servant – ritual acts of worship – the Old Law also con- *ceremonial* tained ritual or ceremonial injunctions regulating God's worship. The *injuncts* injunctions of the law that is in us by nature are general and require particular specification. Such specifications made by human law form part not of the law in us by nature but of positively enacted law, and in a similar way the specifications made by God's law remain distinct from the moral injunctions that belong to the law that is in us by nature. Thus the worship of God is virtuous behaviour commanded by a moral injunction, but the specifications put on this command – that God must be worshipped with such and such sacrifices and gifts – are ritual injunctions. Pseudo-Denys says God can't be revealed to men except through sense-images; so the scriptures express him not only verbally in figures of speech, but also symbolically to the eye in prescribed rituals.

And just as the Old Law specified the general command to worship 4 God by ritual injunctions, so it specified the general command to be just to one's fellowmen by judicial injunctions. Judicial injunctions *judicial* share with moral injunctions a dependence on reason, and with ritual *injuncts* injunctions the character of specifying general commands. That we must act justly in general is a moral injunction, but the specifications put on this are judicial injunctions.

In the scientific pursuit of truth men are led to assent to conclusions 6 by logical argument, but in the area of law men are led to observe injunctions by penalty and reward. So, just as we need to learn sciences in an orderly manner beginning with what we best know, whoever wants to lead men to observe injunctions of law should build on their inclinations: we persuade children to do things by offering the kind of presents that appeal to them. When men are perfect they think nothing of temporal goods and stick to spiritual things; when imperfect they still desire temporal goods though in subordination to God; only when they are gone astray do they make temporal goods their goal. So it was fitting for the Old Law to make use of the imperfect man's inclination to temporal goods to lead him to God.

100 1 Moral injunctions of the Old Law. The judgments reason makes
when planning action spring from naturally known premises. Some
human behaviour can be assessed immediately in the light of these
general first premises with a minimum of reflection. Some however
cannot be assessed without prolonged consideration of different circumstances, needing great wisdom and prudence. Yet other behaviour
requires for its assessment the help of God's instruction: matters of
faith, for example. So, though all moral injunctions belong in some way
to the law that we have in us by nature, some belong immediately like
Thou shalt not kill, some only by way of wise men's instruction such as
Honour the person of an aged man, and some only by way of God's
instruction, such as *Thou shalt not take the name of the Lord your God
in vain.*

2   Human law serves the civil community in which men are linked
together by external activities governed by justice, the virtue directly
concerned with bringing order into the human community. So the
injunctions of human law command acts of justice, and acts of other
virtues only in so far as they relate to justice in some way. But God's
law serves man's community with God now and hereafter, and men are
united to God by way of their mind and reason in which God is imaged.
So the injunctions of God's law command anything which will set man's
reason in order. Clearly then it is appropriate for God's law to command
acts of every virtue: obliging us to behaviour without which orderedness
of reason and virtue is impossible, and counselling us to behaviour which
will perfect virtue.

3   [The primary injunctions of the law are *Love the Lord your God*, and
your fellowman as yourself.] The ten commandments differed from the
other injunctions of the law in being promulgated to the people directly
by God himself. They contain commands that man knows of himself
from God, either because they follow immediately from general first
premises of behaviour with a minimum of reflection, or because they
are known straightaway from divinely instilled faith. But they do not
contain the general first premises themselves (written in man's natural
reason and self-evident); nor such remote conclusions as require long
5 reflection by wise men: e.g. injunctions prohibiting certain interior dis-
6 orderliness in men. The goal of man's natural personal and social life is
God. So the ten commandments direct us first towards God so as to
remove the greatest disorder in our lives: requiring us in order of
seriousness to be his faithful subjects, to have no truck with his enemies,
to respect him and give him service. As regards orderedness to our
fellowmen, our gravest offence against reason is to fail to pay our dues

to our greatest creditors, our parents. And then in order of seriousness
we are commanded to do no wrong, say no wrong and wish no wrong.
Murder which takes away life already given is adjudged worse than
adultery which undermines the secure identity of children about to be
born, and both these are counted worse than theft which relates to
external goods. The ten commandments are inalterably right about 8
what is just, but what can alter are the criteria which decide in particular
cases whether this or that is murder or adultery or theft. Sometimes
only God can alter these criteria since he alone instituted them (e.g. the
criteria for marriage, in the story of Hosea); but sometimes the alteration
is subject to human jurisdiction. In such matters, though not in all, men
represent God.

Does the law oblige us to do virtuous deeds virtuously? According to 9
Aristotle, we act virtuously when we act *knowingly, choosing what we do
voluntarily for some intended goal, and doing it wholeheartedly with a firm
and unwavering commitment*, i.e. from a rooted disposition. Now both
human and divine law take ignorance into account when punishing or
pardoning; but choosing and intending are inner acts subject only to
God's law: human law does not punish those who want to kill but don't.
And neither human nor divine law obliges us to act with a virtuous
disposition. So when law commands us to act justly it obliges us to act
in a way that observes people's lawful rights, but not to possess the
habitual disposition of so acting. Lawmakers have two things in view:
virtue itself, to which we are brought by observing law, and the particular
virtuous acts the law commands, which lead eventually to virtue. For
the content of injunctions and their goal are not the same, just as in
other matters goals and means are different. In this connection loving 10
can be thought of in two ways. It is on the one hand the content of a
special injunction: *Love the Lord your God and love your fellowman*. But
it is also the goal of all the commandments, and the manner in which
all other virtuous acts should be done in pursuit of that goal. In this
respect love is not part of the content of injunctions commanding
particular acts of virtue. Somebody who honours his parents and yet is
devoid of the love of charity does not infringe the particular commandment regarding parents; but he does infringe the commandment to
love and so earns punishment. Both these commandments are affirmative
commandments that cannot oblige us to be always obeying them, but
only at such times as are appropriate. So it can happen that someone
fulfilling the injunction of honouring parents might not at that time
infringe the commandment to love with charity. But observing every
injunction of the law includes observing the particular one commanding

love of charity, and that needs grace to do. So Pelagius' view that one can fulfil the law without grace is wrong.

11   Judicial and ritual injunctions derive their force solely from their enactment, and before they were enacted it didn't matter how you did such matters. But moral injunctions derive their force from what reason tells us by nature, and that would bind even if never enacted into law. Yet because the reasons for some of these injunctions are only clear to wise men, they were not part of the ten commandments but additions handed on from God to the people by way of Moses and Aaron. Thus to the first commandment, forbidding worship of foreign gods, were added injunctions concerning idolatry. To the second commandment, forbidding perjury, were added prohibitions of blasphemy and false teaching. To the third were added all the ritual injunctions. To the fourth, on honouring parents, were added commands to honour the aged, to respect superiors, and show kindness to equals and inferiors. To the fifth, forbidding murder, were added prohibitions of hatred and all kinds of violence against our fellowmen. To the sixth, forbidding adultery, were added prohibitions of prostitution and unnatural vice. To the seventh, forbidding theft, were added prohibitions of usury and fraud and every kind of sharp practice and robbery. To the eighth, forbidding false testimony, were added prohibitions of corrupt judgments, lying and disparagement. But to the last two commandments no others were added, since they already forbade all manner of evil desire.

12   The primary and strict meaning of *justifying* is making just; though secondarily, and somewhat loosely, it can mean symbolizing justice or disposing towards justice. In these last two senses the injunctions of the law justified and reconciled men by preparing them to be justified and reconciled by the grace of Christ, which those injunctions prefigured. But strictly speaking true justice is a virtue instilled in us by God's grace, and cannot be caused by moral injunctions which govern human action; though the injunctions of human law can generate in us an acquired virtue of justice, which is not our concern at the moment.

101 1 **Ritual and judicial injunctions.**   The ritual injunctions regulated the sacrifices by which God was worshipped, the sacred things employed in worship, the sacramental actions which consecrated men to God's worship, and the sacred observances which distinguished the way those

2 worshippers lived. The worship of God has two parts: the first – external bodily worship – is at the service of the second – an interior worship uniting our minds and hearts to God. In the life to come our minds will see the true God himself, and our outer worship will need no symbols

but consist in praise of God from heart and mind. At present however God's truth can only express itself to us in symbols we can sense. At the time of the Old Law, when the way towards seeing God was still closed, man's external worship not only prefigured the revelation of truth to come in our heavenly home, but also Christ, who was to be our way home. Now, in the New Law, when this way has already been revealed, it is no longer prefigured as something to come, but remembered as something past and present; only the truth of glory yet to be revealed is prefigured. As Hebrews says: *the law foreshadowed the good things to come, but it did not reflect them.* A shadow is less clear than a reflection, the Old Law less clear than the New.

There was no natural reason for the Old Law observances, e.g. for 102 1 refusing to make garments of wool and linen. The reason was symbolic. But New Law decrees, since they chiefly command us to believe and love God, are of their nature reasonable. However, just as Old Testament 2 history has a literal sense besides the figurative sense in which its happenings symbolize Christ, so too the ritual injunctions of the Old Law have literal as well as symbolic reasons. The literal reasons explain the ritual injunctions in terms of what the divine worship meant at that time. The symbolic reasons relate rather to Christ and the church to come. So, just as to understand metaphorical turns of phrase in scripture as metaphors is to grasp their literal sense (since that's what the words were used to mean), so the literal significance of Old Law rituals is to be found in the symbolic reason for instituting them at the time, namely, to commemorate some deed of divine favour. The literal significance of the Passover is that it symbolized the liberation of the Jews from Egypt, and of circumcision that it symbolized God's pact with Abraham.

The Old Law distinguished two kinds of uncleanness: the spiritual 103 2 uncleanness of sin and the bodily uncleanness which made men unfit to take part in the worship of God. There were Old Law rituals of purification from this latter uncleanness, since the law could prescribe remedies to take away uncleanness it had itself established. But only Christ has the power *to take away the sins of the world*; and since the mysteries of Christ's taking flesh and dying to it had not yet become reality, no Old Law ritual could yet contain the power that flowed from Christ's crucified flesh as New Law sacraments do. Nevertheless, believers could at that time join themselves in mind to the Christ who was to suffer, and so be reconciled to God through their faith in Christ. Indeed the Old Law rituals prefigured Christ, and observing them was a sort of proclamation of faith in him. The sacrifices for sin offered in the Old Law didn't themselves cleanse from sin, but they nevertheless proclaimed a faith which did cleanse.

3   In the state of bliss to come symbolic worship of God will yield to direct *thanksgiving and the sound of praise*: John *saw no temple in the city of the blest: for the Lord God almighty is its temple and the Lamb*. In the same way, when the New Law came, the rituals of the Old Law were supposed to give way to others appropriate to the new state of divine worship, in which though heavenly goods are still to come, the actions of God's grace which lead to them are already present. The mystery of the freeing of the human race was completed in Christ's passion when he said: *It is finished*. That was when the injunctions of the law ceased entirely to bind, their truth fulfilled; and as a sign of this the veil of the temple was torn in two. Before that, while Christ was preaching and doing miracles, when the mystery of Christ was begun but not yet completed, the law and the gospel were in force together. That is why Christ our Lord, before his passion, commanded the leper to obey the rituals prescribed by law. Abraham's faith was commended because he believed God's promise that all nations were to be blessed through his future seed. As long as this lay in the future Abraham's faith had to be proclaimed by circumcision, but once it had come about, that had to be expressed in another sign – baptism – which replaced circumcision. In the same way the Saturday sabbath commemorating the first creation was changed into the Lord's day commemorating the new creation begun in Christ's resurrection; and new feasts replaced other Old

4   Law feasts. The rituals of the Old Law symbolized a Christ who was to come, whereas our sacraments symbolize him as already having been born and having suffered. So just as now it would be fatally wrong to proclaim faith in a Christ still to be born, though that for our forefathers was a devout and truthful act, so too it would now be fatally wrong to observe rituals which they observed devoutly and truthfully.

104 2   Ritual injunctions were primarily figurative, but judicial injunctions were not: they were enacted to regulate the state of God's people with justice and equity. But inasmuch as the whole state of that people was figurative, judicial injunctions also were. God chose the Jews as the people from whom Christ would be born; so their judicial injunctions are more figurative than other peoples'. Even their wars and history have figurative meanings, whereas those of the Assyrian and Roman peoples, though humanly more famous, have none.

The New Law.   The law of the New Covenant is implanted in people's [vol 30] 106 1
hearts: *The days are coming, says the Lord, when I will draw up a new
covenant with the people of Israel: I will put my laws in their minds and
write them on their hearts.* The New Law is first and foremost the gracious
gift of the Holy Spirit to those who believe in Christ: *the law of the spirit
of life in Christ Jesus has set me free from the law of sin and death. What
are the laws of God written by God himself in our hearts,* Augustine asks,
if not the very presence of the Holy Spirit? The words and writings of the
New Law are secondary: instructing Christ's faithful in what they should
believe to dispose themselves to the grace of the Holy Spirit and how
they should behave when exercising that grace. The New Law is first
and foremost a law planted within, and only secondarily a written law.
The law we have in us by nature is inwardly implanted in us in the way
human nature is: the New Law is inwardly implanted by way of a
gracious gift added, so to speak, to that nature, not only telling us what
to do but actually helping us do it. No one ever had this grace of the
Holy Spirit except by believing in Christ, explicitly or implicitly. To
have the law of grace implanted in one is to belong to the New Covenant.
Because the New Law of the gospel consists first and foremost in the 2
inward gift and grace of the Holy Spirit, it reconciles man to God.
Merely as witnessing to the faith and commands that regulate our
affections and behaviour, it does not reconcile: *the letter kills but the
spirit gives life,* where *the letter means any written text existing outside men, even the moral commandments in the gospels.* Even the gospel
letter kills unless there is the inward presence of the grace of faith to
heal us.

  The New Law was not given from the beginning of the world because 3
the gracious gift of the Holy Spirit could be given in abundance only
after the completion of Christ's work of redemption and the removal
from mankind of the impediment of sin. In any case, perfection usually
comes not at the beginning but gradually with time: we start as children.
Men had to be left to themselves at first under the regime of the Old
Law, so that by falling into sin and recognizing their weaknesses
they could see their need of God's gracious gift. God showed no partiality in not proclaiming the law of grace from the beginning of
things: the human race deserved to be without the help of his grace
because of Adam's sin. But the situation of mankind doesn't differ
from place to place, as it has differed over time. So the New Law is
to be proclaimed in all places, though it was not proclaimed at all
times. At all times nevertheless some men have belonged to the New
Covenant.

*contra
Joachim of Fiore*

4 [Joachim of Fiore argued that we should look forward to] a third and more perfect age in which the New Law itself will be done away with; all truth will be revealed by the Holy Spirit, spiritual men will rule, and the gospel of Christ will yield place to a gospel of the kingdom to be preached throughout the world, after which will come the consummation. But none of this is true. No law could bring the present situation of the world nearer our ultimate goal than the New Law has brought it. We can of course expect the grace of the Holy Spirit to be more or less perfectly possessed at different places and times by different persons, but we can hardly expect there to be a time when it will be more perfectly possessed than it was by the apostles, who received the first fruits of the Spirit, first in time and plentifulness. The Holy Spirit was given as soon as Christ entered into glory by his resurrection and ascension. He taught the apostles all truth needed for salvation, what they should believe and how they should behave. He did not teach them everything that was to happen, because that was none of their business. It is absurd to distinguish the gospel of Christ from the gospel of the kingdom. This was the gospel, proclaiming the good news of Christ, that was preached to the world at large even in apostolic times, after which came the consummation, namely, the destruction of Jerusalem. And after the church is founded in every nation the consummation of the world will come.

107 1 Laws can differ by serving distinct goals, or by serving one and the same goal more or less directly (as adult laws serve the goal of virtue more directly than laws for children do). The Old Law and the New Law do not differ in the first way, because they both serve the same goal of subjecting man to God: *It is one God who reconciles the circumcised on the ground of their faith and the uncircumcised through their faith.* But the Old Law is a tutor for children whereas the New Law is a law of perfection, the law of love of charity. The two covenants proclaimed one faith in one ultimate goal, but what the faithful of the Old Law believed would happen in the future, we of the New Law believe has already happened. The Old Law, given to those who had not yet obtained spiritual grace, was called a law of fear because it persuaded men to observe its injunctions by threat of penalties. But virtuous men incline to virtuous behaviour from love of virtue, not because of extrinsic penalties and rewards. So the New Law, which consists primarily of spiritual grace implanted in men's hearts, is called a law of love. The Old Law commanded the love of charity, but it did not give the Holy Spirit who pours out that charity in our hearts. The New Law like the Old enjoins moral and sacramental activity, but only secondarily, not

*OT as law of
fear*

*New Law is
law of love*

primarily as in the Old Law. Those under the Old Law who were accepted by God because of their faith belonged in that respect to the New Covenant; for their faith was faith in Christ, the author of the New Covenant.

The New Law fills up what the Old Law lacked. The goal of the Old Law was to reconcile men and set them right, though it could not actually do this but prefigured it in ritual practices and promised it in words. The New Law fulfils the Old Law by setting men right through the power of Christ's passion. So the New Law is called the law of truth, the Old Law the law of shadow or figure. Even the injunctions of the Old Law were fulfilled by Christ in his actions and his teaching. He chose to be circumcised and to observe whatever other legal prescriptions had to be observed at that time, he gave true interpretations of the law showing that interior wrongdoing was also forbidden, he showed how to observe more safely what the Old Law prescribed, adding to it counsels of perfection. Only the ritual practices of the Old Law are abolished by the New, because what they prefigured has come about, and observing them any longer would signify that their fulfilment is still to come. The Old Law was much more burdensome than the New, imposing many more external actions and ritual practices. The New Law as taught by Christ and the apostles added very little to the law that is in us by nature, though things have been added since. But the New Law is more burdensome than the Old in this sense: it expressly forbids movements of the heart which the Old Law forbade only implicitly, and without attaching penalties. So it is very difficult for the non-virtuous; when St John says: *his commandments are not burdensome*, Augustine comments: *not to one who loves*.

The New Law primarily consists of the grace of the Holy Spirit showing itself in faith working through love. That grace comes to mankind through the Son of God made man: grace first filled his human being and then flowed over to us. *The Word was made flesh, full of grace and truth, and of his fullness we have all received, grace upon grace. Grace and truth came through Jesus Christ.* It was fitting then that the grace overflowing from the Word made flesh should be channelled into us by externally perceptible means; and that this inner grace should subject flesh to spirit and bear fruit in externally perceptible behaviour. So grace and external activities are related in two ways: certain external activities – sacramental actions like baptism and the eucharist instituted in the New Law – draw us to grace; and grace interiorly prompts us to other external activities. Some of these, because they necessarily accompany (or run counter to) the inner grace of faith working through love, are commanded (or forbidden) by the New Law : e.g. confessing (or denying) our faith. But other activities which do not necessarily either agree or disagree with a loving faith, are left by Christ the lawmaker to each individual's freedom in proportion to his responsibility for others. And this is why we call the New Law a law of freedom. To act freely is to act from oneself. Acting from a disposition that accords with one's nature is acting from oneself, whilst acting from a disposition running counter to one's nature is acting from some degeneration of oneself. Now the grace of the Holy Spirit is like an inner disposition instilled into us inclining us to right behaviour, and so it makes us freely do what accords with grace and avoid what runs counter to it. Here is another sense in which the New Law is a law of freedom. In the first sense, the New Law was a law of freedom because it constrained us only to what must be done or not done to be saved at all. But in the second sense, it is called a law of freedom because it makes us fulfil freely by inner prompting of grace whatever the law constrains us to. So the New Law is called the law of perfect freedom. The only activities the New Law has to command or forbid are those which lead us to grace and those which must be done if grace is to be used rightly. For since we cannot lay hold of grace for ourselves but must receive it through Christ, the Lord himself has to institute the sacramental activities through which it is obtained. The right use of grace, however, is in the loving activity of charity. In so far as such activity is a necessary part of virtue it is already governed by the moral injunctions of the Old Law; though in so far as that law specified general injunctions in particular ways (that God was to be worshipped with such and such rituals, and justice done to our fellowmen through such and such judicial actions) such specifications are not necessary to the inner grace of the New Law and are left to human decision: what concerns the individual to the individual, and what concerns the community to the relevant secular or spiritual authority. So the New Law does not need to command or forbid any external activity other than that of the sacraments and what the moral injunctions essential to virtuous action enjoin, such as not committing murder or stealing. Injunctions imply a *must*, but counsels leave things to the free choice of those counselled. So fittingly the New Law – the law of freedom – contains counsels not in the Old Law – the law of servitude. A man doesn't have to abandon totally the affairs of this world in order to arrive at eternal blessedness; he can arrive there by using the things of this world as long as he does not make them his goal. But he will get there more expeditiously by totally abandoning this world's goods, and such is the gospel's counsel. Such goods are threefold:

external possessions, sensual pleasures and honours – the desire of the
eyes, the desire of the flesh and the pride of life. The gospel advises us
to leave these behind as far as possible; thus laying the basis of every
form of religious life established to pursue a state of perfection, all of
which prefer poverty to riches, perpetual chastity to sensual pleasures,
and the service of obedience to the pride of life.

basis of religious life [handwritten marginal note]

Grace

God influences our behaviour from outside, [not only by instructing us
with *law*, but also] by helping us to act rightly with *grace*.

Why we need God's grace.   All movement and activity presupposes   109 1
in the agent a quality [enabling it to act that way], and an initial
activation. For physical movements this initial activation comes from
some body in the heavens acting by necessity of its nature, but in the
universe as a whole – bodily and spiritual – the absolute initiator of all
activity is God, acting according to his own plan. However perfect the
nature [disposing it to act], an agent cannot bring itself to act without
God's initial activation. Our spiritual activity then (like any other
activity) needs God in two ways: to give us a form disposing us to such
activity, and to activate us.

The form God implants in a creature is sufficient to enable activity
specific to that form, but activity beyond that will need a supplementing
form: water as such cannot heat unless it is first made hot. Our human
mind has a form, its own light of understanding, sufficiently enabling
us to know and understand whatever we learn about through the senses;
but to know anything beyond that the human mind needs completing
by some stronger light (the light of faith, say, or prophecy): and that
light must be grace-given, since it is beyond nature.

To sum up then: to know *any* truth we need God's help to activate
our minds; but we need new light supplementing the light we have by
nature only to know truths beyond our natural ability to know. *Every
truth men utter comes from the Holy Spirit* bestowing on us the light of
our nature and activating us to understand truth and utter it; but not
every truth comes from the Holy Spirit dwelling in us himself by grace
to make us holy and bestowing on us a disposition supplementary to
our nature. We need this only when certain truths like the truths of faith
are to be understood and uttered.

all truth comes from / Holy Spirit / but in different ways [handwritten marginal note]

Before Adam sinned man's nature was integrated, but since that time   2
it has been in disorder. Man's nature always needed God's help to

fall

activate the doing or willing of any good whatever. But when his nature was integrated, it sufficiently enabled him to will and do what was by nature's standards good for him (the goodness of acquired virtue), though not any good beyond that (such as the goodness of instilled virtue). Now his nature is disordered, however, man falls short even of the goodness natural to him, and cannot wholly achieve it by his own natural abilities. Particular good actions he can still perform in virtue of his nature (building houses, planting vineyards and the like); but he falls short of the total goodness suited to his nature. He is like a sick man able to make certain movements by himself, but unable to move like a man in perfect health until he has had medicine to heal him.

fallen, man needs help even to achieve his natural potential

In its integrated state, then, man's nature required strengthening by grace-given powers to do and will goodness surpassing nature. But in its disordered state it first needs even its natural strength healed, before it receives added strength to do what is supernaturally good and deserving. And in both states man needs God's help to activate him to act well.

human agency is dependent on God's but is agency

Man is master of his own activity, willing or not willing it by making up his mind to turn this way or that. But if he is also to be master of making up his mind, this must come from some previous making up of mind, and so on endlessly, unless there is (as Aristotle argued) a point at which man's free decision is initiated from above and outside his mind by God. Even the mind of a man in health is not so much master of its activity as not to need God to activate it; but free decision by a man made sick by sin needs God even more, to overcome the obstacles to choosing good that are posed by disordered human nature. Man can run counter to his nature and commit faults on his own, but he is unable on his own to do and will good suited to his nature. For all created things exist by another's power and left on their own are nothing, needing another's help even to conserve in themselves their own natural good. Left on their own they can fail to be good, just as left on their own (without God to conserve them) they can fail to exist.

it is natural to man to love God

3   With an integrated nature man could achieve the goodness suited to his nature without additional gifts of grace, though not without God's help to activate him. Now to love God above everything else suits man's nature just as it does that of all other creatures – reasoning, non-reasoning or even non-living: interpreting love in a way appropriate to each creature. For things are naturally desired and loved for what they naturally are; so, since parts are good when serving the whole, each

particular thing naturally desires and loves its own good as serving the general good of the whole universe, which is God. *God draws all things to love him.* When man's nature was integrated, he related his love of himself and all other creatures to love of God, loving God above himself and above everything else. But now that man's nature is disordered, his will fails to be reasonable in this respect and, unless God heals the disorder by his grace, pursues its own private good. To sum up then: in order naturally to love God above everything else man, when his nature was integrated, needed no gift of grace supplementing his natural gifts, though he needed God's help to activate the love. But now his nature is disordered, he also needs help from God's grace to heal his nature. Nature loves God above everything else as the source and goal of all natural good; charity loves him as the object of all happiness with whom we enjoy a kind of spiritual community. Charity moreover adds to our natural love the readiness and delight which virtuous dispositions add to all our good actions, for without such dispositions such actions are done merely from natural reason.

When his nature was integrated, man kept every commandment of the law in the sense that he did everything commanded; but now his nature is disordered he can't even do that unless grace heals him. Neither then nor now could he keep the commandments lovingly and charitably without grace; and both then and now he needed God's help to activate and initiate his keeping of them. *God doesn't command the impossible*; but what God can help us do is not altogether impossible: as Aristotle says, *what we can do through friends, we ourselves, in a sense, have the power to do.*

Eternal life is a goal out of all proportion to human nature; so man has no natural ability to earn it; for this he needs a greater grace-given ability. He is only able to achieve what is naturally good for him, by doing things like working the land, drinking, eating and making friends. Man does however will and do things which earn him eternal life, but only because his will has been prepared for it by God through his grace. *Eternal life is certainly a reward for good works; but those works themselves are done by God's grace*; for keeping the commandments of the law with charity in a deserving way needs grace. It is a mark of the dignity of human nature that it can, at least with the help of grace, achieve a higher goal than lower natures can in any way achieve.

There are two senses in which a man must prepare himself to will good. Firstly he must be willing to behave well and attain God, and for this he needs the gift of grace as a lasting disposition enabling him to earn [God] by his behaviour. So secondly, man must be willing to receive this gift of grace-as-disposition. Now for this it is not necessary to presuppose the gift of yet another disposition. For where would the process end? What we must presuppose is rather some gracious help from God activating our will from within, inspiring the good we propose. For when agents are acting in subordination to one another, their goals are correspondingly subordinated, the initial agent acting towards the ultimate goal and the secondary agents to the nearer goals. Thus God as absolute initiator of all activity is drawing all things to himself by initiating that general tendency to goodness through which everything tends to be as like God as in its own way it can. And he is also drawing good men to himself as to some special good they themselves aim to achieve and desire *to cling to as good for them*. So man can turn to God only if God draws him. And since willing grace is a sort of turning to God (like men turn to the sun for light), clearly we can't be willing to receive the light of grace unless God graciously helps by activating us within. *Turn to me*, God says to man in Zechariah, *and I shall turn to you*: and man does turn to God by his free will; but since his free will cannot turn to God except God turn it, in Jeremiah man says to God: *Turn me, and I shall be turned*. If a man does what he can, people say, God will not deny him grace. Yes, but a man can do whatever God moves him to do. We need our will to be prepared for grace-as-disposition in the way matter needs preparation to take on a new form; but to be acted on by God we don't need previous activation, since God is the initial activator. So the process of preparation is not endless. Man prepares himself by his own free will, but not without help from God activating him and drawing man to himself.

7 Man cannot rise from sin without the help of grace. When the actual sinning has stopped, certain damage has been sustained; so to rise from sin is not simply to stop sinning, but to have that damage repaired. The damage is threefold: a stain, by which we mean an eclipse of the brightness of grace by the tarnish of sin; a disorder of nature, in which man's will is no longer subject to God; and a liability to punishment, since fatal sin deserves to lose God for ever. Only God can repair such damage: he alone can shine his light on the soul again and restore the gift of grace-as-disposition; he alone can draw man's will to submit itself again to him; and he alone as plaintiff and judge can remit the liability to eternal punishment. So to rise from sin man needs the help of grace, both as disposition and as inner activation from God. Men cannot recuperate from sin on their own, because the light of grace has to be instilled in them afresh; just as a body cannot recover from death unless its soul is instilled afresh. Even an integrated nature couldn't have

restored itself to a state beyond its natural capacity without external help. Human nature is now dissipated by an act of sin, no longer integrated but in disorder; so it cannot even restore itself to its own natural goodness, never mind to a state of rightness beyond its nature.

When his nature was integrated, man could refrain from sinning 8 either fatally or non-fatally, even without any grace-as-disposition; for we sin when we deviate from the standards of nature, and men with integrated natures could avoid doing that as long as they had God's help conserving them in goodness (without that, of course, man's very nature would collapse into nothingness). But now that his nature is disordered, man also needs grace-as-disposition to heal the disorder, if he is wholly to refrain from sin. In the present life this healing already starts in the spirit, but the appetites of our flesh are not yet fully renewed: so we can refrain from fatal sins which need reasoned consent, but because of the disorder in our lower sensual appetites cannot avoid all non-fatal sins. Reason can indeed put down each individual movement of appetite (and that is enough to characterize such movements as voluntary and therefore sinful), but it (cannot control all of them at once:) while it is trying to resist one another arises, and reason can't always guard against that. In the same way, after fatally sinning and before being reconciled by grace, reason can avoid each individual fatal sin for a time – we don't have to sin continuously – but before long sins fatally again. For just as our lower appetites should submit to reason, so our reason should submit to God and make him the goal of our will; and just as our lower appetites, when not wholly subject to reason, are subject to disordered movements, so our reason, when not stably fixed on God, is the seat of much disordered activity. Many things arise to obtain or avoid which a man will deviate from God, rejecting his commands and thus sinning fatally. Especially when things happen unexpectedly, we follow preconceived goals and pre-established dispositions, whereas if we had had time to think we would have acted otherwise. We cannot always be thinking ahead, and unless grace restores us quickly to proper orderedness, before long we will follow the lead of a will not submitted to God. It is our own fault if we are not prepared for grace, so the fact that without grace we cannot avoid sin doesn't excuse us from the sin.

A man established in grace has all the help he needs in the way of 9 instilled dispositions, but still needs the help of God activating him. For it is a general truth that no created thing can act at all except in virtue of God initiating the action; and in man's specific case, though his nature is healed in spirit by grace, it is still disordered in the flesh and darkened by ignorance (things never happen the same way twice, and we don't even fully know ourselves, so how can we always know what is the best thing to do?). We need God, who knows and can do all things, to direct and protect us. We are not given grace-as-disposition to preclude all further need of help from God; for all creatures need God to conserve them in the good they have already received. Even in the state of glory, when grace has reached its full perfection, man will need such help from God. The Holy Spirit moves and protects us not only through the disposition he gives us; but together with the Father and the Son in other ways as well.

110 1 **What is grace?**   In common speech we use the word *grace* in several ways: of love and favour as when we say a certain soldier is *in the good graces of the king*, i.e. pleasing to him; of a free gift, as when we say *I confer this grace on you*; and of gratitude for such free gifts, as when we talk of *saying grace*. The third use derives from the second, and the second from the first. The second and third uses of the word *grace* name something in the person favoured: the gift freely given or the acknowledgement of the gift. But whether grace in the first sense names something in the person favoured depends on whether we are thinking of God's grace or man's.

Creatures are good because God wills them so: their goodness derives from the love with which God wills their good; but man's will is moved by good already there in creatures, and man's love of things doesn't cause their good but presupposes it, in whole or in part. So if God loves a creature, some goodness will result at some time in that creature, though not co-eternally with the love itself. And because of differences in such goodness, we distinguish different loves of God for creatures. One is the general love with which he loves everything there is, and which gives natural existence to all created things. Another is the special love with which he draws reasoning creatures above their natural condition to share in his own good; and this is the way God loves creatures in an unqualified sense, willing them an eternal good which is nothing other than himself. To say then that a man is in God's grace implies some supernatural gift flowing out from God into that man. Although sometimes we refer to God's eternal love itself as his grace: the *grace of predestination*, for example, is God's free choosing of people without them earning it. As St Paul says: *He predestined us to be adopted sons, to the praise of the glory of his grace.*

2   So saying someone is in God's grace implies that God's gracious will is causing something in him. Now God's gracious will helps men in two

ways. Firstly, God activates our every act, stimulating us to know and will and do things, causing in us not a disposition but an actual movement: as Aristotle says, *the act of a mover is the movement of what it moves*. Secondly, God's gracious will helps us by instilling in us dispositions. For fittingly God's love is as thorough in caring for those to whom he wills good beyond their nature as he is for those to whom he wills natural good. He not only stimulates natural behaviour in creatures but bestows on them the natures and powers which make that behaviour natural and easy, disposing them to behave in that way of themselves; for *Wisdom orders all things sweetly*. All the more then does God instil into those he stimulates to achieve an eternal good beyond their nature, forms or qualities beyond nature whereby they move to that eternal good sweetly and readily. Grace given in this way is therefore a sort of quality or disposition. Grace is beyond human nature, so it cannot be man's substance or the form that makes him man, but some form supervening on that. For whenever man shares some divine good (like knowledge) what is God's substance in God becomes something supervening on substance in us. Grace is a sharing of God's good, and exists in the soul in a less perfect way than the soul itself, which exists substantially. As expressing and sharing God's goodness, grace is of a higher order of reality than the soul, but not in its mode of existing. Strictly speaking, a supervening quality is not so much in existence itself, as a way in which something else exists; and so grace is not created, but men are created in it, established in a new existence out of nothing, without earning it: *Created in Christ Jesus in good works*.

The virtues we acquire by human activity dispose us in ways in keeping with our nature as men, but the virtues instilled in us by God dispose us in higher ways to the goal of sharing God's nature, into which we have been reborn as sons of God. So, just as our acquired virtues presuppose a natural light of reason, instilled virtues presuppose a light of grace, which is our sharing in God's nature. *Once you were darkness*, St Paul wrote, *but now you are light in the Lord; walk then like sons of light*. Acquired virtues strengthen us to walk according to the light of natural reason; instilled virtues strengthen us to walk according to the light of grace. St Augustine calls *faith acting through love* grace, because that is the activity which first manifests in us the grace that makes us pleasing to God. Grace then is a disposition presupposed to instilled virtues as their origin and root. And since by grace we are reborn as sons of God, grace must modify our very nature in some way: it is presupposed to virtues, so affects what is presupposed to every ability of the soul, namely its nature. We share God's knowledge through the virtue of faith strengthening our mental ability, and God's love through the virtue of charity strengthening our power to will; we share some likeness to God's nature through a kind of rebirth or recreation taking place in the nature of our soul. The soul's abilities to act derive from its nature, and the virtues which strengthen those abilities derive from grace itself.

111 1   St Paul talks of grace both as making us pleasing – *He has taken us into his good grace through his beloved Son* – and as freely given – *If by grace then not by works, otherwise grace would no longer be grace.* So we should be able to distinguish graces that have both these elements from graces that have only one. And indeed God plans to draw men back to himself by grace through others. So there is not only grace-which-makes-pleasing, which unites its recipient to God; but also grace which allows its recipient to help draw another to God. This is a grace-freely-given since it surpasses natural abilities and personal deserts, but not grace-which-makes-pleasing since it is not given to set the recipient himself right with God but rather to enable the recipient to work for the setting right of someone else. This is the grace St Paul says *shows the Spirit is present in some way in that person for the good of all.* To say grace is freely given is to say it isn't owed either to personal desert or to nature (as man is owed a mind or whatever else is part of his nature). Not that God owes anything to creatures in either of these ways, but creation owes God submission to his plan, according to which this nature should possess these properties and dispositions, and doing this should earn that. Natural gifts are owed not as personal deserts but owed to nature; gifts beyond nature are owed in neither sense and so are specially entitled to the name of *graces*. Grace-that-makes-pleasing, then, adds another meaning of grace to this general notion of grace-freely-given. Only graces that don't do this retain the general name of grace-freely-given; so the distinction is really between graces that do or do not make pleasing.

2   Grace can mean God's help stimulating us to will and act well, or the gift of a disposition implanted in us by God. In both cases we can fittingly distinguish grace working in us and with us. The working of an effect is never ascribed to what is acted on, but to the agent; so if our mind is stimulated to activity by God without activating itself – God being the only activator – we talk of what is done as the work of God alone, and of his grace as working in us; but if our mind, activated by God, activates itself, we talk of what is done as the work of both God and the soul, and of grace as working with us. Now we distinguish

two levels of activity in man. We will interiorly, activated by God's activating (especially when the will is first starting to will good after previously having willed evil); so here grace is said to work in us. But we also engage in external behaviour under will's control, so that our will is at work and God is also helping, strengthening the inner will and providing the external means to act; and there grace is said to work with us. As Augustine says: *Working with us God completes what he started working in us; for at the beginning he works to make us will and at the end works with us when we will.* Grace then, thought of as the freely given activation of God moving us to act well and earn heaven, can fittingly be distinguished as working in us and working with us.

But also when grace is thought of as a disposition God gives us, we can distinguish two things it does: like every form it determines a way of existing and a way of doing things. Just as heat first makes something hot, then makes it able to heat other things, so grace-as-disposition first works in us to heal or set the soul to rights, making it pleasing to God, and then works with us as a source of those works of our free will which earn us heaven. (Grace-as-quality *does* things only in the sense that forms do things, not in the sense agents do: in the sense, that is to say, in which whiteness is said to make things white.) God does not set us to rights *despite* ourselves, for at the moment we are set right our free will consents to it. But that consent is not a cause of the grace but an effect of it, so the whole process is worked in us by grace. It is not only secondary agents involved in an action that are said to *work with*, but any agent that is helping towards an already presupposed goal. So God by grace works in us helping us to will good; and then, once that goal is presupposed, his grace works with us for its achievement. It is one and the same grace that works in us and works with us: the distinction lies solely in what the grace is doing.

Grace does five things: first it heals our soul, so that secondly we will to do good, thirdly actually do the good we will, fourthly persevere in doing good, and finally come to glory. Grace by causing one of these effects can be said to lead to the next effect; and in causing the next effect can be said to follow on from the first. And since these effects come before and after one another, grace can lead to and follow on from the same effect as related to different effects. As Augustine says: *It leads by healing and follows on when what is healed lives and grows; it leads by calling us and follows on by bringing us to glory.* God's love, being eternal, can never itself do anything but lead; but grace, its effect in time, can lead to one thing and follow on from another. It is the same grace that leads and follows; but doing different things, just as we said of grace working in us and with us. Even the grace which brings us to glory is the very same grace that now leads by setting us to rights. The love of charity we had on the way is not made void but comes to fulfilment when we come home to glory, and so it is with the light of grace; for neither charity nor grace is defined by its incompleteness [as faith and hope are].

4   St Paul distinguishes various graces-freely-given saying *The Spirit gives one person a message of wisdom, another knowledge. One and the same Spirit gives faith to one person, to another the gift of healing, to another power to work miracles, to another prophecy, to another reading the mind, to another speaking strange languages, to another explaining what is said.* Graces-freely-given are bestowed on men so they can help bring others back to God. Men can't work on others inwardly; only God can do that. But they can teach and persuade externally, and for this they need full knowledge of God (faith, wisdom and knowledge), the ability to confirm or prove what they say (the gifts of healing, miracles, prophecy and reading minds), and the ability to express their thoughts well (speaking

5. languages and explaining what is said). Graces-freely-given serve the general good within the church, but grace-that-makes-pleasing serves that universal good beyond the church which the church itself serves, namely God. So the grace-that-makes-pleasing is the more precious.

112 1 **Sources of grace.**   Only God can give grace, since it surpasses the abilities of any created nature, and shares in the nature of God. Only God can make gods of us, sharing his nature and living like him in some way. Christ's human nature is *a sort of tool of his divine nature*, to quote Damascene, and tools don't do what we use them to do by their own power but by the power of the tool-user. So Christ gives grace not in virtue of his human nature but in virtue of the divine nature with which it is united, and which gives to Christ's human actions their power to save. And just as Christ's human nature gives grace only in virtue of being used by his divine power, so also the sacraments which Christ instituted in his New Law give grace only as tools used by the power of the Holy Spirit.

2   Sometimes grace means God's gift of a disposition, and sometimes God's active stimulation towards good. Grace in the first sense must be prepared for, since matter can only take on forms for which it is ready. But grace in the second sense, God's help, needs no preparing; rather whatever preparation occurs in man comes from God helping him and stimulating him towards good. The very movement of free will by which

someone readies himself to receive the gift of grace is such a good: an act of free will to which he is moved by God (and in that sense it is *up to man to prepare his spirit*), and an act of God moving our free will (and in that sense *man's will is prepared by God*). There is a preparation of man to receive grace which occurs at the same moment as grace is instilled: such activity cannot earn a man the grace he already possesses, but can earn the glory which is still to come. The incomplete preparation which God stimulates in us before the gift of grace-which-makes-pleasing, does not earn however, for only when grace has already set us to rights can we earn. Infinitely powerful agents don't need matter to work on, nor other agents predisposing matter for them. Though the circumstances of the thing being caused may require the infinite agent itself to create matter for the thing and dispose it in the way the form needs. So, when God instils grace in the soul he needs no other preparation than that which he himself provides.

We are prepared for grace by God activating us and by our free will thus activated. Grace does not have to follow the preparation regarded as an act of free will, since the gift of grace is beyond anything human power can do. But grace has to follow the preparation regarded as an act of God. That doesn't mean God's grace is coerced, but that what God intends happens, and if God intends the man whose heart he moves to obtain grace he will. Every man's grace unites him to God, the highest good, and in this respect one man's grace is equal to another's. Nevertheless one man may be more enlightened by grace than another; part of the reason being that one man is more prepared for grace than another. But this doesn't get to the root of the matter, since this preparation is man's doing only inasmuch as his free will has itself been prepared by God. So in the last analysis it is God who dispenses his gifts of grace unequally, to enhance the beauty and perfection of his church, just as he creates different levels of natural things to enhance the perfection of the universe. *Grace is given to every man in the measure Christ gives it, for perfecting the saints and building up Christ's body.*

God sometimes reveals to specially privileged people their graced state, but no one can make certain for himself that he is graced. To be certain of something we must know the grounds for it, and the ground of grace is in God himself, whose sublimity is beyond all our knowing: *if he comes to me, I shall not see him.* We might guess from indications: seeing ourselves delight in God and despise worldly things, and being unconscious of any fatal sin. But such knowledge is incomplete: *I am not conscious of anything but I am not thereby justified.* For *who can discern his own sins?* Whatever is there in the soul can be experienced, for man experiences the inner springs of his action through acting; the will through willing, life through exercise of the activities of life. And since perfections of the mind involve certainty essentially, people possessing knowledge or faith can be sure they possess them. But the same doesn't hold for grace or love which are perfections of our faculty of desire.

113 1 **Grace works in us to set sinners right.**   Justification is God setting man to rights. Now being right can simply mean being personally just in our dealings with other people, and legally just and observant of the general good. But more broadly, it means being rightly disposed within ourselves with our lower powers subject to the higher power of reason, and that higher part subject to God. Such rightness is either a straight gift from God, as his original state of integrity was to Adam before he sinned; or it is a transformation from unrightness – *the justification of*
2 *the unrighteous* – when a man who has sinned has his sins forgiven. Now sin is forgiven when God is again at peace with us. This peace is God's love, which, though eternal and unalterable as an activity in God, imprints an effect in us which is interrupted from time to time as we fall away from God and then recover. That effect is the grace that fits man for eternal life, with which fatal sin is incompatible. So forgiveness of sin must be accompanied by instilling of grace. Men can be neutral towards one another, neither loving nor hating; but if one has offended the other then forgiveness of the offence will involve the other's special favour. So, although before man sinned he could have been in a neutral state, neither in God's graces nor guilty of sin, after sinning he can only escape guilt by possessing grace. Sin itself is a transient action, but a liability to punishment remains. Someone might stop one sin by passing on to another opposed to it, but then not only would the liability still be there, but the sinner would become liable for two opposed sins at once (for in that respect – as turning away from God and attracting punishment – they are in fact not opposed). God moves things in keeping
3 with their own way of moving: men, therefore, in a human way, by means of their own free choice. So in moving them towards rightness, he so instils his gift of reconciling grace, that he moves all those
4 capable of receiving his movement to accept his grace freely. Setting the unrighteous to rights, then, requires a free turning of man's spirit to
1. God, the first step of which is an act of faith: for *whoever draws near to God must believe that he exists.* If the movement of faith is to be perfect it must be inspired by the love of charity, so in setting the unrighteous
2. to rights two movements, of faith and love, occur together. One and the

same act of free choice exercises two different virtues, one controlling the other, since actions can serve more than one goal. We cannot turn to God as object of our eternal happiness and cause of our reconciliation sheerly by natural knowledge: for reconciliation we need to make an act of faith that God is reconciling us to himself through the mystery of Christ. And the movement of free will has another side: in desiring God's rightness it also renounces sin; for since charity is love of God, it is also renunciation of the sin which separates us from God.

So, since God in reconciling us, moves us from a state of sin to a state of rightness, we can describe that reconciliation in four ways: the one act of God instils grace, moves our free will away from sin by renunciation and towards God by faith, and ends up by achieving forgiveness of sin. In substance this is one action of God bestowing grace and forgiving sin. In the physical world, too, though coming is not going, the coming to be of one thing is identically the going away of another.

The start of the whole process is the instilling of grace, by which the free will is moved and sin forgiven. That instilling of grace is instantaneous and takes no time. The only disposing the soul needs to receive God's grace is the disposing he himself gives, and this need not be gradual: God has infinite power and can dispose any matter he himself creates to its form in an instant; especially man's free will which by nature acts instantaneously. Reconciliation as a whole, then, is instantaneous. A man may take time to consider his act of consent beforehand, but that is on the road leading up to reconciliation, which then happens instantaneously. There is nothing to stop us thinking two things at once when they form some kind of unity: for example, the subject and predicate of one affirmation are understood simultaneously. In the same way our free will can choose two things at once if they are related to one another; and that is how free will simultaneously renounces sin and turns to God, since the renunciation of what sets us against God serves our willing unity with him. There is no timelag between acquiring a form, starting to act in keeping with it, and – if the act is instantaneous – finishing it. Now willing doesn't take time, so neither does reconciliation. In processes that do take time there is no instant immediately prior to any given instant, though there is a period of time ending at the given instant. When something is changing towards a given state, during the whole of the preceding period it is in some other state, and then at the last moment of that period (which is also the first moment of the next period) it is in the state it was moving towards. Only if the process is not in time will states succeed each other discretely rather than continuously; and then there will be a last instant in one state and a first instant in the next, without need of a time between, since no continuity will require it. Now the human spirit, though beyond time itself, is subject to time incidentally, since it understands the meanings of things as reflected in images involving space and time. So any changes in human minds must be thought of as subject to the same conditions as temporal processes; there is no last instant in which sin is present in the process of reconciliation, but only a last period of time, and then a first

8 instant in which grace is present. So the four elements we distinguished in the reconciliation of sinners are temporally simultaneous, even if they have a natural order of priority: first the instilling of grace, then the free willing of God, motivating the freely willed renunciation of sin, and finally the forgiveness of sin. For in any movement, the movement by the mover naturally precedes the change in what is being moved, and that precedes the achievement of the goal of the change. From the point of view of the thing being changed, leaving a previous state must naturally precede arriving at an opposite state; but from the agent's point of view the reverse is true. The agent expels the previous form because it already possesses the second. Thus the sun has to be luminous in order to expel darkness; but the atmosphere must lose its darkness before it can become light (though these processes are temporally simultaneous). Now the instilling of grace and the forgiveness of sins are described from God's point of view, so the instilling of grace precedes forgiveness of sins by definition. But from the sinner's point of view the reverse is the case, and liberation from sin by definition precedes the obtaining of reconciling grace.

9 Judged by the way he does it – producing things out of nothing – creation is God's greatest work. But judged by what he does, reconciliation is his greatest work: for what is achieved is the eternal good of sharing in God's nature, rather than the good of changeable nature, earth and sky. Absolutely speaking, the gift of glory is greater than the gift of reconciling grace, but proportionately speaking, the gift of grace is greater, exceeding the worth of the unrighteous man (who deserves punishment) by more than glory exceeds the worth of the righteous man (who as righteous deserves it). The good of one individual person's grace is greater than the natural good of the whole universe.

10 But the reconciliation of the unrighteous is not a miracle, outside the power of nature: for as Augustine says *to be able to have faith or the love of charity is natural to man, though actually having them is a grace reserved*

to believers. If we characterize miracles – or marvels – as things that need a marvellous cause like the power of God, then the creation and all the other things only God can do are miracles. But if we limit miracles to cases of matter taking on some form beyond its natural capacity (e.g. dead bodies coming to life again), then the reconciliation of the unrighteous is not miraculous, since the soul has a *natural capacity for grace being made in God's image.* And if miracles are defined as events outside the usual customary order of cause and effect (e.g. instantaneous healing), then the reconciliation of the unjust is sometimes miraculous and sometimes not. The common and customary course of reconciliation starts with God moving the soul inwardly so that man turns to God firstly imperfectly and then more perfectly. But sometimes God moves the soul to perfection instantaneously (as in St Paul's case), and such a reconciliation is miraculous. Not every movement of natural things against their natural inclination is miraculous, otherwise water boiling and stones being thrown upwards would be miracles. But if such movements happen outside the established order of causes that normally cause them, then they are miraculous. Now only God can reconcile sinners, just as only fire can heat water. So in this sense God's reconciliation of sinners is not miraculous.

Grace works with us to earn heaven. What we earn we call wages: a recompense made in return for work done, a sort of price paid for it. Justice demands we pay a proper price for goods bought, and pay proper wages for work done. But justice, strictly speaking, is the preservation of equality between equals; so earning wages is something that can only happen, strictly speaking, between equals; not between son and father, or slave and master. Between God and man there is no equality at all – the whole of what man has comes from God; so justice between God and man must be proportionate, each working to his own measure, a measure set up by God himself. Man can earn from God only what in God's plan God has allotted him power to earn. In the physical world too things achieve by their own power just what God has planned they can; but since reasoning creatures act freely, what they achieve is said to be earned. Man earns when he does freely even what he is obliged to do, otherwise acts of justice like repaying debts would not earn anything. God is not seeking profit for himself from our good works, but only the glorious revelation of his goodness. So we earn from him not by adding something to his store but by glorifying him. Our actions earn only because God has planned it so, so that God is not in our debt, strictly speaking, but rather in debt to himself, in the sense that he owes it to himself to fulfil his plan.

2   In the state of mankind before sin there was already one reason why man couldn't earn eternal life by his own purely natural abilities; for in God's plan things can't act beyond their abilities, and eternal life is a good quite out of proportion to created natures, unaided by grace. But when man sinned the obstacle of sin added a second reason, since we needed grace to forgive sin and reconcile us to God first; for *the wages of sin is death* not life. In God's plan, human nature attains the goal of eternal life not by its own power but aided by grace; and that is the way its actions earn eternal life. Men earn from God by God's gift; but we earn from men without any gift on their part, by means of gifts we have from God. Though we cannot earn from a man we have offended until we have first made recompense for that and been reconciled to him.

3   As acts of free will, our acts of earning from God are not commensurate with what they earn because there is no equality between God and man; but a certain proportion exists, God recompensing to the excelling measure of *his* power what we do to the measure of ours. But as acts of the Holy Spirit, our acts earn eternal life commensurately. For the worth of these acts is now measured by the power of the Spirit moving us to eternal life, *becoming in us a fount of water springing up to eternal life*. Or we can measure the price of what we do by the worth of grace, through which we share in God's nature through adoption as sons, to whom inheritance is owed by the very law of adoption – *if sons, then heirs*. The grace of the Holy Spirit possessed in this life, though not the actual equal of glory is its virtual equal – as the seed is the equal of the tree. And through that grace the Holy Spirit dwells in man: cause enough of his eternal life, *the pledge of his inheritance*.

4   Our actions earn the good God has planned as man's reward. But what moves man's spirit towards the enjoyment of God is love of charity, which directs all the acts of all other virtues to that goal. So earning eternal life primarily belongs to love of charity, and to other virtues as controlled by that love. Also, because earning must be voluntary it primarily belongs to charity, since clearly acts are most willed when done from love. Work is laborious and difficult either because there is a lot of it (and the greater the labour is in this sense the more it earns, and charity doesn't lessen our labours but urges us to attack even greater ones), or because the worker lacks skill and fitness or a ready will (and such labour lessens our earning capacity, but is removed by charity).

Earning is incompatible with the free gift character of grace (*if by* 5 *works then no longer by grace*). And in the nature of what we are given, someone without grace can't earn it; firstly, because it surpasses nature, and secondly, because in the state of sin before grace, sin itself is an obstacle to earning grace. But once one has grace – to begin good works – one can earn further grace as a result of those works. Such further graces are not, however, the first grace; nobody earns that for themselves. Man is reconciled by faith, not because believing merits reconciliation, but *believing as such* because reconciliation involves belief, the movement of faith being a *does not merit* necessary element in the reconciliation. *reconciled*

What we do earns commensurately to God's movement within our 6 actions, and proportionately to our free willing of them. Clearly then only Christ can earn the first grace for others; only his soul is moved by God's grace to the glory of an eternal life for others, as well as for himself, being constituted head of the church and author of salvation for all men. *For it is fitting that he who brought many sons to glory should perfect the author of their salvation.* Though we can earn someone else's ✕ *true intercession* first grace in a proportionate way. For if we do God's will in a state of *of / saints* grace, it is a fittingly friendly thing that God should do man's will in return and save the other person; though sometimes of course that other person impedes his own reconciliation. Prayers rely on mercy; only works of commensurate earning rely on justice. No one can earn a right 7 to his own restoration from any future fall, neither commensurately nor proportionately. Commensurate earning depends on God moving one, and that sin has interrupted; whilst proportionate earning of a first grace can be impeded by the one it is earned for, and certainly will be in this ! ! case when the one earning and the one earned for are the same. Some have held that a man can unconditionally earn eternal life only with the last graced act he does; and that all earlier earning is conditional on perseverance. But this is absurd: indeed sickness sometimes makes our last graced acts less deserving than previous ones, not more. We hold that every act of charity earns eternal life unconditionally; but that later sin can impede the effect of such earning, just as obstacles can hinder the effects of natural causes.

The end that grace moves towards is eternal life, and the movement 8 develops by growth in charity and grace. So growth in grace can also be *growth in* earned commensurately. A tree is not beyond the seed's power just *grace* because it's bigger. Any deserving act earns man growth in grace just as it earns him that fulfilment of grace which is eternal life. And just as eternal life isn't given immediately but in its proper time, so grace will not grow immediately but in its proper time when a man is sufficiently disposed to receive it. What man can earn is the appointed end towards which God moves his free will. So perseverance in glory (which is the end in question) can be earned. But perseverance in grace throughout life cannot be earned, since it depends only on God's movement, the source of all earning. God is free to bestow perseverance on whomsoever he wills to bestow it. But what can't be earned can always be prayed for.

Chapter 10

LIVING WITH GOD – FAITH, HOPE AND LOVE

In moral matters generalizations of the sort we have been making are of [vol 31] limited usefulness, since every action is a particular case; so now we shall consider each virtue and vice in detail, and later each walk of life. To avoid repetition we shall treat, together with each virtue, the related gift of the Spirit, the opposing vices, and any related precepts; and the virtues will be listed under seven main virtues: three *deiform* (or theological) virtues uniting us to God – faith, hope and charity, and four *cardinal* moral virtues – prudence, justice, courage and moderation.

> **Introductory comment.** The next three chapters form a kind of large parenthesis in the structure of the *Summa*, caused as Thomas explains by the need to cover moral questions in a detail sufficient to make them useful in daily life. What Thomas does in these chapters is to expand the brief introduction to the virtues (and vices) that he gave in chapter 8 above, so that it comprehends the wealth of diverse writing on sin and virtue to be found in the Christian tradition. He introduced in chapter 9 the notion of an act of grace whereby God salvaged creation, the act of love performed on Calvary to bring back man to integrity; from chapter 13 onwards it will be the detail of that act of salvaging that shall occupy our attention. In the meantime the life of integrity that was made possible to man by that act of grace is studied.
>
> And firstly, Thomas turns his attention in this chapter to the *theological* or *deiform* virtues, and in the next to the *moral* or *human* virtues. These are virtues in different senses of the word. The moral virtues dispose men's abilities of mind and will and emotion into an integrated whole to serve the good to which he is naturally drawn, the good of a human life fulfilling itself by fulfilling its role in creation as a whole. But as we have seen Christians believe that man is also called to share in God's life and God's nature, to share indeed in that creative and redemptive act of love which God is, and which he made available to men through Christ on Calvary. Man's nature is called not only to an inner integration with itself

but to an integration, unity and identification with God himself. When this life is seen from outside, so to speak, from the point of view of the life which it fills out and replaces as man's ideal, then it is seen as something more-than-natural, supernatural not in the sense of unnatural but in the sense of bringing with it its own connaturality to man, the tapping of a new spring *within* him where God dwells, springing up to eternal life. Thomas quotes with approval the saying of Augustine that even if knowing and loving God face to face is impossible without God's grace, nevertheless to be able thus to know and love him, to be able to receive such a grace, is in man's nature. For what is possible through friends, he says, quoting Aristotle, is in some sense possible to us. And in his discussion of faith Thomas gives an analogy which helps to make this intelligible.

Grace is natural to men in the sense that tides are natural in the ocean: they are the natural effect in a natural object of a natural cause with which that object is in an immediate natural relationship. The nature of the ocean lies not simply in its internal physical and chemical and biological constitution, but in its natural place on the earth's surface under the sun and moon. In the same way, Thomas says, man's natural place is under God. So man is able to be moved by God to friendship and disposed by God to a life of love in common with him. The function of the deiform virtues is to be the first seeds of that new nature in us, that life of friendship which is our way of living what God lived on Calvary.

The fundamental virtue is the one called **charity** then, the historical translation of the Greek word *agape* used in the New Testament: love, or, as Thomas always spells it out, the love of friendship, a love which wants to share life and the doing of good. Charity however presupposes **faith and hope**. In one sense *all we need is love* (as the Beatles sang); or, as Augustine is supposed to have said: *Only love, and you may do what you like.* This is indeed the message of John's first letter in the New Testament, but by love is meant true love, something that truly is love, for then *what you like* will be *what is good to do.* John maintains that the paradigm of true love is the act of love of God for creation and man displayed in Christ on Calvary, and that our love keeps itself true by faithful response to and imitation of that love, by a faith in that love's genuineness and a hope in its power. And this is the sense in which charity presupposes the two lesser deiform virtues of faith and hope.

Thomas talks of these virtues as our contact with God, the means by which he is brought into our lives as a new standard of action added to that of our own right reason. They are virtues, not because they dispose us to actions which measure up to a standard, but because they dispose us to actions in which we embrace and adopt a new standard – God himself. Thomas points out that these virtues all have two objects: faith believes what it believes because it believes who it believes (it believes God's truths because it believes God's truthfulness); and hope is confident of what it expects because it is confident of the person in whom it places reliance (it hopes for God's life because it relies on God's power and friendship); and charity is not only love but friendship, not only love of the good life we share with our friend, but love of sharing it with the friend and his friends, love then of the friends themselves. Faith and hope are virtues of this life only, for in themselves they carry an element of imperfection: in the life to come they will be replaced by other gifts of God's friendship, vision replacing faith and possession hope. But the love which is the friendship will remain: love is as perfect in the friend's absence as in his presence, and indeed it is a mode of presence.

Two concluding points: one on self-love, and the other on heresy. Thomas refuses to condemn self-love, and indeed believes that true friendship for God involves us in loving his whole creation in an ordered and truthful way. For him even our natural love of life is love of the world as God has made it, with its natural order in which the one loving also has a place and must be loved as everything else is loved. So his conception of natural love is at once more selfless and his conception of charity more self-ful than spiritual writers sometimes allow. Natural love already loves God above all things since in the natural order of things that is where God ranks; and in charity we love our friend's world because we love him, and that means loving ourselves and our fellowmen as ourselves, and not only as *we* love ourselves but as *he* does.

It is difficult for us nowadays to sympathize with Thomas's attitude to disbelievers: pagans, Jews and heretics. We feel something false about Augustine's claim, quoted by Thomas, that the church, in punishing heretics, is moved by love for her erring children. In Thomas's case, the attitudes taken over from the culture he inhabited seem to be strengthened by his assumption that explicitness is essential for faith. The degree of explicit faith in Christ to come which Thomas attributed to Moses and Abraham and the Israelites astonishes us today, because it lacks the historical sense that is now a part of our culture. The principles that Thomas enunciates, on the other hand, would seem compatible with a faith almost completely implicit: since he quotes the saying of the letter to the Hebrews that he who believes must believe that God exists and that he rewards those who seek him. Who would dare to say what degree of explicitness is involved in a belief in God existing, since God defies definition in the first place (cf ch 1 pp 45, 59)? Thomas does not envisage a culture in which Christ is so preached that people hear not of him, but only of the preacher's self and attitudes; and he hardly envisages cultures in which Christ has not explicitly been preached at all. So he understands heretics to be people who know that they should believe, and are stubbornly refusing a faithfulness that they had promised. Where Jews and pagans are concerned – non-Christians – he is always careful to take his stance on natural law: no amount of special pleading by Christian emperors with friends in the episcopate, he says, can subvert the natural law that a man must be free to make his own decisions, and a parent must be free to make decisions for his immature children. In many cases he does allow to the church more than he should, but he is poles removed from the born-again insistence on explicit faith, which often involves a rejection of all natural responsibility, and the belief that it is faith, not love, that covers a multitude of sins.

a little dig at 'born-again'

Faith

We begin with the virtue of faith: what we believe, the act of believing and our disposition to believe.

1 1 **What we believe.**   With regard to any disposition to know, we can distinguish what it disposes us to know from what makes that knowable; for example, in geometry what we know are proved conclusions, but what makes them knowable is the means by which geometry proves them. Now what makes things objects for faith is Truth himself, for faith believes only things God has revealed: his truth guarantees their truth. And what Truth makes believable includes God but also much else related to Truth himself, namely, the works of God which help us attain him: e.g. the manhood of Christ, the sacraments of the church, creation itself.

Human minds know truths by making connections or disconnections. 2
So by objects for faith we can mean either the realities believed in, or
the mode in which they are presented to the believer: namely, through
propositions stating certain connections. We formulate propositions
only in order to know reality through them, so the act of believing moves
through the propositions to rest in the reality – *I believe in God, in his
only-begotten Son, in the church.*

Sometimes the mind's assent is determined by what it assents to, 4
which is either self-evident (like first premises) or provable (like conclusions from such premises). Sometimes however what we assent to is
insufficiently convincing, and our assent is determined by a voluntary
choice between alternative positions. If the choice is made tentatively
we call it *opinion*, but if with certainty and without doubt we call it *faith.*
But we talk of seeing things only when those things themselves determine
the mind or the senses to know them; so neither faith nor opinion
concerns what we see. Though a man sees what he believes under the
general aspect of being believable, since he wouldn't believe it unless he
saw it as requiring his belief, evidenced by miracles or in some other
way. Indeed, any virtuous disposition enables us to see what is in keeping
with the disposition; so faith is an inclination to assent only to what it
is right to believe, and to nothing else. Unbelievers see neither the 5
things that believers believe nor their believability. Believers however
do see that; they cannot prove it but see it by the light of faith. Believers
prove things from the premises of faith (the authoritative sources of
sacred scripture) in the way everybody proves things from naturally
known premises: as we said at the start of this book, theology is a science.
You can't *know* what you simultaneously hold as an opinion, because
knowledge (like faith) rules out the alternatives which opinion allows to
be possible. You can't *know* what you simultaneously put faith in,
because knowledge sees and faith doesn't.

Creeds articulate the faith of Christians into different *articles* so- 6
called, into connected parts. Where things we believe are unseen for
different reasons they constitute separate articles; where many truths are
unknowable for the same reason they join in one article. Thus we
distinguish the article of Christ rising from the dead from the article of
his suffering, because it gives rise to different difficulties; but that he
suffered, died and was buried all raise the same difficulty and constitute
one article. The matters essential to faith are those directing us towards
eternal life, so it is these that are articulated in the creeds. Scripture
asks us to believe other things, like Abraham having two sons, but only
in order that the essentials of faith should get revealed, not as if such

truths were themselves articles of faith. What makes all the articles
matters of faith is that though we cannot see them God's truth guarantees
them. God's guarantee unites them as objects of faith; our not being
7   able to see them differentiates them as articles. Articles of faith have the
same role in the teaching of the faith as self-evident premises in teaching
what reason discovers naturally. And just as such premises are subordinate to one another, some implicit in others, so the articles of the
faith are all implicit in a first belief *that God exists and rewards those
who seek him.* God's existence implicitly includes everything existing
eternally in him and constituting our eternal happiness; God's providence includes everything God does in time to lead men to that happiness. The reality faith believes in has never changed, but the number
of explicit articles has grown as later believers have become more
explicitly aware of what earlier believers held implicitly. In the sciences
that human reason discovers the knowledge of teachers grows with time;
but when men grow in knowledge of the faith they are learners gradually
absorbing over time what their teacher always knew. God is the eternally
knowing agent of revelation, and man is the material acted on, gradually
knowing more and more. The last fulfilment of grace came through
Jesus Christ: that was *the fullness of time.* So those nearest that time,
whether just before like John the Baptist, or just after like the Apostles,
knew most fully the mysteries of faith.

8   The creed proposes for our faith the hidden depths of the godhead,
which we shall see when we enter bliss, and the mystery of Christ's
manhood, through which *we enter the glory of the sons of God. This is
eternal life: to know you, true God, and Jesus Christ whom you have sent.*
Seven articles of faith concern the godhead: God's unity, the three
persons in God, and the three works God alone does – creating nature,
making us holy by his grace, and raising us to live for ever in his glory.
Seven articles concern Christ's manhood: his taking flesh, his birth, his
suffering through death to the tomb, his descent into the underworld,
his being raised, his ascending into heaven, and his coming in judgment.
Knowing the Father involves knowing his Son and their union in the
Holy Spirit; and this favours those who talk of one article of faith in all
three persons. But because separate errors arose about each person –
Arius about the Son, Macedonius about the Spirit – three articles
9 became necessary. To extract the truths of faith from sacred scripture
requires long study and practice, something not possible for everyone
who needs to know such truths; many people are too occupied with
other business to find the time for study. So there was a need to make
a clear summary of scriptural theses that all could profess. The creed is

not added to scripture but extracted from it. Gratian's Decretals declare 10
that making new versions of the creed is reserved to the Pope, along
with everything else that affects the whole church, like the invoking of
general councils, and so on.

The act of believing. Believing, Augustine says, is giving assent to 2 1 *believing*
something one is still thinking about. Strictly speaking, we think about
what we cannot yet fully see to be true. Mind sometimes firmly assents
to things it is no longer thinking about in this way since it now knows
or sees them to be true by self-evidence or proof. At other times it hasn't
finished thinking about something so withholds firm assent: leaning
towards neither alternative (doubting), or trying out one alternative
(suspecting), perhaps accepting it but not firmly (holding an opinion).
Believing, however, means putting faith in something, and this resembles
knowing in giving firm assent, but resembles doubting, suspecting and
holding opinions in having no finished vision of the truth. So we
characterize it as assenting to something one is still thinking about. Not
that faith is engaged in thinking about something hoping to prove what
it believes by reasoned inquiry. Though it does inquire in a way into
the credentials of what it believes: whether God said it and confirmed
it by miracles. Faith's assent is an act of mind not determined by reason *? l'o seen dogeuros*
but by will. In Augustine's words God is what, who and why we believe, 2
the object of our faith in three different ways. He is what we assent to,
the Truth guaranteeing what we assent to, and the goal our will is
pursuing when it determines our mind to assent.

   Without faith we cannot please God. When one thing is naturally 3
subordinate to another, its perfection consists not only in what it can do
on its own but also in what it derives from the higher nature: thus the *orel,- fides*
sea not only moves downwards with water's natural heaviness, but also
moves in and out tidally under the influence of the moon. Now the only
nature that relates immediately to God is that of reasoning creatures;
they grasp the meaning of good and existence in general and so can
relate immediately to the source of existence as such. The perfection of
such creatures consists therefore not only in what they can do naturally
on their own, but also in what they can do by supernaturally sharing
God's own goodness. So man's ultimate happiness consists in a sort of
supernatural sight of God, which he must learn from God as from a
teacher, step by step as is man's natural way. But, as Aristotle says,
learners, if they are to attain full knowledge, must put faith in their teachers.
So to see God man must first believe him, as students believing a teacher.
It is dangerous to assent to things one has no way of verifying; but just

as men assent to first premises by a natural light of intelligence, and virtuous men are disposed by their virtue to judge rightly about what is in keeping with that virtue, so believers, by the light of faith divinely instilled into them, assent to what is worthy of faith, and to nothing

4 else. Men must hold by faith many things discoverable by reason if they are to know God quickly, generally and surely: for proving things about God presupposes long study in many different fields, many people can't follow such proofs anyway, and men make mistakes whereas God can't be doubted. The truths one person can prove, another must take on faith.

5   *Whoever approaches God must believe that he exists and that he rewards those who seek him.* The essential matters of faith are those that contribute to men's eternal happiness; whatever else sacred scripture hands down from God (Abraham having two sons) is secondary. Man's obligation to believe obliges him to believe the primary matters of faith – the so-called *articles* – explicitly; but secondary matters only implicitly, by being ready in soul to believe whatever scripture contains. Only when it becomes clear to him that such matters are part of what faith teaches is he obliged to believe them explicitly. We might ask *How can anyone believe in someone he has never heard of? And how can he hear of him without preachers? And what if no preachers are sent?* But men are obliged to do many things that they can do only when healed by grace: they must love God and their fellowmen, and they must believe the articles of faith. They can do these things with the help of grace, which when given is mercifully given, and when withheld is justly withheld as penalty for earlier (if only inherited) sin.

6   Revelation is handed down from the more knowledgeable to the lesser. The faith of the more knowledgeable teachers must be more explicit. The less knowledgeable learners are obliged to believe implicitly whatever their teachers are truly passing on from God, but only that. If some teachers teach falsehood this cannot harm the faith of the simple people who believe them to be teaching truth, unless they stick to the errors of some particular clique in the face of the universal teaching of the church. For that teaching can never fail, the Lord having said *I myself have prayed for you, Peter, that your faith will never fail.* Lk 22:32

7   Man's road to happiness lies in the mystery of Christ's coming in the flesh and dying for us: *there is no other name given to men to save us.* So in all periods everyone had to believe this mystery of Christ in some way or another. Adam, before he sinned, had explicit faith in Christ's coming in the flesh as the road to final glory (for Adam and Eve, as St Paul says, were *a great sacred symbol of Christ and his church*, and the

first man must surely have known his own sacred significance); but only after sinning could man believe explicitly in the sufferings and resurrection of Christ that were to liberate mankind from sin and death. Because of this faith, sacrifices before and under the Law could prefigure Christ's sufferings, though the reality prefigured was known explicitly only to the leaders, and to others under the veil of sacrificial actions that they believed divinely heralded a coming Messiah. Now that grace has been revealed, all, leaders and led, are obliged to believe explicitly the mysteries of Christ; particularly those articles of Christ's coming in the flesh that are commonly celebrated in the church and publicly preached. Christ was revealed to many pagans too: Job *knows that his redeemer liveth* and the Sibylline oracles (so Augustine says) predicted him. In any case, even people saved without such revelation were saved by faith in God's go-between; for they had implicit faith in God's providence, believing God would deliver men in ways of his own choosing that his Spirit would reveal to some knowers of truth. Explicit belief in Christ's 8 coming in the flesh presupposes faith in the three persons: in a son of God taking flesh and renewing the world by the grace of the Holy Spirit through whom he was conceived. We can know God's goodness in his effects without understanding that he is three persons, but not in himself as the blessed in heaven know him. To that blessed happiness we are led by the sending of those three persons.

Through faith the blessed did what was right and received what God 9 *promised.* All human behaviour freely willed and directed towards God earns a reward, and believing is such behaviour, mentally assenting to God's truth in obedience to a will activated by God's grace. Our natures are like matter that the love of charity (the source of all earning) gives life to; and faith is the final disposition which prepares nature for charity. So neither nature nor faith can earn without charity, but given charity, acts of faith and nature and natural free will all earn. Our assent to what we prove scientifically is forced, not freely willed, and cannot earn; but reflecting about such things is under our control, and when it serves the goal of charity – the honour of God and the well-being of our fellowmen – it can earn a reward. In believing, however, both assent and reflection are freely willed and can earn. Opinions though are assented to only weakly with an undecided will, and that cannot earn much, though actually thinking about them can earn. Believers do not believe frivolously; they have inducement enough to believe: the authority of God's teaching confirmed by miracles and (more importantly) by the inner inspiration of God attracting them. But because the inducement is not enough to prove what is believed, the believers' assent

10 can still earn a reward. Human reasons for believing may lead to our act of will or follow from it. They lead to willing when we wouldn't so easily will without them, and then they detract from faith's merit; for just as acts of virtue should be done from judgment rather than passion, so we should believe on the authority of God rather than human reason. On the other hand, the readier our will to believe the more we love what we believe, meditating on its truth and cherishing any reasons for it we discover. So human reasons that follow on faith are an indication of additional merit; just as passion following on virtue indicates greater readiness of will. Reasons supporting faith's authority cannot prove what we believe and remove its unseenness or its meritorious character as faith, but they can remove obstacles to believing. When reason proves certain preliminaries to the articles of faith, those preliminaries are no longer matters of belief but are *seen* to be true. That however doesn't detract from the love of charity which made our will ready to believe them even when they were unseen; so there is no loss of meritoriousness.

3 1 We speak externally in order to express our inner thoughts; so since inner belief is an act of faith so too is its external profession, just as professing thanks and praise is an act of worship, and confessing sins an act of repentance. All external virtuous behaviour is the work of our inner faith working through love, commanding other virtues to evoke that behaviour rather than evoking it itself; professing the faith is faith's
2 own external act, unmediated by any other virtue. [What precepts prohibit we must never do;] what they positively command we need not always do, but only when circumstances make the act a virtuous one. So professing the faith always and everywhere is not necessary for salvation, but only when omitting to do so would jeopardize God's honour or our fellowmen's well-being.

4 1 **The disposition to believe – faith.** *Faith is the substance of what we hope for, the evidence of what we cannot see,* says the letter to the Hebrews. Faith is a disposition we characterize by the activity of believing it disposes us to, and that activity we characterize by the object believed in. Now believing is an assent of mind commanded by will, so faith's activity relates to its object both as to a good willingly pursued and as to a truth mentally assented to. Moreover, being a theological virtue in which goal and object are identical, the way the object is faith's goal will correspond to the way it is its object. Now faith's object is unseen Truth itself and whatever else we assent to because of that Truth. So faith's goal is also Truth itself as unseen, that is to say, as still unachieved yet hoped for. So Hebrews expresses the way faith relates to Truth as goal,

the object willed, by saying *Faith is the substance, or seed, of what we hope for*, since what we hope for is to see openly the Truth we already assent to by faith. And the epistle expresses the way faith relates to Truth as object of the mind by calling faith *the evidence*, or conviction, *of what we cannot see*. Throwing this into the form of a definition, we could say that faith is the mental disposition through which eternal life starts up in us, causing our mind to assent to what it does not see. Calling faith *conviction* distinguishes it from opinion, suspicion and doubt; saying it is *of things unseen* distinguishes it from both proven and self-evident knowledge; and calling it *the substance of things hoped for* distinguishes it from all faith unrelated to our hoped-for happiness.

Believing is an act of mental assent commanded by will, perfected by dispositions both of will and of mind; but since its object is truth (the object of mind) believing is more immediately an activity of mind and the disposition proper to it – faith – disposes our mind. For the will to be disposed to obey would not be enough unless the mind was ready to follow the will's command; so we need a strengthening disposition not only in the will commanding, but in the mind assenting. Every voluntary act is given life, so to speak, by the goal it serves; that goal determines its species and mode of activity. Now the goal of faith is the good God himself, the object defining the love we call charity. So charity gives life to faith, perfecting and enlivening faith's activity. Faith as such is a perfection of mind and what defines faith is its relation to mind; its relation to will does not define it and cannot be used to differentiate types of faith. Now the distinction of faith as living or lifeless relates to the will and the love of charity; so this distinction doesn't differentiate two dispositions. Only dispositions that dispose us always to act well are human virtues, and living faith is such a disposition. Believing is an act of mental assent commanded by will, and to believe perfectly our mind must tend unfailingly towards the perfection of truth, in unfailing service of that ultimate goal for the sake of which our will is commanding our mind's assent. Both elements are present in living faith: as faith it sets the mind always on course to truth, and as living by the love of charity it sets the will always on course to a good goal. But lifeless faith is no virtue: it has the perfection needed on the part of the mind but not the perfection needed on the part of the will. And faith that does not rely on divine truth can fail and believe falsehood, so such faith is also no virtue.

The goal is the first thing in behaviour, so theological virtues, which have our ultimate goal as their object, precede other virtues. And since we must have our ultimate goal in mind before we can will it (for we

faith is 1st of all virtues – 1st of / mind

can only will what we perceive), faith must precede hope and love, making it the first of all virtues. Natural knowledge can't substitute, since it can't embrace God as source of our ultimate happiness, which is the way we hope for him and love him. We cannot, for example, hope for eternal happiness unless we believe it possible; what is impossible can't be hoped for. A building's foundation, however, is not only its beginning but that to which all its parts are made fast. Now what ties the whole spiritual building together is charity: *above all things have love, which is the bond of perfection.* So without charity faith can't be a foundation, though that doesn't mean charity precedes faith. Faith presupposes an act of will but not necessarily an act of charity; but acts of charity presuppose faith, since will cannot tend to God in perfect love

8 unless the mind has a right faith about him. Two virtues of mind are concerned with variable and uncertain events, namely prudence and technical skill. Faith has greater certainty than these since its matter is eternal and invariant. Three other mental virtues are also concerned with the invariant: wisdom, scientific knowledge, and understanding. Now if we judge certainty by its cause, faith which relies on divine truth is more certain than these three which rely on human reason. If however we judge certainty by the degree to which the mind takes hold of what it knows, then faith is less certain since it deals with things beyond the mind's grasp. But it is the cause which matters, simply speaking, so faith has the greater certainty simply speaking though not in regard to

I not judge'd reasoning but seems pretty fast & loose

our grasp of it. Other things being equal sight is more certain than hearing; but if the person one is listening to can see more, then hearing gives the better certainty. So what we hear from God, who cannot be mistaken, is much more certain than what we see by reason, which makes mistakes.

5 1   Believers assent to what they believe not because their minds see it to be true, either directly or by reduction to self-evident premises, but because their wills command their minds to assent. And this is either

Christian vs Satanic reasoning

because believing is willed as a good (the way Christians believe) or because the mind, though not seeing what it believes, is somehow convinced of its truth: and this is the way the devil assents, seeing clearly that the teaching of the church comes from God, though not seeing the realities taught: the three persons, for example. The devil's faith is forced from him by the evidence of signs. Faith given by grace inclines men to believe from love (even if not always the love of charity); but

cf Milton's Satan

the devil is not inclined by grace but forced to believe by his natural
3 intelligence of mind. Heretics who disbelieve one article of faith lose all faith, living and lifeless. For what makes something a matter of faith is

God's truth revealed in sacred scripture and the church's teaching. So whoever does not adopt the church's teaching, derived from the truth revealed in scripture, as an infallible and divine rule, doesn't have the disposition of faith, but is holding matters of faith in some other way than by faith. Because he picks and chooses from the church's teaching what he takes as his infallible rule is his own will. When such a person is not stubborn he is not a heretic but only mistaken; but a heretic who stubbornly disbelieves one article clearly doesn't have faith in the others, but is only following his own wilful opinion.

Truth itself, one and simple, defines what are matters of faith, and from that point of view we all have one faith. But since matters of faith can be held more or less explicitly, one man's faith can be more explicit than another's. And also deeper: either because his mind assents more firmly and certainly, or because his will has a more ready devotion and trust.

If it is to be explicit, faith needs matters of belief to be proposed to it, which it can then assent to. Clearly the proposing must come from God: to apostles and prophets immediately, and to others by *preachers sent* from God. But as to the assent, all external inducements and persuasions of men and witness of miracles are insufficient, for faced with such things some believe and some don't. So there has to be some other inner cause moving us to assent, which Pelagians held to be our own free will. We begin our faith, they said, by being ready to assent, and God completes it by proposing to us what we should believe. But that is a mistake. To assent to matters of faith is something surpassing our natures, and requires supernatural interior stimulus from God. So our assent, the chief act of faith, is an interior movement of God's grace. Even lifeless faith is essentially faith, so God is its only cause too.

Knowing and understanding the faith. Understanding implies [vol 32] 8 1 depth of knowledge, penetrating under the surface. Thus, though our senses perceive the outer qualities of things, we need understanding to penetrate what those things are. However, there are many ways of being *under*: the essences of things underlie their outer supervening qualities, meanings underlie words used to express them, truth lies behind images and figures, spiritual realities behind the things we sense, effects lie hidden in their causes; and in all these cases penetrating beyond the surface is called *understanding*. Our natural light of understanding has limited powers of penetration, however, so we require a supernatural light to penetrate further; and this is appropriately called *the gift of understanding*. Reasoning is a process that starts from something we

*grace adds to &
perfects under-
standing*

already understand and leads to the understanding of something new; but grace doesn't issue from natural understanding but adds to it perfecting it. So such an addition is better called understanding than reason, its relation to what we know supernaturally being the same as that of our natural understanding to the fundamentals of our knowledge.

3 It shows the worth of the gift of understanding that it penetrates eternal realities not only in themselves, but as setting the standard for human behaviour. Human reason and eternal law both set us such standards, but eternal law so surpasses human reason that its understanding requires the

2. charity

4 supernatural light of a gift of the Holy Spirit. The Holy Spirit by the gift of charity disposes our wills directly to intend supernatural good, and by his gift of understanding enlightens our minds to know the supernatural truth on which our good will must be intent. Not all believers fully understand what is proposed for their belief, but they must at least understand that it is to be believed and never abandoned.

5 Such enlightenment of the mind is called a gift of the Holy Spirit because it makes our mind responsive to the Spirit's stimulus, rightly appreciative of our ultimate goal, making no mistakes about it, and cleaving firmly to it as our greatest good. This needs grace-that-makes-pleasing, just as dispositions of virtue are needed to judge our moral goals rightly. Faith implies only assent to what is believed, but under-standing adds a certain perception of truth, which we cannot have about

*response to what
we believe –*

3. wisdom

4. knowledge

5. counsel

6 our ultimate goal unless we have grace-that-makes-pleasing. We need to respond to what we believe in two ways: to grasp or penetrate it soundly with our mind we need the gift of understanding; to judge rightly what to accept and what to shun we need the gifts of wisdom (in divine matters), knowledge (in creaturely), and counsel (when applying judgment to particular actions).

9 1 We need *the gift of knowledge* to enable us to discern rightly and surely what and what not to believe. Man's knowledge comes by reasoning and proof, but God's by simple insight, and the Holy Spirit's gift is a shared likeness in God's knowledge. All people with grace-that-makes-pleasing share this gift of knowing what is and what is not to be believed. But not all have the grace-freely-given (also called knowledge) which would enable them not only to know what to believe, but also how to witness

2 and preach and argue it. When a class of objects includes one more perfect than the rest that object is often given a special name while the rest are known by the common name of the class. Thus in logic one of the characterizing attributes proper to a thing actually states what it is and is specially called its definition; whilst the rest are collectively known as its characteristic properties. Similarly, all knowledge implies certainty,

but, when the certainty is based on the deepest possible grounds and causes, we give the knowledge the special name of wisdom: so knowledge of divine things is called wisdom, and all knowledge of human things shares the more general term of knowledge. Wisdom knows – by a kind of unity with them – the actual things in which we believe, and so corresponds to the virtue which unites us to God – charity. But knowing how and what to believe is knowing something temporal about the human mind[, so corresponds to faith]. Every cognitive disposition is a disposition to know certain things by way of something that makes them knowable, and this latter is what decides the type of that disposition. Thus sciences which prove truths about natural things by mathematical arguments are more akin to mathematics than to natural philosophy. In the same way, knowing God through creatures is more knowledge than wisdom, whilst judging creatures in God's light is more wisdom than knowledge. Faith is first and foremost a fidelity to truth, indeed to Truth himself; but since Truth himself is the ultimate goal of our activities faith also directs our behaviour. In the same way the gift of knowledge first and foremost tells us what we should believe but secondarily directs our behaviour. Only when our judgments about what should be believed and done come from instilled grace are we said to have the gift of knowledge.

Disbelief.   Disbelief in the strict sense is an opposition to faith, resisting it and even despising listening to it; so it is a sin. But disbelief as sheer absence of belief because we haven't heard about it is not so much a sin as a penalty consequent on Adam's sin. And if men who lack faith in this sense are lost, that is because of other sins that cannot be forgiven without faith, rather than because their disbelief is sinful. Strict disbelief, like faith, is a disposition of mind under the influence of will. It distances us from God by depriving us of true knowledge of him, and as such is a greater sin than any moral wrongdoing, though not than wrong against the other theological virtues. There are several types of disbelief: pagans resist a faith they have never accepted, Jews a faith they accept in figure, and heretics a faith that was clearly revealed to them. But there are numberless mistaken positions contrary to the faith. What makes a sin the type of sin it is is what the sinner intends; but what makes it evil and a sin at all is the good it rejects, which does not so much decide the sin's type as deprive it of all type. So, though faith is a single virtue unified by adherence to the one Truth himself, there are as many types of disbelief as there are false opinions to follow. Disbelief of heretics, who resist and distort a gospel they once professed, is a worse sin than the disbelief of Jews who never accepted it; but because Jews accept the gospel faith in figure in the Old Testament, but distort it by bad interpretation, their disbelief is worse than that of pagans who have never accepted the gospel at all. Nevertheless pagans are more mistaken than Jews, and they than heretics: except perhaps for the Manichean heresy which is more mistaken about the faith than even pagans are.

7   When arguing about the faith we should remember two things: our intention in arguing and the danger to those listening. If genuine doubt leads us to test out the faith with argument, this is clearly a sin of disbelief; but arguing to repel error, or even as an exercise, can be praised. As to those listening, there is no danger if they are firmly educated in the faith, but uneducated listeners with an unstable faith should not be disturbed by argument unless they live where they are already bothered and attacked by disbelievers distorting the faith, in which case people suitably trained for the job should publicly argue for the faith before them.

8   In Luke we are told: *Go out into the country roads and lanes and compel people to come in, that my house may be full.* So some people are to be compelled to believe and enter the church. But only people who had once accepted the faith: pagans and Jews can't be forced to believe, since believing is a matter of will. The faithful, if they have the power, may use it to stop such disbelievers hindering the faith by blasphemy or propaganda or openly persecuting it. This is the reason Christians frequently wage war on disbelievers: not to force them to believe (because even if conquered and held captive they must be left their freedom to believe or not as they will), but to stop them hindering the faith. However, disbelievers who once accepted and professed the faith – heretics and apostates – can be compelled, even physically, to fulfil their promises and hold to what they once professed. For even though making a vow is a voluntary matter, keeping it is an obligation. So adopting the faith is voluntary, but sticking to it once adopted is obligatory. As Augustine says, *none of us would want a heretic to die. But the house of David could not have had peace if Absalom had not died in the war he waged against his father. And in the same way, if the catholic church loses some in gathering others, freeing the many heals the wound in her maternal heart.*

9   The faithful are forbidden communication with certain persons partly to punish those persons and partly to safeguard the faithful. The church therefore visits the penalty of excommunication on heretics and apostates, but not on disbelievers who have never accepted the Christian faith – Jews and pagans – since over them she has no spiritual juris-

Margin notes:
which is most mistaken? "heretics" include I dont arguing about faith

even: conquered disbeliever must be left free to believe or not – but heretics & apostates may be compelled

Ep. 185.8.807

diction, and temporal jurisdiction only if they live in a Christian community and when in fault are punishable by Christians. But as regards the safety of the faithful: if their faith is strong enough one can hope more for conversion of the disbelievers than subversion of believers, and in this case the faithful should not be forbidden communication with Jews or pagans. But if the faithful are weak and uneducated they should be forbidden such communication, especially in intimate or unnecessary ways.

Authority is instituted by human law, but believers and disbelievers 10 are distinguished by God's law. Since the law of grace does not abrogate human law based on reason, being believers does not as such exempt us from the already established authority of disbelievers. The church, however, does have God's authority to take authority away from disbelievers, since their disbelief makes them unworthy to exercise power over believers, who have become sons of God. And sometimes the church exercises this right, sometimes not. As regards disbelievers subject to the temporal authority of the church or its members, church law states that slaves of Jews must be freed immediately on becoming Christians, with no ransom paid if they were born slaves or sold into slavery. But if in the market they must be offered for ransom within three months. The church has the right to dispose of the Jew's goods since he is subject to the church. And secular princes have enacted similar laws for their own subjects, favouring freedom. But as regards disbelievers not subject to the church's temporal authority the church – in order to avoid scandal – has made no such law, though it has the right to. The church permits Christians to work Jewish lands, because that doesn't involve living together; but if such contact did hold dangers for the faith of Christians it would be altogether forbidden.

God, despite his omnipotence and supreme goodness, allows evils he 11 could prevent to exist in the world, if removing them would cause greater goods to be lost or greater evils to ensue. So human rulers may also tolerate some evils for the same reasons; *forbid prostitution*, says Augustine, *and lust will turn everything upside down*. The religious rites of disbelievers, though sinful, can be tolerated if doing so brings good and avoids evil.

The greatest authority of all is church tradition, which should always 12 be jealously observed. Even the teaching of the great Catholic theologians gets its authority from the church, the authority of which is greater than that of Augustine or Jerome or any other thinker. Now it has never been the church's custom to baptize Jewish children without their parents' permission; though in past ages many powerful Catholic princes with

[margin note: Jewish children should not be baptized against their parents' wishes]

[margin note: repugnant to natural justice]

holy bishops as their friends – Constantius with Sylvester, Theodosius with Ambrose – would surely have claimed authority to do it if they had thought they reasonably could. But it is a practice dangerous to the faith, for when the children grow up their parents will easily persuade them to abandon what they unknowingly received. And it is also repugnant to natural justice, since children belong by nature to their parents, and to remove them from their parents' care or arrange things against their parents' wishes while the children are still without use of their own reasons is an offence against natural justice. When children start to use their own free will they begin to belong to themselves, and then they can be brought to believe – but by persuasion, not by coercion – and be baptized without their parents' permission. People married to each other have free will, so can assent to the faith without each other's permission.

11 1 **Heresy.**   People deviate from the straight path of the Christian faith in two ways: pagans and Jews, by being unwilling to assent to Christ, get the goal wrong; heretics, however, intend to assent to Christ but make a wrong choice of what to assent to, choosing what their own mind 2 proposes rather than what Christ handed down. Canon law quotes Augustine: *However false and perverse people's opinions are, we mustn't accuse them of heresy when they aren't stubborn in those opinions, but seek truth with anxious care and when they find it are ready to change their minds.* Such people are not choosing to contradict the teaching of the church. Even doctors of the church have disagreed about matters of no consequence to the faith or not yet decided by the church; but when such matters are decided by the authority of the universal church (vested principally in the Pope) anyone who stubbornly resists the decision must 3 be adjudged a heretic. About heretics there are two things to say. Their sin deserves banishment not only from the church by excommunication but also from the world by death. But the church seeks with mercy to turn back those who go astray, and condemns them not immediately but only *after a first or second warning.* If, however, a heretic remains stubborn, the church, despairing of his conversion, takes care of the salvation of others, separates the heretic from the church with a sentence of excommunication, and delivers him to the secular courts to be 4 removed from the world by death. The church, as the Lord commands, extends her charity to all, willing good to her enemies and persecutors as well as her friends. But there is spiritual good and temporal good. Spiritual good is the soul's salvation, the main objective of charity; so heretics who return, no matter how often they have fallen away, are

[margin note: pre-eminence of Pope]

[margin note: heretics deserve excommunication & death – but only after warning(s)]

readmitted to repentance, the way to salvation. But temporal goods are things like bodily life, worldly possessions, reputation, and ecclesiastical or civil position. Charity does not oblige us to will such things for others unless that serves their, and others', eternal salvation. Now were heretics so received on their return that they kept life and temporal possessions, this might prejudice the salvation of others; and so the church admits them to repentance and to life the first time, and sometimes by dispensation to their ecclesiastical positions, should their conversion appear sincere. Often this is done for the sake of peace. But if they lapse again, on their second return they are admitted to repentance but not delivered from sentence of death. God can read the heart and knows those genuinely returning and always receives them. But the church is not able to imitate this, and presumes that those who lapse a second time did not genuinely return. So though it does not deny them the way to salvation, it does not save them from death. Our Lord told Peter we should forgive *seventy times seven times* – meaning always – offences committed against ourselves; but that does not mean we are free to forgive offences against God and our fellowmen: there the law sets the standard, taking into account God's honour and our fellowmen's well-being.

Apostasy.   Men can turn their backs on God by forsaking religious 12 1 or clerical vows, or by rebelling against his commandments, while remaining united to him by faith. But if they forsake faith then they turn from God altogether. So apostasy in an unqualified sense means forsaking the faith. It is not a special type of disbelief but an aggravating circumstance of it. Being disbelievers does not of itself deprive men of 2 authority to rule, for that is a right recognized by human law, whereas believing or not believing is a distinction made by God's law which does not abrogate human law. But disbelievers can be deposed for disbelief just as for other crimes. It is not the church's job to punish the disbelief of those who have never believed, but she can pass sentence on those who once believed and as a suitable punishment depose them from ruling over believers. Excommunication for apostasy from the faith *a dangerous* automatically releases a ruler's subjects from his authority and from *doctrine* their oaths of allegiance to him. In her early days the church wasn't yet able to suppress earthly rulers, so, to avoid greater dangers to the faith, allowed believers to obey Julian the Apostate in matters not contrary to faith.

13 1 **Blasphemy.** Blasphemy is vilification of God's excellence and goodness. Whoever denies truth or affirms untruth of God vilifies his goodness; sometimes accompanying his false opinion with hatred (as
contrariwise love perfects faith), and sometimes adding blasphemy by
2 mouth to blasphemy in the heart. Of its nature vilification of God's
goodness is a fatal sin irreconcilable with God's love: it cuts us off from
that love, the first source of spiritual life. But blasphemy can burst out
thoughtlessly. Sometimes we don't even realize what we are saying,
because passion breaks out in words we haven't yet weighed in our
minds: and this is non-fatal sin and not really blasphemy. But sometimes
we know what we're saying, and then thoughtlessness no more excuses
a blasphemer from fatal sin than it does a man who in a fit of anger kills
3 the man sitting next to him. The gravity of a fault depends more on
wicked intention than on the deed's actual outcome, so that blasphemy
which intends to harm God's honour is graver, simply speaking, than
4 murder, the gravest sin against our fellowmen. The hatred of the damned
for God's justice is an inner blasphemy of the heart, but after the
resurrection it will probably break out in words just as the blessed in
heaven will praise God with their voices.

[margin notes: O min? / cursing of God / dog / damned?]

Hope

[vol 33] 17 1 The virtue of hope. Human behaviour has two standards: reason at
its own level, and God who surpasses it. Any act that embraces these
standards is good. Now the sort of things we hope for are future goods,
challenging but possible of achievement either by our own power or
with others' help; and in so far as we hope to achieve something by
reliance on God's help, our hope embraces God. That makes hope
a virtue, and the act of hoping good: up to a standard it should have.
No one can misuse a hope that embraces God by relying on his help,
any more than they can a virtue that embraces reason by conforming to it, for the very embracing of the standard is good use of the
virtue. The perfection of hope lies not in achieving what it hopes
for, but in embracing its standard, namely the God on whose help
it relies.

[margin note: 2 standards for behaviour – reason / God]

2   The good we first and foremost hope for from God is an unlimited
good, matching his unlimited power to help; and that is eternal life, the
enjoyment of God himself. Eternal happiness does not *enter into the
heart of man* perfectly, for while en route to it we have no specific idea
of what kind of life it is; but we have a general idea of it as the most
perfect good, and so we can hope for it. *Hope reaches even beyond the*

[margin note: how can we hope for what we can't conceive?]

veil, since what we hope for remains veiled to us. But we hope also for other things in line with eternal happiness, just as primarily we believe God but secondarily many other things related to him. Though nothing else is challenging when measured against the hope for eternal happiness, yet measured against our own powers other things remain challenging and can be hoped for as part of our hope. Love implies some sort of 3 union of lover and beloved, hope some sort of movement or stretching of desire towards the good that challenges us. So, though love can bear directly on someone else united to us, hope bears directly on good desired for ourselves. However, given union with someone else by love, we can desire and hope for that person too as if for ourselves. With one and the same love of charity we love God, ourselves and our fellowmen; and with one and the same virtue of hope we hope for ourselves and for others. All hope relates to a goal – the good it hopes for – and to an 4 agent – on whose help it relies to attain the goal. The virtue of hope has as ultimate goal eternal happiness, and the primary agency on which it relies is God's help. And just as it is not right to hope for anything else as ultimate goal, but only as serving that goal, so we mustn't hope in men or other creatures as if they were the primary agent of our happiness, but only as tools or instruments of that agent. In this sense we can turn to the saints, or ask men's help, or reproach those who can't be relied on for aid.

Hope is a virtue, we said, because it embraces the highest standard 5 of human behaviour: embraces God as the primary agency on which it relies and the ultimate goal in which it seeks happiness. Having God as object in this way defines it as a theological virtue. Things measured by a standard embrace it when they achieve the happy medium between overstepping and falling short of it. But standards as such know no medium or extremes. Moral virtues are concerned with behaviour that must measure up to a standard, the standard of reason. But theological virtues are concerned with adopting a standard, the highest of all standards, which has not itself got to measure up to any further standard; so theological virtues in themselves are not balanced between extremes. Yet, because they relate other objects to the standard, they can inci- dentally strike a balance in this way. Thus on Truth himself faith cannot rely too much, but the truths it believes can lie midway between two false opinions. And similarly hope cannot rely too much on God's help, but in relation to what we hope for, we must strike a balance between presuming to achieve inappropriate things and despairing of achieving even what is appropriate.

Charity embraces God for his own sake, uniting us to him spiritually 6 in love; but faith and hope embrace him as a source of benefit to ourselves: knowledge of the truth in faith's case, enjoyment of a perfect good in the case of hope. Hope inclines us to God as our ultimate goal and as an unfailing source of help in reaching it; but charity inclines us to him by uniting us in affection with him, so that we live no longer to

7   ourselves but to him. To hope for anything we must believe it possible, and, since eternal happiness and God's help are both matters of faith, hope presupposes faith – *whoever comes to God must have faith that he*

8   *exists and rewards those who seek him.* Perfect love loves another person for his own sake as someone to whom we will good, as a friend; but imperfect love loves a thing not for its own sake but as a source of good to ourselves, as desirable. Charity is love of the first type, embracing God for his own sake; hope is love of the second type, hoping to achieve something. So hope precedes charity in time and prepares for it, since hoping for God to reward one inspires one to love him and keep his commandments. But charity precedes hope in worthiness, and once it arises renders hope more perfect, since we especially hope in friends. Hope, like every movement of desire, springs from some form of love of the thing desired; but not all hope springs from charity, only that living hope that hopes for good from God as from a friend.

18 1   The emotion of hope responds to challenging goods perceptible to the senses; the virtue of hope responds to a challenging good that is perceptible only to mind, or to be more accurate surpasses even the

2   mind, God himself. Hope responds to challenging goods that are possible of achievement in the future. So when the saints attain eternal happiness, and have it already present, the virtue of hope disappears just as faith does. Their happiness is called eternal life precisely because, by enjoying God, they share in some way his eternity beyond time: their happiness does not divide into past, present and future. So they do not hope for their happiness to continue, but have it already timelessly. They still hope for others, but with the love of charity, not the virtue of hope. And though the glorification of their bodies is a challenge to human nature, it is not a challenge to the saints in whom the soul's glory is

3   already powerful enough to glorify their bodies. The realization that there is no longer a way to escape damnation and reach happiness is part of the anguish of the damned. They cannot perceive happiness as possible, just as the blessed in heaven cannot perceive it as future. So neither those in heaven nor those in hell hope. Hope is for those en route to heaven, whether in this life or in purgatory.

4   Certainty is primarily a quality of mind, but it extends to anything guided unerringly to its goal by mind, as for example to all natural

activity planned by God. Virtues operate with more certainty even than skills in this sense, since reason moves virtues in the way that God moves natures. It is in this way that hope moves unerringly to its goal, sharing the mental certainty of faith. Hope relies chiefly not on grace possessed but on the omnipotence and mercy of God, who can give grace (and hence eternal life) to those who do not yet have it. Whoever has faith has this certainty of God's omnipotence and mercy. The fact that people who hope nevertheless sometimes fail to achieve happiness is not due to any defect in the omnipotence and mercy on which hope relies, but to a failure of free will, which introduces the obstacle of sin. So this doesn't prejudice the certainty of hope.

Fear of God.   Fear, like hope, has a twofold object: it fears both evil 19 1 and the source of that evil. Now God can't be an evil, but the evils that threaten us can come from him or bear some relationship to him. Evil that comes from him comes as punishment and is evil only in a qualified sense, being simply speaking good. What is evil simply speaking is the evil of fault, which destroys our relationship to God as our ultimate goal and separates us from him. Reflection on God's justice occasions fear in us, reflection on his mercy hope. God is not the author of our faults, *we* are, by withdrawing ourselves from him; but he is the author of our punishment, inasmuch as it is good and just. Sometimes fear of some 2 evil or other turns us away from God in *worldly fear*; sometimes it turns us towards God, and if what we fear is punishment we call such fear *slavish*, but if what we fear is offending God with our faults, we call the fear *filial*. All these fears are morally good or evil, unlike our natural fears which are prior to any moral good or evil. Worldly fear is always 3 evil; for though it is natural to avoid bodily injuries and loss of one's worldly possessions, acting unjustly to avoid these things is against natural reason. The slavishness of slavish fear is evil; for slavery is 4 opposed to freedom, and what we do in fear is done in subjection to outside influence whereas what we do lovingly we do of ourselves. So slavish fear is opposed to the love of charity. However the slavishness of slavish fear is no more essential to it than the lifelessness of lifeless faith. Essentially, slavish fear is fear of punishment: when one lacks charity this punishment is feared absolutely as if it deprived one of one's ultimate goal, but when one possesses charity the punishment is not so feared but referred to God as ultimate goal. This difference is incidental to the punishment as such: so fearing the punishment is essentially a good thing; only the slavishness is bad. Slavish fear regards God as a 5 source of punishment; filial fear regards him, not as source of our faults, but as the goal from which we fear separation because of those faults.

6 The slavishness of slavish fear is incompatible with the love of charity; but the fear as such is compatible with charity in the same way as love of self is.

7   For philosophers wisdom is merely knowledge of God; for theologians it is also a practical guide for human life which uses divine standards. Wisdom as such is based on its own first premises, the articles of faith; but the effectiveness of wisdom starts with fear: slavish fear disposing us to avoid sin and letting wisdom act in us more easily, and filial fear as the first thing wisdom inspires in us, namely a reverence and subjection to God that enables him to rule us in all things. The gifts of the Holy Spirit dispose and strengthen all our abilities to respond well to the Holy Spirit, in the way moral virtues dispose our desires to respond well to reason. Such responsiveness requires lack of resistance to the mover, and this among the gifts is the role of filial fear. Love is a virtue, concerned with good; and hope similarly. But fear is concerned with evil and the avoidance of it, so it is something less than a theological virtue. The gifts of the Holy Spirit function as source of the intellectual and moral virtues, but have the theological virtues as their own source. Growth in hope lessens fear of punishment but increases filial fear, since the more surely we expect help from someone in achieving good, the more we fear offending him or becoming separated from him.

20 1 **Despair and presumption.**   God is truly the source of men's salvation and sinners' forgiveness – *I desire not the death of sinners, but that they turn and live* – and it is false to think he denies forgiveness to repentant sinners. Hoping is an attitude in keeping with the true belief, and is praiseworthy and virtuous; but despair is an attitude in keeping with the false opinion, and is vicious and sinful. [It is no sin to despair of achieving what is truly beyond one's capacity or due, as doctors despair of cures and other people of making money.] Sins against theological virtues, such as hatred of God, despair and disbelief, start by turning away from the eternal God (the object of theological virtues) and as a consequence embrace some temporal good. Other sins start by turning towards a temporal good and in consequence abandon the eternal God: thus a sexual sinner doesn't intend to forsake God but to enjoy sexual pleasure, and as a consequence abandons God. Since mind is concerned with the general and desire with the particular, we can have a right opinion in general, and yet our desires go wrong because our judgment gets distorted by a bad disposition or passion when applying

itself to a particular case. So we can hold the true general belief that sins are forgiven in the church, yet despair of it for ourselves in our present state, because of some wrong assessment of particular circumstances. So like other fatal sins, despair can occur without loss of faith. Hope can be destroyed not only by breakdown in one's general faith (the first cause of a sure hope), but by some wrong judgment in particular (on which hope is secondarily dependent). Disbelief and hatred of God are directly opposed to God in himself; despair to our sharing in him. Not believing in God's truth and hating him are greater sins than not hoping for glory from him.

3

When we are hoping in ourselves, presumption arises from pursuing something beyond our own powers, and is opposed to self-confidence which strikes a balance in such matters. But when we are hoping in God, presumption arises by pursuing something which is not possible to God's omnipotence and mercy as though it were possible: hoping to be pardoned without repenting, for example, or hoping for glory without deserving it. And this is a kind of sin against the Holy Spirit. But it is less sinful than despair, because it is more in God's nature to show mercy and forgive than it is to punish: mercy he is in himself whereas punishment is his response to sins.

21 1 *presumpt* vs *slf-confidnc*

2

Charity

God's friendship. *I no longer call you servants*, Jesus said, *but my friends*; so the love of charity is a friendship. Aristotle defines friendship as the love with which we love those we will good things to, distinguishing that from the love of desire we have for the good things so willed to ourselves: we desire wine and horses, but it would be absurd to call them friends. In addition, friendship must be mutual (friends are friends with friends): a mutual goodwill built on what we have in common. What God and man have in common is the eternal happiness he shares with us, *the fellowship of his Son*; and the friendship between God and man based on this we call charity. We don't share the physical life of our bodies with God and the angels, but we share a life of our spirit: incompletely in this life, for *our common life is in heaven*, but completely when *God's servants serve and see him face to face*. So great can be our love for a friend that for his sake we love those connected with him, even those who hurt and hate us. And this is how the friendship of charity extends even to our enemies, loved for the sake of God, our chief friend.

[vol 34] 23 1

friendship is desire

friendship must be mutual — based on whats in common

we love our enemies fn God's sake

Peter Lombard thought charity was the Holy Spirit himself dwelling

2

in our hearts, not anything created. He didn't mean that our act of loving God was the Holy Spirit, but that the act sprang directly from the Holy Spirit, not by way of a created disposition, as acts of faith and hope and other virtues do. He was wanting to stress the excellence of this love, but in fact belittled it. If love sprang from the Holy Spirit in our heart in such a way that our heart was moved but was not a source of its movement (as often bodies are moved from outside themselves), this would mean the love was not voluntary and did not spring from within. We cannot love merely as tools of the Holy Spirit; tools in a sense cause action, but whether they act or not is out of their control, and so love would be neither voluntary nor deserving. The Holy Spirit then must move our wills in such a way that we actually will our love. But nothing is able to produce a finished act, except because of some form it has that makes it naturally able to produce that act. God, when moving things to their goals, implants in each their own form inclining them to the goal he has set for them: and so *disposes all things sweetly*. Now acts of charity are beyond our natural ability to will; so unless some other form is added to incline us to such acts of love, they will be less finished than acts of nature or of other virtues, neither easy nor pleasurable. But this is clearly not the case: no other virtue is so inclined to act or acts so pleasurably as charity. So these acts more than any others require, beside our natural ability, a disposition implanted in us and inclining us to love readily and with joy. Of course, God is the life of the soul, but in the sense of its life-giver: he gives life to our souls by implanting charity, just as he gives life to our bodies by implanting soul. Charity acts in the sense in which forms act, with the effectiveness of the agent that implants them.

3   Virtue in man consists in embracing a standard of behaviour, be it the standard of human reason (as in all moral virtue) or God himself (in theological virtue). Since in charity we embrace God himself, it is in Augustine's words *a virtue which, as our most ordered affection, joins us to God in love*. Aristotle, too, describes human friendship as *a virtue, or accompaniment of virtue*. One might say that friendship concerns itself with what is given freely, just as justice concerns itself with what is legally owed. But human friendship is virtuous only when based on esteem for virtue, so that it is not so much itself virtue as something consequent on virtue. Charity however is different, because it is based

4   not on men's virtue but on God's goodness. The object of charity's love is the ultimate goal of man's life, his eternal happiness. So charity is involved in every act of life, controlling even acts which are the immedi-

5   ate exercising of other virtues: *love is the goal of law*. Friendships differ

in type according to the goal pursued: profit, pleasure or esteem for virtue; and, as Aristotle says, according to the kind of life the friends have in common: are they kinsmen or fellow-citizens or fellow-travellers? But charity has only one goal – the goodness of God – and one shared life – eternal happiness – so there is only one type of charity which loves God in the first place and our fellowmen for God's sake.

Faith and hope embrace God as source of our knowledge of truth and our achievement of good, but charity embraces him to rest in him, not looking for anything from him. So it is a greater virtue than faith or hope – *the greatest of these is charity* – and as such greater than all other virtues. Among the moral virtues prudence is greatest in a similar way, embracing the rule of reason itself rather than applying it to our deeds and feelings. Knowing brings what is known into the knower; but will, like all desire, goes out from the one desiring to the thing desired. So whatever exists at a lower level outside than it does in mind is better known than loved; whereas whatever exists at a higher level (God especially) is better loved than known.

The ultimate goal of man is to enjoy God, and to this charity directs him. Secondary more particular goals are only genuine when they are compatible with this ultimate goal, illusory when they lead us away from it. So genuine and perfect virtue disposes us to our ultimate goal, and needs charity; in relation to secondary goals virtues are illusory if the good they dispose to is illusory, and genuine but imperfect if the good is genuine but not actually referred to our ultimate goal by charity. Actions can be good of their kind without charity, but are only perfect when done in pursuit of our ultimate goal. Genuine justice and purity require due reference to our ultimate goal by charity, as well as rightness about other things. What gives a moral action existence is its orderedness to a goal derived from will, the function of which is precisely pursuing goals. Charity orders our behaviour to its ultimate goal, and so gives all virtuous behaviour its existence and life. That is why we call charity the life of the virtues, for what makes them virtues is that they dispose us to behaviour which is enlivened in this sense.

Growing in love.   Charity loves a goodness that our senses cannot perceive: God's goodness, which only our minds can know. So charity is a disposition of will, desiring what our mind knows, not of any ability to desire what our senses perceive. The will is connected with reason; but charity is *the love of Christ that surpasses knowledge*, so measured not by reason in the way human virtue is, but by God's wisdom. Charity does not, like prudence, dispose our reason, nor does it, like justice or moderation, dispose the rest of us to the rule of reason; it is a virtue of reason only because of the kinship between will and reason. Will and free will are the same faculty: as will, the faculty to desire goals, and as free will, the faculty to choose what best serves a goal. So charity, which orders us to our ultimate goal, is said to dispose our will rather than our free will.

2   Charity is friendship between God and man based on sharing eternal happiness: something we share not by nature but by *the free gift of God*. So charity is not born in us by nature, nor acquired by our natural powers, but is a created share in the Holy Spirit, the love of Father and Son, instilled into us by him. Of himself God is the most lovable object of happiness there is, but our affections can only incline us towards good we can see, so we cannot love God as what most makes us happy unless

3   he pours his charity into our hearts. Our charity and its degree depends not on the quality of our natures or the capacity of our natural powers but on the will of the Holy Spirit distributing his gifts as he pleases:

4   *giving grace to each of us according to the measure of Christ's giving.* In this life we are on the road to God, approaching him not with bodily steps but by growth of affection and charity. So Paul talks of charity as *a road*, along which we advance, not merely by loving a growing number of things, but in the intensity with which we love them. Like all supervening qualities of things, charity exists by existing in things and grows by becoming more deeply rooted in those who possess it. And since it is essentially a disposition to action, it grows also by gaining

5   effectiveness in producing more and more fervent acts of love. It doesn't grow like our knowledge of geometry does, by embracing new things it hadn't known before; for charity of even the smallest degree embraces every object of God's love. But it grows in intensity, the subject who loves being more and more led to love and more and more subjected to loving. Even bodily quantity grows in two ways: as quantity and as possession. As quantity it is extensive and multiplicable and grows by addition, in the way animals grow; as possession it grows in the intensity with which it is possessed, as when things expand and contract. Knowledge too grows either by adding to the number of objects known or in its certainty and intensity of possession. Charity however doesn't grow

6   in the number of objects loved but only in intensity. Charity doesn't grow with each act of charity though each act prepares for growth by making man readier to act charitably the next time. As this aptitude grows, man will break forth into more and more fervent acts of charity as he strives to grow in love, and then charity actually grows. Not even when we acquire virtues for ourselves does our first act acquire the

virtue, but a sequence of acts disposes us to the virtue and a last one, acting with the power of all the preceding acts behind it, realizes the virtue. Many drips wear away a stone. Nothing in the definition of charity can set a limit to its growth, for it is a sharing in the limitless charity of the Holy Spirit. Moreover, its agent of growth is God with unlimited power. And even on our side, each increase in charity produces an even greater increase in our capacity to grow – *our heart is enlarged.* The goal of charity's growth is in the next life, not in this. No charity except God's own love is ever perfect enough to match his lovableness; and creatures can have perfect charity only in the sense that they love to the top of their powers (In heaven) this means that their whole heart will be actually set on God at all times; in this life it means devoting as much zeal as can be spared from life's needs to God and divine things; though anyone who has charity is already perfect in this sense: that he has his whole heart so disposed to God that he does not think or will anything incompatible with God's love. Non-fatal sin is compatible with the disposition of charity though it excludes its act, so it is compatible with perfection of charity in this life but not with its heavenly perfection.

Aristotle says *many a friendship has lapsed through lack of communication*, for the continuance of things is dependent on their cause, so that when we stop acting virtuously virtues acquired by our own acts fade and die. Charity however is not acquired by our own acts but instilled by God, so that our ceasing to act, as long as it is not itself sinful, neither weakens nor destroys charity. God in his turn causes defects only as punishment for sin, so the only thing that could weaken our charity would be sin, either by deserving or actually causing the weakening. Now fatal sin doesn't weaken charity, it totally destroys it. And non-fatal sin is a disorder in the choice of means to the goal, and doesn't weaken our love of the goal. So charity cannot be directly weakened, though we can say it is weakened indirectly by anything that disposes us to lose it, like non-fatal sin or ceasing to act charitably. The first instilling of charity needs our free will, so that a weakened free will disposes us to have less charity instilled; but the preservation of charity doesn't depend on free will (otherwise we would lose it when asleep), so a less intense free will can't weaken our charity. In heaven charity so fulfils the whole potential of mind and spirit, directing every act we do to God, that it cannot be lost; but in this life charity is not so perfect, and at some moment when we are not actually intent on God something can occur by which charity is lost. For the very nature of the love of charity rules out all motives for sinning; but if we are not always exercising it in act, there will be times when such motives find their

12 way in and the man who consents to them will lose his charity. Every fatal sin is opposed to the very idea of charity: the love of God above all things and with everything we have. If charity was an acquired virtue it wouldn't succumb to a single act, since acts directly oppose acts, not dispositions, and continuance of a disposition doesn't need continuance of its act. But charity is instilled into us and preserved in us by God, in the way the sun gives light. A single obstacle to the sun's rays cuts that light off, and a single obstacle to God's action in the soul cuts off charity. One fatal sin chosen in preference to God's friendship loses charity for us. Faith and hope don't, like charity, imply identification with God; all fatal sins turn us away from God and oppose charity, but only certain fatal sins oppose faith and hope. So fatal sin can leave a lifeless faith and hope behind, but because charity gives virtues their life, relating them to God as our ultimate goal, one cannot have lifeless charity.

25 1 **Whom do we love with charity?** *We have this commandment from Christ: that whoever loves God must love his brother also.* The same act of seeing that sees light, by reason of the light sees colour. Since we love our fellowmen by reason of God, willing their existence in God, we love God and our fellowmen with the same love. Honour respects a particular good of the one honoured whereas love loves all good as such and in general. So the same love of charity loves all our fellowmen as embraced by the common good that is God, whereas different honours are given to each according to their special qualities, and to God the singular honour of worship. It would be a fault to love our fellowman as our principal goal in life, but not to love him for God's sake as charity does. All love loves itself: first, it is in the very nature of will to be attracted to all good as such including its own willing; and then the very spontaneity of love loves to love. Charity moreover is not simply love but friendship, which loves both the friend to whom we will good, and the good we will to him. And so charity loves charity, as a good willed to all we love with charity, just as we will them happiness. Our friendship with God and our fellowmen consists in loving this, that we and our fellowmen love God. For since charity is the spiritual life leading to the happiness we shall all share, it is the good we love and desire for all who are our friends in charity.

3 Strictly speaking we cannot will good to creatures lacking reason, since only reasoning creatures possess goods in the strict sense, having authority to use them as they will. Moreover, friendship builds on life in common, which we have with non-reasoning creatures only metaphorically. Charity, especially, is based on sharing an eternal hap-

piness of which non-reasoning creatures are incapable. But we can love non-reasoning creatures as good things to be conserved to the honour of God and the serving of man; which is the way God loves them too.

Strictly speaking we don't have friendship for ourselves but something more: a love of self which is at the root of all friendship, since in friendship we love others as we love ourselves. But charity is friendship first with God and secondly with all who belong to God including ourselves. So we love ourselves with charity, inasmuch as we too are God's. When we blame people for self-love it is because they love and subject themselves to their bodily natures, not loving what is genuinely good for themselves as rational beings. But by charity especially we love ourselves in this latter way. Our bodies were created by God, not as the Manicheans pretend by some evil principle. So we can serve God with our bodies, and should love them with the charity with which we love God. What we shouldn't love is the taint of sin and the damage that its punishment has wreaked in our bodies; we should rather long with charity for an end of all that. Our body helps us to happiness, and that happiness will overflow into our bodies, so that they too can be loved with charity.

Sinners must be loved with charity as human beings capable of eternal happiness. But because their sin is opposed to God and an obstacle to eternal happiness, we must hate them being sinners, be they our own father and mother; for that is loving them with true charity for God's sake. When there is more probability of sinners harming others than of them amending their ways both human and divine law invoke the death penalty. The judge who sentences such sinners does so not out of hate but out of the love of charity which puts the public good above the life of the individual. Though death can also benefit the sinner too, expiating his crime if he is repentant, and otherwise saving him from further crime. We don't love sinners by willing what they will or enjoying what they enjoy, but by willing them to come to will what we will and enjoy what we enjoy. *They shall turn to you, not you to them.* The insecure should not live with sinners for fear of being led astray; but those who are in no danger do a praiseworthy thing by living with sinners to help them turn to God. Our Lord ate and drank with sinners for this reason. But we must all avoid sharing in sinner's sin. All men, good and bad, love themselves with a love of self-preservation. But bad men esteem the outer man, their bodily natures, more than their inner rational being; they do not truly know what they are, and so love not their true selves but only what they think they are. Good men however know themselves and love themselves truly.

how we must love our enemies

8   Charity obliges us to a general love of enemies as human beings, and we cannot exclude our enemies from our love of God and our fellowmen. But charity no more obliges us to a special love of each enemy than it requires special love of any other man. We must be prepared in soul to love particular enemies in their time of need. If we also do it at other times that is a perfection of love. The enmity of enemies opposes us and must displease us; but not the fact that they are men, capable of eternal
9   happiness. Certain expressions of love we show to our fellowmen in general: praying for them or doing some community service; and from such expressions of love we must not exclude our enemies. But the expressions of love we show to particular people we do not have to show to enemies, though we must be prepared in soul to help them in their time of need.

loving God above all

26 1   Charity is the virtue that disposes us to have our ultimate goal as our
2   ultimate goal; no other virtue does this. So what charity loves is first God – the source of our shared eternal life – and secondly our fellowmen, loved as fellow-sharers in that life. From the fact that a person does not love his fellowmen we can argue that he does not love God; not because our fellowmen are more lovable than God, but because they present themselves for our love first. In fact God is more lovable because of his greater goodness. Our likeness to our fellowmen comes from all of us sharing the same things from God; so it should lead us even more to
3   the love of God than it does to the love of our fellowmen. Natural love is based on sharing natural goods from God, and leads not only men of integrated nature to love God above all things and more than themselves, but also all creatures to do so in their own manner, be they intelligent or animal or even without awareness; for by nature parts love the general good of the whole to which they belong more than their own particular goods. This must be much more true of the friendship of charity, based on the sharing of God's grace. So with charity man loves God, the common good of all, more than himself; since eternal life exists in God as in the fount and source of everything that shares it.
4   Unity is stronger than union: a man's own sharing in God's goodness is stronger reason for self-love than others' sharing is reason for loving them. In charity then a man should love himself more than his fellowmen; we mustn't, for example, submit ourselves to sin (an obstacle to eternal life) in order to free from sin our fellowman. A man must put up with bodily harm for his friend's sake, but in doing that he spiritually loves himself more for he is willing his own perfection of virtue. The general good, however, is always more lovable than one's own good; for
5   a part loves the good of its whole more than its own part in it. The

fellowship we have in the fulness of eternal life is more of a reason for loving our fellowmen than the overflow of happiness into our body is a reason for loving it. So we must love the souls of our fellowmen more than our own bodies. Every man bears responsibility for his own body, but not always for his fellowman's well-being. So charity obliges us to sacrifice our bodily life for our fellowman's well-being only in cases where his well-being is our responsibility. Though persons who do this spontaneously have so much more perfect a love. Some people say that 6 though we owe more outward good to some than to others, our inward love for all must be equal. But this does not make sense. The affection of charity, a tendency we have by grace, is no less orderly than natural love, the tendency we have by nature; for both tendencies are the work of God's wisdom. But in the natural world natural tendencies match natural movements or qualities: earth is heavier than water, since its natural place is below water. In the same way, the tendency of grace, our affection of charity, must match our outward activities, being more intense towards those to whom most kindness should be done. Though the good that charity wants for all its friends is the same, namely eternal happiness.

In charity God is loved and we do the loving. A person's closeness 7 to God affects the kind of charity we show him (those closest to God being willed greater good), while closeness to us affects the degree of our charity (so that a kinsman's good is willed more intensely than is a greater good to those closer to God). Moreover, though natural closeness to a kinsman can't vary, the virtuousness that brings men close to God can; so we can will for a kinsman more virtue and a higher level of happiness than others have. Again, those close to us we love not only with charity but with other types of friendship too, depending on the ties of connection. And since every good upon which such virtuous friendships are based can serve the goal of the good on which charity is based, charity can control those friendships and so love those close to us in many more ways than it can others. As we have already said [ch 7 pp 198–9 above], we can will certain things with charity that please us, but which God does not will because they do not please him. In what 8 concerns nature we should love our kinsmen most, in civic matters our fellow-citizens, in military affairs our fellow-soldiers. Of these, family connections and love for kinsmen are the most stable. When engaged in activities we have chosen to participate in, our love for chosen friends will outweigh our love of kinsmen; in such activities we seek the company of such friends. But friendship with kinsmen is more stable and natural, and of more weight in matters which relate to nature; we are for example more closely bound to provide them with the necessities of life.

27 2   Emotions exercise a pull on us, though our emotional love is no sudden pull, but derives from long familiarity with what we love. Good will, Aristotle says, is different: not a pull of desire but a product of judgment, and sometimes sudden, as when we want one of two fighters to win. Nor is good will to be identified with that love in our will which involves union of affection between lover and beloved, and in which the lover feels one with the beloved in some way and is attracted to him. For good will is a simple act of willing good to a person whether we have such union of affection with him or not. The love of charity involves not only good will but also union of affection. Aristotle lists five characteristics of friendship: ①willing the friend's good, ②being glad that he is alive, ③taking pleasure in living with him, ④having the same preferences, ⑤sharing his griefs and joys. And all these, as Aristotle also says, spring from loving the friend as one loves oneself, the union of affection we mentioned.

3   We love one thing because of another in all the different senses of *because*. We love medicine because of the goal of health, men because of some virtue making them lovable, sons because of their father who gave them birth, benefactors because of some gift disposing us to love them. In the first three senses we don't love God because of anything else but himself; but other things can dispose us to love God: favours

4   received, hoped-for rewards, or sufferings we need his help to avoid. In the nature of things God is knowable and lovable of himself, being the Truth and Goodness by which other things are known and loved. So even in this life love, which desires things as they are in themselves, is attracted first to God and through him to other things: charity loves God without intermediary and other things by way of God. But knowledge is quite the opposite: because our knowledge starts with sensation, we first know what is closest to our senses, and God only in relation to other things, as their surpassingly different cause. So love begins where knowledge ends, with what we come to know through other things. Just because loving God is something greater than knowing him, especially in this life, it presupposes knowledge. And since knowledge does not stop at created things but pushes through to something higher, love starts there and flows back on to other things completing a sort of circle. Knowledge starts from creatures and reaches God; love starts with God, our ultimate goal, and flows back on creatures.

5   *Love the Lord your God with your whole heart.* The whole of God is to be loved, with the whole of one's ability; but the manner of our loving never equals the degree to which God is lovable, for the one is finite

and the other infinite. Goals are the measures of action, and whatever 6 *loving God*
serves a goal must measure up to it; *no craft lays down rules for its goal,
only for the means of achieving it.* In the same way there is no measuring
the love of God, no adjusting of it this way or that way. It is itself the
measure, which we cannot overdo, because the more we have of it the
better. Reason can measure our affection for the objects reason can
appraise; but God, the object of divine love, is beyond the appraisal of
reason. Moreover, our inner act of love of charity is a sort of goal, since
man's ultimate goal consist in cleaving to God: *to cleave to my God is
my good.* Our external activity, which serves this goal, must measure up
both to charity and to reason. The words of Jesus – *if you love those who* 7
love you, what will it profit you? – must be interpreted formally. Loving
only friends to the exclusion of enemies goes unrewarded by God. But
to love friends not only as friends but because of God reaps a reward.
Love of friends is less deserving when they are loved merely for them- 8
selves, for the love falls short of the friendship of charity which loves
God in them. But loving God for himself is not less deserving, and
indeed is the source of all deserts. What makes things virtuous and
deserving is not their difficulty but their goodness. The fact that something is difficult does not automatically make it more deserving, but
only if the greater difficulty results from its being better.

Joy and peace.   One and the same disposition can dispose us to 28 4
several mutually ordered acts. The disposition is defined and named
after the most fundamental of these acts. Thus our fundamental affection
is love, from which follow desire and joy; so the same disposition of
charity disposes us to love and to desire and to enjoy what we love,
though it receives its name from love. Joy then is not a different virtue *joy is . fruit*
from charity, but an act or effect or *fruit* of charity. Hope follows from *of charity*
love, as joy does, but relates to what is loved under a new aspect, as
something challenging yet possible of achievement; so hope ranks as a
special virtue. Joy, on the other hand, adds no such new aspect.

Peace requires more than communal concord; for even one person's 29 1 *peace*
heart can be divided, with desires at war with one another – *the flesh
lusting against the spirit* – seeking incompatible objects. Concord harmonizes different people's desires; peace also harmonizes one and the
same person's desires. All desire is desire of peace, a desire to enjoy 2
what we desire tranquilly and without hindrance; and that is how *Aug:– peace is /*
Augustine defines peace: *the tranquillity of order.* To be in concord with *tranquillity of order*
another against one's will is not peace, and men wage war to break up
such concords and arrive at a more perfect and acceptable peace. But

just as we can desire true and false goods, so we can seek true or false peace. True peace may be perfect or imperfect: <u>perfect peace</u> is the enjoyment of God in whom all desires are fulfilled, the ultimate goal of reasoning creatures; but only imperfect peace can be had in this world, in which, even if the innermost heart of man rests in God, all sorts of

3 obstacles outside and inside disturb our peace. <u>Peace then involves</u> two <u>kinds of harmony</u>: order among one's own desires, and harmony of those <u>desires with other people's.</u> Charity causes both kinds of harmony, unifying all our desires in the love of God with our whole heart, and making us want to fulfil our fellowman's will as if it were our own. There <u>is nothing to stop people with charity having different opinions, yet being at peace; for opinions are mental matters prior to the desires that peace harmonizes.</u> Nor will dissension over trivial matters, arising from such differences of opinion, destroy peace, as long as there is agreement on vital issues. For though such dissension is incompatible with the perfect peace in which all truth will be known and all desire

4 fulfilled, it is compatible with the imperfect peace of this life. When related actions issue from an agent, following one on another, then they are actions of one virtue, not several; just as in the bodily world fire melts things and vaporizes them with one and the same virtue of heat. So peace and joy are both effects of charity's love of God and fellowman.

30 1 **Compassion.** *Compassion is heartfelt identification with another's distress, driving us to do what we can to help.* (Distress) is anything a man suffers against his will: what first moves us to compassion is some evil of destruction and pain opposed to natural desire, but this is more likely to excite compassion if it has the character of misfortune, of a mischance defying our free will. And especially if it befalls those whose whole will

2 has followed good. We are saddened by others' misfortunes in so far as we regard their distress as our own. So <u>what moves us to compassion is a lack: a lack which might affect us in reality, or which we feel as affecting us through love.</u> God's compassion is entirely of this second sort, for he

3 loves us as something belonging to himself. Joy and peace add no additional virtue to charity, since they delight in the same aspect of goodness as charity loves; but compassion introduces a new aspect, the

4 distress of the one for whom we have compassion. As far as outward activity is concerned, compassion is *the Christian's whole rule of life*; but <u>the inner affection of charity, which binds us to God, is more than just love and compassion for our fellowman.</u>

Doing good for people.   Love involves willing good to one's friends, 31 1
and consequently doing good for them. So doing good for people is in
general an activity of charity, though particular kinds of good deed also
need their own special virtues. *Love inspires the lesser to seek completion*
in the greater, and the greater to provide for the lesser by doing good for
them. So love inspires us not to do good for God, but to honour him
and subject ourselves to him; while he, out of his love, does good for
us. The function of generosity is to moderate our inner passion for
possessions and stop us desiring and loving them too much; so it is not
generous to give away a handsome gift yet still hanker after it. But
outward giving is a mark of friendship, and wanting what one gives for
oneself doesn't detract from the friendship, but rather shows just how
deep it is. Friendship and charity look to the general goodness of what
we do, justice is concerned with whether it is owed, compassion with
whether it relieves distress or want. Since the love of charity extends 2
to all men at every level, so too must doing good for them, given the
right time and place. Charity obliges us to be ready in spirit to do good
to anyone as the occasion arises; and one kindness we can do to everyone
in a general way is to pray for them, unbelievers as well as believers.
We must help a sinner maintain his humanity without encouraging his
sin, for that would be doing evil rather than good. *Since you can't do* 3
good to everybody, first care for those who by chance of place or time or any
other circumstance are closest to you. When our Lord told us not to invite
our friends, brothers and kinsmen to our banquet, but rather the poor
and the disabled, he was not forbidding us to invite kinsmen as such,
but rather forbidding the kind of inviting that wants to be invited back,
and stems from greed rather than charity. In particular cases, strangers
may have greater claim to be invited because of greater need; for the
obligation to do good first to those closest to us holds only when all
other things are equal. As to whom first to help if one person is closer
to us but another more in need: because kinship and need have many
levels no general rule can decide the matter, and the prudent man must
make his own judgment. What we owe to others cannot usually be given
to relatives: it was stolen or borrowed or held in trust, and must be
returned. (Unless of course our relatives are in such need that we are
justified in relieving them with the property of someone else not in so
great a need; and that no general rule but only prudent judgment can
decide.) But what we owe is sometimes ours to give away: because we
owe it not in strict justice but in fairness to those who have done good
to us. Now parents are the greatest such benefactors, and so they
outweigh every other person, unless need or the common good of church

or state demand otherwise. With our other benefactors no general rule
4 can decide the matter. Doing good to people is an activity of charity,
not a separate virtue.

32 1 **Giving alms.**   We give alms to relieve need, so almsgiving is an activity
of the virtue of compassion. Activity can be virtuous, either materially
or formally. We can do the materially just thing without any disposition
to act justly, from a judgment of reason or from fear or hope of reward.
But to do such a thing readily and pleasurably is to do it as men disposed
to act with justice do it, as a formally just action. In the same way
almsgiving can be done materially without charity, but not formally for
2 God's sake, readily and pleasurably. Traditionally seven bodily and
seven spiritual acts of almsgiving have been distinguished. The verse
sums them up as: *visit, sup, feed, clothe, ransom, shelter, bury; teach,
advise, reprove, comfort, forgive, support and pray.* These acts answer to
various bodily and spiritual needs of our fellowmen. In life there are the
general needs for food and drink internally and clothing and shelter
externally; the sick and the captive have special needs; and after life we
need burial. Our spirit too needs help from God, solicited by prayer,
and from man teaching and advice for the mind, comfort for the
feelings, reproof and forgiveness for sins, and support in bearing sin's
3 consequences and other troubles. In general spiritual almsgiving out-
weighs bodily, but in particular cases the reverse may be true: it is better
5 to feed the starving than give them advice. *Let us not love in word and
talk but in deed and truth*: charity obliges us not only to will good to our
fellowmen but to do good to them and help them in their need. Almsgiving is compulsory under two conditions set by virtue and right reason:
that the giver has resources available after his own and his dependents'
needs have been met, and that the recipient's need is a matter of life
and death. Even when these conditions are not met, almsgiving is
advisable though not compulsory. Perhaps you say: my property is my
own to use and to keep. But though the earthly goods God gives us may
be ours to own, the use of them in excess of our needs must be shared
with anyone who can benefit from it. As Basil says: *It is the bread of the
hungry you are hoarding, the clothes of the naked that hang in your
wardrobe, the shoes of those who go barefoot that fall to pieces in your house,
the money of the poor that you possess and do not use. You commit as many
injustices as there are things you could give away.* And Ambrose says the
same. For we have no need to insure against every future contingency:
our Lord forbids us to *take thought of the morrow.* We must work out
what we need or can do without by considering what will normally crop

up. *If you want to be perfect, go and sell all you possess and give to the* 6
poor. In one sense we need what we cannot survive without, and this
should never be given away in alms, for then we would be taking the
lives of ourselves and our dependents (though exceptionally perhaps
this might be allowable for the general good). In another sense we need
that without which we cannot keep up our and our dependents' social
position, a difficult thing to assess. To give this away in alms is not
compulsory, but it is the Lord's advice; and in three cases position ought
to be sacrificed to alms in this way: when we enter religious life, when
what we need in this way can easily be recouped, and when the need
for alms is extreme. Ill-gotten goods are sometimes owed to the person 7
from whom they were acquired (by robbery, theft or usury, for example);
and such goods must be returned and not given in alms. Other ill-gotten
goods may have been given and received unjustly (as a bribe, for
example); and such goods must be given in alms and not returned.
Finally, some goods are ill-gotten because they come from an unlawful
source though the getting was not unlawful (like money earned for
prostitution); and such goods can be either kept or given in alms.
Gambling winnings are against God's law if won by cheating or from
minors or madmen or people one seduced into gambling. Such winnings
must be returned, not given in alms. And where gambling is forbidden
by civil law the same is true for those subject to that law, unless custom
has decreed the contrary (or the money was won from the seducer, in
which case it should not be kept or returned but given in alms). In a
case of extreme need everything becomes common property; and a man
in such need is entitled to take what he needs from others if no one will
help. To such a man one can give alms out of what one has kept or
taken from another; though the owner's consent should be sought first
if that can be done safely. A monk cannot give alms unless he has the 8
express or reasonably presumed permission of his superior, or unless
the need is so great that it would even be lawful to steal for the purpose.

Brotherly correction. There are two ways of correcting wrongdoing: 33 1
brotherly correction treats it as bad for the wrongdoer, and is an act of
charity towards him as a brother aimed at his recovery; another kind of
correction treats the wrong as harmful to others and to the general good,
and is an act of justice maintaining law and order between people.
Negative commands prohibit wrongdoing; positive ones foster acts of 2
virtue. Now wrongdoing is bad in itself, and no circumstance of time
or place can make it good, so prohibitions bind at all times. But acts of
virtue are good only when done in the proper circumstances (where and

when and how they should be) and for a good goal; so in certain circumstances doing the act might be against the command. Now brotherly correction is meant to serve our brother's recovery, so it is commanded only when it is necessary for that purpose, not everywhere and at every possible opportunity. Just as a man who owes money must seek his creditor out when the time comes to repay him, so a man spiritually responsible for another must seek him out to correct him. But the good turns we owe to all in general don't have to be sought out; it is enough to be ready when they seek us out *as though by chance*, as Augustine puts it. Otherwise we would go round prying into other people's lives and that is forbidden. Brotherly correction is an act of charity, and we all owe it in charity to anyone we see doing wrong. But the circumstances must be observed, and when subjects correct superiors they should do it modestly and reverently, not impudently and harshly. When pseudo-Denys reproved the monk Demophilus for correcting a priest, it was because he did it irreverently, hitting him and throwing him out of his church.

[vol 35] 34 1 **Hatred, apathy and envy.** In himself God is unqualified goodness, and no one who sees him as he is can ever hate him. Some of his effects too (existence, life, knowledge) cannot but attract us; so we cannot see God as their author and hate him. But other effects such as punishment and God's laws against sin do repel disordered wills, and when God is
2 seen as their cause he can be hated. When someone hates God he explicitly turns his will away from God, but in other wrongdoing, sexual sin for instance, the turning away is only implicit in the disordered turning towards pleasure. Hatred of God is thus worse than other sins; even than disbelief, which is not sin unless it is willed, and can only be willed by hating the truth faith proposes. Many people hate punishment but bear it patiently with reverence for God's justice: *God tells us to bear punishment, not to love it*. Giving way to hatred of God because he punishes us is hating the very justice of God, the worst sin of all.
3 *Whoever hates his brother is in darkness.* To hate wrongdoing in one's brother and everything that falls short of God's order is part of loving
4 our brother; but to hate his nature or his grace is wrong. Hatred is a disorder of the will, which is the source of all power in man and the root of all sin. If actions are disordered outwardly but not inwardly then they are not sins; the sinfulness of outer actions against our fellowmen derives from inner hatred. So in this respect hatred is worse than outward sin, though outward sins are worse in the harm they do to our
6 fellowmen. We love good, and since God is the source of that in all

creatures, love loves God first and then our fellowmen. But we hate evil, and that exists not in God but in his effects; so we hate our fellowmen first (envying their good), and then transfer that hate to God.   *is that true?*

Apathy is *a sort of depression* which stops us doing anything, a   35 1 *apathy* weariness with work, a *torpor of spirit which delays getting down to anything good.* Spiritual goods are real goods, and taking no joy in them is bad in itself; and it is bad in its effects if it so depresses a man as to keep him back from good works. Apathy then is doubly wrong. Sadness as such merits neither praise nor blame; what we praise is a controlled sadness at evil, what we blame is sadness that is either uncontrolled or is sad about good. Our sense-desires are exercised through bodily organs, so bodily changes can increase our susceptibility to wrong desire and affect us at set times. Apathy for example bothers us most at midday when we begin to feel the heat of the sun and need our food. Every   2 virtue takes pleasure in its own activity, the particular spiritual good it aims at; but charity takes a special joy in the goodness of God. In the same way every vice breeds sadness and depression at the spiritual good of virtuous acts; but apathy is a special vice saddened by the very goodness of God in which charity rejoices. Sins that by definition exclude the love of charity are of their nature fatal. Since joy in God necessarily follows on charity, and apathy is sadness about spiritual good as a facet of God's goodness, apathy is of its nature fatal. But sins are completed only when reason consents to them, and if apathy arises in our sense-appetites – the flesh rebelling against the spirit – but does not get at our reason – by turning into horror and loathing of God's goodness – then the sin is incomplete and non-fatal.

Damascene describes **envy** as *discontent with another's good.* Some-   36 1 *envy* times we regard another's good as our evil because it bodes harm to us, and being sad about it for that reason springs from fear rather than from envy; but sometimes we regard the good of others as lessening our own status and prestige, and that is the sadness of envy. We don't envy people far away from us in place, time or status, but only those who are near to us and whom we hope to emulate or outdo. The people most prone to envy are on the one hand the ambitious, and on the other the fainthearted who make mountains of molehills and think themselves bested by any good in others. Being sad about someone's good fortune   2 because we fear our own harm is not envy and may not even be a sin. Being sad that he had it rather than us is properly speaking only rivalry and may or may not be sinful. Being indignant because we think the man unworthy of such temporal good fortune is a sadness that Aristotle thought just but that scripture forbids, since God in his justice orders things the way he does for the condemnation or correction of sinners, and since temporal goods are as nothing in comparison to what is in store for those who do good. But being saddened by another's good precisely because it surpasses our own is envy and is always wrong, because we are being sad about what should give joy, our fellowman's

3 good fortune. Envy is fatal of its nature, opposed by definition to God's love which is our spiritual life: *we know we have passed from death to life because we love our brothers.* Love of charity rejoices in the good of our fellowmen, but envy is despondent. Though the first stirrings of envy are non-fatal sins, and may be found even in holy men.

37 1 **Dissensions and war.**   Direct dissension between men is a knowing and deliberate resistance to the good of God and our fellows to which we ought to consent. It is a fatal sin directly opposed to the love of charity. But if several people intent on the good of God and their fellowmen differ in opinion about what best serves that good, then that dissent only indirectly opposes the good itself, and will not be sinful. As we said above, concord is union of wills, not opinions. Dissension which destroys true loving concord in charity is a grave sin, but dissent which destroys false and badly-intentioned concord is praiseworthy: *I*

38 1 *came not to bring peace but the sword.* Dissension is opposition of wills, but quarrelling is opposition in words. Here we must attend both to the speaker's intention and his manner: if the intention is to oppose truth, or the manner is offensive to the persons and matters involved, then the quarrel is blameworthy and indeed a fatal sin; but if the intention is to oppose falsehood and the manner is in keeping with the persons and matters involved, then it deserves praise. Opposing falsehood in an immoderate manner can be non-fatally sinful.

39 1   Charity unites one person to another in bonds of spiritual love, but also first and foremost binds together the whole church in unity of spirit. So schismatics, properly so called, are those who of their own free will separate themselves from church unity: the association between the members of the church, and the ordering of all these to their one head, Christ himself, represented in the church by the Pope. So schismatics are people who refuse to obey the Pope or to communicate with people

2 who do obey him. The particular circumstances in which sins are committed are infinitely various, and if you ask in general which of two sins is graver you must be thinking of the type of the sins abstracted from all such circumstances. Disbelief as such sins against God, upon whom as Truth himself faith relies. Schism sins against church unity, which is a kind of good we share from God, but less than God himself.

Spiritual power can be sacramental or jurisdictional. Sacramental power 3
is conferred by an irrevocable consecration and lasts as long as the *sacramental*
consecrated persons do, even if they fall into schism or heresy; and such *power*
people if they return to the church do not have to be reconsecrated. It
is illicit for them to use their power except in submission to higher
authority, but if they do the sacramental effect follows because they
operate as God's instruments despite the blameworthiness of their
action. Jurisdictional power is conferred by simple human command, is *jurisdictl*
not permanent, and is lost by schismatics and heretics who cannot *power*
absolve or excommunicate or grant indulgences or anything of that sort;
and if they tried nothing would happen.

If a **war** is to be just three things are needed. It must be waged by 40 1 *just*
the due authorities, for those who may lawfully use the sword to defend   *war*
a commonwealth against criminals disturbing it from within may also *1. wagd by 1 due*
use the sword of war to protect it from enemies without. But the cause *autorities*
must be just (those whom we attack must have done some wrong which *2. cause must be*
deserves attack), and those waging war must intend to promote good *just*
and avoid evil. The Lord's words: *I say to you, offer the wicked man no* *3. tos waging war*
resistance, must always be borne in mind, and we must be ready to *must intnd good*
abandon resistance and self-defence if the situation calls for that. But *xt evil*
sometimes the common good demands resistance. All the clerical holy 2
orders are services of the altar on which Christ's sufferings are made
present in sacrament. So their office is not to kill or shed others' blood ,
but rather to be ready to shed their own for Christ, imitating in very
deed what they sacramentally re-enact. To wage a just war is a deserving
act, but it is not allowed to clerics who have been deputed to an activity
more deserving. (The marriage-act is also deserving, but condemnatory
for those obliged by a vow of virginity to a greater good.) To fool our 3
enemy by telling him lies or not keeping our promises is always unlawful:
rights must be observed in war and agreements with enemies kept, as
Ambrose said. But we are not bound to tell our enemies everything in
our mind (even in God's teaching many things are hidden) and we may
quite legitimately conceal our plans from him. This is not deception
properly speaking and does not offend justice nor a regulated will; indeed
it is unregulated wills that want to know everything about everybody.
One may wage a just war on feastdays if that is needed to protect the 4
Christian commonwealth; indeed to act otherwise in the face of peril
would be testing God out. Quarrelling implies opposition in words, but 41 1
fighting opposition in action. Fights are like private wars, conducted not *fighting*
by a public authority but by the unregulated wills of private persons.
They are always sins; though the party defending himself can maybe

avoid fatal sin, even any sin, if he is restrained in his defence and so does not, properly speaking, fight.

42 1   Sedition is a disturbance of the unity of the state in preparation for
2 a physical uprising. Tyrannical governments are unjust, opposed to the general good and serving the private good of the ruler. So disturbing such a government is only seditious if the people suffer more from it than the tyrant does. Indeed it is the tyrant that is guilty of the sedition, properly speaking, fomenting discord in his people in order to lord it over them more safely. For that is what tyranny is: government for the ruler's personal advantage and the people's harm.

43 1   **Setting (and following) bad example.** [Bad example is called scandal in the New Testament, and] in Greek *skandalon* means *stumbling-block*, so the word is well-used for *any not so right word or deed occasioning someone's spiritual downfall.* Evil thoughts and desires lie hidden in the heart, so can't set a bad example for others; but *not so right* includes under bad example not only words and deeds which are actually evil but also those which appear evil. However, since the only thing sufficient to cause a man's spiritual downfall or sin is his own will, bad example
2 is not said to cause his fall but to occasion it. Willingly to follow a bad example is a spiritual fall and so always a sin; though sometimes the action that occasions the fall may not itself have been sinful. Wilfully setting a bad example is always sin, even when what is done is not a sin but only looks like one; it should have been avoided out of love for one's fellowman's welfare. And in this case following bad example need not
3 always be a sin. Willingly following a bad example is not a distinct type of sin: a man can fall into any kind of sin as a result of another's words or deeds. Willingly setting a bad example, if unintentional, is also not distinctive: for what is coincidental to an act can't define it; but if
5 intentional the special intention gives the act a special sinfulness. Neither the willing setting nor the willing following of bad example is to be found in those who are joined to God in perfect love; for willingly following bad example presupposes some shakiness in holding to the
7 good. Spiritual goods needed for salvation cannot be given up without fatal sin, so mustn't be foregone from fear of setting [apparent] bad example. But when spiritual goods are not so needed, and some people might take bad example out of weakness or ignorance – *the scandal of the little ones* – we ought to conceal or put away such goods until explanation has removed the bad example. If no amount of explanation will do that, then the taking of bad example would seem to be an act of malice – *the scandal of the Pharisees* – and should be ignored.

The commandments to love.   Command implies obligation; and 44 1
within any activity goals oblige of themselves and means because of
goals. Now the goal of the spiritual life is man's union to God in love
of charity, and everything else in the spiritual life serves that: *the goal
of the commandment is charity from a pure heart and a good conscience and
an unfeigned faith.* As a result we are commanded to perform those
virtuous acts which cleanse the heart from unregulated passion, and
maintain a good conscience in acting and a right faith in worshipping
God. So since what obliges of itself obliges more strongly than anything
serving it, *the greatest of all* commandments is love. *Where the spirit of
the Lord is there is freedom*, but the obligation of commands is only
opposed to freedom when men are averse to what is commanded. Indeed,
the command to love can only be fulfilled by one's own act of willing
and that is totally free. *This is the command we have from God, that* 2
whoever loves God love his brother also. Commands function in law like
theorems in science, but not everyone can see what is implicit in the
starting-points of a science until science draws it all out in conclusions.
Similarly, in practical matters, when we are guided by the law and its
commands, the love of God functions as our goal and starting-point,
and in that is implicit love of our fellowmen. But for those who can't
see it, this second command must be made explicit. Charity is a single
virtue but it has two acts, the one ordered to the other as to its goal; so
because commands command acts, not virtues, there is more than one
command of love. God is loved in our fellowmen as the goal is loved in
whatever serves that goal. *On these two commandments hang the whole of* 3
the Law and the Prophets. Other acts of charity are effects of the act of
loving, so commands to love implicitly command them, though for those
slow to grasp this the scripture makes them explicit: *Rejoice in the Lord
always, Keep peace with everyone, While you have the chance do good to
all,* and other commands to do special acts of beneficence. Similarly,
against the vices opposed to charity we have prohibitions: *Do not hate
your brother in your heart, Do not lie down [apathetically] in your bonds,
Stop being envious,* and so on.

Love the Lord your God with your whole heart. God is to be loved as 4
our ultimate goal, to which everything is to be referred. Rightly then a
certain totality is commanded in our love of God. In heaven we will
love God with all our heart actually intent on him at all times; on the
way there the whole of our heart is to be disposed to God, in such a
way that it will not receive into itself anything opposed to God's love.
Non-fatal sin is not opposed to this disposition, since it does not take
away love by tending in the opposite direction, but only hinders its

exercise. There is a perfection of charity to which we are advised which lies halfway between the two mentioned above: namely, that we should as far as possible refrain from even licit temporal preoccupations if they 5 distract and impede the actual movement of our hearts to God. *With all your heart and all your soul and all your mind and all your power.* Love is an act of will, called here the heart, since the heart is the root of bodily movements just as the will – and especially the willing of our ultimate goal, the object of charity – is the root of all spiritual movement. And there are three further sources of action which are themselves moved by the will: the mind, the lower appetite (here called the soul) and our external powers.

7   *Love your fellowman as yourself.* The reason for loving him is that he is our fellow both as naturally imaging God and as capable of glory: call him *neighbour* or *brother* or *friend* as you will. The manner of loving him is as ourselves: not equally but in like manner—holily (for the same goal as ourselves: God), justly (according to the same rule as ourselves: in good but not in bad), and truly (for the same reason as ourselves: not 8 just for profit and pleasure). The order in which we love is part of the very meaning of love, proportioned to what is loved: God above all (because *with one's whole heart*), self above fellowman (because *him as ourselves*), fellowman above our own bodily life (since we *lay down our life for our friends*), and – among our fellowmen – especially *our brethren in the faith* and *our own relations.*

45 1 **The gift of wisdom.**   A man is wise in some field like medicine or architecture when he knows the most fundamental causes in that field and can therefore judge and plan over its whole extent. Those who know the deepest cause of all, God, and judge and plan by him are called absolutely wise. Such knowledge and judgment comes from the Spirit *who reaches into the depths of everything, even the depth of God.* Clearly then wisdom is a gift of the Spirit. Even in wrongdoing something constitutes an ultimate goal, and the man knowledgeable of it is 2 wise in evil. To judge well about the things of God through reasoned investigation is an act of the mental virtue of wisdom, but to do so through a certain oneness in nature with God is an act of the Spirit's gift of wisdom. Such sympathy or connaturality with divine things is an effect of the love of charity uniting us to God, so that wisdom's cause is love in the will, even if in essence wisdom is a disposition of mind to judge well. The gift of understanding guides the mind's perceptions, but the gifts of wisdom and knowledge form its judgments, according 3 to divine and human reasons respectively. Since we must consider things

in themselves before comparing them with other things, wisdom first contemplates divine things, then plans human actions according to God's plan. This is a wisdom which presupposes charity and can't co- 4 exist with fatal sin. But there are degrees in it according to our degree 5 of union with divine things. For some the measure is no more than is necessary for salvation, and such wisdom belongs to all who possess grace that makes them pleasing and who do not commit fatal sin. Others possess wisdom to a higher degree, passing on their contemplation of the higher mysteries of God to others, and planning for others as well as themselves: and this wisdom is rather one of those graces freely given that the Holy Spirit *distributes as he wills*. Even children and madmen, if baptized, possess wisdom as a disposition given them by the Holy Spirit, though they can't exercise it because of the physical impediments to their exercise of reason.

Stupidity implies a dull heart and blunted senses; madness complete 46 1 loss of our mental senses. Stupidity is opposed to wisdom, madness just its absence. Judgment can be blunted in two ways: by natural disposition 2 as in the mad (and that is no sin), or from so burying our senses in earthly things that we cannot see divine ones, and such stupidity is a sin.

Chapter 11

LIVING IN THE WORLD – MORAL VIRTUE

Introductory comment. In this chapter Thomas attempts to summarize the moral teaching of the Christian tradition under headings derived from the Greek philosophical tradition going back to Socrates, Plato and Aristotle. This is not as strange as it might seem since the early Christian tradition, through Roman writers, had already assimilated that philosophical tradition. But it does mean that the structure doesn't stress headings like the seven deadly sins, but rather the four cardinal or *political* virtues to be found in Aristotle. The background is to be found in chapters 7 and 8 above, which dealt with moral behaviour and moral virtue. Morally good behaviour is behaviour in which our voluntary actions are concordant with their objects in ways which reason can accept: externally concordant in the sense that those who have a right to live are not killed, what belongs to another is not appropriated, and so on; and internally concordant in the sense that our interior consent to any act accords with our natural desire to achieve the good human nature is capable of achieving. For us to act well in this way in the multitude of different circumstances with which we are faced requires dispositions to act well: a disposition called prudence to choose what in the circumstances will implement our right desires, and the dispositions of justice, moderation and courage to desire rightly (and so choose rightly) in the face of specially difficult circumstances, such as the fact that though an action is owed to others we will get nothing out of it, or that it goes against our desires, or brings us face to face with things we deeply fear. Such dispositions are the cardinal moral virtues and they and their satellite virtues are the subject of this chapter.

We should notice to begin with that for Thomas these virtues are in a real sense all one virtue: Thomas certainly believes that no partial skill in one area is a virtue unless we have skill in all areas, for what makes such skills virtuous is their ability to serve the final prudent choice of a good action. Prudence able to be prudent only in certain areas is not prudence at all but an approximation to it; either virtue grows in all areas at once or it is not true virtue. Secondly, virtues develop their own identities in various areas because virtue meets with special difficulties there, and it is in terms of those special difficulties that the virtues tend to be defined. Thus courage is especially defined in relation to fear of death, since that is the emotion most likely to make us timid; and moderation is especially defined in relation to the pleasures of touch – of food and sex – since those are the emotions most likely to make us unreasonably attracted to things. And prudence – though it must know how to investigate and plan – is nevertheless defined by what is most difficult for the mind in moral matters, namely, getting ourselves to act. Thirdly, all other individualities of virtue can be related in some way or other to these four main virtues as parts of those virtues: but the word *parts* can take on three senses: that of the component actions that make up any action of the virtue (for example, justice must pursue good and avoid evil), that of subdivisions within the area of difficulty defining the virtue (for example, the prudence of the teacher or the prudence of the statesman), and that of satellite virtues imitating the main virtue in areas slightly off-centre (for example, the virtues of religion and family loyalty, of truthfulness and friendliness, regarded by Thomas as satellite or allied virtues of justice).

Prudence, as the central moral virtue in which all the others constitute so to speak one virtuous whole, is treated first. Then comes the largest section, dealing with a virtuous will: **justice**. Thomas distinguishes two levels of justice: justice to society as a whole, and justice to individual persons in society. The first justice is solicitous of the common good, and is commonly implemented by a disposition to obey the law, which Thomas calls legal justice. Justice directed to the community at large he also calls *general justice* at times, and notes that all other moral acts in their special areas can become subject to it by becoming matters of law. Examples of such moral acts in special areas are the two types of *particular justice* or justice to individual persons: firstly, justice between person and person in exchanges – buying and selling, loaning at interest, observance of a person's right to life and liberty; and secondly, justice towards the person by the community at large, as for example in the proper and equitable distribution of the wealth of the community. And here it is worth stressing that

Thomas's conception of private property is in tune with a long and consistent Christian and Jewish tradition which, if obscured at the moment by post-Christian values, is nevertheless surely the only reasonable one. Private property he regards as a reasonable way of caring for things as long as those things when used by their owners are used in accordance with the common good. Nothing can ever be so privately owned that the common need cannot direct its use. And since the poor are always to be with us, it will always be true that in case of extreme need the ownership of the necessities of life reverts to whoever needs them, and the appropriation of them in such circumstances by the needy is never stealing, whereas the appropriation of them by their legal owner is. What Thomas calls particular or individual justice, then, deals with contractual rights and wrongs. Society, however, for Thomas, is not exclusively a matter of contracts entered into by equals; so, after treating of justice in the strict sense, Thomas deals with **virtues allied to justice** – justice's satellite virtues – the kinds of justice which hold between people who are not equals, like religion and family loyalty. Towards the end of his treatment – after having talked of truthfulness and generosity and the like – he mentions a virtue called here *equity* or equitableness, the virtue of being able to temper one's obedience to the letter of the law by other actions if they are seen to be more solicitous of the common good. Thomas esteems equitableness more highly than a legal justice which allows equity no place, calling it the more important part of legal justice.

Disposing us to virtuous emotion are the twin cardinal virtues of **courage** and **moderation** (and their satellites): virtues which dispose us to virtuous affective emotions and virtuous aggressive emotions respectively. For an explanation of this distinction we must look back to ch 7 p 201. We have to note here that Thomas follows Aristotle in not finding self-discipline a virtue (below pp 432ff) The self-disciplined man is one who struggles to control his unruly emotions with will-power, whereas Thomas's conception of the virtuous man is one in whom the power of love has so permeated the emotions themselves that they have themselves become disposed to ruliness, so that the body itself sympathizes and cooperates with what the whole man feels reasonable and integrated behaviour.

This perhaps is a good place to make a comment on Thomas's attitude to sex. The subject crops up in several different places: for example, in chapter 5 in connection with the nature of man and the distinction of the sexes (p 143 and p 148); at various places in chapter 7 when Thomas raises the question whether passions are good or evil; in this chapter when the subdivision of the virtue of moderation called chastity is discussed (pp 429ff); and under religious life in chapter 12 in connection with the vow of continence (p 461). In general, one should note that Thomas has nothing against sexual pleasure. He refuses to connect the transmission of inherited sin with taking pleasure in the sexual act as Augustine apparently does; he states that not only would an innocent Adam and Eve have enjoyed their intercourse in the garden of Eden, but that they would have got more pleasure out of it than their banished successors; and though he accepts that genital motions do not obey reason and that the moment of intercourse tends to distract our mental attention, he will not accept that indulging in sex is therefore unreasonable – one might as well call going to sleep immoral, he says. Careful study of the passage on sexual sin in this chapter will show that his severity, and he is severe in his judgments, is based not on distaste for pleasure or even for excess of pleasure as such, but for the consequent injustice towards sexual partners, children and families that he believes it involves. This is also the criterion he adopts when assessing the relative gravity of sins; whatever else can be said of Thomas he was not a prude. Was he however sexist? He inherited an unfortunate biology: he quotes Aristotle's opinion that a female is a male *manqué* in the sense that human seed as such *intends* to produce males but due to unfavourable circumstances such as the dampness of the south wind occasionally produces females. But at that very point his innate reasonableness causes him to point out that whatever may be said of the human seed's intentions, the intentions of nature as a whole are clearly to produce as many women as men, even if this entails quite a bit of damp in the wind; and that that in turn means that it is God's intention. And he also quotes Paul's statement that in the body of Christ – the new graced world ushered in by Christ – there is no male or female. However, like Paul before him and modern popes after him, Thomas belongs to his culture, and believes that men and women have different roles in society; thus he allows only men to teach openly in church, saying that women anyway do the teaching of the children in the home. The fact is that Thomas is a man of few prejudices and very fair mind, but a man at that, and not a woman. Here may also be the place to mention that Latin does not suffer from the weakness of English in having only one word *man* to translate *homo* – human being, and *vir* – the husband or male man. Nor does Latin have to express the personal pronoun as either *he* or *she*. So no conclusions can be drawn about Thomas from the very frequent use of *man* in this translation to mean *human being* or from the use of masculine pronouns. This is a choice to which the editor must plead guilty, knowing quite well that if he had been a she, she might well have chosen differently.

Prudence

[vol 36] 47 1 **Function of prudence.** *Prudence is knowing what to want and what not to want.* The word *prudence* [a doublet of *providence*] means *looking ahead*; and since knowing the future by way of the present and past involves making connections, prudence is characteristic of reason. Prudence directs means to ends, and that requires mind to deliberate and will to make choices. Of those two activities, deliberating is the more characteristic of prudence: *a prudent man is a well-advised one*, says Aristotle; choice, as *advised desire* (desire guided by deliberation), is a consequent effect of prudence. Aristotle says *intentional breaches of rule are praised in artists and craftsmen but blamed in men of prudence and virtue.* This is because prudence is praised not simply for the plans it makes but for the use it makes of those plans. As Aristotle goes on to say, *all art involves reason*, but only prudence applies it to conduct

2 through will. *Prudence is reasoned regulation of conduct*, reasoning well about the whole business of living well. All regulation by reason of the making of things can be called art or craft; but only regulation by reason when there are no fixed rules for achieving the goal and deliberation is needed, can be called prudence. There is an art of constructing syllogisms and propositions according to fixed and certain rules, but no prudence of that. Arts can be speculative; but not prudence.

3 *Prudence explores not only general rules but particular cases.* It not only makes plans but makes use of plans, and that you can't do unless you know both the general principles of reason and the particular practical situations in which they must be applied. Reason first and foremost grasps general truths, but it also applies them in particular cases; from general premises it argues particular conclusions, turning round, so to speak, to consider matter. Human experience reduces the unmanageable infinity of particular cases to a finite set of usual situations adequate enough for human prudence. Our interior senses are perfected by

memory and experience so as readily to judge particular situations as they arise; not that prudence is primarily a disposition of our sense-powers, but of reason applied to those powers.

When treating virtue in general we defined it as making us and what 4 we do good. Now *good* may mean goodness of some particular type, or goodness as such, the quality of being good or desirable. Dispositions which make for rightness of reason abstracted from rightness of desire, dispose us to a particular type of goodness without disposing us to goodness as such; these are less truly virtues than dispositions which dispose us to desire rightly and thus incline us to the goodness of things as such. Prudence is right reason using itself in conduct, and that presupposes rightness of desire. It is not only a virtue in the lesser sense of mental virtue, but also in the sense that moral virtues are.

We distinguish different types of activity wherever there are different 5 ways in which things can be objects of activity; big differences in type of activity distinguish different abilities to act, but lesser differences distinguish different dispositions of one ability. Thus there are various dispositions strengthening our ability to reason: wisdom, insight and the sciences concern truths that are necessarily true, art and prudence things that could have been otherwise (art concerns itself with what can be made with external material, prudence with what we can make of ourselves). Prudence differs from the moral virtues by a distinction big enough to distinguish abilities: prudence strengthening our ability to reason, the moral virtues our abilities to desire. Nevertheless, all powers strengthened by moral virtues share reason in some way; and the moral virtues themselves derive their virtue from sharing in the virtue of prudence. Our conduct is the object of prudence as a truth we must reason about, but the object of moral virtue as a good to be desired.

The function of prudence is not to set the goals of moral virtue, but 6 simply to determine means to those goals. Just as reason when pursuing truth starts from certain premises known by natural insight and ends up with scientific conclusions known in the light of those premises, so too when directing behaviour reason starts from certain naturally known goals of moral virtue (goals function in activity like principles do in knowledge), and concludes to what we ought to do to achieve those goals. Prudence presupposes the goals of moral virtue as general starting-points and determines what to do in particular. The goals are set by natural reason, for the proper goal of every moral virtue 7 is conformity with right reason, and that is prescribed to man by his natural reason bidding him act reasonably. How a man must strike that reasonable balance is the business of his prudence to determine. Striking

the balance is the goal, achieved when the means are disposed rightly. Just as physical agents cause matter to take on some form but don't invent the essential structure of that form, so prudence introduces balance into our feelings and activities without itself introducing the notion of virtue as balance. Moral virtues tend to a balance instinctively and naturally; but because the balance is different in every situation, such natural tendencies (which have only one way of operating) need
8 the help of prudent reasoning if they are to find that balance. *Prudence commands our behaviour*. Reason has three main functions in regulating conduct: the two it already exercises when pursuing truth – namely, investigating and then passing judgment on its findings – and a third function of putting what it has investigated and decided upon into practice. This third act finally implements the goal of reasoned direction of conduct, and is prudence's main activity.
10   The idea that man need only seek his own private good conflicts with charity and with right reason, both of which prize the general good above all. So men need a political prudence aiming at the general good, and bearing the same relation to legal justice as ordinary prudence does
11 to the moral virtues. The good of the individual, of the family and of the state differentiate types of prudence: ordinary, domestic, political. But since the good of the whole people comes first, political prudence
12 is primary and in control of the other types. Prudence is for people entrusted with rule and government: it is not a virtue of slaves or subjects as such. But since every man's reason shares in government whenever he makes a rational decision, every man shares in prudence. There are seeming prudences which contrive means for bad ends, like the prudence of the thief planning to thieve well. There are genuine but partial prudences: particular and not general like prudence in trade, or general but incomplete like that of men who investigate and decide well but don't implement their decisions. Prudence that is genuine, general and complete is the virtue of prudence, and cannot exist in sinners. For prudence involves right inclinations: it needs them to provide it with right goals as starting-points (through the moral virtues), and it needs
14 them for the right deeds which it is its function to command. Whoever has grace has charity, and since all the virtues are connected, prudence. The prudence men acquire needs time and experience, so the young have it neither in act nor in disposition, but the prudence God instils is a disposition of every baptized infant or madman, though only those
15 who can use their reasons can exercise it. Prudence's knowledge of what to do in general begins with principles that are even more natural to man than those of the speculative sciences, and other principles are

developed through experience and teaching. Prudence's knowledge of
what to do in particular cases is different: for the right goals for man
are determinate and we can be naturally disposed to them, but the means
are as various as the people and undertakings involved, and knowledge
of them cannot be natural.

Prudence involves not just knowing but desiring, because its main 16
activity is putting what we know into practice through desire and action.
So prudence is lost not so much through forgetfulness as through being
obscured by feeling and passion. The experience prudence presupposes
is not memory so much as the practice of directing conduct well.
Forgetting moral truths doesn't destroy prudence's main activity, though
it causes obstacles to it.

Analysis of prudence.   Parts are of three sorts: component parts such 48 1
as the walls, roof and foundations of a house; subdivisions such as the
species of animals; and functional parts such as the different abilities of
a man.

The component parts of a virtue are the qualities which together
contribute to a perfect act of the virtue: a prudent act, for example,
must be both perceptive and preceptive: perception demands a good
memory for the past, insight in the present, readiness to learn, inventiveness and soundness of inference; and effective government demands
foresight of the goal, circumspection about circumstances, and caution
about obstacles. **Memory** is the foundation of experience, the know- 49 1
ledge of what usually happens, a natural ability which we can cultivate
by technique and hard work. Some hints: match unusual, and therefore
striking, images to what you want to remember, since sense-images are
mastered more readily than spiritual ideas; connect the images so that
remembering one brings back the next; be interested in what you must
remember and frequently ponder it. **Insight** means not our natural 2
understanding of general premises, theoretical and practical, such as *Do
no evil*: though that is presupposed by prudence. Rather it means insight
into the individual cases to which we apply such general premises when
deciding our behaviour, a sense of the particular goal. It is called insight
because it throws light on our action, and good sense because it does
this in the particular case, exercising the judgment of our interior sense-
faculties. **Readiness to learn** from the experience of others, above all 3
from the old, is especially characteristic of prudence, since one man
alone can't sufficiently consider all the infinite variety of possible action.
We should attend to tradition carefully, constantly and respectfully,
without lazy neglect or proud disdain. **Inventiveness** is a sort of shrewd 4

5 ability to light quickly on the best course to follow. **Soundness of inference** is needed to apply general principles to the variety and uncertainty of particular cases.

48 1   [The subdivisions of prudence are the prudences needed to govern one's own life, those united in special undertakings (like the soldiers of an army), and those living the whole of life in common (like families or

50 1 states).] **Statesmanship** and **lawmaking** belong to rulers in authority over self-contained communities and is the most perfect form of

2 prudence. **Political prudence** differs from ordinary common prudence whereby man rules himself for his own personal good; by political prudence he rules himself for the general good. Things without life or reason act at another's stimulus and not their own, since they are not masters by free choice of their own behaviour. Whether they are ruled rightly depends not on them but on what stimulates them to action. But men who are subject to the authority of others are so acted on by their commands that they cause themselves to act by free choice. So in obeying

3 their rulers, they need to rule themselves rightly. **Domestic prudence** is household economy, the aim of which is not wealth: wealth is only an instrument with which we aim at the true goal of living well in a domestic environment.

48 1   [The functional parts of a virtue are its closely allied virtues, which fulfil secondary functions allied to the virtue's main function. Thus prudence's main function is government, and its allies are good counsel or well-advisedness in investigation, judiciousness (in judging common

51 4 cases) and farsightedness (in judging uncommon ones).] **Farsightedness** is a special virtue. Clearly things that escape the control of lower causes are sometimes subject to higher ones: birth deformities signify failure of the active semen, but are subject to the heavenly bodies and God's providence. In the same way we must sometimes do things outside the ordinary rules of conduct (not returning something entrusted to us by a traitor, for example); and here we have to appeal to higher principles by means of a higher virtue, farsightedness. Judgment must be faithful to a thing's peculiarities; but inquiry often throws up general questions. Thus dialectical inquiry pursues truth guided by general logical principles, but final demonstrative proof must attend to the peculiarities of the subject-matter in question. So, though we need only a single virtue of well-advised counsel to regulate inquiry about what to do, we need two virtues of judgment. Prudence is also single, attending to commanding one goodness in all it does. Things outside the common run are ruled by God's providence alone; but farseeing men can form reasonably good judgments about them.

Because our mind cannot grasp all and every individual contingency 52 1 *the thoughts of mortal men are fearful and our counsels uncertain.* In our searchings we need the guidance of God, who knows all things; and this is given through a gift of counsel in which we take as rule God's advice, so to speak. Judgment and command belong to the one directing rather 2 than the one directed. So since under the gifts of the Holy Spirit we are more moved than moving, the gift corresponding to prudence is not called judgment or command but counsel, as though to stress we are receiving advice from another. When a cause of some change is not 3 cause of the form acquired by the change the cause ceases to act once the change is accomplished: the builder doesn't go on building the house once built. But if the cause also causes the form that is acquired then it continues to act even after the change is accomplished, as the sun goes on illuminating the atmosphere all day. And this is the way God causes knowledge and virtue in us, not only when we acquire them but as long as they last. So the blessed in heaven go on receiving the gift of counsel from God, inasmuch as God preserves the knowledge they already have of what to do, and enlightens them about things they do not know.

Imprudence. Just as prudence plays a guiding part in all moral 53 1 virtue, so imprudence is at work in all sin and vice, for you can't sin unless reason fails to guide in some way, and that is imprudence. And vices allied to imprudence oppose prudence's allied virtues: headlong haste opposes deliberate counsel, thoughtlessness judgment, and neg-ligence prudent government itself. Reason occupies the summit of the 3 soul and descends to commanding bodily action down many steps of deliberation: memory of the past, insight into the present, inventiveness as to the future, sound inference in making connections, readiness to learn from the judgment of those more experienced. If somebody driven by wilfulness or passion hurtles down these steps we have the vice of headlong haste. Negligence arises from slackness of will and results in 54 3 reason not being attentive enough to govern what and how things are done. If the will is so slack that it falls short of God's love, or if reason omits something necessary for salvation, then negligence is fatal. Some 55 3 faults against prudence counterfeit it: when reason becomes intent on a goal which only seems good, we have worldly prudence; when the means to a goal, good or bad, is counterfeit, we have cunning; and cunning 5 shows itself in guile and fraud.

The immediate concern of prudence is not our ultimate goal but the 56 1 means to that goal, so no injunction in the ten commandments deals directly with prudence. But all ten commandments are relevant to it, because prudence governs all our moral behaviour. The gospels, on the other hand, teach perfection; so they have to instruct us in everything related to right living, goals and means. That is why we are told in the gospel to *be prudent as serpents*.

Justice

[vol 37] 57 1   **Doing the just thing.**   Justice governs our dealings with others; the very name *justice* signifies equality – to adjust something is to make it equal to some standard – and equality is a relationship to something other. Other moral virtues fit a man to himself: they aim at action right for the doer. Justice, over and above that, aims at action right for someone else, adjusted to match another: for example, paying someone the due wage for services rendered. The *just thing* is what is objectively right and equitable, abstracting from how it is done; other virtues aim at what is right in the way it is done. The virtue of justice is peculiar in observing this objective criterion, which we call the *just thing*. Just as art produces things in accordance with some idea or plan pre-existing in the artist's mind, so prudence determines the just thing with the help of a pre-existent rule or plan, which, when written down, we call *law*. Law is not itself the just thing, but a plan for it.

2   The just thing then is something done to be equitable to someone: either naturally equitable (giving as much as one receives), or equitable by convention or mutual agreement (giving what the parties deem sufficient). Such conventions can be private and personal contracts or public, enacted by the whole people or their representative authorities. Human nature is unstable, and what is natural to man can nevertheless sometimes fail. Natural equitableness says deposits must be returned to depositors, and if man's nature was always right that would always bind. But often men's wills are disordered, and there occur cases in which you can't return a man's deposit for fear he might use it badly: a man in a fury asking for his weapon back. If what men by mutual agreement lay down to be the just thing does not conflict with natural justice, then we call it enacted or positive justice. But if it conflicts with natural justice, human will cannot make it just: you can't decree stealing or adultery licit. *Woe to those who make wicked laws*, says scripture. There is also a justice promulgated by God. It consists partly of things naturally just but obscure to man, and partly of things God decrees to be just. For in divine as in human law some things are commanded because good and forbidden because bad, and other things are good because commanded and bad because forbidden.

The naturally just is what matches up to something else by nature: 3
either in itself (as males are in themselves the natural reproductive
partners of females and parents the natural rearers of children), or on
account of some consequence accruing (though there is nothing in this
particular field itself to match it to either of us, considerations like
availability to cultivation and peaceful use naturally match it to you
rather than to me). Animals as well as men perceive things in themselves,
and the first kind of natural justice is shared with animals; but only
reason can relate a thing to its consequences, so the second kind of
natural justice is restricted to men (the so-called *ius gentium*: universal
human custom). There is no reason in the nature of a man himself why
he rather than another should be a slave; it happens because of some
consequent utility to both slave and master. So slavery is natural only
in the sense of being a universal human custom. The *ius gentium* is not
enacted law: the peoples of the world never came together to agree it;
such universal customs are rather dictated by natural reason as being
close to natural equitableness.

In the respects in which people are quite distinct from one another 4
strict justice must govern their mutual dealings. Sometimes people also
belong to one another in some way – children to parents, servants to
masters – and then special forms of justice govern them in that respect.
Things are not quite the same with wives and husbands, for although
there is a way in which a wife belongs to a husband (she is related to
him as his own body), that relationship is more like a companionship or
society. Considered as human beings, children and servants are self-
subsistent distinct individuals; and in that respect strict justice applies
to them.

Being just. *Justice is a stable and lasting willingness to do the just thing* 58 1
for everyone. Every virtue disposes us to do good deeds, and is defined
by the good deeds appropriate to its particular field. For justice that
field is our dealings with others, which is why the definition above refers
to doing the just thing for everyone. For such acts to be virtuous they
must be done *knowingly, from choice for a due goal, and stably.* So our
definition starts with willingness (which involves knowing), and qualifies
it as stable and lasting. The definition is complete, though it might be
articulated more formally as *justice is a disposition to do the just thing for
everyone with a stable and lasting willingness.* Aristotle gave much the
same definition: *Justice is a disposition to act by choosing the just thing to
do.* The virtue of justice is not sufficiently displayed by doing the just
thing on one occasion in one matter, since it would be difficult to find

anybody who didn't do that. Rather a just man is one willing to do the just thing always in all cases.

2   Justice implies equality, and that implies a relationship to others, since things are equal to other things, not themselves. Since it is human deeds that are being adjusted, the particular equality implied by justice must be between different doers of such deeds. Such doers are whole and complete substances, not parts or forms or powers: strictly speaking, hands don't deliver blows but men with their hands. So justice strictly speaking is exercised by men in relation to each other. Actions relating a man to himself are sufficiently right when the other moral virtues have put right order into his emotions; but actions that relate us to other people must observe rights in a special sense, and be right not only in respect of the doer but also in respect of whomsoever they are done to.

3   That needs a special virtue: justice. Human virtues *make human deeds good and human beings good*. Justice is a virtue because it regulates human action according to a standard of right reason, and so renders it good. Actions necessitated by constraint cease to be voluntary or deserving, but actions necessitated by legal obligation, prescribed by a goal which cannot be attained without them, can be done voluntarily and are then deserving. Though their obligatoriness does exclude any notion of

4   supererogatory credit. Being just is doing something rightly, and since our immediate ability to do things lies in our capacity to desire them, justice must perfect some capacity to desire. Now rendering a person his due can't be a movement of emotional desire, because reason alone can grasp the proportion of things to each other, not the senses. Justice then perfects not our capacities for affective and aggressive emotion, but our rational will.

5   Justice directs our conduct in relation to others, both individually and in general, since by serving a community we serve everyone in that community. Justice properly so-called deals with both. Moreover, every member of a community is part of that community, and the goods of parts serve the good of the whole; so the good of each man's virtue, whether governing his conduct in relation to himself or to others, serves the general good that concerns justice. So every act of every virtue is an act of justice when so related to the general good; and justice, thought of in this way, comprehends every other virtue. Because the general good is regulated by law, justice in this general sense is often called *legal*

6   *justice*. Legal justice is the virtue of being a good citizen. It is not a general nature entering into the definition of every virtue (as animality enters the definition of men and horses and all other animals), but it exercises a generality of causal power over the acts of every virtue (like

the sun has a general influence over all the earth). Legal justice directs the acts of all other virtues to its own goal of the general good, just as charity directs them to God's good. Both virtues are causally general, though special in their definition with their own special object: God's good in the case of charity, and the general good in the case of legal justice – whether we think of that virtue as a master-virtue present in the ruler of the society, or present apprentice-like in his subjects. Any virtue ordered to the general good by this virtue special in definition but general in power, could itself be called legal justice; but understood in that way legal justice doesn't really differ from all the other virtues, though it considers them from a different point of view. Considered under its own special aspect each virtue directs its act to its own goal; that the action is sometimes or always directed to a further goal comes not from that special virtue as such, but from the higher virtue directing all virtues to the general good: the special virtue of legal justice. Legal 7 justice relates a man directly to the general good; his other virtues relate him directly to particular goods, be it to his own good (as do the virtues of moderation and courage) or to the good of other individuals (as does the virtue of justice to individuals). Legal justice governs our dealings with others to the degree that such dealings are included in our pursuit of the common good; but only indirectly. So we need a justice to individuals to look after such dealings directly.

Men relate to each other through external actions and the external 8 things they must share; a man's interior feelings relate him to himself. So justice has as its special field external deeds and objects inasmuch as they relate men to one another. Regulation of actions as effective in 9 the external world belongs to justice; regulation of them as expressive of interior feeling belongs to other moral virtues. Justice stops us stealing because it upsets the external balance of things; generosity stops us stealing because it expresses an immoderate love of wealth. Since external actions are defined more by their external objects than by the interior feeling they express, in themselves they concern justice more than they do the other moral virtues. Those other moral virtues govern 10 feelings, determining the right balance of feeling for this man in these circumstances. That balance is not something we can objectively measure by a proportion between things; it must be determined by reason taking into account the man himself. The balance of justice is an external matter, matching external things to external people; though this external balance is discovered by reason, so that justice retains the character of a moral virtue. The act proper to justice then is to render to each 11 man what belongs to him, according to a certain proportionate equality.

12 Legal justice evidently outshines other moral virtues, since the general
good surpasses the goods of individuals: *neither morning nor evening star
is as worthy of admiration.* But justice to individuals also excels other
virtues: for it perfects our will and not just our feelings; and is not only
good for us but good for others: *courage serves others in war, justice serves
others in war and in peace.*

59 2   One can do an injustice without being an unjust person: either because
the action is not directed at the external injustice as such, which is
unintentional due to ignorance; or because the action proceeds neither
from a disposition to injustice nor from choice of injustice but from
sudden passion. An unjust person strictly speaking is one disposed to
injustice, intending and choosing it. People do not easily do injustice by
choice, as something they find agreeable, but for other reasons; to do it
by choice is peculiar to those who are disposed to injustice. What is
unintended and coincidental cannot be either externally or interiorly
immoderate. But it can be externally (though not interiorly) unjust.

3 The proper spring of human action is will; only what a man does
willingly is properly his doing, and only what he suffers unwillingly is
strictly speaking suffered. Strictly speaking then, only the willing can

4 properly do injustice and only the unwilling can properly suffer it. Fatal
sin is wrongdoing opposed to God's friendship, the life of the soul. Now
every injury we inflict on others is of itself opposed to God's friendship,
which moves us rather to will good to our fellowmen. So to do injustice
is of its nature a fatal sin.

60 1   Judgment is primarily the definition or determination of what is just.
Such determinations in matters of virtue properly proceed from that
virtue as disposition (chaste men decide what is chaste). So judgment is
primarily an act of the virtue of justice. The word has been stretched to
cover any determination of what is right, whether in speculative or
practical matters. Nevertheless it always requires an ability to pronounce
judgment (and in this sense judgment is an act of reason), and a
disposition to judge well. In our case it is the virtue of justice that
inclines us to judge well, and prudence pronounces the judgment. Man
is master of his own affairs but not those of others. So other virtues
need only the judgment (in the stretched sense) of the virtuous man,
but justice requires further authoritative judgment from *some umpire
appointed to put his hand between us both.* That is the special judgment

2 belonging to justice. Judgments are illicit and unjust if they are perverse
(going against the rightness of justice) or *ultra vires* (beyond the judge's

4 authority) or rash (based on uncertain evidence). In the absence of clear
evidence of another's wickedness we must presume him innocent, giving

him the benefit of every doubt. To make many mistakes by thinking well of the wicked is preferable to making few by thinking badly of the innocent; we do injustice in the second case but not in the first. Judgments on men differ from judgments about things. In judging things we do them no harm, however we judge them; only the quality of our judgment is at stake. But when we judge men, it is their good or harm, honour or dishonour, that is at stake. So we must be biased towards judging well of them unless there is clear evidence to the contrary. If we are mistaken, that is no black mark against our mind (for to know the truth in individual contingent cases is no part of the mind's perfection); but it is a good mark for our affections. Legal codes may contain 5 some natural justice, but they don't give natural justice its force; they both contain and give force to enacted justice. So a code containing something contrary to natural justice is unjust and does not oblige, enacted justice only prevailing in matters where natural justice is neutral. Even rightly enacted laws can fall short in particular cases and decree something opposed to natural justice. One must not then give judgment according to the letter of such laws but fall back on equity, since equitableness is the legislator's intention.

Distributive and commutative justice. Individual justice is 61 1 directed to private individuals, towards the parts making up the community as a whole. Dealings which relate part to part, one person to the next, are the field of commutative justice: justice in exchanges. But the whole must also relate to its parts, the community to its members, and such dealings are the field of distributive justice: justice in apportioning out proportionately what is common. So these are two types of [individual] justice: commutative and distributive. The whole belongs to its parts in a way, so when goods held in common are distributed, each is receiving something that in a sense belongs to him. Legal justice determines the way in which the goods of private individuals are subordinated to the general good; the way the general good is distributed among private individuals is determined by one type of individual justice. The distributive-commutative distinction is a distinction of type of dues, for a person's share of the general good is his due in a different sense from his private goods.

In distributive justice the common goods are distributed according 2 to the status in the community of the person receiving. In an aristocracy this status is judged by virtue, in oligarchies by wealth, in democracies by freedom. The balance is assessed not by equality of thing to thing, but by a proportion of thing to person called by Aristotle geometric. In exchanges however there is a balance of things given to things received (which we observe chiefly in buying and selling, the archetypal exchange) and such repayment Aristotle calls arithmetic. A person's status is directly relevant to distributive justice; it may indirectly affect commutative justice in so far as it affects the balance of actions to one 3 another. Commutative justice governs exchanges between two people. Some of these are involuntary, one man making use of another's property or person or labour without his consent, either secretly and deceitfully or openly by use of force: examples are theft and robbery, hidden or manifest bodily harm, false witness and public accusation, adultery and enticement of servants. Other exchange transactions are voluntary: simple gifts without debts attached are not matters of justice, but buying and selling, loans and usufruct and hiring, deposits and pledges, must all be governed by it. Despite all their differences one sort of balance is sought in all these exchanges: equitableness of recompense; so all belong 4 to the one type of justice, commutative justice. *Quid pro quo* implies recompensing action with reaction: loss for loss and, especially when injury is suffered, blow for blow. And the term is also used in voluntary exchanges. In all cases commutative justice demands equality of recompense; but not necessarily *an eye for an eye*, i.e. returning the identical action: status differences enter in, and simple restitution of property stolen would not inflict a loss on the thief nor compensate for the damage done to public safety. *Quid pro quo* rather implies a certain proportionate correspondence, to measure which money was invented. In distributive justice *quid pro quo* of action and reaction has no place; here things are measured against persons, what is received corresponding not to what was spent but to what others receive, taking into account their persons.

62 1   The act of restitution is characteristic of commutative justice: the return to its owner of something held by another, whether loaned or deposited voluntarily, or taken without permission. Just as we stretch the notion of exchange to cover actions and reactions benefiting and injuring people, so we extend the notion of restitution to cover repayment for the physical and psychological effects of action. Notice that even restitution made to one who received less than he should have done in a distribution is judged to be an adjustment of thing to thing and so 2 a matter of commutative justice. When one can't restore the equal of 3 what has been taken, recompense must be made as far as possible. And when property is taken unjustly, not only the imbalance of property must be put right by restitution, but also the fault of injustice by a 4 judicially imposed penalty. Actual loss must be fully indemnified, but loss of expected revenue need not be, since a man does not fully possess

his expectations. But some restitution must be made, appropriate to the situation and people involved.

Injustice.   Unfair discrimination is opposed to distributive justice. [vol 38] 63 1 The equitableness of such justice consists in different people receiving different things in proportion to their social worth. But if someone is appointed to a teaching post, for example, not on the basis of his qualifications and professional competence, but because he is John Smith, that is discrimination. Worth is here assessed with respect to the 2 general good, and it can happen that someone less holy or less learned can contribute more to the general good because of his worldly wisdom and influence and suchlike. When a judge busy with commutative justice 4 takes something from one person and gives it to another his judgment is an act of distributive justice; and that is why it can be flawed by discrimination.

Injurious deeds – Killing. Plants – the lowest level of life – exist 64 1 for animals, and animals for men; so there is nothing wrong in using plants for the sake of animals, or animals for men's sake. However, what animals most need plants for, and men animals, is food, and for that they must be killed. So it is legitimate, as Genesis teaches, for animals to kill plants and men to kill animals for their respective benefits. Moreover, every individual person is as it were a part of the whole 2 community. If a man is a danger to the community threatening it with disintegration by some wrongdoing of his, then his execution for the healing and preservation of the general good is to be commended. In doing wrong men depart from the order laid down by reason, falling away from their human dignity in which they are by nature free and exist for their own sake into the subject state of animals that must serve the needs of others. So it becomes justifiable to kill a malefactor as one would kill an animal. *An evil man*, says Aristotle, *is worse than an animal and more harmful.* But the care of the whole community is entrusted to 3 those exercising public authority, and so only they, not private persons, may licitly execute malefactors. We cannot distinguish malefactors from just men by nature; they can only be differentiated by a public judgment.

Suicide is altogether wrong for three reasons. Firstly, it runs counter 5 to the inclinations of nature and charity to love and cherish oneself. As such it is a fatal sin and against nature. Secondly, it does injury to the community to which each man belongs as a part of the whole. And thirdly, it wrongs God whose gift life is and who alone has power over life and death. What gives man mastery over himself is free will. So he may licitly manage his own life in respect of everything that contributes to it; but his passage out of this life to a happier one is not subject to his own free will but to the authority of God.

7   An act of self-defence may have two effects: it may save one's own life and cost the attacker his. Now intending to save one's own life can't make an act illegitimate, since it is in the nature of all things to want to preserve themselves in being as far as they can; but an act that is properly motivated may nevertheless be vitiated by not being proportionate to its goal. Somebody who uses more force than necessary to defend himself will be doing wrong, though moderate use of force can be legitimate. For men are not obliged under pain of losing eternal life to renounce moderate force for fear of killing another; our responsibility for our own life is greater than our responsibility for another's. However, it is not licit for a man actually to intend to kill another in self-defence, since the taking of life is reserved to public authorities acting for the general good. The only people who may deliberately kill in self-defence are those with public authority to do so for the general good, namely, soldiers fighting the enemy and policemen fighting crime; and even they do wrong if they are influenced by private passion. And nobody is allowed to commit adultery or a sexual sin in self-defence: such acts haven't the same necessary connection with saving one's life as the acts

8 of self-defence which can lead to homicide. Accidents as such can't be sins. But what we do not will or intend as such we may nevertheless coincidentally will or intend by removing an obstacle to its happening. Somebody who doesn't avoid circumstances in which a homicide might occur, circumstances which he could and should have avoided, will in a way have willed the homicide. Maybe he killed a man while engaged in nefarious activities he should have refrained from, or maybe he was guilty of negligence in a situation.

65 3   There is a hierarchy of bodily goods: the physical integrity of the body itself which can be damaged by killing or grievous bodily harm; the tranquillity and delight of our senses, which can be disturbed by blows and the infliction of pain; the free movement and use of our limbs, which can be inhibited by imprisonment and detention. All such hostile actions are illegitimate unless done with due process of justice by way of punishment or warning.

66 1   **Injurious deeds – Robbery and theft**. The natures of external things are not subject to man but to God whom they obey without question. But man has a natural dominion over the use of such things, and his mind and will can exploit them for his benefit as things made for him, the less perfect for the more perfect. This is Aristotle's argument

2 to prove possession of external things natural to man. Man in fact

exercises a twofold competence where external things are concerned. Firstly, he is entitled to take care of them and share them out; and in this respect private ownership is both legitimate and necessary. Firstly, because everyone takes more care of the things for which he is privately responsible than of things held in common, the responsibility for which is left to the next man. Secondly, because human affairs are more efficiently organized when each person has his own distinct responsibility to discharge. Thirdly, because there is a greater chance of keeping the peace when everyone is content with his own matters. Man's other competence in relation to external things is their use; and in this regard men should not treat things as exclusively theirs but use them for the good of all, ready to share them with those in need. The distribution of property is not determined by natural justice, but by human agreement and enacted law. Private ownership is not against natural law, but it is something invented by human reason over and above natural law.

The essence of theft is the surreptitious taking of another's property. 3 Concealment can contribute to wrongdoing by making it possible, as in cases of deceit and fraud. In such cases concealment does not lessen the wrongdoing – as it might if it was just a circumstance indicating shame – but rather constitutes it as a special type of wrongdoing. This is what happens with theft. Theft and robbery are wrong because the taking is 4 against the owner's will. But things happen against our will either because we are ignorant of them (and that defines theft) or because force is used (and that defines robbery); so here there are two different types of sin. Even a person who takes back by stealth property of his own 5 unjustifiably held by another is doing wrong: not because of any harm he does the holder (and so he has no obligation to restitution or compensation in that regard), but because he offends against ordinary justice by taking the law into his own hands and bypassing due legal processes. So he is bound to make amends to God and see to it that he mitigates any possible scandal to others. Human society would perish if everybody 6 started stealing from everybody else. Theft then is a fatal sin, opposed to the love of charity. Penalties imposed in this life are corrective rather than retributive, for retribution is reserved to God's judgment. So men should not be sentenced to death in this life for fatal sins, unless they cause irreparable harm or are particularly perverted. Theft is not normally a capital offence since the damage it does can be repaired, though it may be capital if there is some aggravating circumstance like the property being sacred or public, or the stealing being kidnap.

In need everything is common property. In the natural order estab- 7 lished by God's providence lower things are intended to serve men's needs. The division and apportionment of these by human law must not interfere with this purpose. So that goods possessed over and above our requirements should in natural justice be used to support the poor. Those who suffer want are so numerous that they cannot all be supported from one source, and each individual must decide how to manage his property in such a way as to help in supplying the needs of those who suffer. But in cases of urgent and blatant necessity immediate needs must be met out of whatever comes to hand, and then a person is allowed to supply his own needs out of another's property, secretly or openly. Such action is neither theft nor robbery, for need of that sort renders what a person takes to sustain his life his own.

8   Any private and unauthorized person who takes something from another by force is guilty of robbery. Even public authorities may only use force or coercion to the extent justice permits, when fighting enemies or punishing malefactors. If they confiscate the property of others by force in ways opposed to justice then they commit robbery and are bound to restitution. Indeed they are worse than robbers, inasmuch as they jeopardize more generally the public justice of which they have
9 been made guardians. In theft something is taken against the owner's will through his ignorance, in robbery because force is used. Because force is more directly opposed to the will than ignorance, robbery is a graver sin than theft.

67 1   **Injurious words – Court cases.** A judge's judgment is like a particular law passed for a particular case, and enjoys similar coercive power; so a judge must have the public authority entitling him to such
2 coercion. It follows that his judgment must be formed by what he learns in his public, not in his private, capacity: through his general knowledge of the law, divine or human, which he must treat as incontrovertible, and in particular cases through the evidence of witnesses, affidavits and other admissible documents. He can allow privately acquired knowledge to lead him to scrutinize this evidence more strictly, looking for possible flaws; but if he cannot fault it by due process of law he must give
3 judgment in accordance with the evidence. A judge is a mouthpiece of justice, *justice personified*, and justice is concerned with relationships to others, not to oneself. So there must be two parties for the judge to adjudicate between: accuser and accused. In criminal trials a judge is not entitled to convict someone who has not been duly charged.

68 1   Anyone is bound to lay a public complaint in cases where a crime tends to harm society, provided he has the evidence required of a complainant. But if the crime does not impinge on society or there is not enough evidence to substantiate a complaint, no man is obliged to

initiate something he cannot properly complete. An accused is under 69 1
obligation to give the judge such evidence as the rules of evidence
require. He commits a fatal sin if he refuses to confess or denies any
truth he is bound to tell. But if the judge asks for something not allowed
by the laws of evidence the accused is not bound to reply and he can
either appeal or resort to some other technicality. But he is not allowed
to lie. One is not obliged to tell the whole truth, but only such truth as 2
a judge can and should require to be told under the laws of evidence.
If required to give evidence by a person authorized to require it, we 70 1
must give such evidence whenever the law says we must, namely when
the crimes are public and notorious. Otherwise we are not bound to give
evidence. If on the other hand we are asked to give evidence by someone
without the requisite authority then, if it is to free a man from unjust
penalties of death or loss of reputation or other damages, we are bound
to give evidence; for then, even unasked, we are bound to do what we
can to reveal the truth to those who can best make use of it. But evidence
needed to condemn a man we can only be obliged to give by proper
authority according to the rules of evidence. False evidence is wrong on 4
three counts: because witnesses have to swear to what they say, false
evidence involves perjury and is always fatally wrong; it is also directly
unjust and, like all injustice, in principle fatal; and finally it is a lie and
like every lie a sin, though not necessarily fatal.

Lawyers are not always obliged to offer their services free to the poor 71 1
but only on certain conditions. Otherwise they would have to give up
all other work and devote themselves exclusively to the cases of the
poor. The same considerations apply to doctors. It is wrong to be an 3
accomplice in wrongdoing, whether by advice or active help or consent
of any sort, for advisers and abetters are in effect doers. So if a lawyer
defends a cause knowing it to be unjust, he is undoubtedly committing
a grave sin, and he is bound to make good the loss the other party incurs
through his action. If however he took up the cause not knowing it to
be unjust he is excused to the extent that ignorance excuses. A lawyer's
professional skill may draw praise, but if he uses it for wrong ends he
wills injustice and does wrong. If he begins thinking his cause just and
discovers during the proceedings that it is not, he mustn't betray the
cause by helping the other party or giving away confidential information;
but he can and must give up the case, persuading his client either to
concede or settle without loss to the other party. A lawyer defending a
just cause is entitled to conceal what might prejudice his case, but not
to make use of falsehood. A man is entitled to recompense for any 4
services he is not obliged to offer. And clearly a lawyer is not always

obliged to give his services and advice to others. The same goes for doctors rendering medical services, as long as they charge fees suited to their clients' status and occupation and the customs of the country. But anyone dishonest enough to charge excessive fees sins against justice. Judges and witnesses must be impartial, with the judge bound to give just judgment and the witnesses bound to give true testimony; for justice and truth are unbiased. So judges' salaries are fixed by statute, and witnesses receive expenses (but not payment for their testimony) either from both parties or from the party summoning them. A lawyer however defends only one party, so is entitled to receive payment for his help from that party.

72 1   **Injurious words out of court. Defamation** strictly speaking is taking away a person's character by drawing attention to anything that 2 detracts from that character. What words mean depends on interior intention. Words uttered with the intention of taking away character constitute an insult or defamation in the strict sense and are sins no less fatal than theft or robbery, since a man prizes his character just as much as his material possessions. But if the intention is admonishment, the words, though materially defamatory, are not formally so, and may be non-fatally sinful or not sinful at all. All the same, a man should pick his words carefully, since uttered incautiously they might take away a person's character, and a fatal wrong might be done without even intending it. In just such a way men must bear responsibility for any serious harm that results from a careless blow, even one delivered in play. But a mild insult which does little discredit to a man, thrown out lightly from annoyance, without any firm intention of discredit but only of discomfort, can well be excusable.

76 1   **Cursing** is one way of speaking evil: not by way of report in the indicative mood (which is rather defamation), but by way of command in the imperative mood or desire in the optative. When a person commands or desires evil for another and intends the evil as such, that is cursing, and wrong. But commanding or desiring another's evil for a good reason is not strictly speaking cursing and is licit. Judges, for example, in pursuit of justice command evil for persons when they sentence them to a just penalty; and someone can legitimately wish a sinner fall ill or be otherwise prevented from sinning, so that he becomes 4 a better man or at least is prevented from harming others. Those who spread defamatory remarks, malicious gossip, slander or even ridicule report the evils that men do, whereas those who curse command or wish men to suffer evils, not to do them. Reporting evil that men do is a sin inasmuch as it harms them; and other things being equal it is more

serious to inflict harm than merely to desire it. But commanding evil is also a sort of causing it, and can be more or less serious than defamation, according to the degree of harm it causes.

Unjust sales and loans. Any fraudulent practice enabling one to   77 1
sell a thing for more than its real worth is altogether wrong: it is a deception which harms. *The seller mustn't plant a sham bidder, or the buyer someone who undercuts the sale price.* In the absence of fraud, however, there are two ways of regarding a **contract of sale**. In itself it should equally benefit both parties, so should be based on an equality of material exchange: to sell a thing for more or buy it for less than it is worth is in itself unjust and illicit. But in certain circumstances a sale may be of advantage to one party (the buyer, say) but disadvantage the seller; and in such a case the price should be adjusted to take into account both the commodity to be sold and the loss the seller incurs by selling. In other words the commodity can be sold for more than it is worth in itself, though not for more than it is worth to its possessor. But if the seller is not disadvantaged by the sale he cannot charge more simply because the sale means a lot to the buyer; you can charge for your own loss, but you can't sell the buyer what belongs not to you but to his situation. Human law can't prohibit everything opposed to virtue; it is enough if it prohibits whatever destroys social intercourse and allows other things, not approving them but not penalizing them either. So the law doesn't penalize a seller who overcharges or a buyer who underpays unless there is fraud involved or a gross disparity, say, over fifty per cent of the just price. But God's law punishes everything contrary to virtue, and obliges profiteers to make restitution in cases where the loss is significant. I add this last phrase because we cannot always fix a just price exactly; sometimes we must make the best estimate we can, give or take a small amount.

An object for sale can be flawed in three ways: sometimes it is not 2
what it claims to be, sometimes its amount is defectively measured, sometimes its quality is not up to scratch; and in all these cases if the seller is aware of the flaw he commits a fraud and the sale is illicit. Commercial measures are bound to differ from place to place according to supply: where there is an abundance measures are more generous. In any given region it is the government's business to determine what will be a just measure in the local conditions. When there are hidden flaws 3
in something offered for sale and the seller doesn't disclose them the sale will be fraudulent and illicit, and the seller bound to restitution. But when the flaws are obvious, or when other people than the buyer could make use of the object, and a fair amount has been subtracted

from the price, the seller need not draw attention to the flaw. Under such conditions he is entitled to consult his own interest, lest the buyer be tempted to subtract even more from the price. A man is not bound to advertise publicly the flaws in what he sells, since that might frighten off potential buyers before they have a chance to see its good and useful qualities for themselves. But he must inform interested buyers privately when they are in a position to assess its good and bad points together. A seller selling something at its market price would not seem to act unjustly if he keeps quiet about what may happen to the market in the future. It would be much more virtuous not to, or to reduce the price, but strict justice does not require it.

4   There are two sorts of exchange: those that seek commodities in exchange for other commodities (or for money) in order to maintain life, and those that seek money in exchange for money (or commodities) for the sake of profit. This last is characteristic of people in business, according to Aristotle. The first sort of exchange is praiseworthy because it supplies natural needs, but the second sort can be justly criticized for feeding the acquisitive urge, which knows no defined bounds and grows without end. Commerce then as such has something shameful about it, being without any honourable or necessary defining goal. However, the goal of profit, though neither honourable or necessary, is not in itself opposed to virtue. So it can be made to serve honourable and necessary goals, and in this way business can be justified. As for example when a business generating modest profits supports a family, or helps the poor; or when commerce ensures that a country doesn't run short of essential supplies, profit being not a goal but a sort of reward for the service provided. Not everyone who sells something for more than he paid for it is engaged in commerce, but only those who buy simply in order to sell at a profit. People are entitled to sell at a higher price when they have made improvements, or if prices have gone up generally in the meantime, or the seller has incurred risks in transport and delivery. In such cases neither the purchase nor the sale is unjust.

78 1   Charging for the **loan** of money is unjust as such, for you are selling something that doesn't exist. Some things like food are consumed by use, so that the use can't be separated from the thing. When we let someone use such things then we transfer the ownership of the thing itself. If we tried to sell wine and its use separately we would be selling the same thing twice over or selling something non-existent, and that would clearly be unjust. By the same token then it is unjust to lend wine and then ask for a twofold recompense: the restoration of some equivalent and a charge for its use. This is what usury is – a use-charge in such

cases. There are however things which are not consumed by use: a house is used by living in it, not by pulling it down. So here we can separate the thing from its use, transferring the ownership, for example, while reserving the use for a time, or vice versa allowing someone the use while retaining the ownership. This is why one can licitly charge for a house's use and later ask for its return, as happens in letting and renting. Now Aristotle tells us that money was invented for purposes of exchange, and that its prime and proper use is in its consumption and disbursement by being spent in transactions. It follows that it is in principle wrong to charge for the loan of money, as is done in usury. A man is obliged to restore money obtained in this way, just as he must make restitution of any other ill-gotten gains. Men are not bound to make loans, but if they do they are bound not to make profit from them. Silver plate is not primarily meant for consumption, and one can licitly sell the right to use it while retaining ownership. But silver coin is primarily meant for spending, and one cannot licitly charge for its use and then expect it to be restored. Of course, one could use silver plate for barter, but then one couldn't charge for its use; just as one could use silver coin for ornament or security, and then one could charge separately for its use. A man paying interest on a loan isn't doing it voluntarily but under pressure; he is forced to by his need to borrow from lenders who won't lend except at interest.

Anyone who lends money and, by explicit or tacit agreement, accepts 2 in return something on which one can put a money price, commits usury. But if he accepts it not as a condition of lending nor as part of any agreement, expressed or tacit, but as a free gift, then there is no sin: he would have been entitled to accept a gift before the loan and the lending can't worsen his situation. And a lender is entitled to seek the sort of compensation that cannot be measured in terms of money – things like benevolence and friendship. A lender is within his rights to settle terms of compensation for loss resulting from his not having the money. But not for loss of profit he might have made with the money, because one can't sell what one doesn't yet have and which one might have been prevented in many ways from getting. When you lend money you transfer ownership of it to the borrower and with it all attendant risks and the obligation to complete restitution. So you can't ask for more. But if you entrust your money to a merchant or craftsman in a sort of partnership you don't hand over the ownership, and it is at your risk that the merchant trades or the craftsman works. So you can licitly ask for part of the profit of the undertaking: it is yours. If a seller wants to charge more than the just price for his goods in return for a postponement of payment then he obviously commits usury. By the same token, if a buyer wants to buy something for less than its just price in return for pre-payment that is also usury. If, on the other hand, the seller is willing to take the lower price in order to have the cash in hand

3 that is not usury. Some things are consumed in use and cannot therefore be the subject of usufruct in law. So a lender who extorts such things as money or food by way of interest on a loan need restore only what he has actually received from the borrower; anything that has been made out of the commodity is the fruit not of that thing itself but of human labour. Unless the lender's holding on to the thing resulted in loss for the borrower, in which case the lender must recompense him for that loss. But if what was extorted as interest was a subject of usufruct, like a house or a field, then the lender is bound to restore not only the thing extorted but also all the fruits thereof, which belong to the owner of

4 the thing in question. It is never right to induce anyone to lend at interest, although it is permissible to accept a loan from someone prepared to make it and already in the business of moneylending, if the object is some good like relieving one's own or another's needs. Just as a man fallen among thieves has a right to tell them where his money is in order to save his life.

79 1 **Component parts of justice.** Taking good and evil generally every virtue does good and avoids evil. But justice to individuals involves doing the specific good owed to one's fellowmen and avoiding specific evils harmful to them; and legal justice involves doing the good owed to the community or God and avoiding evil opposed to that. In this sense avoiding evil and doing good are component parts of justice, required for its wholeness in action. By doing good and so giving others what we owe them we establish the equality justice requires; by avoiding evil that harms our fellowmen we preserve that established equality. Other moral virtues deal with emotions, and there doing good is a matter of achieving a balance between extremes, the evils we must avoid; so for these virtues doing good and avoiding evil come to the same thing. But justice is concerned with external transactions and commodities, where establishing equality is one thing and keeping it intact once established is another.

2 A transgression or overstepping in the strict sense is an infringement of a prohibition. Every type of fatal sin infringes some divine prohibition so is materially a transgression. But formal transgression of a prohibition as such defines a distinct type of sin: distinct from the sins opposed to other virtues (for just as legal justice attends to the *ought* of a command

as such, so a transgression disregards the *ought* as such); distinct also from omissions, which disregard not prohibitions but positive commands. Omission is failure to do a good one ought to do; but goods owed are 3 strictly speaking the concern of justice. So just as justice is a special virtue, omission is a special category of sin, distinct from sins opposed to other virtues. Moreover, since doing good (opposed by omission) is one distinct component of justice, and avoiding evil (opposed by transgression) another, omissions and transgressions are distinct. Transgressions oppose prohibitions and the avoiding of evil; omissions oppose positive commands and the doing of good. Now positive commands bind only at determined times, and it is at such times that omissions can occur. A person may, of course, be incapable at such a time of doing what he ought to do, and if the incapacity is not his fault then he is not guilty of the omission. But if the incapacity is due to some previous fault of his then he starts to be guilty of an omission when the time comes for obeying the command, though the cause that makes the omission voluntary lies in the past. Clearly transgression is in general 4 more serious than omission, though particular omissions may be more serious than particular transgressions. Doing good is the contradictory of not doing good (omission) but the contrary of doing evil (transgression); contrariety involves the greater distance and transgression is the greater sin.

Virtues allied to justice

Since justice is concerned with rendering to others the equivalent of [vol 39] 80 1 what we owe them, all virtues concerned with rendering to others are allied to justice, falling short of it because what they render is either not equivalent or not owed in a strict sense. Virtues which render what is not equivalent are **religion** owed to God, **family loyalty** owed to parents, and **respect** owed to virtue. Virtues which render what is not owed in a strict sense are those which fulfil moral debts (requirements of decency) rather than legal ones (laid down by law). In some virtues the moral debt is such that no honourable man could disregard it: **truthfulness** requires a man show himself to others in word and deed just as he is, and we must repay others with **gratitude** for good done and **retribution** for evil. But some virtues, though adding to honour, are such that honour could be maintained without them: **generosity**, for example, and **friendliness**. And then, allied not to particular justice but to legal justice, we have **equity**.

81 1 **Religion.**   Religion consists in performing services and rites in honour
   2 of a superior nature called divine. *Virtues make men and their actions
   good. Since paying our debts is good, religion, which pays our debt of
   4 honour to God, is a virtue. Where there is a special kind of good we
   need a special virtue. Now honour is owed to people of excellence and
   God's excellence is unparalleled, so religion must pay him special
   honour and be a special virtue. Everything we do, if done to the glory
   of God, is an action subject to the command of religion, even if not
   primarily an exercise of religion. For only those deeds are primary
   exercises of religion which are defined as acts of reverence for God.
   Love loves the good; reverence honours the excellent. God's goodness
   he shares with his creatures, but the excellence of that goodness is his
   alone. So the charity with which we love God is the charity with which
   we love our fellowmen; but religion, which honours God, is distinct
   from the virtues which honour our fellowmen.

   5   Religion offers to God honour owed to him. But acts done in God's
   honour don't embrace God in the way acts of faith do. God is the object
   of our faith: not only what we believe but also the person in whom we
   believe, the person we put our faith in. But God is only the goal of
   religion, and its matter or object is the acts of service, sacrifices and
   offerings we make to show him reverence. Religion is not a theological
   virtue like faith, hope and charity taking our ultimate goal as its object,
   but a moral virtue concerned with actions that serve that goal. The acts
   of theological virtues have God as their proper object, and employ
   religion as an instrument, directing its acts to God. That is what
   Augustine means by saying *we honour God through faith, hope and charity.*
   Religion in itself is a moral virtue, allied to justice, seeking out not a
   balance of emotions but an equality of actions directed to God. The
   equality is not absolute since we cannot give God as much honour as
   we ought, but only as much as is possible to us and acceptable to him.
   We can't offer God more honour than he warrants, but the honour we
   offer can be excessive and unbalanced in other ways: shown to false
   6 gods or at the wrong time. Moral virtues are concerned with everything
   done to serve our ultimate goal, which is God. Religion approaches God
   more closely than other moral virtues, since what it does directly and
   immediately honours God. So religion is the greatest of the moral
   virtues.

   7   We show God reverence not for his benefit, since creatures can add
   nothing to the fullness of glory he already has in himself; we do it for
   our benefit, so as to subject our spirit to him and perfect it. Every
   creature gains perfection by subjecting itself to higher ones: the body

gets life from the soul, and the air light from the sun. The mind needs leading to unity with God by way of the world we sense, and in the service of God this means using bodily things as symbols and signs, to arouse our mind to the spiritual acts that unite it to God. So there are interior acts of religion (and in these religion primarily consists), and secondary external acts subordinate to the interior ones. Not only men 8 but also things like churches and sacred vessels are said to be made holy by being devoted to God's honour. Man's holiness consists in devoting himself and his actions to God, and doesn't differ essentially from religion. We call it religion when it offers God the service owed him in ways specially adapted to honouring him: things like sacrifices, offerings and suchlike; we call the same virtue holiness when it offers to God not only such works but every work of virtue, or when man disposes himself to honour God by doing virtuous works. In essence holiness is a special virtue, that of religion, but it can embrace virtue in general in so far as it directs the actions of all other virtues to the divine good in the way legal or general justice directs them all to the general good.

Interior devotion and prayer. **Devotion** is a ready willingness to 82 1 give oneself to the service of God: a special act of will. It is present in all sorts of other acts as a mood or manner of such acts, derived from this special act of will, just as any causal stimulus is virtually present in the movements it causes. Devotion is a vowing, and therefore an act of 2 religion. Giving oneself to God, cleaving to him in a union of spirit, defines the act of loving God; giving oneself to God by devoting oneself to honouring him defines religious activity, though this is directed by love, the source in us of all our religion. God is the most lovable of all 3 things, and meditation on his nature is the strongest incentive there is to love and devotion; but because our minds are not strong in themselves, we need to be led to knowledge and so to love of God by way of the world we sense, and above all by thinking of Christ the man, so that *by seeing God with our eyes we can be lifted up to love what we cannot see.* Knowledge, like all accomplishments, leads men to trust in themselves rather like give themselves totally to God. Sometimes that interferes with devotion, so devotion is more prevalent in simple souls and in women, who don't think so much of themselves. But when a man perfectly subjects his knowledge and other accomplishments to God, they help increase his devotion. Consideration of God's goodness is the 4 goal of devotion, and though in itself a cause of joy, can be accompanied by sadness because we haven't yet fully achieved that goal. The consideration of our own inadequacies is the starting-point for devotion, and though in itself a cause of sadness, can be accompanied by joy in God's help. In Christ's sufferings there is cause for sorrow – the human weakness that needed such suffering to remove it – and cause for joy – God's loving kindness that provided this way to set us free.

83 1   In pursuing truth reason merely perceives, but in directing behaviour it not only perceives but causes: commanding action from whatever it totally controls (our lower powers, limbs and human servants), and persuading and inclining whatever it doesn't totally control (making appeals and requests to equals and superiors). Commanding and appealing both imply directing, arranging that someone does something, and that is a function of reason. **Prayer** is a sort of appeal, and so an act of reason. Mind sees what things are, makes connections (sees that things are thus or not thus), and reasons from things it already sees to things it doesn't. These three acts characterize reason in pursuit of truth; but when mind is directing behaviour we must add another action of mind:

2 that of causing, either by command or by request. Some early thinkers thought human affairs were not governed by any divine providence and that it was altogether pointless to pray to or honour a God. Others thought everything, even human behaviour, totally determined, and so again thought prayer quite useless. Yet others disagreed with both these opinions and said that divine providence was not fixed, and that prayers and acts of worship directed to God could make it change course. All these opinions we refuted in the first part of this book [ch 2 p 56 and ch 6 pp 160–1]; here we must rather defend the usefulness of prayer in such a way that we fall into none of these errors: neither subjecting human affairs governed by divine providence to total determinism, nor implying that God's arrangements can be changed. We do this by noting that divine providence not only plans what effects will happen but also what causes will cause them to happen and how. Human actions are themselves included among such causes, so they don't change God's arrangements but rather achieve their effects in accordance with God's arrangements, as do natural causes. And this is true also of prayer. We don't pray in order to change God's arrangements, but in order to obtain effects that God has arranged will be achieved through the prayers of his chosen people. God arranges to give us certain things in answer to requests so that we may confidently have recourse to him, and acknowledge him as the source of all our blessings; and this is all for our good.

3 Praying is an act of reverence for God, which subjects us to him and professes that we need him as source of our blessings; so clearly it is an act of religion. Charity commands us to desire what we need, and religion commands us to ask for it: *Ask and you shall receive.* The Trinity we

beseech to have mercy on us; the saints we simply ask to pray for us to the Trinity.

Socrates thought we should simply ask the immortal gods for good gifts, 5 *since they knew better than us what those good gifts should be.* And this opinion has some truth in it in regard to things which can turn out badly or which we can make bad use of, but not in respect of goods we can't misuse and which can't turn out badly, such as the blessings that lead us on to eternal happiness. Moreover, it is lawful to desire the goods of 6 this world, not indeed as our chief goal in life but as helps towards eternal happiness, supporting our bodily life and serving as instruments of virtuous action. So it is lawful to pray for them as long as we ask for them to be granted us only in so far as they are profitable for salvation. The love we must have for our fellowmen leads us to desire good things 7 for them as well as for ourselves. So charity demands we also pray for others: for sinners to return, and for just men to persevere and progress. Not all our prayers for sinners will be answered: for those predestined to eternal happiness they will be heard, but not for those whom God foreknows will never gain that happiness. But since we do not know the predestined from the lost we cannot refuse anyone the help of our prayers. We pray for the just so that God may receive our thanks for the blessings he conferred on them and which profit us all. In our 8 treatment of charity we saw how we are bound to love our enemies. In a parallel way when we pray in common for others we are forbidden to exclude our enemies; to offer special prayers on their behalf is a perfection not demanded of us, but we must be ready in soul to help them in time of need or when they beg our pardon. The imprecations against enemies in the scriptures can be interpreted as prophecies, as prayers for our enemies' correction or against the kingdom of sin as such, and as expressions of our consent that God's justice act against those who persevere in sin.

Prayer is a sort of representation to God of our desires. In the Lord's 9 prayer – *Our Father* – we are taught not only what we should desire but also in what order, so as to build up the whole structure of our affections. The first thing to desire is our goal, God himself: we will his glory – *hallowed be thy name,* and our enjoyment of it – *thy kingdom come.* Then come those things which of themselves lead to the goal: directly and primarily, obedience to God which deserves to achieve the goal – *thy will be done;* secondarily and instrumentally, our sacramental and even earthly food – *give us this day our daily bread.* Finally, we must desire the removal of all obstacles to our goal: sin – *forgive us our trespasses,* temptation – *lead us not into temptation,* and hardship – *deliver us from*

evil. This order is not the order things happen in but the order in which things are to be desired or intended: the goal before the means, the
11 achievement of good before the removal of evil. Praying for others is a sign of love; and the more love the saints in heaven have, the more they pray for those on earth who can be helped by their prayers. And the closer they are to God, the more effective their prayers are.

12   Communal prayer is prayer offered to God by ministers of the church in the name of all his faithful people. Such prayer must be made known to all the people on whose behalf it is offered, so it is spoken aloud. Individual prayer, on the other hand, is offered by a single person praying for himself or others. There is no need for us to speak such prayers aloud, though sometimes we do in order to excite interior devotion. But if it actually distracts us then we should stop it. Sometimes too we speak prayers aloud in order to serve God with our whole self, mind and body; or because the intensity of our affection flows over from
13 our soul into our body. If spoken prayer is to be properly effective we must attend to what we are saying. But there are three effects of prayer. The first effect, the deserving of eternal life, is an effect of all acts enlivened by God's love; and for our prayers to be effective in this way it is not necessary for us to attend throughout to what our prayers say, since our initial intention to pray renders the whole prayer deserving. The second effect, the obtaining of what we ask, is specific to prayer, but again the original intention is what God chiefly attends to. But the third effect of prayer, the spiritual renewal of mind that is produced as we pray, needs attentiveness. There are however three levels of attentiveness: attending to saying the correct words, attending to their meaning, and attending to the goal of prayer, God himself, and whatever we are praying for. This last is the most necessary level of attentiveness, available even to the feeble-minded; and sometimes this level can be so intense that everything else gets forgotten. However, the human mind is too weak to stay aloft for long. Sometimes in the middle of prayer, when the mind is lifted up to God in contemplation, it suddenly wanders.
14 But unintentional wandering cannot deprive prayer of its fruit. Loving desire is the cause of prayer and ought to be with us constantly, either actually or virtually, making itself felt in everything that we do out of love. But prayer itself cannot be constant, since there are many other things we must do. The amount we do of anything (like the amount of medicine we take) corresponds to our goal. The fitting thing is that prayer should last as long as is found useful in arousing the fervour of interior desire. When it goes on longer than that and starts to weary us we should stop. And just as individual prayer must be measured by the

individual's ability to concentrate, so communal prayer by the people's devotion.

Besides the immediate effect of prayer – spiritual consolation – there 15 are two future effects: it is deserving of eternal happiness and it obtains what it asks. Its capacity to deserve derives from its root in love (for though the offering of prayer is itself an act of religion, it is charity which desires what the prayer requests); and prayer's effectiveness in obtaining what it asks for comes from the grace of God. The prayer of 16 the sinner can't be deserving, but it can effectively obtain what it requests; for deserts are a matter of justice, whereas obtaining what we pray for is an effect of pure graciousness. Prayer has four parts: 17 consecration, address, petition and thanksgiving. We see this in many of the communal prayers of the church: in the collect for Trinity Sunday, for example, we pray: *Almighty eternal God* (an address that raises up the mind to God), *who has given to thy servants,etc* (a thanksgiving), *grant we beseech thee, etc* (a petition), *through our Lord, etc* (a consecration).

External religious behaviour. Just as prayer is primarily mental 84 2 but secondarily expresses itself in words, so **adoration** is primarily an interior reverence for God expressing itself secondarily in bodily signs of humility: bending the knee (to express our weakness compared to God) and prostrating ourselves (to show that of ourselves we are nothing). Natural reason tells us that because of the inadequacies we 85 1 perceive in ourselves we need to subject ourselves to some superior source of help and direction. And whatever that source might be, everybody calls it *God*. Our natural way of expressing such things is by using sensible signs, since we derive our knowledge from the senses. So natural reason leads us to offer sensible things to God as a sign of the subjection and honour we owe him, rather as we offer things to our temporal masters in recognition of their authority. This is what we call **sacrifice**, so offering sacrifice is an act of natural justice. The particular sacrifices offered are determined by human or divine institution, and for that reason differ from people to people. External offering of sacrifice 2 symbolizes an interior spiritual sacrifice in which the soul offers itself to God, the source of its creation and goal of its happiness. So just as we ought to offer the spiritual sacrifice of ourselves only to God, so we ought to offer external sacrifices to him alone. The very wanting to 3 cleave to God in a sort of spiritual society is an act of reverence to him. So the act of any virtue takes on the character of sacrifice inasmuch as it aims at participating in this holy society with God. Man possesses

three sorts of goods. First, his soul, which he offers to God in a sort of interior sacrifice by devotion, prayer and other interior acts; and this is his primary sacrifice. Secondly, his body, offered to God through martyrdom and sexual abstinence. Thirdly, external things which are sacrificed to God directly when offered straight to him in worship and indirectly when shared with our fellowmen for his sake. Strictly speaking, sacrifice means doing something to the things we offer to God (killing and burning an animal, or blessing, breaking and eating the bread); for the word derives from *sacrum facere*, making something sacred. An offering however needs nothing done to it, so all sacrifices are offerings but not vice versa. Tithes properly speaking are neither sacrifices nor offerings, because given not directly to God but to the ministers who
4 serve him. Everyone is obliged to offer God the primary interior sacrifice of a devout mind. As to external sacrifices that are simply signs of subjection to God and nothing more: those bound by God's Old or New Laws must offer the particular sacrifices laid down by those laws, whilst those not so bound must offer things in accord with the customs of the people they live among. As to those external sacrifices which are the external acts of other virtues done out of reverence for God, some are morally obliging and must be done by all, and some are supererogatory and do not bind everybody.

86 1   Whenever a thing offered to God is made sacred, so to speak, and consumed, we call it a sacrifice; but if it remain intact to be devoted to the service of God or used by his ministers it is simply an **offering**.

2 Priests are *appointed trustees and mediators* between the people and God, presenting God's teaching and sacramental mysteries to the people, and the people's prayers, sacrifices and offerings to God. So the offerings of the people to God are entrusted to the priests, not simply for their personal use but as faithful stewards who must use them partly on things needed for the service of God, partly on keeping themselves alive, and partly on the poor who as far as possible must be maintained from church funds, just as the Lord had a purse for the poor.

87 1   The injunction to pay **tithes** is partly of moral force derived from natural reason and partly of judicial force deriving from divine institution. Natural reason tells us that those who minister in the service of God to the spiritual health of the whole people should be ministered to in the necessities of life by the people; just as men ought to contribute to the upkeep of their rulers and soldiers and all those who watch over the general good. But natural justice does not determine the particular portion to be set aside for those ministers; that was laid down by divine institution according to the conditions of the people to whom the law

was given. And though the determination had ritual significance it was primarily judicial. The difference between ritual and judicial injunctions of the law, is that now in the time of grace it is unlawful to obey the ritual injunctions (which expressed faith in a future Christ still to come); whereas judicial injunctions, though abrogated, may still be observed without sin, and indeed must be observed if re-instituted by those with legislative authority. Clearly then men are bound to pay tithes partly out of natural justice and partly by institution of the church (though the church can vary the proportion to be paid to suit the times and the people).

A vow is an act of reason arranging things. For just as a man with 88 1 commands and requests arranges things to be done for him by others; so with promises he arranges things to be done for others by himself. But promises arise from resolves which are acts of will that in turn presuppose deliberation. Vows therefore necessarily involve deliberation, resolve of will, and a final act of promising. To which are sometimes added the speaking of the promises aloud in the presence of witnesses. A vow implies a voluntary promise, so you can't vow what is 2 already necessarily determined: vowing to die or not to sprout wings would be ridiculous. But what is necessary not absolutely but only for the achieving of some goal like salvation can be vowed in so far as it is voluntary; and what is not necessary in either sense but absolutely voluntary is the most proper matter for a vow. This is what people have called *a greater good* in contrast with the good that must be done for salvation. And so they say that what is vowed must be some better good. Enfeebling one's own body by nightwatches and fasting is only acceptable to God if it can claim some virtue; if it is done with due discretion and curbs our passions without overburdening our nature. Only then can it be made the matter of a vow. After saying *Present your bodies as a living, holy and pleasing sacrifice to God*, Paul added: *your reasonable allegiance*. However, because man easily makes mistakes when judging what is best for himself, vows are better observed in accordance with some superior's judgment. In such a way however that if observing the vow becomes exceedingly burdensome and one can't contact the superior one should stop observing it. Vows about empty and useless things are better ridiculed than observed. A faithful man must keep his 3 promises, above all to God because we belong to him and have received from him so many benefits. We are especially obliged then to keep vows made to God. We promise things to men for their benefit, since it is 4 useful for them to know beforehand what we are going to do for them. But we promise things to God not for his benefit but for ours, since by vowing we fix our wills stably on what we should do. Inability to commit sin doesn't lessen our freedom, and neither does any necessity that results from firmly fixing one's will on good. We see this in God himself and the saints in heaven. *It is a happy necessity that compels us to do a better thing.* A promise is one way of putting what we promise at the disposal of the person to whom it is promised. A vow puts what we vow at the service of God, and thus vowing is properly an act of worship or

6 religion. To do something under vow is better and more deserving than to do it without, for three reasons. Firstly, when vowed, the acts of lesser moral virtues like fasting and abstaining from sex are directed by a higher moral virtue to the service of God, giving them the character of a sacrifice to him. Secondly, a vow subjects to God not only the act itself but our power to act, since we can't act differently in the future. And thirdly, a vow gives stability and firmness to our willing of good, and that is one of the perfections of virtue.

7   Solemnization usually accompanies our acts of total dedication: for example, marriage in which the spouses surrender power over their bodies to one another. In the same way we solemnize vows that dedicate people to God's ministry by the reception of holy orders, and the profession of a certain rule of life, when people renounce the world and their own will to take on a state of perfection. Vows of particular things like pilgrimages or special fasts are not fittingly solemnized, but only vows in which a new state of life is taken on, when someone dedicates himself totally to God's service, as to something universal com-

9 prehending many particular works. Solemnization consists in a sort of spiritual blessing and consecration performed by ministers of the church. The efficacy of a simple vow comes from the mind's own deliberate obliging of self and it fails if the one making the vow is mentally defective

10 or under the authority of another. A person who vows something makes so to speak a law for himself obliging himself to something which is in itself and in most cases good. Though it can happen that in a particular case it might be bad, or useless, or obstructive of a greater good. So it is necessary to be able to decide not to observe the vow in such a case – either to dispense it so that it is not observed at all, or to commute it into some other obligation. Both dispensation and commutation are in

11 the power of the church to do. But no church prelate can deconsecrate what has once been consecrated: not a chalice even, much less a man. So no church prelate can undo the consecration attached to a solemn vow: make a priest not a priest, though he can stop him exercising his orders. Sexual abstinence is connected with sacred orders not essentially but by a law of the church, and the church can dispense from a vow of

sexual abstinence solemnized by reception of sacred orders. But such a vow is essential to the religious state by which man renounces the world and binds himself to total service of God, and which is incompatible with the married state in which man is under obligation to care for his wife and family and provide for their needs. So the church cannot dispense such a vow when solemnized by religious profession.

Man can also receive things from God in external religious acts: 89 1 sacraments, which we shall discuss in our third part, and God's own name, which we shall discuss here. You can't prove particular contingent human facts by rational argument, so you appeal to witnesses. But human witnesses fail, because many men lie and because none know future or secret thoughts or what goes on in their absence. So we have recourse to the testimony of God, who cannot lie and to whom all things lie open. To call God as witness is to swear an oath. Oaths aren't employed to substantiate necessary truths which reason could demonstrate; it would be laughable for a man to try to justify a point in a scientific proof with an oath. Oaths in themselves are lawful and honour- 2 able both in origin and purpose. But if used wrongly without necessity and proper caution they become bad things. To be used well an oath must not be used lightly but only when necessary and with discretion; and what is sworn to must be true and not itself unlawful. Incautious oaths lack judgment, lying oaths truth, and unlawful oaths justice. By 4 invoking God in an oath we confess his greater power, his unfailing truth and universal knowledge, and in so doing show him reverence. So clearly taking an oath is an act of religious worship. Oaths are there to 5 remedy weakness, like medicines. They are desirable not for their own sake, but as necessities of life which are wrongly used unless only used when necessary. The obligation of vows arises from faithfulness owed 8 to God, the debt of keeping our promises. The obligation of oaths arises from reverence owed to God, which obliges us to verify whatever we swear to in his name. Now unfaithfulness includes irreverence, but not vice versa; so vows oblige more than oaths.

When speaking to God we aren't revealing our thoughts to him – for 91 1 he always sees our hearts – but bringing ourselves and our listeners to reverence him. That we praise him out loud is not for his benefit, but for our own, since the praise arouses love for him in the hearts of ourselves and others.

Too much religion.   Superstition is the vice of over-doing religion. [vol 40] 92 1 That doesn't mean it gives God more honour than true religion; one 2 type of superstition gives him honour in unfitting ways, and other types extend the honour to creatures: worshipping them (idolatry) and looking to them for knowledge (divination and fortune-telling) or guidance

93 1 (magical practices). External worship is most unfitting when it expresses something untrue: for example, worshipping God with Old Law rituals that foreshadow the mysteries of Christ as still to come even though Christ has already redeemed us; or a minister in the communal liturgy claiming to represent the whole church yet celebrating in a way not

2 established by the church's God-given authority and custom. If we worship in ways not conducive to God's glory or man's devotion, ways which are not emotionally balanced, or run counter to the institutions of God and his church or to common custom (which, as Augustine says, has the force of law), then our worship must be reckoned excessive and superstitious, external worship without the inner virtue of true religion.

94 1   **Idolatry** – offering divine worship to idols – has taken various forms. Some people have treated idols themselves as gods; others thought the creatures the idols represented were divine: be they men like Jove, Mercury and the rest, or the whole world and its component parts of sky and sea and so forth, or (in the case of the Platonists, who did believe in one ultimate god and cause of all things) subordinate spiritual beings whom we call angels, and below them souls of heavenly bodies, ethereal demons and finally the souls of men whose virtue gains them entry into the society of gods and demons. The Platonists' opinions and world-worship or nature-theology were studied by philosophers and taught in their schools; men-worship or myth-theology was invented by poets and acted out in the theatre; and idol-worship as such was a political theology celebrated by state priesthoods in temples. All of them were forms of superstitious idolatry. The word *worship* sometimes describes the human actions we do when worshipping the true God or idols: to whom it is offered doesn't enter its definition, just as whether a government is legitimate or not doesn't enter the definition of tax. But we can also use the word to mean true religion as such, the virtue which by definition offers worship only where it is due. Idolatry is then a different disposition from worship or religion, just as worldly prudence is a different dis-

3 position from the virtue of prudence. In itself idolatry is the most serious of sins since it sets up another god in the world, diminishing God's primacy. But knowing heretics sin more grievously than ignorant idol-aters. And other sins too, committed with more contempt, can be more serious for the sinner than idolatry. The Manichean heresy as such is more serious than any idolatry, because it dishonours God more, setting up two opposing gods and inventing a multitude of empty fables about them. Other heresies are different, since they acknowledge and honour

one God. There are two causes of idolatry: firstly, men, preparing the 4
way for idolatry by exaggerating into worship their great affections for
some men, or their natural delight in skilfully fashioned images, or
(because of ignorance of the true God) their wonder at the beauty and
strength of God's creatures; and, secondly, demons, completing the
process by presenting themselves for worship in the idols men have
made and supplying a confused mankind with oracles and miracles.

By **divining the future** we mean predicting it. Causes can relate to 95 1
their future effects in three ways. Some produce their effects always and
necessarily, so that their future effects can be predicted with certainty
by inspecting the causes, in the way astronomers predict eclipses. Some
causes don't always or necessarily produce their effects, but on the whole
they do, rarely failing; and from such causes one can conjecture the
future though not with certainty, in the way meteorologists predict the
weather and physicians whether their patients will live or die. But some
causes are not in themselves determined one way or another, the main
example being the powers of reasoning creatures, which can go either
way. The effects of such causes, as also the particular chance effects of
natural causes, cannot be predicted from inspection of the causes and
can only be known in the effects themselves. Men do that by seeing
them happen in the present; to know events in themselves before they
happen is God's prerogative, since he alone in his eternity sees future
things as though they were present. If anyone else claims to foreknow
or foretell the future without God having revealed it, then clearly he is
arrogating to himself what belongs to God. So by divining the future
we don't just mean predicting what will happen necessarily or normally,
for that can be reasoned out; nor knowing non-determined future events
by divine revelation, for that is not so much divining them as receiving
them from the divine. Divining means arrogating to oneself without
justification the prediction of future events, and this is clearly a form of
wrongdoing. Divining the future needs demonic advice and help, either 3
expressly enlisted or covertly supplied. In the covert case, men sometimes consult the way certain things are arranged: astrologers cast
horoscopes by consulting the position and motions of the stars, augurers
observe the flight and calls of birds and the sneezes and involuntary
spasms of men, omens make meanings out of words said unintentionally,
palmistry inspects the lines of the hand. But sometimes men base their
divinations on the outcome of actions specially engaged in for the
purpose: drawing lots, pouring molten lead into water and examining
the shapes, picking out different-length sticks, throwing dice, opening a
book at random. No worldly usefulness can ever outweigh the spiritual 4

harm of invoking demons in this way to uncover secret things.

5   Clearly events which happen necessarily can be predicted with the help of the stars, in the way astronomers predict eclipses. But the stars neither signify nor cause future contingent or chance events. They can't signify them, because signs have to be either effects of what they signify (which stars are not) or co-effects of the causes of what they signify. Now although future events and the motions of the stars both derive from a single cause – divine providence, they do so along quite different lines: the former created to exist contingently, here one moment, gone the next; the latter created to exist necessarily, always happening in the same way. But neither can stars cause future events. Chance events don't have causes at all, and especially not natural causes. For chance events as such have no unity; they are mere coincidences. But all natural causality is based on unified natural forms determined to unified effects. Nor can the stars cause free acts of reason and will; bodies cannot directly affect our mind and will, which are neither bodily nor functions of bodily organs. The stars can cause changes in human bodies, and so influence our sense-appetites which are functions of bodily organs. So the stars can incline us to certain behaviour; but since, as Aristotle says, our sense-appetites obey reason, man still has a free will to act against the influences of the stars. To sum up then: trying to predict chance events or human behaviour from an inspection of the stars is pointless, and leaves one open to the influence of demons; fortune-telling of this kind is superstitious and unlawful. This doesn't preclude prediction of things which are truly effects of the stars, like drought and rainfall and suchlike. The stars cause changes in our bodies and influence our emotions, and since most men follow their emotions without controlling them, astrologers often get things right, especially when predicting group behaviour. But the demons also have a hand in it.

6   Dreams sometimes influence future events, alerting the dreamer to do this or that; and sometimes they are signs of what is going to happen, caused by whatever does cause or know the future. Now dreams are caused partly by memories of what we felt and thought while awake, partly by internal and external bodily stimuli occurring while asleep, partly by God or demons influencing our imaginations. Any match between future events and memories would be coincidental; but bodily causes might conceivably influence future action. So it would be legitimate to consult dreams which are of divine origin, or which have a physical cause (to just the extent that such a cause could influence future events). But to rely on demons expressly, or tacitly by stretching natural causes to what they can't stretch to, is unlawful and superstitious.

The flights and calls of birds and suchlike patterns in events can't 7
themselves be the causes of future events, but could they be caused by
those causes? Such animal behaviour is instinctive, not freely willed,
and since instinct, being partly bodily, is dependent on the stars and the
environment, animal behaviour sometimes helps us predict the future
events such causes cause (especially things relevant to animals like rain
and winds, since animal instincts are given to them for just that purpose).
Sometimes too animal behaviour is influenced directly by God or
demons; and this would apply to human babbling of omens, which
couldn't be caused by the stars. So again, prediction within the order
of nature or divine providence is legitimate, but outside that order
unlawful and superstitious.

Casting lots covers all sorts of human behaviour with outcomes from 8
which we hope to learn secret things: how to distribute rewards and
punishments, what to do next, what is going to happen. Now human
behaviour and its outcome is not subject to the stars, as we have said;
rather the outcome is planned by a mind, or happens by chance. It
doesn't seem wrong in any way (only trivial) to use chance to decide
how to distribute things, given that all concerned agree. But to appeal
to demons is unlawful and forbidden by church canons; and to appeal
to God, though not bad in itself, may be wrong if done unnecessarily
to try God out, or irreverently, or for mundane profit, or to substitute
in church elections for inspiration by the Holy Spirit. But urgent
necessity could justify reverently calling on God by the casting of lots.
Trial by red-hot irons and boiling water in interrogation of hidden
crimes is akin to casting lots, but has the extra peculiarity of expecting
a miracle: it is unlawful and explicitly forbidden by papal decree. Trial
by combat is much the same though it doesn't expect miracles, except
perhaps when the combatants are very ill-matched in strength or skill.

The **magic arts** are unlawful and useless. They don't follow the 96 1
methods of acquiring knowledge which are natural to man, research and
study, and so must expect intervention from God or demons. Now
God's gift of wisdom is not given to those who try to conjure it up with
magical rites and incantations, but to those whom the Holy Spirit
chooses. And demons aren't in the business of enlightening human
minds. There is nothing superstitious or unlawful about applying natural 2
causes to produce what appear to be their natural effects. But adding
marks or words or other ritual observances which clearly have no
natural efficacy is superstitious and unlawful. Natural things exert power
because they are substances formed naturally under the influence of the
heavenly bodies. But artificial things derive their form from the mind

of their designer structuring, ordering and shaping natural material; what natural power they have from the heavenly bodies comes from their natural material only, and precisely as artificial things they have 3 no power at all. The causes of illness produce early symptoms of sickness that doctors can diagnose. There is nothing unlawful about such foretelling of future events from their true causes; it is like slaves seeing their master's fury and fearing the whip, or parents fearing for their child when they see someone with an *evil eye*.

97 1 **Too little religion.   Trying God out.** We test people to find out what they know or want or can do. Our words test God when we pray for something with the aim of finding out what he knows or is able and willing to do. And our deeds put him to the test when we do something that has that explicit aim, or must be construed as having that aim because there doesn't seem to be any other reason for the deed. But entrusting ourselves to God's help in time of need is not a case of testing 2 him out. Tests are made to remove ignorance or doubt. Now it is wrong to be in ignorance or doubt of God's perfection. But we would not be testing God in any bad sense if we needed to show others his knowledge and power. It is the truth of God's goodness and intentions we mustn't doubt. But there is also an affective and experiential knowledge of God's goodness obtained by tasting in ourselves the sweetness and pleasantness of his love. That is why the scriptures tell us to *prove to ourselves his* 3 *will* and *taste his sweetness*. Just as professing our faith with religious symbols is an act of religion, so irreverently putting God to the test because we doubt the faith is a type of irreligion. To start praying without first preparing oneself by forgiving others and doing whatever else one can to reach God's ear, is construable as testing God out. 4 Superstitious men profess an error, but the man who tests God out professes a doubt; so superstition as such is the graver sin.

98 1   Jerome said oaths should possess truth, justice and judgment. The primary thing that goes wrong with oaths, and merits the name **perjury**, is lack of truth. The purpose of oaths is to confirm assertions, and this becomes pointless just when the assertions are false. So oaths are perverse precisely when false. The other wrongnesses of swearing to something unjust and unlawful lead to falsehood, since the oath must be disobeyed; and swearing indiscretely without judgment puts ourselves in danger of 2 falsehood. To call on God to witness to falsehood is irreverent and clearly irreligious, since it implies either that God doesn't know the truth or would be willing to witness to falsehood.

99 1   A means to a good end is itself good, and whatever is consecrated to

God's service is itself worthy of reverence. Showing irreverence for consecrated things, then, is an offence against God's reverence, called **sacrilege**. But the consecration of holy places is subordinate to the consecration of those who worship there, and irreverence towards them is worse sacrilege than irreverence towards the place. Among consecrated things the highest reverence is owed to the sacraments, and especially the sacrament of the eucharist which contains Christ himself; next in order come the sacred vessels consecrated for use in the sacramental rites, then holy images and relics of the saints, church furnishings and vestments, and last of all whatever serves the upkeep of the ministers. Irreverence against these are all various types of sacrilege. 3

Simony is *a deliberate will to buy or sell something spiritual*. The buying and selling of spiritual things is wrong firstly because one can't set an earthly price on such things, secondly because those who have charge of them in the church do not own them, and thirdly because God gives them freely. So whoever buys or sells them is irreverent and irreligious. To take money in return for the spiritual grace of the sacraments is a sin of simony which custom can't in any way excuse, since *custom can't prevail over natural or divine justice*. Those who administer the sacraments should be able to receive something for their upkeep, in accordance with church statute and approved custom; but such money must not be payment for goods received, but a stipend to cover needs. 100 1

2

Loyalty, respect and obedience.   Our existence and guidance in life comes primarily from God, but secondarily from our parents and our native country. As religion honours God, so at a secondary level **loyalty** honours parents and country. Parents give and children receive existence, so parents as such provide for their children's lives as a whole, whereas children provide for parents only as an exceptional response to special need. By nature children are parents' heirs, not vice versa. Religion gives expression to the faith, hope and charity which fundamentally unite us to God; in the same way loyalty expresses the love we have for our parents and native country. Loyalty is respect for our native country as giving us existence in some way; legal justice pursues the country's good in another sense, as the general good of its citizens. If honouring our parents held us back from honouring God it would no longer be an act of loyalty; so we never have to desist from loyalty for religion's sake. A layman with parents in need of his support would transgress the commandment to honour them if he abandoned them to enter a religious order. It would be trying God out, since against all [vol 41] 101 1

2

3

4

human prudence he would be exposing his parents to danger in the hope that God would help them. But a man may leave parents that can manage without him and enter religious life, since children owe parents support only in time of need.

102 1   Authorities are sources of guidance in particular fields: heads of state, army commanders, masters of schools. Just as loyalty honouring parents is a sort of offshoot of religion honouring God, so **respect for authority**
 3 is a sort of offshoot of loyalty. A head of state may be more universally powerful than a head of a family in governing our external life, but not as a giver of existence. Here the comparison must be with God's power which brings everything into existence. In their own persons virtuous men may be more worthy of honour than parents, but children are more obliged to honour parents because of the benefits received from them and the ties of blood.

103 3   The services men pay earthly masters differ from the worship we owe as service to our divine master; the former services are a type of respect. Just as religion is loyalty *par excellence* (since God is our father *par excellence*), so worship is service *par excellence* (since God is our master *par excellence*). No creature takes part in creating (the reason for which God is worshipped), but because they do share God's rule in a way, they can command service.

104 1   The natural order established by God subjects lower things to the influence of higher things, and in the same way natural and divine justice in human affairs require subordinates to obey their higher authorities. *God left man to his own devices*, not in the sense of leaving him to do as he liked, but in the sense of not compelling him like a non-reasoning creature to do what he should by natural necessity, but letting him respond with a free act of his own devising. We should obey our superiors
 2 as we do everything else, by our own decision. Of the many duties inferiors owe superiors, obedience to their commands is one specific
 3 duty calling forth a special virtue. **Obedience** springs from the respect and honour due to a superior. And so, although in itself it is a special virtue relating to commands, it comes under the aegis of several others: under respect when it obeys authorities, under loyalty when it obeys parents, under religion (and especially the chief act of religion, which is devotion) when it obeys God. It is in that context that we read that
 4 *obedience is more praiseworthy than sacrifice*. God never acts against nature, since *the nature of things is what God does within them*; but he can act against the usual course of nature. In the same way God never commands things against virtue, since virtue and right consist primarily in accord with God's will and response to his commands, even when

that runs counter to the usual measure of virtue. Thus the command to Abraham to kill his innocent son did not command something unjust, since God is the author of death and of life. Nor was it against chastity to order Hosea to take to himself an adulteress, for God is the designer of human procreation and whatever way he relates man to woman is a right way. These men did not sin in obeying or being willing to obey God. Physical things escape causal influences either because a stronger 5 cause intervenes (water quenching burning wood, for example) or because they are not fully subjected to the cause's influence (fire able to warm water but not evaporate it, for example). In the same way subjects may escape the obligation of obedience, either because a more powerful authority intervenes, or because the subject is not the superior's subordinate in every respect (as Seneca says, *the thoughts of slaves are free*). In the inner movement of his will man is not obliged to obey men but only God; he must obey men only in his outward actions. And then not in what pertains to his bodily nature, in which all men are equal and only God is master (keeping his body alive, begetting children, contracting marriage), but only in those areas of human conduct and affairs over which the superior has authority: army commanders in military matters, masters of servants in what pertains to their service, parents of children in matters of upbringing and household order. The 6 order of justice is not abolished but strengthened by faith in Jesus Christ. So our faith does not exempt us from our duty to obey civil authorities. But where regimes hold power illegitimately, or command what is wrong, subjects have no duty to obey except for extraneous reasons like avoiding scandal and risk.

Debts of honour.   We are indebted primarily to God, the first source 106 1 of all our good; secondarily to our parents, the direct source of our birth and upbringing; thirdly, to the authorities, the sources of our public welfare; and finally, to all our private benefactors. So after religion which pays our debt of service to God, loyalty which honours our parents, and respect for authorities, comes **gratitude** for the kindness of benefactors. There could be a vice of over-gratitude, making unnecessary or over- 107 2 eager recompense for things. But more opposed is the vice of ingratitude: failing to return a favour or, more seriously, not showing any sign of gratitude for it, or, more seriously still, not even noticing it and forgetting it. Someone who fails to recognize or praise or repay a favour does not 3 always sin fatally, for the debt of gratitude is precisely not owed in strict justice. But contempt in the recipient or need in the benefactor might in certain cases make the sin fatal; and to do something positively opposed to gratitude, depending on what is done, could also be fatal.

108 1   Our attitude when exacting **retribution** makes a difference. If the only thing we want is to inflict punishment on the sinner, then we act altogether unlawfully; but if our primary aim is the good to be achieved through such punishment – the sinner's correction, or at least his restraint so that others may enjoy peace and justice be defended and God honoured – then in the right circumstances retribution can be
2 lawful. When public justice demands punishment of an offence the punishment is an act of commutative justice; but individual avenging of
3 injury is an act of the virtue of retribution. Fatal sins are sins deserving eternal death in the future retribution when God delivers his unerring judgment; but in this life punishments are meant to be medicinal, and only those crimes should be visited with the death penalty that involve the direst ruin for others.

109 1   To acknowledge the truth about oneself is in itself a good thing, but to be virtuous it must be done only in the right circumstances. Being truthful must not only have a balanced object (the truth, balanced between boasting and understatement) but be performed in a balanced way (not overdoing the revelation at the wrong moment, nor underdoing
3 things by hiding what should be revealed). The virtue of **truthfulness** resembles justice in relating to other people and setting up some sort of equality: between thing and thing in justice's case, between sign and thing in the case of truthfulness. But truthfulness differs from justice in dispatching not a legal debt but a debt of honour, for it is honour that demands one reveal the truth about oneself. So truthfulness is a virtue allied to justice. Man is a social animal, and men owe one another by nature whatever is needed for the survival of human society. Since men can't live with one another unless they can rely on each others'
110 1 truthfulness, the virtue of truthfulness renders a sort of debt. Whenever we say something false we utter a material or factual falsehood; if we purposely say that falsehood then we utter a formal or moral falsehood; and if we say it in order to deceive then we utter an effective falsehood. Lies are formal or moral falsehoods. Uttering a material falsehood that one believes true is not a lie in the complete sense, but uttering a material truth that one believes false is. The intention to deceive is not however included in the definition of a lie. Deception is a natural but not a necessary consequence of lying, just as actually falling downwards isn't
2 part of the definition of being heavy and doesn't always occur. Lies divide intrinsically into boasts (which overstate) and understatements. But their gravity varies according to their purpose: the most serious, called pernicious lies, intend harm to others, whilst the less serious are

those that pursue the goods of pleasure (the so-called jocose lie) or usefulness (aimed at helping or protecting others). All lies are by defin- 3 ition wrong, acts out of tune with their matter, since words should by definition signify what we think, and it is perverse and wrong for them to signify what is not in our mind. So since lies as such are out of order, they can't be used to rescue others whatever the peril; rather the truth must be cleverly masked in some way. Even a jocose lie of itself could deceive, though it is not meant to and won't because of the tone of voice. Hyperbole and figures of speech such as are found in scripture are quite different: as Augustine says, *statements must be related to what they say, and what figurative statements say is what they convey to those to whom they are spoken*. A lie is already contrary to the love of charity because 4 of its falsity, and if the falsity deprives man of some good (some perfection of knowledge or moral perception) then lying can be fatal, bringing damage on our fellowman; but if it is about factual matters which it matters little whether he knows or not then the lie is not of itself fatal. However a lie may also be contrary to charity because of its purpose: this is the case with pernicious lies though not usually with jocose or useful lies. And finally a lie may be contrary to charity for some extraneous reason like scandal or ensuing harm. Pretence is 111 1 communicating a lie by doing something. *Makebelieve can have a genuine significance and be not a lie, but truth in figure*. Hypocrisy is posing as 2 someone one isn't: for example, sinners pretending to be just men.

All men are friends in a general way: *every beast loves its kind*. 114 1 The marks of friendliness we should show to strangers express that friendship, and no pretence is involved. **Friendliness** is a debt of 2 honour, which our own honourableness demands of us. We are by nature social animals and owe in honour that truthful revelation of ourselves without which human society could not survive. And just as we can't survive without truthfulness so we can't survive without agreeableness: *no one can put up with a gloomy and disagreeable companion all day long*. So we are obliged by a certain natural honour to be agreeable to those we live with, unless there is a good and useful reason on occasion for making them sad. Flattery in a broad sense covers all use of words and 115 1 deeds in our daily lives which aims at pleasing others without regard to a virtuous balance.

Generosity properly concerns money: its immediate concern is our 117 2 passions, but passions concerned with money, where *money covers anything that can be measured in cash*. Generosity disposes us to good use of 3 wealth as such, justice is concerned with wealth as something owed to others, munificence with wealth as something to be expended in great enterprises. Generosity is chiefly concerned to see that a man's passion for wealth doesn't hinder its proper and just expenditure and donation.

118 1 Material goods are useful for certain ends, and we should seek them in a balanced way, to the degree that they are necessary to our particular status in life; but to want to acquire and retain goods in excess of this measure is wrong and avaricious: avarice is *an unbalanced love of possess-*
2 *ing*. All such material goods useful for human living we sum up in the
3 one word *money*. Avarice as an unbalanced acquisition and retention of wealth steals what belongs to others and contravenes justice, and as an
4 unbalanced interior passion for wealth it is opposed to generosity. As opposed to justice it is fatal by nature, involving one in robbery and theft; as opposed to generosity it is fatal when the love of money ousts
119 1 love of charity for God and our fellowmen, but otherwise non-fatal. The avaricious man goes too far in the love of wealth, loving money more than he ought; the prodigal doesn't go far enough, showing too little responsibility in its use. Or one could say that the avaricious man under-does giving and the prodigal man over-does it.

120 1 **Equity.**   The human actions which laws are intended to govern are all individual happenings, so infinitely various that no rule of law can cover every case. Legislators concern themselves rather with what is ordinarily the case and formulate their laws accordingly. That means that in some cases observance of the law can militate against the equality sought by justice and against the general good at which the law aims. Thus the law which tells us to return deposits to their depositors because this is usually the just thing to do, can in some cases be harmful – the madman who wants his sword back. In such cases it would be wrong to comply with the letter of the law, but right to comply with what justice and the general good require. Equity is the virtue that disposes us to do
2 this. The parts of a virtue can be component parts, subdivisions or allied subsidiary virtues. Subdivisions of a class share the general definition of the whole class but are less extensive than it. Such sharing is sometimes equal (cattle and horses are equally animal) and sometimes weighted (substance is the primary subdivision and accidents secondary subdivisions of being). Equity is a part of what we broadly call justice, yet *is itself justice of a sort*; in other words, equity is a subdivision of justice. And it is the primary subdivision, with legal justice secondary to it, guided by it as by a higher rule of human behaviour. If by legal justice we mean our disposition to comply not only with the letter of the law but also with what is more important, the legislators' intentions, then equity is the primary subdivision of legal justice. If we restrict legal

justice to compliance with the letter of the law, then equity is the primary subdivision of justice broadly so-called, and legal justice its secondary subdivision.

The ten commandments.   The ten commandments are the primary 122 1 premises of all law, those that natural reason finds most evident and to which it gives immediate assent. Now the *ought* that characterizes commandments is most evident in matters of justice *owed* to others; for at first sight a man seems master of his own individual affairs and able to do what he likes in such matters. So the ten commandments relate to justice: the first three to religion, the most important part of justice; the fourth to loyalty, its second part; and the other six to ordinary justice as observed between equals.

One of the commandments relating to religion is a positive command: 2 *Remember to keep holy the sabbath day*; but it is preceded by prohibitions removing obstacles to religion. For obstacles must be removed first, especially where God is concerned, since in our inadequacy negations mean more than affirmations in relation to God. So the first com- 3 mandment forbids superstition – the over-doing of religion – and the second perjury – an act of irreligion. Man is led to prayer and devotion, 4 the inner worship in his heart, by inner promptings of the Holy Spirit. The commandment of the law concerns rather what symbol to use in external worship, and sets up one to represent God's most manifest work of goodness to all mankind, namely, the creation of the world. *From this work God rested on the seventh day*, and we are therefore commanded to keep that day holy, set aside for God, as a symbol. Man is naturally inclined to set aside portions of his time for each thing he needs to do – eating, sleeping and so on. Setting aside time for God is a natural moral obligation; that the particular time should be the seventh day was a ritual prescription symbolizing creation, but it is included in the ten commandments as a moral not a ritual obligation. *You shall do no servile work on that day*. There are three types of servility: to sin, to other men through bodily work, and to God through worship. The first two are obstacles to man's concentration on God and contrary to the observance of the sabbath, the first more than the second. But bodily works such as both slaves and free men do, providing necessities of life for oneself and others, are not servile and do not violate the sabbath. In the New Law the observance of the Lord's day has replaced the observance of the sabbath, not by command of a law, but by church decision and the custom of the Christian people. And because it is no longer a figurative command concerned to protest a truth, the prohibition of work is not so strict and dispensations are more easily granted.

5   Among all our fellowmen we are most obliged to our parents, the particular causes of our existence as God is the universal; so the next
6 commandment prescribes honouring them. The prohibitions on doing injury to our fellowmen are general prohibitions such as can find place in the ten commandments. All injuries to the person are to be understood under the heading of murder; all injuries to people connected with us, especially such as are prompted by lust, come under the heading of adultery; all damage to property under theft; and every wrongdoing by way of speech under false witness. The prohibitions against coveting are not directed against the initial stirrings of such desire in our sensory appetites; what they forbid is the will's consent not only to deeds but to delight in them.

Courage

[vol 42] 123 1 **The virtue of courage**   Mental virtues set reason itself right, justice applies right reason to human affairs, the other moral virtues remove the obstacles to that application: moderation stops us from being attracted unreasonably by pleasures, **courage** from being repelled unreasonably by difficulties. This courage is a spiritual bravery to overcome spiritual difficulties, in the way physical bravery overcomes and repels physical difficulties. Aristotle lists five imitations of courage, which perform brave acts but not out of bravery. Sometimes the difficult isn't felt as difficult, through ignorance or optimism or skill; sometimes passion is the motive (flight from sorrow, or anger) and sometimes some calculation of profit. Some people's natural temperament inclines them to courage, but
2 courage properly is a virtue: a condition characterizing all virtue if by courage we mean a steadfast spirit, but a distinct virtue with a special field of action, if we mean a spirit steadfast to endure when steadfastness is particularly difficult, namely, in situations of extreme danger. For if you can hold your ground in the most difficult conditions you will be able to resist less difficult situations. So courage is primarily concerned with the fears of difficult situations that hold our will back from following reason's lead. Courage doesn't merely endure the pressures of such situations without flinching, by restraining fear, but also in a measure attacks them if future safety demands elimination of the difficulty. This requires daring. So courage deals with fear and daring, restraining the
4 first and imposing a balance on the second. Courage of spirit keeps the will steadfastly attached to the good that reason proposes in the face first of greater and then of lesser evils. We define virtue by the utmost

of which it is capable, and since the most feared of all bodily evils is
death, which takes away all our bodily goods, the virtue of courage is
concerned with fears of the dangers of death. Any virtue that ensured
balance in our love of some good would ensure balance in our fear of
the opposing evil, but our love for our own life is a natural love, so here
there has to be a special virtue to ensure balance in our fear of death, 5
instilling steadfastness of spirit against this danger which threatens not
merely in a general war, but also in individual cases of assault. Restrain- 6
ing fear is more difficult than controlling daring, since the very danger
feared tends to restrain daring but increases fear. So the principal activity
of courage is not so much attack as endurance, standing one's ground
in the midst of danger. Virtue is by definition concerned not with the 12
difficult but with the good. The stature of a virtue is to be measured by
how it contributes to good, rather than by how difficult its matter is.

In the very nature of **martyrdom**, the martyr stands firm in truth 124 1
and justice against the assaults of persecutors. Clearly then martyrdom
is a virtuous act, an act indeed of courage. The courage of good citizens 2
is a steadfastness in human justice, to preserve which they will endure
mortal danger; and the courage given by God is a steadfastness in *God's
justice, which comes through faith in Christ Jesus.* So faith is the goal to
which martyrs remain steadfast, while courage is the virtue disposing
them to do so. Charity is the primary motivating power behind the act
of martyrdom, the virtue commanding it; but the immediate motivation
evoking the act is the virtue of courage. But martyrdom as such, the 3
dutiful endurance of death, cannot be the most perfect of all virtuous
actions; for endurance of death is praiseworthy only when directed
towards some good action of faith or love for God. So that action – the
goal of martyrdom – must be better than martyrdom itself. Martyrdom
is however a mark of most perfect love of God, and in that sense the
most perfect of acts. *No man has greater love than this, that he lays down
his life for his friend.*

Evils of the soul are more to be feared than those of the body, and 125 4
those of the body more than external misfortunes. So men who sin to
avoid bodily evils like whipping or death, or external misfortunes like
loss of money, or who prefer suffering bodily evils to losing money,
cannot be altogether excused from their sin. But it is lessened in the
degree that fear lessens voluntariness: for pressing fear imposes a sort
of necessity to act. One may also fear death and other worldly evils less 126 1
than one should, by not loving life and its goods enough. So clearly
there is a vice of **insensitivity to fear**, whether it arise from lack of love,
or swelled head, or sheer stupidity (though this last, if unconquerable,

2 excuses from sin). Just as fearfulness over-does fear, fearing what it ought not to, so insensitivity to fear under-does fear, not fearing what
127 1 it ought to; and both are opposed to the virtue of courage. We lack names for certain vices (and virtues) and use names of feelings for them: for vices the names of feelings against evil: hate, fear, anger and daring;
2 and for virtues the names of feelings for the good: love and hope. Daring sometimes names the vice of rashness, and implies excess of daring. Clearly it then opposes courage, which must put order into both fear and daring.

128 1 **Virtues allied to courage.**   Virtues have three sorts of parts: subdivisions, component parts and subsidiary allied virtues. Because courage is a special virtue concerned with a very special field it has no subdivisions or species, but it has component parts which go together to make up a courageous action, and allied virtues concerned with subsidiary perils and challenges. Courage must be aggressive in attack and able to endure. Its aggressiveness requires *confidence* to start with and *drive* to follow through: these qualities in the face of the dangers of death constitute component parts of courage, but in face of secondary challenges define its subsidiary virtues of *enterprise* and *munificent grandeur* (thinking big and acting big). Courage's ability to endure requires *patience* to remain unbroken by sorrow and *perseverance* to remain undefeated by hardship: and these too are both component parts of courage and its subsidiary virtues. Confidence is hope in oneself, though in subordination to God, of course.

129 1   **Enterprise** is in a sense concerned with recognition: not so much with recognition itself as seeking to do things worthy of recognition.
2 Virtues are concerned with two sorts of difficulty: finding and maintaining a balance is already difficult for reason (and this is the only difficulty attaching to mental virtues and to justice), but in the other moral virtues there is also difficulty arising from the virtue's matter,
3 since *our feelings resist reason.* All virtues are connected at their root, be that prudence or grace, and co-exist as dispositions, either actually there or ready to show themselves. So a man can have an enterprising disposition even though he cannot act enterprisingly until his position
131 1 in life enables him to do so. Desire for recognition can be excessive in three ways: one can seek it without deserving it, or without acknowledging God's part in it, or without using it for the good of others. Ambition covers all these types of excessive enterprise, and is clearly
2 sinful. Enterprise aims at great achievements appropriate to one's resources, but over-confidence over-estimates the resources, and

ambition seeks excessive recognition. Conceited men are in truth less 132 1
confident than men of enterprise, glorying in things enterprising men
would disdain. They think too much of themselves, over-valuing their
worthiness for recognition. Pusillanimity opposes enterprise, as small 133 2
aims oppose large ones. Its cause is mental ignorance or fear, and its
effect indolence.

Anything we produce we produce by craft, and we consider a crafts- 134 2
man's work specially good if it has some sort of greatness, be it in
quantity or value or worthiness. The production of such great works is
the province of the virtue of **munificence** or grandeur. The really great
works are those directed to the honour of God. So *grandeur and holiness*
are mentioned together in the psalm when thinking of such works. The 3
chief act of any virtue is its interior willingness and choice, and that
can be exercised without external fortune; so even poor men can act
munificently in this sense. But external actions need means; so poor
men can't perform munificent acts with great materials in an absolute
sense, but only with materials great proportionately to the field open to
them. Small and great are in fact relative terms. Justice is concerned with 4
transactions in themselves: as involving indebtedness. But generosity and
munificence consider them in relation to the passions: as involving
expense. Generosity relates that expense to love and desire for money,
which must not hinder a generous man's giving and spending. Munificence relates the expense to hope of achievement in a particular field of
expenditure. So generosity seeks a balance in our affective feelings and
munificence in our aggressive ones. The munificent man aims first at a 135 1
great undertaking and, for that undertaking's sake, boldly confronts the
great expense involved. The petty man looks first at keeping expenditure down, and so aims at small undertakings that are acceptable
because they don't cost much.

Sorrow is a passion that greatly hinders reason. So it is essential for 136 1
us to have a virtue which ensures that reason is not overcome by grief.
Courage primarily concerns the aggressive feelings, and resists flight 4
from fear. **Patience** primarily concerns the affective feelings, and
endures sorrows already present; nevertheless, it is a subdivision of
courage, because virtues are allied to one another not because of the
faculty they dispose, but because of what they are about and what they
aim to do.

Perseverance is a special virtue with the function of enduring as 137 1
long as is necessary for certain acts of virtue to be performed. As a form 137 2
of endurance perseverance is allied to courage, but because it is not so
difficult to keep at a thing as it is to brave death, perseverance is

138 1 subsidiary to courage. The opposed vices are spinelessness – under-persevering – and obstinacy – over-doing it.

Moderation

[vol 43] 141 2 **What is moderation?**   Moderation is a condition characterizing all virtue. But it is also the name of a special virtue of restraint operating in fields in which we find ourselves specially and exceptionally attracted.

3 What our body feels is good for it is not as such inimical to reason, but rather serves reason; what causes trouble is that the sense-appetites respond to stimuli in ways not measured by reason, so that we need a special moral virtue to moderate and bring balance into our attraction to such goods. Contrast our revulsion from things we feel are bad for our body: that can be inimical to reason not so much because it is immoderate as because it arouses aversion to what reason sees as good, and here a moral virtue is required to withstand such aversion. So the virtue of courage makes us steadfast in the midst of feelings of aversion for bodily evil, dealing with our fears (and in consequence with the feelings of daring with which we attack what we fear in the hope of achieving good). But the virtue of moderation introduces restraint in the midst of feelings of affection for goods, dealing with our desires and pleasures (and in consequence with the feelings of sadness which arise in the absence of such pleasures). Desire implies impetus towards the pleasurable and needs moderation to rein it in; fear implies shying away from the harmful and needs courage to resist it firmly. Moderation properly controls desires, courage fears.

4   Pleasure follows congenial activity, and the more natural the activity the stronger the pleasure. The activities most natural to animals are those which serve their survival: eating and drinking to keep individuals alive, and sex-activity to preserve the species. So moderation is chiefly concerned with the pleasures of eating, drinking and sex: pleasures all

5 connected with the sense of touch. Moderation then is principally concerned with the tactile pleasures accompanying use of things essential to life. But moderation and immoderateness extend secondarily to pleasures of taste and smell and sight, inasmuch as they too contribute to the pleasurable use of the tangible necessaries of life: taste more than the other senses since that is closest to touch, though the pleasures of the table lie only secondarily in fine taste and preparation of the food,

6 and primarily in its nourishing substance. Moderation's rule for using pleasurable things derives from how much we need them to live. The doer's goal may differ from the deed's: the goal of building is the house,

but the goal of the builder may be profit. In the same way, the goal and rule of moderation itself is happiness, but the goal and rule of the things moderation makes use of is their need in human life. Under needs we include everything we must have in order to survive decently. *The moderate man desires some pleasures for health's sake and some for his welfare.* Everything that hinders health and welfare the moderate man will avoid; what is not needed but doesn't hinder, he employs with regard to the place and the time and the convenience of those he lives with. Virtue is concerned with the good and the difficult; but a virtue's 8 status is judged by its relation to good (in which justice excels) rather than to difficulty in which moderation excels.

Someone who so avoids pleasure that he omits to do what is needed 142 1 to survive does wrong, and runs counter to nature; he is guilty of the vice of insensitivity. Sometimes, however, abstaining from such pleasure may be praiseworthy and even necessary for some goal: we diet for bodily health or as a part of athletic or military training, or sometimes to help us repent sin and recover spiritual health, or to give us time to contemplate divine matters. The body however is kept going by activities which are pleasurable, so it cannot possibly be reasonable and good for man to abstain from all such pleasures.

Cowardice runs away from danger of death, impelled to do so by the 3 great need of saving one's life. Immoderateness desires pleasure without such great need, so immoderation is the graver sin as far as matter is concerned. And the same is true when we consider the doer. For the immoderate man is more composed than those who are out of their minds with anxiety and fear of death; his actions are more willing, unmixed with external pressures of fear, willing particular acts of intemperance despite not wanting intemperance in general, whereas cowards will the particular throwing away of their shields only because in general they want to save their lives. Finally, immoderation is easier to avoid than cowardice: all one's life one can practise moderation in food and sex without running any risks, but you can only practise confronting the dangers of death by living dangerously. Immoderation 4 is a shameful vice. It debases a man: pleasures are what we share with the beasts, whereas the light of reason, the shining loveliness of all virtue, shines forth in man alone.

There are three kinds of parts to a cardinal virtue: component parts, 143 1 subdivisions, and subsidiary virtues. The component parts that go to make up moderation are *shame* for the ugliness of its opposing vices, and *honour* for its beauty. Its subdivisions are related to distinct pleasures of touch. *Abstinence* concerns the pleasures of food, *sobriety* the pleasure of drinking; *chastity* concerns the pleasure of the sex-act itself, *purity* the surrounding pleasures of kissing, fondling and embracing. Subsidiary virtues apply the measure of the principal virtue in less difficult areas. Moderation puts balance into our sense-desires as such, but *self-discipline* deals with a will already disturbed by immoderate sense-desire, *humility* moderates our hopes and boldness, *mildness* our angers and desire for revenge, *modesty* moderates our bodily actions, and in external things *frugality* eschews superfluity and *simplicity* over-elegance.

144 1   Shame, being praiseworthy, is either itself a virtue or contributes to virtue. But not prudence, because it is not a knowledge; not justice, because it is a feeling; not courage, because it is a feeling of recoil; and not (it would seem) moderation because it is not a desire. Shame is in fact a recoiling from what is dishonourable and disgraceful, and since lack of moderation is the most dishonourable and disgraceful thing there is, shame contributes more to moderation than to any other virtue, though not because of the sort of reaction it displays (which is fear) but
   4 because of the sort of thing that prompts that reaction. Shame is not so much an essential constituent of moderation as a preparation for it: laying its first foundation by instilling in us horror of what dishonours
145 4 us. Honour in contrast is a certain gracefulness and beauty of spirit, opposed to the disgraceful; and it contributes to moderation by involving repulsion to what is most disgraceful and unfitting for men, namely the pleasures of beasts. It is a condition of moderation, and in that sense a component part of it.

146 1 Moderation in food and drink.   Not eating, as such, is neutral: only virtuous if the abstinence is reasonably regulated. Courage urges us onward, moderation draws us back. So **abstinence** has a name which suggests doing without, though in fact what it names is a balanced attitude to not eating, regulated by reason. For right reason leads us to abstain only when and as we ought, with a cheerful heart, and for God's
147 3 glory not our own. Fasting as such is a sort of punishment, not something one would choose to do unless it had a useful purpose. So no precept obliges us to fast unless we need such a medicine. But since most people do need it, the church has laid down certain fasts to be observed by all. It is not trying to turn a work of supererogation into an obligation, but simply laying down how to go about doing something we already need
148 1 to do. The vice of gluttony does not lie in food as such, but in unregulated and unreasonable desire of it. Eating too much thinking one needs it is not gluttony but inexperience. Gluttony is knowingly eating too much pleasurable food for pleasure's sake.

Sobriety specially concerns drink, and not any sort of drink but 149 1 spirituous drink like wine, which muddles the head and leads to drunkenness. Intoxicating liquor has a special facility for hindering our 2 reasoning processes by muddling our brain, and so it calls for a special virtue, sobriety, to stop this happening. Immoderate pleasure of any sort can so occupy reason as to hinder it in a general way, but intoxicating drink hinders reason in a special way and so requires a special virtue to control its use. No food or drink is unlawful in itself. Wine is not 3 unlawful as such, and becomes so only because of other factors: the fragile condition of the drinker, the immoderateness of the drinking, the scandal given. Being drunk and befuddled is not itself the fault but a 150 1 consequence we must suffer. The fault is the act which makes us drunk. If a drinker is unaware of a drink's potency, and not negligent, then there is no fault; the fault comes from unregulated desire and consumption of wine. There is an opposite extreme to drunkenness which has no name: when someone knowingly abstains from wine to such an extent that he damages his health. If a man gets drunk quite unwittingly there is no 2 sin; if he is aware of drinking a lot but unaware that the drink can intoxicate him, there can be sin but only a non-fatal one; but knowingly to prefer being drunk to abstaining is true drunkenness, intended and therefore a fatal sin, by which the drinker willingly and wittingly deprives himself of the use of his own reason, the power that enables him to act virtuously and avoid wrongdoing. A drunken condition can excuse from 4 sin, rendering one's acts involuntary because one doesn't know what one is doing; though, if the condition itself is culpable, the consequent acts committed while drunk will not be altogether free from blame, since they are voluntary in their cause. How less sinful they will be will depend on how less voluntary.

Moderation in sex. The pleasures of sex are more vehement than 151 3 the pleasures of food and exert more pressure on us; they need more whipping into line, for the more we give way to them the more they dominate us and the more able they are to overthrow our strength of mind. Even married sex, adorned with all the honourableness of 4 marriage, carries with it a certain shame, because the movements of the genitals unlike those of other external members don't obey reason. The virtue that deals with the sex-act we call **chastity**, and the virtue concerned with more public actions such as looking and kissing and caressing we call **purity**. Purity is a sort of adjunct serving chastity, not a separate virtue but a sort of environment to chastity. Sexual sin is thought of as more disgraceful than other immoderate action, partly because of the uncontrolled movements of the genitals, but also because our reason gets submerged.

152 1   There are three levels to be considered in the act of sex: the physiological level (the breaking of the hymen, etc) has no moral content as such; at the psychological level shared by body and soul, emission of seed brings sensory pleasure (the material side of the human moral act); and at the deepest level there is an act of intention in the soul aiming at such pleasure (and making the act a human, moral activity). Now **virginity** is defined by a moral integrity: not then the integrity of the hymen as such, but a material immunity from the pleasures of orgasm, wedded with a formal purpose of perpetual abstinence from such pleasures. A hymen broken from some other cause is no more a loss of virginity in this sense than a broken arm or leg. And the pleasure of orgasm can be experienced unintentionally during sleep or externally forced without a person's consent. In no such case is virginity lost.

2   External goods are meant to serve our body's good, our body to serve our soul, and in our soul the active life should serve the contemplative life. So it is not a bad thing, but reasonable and right, to abstain from external possessions, which are otherwise good, for the sake of the body's health or the contemplation of truth. And in the same way abstaining from bodily pleasure so as to make ourselves more freely available to contemplate truth, is reasonable and right. The injunction of the law in us by nature to *eat* must be observed by everybody if individuals are to survive; but the injunction to *be fruitful and multiply* obliges the community of mankind as a whole, and that must be spiritually fruitful as well. So it will be enough if some people in the community of mankind reproduce whilst others, abstaining from that, give themselves up to the contemplation of God, and so bring a beauty and health into the whole human race. To refuse all pleasure as such because of dislike for it and without any good reason is to be insensitive and boorish. The practice of virginity doesn't refuse all pleasure, but

4   only that of sex, and that only for a good reason. Virginity seeks the soul's good in a life of contemplation *mindful of the things of God*. Marriage seeks the body's good – the bodily multiplication of the human race – in an active life in which husband and wife are *mindful of the things of this world*. Without doubt then the state of virginity is preferable to that of even continent marriage, though married people may well be better people than those practising virginity: more chaste, having a spirit that would have made them better virgins were they called to it than those actually practising virginity, and more virtuous in general. The general good ranks above the good of a private person when those goods

are of the same sort. But the private good may be of a higher sort; and this is what happens when virginity dedicated to God is compared with bodily fruitfulness. However, the theological virtues and even the virtue 5 of religion, being directly occupied with God, are to be preferred to virginity. Again martyrs cleave to God more mightily, because they lay down their own lives, whilst those who dwell in monasteries lay down their own wills and all they possess; virgins lay down only the pleasures of sex. Simply speaking then virginity is by no means the greatest of virtues.

Use of food properly ordered for the body's welfare is no sin; and in 153 1 the same way, use of sex properly ordered for its purpose of human reproduction is no sin. Virtuous balance is not measured quantitatively but by rightness of reason, so the high degree of pleasure that attaches to a properly ordered sex-act doesn't stop it being balanced. In any case virtue isn't concerned with how much external sense-pleasure accompanies the act (that depends on the body's temperament), but with the way that pleasure interiorly affects us. Though not even our distraction from spiritual matters at the moment of enjoying such pleasure makes it unvirtuous; for it is not unvirtuous to suspend reason for a time for a good reason, otherwise sleeping would be a vice. Sexual sin consists rather in a breakdown in proper reasonable order in 3 exercising the sex-act, and that can happen in several ways. Sometimes 154 1 we seek pleasure in a sex-act with an object naturally unsuited to the act's purpose: unnatural vice, for example, rules out reproduction by nature, and sex outside of marriage rules out proper provision for the bringing up of any offspring of the act. Sometimes the object of the act is unsuited because of relationships with other human beings. To have sex with this particular woman may dishonour a blood or kin relation-ship, as in incest; or do injustice to her guardian – her husband in adultery, her father in seduction and rape. (We differentiate with respect to the woman rather than the man since in sex-acts she is acted on, and he the agent). The injustice of adultery is not altogether irrelevant to the act's lack of chastity, since that must be judged all the worse for provoking us into injustice.

Observation of animals shows that when care for the young involves 2 both male and female, the male mates with a determinate female or females, as in the case of birds. But when the care involves only the female, mating is promiscuous, as with dogs. Now human children need not only a mother to nurse them, but even more a father to protect and guide them interiorly and exteriorly. So promiscuity is contrary to human nature: the husband takes to himself a determinate wife and lives with her not for a short but for a long time, even for life. Husbands have a natural wish to be sure who are their children, for they have a responsibility to bring them up; and it is such sureness that is damaged by promiscuity. The commitment to a particular woman we call *marriage* and it is dictated by the law that is in us by nature, though, because intercourse serves the general good of mankind and that general good is the subject of enacted law, so too is the union of husband and wife in marriage. (What law that is for Christians we shall discuss when we talk in the third part of this book about the sacrament of marriage.) As such, then, the exercise of the sex-act outside marriage is promiscuous and disadvantageous to the care of children, and for this reason a fatal sin. It doesn't matter that sometimes people who act this way do provide sufficiently for the consequent offspring of their actions: laws are laid down to cover the general run of things, not particular cases. One act of intercourse can beget a child, so any disorder in that act which disadvantages a child that could be born of it is a fatal disorder as such, quite apart from any disordered desire. And disordered desire is in any case not at its lowest in such a sin, for too lustful an intercourse with

4 one's wife is also a sin, though a lesser one. Kisses, embraces and caresses are not of their nature fatally sinful. Indeed they sometimes occur without lustful feeling, according to the custom of the country or some other need or reasonable cause. But since unmarried sex is a fatal sin (and other species of sexual sin even graver), it follows that consent to the pleasure of such a sin is as fatal as consent to the deed. And kisses and embraces directed towards such pleasure can also be fatal. Indeed those are the kisses we call *lustful*, so we can say that lustful caresses are always fatal.

[vol 44] 155 1 **Virtues allied to moderation.   Self-discipline** has some features of virtue, being a steadfastness of reason against seduction by feelings; but it is not a full moral virtue, since it does not so subject our passions to reason that no passion contrary to reason arises. To be man is to be reasonable, so self-discipline aims at a steadfast possession of a self in harmony with reason, not at one which is steadfastly perverse. The truly self-disciplined man abstains from perversity of desire to stand firm in reason; to stand firm in perverse reason and abstain from good desires

2 is rather obstinacy. Our natural desires are the basis of all our subsequent desires, and the closer these are to natural desire the more urgent they are. Nature inclines us above all to the necessities of life: food and drink for the individual's survival, and sex for the survival of the species: both associated with pleasures of touch. So self-discipline is properly speaking

discipline of the pleasures of touch, but secondarily and broadly speaking of any other matters in need of control. In regard to fears we speak rather of steadfastness than self-discipline; and since anger is not so much a natural as a partly rational drive consequent on apprehension of injury, we talk of self-discipline there only in a qualified sense. The main area of self-discipline is sex, since those pleasures are more vehement than the ones associated with food and drink. The capacity 3 for affective emotion in self-disciplined men is no differently disposed from that of undisciplined men: both are capable of breaking out in strong and unruly desires. So self-discipline is not a disposition of this capacity. Neither does a disciplined man's reason differ from that of the undisciplined: each admits what is right, and when not under the sway of passion will choose not to follow unlawful desires. The basic difference between the two lies in the act of choice: self-disciplined men experience strong pleasures and desires, but choose rather to follow reason, whereas men without discipline choose to follow desire against the advice of reason. So self-discipline is a matter of will, affecting choices. Self-discipline is concerned with desire of the tactile pleasures, resisting it but bringing no balance to it (that is the function of the virtue of moderation, a disposition of our capacity for affective emotion itself). So self-discipline must be in another faculty than the emotions, since resistance implies one force acting against another. The will lies between reason and our emotional capacity, and can be set in motion by either. In self-disciplined men it is controlled by reason, in men without discipline by desire. The initiation comes from reason in self-disciplined people, from desire in others, but *what* is disciplined is the will. Reason's 4 influence for good is greater in moderate men in whom the very capacity for emotion is subjected to reason – *tamed*, as it were – than in self-disciplined men in whom the emotions strongly resist reason. So self-discipline is less perfect than moderation. The will lies closer to reason than to our capacity for emotions, so the influence of reason for good which gives virtue its value, shows itself more powerful when it reaches past the will to the emotions (as it does in moderate men) than when it only reaches the will (as in self-disciplined men).

The will of an immoderate man has a lasting bent towards choosing 156 3 wrongly, a habitual disposition acquired by repeated usage; but the undisciplined man's will is swayed by temporary passion. He quickly repents when passion is spent, whereas immoderate men rather enjoy having sinned, this sort of activity having become second nature to them. Both types of men don't know what they are doing, but the immoderate man's ignorance is longer lasting and, where undisciplined men are mistaken in their choice of particular acts, immoderate men are mistaken about their very goal, thinking it good to follow unrestrained passion. Ill-discipline can't be remedied by knowledge alone, but needs inward help from grace to temper desire and outward admonition and correction to wake resistance to desire. The same cure is required by the immoderate man, but for him it is more difficult, for his mind has lost touch with his ultimate goal, and his capacity for emotion has been lastingly disposed. There is greater wantonness in immoderate men's wills than in those of ill-disciplined men. Though the wantonness in ill-disciplined men's emotions is sometimes greater, since men without discipline give way only to strong desires whereas immoderate men give

4 way even to weak ones and indeed may even provoke them themselves. Ill-discipline in desire is more squalid than ill-disciplined anger, because, as Aristotle points out, desire is more disorderly than anger. Anger is already partly rational, being bent on avenging a wrong, and it is also more a matter of genetic temperament and therefore more excusable; anger is also more open than desire, and it acts under compulsion from unpleasantness, rather than from pleasure. Nevertheless ill-disciplined anger is usually more grave in its consequences and more harmful to our fellowmen.

157 1 **Mildness and clemency.**   Our external behaviour is aroused (and also hindered) by inner emotion; so virtues that integrate our emotions cooperate with those that bring balance to our outward actions. Justice, for example, prevents us stealing, to which an unbalanced desire for money, unless moderated by generosity, would incline us. So generosity cooperates with justice in stopping us stealing. And so it is with punishing: **clemency** directly mitigates the external act of punishment itself, whereas **mildness** moderates the excessive anger which would

3 oppose such mitigation. Allied virtues seek the same kind of balance as the virtues they are allied to, but in subsidiary matters. Now justice seeks a sort of equivalence, courage a certain steadfastness, and moderation seeks restraint. Clemency which mitigates punishments, and mildness which mitigates anger, being restraining virtues, are allied to moderation, even though that virtue's restraint is exercised on our most vehement tactile pleasures. Mitigation of penalties to suit the intent rather than the letter of the law is a function of equitableness; but the restraint of feeling which leads us not to use our own power of inflicting

158 2 penalties is properly the function of clemency. Reason introduces balance into our anger and ensures that the retaliation it seeks is deserved, legitimate, rightly-intentioned, and not sought too fiercely. Man exer-

cises mastery of his behaviour by way of reasoned judgments; movements which arise before reason can make a judgment are not in general in man's power to prevent. Nevertheless each one in isolation could be stopped as it arose, and so they are in some way within man's power and, if disordered, can't altogether escape being sins. Anger that seeks 3 unjust retaliation is as such fatally wrong, opposed to charity and justice; but if incomplete it can be non-fatal: for example, a movement of passion forestalling our reason, or a petty tit-for-tat, tweaking a child's hair or the like. But if the anger is too fierce, it could be enough to cut us off from the love of God and our fellowmen, and then it would be fatal. Hatred is worse than envy and envy than anger, since it is worse 4 to desire evil as such than to desire it under the guise of a good; and worse to desire it for our external honour or glory than as something owed in justice. If anger meant the simple will to punish reasonably and 8 without passion, being without anger might sometimes be sinful. Since normally anger also involves some emotion and bodily disturbance, naturally consequent on that simple will, being entirely without emotional anger might also be wrong, implying absence of a will to exact reasonable retribution. The emotion of anger, like all emotions, helps man to execute promptly what his reason commands. What else is the point of emotions? In a man of ordered behaviour a reasoned judgment causes movements of will and of emotion. Absence of effects implies absence of their cause, so lack of anger can be a sign of lack of reasoned judgment. Just as equitableness can mitigate punishment and 159 1 clemency sweeten our temper to dispose us to that, so injustice can overdo punishment and cruelty give us a harshness of soul prompting us to such excess. Mercy and clemency both abhor another's distress, but mercy relieves it with good works whereas clemency reduces it by mitigating penalties. So cruelty is more directly opposed to clemency than to mercy, though sometimes cruelty means lack of mercy in the strict sense. Properly speaking, ferocity or savagery is the infliction of 2 pain not in retribution for some fault but out of delight in another's torment. And so we call it inhumanity, arising from bad custom that has corrupted our humanity. Cruelty however is excessive punishing of faults, and so not an inhuman but a human wickedness. Remission of punishment is wrong only if it disregards the order of justice that crimes ought to be punished. It is opposed to cruelty, which is an excessive regard for such an order; savagery, note, pays no attention to justice at all.

160 2 **Modesty: humility, studiousness, decent behaviour.** Modesty
covers restraint in all matters not too resistant to restraint. This excludes
tactile pleasures which present a special challenge and are the matter of
a special virtue, moderation. And Cicero also excluded clemency. So
modesty is left covering humility, which restrains our desire for self-
excellence, studiousness which restrains curiosity, and all restraint in
external display.

161 1   Our desires for difficult and challenging goods need virtue in two
different ways: to moderate and restrain desire lest it tend too high
(humility's function), and to stiffen our spirit against hopelessness, and
hearten it to push forward with great things in accordance with right
reason (and this is the function of enterprise). **Humility** restrains desire
from unreasonable heights; enterprise encourages it to reasonable ones.
So they are not contraries, but cooperate in the pursuit of right reason.

2 By humility a man restrains himself from getting above himself, and for
this he needs to know the limit of his abilities. Knowledge of that
provides a standard for one's desires, though humility essentially is
regulated desire itself. Courage restrains our boldness and stiffens us
against fear, for the same reason: so that we will prize the good of reason
above the dangers of death. But humility restrains our presumption and
enterprise stiffens us against hopelessness for two different reasons:
enterprise aims at our own due good, of which hopelessness might
otherwise deprive us; whereas humility aims at prompting us to be
submissive to our divinely appointed place in things. So courage exploits
rather than quells our feelings of boldness, over-doing rather than underdoing them; whereas humility quells rather than exploits our self-

3 confidence, under-doing rather than over-doing it. Humility reverences
God and esteems what we have from ourselves less than what our
fellowmen have from God. It does not require us to esteem what we
have from God less than what others have from him, or what we have
from ourselves less than what they have from themselves. Though we
would always do well to admire in our fellowmen good qualities we lack,
and notice bad qualities in ourselves that others lack, and judge ourselves
less than others accordingly. Humility, like other virtues, is mainly
something within the soul. External acts of humility should be moderate,
as with other virtues, so as to avoid exposing others to the dangers of

4 pride. All virtues which restrain our affections and moderate our actions
are allied to the virtue of moderation. Mildness restrains angry feelings,
humility restrains hopes of greatness; they share a mode of action even
if they differ in their matter. Enterprise and humility however share the
same matter but have different modes of action: for enterprise is a branch

of courage, humility of moderation. Human virtue is valued for the 5 reasonable order it brings about. First in relating us to our goal, the theological virtues that set up our ultimate goal being the most important virtues. Secondarily, ordering things to this goal: reason itself [by prudence], and the faculties of desire regulated by reason [the will by justice, our emotions by courage and moderation]. The communal order is laid down by justice, especially legal justice, and men are made submissive to this order by humility in general and by other virtues in particular. So we can rank humility immediately after justice in this order of virtues. The reason Christ especially recommended humility to us is because it most effectively removes the main obstacle to our spiritual welfare, the preoccupation with earthly greatness that holds us back from striving for spiritual and heavenly things. Humility frees and disposes us to receive God's blessing: charity and the other virtues which will move us directly to God and are therefore more to be prized than humility.

Pride is wanting to get above oneself. Right reason sets one's will on 162 1 what is appropriate to oneself, so pride goes against reason and that is sinful: *to act unreasonably is an evil of soul*. Pride directly opposes humility, which shares the same matter as enterprise. The function of enterprise is to push on against hopelessness to great things, the function of humility to restrain our presumption from pushing on too far. Petty-mindedness, if it means failing to will great things, is a defect in enterprise; and if it means attachment to things below our level it is a defect in humility. Pride on the other hand opposes both these virtues by excess: humility by disdain of submissiveness, enterprise by disordered desire for greatness. But since pride implies uppishness it is more directly opposed to humility, whilst smallmindedness is more directly opposed to enterprise. Pride is a special sin with a special object: a disordered 2 desire for one's own excellence. But it has a certain generality inasmuch as it can give rise to every other sin: directly, since all sins can be made to serve the goal of our own excellence, and indirectly, since pride breeds contempt for God's law which keeps us from sin. Not that pride is always the source of our sins, but it can be on occasion; sins often arise from contempt of the law, but also from ignorance and from weakness. Transgressing a commandment of God is often called an act of pride even when the affection of pride is not present. Pride directly destroys humility, being its direct opposite; but it can corrupt all virtues by making them excuses for pride. Pride has a challenging object – our 3 own excellence – and so is an unbalance in our aggressive attitudes; if the challenge was only to the senses these attitudes would be simply

emotions, but since the challenge is also spiritual, pride is also something
5 you can will: the demons sinned by pride. Humility is submissiveness
to God; pride lacks that submissiveness and raises itself above the level
God has set us. This is a turning away from God, so pride is as such a
fatal sin, though some movements of pride can be non-fatal if reason
6 has not consented to them. What pride aims at is not in itself the most
unvirtuous thing there is; but in acting it turns away from God, and not
just out of ignorance or weakness, or coincidentally because it is seeking
something else, but precisely as not wanting to submit to God's order.
In other sins turning away from God is a sort of consequence, but it is
essential in pride. So from this aspect pride outmatches all other sins.

163 1   Many elements conspire in a sin, and the primary one will be the one
that first introduces disorder. That will be an inner movement of soul,
rather than an external bodily movement, and a movement to a goal
rather than to what serves the goal. So a first sin is always a first desire
for a disordered goal. Now Adam's flesh in the state of innocence could
not rebel against his spirit, so the first disorder could not be unreasonable
desire of some sense-good, but has to be disordered desire for something
spiritual. Adam had to desire some spiritual good without regard to
God's order, and that was an act of pride. He didn't desire to disobey
as such; he couldn't do that unless his will was already disordered by a
desire of his own excellence. Pride caused his disobedience. Gluttony
played a part in the sin of our first parents: *The woman saw that the tree
was good to eat and pleasing to the eye.* But the prime motive was not the
tree's goodness and beauty, but the serpent's persuasion: *Your eyes shall
be opened and you shall be like gods*, and by desiring this the woman fell
into pride. So the sin of gluttony derived from the sin of pride. The
itch to know was caused in our first parents by their disordered desire
for excellence. So when the serpent said *You shall be like gods* he added
2 *knowing good and evil*. Adam sinned primarily in wanting to be like God
in knowing good and evil: he wanted to determine by his own natural
powers what was good and what was bad for him to do, or he wanted
to predict his own future destiny for good or for evil. And secondarily
he wanted to be like God in power, making his own happiness by his
own natural power, as the devil had also wanted to do.

164 1   In his original state man was divinely graced so that as long as his
mind remained submissive to God the lower powers of his soul remained
submissive to his reason, and his body to his soul. But when by sin his
mind ceased to submit itself to God, as a consequence his lower powers
lost their total submission to reason (hence the rebelliousness of our
flesh) and his body lost its total submissiveness to his soul (hence death

and all our bodily weaknesses). Just as we count rebelliousness of the flesh against the spirit as a penalty of our first parents' sin, so also death and bodily defects. Death is not natural to man's form, but man's body is composed of warring elements, and in this respect death is natural. This condition is not appropriate to his form, but is a necessary consequence of the human body having to be an organ of the sense of touch; just as the liability of a saw to rust doesn't suit its purpose but is a necessary consequence of the material needed to make it hard. The rustiness was not chosen by the maker of the saw. God, however, who makes man, is all-powerful. So, when he first created man, he exempted him by grace from the death which necessarily accompanied the matter he was made from. The sin of our first parents removed that grace, so that death is now both a natural condition of the matter we are made from, and a penalty resulting from loss of God's preserving gift. Our first parents were created by God not simply as individual persons but as progenitors from whom the whole of mankind was to derive its human nature, together with the grace that was to preserve it from death. By their sin the whole of mankind was deprived of this grace and sentenced to death. Sin has two sorts of deleterious effect. Firstly, the penalties imposed by a judge, which must bear equally on all who are equally guilty. And secondly the consequent indirect effects, such as the falls that a man blinded for his crime will experience. Such effects are not proportionate to the crime, and no human judge can foresee them or take them into account. The proportionate penalty for the first sin of man was the withdrawal of the gift which conserved human nature's original rightness and wholeness. But the indirect effects were the deaths and other penalties of our present life, not equally borne by all subject to the first sin. God however knows the future, and the diversity of these penalties in different people accords with his foreknowledge and providence: they do not, as Origen thought, follow on our deserts in some previous life, but either they result from faults of our parents or God intends them as medicines for our welfare.

Study is close mental application to anything: firstly, knowledge, and 166 1 secondly, anything knowledge can control. Just as men's bodies naturally 2 desire food and sex, men's souls desire knowledge. The moderation of this desire is the function of **studiousness**, a virtue allied to moderation and included under modesty. Mental virtues ensure the goodness of the act of knowing as such, that it knows truly; but studiousness is a moral virtue ensuring a right desire in the use of knowledge. The soul has an urge to know, and the body an inclination to shirk the effort involved. So studiousness must restrain the first urge lest it become immoderate,

and encourage an eagerness to work for it; and it is from this last that its name has come, though the first function is nearer its essence as a
167 1 virtue, a branch of moderation. The studious desire to know truth can be unbalanced: either because it is directed towards something which is incidentally bad for us (an occasion of pride, or something teaching us bad ways), or because the desire itself is disordered, distracting us from necessities towards trivialities, or seeking knowledge from unlawful sources, or seeking to know creatures without reference to God, or
2 seeking knowledge beyond our capacities. Sense-knowledge has two purposes: bodily welfare (a purpose shared with animals) and the service of theoretical and practical intellectual knowledge (a purpose peculiar to man). So we may sin with a curiosity of the senses in two ways: when our knowledge serves no useful purpose, and when it serves a harmful purpose (eyeing a woman with lust in mind, or watching the behaviour of others with the intention of calumny). Curiosity seeks the pleasures of knowledge that accompany all the senses; lust and gluttony the tactile pleasures that accompany the use of certain things.

168 1   Our outward gestures betray our inward disposition: *the apparel on our bodies, the smile on our face, the way we walk, all show what we are.* Insofar as such gestures are directed towards others they must be controlled by friendliness and affability; insofar as they express our
2 inward dispositions they must be controlled by truthfulness. Just as we relieve bodily tiredness by bodily rest, so we relieve tiredness of soul by pleasure, which is rest to the soul. We take a break from serious intent and take refuge in words and deeds which are playful and humorous, giving us the pleasure we seek. Ambrose condemned jocularity in theology, but not in all social converse: *Jokes are decent and pleasant in their place, but not in church, just as not in scripture.* What we actually do in play has no other goal; but the accompanying pleasure serves the
3 soul's recreation and rest. Play can go over the top if it becomes obscene or harmful to our fellowmen, or if the circumstances are wrong. And if we then persist in it to the detriment of God 's love and commandments
4 it could be a fatal sin. But it is also unreasonable to be a burden to others, never agreeable but always a wet blanket, *never saying anything nonsensical and reacting grumpily when others do.* Aristotle calls such people rough boors. But rest and pleasure are not themselves the goal of human life; they serve living. Too little play is not as bad as too
1 much; like salt, one needs only a little to give savour to life. The way we dress represents our state in life, and excess, defect and balance
2 in these matters involves truthfulness. This applies to women's adornments too although something special is involved here: the attracting of

men. This can be done lawfully as when women set out to please their husbands, or unlawfully as when an unmarried woman tries to provoke sexual desire. That would be a fatal sin, unless it were done simply from frivolity or a little boasting. And the same applies to men too. It is one thing to pretend to a beauty one doesn't possess, and another to hide some ugliness that has arisen from disease or the like. That is lawful.

Chapter 12

SPECIAL WALKS OF LIFE

[vol 45] We have been considering in detail the virtues and vices common to all men in all walks of life. Now we turn to what distinguishes the moral acts and dispositions of particular men: *diversity in charisms*, i.e. graces freely given to some; *diversity in activities*, some leading active and some contemplative lives; and *diversity in ministries*, i.e. in function and status. [vol 45]

> **Introductory comment.** Chapters 10 and 11 discussed the general shape human life should take, the activities and dispositions required in all men pursuing unity with God as their goal. Now we consider the special shapes life takes in certain individuals, shapes dictated by the special roles those individuals play in the organized pursuit of the general goal by mankind as a whole. For the quotations about diversity of charisms and activities and ministries come from chapter 14 of St Paul's first letter to the Corinthians, where he argues that spiritual gifts are given to individuals for the good of the church as a whole: that the church is an organized body in which the particular functions of each limb and organ are designed for the whole body's welfare. There are indeed different charisms, but all are gifts of the one Spirit; different activities, but all the working of one God; different ways of serving, but one Lord.
>
> The **charisms** referred to are the graces freely given, which were distinguished in chapter 9 from the grace which makes pleasing: gifts of tongues, of healing, of interpretation, all of which, as St Paul says, are worthless to the individual without charity. Thomas regards all these charisms as subsidiary to the gift of *prophecy*. Prophets are seen as the church's main organ of revelation, beneficiaries of a transient sharing in the light of glory which will be the permanent possession of those who see God face to face in heaven. The word *prophecy*, Thomas admits, suggests a sort of obscure seeing and saying of faraway things, clad in symbols, bearing on the contingent future. But the theologically purer centre

of prophecy consists primarily not in visions or imaginations, though these may accompany it, but in the ability to judge things in God's light of judgment; the prophet may even be unaware of his gift, though Thomas argues that the great prophets through whom the church received its revelation must have had explicit awareness, proclaiming their vision in words and working miracles to give it authority. This treatment of prophecy provides the missing link, so to speak, between Thomas's discussions of faith (chapter 10), of theology (Introduction), and of how the blessed see God in heaven (ch 1 pp 26ff). Thomas sees the prophet's gift as a transient share in the heavenly vision, proclaimed to the rest of the church for their acceptance in faith. It serves the good of the church, but not necessarily the good of the prophets themselves: prophecy might conceivably go together with wickedness though this would be inappropriate.

The next part of the chapter deals with the different ways of life of actively-inclined *Martha*s and contemplatively-inclined *Mary*s, and might seem to be about temperament more than anything else. But there is a message for the church as a whole, which in the course of its history has developed many bands of people living predominantly active lives or predominantly contemplative ones. There has been an inclination to play these lives off against one another – Thomas in the next part of this chapter will decide that those who band together to teach (like his own band of Dominican friars) have the best of this argument, because they have to be contemplatives sharing the fruit of their contemplation with others; they combine the intimacy of a contemplative life with God (which Thomas conceives of as not simply knowledge but a love of God's truth, bringing with it moral virtues) with the merit of an active life of charity, planning good for others. Perhaps the true message is that all these groups are dependent upon one another and organs of the one body of Christ: that the full active life of the church demands that some go into the desert in order that others may gain spiritual support to go into the city, and that some go into the city to provide physical support for the contemplatives.

The final part of the chapter talks of different ways of serving or ministering in the church. Here one could expect some discussion of the administration of the church perhaps, but this is separated off early as a matter of function and rank. The functions of administering the sacraments are reserved for later discussion (though the author died before he could fulfil that promise); and other administrative matters are left to the canon lawyers. So what we are left with is a discussion of two **states of life** – that of bishops, and that of religious. These are called states because bound to special levels of perfection, and this is explained by reference to what was then secularly understood as state or status: namely, being a freeman or a serf. The state of perfection as Thomas understands it is not simply the perfection to which all Christians are bound – loving God above all things and our fellow-men as ourselves; nor is it the perfection possible only in heaven – total undistracted active loving all the time. Indeed the state of perfection is not a state of being perfect as such, but of binding and devoting oneself to pursue perfection, a vowed enslavement to a life of love and freedom, by masters of the art (the bishops!) and apprentices (vowed religious). This requires Thomas to distinguish God's commandments and his counsels of perfection (the vows of voluntary poverty, perpetual continence and obedience), to discuss the morality of taking vows at all and the immorality of letting children take them, to see the bishop not simply as an administrator or a priest *par excellence* but as a man vowed totally to pastoral care of others as religious are vowed totally to develop themselves in God's service. There are also discussions of more mundane matters such as the amount of money that bishops and religious can reasonably amass, all of it deriving from bitter wrangles in Thomas's own time about the relative merits of religious and pastorally-devoted lives.

Charisms

171 1 **Prophecy.**   Some charisms freely given relate to knowledge, some to words, some to deeds. Those relating to knowledge can be summed up in the word *prophecy*: *Those we now call prophets were once called seers.* Prophecy consists first and foremost in knowing certain far-off things outside the normal knowledge of men. But secondarily it involves speech, since a prophet proclaims to others what God has taught him in order to build them up. And finally prophets sometimes work miracles to confirm their prophecies. The prophet must first be lifted up and inspired by the Holy Spirit to attend to God; then the prophecy is completed by revelation, the removal of the veils of darkness and

ignorance so that the prophet can see what God is revealing. Bodily eyes 2 need physical light to reveal things and the mind needs a mental light, the revelation being proportionate to the light which causes it. Since prophecy involves knowledge beyond the power of natural reason it needs light beyond the natural light of reason to make it knowable: *when I sit in darkness the Lord will be my light*. But light can be present permanently as in the sun, or transiently as in the atmosphere. The prophetic light is transient: prophets can't always prophesy. A permanent light would enlighten the principles and grounds of what it revealed; but in prophecy that is God himself, and he is seen in substance by only the blessed in heaven, where the same light is permanent. In prophets the light is a passing light: *the Lord will pass before you*; and just as the atmosphere needs continuous illumination from the sun, so prophets need fresh revelation continually, like apprentices who have not yet mastered the principles of their art and need everything explained to them. The very way scripture talks of prophecy shows it: *God spoke to the prophets*, or *the word of the Lord came to them*, or *the Lord's hand was upon them*. Clearly prophecy is not a lasting disposition in the prophet. Nevertheless in prophetic knowledge the mind of man is illuminated by God's light in the way a man's receptive mind is illuminated by his own active mind in natural knowledge. Though even when the prophet's mind is not actually being illuminated, he is still called a prophet because he has been deputed to prophesy by God: *I appointed you as a prophet to the nations*. Every gracious gift of God raises men to something beyond their nature: sometimes to do something substantially beyond human nature (like working miracles, or knowing the hidden mysteries of God's wisdom) and then the gift is not a lasting disposition; sometimes to do at a supra-natural level something not substantially beyond nature (like loving God or knowing him through the mirror of creation) and for that men receive lasting dispositions of grace. Prophetic knowledge relies on 3 God's light in which all things are visible, human and divine, bodily and spiritual, so that anything whatever can be the subject of prophetic revelation. But the further away something is from ordinary human knowing the more appropriate it is as a subject of prophecy. A first level of such things consists of things unknown to some though not unknown to all; a second level consists of things beyond the knowledge of all men, but because of man's, not the things', deficiencies (as for example the mystery of the Trinity); and a final level consists of things unknowable in themselves, such as future events which may yet happen or not happen since their truth is not yet determined. So it is in the revelation of future events that prophecy above all consists and to which it owes its name. But in a broad sense the subject of prophecy is whatever man knows by God's revelation. It differs from other charisms such as wisdom and knowledge and understanding of speech, the subjects of which man can know by natural reason, though not as perfectly as by God's light. It differs also from faith which, though concerned with things beyond human knowledge, doesn't know them, but unshakeably assents to them because God knows them. Knowing such things by God's light defines prophecy as distinct from everything else, and gives it a single identity despite the diversity of things God's light can reveal.

4   To understand in depth the starting-point of some area of knowledge is to know all that can be derived from that starting-point. But when we don't know the starting-point, or know it only superficially, then the area is known only in part. Now the starting-point of prophetic knowledge is the first Truth, God himself, who remains invisible to prophets as such. So a prophet doesn't automatically know everything that can be the subject of prophecy, but only what is specially revealed to him

5   on some occasion. God enlightens prophets either by explicit revelation or by *a mysterious inner stimulus which human minds undergo without even knowing it*. What prophets know by explicit revelation they know most surely, certain that it is revealed to them by the spirit of God; so that the faith that relies on what prophets say can itself be certain. (An indication of the certitude produced is Abraham's readiness to sacrifice his only son because of a prophetic vision, a thing he could never have done unless the certainty of God's revelation had been absolute). But when prophets know something by hidden stimulus they sometimes can't decide whether they thought of it on their own or because God

6   prompted them. Prophecy is knowledge imprinted on the prophet's mind by the teaching of God's revelation. Now the teacher, in sharing what he knows with his student, shares whatever truth it has. So a prophet's knowledge and proclamation shares in the truth of God's own knowledge, which is infallible. But God's foreknowledge relates to future events in two ways: he sees them as they exist in themselves, present to him; and he sees them as they exist in their causes, seeing how those causes will produce those effects. Now although contingent future events when existing in themselves must determinately be what they are, in their causes they are not yet determined and may turn out differently. Prophetic revelation sometimes shares one type of knowledge and sometimes the other, and in the first case what is prophesied will happen, but in the second it may not. That is not to say the prophecy is false: for the meaning of the prophecy in that case is that the worldly causes (natural or human) of the event are disposed to bring it about. Jonah

prophesying *Yet forty days and Nineveh will be destroyed* meant that Nineveh deserved such a fate; but, metaphorically speaking, God repented this decision, in the sense that he changed the way things worked out though not his plan.

Prophets don't have to have the love of charity. Prophecy is in the 172 4 mind, and the mind's activity precedes the will's which charity perfects. Moreover, prophecy, like other charisms freely given, serves the church, and is not for the benefit of the individual prophet's unity of heart with God in charity. So prophecy doesn't depend on any roots of moral goodness. Nevertheless morally wicked feelings and behaviour can hinder it; for a prophet's mind must be lifted up wholly to the contemplation of spiritual things, and strong passions and inordinate concern for external things are obstacles to that.

In knowing something we first take in its representation, and by 173 2 means of that we judge it. Now a thing is represented first to our senses, then to our imagination, and finally to our receptive mind, which takes in the thing's species as abstracted by the light of our agent mind from our images. Our imagination contains forms taken in from things we have sensed, and transformations of these induced either by some bodily agency (as when we dream or hallucinate), or by our own reason putting together images to help us understand something. But our power to judge comes from the light of our mind. The gift of prophecy raises man's mind above its natural ability in both ways: it instils a more powerful mental light to judge by, and it provides the mind with further species representing things. Human teaching resembles prophecy only in the latter function: a teacher represents things to his students with words, but he cannot like God instil light from within. This instilling of light is the most important element in prophecy, since knowledge is only complete when we can judge. So no one is accounted a prophet simply because God has represented something to him in an image (like Pharaoh or Nebuchadnezzar) or by a bodily likeness (like Belshazzar), but only when God enlightens his mind to make judgments. Even enlightenment to judge something others have imagined is enough to make a man a prophet: Joseph, for example, expounded the dreams of the Pharaoh. When God does represent things to a prophet's mind he does it either by way of the external senses (Daniel saw the writing on the wall), or by way of images directly imprinted on the imagination (a blind man shown colours) or put together from other images (as Jeremiah *saw a pot boiling over from the north*), or finally by way of species directly imprinted in the mind itself (as Solomon and the apostles received instilled knowledge and wisdom). And when God instils a light in the prophet's mind, this may enable him to judge what others have seen (Joseph and the apostles interpreting the speech of others), to judge what he has naturally observed, or to decide truly and effectively what ought to be done. Prophetic revelation, then, is sometimes instilling of a light, and sometimes a new imprinting or arrangement of representations.

3   Clearly if something is to be represented to the prophet through his external senses he mustn't be in an abstracted state. Nor must he be abstracted from his external senses when receiving an inner mental light or a new species in the mind, since men complete judgments by coming back' to what is the starting-point of their knowledge, the senses. But when prophetic revelation is made through inner sense-images prophets must be in an abstracted state, so that they don't mistake the images for things externally sensed. The abstraction is total when the prophet is insensible, and partial when outer sensing cannot be properly distinguished from inner imagination. In prophets such abstraction occurs in natural ways, through sleep or the trances induced by intense contemplation, without any natural disorder such as characterizes those possessed or hallucinating.

4   When the Spirit stimulates prophets to judge or grasp something, sometimes he stimulates them simply to grasp it, but at other times also to recognize what they grasp as revelation from God. Similarly when he moves them to speak, sometimes they understand what the Spirit means by their words (as David did) and sometimes they don't (as Caiphas didn't). And when moved to do something, sometimes they understand what they do (as Jeremiah did) and sometimes not (as with the soldiers dividing up Christ's garments). When the understanding is missing the prophecy is not fully prophecy, but a sort of prophetic stimulus; though because the minds of prophets are always imperfect tools of the Spirit, even true prophets don't understand everything the Spirit intends by their visions and words and deeds.

174 2   Prophecy involves a sort of obscurity and remoteness in the truth seen by the mind, and that is why it is more usual to call those who see by imaginative visions prophets, despite the fact that prophecy seen in

3   the mind is more estimable, given the same revealed truth. The lowest level of prophecy is when someone is interiorly stimulated to external activity, like Samson. The second level is when someone is interiorly enlightened to know what is naturally knowable, like Solomon. But these two levels fall short of prophecy properly so–called, because they don't attain supernatural truth. When prophecies do reveal such truth through images we rate waking visions above dreams, the hearing of words that

express the truth above the seeing of symbols of it, especially if the speaker is seen in the guise of a man or an angel or, better still, as God himself. But above all these there is a third level of prophecy in which the supernatural truth is communicated without images; although this surpasses prophecy as we normally use the word.

Proclamation of prophecy is done both by word and deed, but such proclamation, like the working of miracles, is secondary to prophecy itself. So in prophecy there is first knowledge, mentally or imaginatively 4 presented, then proclamation, then miracle-working. Moses was the most excellent of prophets in all three respects. *He saw God clearly, not as in a mirror*; and *the Lord spoke to him face to face, as a man speaks to a friend.* He proclaimed what he knew to the whole believing people as God's mouthpiece, and original propounder of God's law. And he worked miracles on a whole people of unbelievers: *never has there arisen in Israel a prophet the equal of Moses, whom the Lord knew face to face, in all the signs and wonders that God sent him to do in the land of Egypt.* Prophecy, the basis of our faith in the one true God, grew through three 6 periods: before the law, under the law, and under grace. In each period the greatest revelation came first: before the law the revelation to Abraham, in whose time men had begun to fall away from faith in one God and into idolatry; under the law the revelation to Moses, which formed the basis of all subsequent prophecy; and in the time of grace the revelation to the apostles of the God who is three in one, on which the whole faith of the church is based. As to faith in the incarnation of Christ, in general the closer prophets were to Christ, before or after, the more instructed they were; but after more than before.

Charisms related to prophecy.   What we carry away we transport 175 1 by some external force against its natural inclination; so we talk of a soul being carried away when it is carried out of its natural way of grasping truth through the senses. Such abstraction from the senses need not lead to any knowledge we couldn't achieve naturally, but it doesn't happen naturally (in contrast to sleep) and must have some external cause, sometimes physical (as with people out of their mind), sometimes demonic (as with those possessed), and sometimes God, as when Ezechiel says that *the Spirit lifted me up between earth and sky and transported me in visions of God to Jerusalem.* That man can be raised to God's level is a mark of his natural excellence, made in God's image; but because God's goodness infinitely surpasses man's abilities, to achieve it man needs the supra-natural help which God provides in his gift of grace. So when God carries man's mind away, that is not against man's

3 nature, but simply beyond his nature's abilities. Man can be mentally carried away by God to contemplate his truth in images and likenesses, as Peter was in a trance, or to understand God in his works, as David was, or to see God's own substance, as Moses and Paul were. Fittingly enough, Moses was the first teacher of the Jews, and Paul the first teacher of the gentile nations. Created minds can see God's substance only by that light of glory which dwells permanently in the blessed in heaven and transiently affected Paul in his ecstasy, as it does prophets.

5 Because soul is the natural form matter takes on in men, souls naturally understand by means of images; and this natural state of things is not altered by ecstasy. As long as the ecstasy endures, there is no actual turning to images and sense-objects, lest the soul be hindered from rising to what lies beyond all imagery; but Paul's ecstasy didn't mean his soul stopped being the form of his body, only that his mind was abstracted from the perception of images and sense-objects. Our nutritive and vegetative powers do not need attention and control as our sense-powers do, but operate by nature; so ecstasy doesn't abstract us from those activities, but only from the sense-activity that would distract our attention from what our mind is seeing.

176 1 Christ chose his first disciples to go out into the whole world preaching everywhere faith in him; so they needed from God a gift of tongues or languages. Just as God *scattered their languages* when the nations started to turn to idolatry, so his gift of languages served as a remedy to recall

2 them to the worship of the one God. The gift of prophecy is a greater gift than that of languages. Languages are means of expressing truth in signs, prophecy enlightens the mind itself to know that truth. Prophecy gives knowledge not just of words but of things, and as such it is more useful: speaking in tongues doesn't profit the church unless there is someone to interpret, nor does it profit the speaker himself. And unbelievers thought the disciples mad or drunk when they spoke in tongues, whereas prophets would have impressed them by telling them the secrets

177 1 of their own hearts. The gift of tongues is the gift of speaking so as to be understood by many peoples, but what St Paul calls the gift of utterance is the gift of speaking effectively so as to instruct, delight

2 and persuade one's listeners. St Paul says it is not for women to utter publicly before the whole church: partly because the female sex was made submissive to the male, as Genesis says, and public instruction and persuasion is a task for leaders not subjects; partly lest men's sexual desires be aroused; and partly since women generally haven't the fullness of wisdom required for public instruction. The grace of prophecy enlightens the mind, and knows no difference of male or female, as St

Paul says; but utterance concerns public instruction of others, and there
sex is relevant. Women exercise what wisdom or knowledge they have
in private instruction of their children, not in public teaching. The 178 1
knowledge a prophet receives from God must be communicated to
others through the gifts of languages and of utterance, and that utterance
must be confirmed as believable by the **working of miracles**: God
confirming the message with attendant signs.

Ways of life

The life of every living thing is displayed in the activity specially [vol 46] 179 1
appropriate to it on which it is bent: plants feed and propagate, animals
feel and move, men understand and act rationally. And among men the
life of an individual man seems to consist in what delights him and
occupies him most: the life he most wishes *to share with his friends.* Since
for some men this is chiefly contemplation of truth, and for others chiefly
external activity, we distinguish two main styles of human life: active
and contemplative. Aristotle also mentions *the life of pleasure* which 2
places its goal in the bodily pleasures we share with animals. At present
however we are concerned only with styles of truly human life. All
human occupations that serve the needs of the present life in reasonable
ways are classed as active lives, all those that serve our craving for
pleasure are classed as lives of pleasure, and all those that pursue truth
are classed as contemplative.

In essence the contemplative life is a life of mental activity, but what 180 1
stimulates us to live in this way is our will which activates all our powers
including mind. St Gregory identifies the contemplative life with the
love of God inflaming us to gaze on his beauty. Since achieving what
you love gives delight, the contemplative life leads to delight and
affection which in turn intensify our love. Aristotle says that con- 2
sideration of truth doesn't play much part in moral virtue, and he assigns
such virtue to the active rather than the contemplative life. But moral
virtues are dispositions to the contemplative life: for the essential activity
of that life, contemplation, is hindered both by strong passions which
distract our attention from mind to sense, and by external worries. The
moral virtues restrain such passions and quell worries arising from
external concerns. Beauty consists in a certain clarity and due
proportion, and both derive from mind as source of light and order. So
beauty is an essential feature of the contemplative life, which consists
in activity of mind. But the moral virtues also share in reason's order

and beauty, especially moderation which restrains those cravings which most obscure the light of reason. That is why chastity above all prepares a man for contemplation, since sex-pleasure is the main thing attracting

3 man's mind to the sensual level. The goal activity of the contemplative life is the contemplation of truth, but there are several activities which prepare for this: activities which imbibe the principles on which our contemplation will rest, and activities which derive truths we seek

4 to know from such principles. Contemplation is first and foremost contemplation of God's truth, the goal of all human life. But we are led to such contemplation by observing what God does in the world, so contemplation of God's works belongs to the contemplative life in a secondary way, and leads us to know God. Four elements then contribute to the contemplative life: the moral virtues, the activities preparing contemplation, the contemplation of God's works, and the contemplation of God himself.

5   No person living this life can contemplate the very substance of God, if by living this present life we mean actually using our bodily senses. But if we are living this life only in the sense that our soul is present in our body as its form, though we are carried away in ecstasy so that we are not actually using our senses or imagination, then the highest degree of contemplation in this present life is indeed the contemplation of God's substance in ecstasy, in the way Paul saw it, existing so to

7 speak half-way between the present and the future lives. Contemplation delights us in two ways. First, the activity itself is delightful, agreeable to man's nature as a rational animal, and to the dispositions of wisdom and knowledge which facilitate contemplation. Secondly, the object contemplated gives delight, because it is so lovable: contemplation's principal object is God to whom we are attracted by the love of charity. The ultimate fulfilment of the contemplative life therefore lies not in merely seeing God's truth but loving it.

181 1   Moral virtues do not pursue contemplation of truth, but the planning of action; as Aristotle says, knowing influences virtue very little. Clearly then virtue belongs essentially to the active life, and leads, as Aristotle

3 also says, to happiness in action. Teaching is something done by word of mouth, an audible expression of ideas in the mind. One object of teaching is what is in the mind, and in that respect teaching may belong either to the active life (if it is teaching of what to do) or to the contemplative life (if it is teaching of a truth to be considered and enjoyed). The second object of teaching is the hearer of the teacher's words, and in this respect teaching is an external activity belonging to

4 the active life. In the future life the blessed cease to occupy themselves

with external activity, and any external activity that does exist will be at the service of contemplation.

Aristotle gives many reasons for preferring the contemplative to the 182 1 active life. It agrees with what is best in man, his mind, and with its most appropriate objects, the things mind can understand; whereas the active life is busy with external things. The contemplative life can be loved for its own sake, whereas the active life is directed to something other than itself. Moreover, the contemplative life concerns itself with God, but the active life with human affairs. In a secondary sense, however, the active life should be preferred in certain circumstances because of present need. As Aristotle says: *It is better to pursue wisdom than riches, though riches are more useful when you are in need.* Con- 2 templative life directly and immediately relates to love of God; the active life to love of our fellowmen. So contemplative life is more deserving of its nature. Nevertheless it can happen that one person may deserve more from his active works than another from his contemplative activities; for example, when someone out of a fullness of love of God consents to separate himself for a time from the pleasures of contemplating divine things in order to fulfil God's will and give God glory. Inasmuch as the 3 active life occupies itself with external activities it clearly hinders the contemplative life, because one can't at the same time be occupied with external activity and free for contemplation of God. But inasmuch as the active life integrates and controls the interior emotions it fosters the contemplative life, which would be hindered by disordered emotion.

States of life

The notion of a state of life.   We don't count as a state of life any 183 1 condition that is external or easily changed: being rich or poor, a dignitary or an ordinary citizen. A state of life implies some obligation, some area in which a man is or is not his own master, and that in some permanent way, not transiently or trivially. The notions of freedom and slavery are relevant to such states: properly a man's state of life is determined by whether he is free or enslaved, in the spiritual or the civil order. Functions in life are defined by some activity to be performed, ranks by divisions into high and low, states of life by some stable situation persons are in. There are different functions and states in the 2 church. Firstly, the perfection of the church requires that the fullness of grace found in Christ, the one head, should be variously distributed through the members of his body: *Some he established as apostles, others as prophets, some as preachers of the gospel, others as shepherds and teachers,*

to give fullness to his holy people. Secondly, the proper performance of the functions of the church requires that different functions be assigned to different people, so that everything can be clearly and efficiently executed: *as our one body has many organs with different functions, so we, being many, constitute one body in Christ.* And thirdly, the beauty and dignity of the church gains from such order. Diversity of states and functions in the church doesn't hinder its unity; indeed that is rather perfected by faith, love and mutual ministry to one another: *from him the whole body is compact* in faith, *joined* in love, *through all its supporting links,* one member serving another. The various members are at peace within the body of the church, brought into harmony by the power of the Spirit which gives the body life. The distinctions of state and function help to preserve this peace, by involving many people in public activity: *God so orders things that no divisions occur in the body, but the*
3 *members care for one another.* So diversity among the members of the church contributes to its perfection, its efficient functioning and its beauty. The states of life relate to diversity in perfection, the offices to diversity of function, and the beauty of the church is enhanced by the levels or ranks occurring in each state and office. Styles of life are distinguished by activities proper to individuals in themselves; the offices of the church by activities which serve others.

4   States of life in the church relate to our freedom and slavery, with respect both to sin and to justice. We are constituted *slaves to sin* or *slaves to justice* by dispositions which incline us to evil or to good. We are free from sin when not enslaved by inclinations to evil; free from justice when not restrained from evil by love of justice. Natural reason inclines us to justice rather than sin, so freedom from sin is true freedom, enslaving us to justice, inclining man to what is appropriate to his human nature. True slavery is slavery to sin and freedom from justice, and hinders us from what is humanly appropriate. There are three states of spiritual freedom and slavery consequent on our own efforts: the state of beginners, the state of the practised and the state of the perfect. Here we shall concentrate on the state of perfection, to which all three states relate. The offices of the church in so far as they involve holy orders will be considered when we come to that sacrament, and in all other respects will be left to the canon lawyers.

184 1 **Perfection in Christian life.**   Charity unites us to God, the ultimate goal of man; so perfection of Christian life consists primarily in the love
2 of charity, and secondarily in the other virtues. Absolute perfection of love involves not only the whole of the lover but the whole of what is

loved, so that God, to be loved perfectly, must be loved to the full extent he could be. But only God can love God so perfectly. A lesser level of perfection is one that realizes the lover's whole capacity for loving in acts of love at every moment; and this, though not possible in this life, will be possible in heaven. A third level of perfection is possible in this life, involving the whole of the lover only in the sense of excluding everything opposed to God's love; at its least this means excluding fatal sin – a level of perfection which is required if we are to have charity and deserve eternal salvation – whilst at its highest level it will exclude everything that hinders us from directing our whole heart to God. The beginners and the practised have not yet reached this last level of perfection; and those who have reached it in this life still *offend in many ways* with non-fatal sins that are inseparable from the weakness of our present life, and which make them imperfect relative to the perfection of heaven. The state of our present life doesn't allow continuous, actual loving of either God or our individual fellowmen. It is enough if we are inclined towards all of them in general, and disposed to respond to each individual as the need arises. The first level of perfection in love of our fellows, without which charity cannot exist, is that of harbouring no affection hostile to them; but a second level is possible: more extensive (loving not only friends and acquaintances but strangers and even enemies), more intense (preferring our fellowman not only to external possessions but also to our own bodily suffering and even death), and more effective (bestowing on him not only earthly benefits but also spiritual ones and even ourself). The perfection of Christian life consists 3 essentially in charity: primarily in the love of God and secondarily in the love of our fellowmen as prescribed by the commandments of God's law. There is no boundary set beyond which love is counselled rather than commanded: *You shall love the Lord your God with your whole heart* (*wholeness is perfection*, says Aristotle), *and your fellowman as you would yourself* (that is to say, without limit). This is because *charity is the goal of law* and limits are set not on goals but on means to goals. Perfection then consists essentially in obeying God's commands. But it also makes use of God's counsels as instruments of perfection. Like the commandments these are meant to increase our love, but unlike the commandments, which command love itself and aim at removing everything incompatible with it, counsels aim at removing even things compatible with charity but which hinder its actual exercise: things like marriage, preoccupation with earthly affairs, and so on. The lowest degree of love of God consists in not loving anything as much as him: if we fell short of perfection in this sense we would fail to obey the commandment of love. Man is born with the natural perfection of being human, yet must grow. In the same way, though the very nature of charity is perfection (the love of God above all things and of nothing opposed to God) there is another perfection towards which we must grow spiritually even in this life, a perfection in which we refrain from even lawful things in order to devote ourselves more freely to God's service.

4 **States of perfection.**   Man's spiritual state as represented by his interior disposition is God's to judge; the church can only judge it as represented in his external activities. It is the diversity of men's state in this sense that contributes to the beauty of the church. Now properly speaking slaves are people obliged to give service to another, and free men people exempt from such service. So we assess someone's state of perfection not by whether he actually loves perfectly but by whether he has obliged himself to perpetual perfection with a certain external ritual solemnity. You can, of course, be perfect without being in a state of perfection in this sense, and you can be in such a state of perfection

5 without being perfect. A state of perfection is a state of perpetual obligation to perfection, ritually solemnized, such as characterizes members of religious institutes and bishops. When men embrace such a state they are not professing themselves perfect already, but declaring

6 their will to strive after perfection. People in holy orders receive power to perform certain sacred functions, but aren't on that account pledged to perfection, although the western church has joined to reception of orders a vow of continence, which is one of the elements of a state of perfection. Nor does receiving the care of souls place someone in a state of perfection; for he is not by that fact pledged by vow to care perpetually for souls, and can abandon his care, or transfer to a religious institute, even without the bishop's permission. He would not be allowed to do this if he were in a state of perfection: *no one putting his hand to the plough and looking back, is worthy of God's kingdom.* Bishops however are in a state of perfection, and cannot abandon their episcopal charge except for certain defined reasons which we shall examine, and unless they are given permission by the Pope who alone can dispense from perpetual vows. Clearly then not all people with care of souls are in a state of perfection, but only bishops. In apostolic times the names *priest* and *bishop* were used interchangeably, though, as pseudo-Denys witnesses, there was always a distinction in fact. To avoid schism the names were later separated, *bishop* naming the higher authority, and *priest* the lesser rank. (Saying priests and bishops do not differ was listed as an Arian heresy by Augustine.) Parish priests and archdeacons do not

have the primary care of souls, though they have a limited charge
committed to them by a bishop. They are not the primary incumbents
of the pastoral office, and are obliged to lay down their lives for their
sheep only to the extent that they share in the bishop's care of souls.
They possess an office relating to perfection rather than themselves
belonging to the state of perfection. Denys says bishops are the agents 7
of perfection whilst religious are recipients of it. Parish priests and 8
archdeacons possess state, orders and an office: by their state they are
non-religious, by their orders priests and deacons, by their office they
have care of souls. When we compare them to religious in sacred orders
our problem is to determine which is more important, the religious state
or the parish priest's office. We must take as criteria goodness and
difficulty. In goodness the state of the religious is preferable to the office
of the parish priest, since the religious pledges to strive for perfection
all his life long, whereas the priest or archdeacon (unlike a bishop) does
not take a lifelong pledge to the care of souls. We are comparing only
the nature of the activities involved: the love with which the activities
are performed might well make activities which are less deserving by
nature more deserving in the particular case. As to difficulty, living the
religious life is less externally dangerous than caring for souls, but
involves more rigorous and regular observances. If our comparison had
been made with religious who are lay brethren, without holy orders,
pre-eminence would clearly lie with those in orders, since they are
committed to the worthiest service of Christ himself in the sacrament
of the altar, something which requires even greater interior holiness than
the religious state. Any difficulty of the religious state arises from the
arduous character of the works performed; those who live in the world,
whatever else may be said of them, suffer difficulties from obstacles to
virtue which the religious have carefully avoided.

The episcopal state.   Three things characterize the state of a bishop: [vol 47] 185 1
his function is to care for his fellowmen – *feed my sheep*; as a consequence
he has rank; and that wins him reverence, honour and a sufficiency of
earthly goods. Clearly it would be unlawful – avaricious or ambitious –
to desire the episcopacy because of its accompanying benefits; and to
desire it for its rank would be presumptuous. And though in itself a
desire to help our fellowmen is praiseworthy and virtuous, it would
seem presumptuous to desire a bishop's pre-eminence in order to help
them as subjects unless there was some evident necessity. But it would
not be presumptuous to want to go on exercising the activities of the
office once we hold it, nor to wish to be worthy of performing such

activities, as long as it is the good work that we want, rather than the high dignity. To desire to enter the religious state is a different matter. The episcopal state presupposes perfection of life (the Lord, before committing to Peter the office of shepherd, asked him whether he loved him more than others did); but the religious state is only a road to perfection: *if you want to be perfect*, says the Lord, *go sell what you have*. Pseudo-Denys explains the difference: the bishop is leading others to perfection, the monk is being made perfect himself. The leader to perfection must be already perfect; but not so the one who is being led to perfection. It is presumptuous to consider oneself already perfect, but not to desire to move towards perfection.

2   Although simply and absolutely speaking the contemplative life is of more value than the active, and the love of God of more value than the love of fellowmen, nevertheless the good of the many is to be preferred to the good of an individual. And all the more so since the exercise of pastoral care over Christ's flock is itself loving God.

185 3   Those who choose bishops are obliged to select not the man who is best in the ordinary sense of most perfect in charity, but the man best able to rule the church, able to instruct, defend and govern it peacefully. And the man selected does not have to consider himself better than others, for that would be pride and presumption; but he should find nothing in himself that would make reception of the office unlawful.

4 The perfection of the episcopal state consists in the bishop having pledged from love of God to devote himself to the eternal welfare of his fellowmen. So he must persevere with that pastoral care as long as he is able to contribute to the welfare of those committed to his care. He must not neglect it even for the peace of contemplating God, since Paul endured even the deferment of eternal contemplation for the sake of those committed to his care. Sometimes however a bishop may be prevented from caring for his flock by some personal obstacle of conscience, health, knowledge or canonical irregularity, or by obstacles in those committed to his care, or from some third source such as scandal (though not scandal deliberately fomented to discredit the faith and justice of the church). But just as one cannot assume such an office without the mandate of higher authority, so too one can only abandon it for the above reasons when authority permits. Only the Pope can dispense a bishop from the perpetual vow he took to care for those committed to him. The perfection of the religious state is a pursuit of one's own welfare; the perfection of the episcopal state a pursuit of the welfare of one's fellowmen. As long as a bishop can serve his fellowmen's welfare it would be a step backwards to want to transfer to the religious

state and devote himself simply to his own salvation, for he has pledged
to care for others' salvation as well. When the welfare of the flock 5
requires its shepherd's presence in person he may not physically abandon
them, be it for worldly advantage or because of some threat of personal
danger: *the good shepherd gives his life for his sheep*. But if the welfare of
his subjects can be well enough looked after in his absence by someone
else, then because of personal danger or some benefit to the church a
shepherd may lawfully leave his flock.

The perfection of the Christian life does not consist essentially in 6
voluntary poverty, though that is a tool of perfection in life. There is
not necessarily greater perfection where there is greater poverty; and
indeed the highest perfection is sometimes wedded to great wealth, as
was the case with Abraham. Many bishops don't give the surplus of 7
their ecclesiastical possessions to the poor, but invest it to increase the
revenue of the church, and we might ask whether that isn't commend-
able. Now bishops, like other people, are masters of their own personal
possessions, and though they can sin by excessive attachment when
using them, reserving to themselves more than they need and not
helping others as charity requires, nevertheless they will not be bound to
restitution since the things are their own. But bishops are only stewards
and administrators of ecclesiastical possessions, and these must be used
for relief of the poor, divine worship, and the needs of the clergy. If
some are granted to the bishop's own use distinct from those assigned
to the poor and the clergy and the church's worship, then if he also
appropriates some of the latter, without doubt he is contravening his
administrative trust, sinning fatally, and is bound to restitution. But the
possessions assigned specially to his use can be treated like his own
personal possessions, and he can sin only by excessive attachment,
keeping more than he needs and not helping others as charity demands.
If however the ecclesiastical possessions are not already divided in this
way, then the bishop is himself entrusted with their distribution. Any
slight unbalance in this will not reflect on his trust, since men cannot
determine such matters with precision. But any large unbalance of which
he cannot but be aware contravenes his trust and is fatally sinful. *If that
evil servant says in his heart: My master is a long time coming* (disdaining
God's judgment), *and begins to strike his fellow-servants* (pride) *and to
eat and drink with drunkards* (luxurious living), *then that servant's master
will come unexpectedly and cut him off* (from the fellowship of good men)
and send him to join the hypocrites (in hell). Not all church possessions
should be given away to the poor, except perhaps in cases of extreme
need when, as Ambrose says, even the vessels devoted to God's worship

should be sold to ransom captives or relieve other needs of the poor. In such cases clerics would sin if they lived off ecclesiastical possessions while having patrimony of their own to support them. As long then as there is no immediate need to provide for the poor a bishop can commendably use surplus church revenue to buy other goods or invest it against future needs of the church or of the poor. But when there is an immediate necessity to help the poor, to save for the future is a superfluous and unbalanced concern of the sort forbidden by the Lord when he said *Have no concern for tomorrow*.

8   The religious state is compared to the episcopal state as learning to teaching, apprenticeship to mastery. When pupils become teachers they no longer sit on the student benches, though they must go on reading and meditating, in fact even more than before. So a religious who becomes a bishop remains obliged to whatever religious observances are compatible with his episcopal office and will help to safeguard its perfection (continence, poverty, etc); and as a sign of that obligation he should continue to wear his religious habit. But he is not bound to observances incompatible with his office (solitude, silence, rigorous fasts and vigils which might render him incapable of fulfilling his duties). And he can dispense himself from other observances in the way religious superiors do, as personal need or the demands of office or the customs of those he lives with dictate.

186 1 **The religious state.**   Religion is a virtue by which we offer God things in service and worship. So those people are called *religious* in a special sense who consecrate themselves entirely to God's service as though they were burnt offerings to God. And the religious state, in this sense, is a state of perfection, by reason of the goal intended. It is not required of people in the religious state of life that they should be already
  2 perfect, but that they aim at perfection. Essential to perfection is the perfect observance of the command to love. And since whatever flows from perfect love – blessing men who curse you, for example – is a consequence of perfection, we are commanded to be ready to do such things when necessary, and a superabounding charity will do them even without necessity. Finally, there are certain tools of perfection, such as poverty, continence, abstinence and so forth. Perfection of charity is the goal of the religious state, which is a kind of training and practice for attaining such perfection. So someone entering the religious state is not already obliged to possess perfect love, but he is pledged to tend towards it and work to achieve it. Nor is he obliged already to the full consequences of perfection, though he is obliged to aim at fulfilling

them; he would not sin by omitting to do them, but he would by disdaining even to aim at them. Neither is he obliged to every practice that disposes to perfection, but only to those laid down explicitly in the religious rule he professes; just as somebody entering a school does not profess to be learned already but must be willing to study to acquire learning. Not observing certain counsels involves a man's whole life in worldly affairs: having personal possessions, getting married, and other things which the essential vows of religious life exclude. So religious oblige themselves to observe such counsels. But other counsels concerning particular activities that have extra goodness can be ignored without involving a man in worldly affairs, and to the observance of such counsels religious are not obliged.

The foundation for perfect love is **voluntary poverty**, whereby one 3 lives without any private property: *if you want to be perfect, go and sell what you have and give it to the poor, and come, follow me.* Involuntary poverty holds spiritual dangers, and men fall into many sins striving to escape it. Though the desire to accumulate riches is usually stronger in those who already possess them. It is difficult to preserve charity in the midst of riches: *a rich man finds it hard to enter the kingdom of heaven.* This is said about the mere possession of riches; someone who loves riches, according to Chrysostom, will find charity impossible: *it is easier for a camel to pass through a needle's eye.* We can compare renouncing personal possessions to a sort of universal almsgiving, a burnt offering compared to an ordinary sacrifice.

The use of the sexual act also distracts us from entire devotion to the 4 service of God; partly because of its intense pleasure, which we the more crave the more we experience it, and partly because looking after a wife and children and the earthly possessions needed for their support preoccupies us. Religious perfection requires **perpetual continence**, as it does voluntary poverty. Husbands however cannot without injustice abandon their wives as they can renounce possessions. Christ therefore did not require Peter to separate from his wife, but he kept John from the marriage he had intended to contract. Because the early patriarchs preserved perfection of soul alongside riches and marriage (a proof of great virtue), weaker people shouldn't presume they too will have enough virtue to achieve perfection while remaining married with possessions: no man would presume to attack his enemies unarmed just because Samson slew many of his with the jawbone of an ass.

Religious must submit themselves to instruction and direction in 5 matters relevant to their religious life. Such subjection to the commands and instruction of others is an obedience. So **obedience** is also required for religious perfection. Those already perfect are the most prompt to obey, not because they need guidance to acquire perfection, but because they wish to preserve what they have already acquired. Religious are subject primarily to bishops, as people still to be perfected to the agents of their perfection. Neither hermits nor religious superiors are exempt from this obedience to bishops. Even if they are totally or partially exempt from their diocesan bishop, they are nevertheless obliged to obey the Pope, not only in those matters in which all are obliged, but also specially in the discipline of their religious life. The obligation consequent on obedience is not coerced but free, since the obedience itself is willed even if perhaps a man would not have done what he is commanded to do considered in itself. If a man obliges himself by a vow of obedience to do for God's sake what does not please him in itself, that makes his doing it all the more acceptable to God, even if it is a small thing; for a man cannot give God anything greater than the subjection of his own will to another for God's sake.

6   A state of perfection obliges perfection, and this obligation must be made to God by vow. So since poverty, continence and obedience dispose us to a Christian perfection of life, the religious state professes these three by vow. No one can actually deliver his whole life to God at each moment, because he can only live it bit by bit; so the only way is to pledge it by vow. Because *God is most pleased with services we could lawfully withhold but offer out of love*, it might seem more pleasing to him for poverty, continence and obedience to be observed without vowing them. But among the things we can lawfully withhold the dearest thing is our own freedom. So when someone freely renounces by vow his freedom to withhold things that would serve God, he does something most pleasing to God.

7   The religious state can be thought of as a training in perfect charity, a freedom from external administrative cares, and a burnt offering of all we are and have to God. The vows of poverty, continence and obedience build up the religious state under all three aspects. To train in perfection we rid ourselves of anything that could hinder the total concentration of our love on God: poverty rids us of desire for external possessions, continence of sensual and especially sexual desire, obedience of any disorders of human will. The vows also free us from the cares of worldly administration: poverty from the administering of external possessions, continence from the administration of a family, and obedience from administering our own actions. Finally, our burnt offering of ourselves includes the offering of external possessions by poverty, our own body by continence, and our own will (and through

that all the powers of our soul) through obedience. The state of religion is built up from these three vows. Obedience is the principal vow: it 8 offers the most (the will itself, of more importance than either one's own body or external possessions), it includes the other vows (poverty and continence being matters of obedience), and it is the most closely related to the goal of religion. Someone who observes voluntary poverty and continence, even by vow, but lacks the vow of obedience, is not in the religious state. In the religious state the rule aims at acts of virtue. If 9 those acts are also enjoined by God's commandments on everyone, transgression of the rule will be fatal; but if the acts are more than God commands then only transgression that involves contempt will be fatal. The rule also prescribes external observances as training, to some of which the religious is obliged by the vows he takes. Transgression of the vows of poverty, continence and obedience is fatal, but transgressions of other observances only if they involve contempt of the rule or directly oppose some directive from a superior. Some religious institutes are careful to profess not the rule but *to live according to the rule*, that is, to strive to behave with the rule as a model. Contempt would offend against this. Other religious institutes, with even greater care, profess *obedience according to the rule*, so that only what contravenes a directive of the rule offends. Transgression or omission in other matters is then a non-fatal sin. In one religious institute, the Order of Friars Preachers, such transgression or omission does not in itself involve any sin, fatal or non-fatal, but merely incurs a set penalty. Accompanying negligence or passion or contempt could of course turn this into a sin, non-fatal or fatal. Sin committed by a religious may be more serious than sin of the 10 same type committed by a layman for three reasons: it may offend against a religious vow, when contempt is involved it would seem to involve a greater degree of ingratitude to God, and it may involve greater scandal. But if a religious sins out of weakness or ignorance, not from contempt or against his vow or with scandal, then the same type of sin may be less grave in the religious, either because it is absorbed so to speak by the numerous good works he does (if it is non-fatal) or because the religious is more easily able to recover from it (if it is fatal).

Monks and clerics may not lawfully engage in secular affairs for 187 2 motives of gain, though they may both engage in and even direct such affairs out of motives of charity, with permission of their superiors and in due moderation. **Manual labour** serves four purposes: first and 3 foremost the obtaining of a livelihood, secondly the avoidance of idleness which is a source of many evils, thirdly the restraining of bodily desires, and fourthly almsgiving. Manual labour for purposes of obtaining a

livelihood is enjoined on us by God's command, but we should remember that it then includes all lawful means of gaining a livelihood, whether with hands or feet or tongue. Watchmen and couriers are also manual labourers. Because the hand is *the tool of tools* all these can be thought of as manual labour, that is, work of the hands. Manual labour for purposes of avoiding idleness or restraining bodily desire is not a matter of precept, since there are many other ways of achieving those purposes; and manual labour for the purpose of almsgiving is only a matter of precept in particular cases where one is obliged to alms and there is no
4 other means available. Anyone can live lawfully on what belongs to him, and what is generously given to us by donors belongs to us. So when monasteries and churches are endowed by the generosity of rulers and the general faithful, it is lawful for religious and clerics to live off such endowments without doing manual labour. This is **living on alms**; and in the same way religious may live on perishable goods donated to them by the faithful, for it would be stupid to say one could only accept great possessions as alms but not bread or small amounts of money. The use of such gifts would be unlawful only if the religious in question ceased to fulfil their religious duties, for then they would be obtaining gifts
5 under false pretences. As for begging, there are two remarks to be made. The act of begging is degrading to a certain extent, but as such it can be a praiseworthy exercise in humility for some people, to be counted with other degrading activities as an effective medicine for pride. As to what is sought by begging, it would be sought unlawfully if one simply wanted riches or food without working for them, but if there is no other way of satisfying genuine needs, or of raising funds for some work for the common good, like building a bridge or a church, or pursuing a course of study, then begging is as lawful for religious as it is for lay people.

188 1   Religious institutes can be distinguished according to their aims (putting up travellers, ransoming captives), or their observances (abstaining from food, manual labour, deprivation). Since the goal
2 always comes first the former differentiation is the most important. The active life engages in activities which serve our fellowmen for God's sake, and so also serve God. If the religious does such works with God in mind then his active life derives from contemplation of God and shares the fruits of a contemplative life. Religious engaged in the active life may be in the world physically but not in their minds and hearts, for they engage in external activity not in order to obtain earthly rewards
3 but in order to serve God. A religious institute could fittingly have a military function, if it were exercised not for worldly motives but to

defend the worship of God or the public good or the poor and oppressed. As the Psalms say: *Rescue the poor, and liberate the needy from the hands of sinners.* Failing to resist evil and condoning an injustice done to oneself can be something perfect if it contributes to the welfare of others, but tolerating injustice done to others is an imperfection and even a sin if resistance is possible. A man can be praised for giving away his own possessions but not for giving away other people's, and still less God's. But the welfare of our fellowmen is better provided for by looking after 4 their spiritual needs than the needs of their bodies. It is therefore especially fitting that religious institutes should be established for preaching and for other activities directed at the welfare of souls. That others beside bishops should take on the task of preaching is a good thing, because of the large numbers of faithful and the difficulty of finding enough people to go out to all nations. Just as military institutes have been established because of a failure of secular rulers to resist the infidel in some countries. Study is also a fitting activity for religious. It 5 promotes the contemplative life directly by enlightening the mind and indirectly by removing the dangers of contemplation: the errors into which it is easy to fall when one doesn't know the scriptures very well. Study is especially necessary in religious institutes established for preaching and suchlike functions. But it can also benefit all religious institutes by restraining cravings of the flesh and desire for riches, and teaching obedience. Philosophers study the sciences of this world, but religious chiefly study *the teaching that is according to godliness.* To study other sciences is not the job of the religious, whose whole life is given to God's service, unless those sciences relate in some way to the teaching of God.

Religious institutes excel each other primarily in goals, and sec- 6 ondarily in observances. An institute aiming at a higher goal is to be preferred, whether it aims at a greater good or at more than one good. But when the goals are identical then we judge by observances; not the amount of them but their suitability for the goal in question. The active life is of two sorts. A life of teaching and preaching deriving from a fullness of contemplation is to be preferred to contemplation on its own: to share what one contemplates with others is better than merely to contemplate it oneself. But an active life consisting wholly of external activities such as almsgiving and putting up guests is less preferable to contemplation, except in circumstances of real need. So religious institutes dedicated to teaching and preaching hold the highest place, closest to the state of perfection of bishops. The second level is that of contemplative institutes and the third of those engaged in external activities.

7 Perfection consists essentially in the following of Christ, not in poverty. Poverty is a tool or a training for perfection, since by renouncing wealth we also remove certain obstacles to charity: concerns, love of wealth, vainglory and pride. Concern is inseparable from possessions, great or small; though not all concern is forbidden by the Lord, only excessive and harmful concern, for the obstacles of loving and glorying in wealth arise only when the wealth is great. It makes a difference however whether the wealth is privately or communally owned. Concern for private possessions is part of man's love for his earthly self; concern for communal possessions is part of the love of charity which *seeks not what is our own* but the general good, though it too can hinder higher acts of charity such as contemplation of God and instruction of our fellowmen. Clearly then communal possession of great wealth, movable or immovable, can hinder perfection even if it does not entirely exclude it. But in relation to the common goal of all religious institutes – dedication to God's service – communal possession of enough external goods to support the community does not hinder religious perfection, though in relation to the special goal of some particular institute more or less poverty may be required. Clearly a religious institute devoted to physical activities such as military service or providing shelter would function imperfectly without common property; whereas institutes devoted to the contemplative life are more perfect the less concerned they are about earthly goods.

8 Solitude is a tool of contemplation, but not of the active life, whether that life be physically or spiritually active, unless the solitude be temporary like Christ's. Solitude suits the contemplative who is already perfect, but life in community is necessary for training in perfection. What is already perfect surpasses what is only working towards perfection, so the life of a hermit, if properly lived, surpasses life in community; but embraced without previous training it can be full of dangers, unless God's grace makes up what others gain from training.

189 5 There are two kinds of vow in religious life: simple and solemnized vows. A simple vow is a promise made to God proceeding from one's own inner decision and binding before God's law. Such a vow can fail either because the person making it has no power of decision (being not yet of the age judged capable of deceit, set normally at fourteen for boys and twelve for girls), or because what a person promises is not in his power to promise (for example, children below those ages of puberty cannot dispose of their own lives, and their father can revoke – or approve – any vow they make). So children under the age of puberty and not yet having use of their reason are not obliged by any vow they may make. If they have use of their reason before the age of puberty,

then they are bound by their vow but their father can revoke it, since law goes by what is usually the case. If they are over the age of puberty the father can't revoke the vow; though if they still haven't full use of their reason they would not be bound before God. Solemnized vows by which one becomes a monk or religious are another matter, since they are subject to the church which solemnizes them. The church goes by what is normally the case, and has made a rule that profession made before the age of puberty, however capable the child is of using reason and practising deceit, is null and void. It is lawful however for religious institutes to accept children before the age of puberty and with permission of the parents for purposes of education. Parents are as such 6 the source of their children, and so must care for them: parents with children cannot lawfully enter religious life without making some alternative provision for their education. But children are not as such responsible for looking after their parents, except in cases of necessity. If children are the only support of their parents then it would not be lawful for the children to neglect to provide for them and enter religious life. But when the parents are not in such need, the children can enter even against their parents' wishes, because, after the years of puberty, every free man can govern his own life, especially in matters relating to God's service. Transferring from one religious institute to another is not to be 8 commended except for some great benefit or necessity. Those left behind are often scandalized, and, other things being equal, it is even more difficult to make progress in a new institute than in the one to which one is accustomed. Three reasons however may commend transfer: desire for a more perfect type of religious life; desire to transfer from an institute whose level of perfection has declined to a more observant, even if less strict, institute; sickness and infirmity. In the first instance one must seek permission in all humility (the permission cannot be refused if the second institute is clearly more excellent, but decision rests with the superior in doubtful cases); the second instance always requires a superior's decision; and the third case requires dispensation.

Part III

THE ROAD TO GOD

Chapter 13

JESUS CHRIST – GOD AND MAN

The Lord Jesus Christ, our saviour, in order *to save his people from their* [vol 48]
sins, revealed himself as the road of truth which will lead us, through
resurrection, to an endlessly happy life. To complete our theological
task, then, we follow discussion of life's ultimate goal and its virtues and
vices by studying the one who saved us all and the benefits he brought
the human race. We will study the saviour himself – God become man
for our salvation – and what in his human flesh he did and had done to
him [chapter 14], the sacramental means by which we achieve salvation
[chapter 15], and the destination of endless life to which we shall rise
through him [chapters never written].

> **Introductory comment.** The last three chapters have been
> a sort of break in the broad lines of the *Summa*'s theological
> development, dealing with particularities of what chapter 8 dealt
> with generally: the life of man as a life of virtue or of vice, of
> theological or deiform virtue over and above human moral virtue.
> At the end of chapter 8 the theological significance of sin as an
> uncreation of God's creation was examined, and chapter 9
> reviewed the broad theological significance of Old Testament
> history – the struggle between sin and the law, and the need for
> grace and the Spirit. In the final chapters of the *Summa* Thomas
> will deal with New Testament history: with the coming of grace
> and the Spirit through the human life of Jesus Christ. Our subject
> is what St John has described as the *coming forth*, from eternity
> into time, of the Word of creation that in the beginning said *Let
> there be light*; the coming forth of that Word into the darkness man
> has made of the world; the taking flesh of the Word, which gathers
> together the broken pieces of the world and implements the original
> creative command, bringing the light. The life of Christ embeds
> in time the eternal issuing of the Word, as Thomas mentioned at
> the end of chapter 3 (pp 100ff). Here, as in the gospels, it is
> referred to as setting up a road for men and the world to follow: a
> road to Jerusalem, a road carrying the cross, a road to death and

to resurrection, a road through the veil of God's hiddenness, a road from the Father to the Father. All this is firmly and traditionally interpreted as the last act in a drama of salvage of creation by God, an undoing of the damage done by human uncreation, but an undoing in which God mercifully and justly invites man to cooperate.

In what follows Thomas attends first to making such statements as precise as human language can. Early church councils had started the process of precision many centuries earlier, just as they had for the scriptural teaching of God as Father, Son and Holy Spirit. Thomas's chapter 3 commented on the early councils' articulation of the Trinity as three *persons* existing in one *nature*, and this chapter comments on their articulation of the **incarnation** as the taking on of a second *nature* by the *person* of the Son. It is a careful treading of the way between opposing errors, and the concluding formulations are so cautiously put together that one can be forgiven for overlooking the boldness of what is actually said. What Thomas works towards in the whole discussion is the unity of the existence of God with the existence of Christ. The reason why we cannot rest content with a model based on the way accidental attributes supervene on the nature of a substance, is that such attributes have an existence over and above that of the substance. We must rather compare the way soul and body unite to make one existent thing: except that there the one existence is achieved by union of soul and body in a substance one by nature, but here we have two births, therefore two natures, yet one existence. The lives of God and of Christ are in a sense identified though the natures of those lives are not. The life of God does, in a sense, animate the life of Christ; it is as if God, who in the world of possibility and nature can exist outside Christ, as a matter of actuality and history does not. Indeed, God, being his own existence, is the very existence of Christ, an existence which in hope and as awaited animates the Old Testament, and which in very effect through the sacraments animates the new history of mankind called into his church.

At the end of chapter 9 (pp 314ff, 318ff), when grace was being defined, a distinction was made in its effects: what God works in a man with his consent but without possibility of his cooperation is the setting right, the salvaging of man from sin, the sowing of the seed of new life within him; but what God goes on to work with man's cooperation is man's own actualization and development of the seed so sown, the earning and reaping of its eternal harvest. This analysis now reappears in the analysis of **Christ's grace**. Though the Son's human nature exists with the existence of God, this existence is natural to him only in his eternal nature, a grace to his human nature (what Thomas calls the grace of union); and over and above this union of existence with God, Christ is also graced with the grace that allows human nature to unite with God through knowledge and love, namely, the grace-as-disposition which graces men for dwelling in heaven with God; and because heavenly union for all men is achieved by sharing in Christ's union with his Father, by being incorporated into Christ's life as if it had been one's own, Christ's grace-as-disposition is the mediating source of every man's grace-as-disposition – the grace that will be shared out through the whole body of Christ from its head.

At this point Thomas develops a concept drawn from John Damascene: that of the human life and nature of Christ as instrument of the divine person who has taken on that nature: **Christ's humanity as God's perfect tool**. A tool is something which lends its form to its agent so that he can shape the effects produced by its means, effects which it cannot produce by itself but only as used by its agent. The clearest discussion of this concept in the chapter is in the section entitled *Christ's activity* (pp 502ff); and the sense in which Christ is a willing tool (and the sense in which he is *un*willing) is covered in the section on *Christ's will* (pp 500ff).

The discussion of what we can say about Christ now proceeds along two parallel paths, so to speak: what his actual life as described in scripture reveals to us (that he wept, suffered pain, was amazed, prayed, and in general was as thoroughly subject to the human condition as any other man; but that he also performed miracles, foretold the future, forgave sins, and in general behaved as though he were God), and in parallel to that what Christ's human nature needed in order to be God's tool for salvaging men and the world. It is sometimes difficult to decide which of these paths in the discussion is the most influential at certain points. The theological role of Christ as God's tool seemed to Thomas to demand perfection from the first moment of his conception: a perfect instilled knowledge, a fully free will, a holiness without compare, even in the embryo an ability to sense perfect enough for his mind to make reliable judgments. And if Christ suffered from weaknesses of body those could not have been incurred weaknesses as they would have been in any other man (inherited with sin by way of a father's seed), but they must have been willed weaknesses, willed positively as constituting the sort of community with other men that his role as tool of their salvation required. Christ's activity was integrated willed activity to a degree hard to imagine: even the natural and normally involuntary movements of his bodily functions were in a sense voluntary, since they were willed by God and perfectly consented to from the moment of conception by Christ's human will. As for Christ's knowledge, Thomas informs us that he has recoiled a little from an earlier position dominated by such considerations. Earlier he had taught that Christ as God knew everything, and as man already had on earth that blissful knowledge of heaven which is God himself existing in the mind, and in addition had all the knowledge that God can instil into men in this life; he did not, however, learn things from experience as other men do. At that time, clearly, Thomas regarded having to learn by experience as an imperfection; the knowledge was the thing, and that could be had more perfectly if the mind was created already formed with ideas directly by God. But here in the *Summa* Thomas corrects himself to this extent: he maintains that it is part of the perfection of man to learn things by his own mind's light, and that if Christ hadn't done so the light of his own human intelligence would have been without any purpose. Thomas cannot however envisage Christ learning from other men's teaching; he thinks Christ turned a deaf ear to that until he could discover those things for himself! It would have been an even greater step for Thomas to adopt the view that the very perfection of the union of humanity with God in Christ would require him to exercise his human powers towards the development of that unity: in his own time Thomas could not, I think, have taken such a step, but modern theologians, encouraged by Thomas's own second thoughts on the subject of acquired experience, have the duty to explore it.

The incarnation

11 **Why did God become man?**   As Damascene says: *By the mystery of the incarnation God showed his goodness and his wisdom, his justice and his strength. His goodness did not disdain the weakness of his own creation;*

his justice did not snatch man from death by force but let man himself vanquish the tyrant; his wisdom found the most apt payment for a most exacting debt; and his unlimited strength performed its greatest work: becoming man. God's very nature is goodness, goodness is by definition self-giving, and the most perfect goodness gave himself to creatures in the most perfect way, *uniting to himself created nature personally: the Word of God taking on soul and flesh.* The mystery of the incarnation involved no change in God's eternal state, but united him in a new way with what he created, or rather, united what he created with himself. What God creates is by nature changeable, so that for it to change its way of existing is not inappropriate. Just as all creation began to exist after first not having done so, so appropriately after first not having been united to God it later became united. The differences between the Creator and what he created are all established by God's wisdom and serve God's goodness: change and matter are creations of the uncreated, unchanging, immaterial goodness of God, and penal evils are instituted by his justice to vindicate his glory; only culpable evil is committed by creatures turning aside from God's wise plan and refusing service to his goodness. So it was appropriate for God to take on a changeable nature, material and afflicted with penal evil, but not to take on culpability of any fault.

We needed God to become flesh if we were to be saved. But notice 2 that some things are needed for a purpose because we can't do without them at all (food for staying alive) and some because we can't do so well without them (a horse for a journey). God needed to become man to restore human nature only in the second sense, since there were many other ways available to God's almighty power, but *none so appropriate for healing our wretchedness.* By this way of doing things God brought us good and took away our evil. He brought us the surest faith by speaking to us himself: *Truth himself, the Son of God made man, established and confirmed our faith*; he immensely lifted our hopes: *What better sign of God's love than that his Son deigned to share our nature*; he most greatly enkindled our love: *if we have been slow to love then at least let us not be slow to return this love*; he has set an example of living life well: *that we might have a model we could both see and follow, God became man*; and he has brought us to the true and happy goal of life, a full share in his own godhead: *God became man that man might become God.* By becoming man he also took away our evil: he taught us not to go in awe of the devil, the author of sin: *Because God joined human nature to himself in one person, no proud and evil spirits dare any longer vaunt over men their fleshlessness*; he taught also the dignity of human nature unsullied by sin: *Acknowledge your dignity, O Christian, and since you share God's nature do not by your conduct degenerate into your former worthlessness*; *the unmerited grace that God showed us in becoming man in Christ* rebukes our presumption; *such great humility on God's part rebuts and cures man's pride*; and finally, God in this way freed us from slavery *overcoming the devil by a man's justice*, since amends which could not be made by man alone and should not be made by God were made by Jesus Christ, God and man, *providing a cure because truly God, and an example because truly man*. And a multitude of other advantages flow from God becoming man which are beyond human comprehension.

Amends are sometimes made perfectly, with adequate recompense for any fault committed. But no one merely human could make amends for sin in this way: sin corrupted all mankind and no individual's goodness could outweigh that; it was infinite in the sense that it offended God's infinite majesty. To make amends adequately and infinitely would need a man who was also God. Someone merely human could however make sufficient amends imperfectly, in the sense of a recompense inadequate but willingly accepted. All such imperfect amends by men are now effective because of the perfect amends made by Christ.

3   Whatever exceeds a creature's due and is decided by God's will alone can only be known to us through holy scripture. Since scripture always gives Adam's sin as the reason for God becoming man, it seems better to presume that had there been no sin there would have been no incarnation. Although we cannot limit God's power by saying it could not have happened otherwise. The perfection of the universe required only that creatures should be ordered to God as goal in the ways natural to them. For we must distinguish the capacities natural to things (which God always fulfils by gifts that accord with those capacities) from the capacity of all creatures to respond to the call of God's power. Capacity for union with God is of this latter sort, and God does not have to fulfil every such capacity: otherwise he could only ever do in creation what he in fact does, and this is false. Nor was it inappropriate for God to raise human nature to a greater perfection after sin than before, for God permits evil precisely in order to draw forth greater good: *where wickedness abounded grace abounded even more*; *O happy fault that deserved so great a ransomer*.

4   But without doubt Christ came into the world to wipe out not only the sin of Adam that we all inherit, but also all subsequent sins. Not that they are all wiped out – some people fail to hold fast to Christ, *the light came into the world and men preferred darkness to the light* – but Christ did enough to wipe them all out. He came principally to wipe

out the greater sin. The sins we commit are more intensely sin than the sin we inherit because more voluntary; but inherited sin is the most extensive, infecting the entire human race and not just an individual, so in this sense Christ came principally to take away inherited sin, *the good of a whole people being more godlike than the good of an individual.*

Fittingly God became man not immediately after Adam's sin, but 5 *when the fulness of time had come.* Adam's sin came from pride, and if man was to be freed from it he had better first become humble enough to recognize his need of a liberator: *God first left us to our free will under the law we have in us by nature, so that we could learn our natural powers; then when we failed we received the Law, but the disease grew worse, so that we could recognize our weakness and call out for the medicine of grace.* Moreover proceeding from imperfect to perfect goodness is a natural pattern of growth: *the physical first and then the spiritual, the man from earth first, earthly, and the man from heaven, second, heavenly.* The fullness of time also fitted the dignity of the incarnate Word of God himself: *the greater the coming judge, the longer should be his file of heralds.* Were a doctor to give medicine to a sick man at the very beginning of the illness, it might benefit him less and even perhaps do more harm than good. So too the Lord did not provide mankind with the remedy of the incarnation straight away, lest it be proudly spurned by men who did not recognize their weakness. All things considered, perfection precedes imperfection in time and by nature, but in each particular thing imperfection, however secondary to perfection in nature, precedes it in time. Thus God's eternal perfection preceded man's imperfect human nature in duration, but the imperfect state of human nature preceded the fulfilment of human nature by union with God. When 6 God became man human nature was raised to its highest perfection, so it was inappropriate for that to take place at the beginning of mankind's history. But because the Word becoming flesh is the cause that brings about our human perfection – *of his fullness have we all received* – it would also have been inappropriate to wait until the end of time. What will come at the end of time is the perfection of glory, to which the Word made flesh is finally leading human nature. God becoming man ended the process from imperfection to perfection, and began that perfection.

Two natures in one person. The Council of Chalcedon laid down 2 1 that *the union of natures in the only-begotten Son in no way removed their distinctness.* The word *nature* originally meant the actual process of birth or coming to be, but later came to name the inner starting-point of that process and in Aristotle indeed of any process: *nature is the inner essential source of change in things*, the material of the thing and the form matter takes on in that thing. But then, since the end-point of all generative processes is the species defining what is generated, that too is called its *nature*: *nature is what specifies a thing and gives it form*. And that is how we are going to use the word here: the essence of a thing, what it is specifically. Now given this meaning of *nature* the union involved in the Word made flesh cannot issue in a single nature. There are three ways in which some single thing can be made up of more than one constituent. Suppose first that the constituents are wholes which remain intact after union: then the form of the whole must be no more than a sort of structured arrangement of these constituents, a form that sets up no new substance but supervenes on existing substances. Such a union would not be essential to the Word made flesh but a coincidental addition; and what resulted from the union would not be one but many simply speaking, and one only in a qualified sense. In any case, because the form in such cases is not natural but artificially contrived, like the structure of a house, such a mode of union wouldn't in fact, as is being proposed, constitute a nature for Christ. Suppose then originally whole constituents are changed by the union in the way chemical elements are combined into a compound. Such a union won't do for Christ either. Firstly, the divine nature isn't subject to change, either into or from something else. Moreover, compounds differ in kind from their constituent elements, so that Christ wouldn't have the nature of either his Father or his mother. Suppose then constituents unchanged by the union, but not originally wholes, like body and soul in man, or the various parts of the body. This again won't explain the mystery of God made man. For in Christ each nature, God's and man's, is a whole; and these natures cannot combine like parts of the body or like body and soul, since God's nature is neither a body nor a form bodies can take on. (And if it was, we would get a nature of which there could be many instances, not one Christ. And it would be a new species, neither God nor man.)

2   The Council of Chalcedon also says: *not divided or separated into two persons*. Some things, especially those in which matter has taken on a certain form, contain elements other than those that define them: supervening forms and features peculiar to them as individuals. In such things one cannot identify an individual with its nature; not because there are two things, but because the individual thing consists of a defining nature plus supervening characteristics. The individual is a whole, and within it it has a nature as its formal part making it whole.

So material individuals are not to be identified with their natures: no man is human nature. Only when there are no such supervening characteristics, as is the case in God, are the individual and his nature not really distinct, but only mentally distinguished by us, our mind conceiving the thing's nature as what defines it, and the individual thing as what exists with that nature. Now whatever is true of individuals is true of persons, things with minds, since a person is nothing else but *an individual existing with a rational nature*. So everything in a person, whether it belongs to him by nature or not, is united to him in person. If the Word of God's human nature were not united to him in person it would not be united to him at all, and that would destroy all belief in the incarnation and undermine the whole Christian faith. So because the Word has a human nature united to himself, which does not form part of his divine nature, that union exists in the person of the Word though not as a union in nature. True, in God nature and person are not really distinct, but the two words signify different ways of conceiving him: person signifying him as something existing with a nature. Now the Word's human nature is united to him in such a way that he exists with that nature, without changing the nature he already has; so that the union of the human nature to the Word of God is made in his person but not by nature. Human nature is of more dignity in Christ than in us, not less, because in us it exists so to speak on its own with its own personality, whereas in Christ it is taken up into the person of the Word. Compare the dignity of the form that contributes wholeness to a thing's species; yet the sensory nature is more noble in man, where it is completed by a greater form of wholeness, than in animals, where it itself completes the whole.

A person is *an individual substance with a rational nature*, and an individual substance we sometimes call a *subject*, meaning something that is a subject of all that can be said about it. If then there was an individual subject in Christ beside the Word himself, then only that subject and not the Word would have been truly born of the virgin, made to suffer, crucified and buried. And that is heresy. An individual subject is a particular substance existing whole and complete. A part of an existent whole, like a hand or a foot, is not called a subject. So Christ's human nature is an individual substance though not an individual subject, because it is only part of the whole Christ, God and man, who is the individual subject. Even among creatures it is not what characterizes us individually that places us in a genus or species; that is done by our nature derived from our form, our individuality being derived from our matter. So Christ too is a member of the human race

not by reason of his person, but by reason of the nature he has taken
4 on. The person of Christ then exists in two natures; one thing existing
in two ways. Only in that sense is his person composite.

6   Two heresies have arisen in regard to this mysterious union of two
natures in Christ. Eutyches and Dioscoros fused the two natures into
one, proclaiming that Christ came to exist out of two natures distinct
before their union, but did not exist with two natures, since they ceased
to be distinct after union. Nestorius and Theodore of Mopsuestia
separated the one person into two: the Son of God and the son of man
united by mutual indwelling, sharing the same intentions and activity
and the same honour and titles: all modes of union, notice, in which the
unity supervenes secondarily. The Catholic faith takes a middle position:
the union of God and man is neither one of nature, nor merely something
secondary and supervening, but a union in subject or person. Whatever
is added to something that already exists complete must supervene as
secondary, unless it is absorbed into that completed existence. At the
resurrection, for instance, our body will be united to our pre-existing
soul, but not as something secondary supervening, but as something
taken up into the same existence, receiving life from the soul. Whiteness
however is a different matter; being white supervenes upon being a man
and is something distinct from it. Now the Word of God has been a
complete person from all eternity, and when human nature came to be
his in time, it was not taken up into the existence of one nature (as body
shares one natural existence with the soul), but it was absorbed into the
existence of one person. So the Son of God's human nature is not
something secondary or supervening. The tools a person takes up do
not usually form part of that person; nevertheless, something that is
taken up into the unity of a person can still be a tool, as are our own
body and its limbs. Nestorius held that Christ's human nature was taken
up by the Word only as a tool, and not into personal unity. But
Damascene held Christ's human nature to be a tool personally united
to him.

7   The union we have been speaking of is a sort of relationship between
God's nature and human nature, which unites them in the one person
of the Son of God. Now all relationships of God to creatures really exist
in the creatures, for they result from some change the creature undergoes,
but exist in God only in our way of conceiving matters, since they do
not result from any change in God. We define a relationship as we do
a change, in terms of its destination or end-point, though in reality its
existence depends on the subject of the relationship. The union we are
talking about really exists in the created nature, and so is itself something

created. Any relationship beginning in time is a result of change, and 8
change implies action and the undergoing of that action. So the first and
principal difference between the two main terms [used in Incarnation
theology] – namely, the *assumption* of human nature, and the *union* of
natures – is that *union* names the relationship, while *assumption* names
the change, either actively as a *taking up* or passively as a *being taken up*.
Hence a second difference: *assumption* signifies the change as happening,
union the relationship as something already there. So what is uniting is
united, but what is taking up is not being taken up. The Son of God
uniting human nature to himself can truly be called man (since the word
man signifies human nature as already taken up into a subject, the divine
person); but he cannot be identified with human nature in the abstract,
human nature signified as what is being taken up. Hence a third difference: relationships, especially those between equals, don't discriminate
between their terms, but action and passion, i.e. the undergoing of action,
discriminate one term as agent and the other as patient. So it doesn't
matter whether we say the human nature is united to the divine or vice
versa; but we can't say the divine nature was taken up by the human,
but only vice versa: for the human nature is joined to a divine person,
as a nature in which that divine person exists. The person of the Father
unites human nature to the person of his Son but not to his own person;
so he unites but he does not take up. *Assumption* expresses who is joined
to what is taken up, since it means *taking to oneself*; *incarnation* (becoming
flesh or becoming man) expresses also what is taken up; *union* expresses
only joining. So *assumption* differs in meaning from both *union* and
incarnation.

   Grace or favour has two meanings: the free will of God bestowing a 10
gift, and the gift thus freely bestowed. Human nature needs God's free
will in order to be lifted up to God, for that exceeds its own natural
abilities; whether the lifting up be by activity, as when people in God's
grace know and love him, or whether it be by the personal existence
peculiar to Christ, in whom human nature is taken up into the person
of the Son of God. Powers need perfecting by dispositions if they are
to be sources of perfect activity, but subjects do not need to be disposed
to their natures. If then by *grace* we mean God's will favouring someone,
then the union of the incarnation is as much an effect of grace as is the
union of holy men to God by knowledge and love. But if by *grace* we
mean a free gift bestowed by God, then in Christ the very union of
human nature to divine person is the grace, being totally undeserved,
and there is no separate disposition called grace mediating the union.
Grace-as-disposition [to activity] is something existing in the soul only;

the grace, or free gift of God, that is union with a divine person, belongs to the whole nature of man: body and soul. *The fullness of godhead dwells in Christ bodily.*

3 1   Even in created persons many natures supervene on one another in a secondary way, as when one man has many qualities. But only a divine person, because of his unlimitedness, can accommodate many natures not as supervening secondarily but as natures according to which that person exists substantially. The Son of God does not exist simply speaking by reason of his human nature, since he has existed from all eternity; he exists as man by his human nature but simply speaking by his divine nature; so he is said to take on human nature but not to take 4 on divine nature. The term *assumption* implies both an action of taking and the destination of what is taken. The action is an act of divine power and in that respect common to all three persons; but the destination implied is the person into whom the nature is taken, the one person of 8 the Son. That it was the person of the Son who became incarnate is altogether fitting. Firstly it produced a fitting union as such, since suitable unions are between like and like. Now the person of the Son has first a general affinity with all creation, being the Word of God, the eternal craftsman's model for creation; so it was appropriate that creation be restored to eternal and changeless perfection by being personally united to the Word of God, the model according to which it was first established. Moreover, the Son has a special affinity with human nature, being the Word of God's eternal wisdom from which all human wisdom derives; so again it suited the finished perfection of man that the very Word of God be personally united with a human nature. Secondly, that it was the Son who became incarnate fitted the purpose of the union, the accomplishment of God's predestined plan for men: in this way men are brought to adopted sonship through him who is Son by nature: *those whom he foreknew he predestined to share the image of his Son.* And thirdly the incarnation of the Son fitted the sin it was remedying: for Adam sinned by craving knowledge, and man is brought back to God by the Word of true wisdom.

4 1   Human nature has no natural capability of union with a divine person but there is a certain suitability based on nobility and need. It is a nature capable of reason, and so open to some sort of contact with the Word of God through knowledge and love; and it needs the union inasmuch as it needs restoration, being burdened with inherited sin. Creatures lacking reason miss out on the score of nobility, angels on the score of 2 need. The human nature taken on is not already the nature of some person, but comes to be such as the result of being taken on. Any pre-

existent person would have to be destroyed by the union (and would therefore have been taken on for no purpose) for otherwise there would be two persons, one taking on and one taken on, which is heresy. The word *man* signifies a concrete instance of human nature, human nature 3 existing in some subject. So one can no more say God took on a man than one can say God took on a person or subject. Only in regard to the 6 fault he came to destroy was Christ separate from sinners, not as regards the nature he came to save: *he was to be like his brothers in everything.* That he took his nature from already sin-laden material makes his purity and freedom from sin all the more marvellous.

Augustine reports that Arius and later Apollinarius believed that the 5 3 Son of God took on flesh without soul, and that the Word took the soul's place. This would imply that Christ had not two natures but only one, since body and soul together constitute one human nature. This is an error: it contradicts the scriptures, for the gospels describe Jesus feeling wonder and anger and sadness and hunger, which just as much proves he had a soul as his eating and sleeping and getting tired proves he had a body; it contradicts too the purpose of the incarnation which was to liberate man, body and soul; and it contradicts the very truth of the incarnation, for flesh is only human flesh, and man's other parts only human parts, because of the soul – without soul flesh and bone are not truly flesh and bone. When we say *the Word was made flesh*, *flesh* there means the whole of man, as it does when Isaiah says *All flesh shall see God's salvation.* The word *flesh* is chosen because that is what makes the Son of God visible, and the text is about to say *And we have seen his glory.* The Word is the primary agent of life, the soul the form in which that life is given to the body. The form is the effect of the agent. So the presence of the Word in a body implies the presence of soul, just as the presence of fire in a body implies that it is hot. Christ had a 4 human mind. The gospel account implies it when it talks of his wonder; the incarnation's purpose requires it, since it is through the mind that man sins and receives grace; and the truth of the incarnation demands it, since if Christ took a mindless soul, he would have taken on animal, not human, flesh.

All men receive from Christ's fullness by believing in him: *the justice* 6 3 *of God comes to all through faith in Jesus Christ.* We believe in him as already made flesh, the Old Testament patriarchs believed in him as one yet to be born. But faith in Christ makes us just *by God's gracious decision*, made from all eternity: so there is nothing to stop some people being made just by faith in Jesus Christ even before the moment when Christ's soul was *filled with grace and truth.* The dissimilarities in origin 4

between Christ and the rest of men precede completion of our human nature: we are conceived from male seed but Christ was not, and conception of the body precedes animation by a human soul in us but not in Christ. But only a difference in the very origin of his soul would
6 make Christ differ from ourselves in nature. We acknowledge two senses of grace in Christ: the grace of union and grace-as-disposition. Neither of these can mediate the taking on of human nature. The grace of union is precisely the personal existence in the person of the Word that is freely given to human nature by God as the result of the Word taking on human nature. Grace-as-disposition, Christ's special holiness, derives from his union with God: *we have seen his glory as of the only-begotten of the Father, full of grace and truth*. That Christ is full of grace and truth derives from the very fact that he is the Father's only-begotten Son, and that follows from union. Our union with God is by the activities of knowing and loving him, and such union presupposes grace-as-disposition perfecting our powers of activity. But the union of human nature with the Word of God is a union in personal existence, and that depends on no disposition but immediately on the nature itself.

Christ's grace

[vol 49] 7 1 **Christ's own grace.** Christ possessed grace-as-disposition. In the first place, his soul was united to the Word of God, and the closer anything is to a cause acting on it the more it is affected. But grace derives from God: *the Lord gives grace and glory*; so the soul of Christ was most fitted of all to receive that grace. In second place, Christ's soul needed to know and love God in the most intimate way and hence needed disposing to that by grace. And thirdly, his position in the human race as *mediator between God and man* required him to be graced with grace that could overflow to others: *from his fullness we have all received, grace upon grace*. Christ is true God in person and in divine nature, but since his oneness of person is accompanied by distinctness of natures, his soul is not by nature divine, but shares in divinity: that is to say, it is graced. As God's Son by nature, Christ is entitled to his eternal inheritance, the uncreated enjoyment of the uncreated activity of knowing and loving God, the same activity as that by which the Father knows and loves himself. But Christ's soul, because it is of a human nature, is not capable of such an activity, so must attain God by a created enjoyment which can only derive from grace. Again, as God's Word, Christ was able to do all things well, acting through his divine nature; but to be able to act perfectly through his human nature he needed

grace-as-disposition to that perfect activity. Christ's humanity is a tool of his divinity: not a lifeless tool unable to move itself, but a tool with a rational life of its own able to involve itself in the doing of what is done through it. Christ needed grace to dispose him to act in such a way.

Grace disposes the soul's nature and virtues dispose its powers; and 2 just as the powers derive from the soul's nature so the virtues derive from its grace. Because grace is at its most perfect in Christ, it gives rise to virtues perfecting every power and activity of his soul. Faith, however, 3 is concerned with God as unseen reality; so Christ, because he saw the substance of God from the first moment of his conception, had no room for faith. Faith, though it ranks higher than moral virtue because it deals with a higher reality, nevertheless implies some falling short of that reality, and that didn't happen in Christ. Just as assent to the unseen 4 defines faith, so firm anticipation of what one doesn't yet possess defines hope. The theological virtue of hope is directed principally to the prospective enjoyment of God, though secondarily, men of hope rely on God for other things too; just as men of faith believe God not only concerning God but concerning whatever he reveals. Since Christ enjoyed God fully from the first moment of his conception he did not have the theological virtue of hope; but he did hope for what he did not yet possess. He did not need to have faith concerning any matter, for he knew everything already, but since he did not already possess everything that was to form part of his perfection – an immortal and glorious body, for instance – he could hope for that. The building up of the church by conversion of the faithful is not part of the perfection of Christ in himself, but is a sharing of that perfection with others. Since, strictly speaking, hope is hope for oneself, one cannot say Christ had hope in that regard.

The gifts of the Holy Spirit make our faculties of soul sensitive to the 5 prompting of the Spirit. Clearly then Christ was outstandingly endowed with such gifts; giving them as God, and receiving them as man. For Christ possessed not only the kind of knowledge we shall enjoy in heaven, but also the kind we need to receive on the way there (though such gifts of the Holy Spirit persist in some form even in heaven). As 6 to *fear of the Lord*, men are afraid not only of evil, but of the person who has the power to inflict it, when that power is overwhelming and not easily resisted. So we can say that Christ feared God: not separation from God through sin or punishment for sin, but the overwhelming might of God, which he reverenced as the Holy Spirit prompted. For what defines the gift of fear is not so much the evils we confront as the overwhelming goodness of God whose power inflicts the evil. *Perfect love casts out the fear* of punishment, and Christ had no such fear.

7   Charisms all serve the proclamation of the faith and spiritual teaching; so Christ as the principal teacher of our faith had these charisms in a surpassing degree. The grace that makes us pleasing to God disposes us to the kind of interior and external action that reaps a reward; charisms dispose us to the kind of external actions that proclaim the faith, like the working of miracles. Christ had both these kinds of grace to the full. The gift of languages was bestowed on the apostles because they were being sent out *to teach all nations.* But Christ willed to preach only to the Jews: *I was sent only to the lost sheep of the house of Israel.* That, however, doesn't mean he didn't know other languages; he knew even the secret thoughts of the heart of which spoken words are the sign; dispositions are not useless simply because no opportunity to use them occurs. A man is a prophet only when he announces things beyond the ken of men whose situation he shares; when God or angels or the saints in heaven know and announce things beyond our ken that is not prophecy. But Christ shared our situation before his death: he was a pilgrim to heaven as well as already enjoying the sight of God. So when he knew and announced things beyond the ken of his fellow-pilgrims he was prophesying. He had full and perfect knowledge on the intellectual plane, and had images in his imagination in which he saw reflected the things of God; for he was not only blessed with seeing God but was also a pilgrim.

9   Grace reached its fullness in Christ, intensively and extensively. Grace existed most intensely in him, because his soul was closest to the source of grace in God and because he was to be the channel of grace to everyone else. And his grace extended to every activity and effect that grace can produce, just as the sun's energy extends into every change that occurs on earth. Whatever is perfect about faith and hope was realized even more perfectly in Christ. His soul was justified by grace working in him in the sense that it was made righteous and holy by grace from the first moment of his conception; this doesn't imply that his soul had any previous sinful existence, lacking in righteousness.

11   Christ's grace of union is the free bestowal on human nature of personal unity with the Son of God, and this grace is infinite as the person of the Word is himself infinite. Christ's grace-as-disposition, however, can be thought of in two ways: as existing in a created subject – Christ's soul – it is finite, but precisely as grace it can be called infinite, for it possesses every feature of grace and is given to Christ not according to some fixed measure but as a universal source of grace for all men: *he has graced us*

in his beloved Son. What measures a form is its purpose, and the purpose 12
of grace is to unite thinking creatures to God. Now one cannot conceive
a greater unity between thinking creatures and God than their union in
one person; so Christ's grace reaches the highest measure of grace. He
could not grow in the possession of that grace, for from the first moment
of his conception he had the full sight of God. Only men who are merely
journeying to heaven can grow in grace: in the form itself since none of
them have it in its highest grade, and in possession of it since none of
them have yet reached their goal. But one can grow in wisdom and grace
in two ways: by growth of the dispositions themselves (and this did not
happen in Christ), and by a growth in their effect, the doing of wiser
and more virtuous deeds. In this sense Christ *grew in wisdom and grace*
with age; for as he grew older he behaved in more mature ways *with
God and with men,* thus showing himself to be genuinely human.

The uniting of human nature to a divine person (the grace of union) 13
didn't precede Christ's grace-as-disposition in time, but it is prior in
nature. Firstly, the source of the grace of union is the person of the Son,
sent into the world to take on human nature; whilst the source of grace-
as-disposition and charity is the Holy Spirit, sent to dwell in our minds
through love. In the nature of things the Son's sending precedes the
Spirit's, since the Holy Spirit comes forth from the Son, love from
wisdom. Moreover, grace in man is caused by God's presence, like light
in the atmosphere is caused by presence of the sun. So grace-as-
disposition in Christ follows the union of his nature with God, in the
way splendour shines forth from the sun. And finally, activity and the
grace that disposes to it presuppose some acting subject; but before
union the human nature had no subject. So in Christ grace-as-disposition
presupposes the grace of union.

Christ's grace of headship.   The whole church is talked of as one 8 1
mystical body by analogy with man's physical body, Christ being its
head, and its different members having different functions in the whole.
Of all the parts of a physical body the head is the first (starting from
the top), the most perfect (containing every sense, internal and external,
whereas other parts contain only the sense of touch), and the most
powerful (controlling the movements and activity of every other part by
means of the sensory and motor faculties seated there). Christ is head
of the church in all these ways: first in grace because closest to God –
*for those whom he foreknew he also predestined to be conformed to the image
of his Son, in order that he might be the first of many brothers,* possessing
grace in its perfect fullness with power to instil it into every member of

the church. As God Christ is the author of grace and giver of the Holy Spirit; and as man he is the tool of this giving, whose actions are used by God's power to bring us salvation, earning grace for us and causing it in us. The head's supremacy over the external limbs of our body is obvious, but the heart's influence is hidden; so the Holy Spirit is likened to the heart, invisibly giving life and unity to the church, while Christ is likened to the head, standing out in his visible nature as man above all others. Christ's whole human nature has active power inasmuch as it is joined to the Word of God, but his body by way of his soul. So the whole Christ, body and soul, acts first on men's souls, and then on their bodies. In one way now when we *yield the members of our body to God as tools of righteousness*; in another when the life of glory will derive from soul to body: *he who raised Christ Jesus from the dead will give life to your mortal bodies also through his Spirit which dwells in you.*

3   The mystical body of the church differs from the physical body of a man inasmuch as its members do not exist all at the same time as those of the physical body do. The body of the church is made up of men from every period of world history, and in each period some members do not yet have grace whilst others already do. So there are potential members of the mystical body and actual members; some potential members will never be actual members, but those who will may be members at three levels: by faith, or by love as we know it on earth, or by the enjoyment of God in heaven. Christ then is head of all men throughout all history, but first and foremost of those already united to him in glory, secondly of those actually united to him in love, thirdly of those united to him in faith, fourthly of those only potentially united but predestined to actual unity, and fifthly of those potentially united and not predestined to be united actually. When these last leave this world they will cease to be members of Christ altogether, no longer able to unite with him in any way. Unbelievers are potentially, even if not actually, members of the church: a potentiality based first on Christ's power to save the whole of mankind, and secondarily on their own free will. And, though a church *in splendour, without spot or wrinkle*, is the ultimate goal to which the sufferings of Christ will lead us when we arrive at our heavenly home, on the way there *if we say that we have no sin we deceive ourselves*. But the sins we call fatal are lacking in those who are actual members of Christ by love; those who are guilty of such sin are only potential members, or perhaps we might say imperfect members, because their lifeless faith unites them in some way to Christ, though simply speaking they do not share his life of grace (for *faith without works is dead*). Their activity is only a kind of life, like that in a

dead limb we can't move. The sacraments of the Old Law related to Christ as *shadow to body*, and this is how the patriarchs regarded them. When you react to an image as an image you are reacting to the thing imaged, and in this way these patriarchs, by their observation of the sacraments of the Old Law, belonged to Christ with the same faith and love as we do, and were members of the same church as ourselves. The 4 analogy of a body applies to any group in which there are a diversity of tasks and activities organized for one goal. Because angels and men have a common goal, the enjoyment of the glory of God, Christ's mystical body includes both men and angels. Christ is the head of the entire gathering, closer to God than the angels and acting on them also. *God the Father seated Christ at his right side in the heavenly world, above all heavenly rulers, authorities, powers, and lords. God put all things under his feet.*

Because Christ received grace in himself in such abundance he was 5 able to bestow it on others, and that is what his headship means. So his own personal grace, by which his own soul is right, is the very grace which makes him head of the church and the source of rightness for others; any difference lies only in the way we consider it. In Adam the sin of his nature, which we inherit, derived from his own personally sinful action: his person corrupted his nature, and because of the corruption Adam's sin was inherited, the nature corrupting the persons descended from him. Christ's grace is not passed on by human nature in this way, but by the personal action of Christ. So we do not distinguish two graces in Christ, one personal and one natural, as we distinguish personal sin and sin of nature in Adam. Christ's personal grace which makes him holy is also the grace which makes others right, and as such is called the grace of headship. The grace of union, on the other hand, produces not activity but Christ's personal existence. So Christ's personal grace and the grace of headship are one and the same disposition, but the grace of union is different. We could, of course, call Christ's personal grace a grace of union in the sense of a disposition required to make union appropriate, and in that meaning of the term all three graces would be identical, though considered under different aspects. The interior flow of grace into us comes from Christ alone, for 6 his human nature alone has the power to make us right, because of its union with the godhead. But as head he guides other members of the body in external ways also, and this headship he has shared with others. They too are heads, though not like Christ: for he is head of the whole church at all times in all places and at all stages, whereas others are local heads (like bishops) or temporary (like popes) or heads only over those at a certain stage (like those still living their earthly life). Christ is head in his own right and strength, others only stand in for him. But through Christ alone *have we access to the grace in which we stand.*

Christ's humanity as God's perfect tool

9 1 **What did Christ know?**   The soul possesses no innate knowledge, but only an ability to know whatever is knowable, called by Aristotle the receptive mind: *a slate on which nothing is yet written* yet *a capacity to become everything.* But it would not have been right for the Son of God to have taken on an imperfect human nature, for through that nature he was to bring the whole of humanity to perfection. So the soul of Christ had its own proper perfection, namely knowledge. It is true that as God Christ knew everything by **divine knowledge**, but that is an uncreated activity to be identified with the divine nature itself, not an activity of Christ's soul, which is of a different nature. If Christ had had only divine knowledge his human soul would have known nothing

2 at all. Man has a potential for the knowledge he will enjoy in heaven and which is his goal in life, namely the sight of God; because he is a thinking creature, made in God's image, he has a capacity for that. But what brings him to realization of this goal is Christ in his manhood: *fittingly he for whom and by whom all things exist, in bringing many sons to glory, made perfect the author of their salvation by suffering.* So, because causes must surpass their effects, the man Christ had already to have that blissful knowledge and sight of God in a supreme degree. He enjoyed uncreated bliss by the union that made him God, but besides that he had to have a **created bliss** in his human nature, bringing his

3 soul to the ultimate goal of human life. Man's receptive mind is an ability to know whatever is intelligible, an ability that is realized when such a mind takes in the species of things and is formed by them. So we must also credit Christ with an **instilled knowledge** in which the Word of God imprinted on the soul personally united to him the species of every thing his receptive mind had the ability to know. So over and above the uncreated divine knowledge and the blissful heavenly knowledge that Christ had (knowing the Word and everything in that Word), Christ also knew things in their own proper natures by way of

4 instilled species adapted to human understanding. But God implanted in human nature not only a receptive mind but also an agent mind, the special function of which is to adapt things to actual understanding by abstracting their species from images. So Christ must also have had such abstracted species in his receptive mind, made understandable by the

activity of his agent mind. What this means is that Christ must have acquired knowledge from experience (something I once denied). Knowledge acquired through experience is distinctively human knowledge, human in the way it is received and human in the way it is caused, for it is caused by the light of the agent mind natural to man. Instilled knowledge comes by a light instilled from above and is an angelic type of knowledge; whilst the heavenly knowledge of those who see God's substance is a divine type of knowledge. Acquired knowledge is humanly acquired, primarily by finding things out for ourselves, and secondarily by learning from others. The first way is more appropriate to Christ, who has been sent to teach everyone. Everything we say of the Son of 10 1 God by reason of his divine nature can be said of the son of man, the same person, by reason of the grace of union; so we can truly say that the son of man fully comprehends God's substance, not with his human mind though, but with his divine nature. And in the same way we can say that the son of man is the Creator.

The human soul, like any other creature, can undergo two types of 11 1 action: the action of appropriate natural agents, and the action of the first of all agents who can, if he wants, realize in creatures things beyond any natural agent's power to which the creature has only a so-called potentiality of obedience. Divinely instilled knowledge realized both types of potentiality in Christ's soul, giving the soul of Christ whatever men can come to know by the light of their own agent mind (all the human sciences) and also whatever God has revealed through wisdom and prophecy and the other gifts of the Spirit. What it did not give was sight of God's substance. Knowledge of particular individual cases adds no perfection to speculative knowledge, but is needed to perfect our practical knowledge which must know how to act in particular circumstances. Prudence, as Cicero says, requires memory of past events, knowledge of present ones, and foresight into future ones. Christ had perfect prudence through the gift of counsel, and must have known everything individual: past, present and future. Up to the time of his 2 death Christ shared both the state of those on earth (particularly in his body's capacity for suffering) and the state of the blessed in heaven (particularly in his rational soul). In the heavenly state the soul is not subject to the body but master of it, and at the resurrection the glory of our soul will overflow into our body; but on earth souls are bound to their bodies and in a way subject to them and dependent on them, and for that reason they only understand by resorting to images. Souls in heaven have no need to do this, either before or after the resurrection, and neither did Christ who shared the ability with those in heaven.

12 1   Nevertheless, we must credit Christ's soul with acquired knowledge so that the activity of his agent mind making things understandable will not be wasted; just as we postulate instilled knowledge so that his receptive mind can be fully perfect. *The receptive mind takes in everything, and the agent mind brings everything to light*; by instilled knowledge Christ's soul knew everything the receptive mind could take in, and by acquired knowledge it knew everything the agent mind could bring to light. By the light of our agent mind we come to understand effects through their causes, causes through their effects, like through like, and opposites through opposites. So although Christ did not experience everything, still, from what he did experience, he could get to know everything. He did not perceive everything the senses could perceive, but by his surpassing power of mind he could come to know everything

2 from the things he did perceive. Could he grow in knowledge? Not in instilled knowledge, for there he knew all things from the beginning. Much less could his heavenly knowledge grow, and his divine knowledge not at all. So if, as I once thought, Christ had no acquired knowledge, there could have been no essential growth in Christ's knowledge at all, but simply a widening of experience and more use of his instilled knowledge to make sense of that experience. But it does not seem right that Christ should lack what is the natural human activity of intelligence, the drawing out of a thing's species as an object of understanding from our images of it; so we must attribute to Christ an acquired knowledge which grew as a result of ever new abstraction of such species. This knowledge he did not begin with, but acquired gradually during the

3 time he was growing up. Christ did not learn it from other men. He has been established by God as head of the church, and indeed of all men, so that they may receive grace and truth through him. What we learn from other people we don't derive immediately from the ideas in their heads, but indirectly by way of the words in which they express those ideas. But just as words express man's ideas so God's creatures express his wisdom. And since it is more dignified to be taught by God than by man, it is more dignified to acquire knowledge from the world than by hearing it from someone else. But we must attain a certain age before we can begin to find out things for ourselves or learn them from others, and the Lord did nothing inappropriate to his age. So although he heard people teaching things, he did not attend until such time as he could reach that level of knowledge by way of his own discovery.

The power and the weakness of Christ.   It is God's nature to exist 13 1 uncircumscribed; and just as other things' abilities to act match the perfection of their natures, so God has the ability to do anything that can meaningfully exist: he is almighty. But the soul of Christ is human and therefore not almighty. In terms of its own nature and abilities, 2 natural and graced, Christ's soul had the power to do everything appropriate to souls: to govern the body, for example, and organize its human activity, and to enlighten in a human way from its own fullness of grace and knowledge all those thinking creatures at lesser levels of perfection. In addition, as tool of the Word united to it, Christ's soul had power to bring about instrumentally miraculous changes which could serve the incarnation's goal of restoring all things in heaven and in earth. Reducing creatures to nothingness however is an activity which matches that of creating them out of nothing, which only God can do. So God alone can annihilate creatures, or preserve them in existence by preventing them from dissolving into nothingness.

Christ shared features of all three states in which men have found 3 themselves: the state of innocence, of guilt and of glory. He shared the sight of God with the saints' state of glory, immunity from sin with Adam's state of innocence, and the necessity of suffering this life's pains with our state of guilt. And *because he himself suffered and was tried, he* 14 1 *has the power to help others who are tried.* It was fitting for the Son of God to take on a body subject to human weaknesses and failings, since he came into the world to make amends for the sin of mankind, and one makes amends for another's sin by taking on oneself the penalty the other has incurred. Our bodily failings – death, hunger, thirst and so on – are penalties of the sin Adam brought into the world, so it was fitting, given the purpose of the incarnation, that the Son of God should take on these penalties on our behalf – *surely he has borne our infirmities.* Moreover, doing this buttressed our faith in his incarnation: we know human nature only with such failings, and if he had taken a nature without them he would not have seemed real but imaginary, as indeed the Manicheans say he was. So *he emptied himself, taking the form of a servant, born in the likeness of men.* By seeing his wounds Thomas was recalled to faith. Thirdly, by courageously bearing human sufferings and failings, the Word of God gave us an example of patience: *Consider him who endured the hostility of sinners, and do not grow weary or fainthearted.* But, whereas the material, so to speak, which makes amends for another's sin are the penalties borne on his behalf, the efficacy of the amends made depends on the disposition of soul which inspired this making amends for others, the love of charity. So Christ's soul needed perfection of knowledge and virtue to give him power to make amends, whilst his body needed weaknesses to give him material with which to make amends. Those weaknesses hid his godhead but they revealed his manhood, which is our road to God: *we have access to God through Jesus Christ*. At her conception Mary's flesh inherited the sin of mankind and the failings accompanying it, but Christ's flesh took from her a nature without fault, and could have taken a nature without penalties had he not wanted to accept them in order to carry out his task of setting us free. He did not inherit these failings but voluntarily undertook them. The remote cause of death and other bodily human failings is the material out of which our body is made, composed of incompatible elements, but in Adam's original state of rightness this cause was prevented from operating; so the immediate cause of death and our other failings is the sin which did away with that state of rightness. Because Christ was without sin we say he did not inherit those failings,

4 but undertook voluntarily whichever of them could be reconciled with perfection of knowledge and grace. He did not take on the kind of failings that occur in particular people for particular reasons (from genetic defect or their own fault), but accepted only those like death, hunger and thirst which are the general lot of men by reason of Adam's sin: what Damascene calls *natural but not degrading afflictions* – natural because common to all humanity, not degrading because involving no failing in knowledge or grace. Christ's soul, united to the Word of God, was entitled to fullness of wisdom and grace. The failings he took on were not an entitlement but a special provision, enabling him to make amends for our sin. So he did not have to take on all failings, but only those needed to make amends for the sin common to humanity.

15 1   *Which of you can convict me of sin?* Christ took on our failings so that he could make amends for us, prove the genuineness of his human nature, and give us an example of virtue. On none of these counts would it have made sense to take on the failing of sin. *Christ took the visible substance of his flesh from the flesh of the virgin Mary; but what caused his conception was not a male seed, but something entirely different, something from above.* So Christ's bodily material came from Adam but his origination did not; he received human nature from Adam only in a material sense, in the active sense he received it from the Holy Spirit (just as Adam himself received his body materially from the dust of the earth, but actively from God). So Christ did not share in Adam's sin, in whom he pre-existed only materially. *God made Christ sin*, not in the sense of making him sinful but in the sense of offering him as a victim for sin. (The word is also used in this sense by Hosea when he says the priests

feed on the sins of my people, meaning that they eat the victims offered for the people's sins.) Isaiah says *the Lord laid on him the iniquity of us all*, meaning that he gave him up as a victim for the sins of all men. Alternatively, *made him sin* could mean made him *in the likeness of sinful flesh*, referring to his body which could suffer and die. The function of 2 moral virtue in the unreasoning part of the soul is to make it responsive to reason, and the more perfect the virtue the more it achieves this. Moderation controls our affections, courage and meekness our aggressive emotions. And since what we mean by our *inflammability* to sin is the tendency of our sense-appetites to go against reason, the greater our virtue the weaker that inflammability is. In Christ, where virtue was at its most perfect, there was no inflammability to sin at all. The lower appetitive powers of sense are by nature amenable to reason; but our physical powers, our bodily metabolism and vegetative powers, are not like that. So perfect virtue responsive to right reason can't stop the body being vulnerable to suffering; but it can exclude inflammability to sin, the resistance of the sense-appetites to reason. Flesh has a natural sensory desire for what delights it, but in man – a reasoning animal – it desires this in a reasonable manner or measure. And that is the way Christ's flesh had a natural sensory desire for food and drink and sleep and whatever it is reasonable to desire. None of this shows inflammability to sin in Christ, or any unreasonable desire for delight. So Christ did 3 not have to suffer interior attack from his own inflammability; but he had to undergo external attacks from the world and the devil, and by conquering those he merited the crown of victory.

Since the soul gives form to the body soul and body share the same 4 existence, and when the body is upset by physical suffering the soul existing in the body is also indirectly affected. So because Christ's body could suffer and die, his soul too was affected by suffering. The soul is also affected, in a different sense, by activities it exercises by itself, or that belong more to it than to the body. Knowledge and sensation are sometimes called *affections of the soul*, but the description applies most properly to emotions of the sense-appetite, which Christ possessed along with everything else natural to men. But whereas in us emotions often bear on unlawful objects, frequently anticipate the judgment of reason, and sometimes draw reason after them, in Christ they were always under reason's control. By the power of Christ's godhead the heavenly 5 happiness of his soul was prevented from overflowing into his body and taking away its vulnerability to suffering and death, or from overflowing into his sense-faculties and excluding all pain. And since sense-appetite naturally rebels against injury to the body – by distress when it is present

and by fear when it is threatening – Christ too felt such distress and fear. But we also fear what we don't know, unexplained sounds in the
8 night, for example, and Christ had no such fears. Christ, however, experienced things as novel and unusual: new things happened to him every day. His divine and heavenly and instilled knowledge could not be surprised, but the knowledge he acquired by experience was
9 compatible with surprise and wonder. In ordinary circumstances our faculties mutually interfere: intensifying the activity of one weakens that of another. Even reasonably moderated anger distracts us from contemplation. But in Christ, by God's provision, *each faculty was allowed its own proper activity* without interference. The delights of contemplation did not prevent him feeling distress and pain at a lower level, and emotions at a lower level were no obstacle to his reason.
10 During his life on earth Christ fully saw God in his mind and consequently possessed heavenly happiness of soul; but because his soul could be affected by suffering, and his body could suffer and die, he did not have the overflow of heavenly happiness that will occur in heaven. He was already in heaven in his soul, yet journeying there in other respects.

[vol 50] 16 1 **Rules for talking about the incarnation.**   All Christians accept that *God is now a man*, but not all understand the proposition in the same way. The Manicheans understand the word *man* to mean not a true man but the appearance of one; and this applies also to those who believe that in Christ body and soul were not united. Photinus accepted the genuineness of the man but thought Christ was not God by nature but, like other holy men only more perfectly, shared in godhead by grace. Nestorius took the words *man* and *God* literally, but not the proposition as a whole, saying that it predicates man of God by some association of dignity or authority or mutual affection and indwelling. And the same error is made by those who talk of two subjects in Christ. But we hold to the truth of the Catholic faith, that the true nature of God and the true nature of man are truly united in one person and subject. So we say that *God is a man* is a true literal proposition, both in the terms it uses and the predication it makes. For any term that signifies a common nature concretely can be used to refer to any individual possessing the nature in question: *a man* can refer to any individual man, *God* to the person of the Son of God. Such terms can also be used as true and literal attributes of any individual subject possessing the nature: Socrates or Plato can literally and truly be said to *be a man*, and so therefore can the Son of God, referred to in this proposition as *God*. In the mystery

of the incarnation the two natures are distinct and cannot be predicated of each other in the abstract – the divine nature is not the human nature; but they can be predicated in the concrete, because they exist in one common subject. In the same way we can refer to the person of the Son 2 of God with the term *a man*, and predicate of him the term *God*: it is true that *a man*, namely Christ, *is God*. Idolaters call sticks and stones God because they think their nature is somehow divine; but we call this man God not because his human nature is divine, but because the subject united to that human nature is an eternal subject. From eternity 3 he has been the subject of a divine nature, and in time, through the incarnation, he has become the subject of a human nature; which is why Damascene talks of God as *made human*. But the reverse is not true: some prior subject of a human nature did not take on a divine nature, so we cannot talk of some man as *made divine*.

Nestorians would not allow terms relating to Christ's human nature 4 to be applied to God, nor terms relating to his divine nature to be applied to the man: *the attribution of suffering to the Word of God is anathema*. But to subject terms like *Christ* or *the Lord* (which can relate to both natures) they allowed predication of the attributes of both natures: so that they could say Christ was born of Mary yet existed from all eternity. Catholics, however, hold that whatever we can say of *Christ*, whether in virtue of his divine or his human natures, we can say also of *God* or of *the man*. Though we must take account not only of the way we identify the subject but also of the aspect under which the predication is allowed. Human nature is said to be taken up, not as already qualifying a subject, but as nature; so we can't say that God is taken up. Attributes of one nature may not be predicated of 5 the other in the abstract. But since concrete terms refer to the subject possessed of the nature, attributes of either nature may be predicated of concrete names for the subject of those natures, be they names relating to both natures (*Christ* – the anointer and the anointed), or only to the divine (*God* or *Son of God*) or only to the human (*this man* or *Jesus*).

A thing can be said to become whatever starts to be newly predicated 6 of it. *Being a man* can now be truly predicated of God, but it has been true of him not eternally but only since the taking on of human nature. So we can say that *God became a man*. Something can start to be newly predicated of a subject because of change in that subject, and this is always the case when the attribute in question modifies the subject intrinsically: a thing can't begin to be called white or of this size unless it has changed colour or size. But when the attribute in question is a relationship, it can start to be predicated of a subject without any change in the subject: a man can start to be on someone's right, not because he moved but because the someone did. We attribute *being a man* to God because of a union, and that is a relationship. And it started to be predicated of God not because of any change in God but because of the change in status of the human nature that was taken on by a divine person. The term *man* refers to that person of God not as some bare it but as a subject of human nature. So although it is false to say that *God became the person of the Son of God* it is true to say that *God became a*

7 *man*, by reason of his union with a human nature. But, given that in Christ there is only one person, one subject who is both God and man, the proposition *A man became God* is false. *A man* stands for a person, and *being God* is true of that man not by reason of his human nature but by reason of the subject he is. The subject of human nature who can truly be called God is the subject or person of the Son of God, and he was always God. So one cannot say that this man started to be God, or became God. If, as Nestorius says, there were two subjects, one God and the other man, and being God could be attributed to the man and being man to the God by some association of the two subjects in dignity or affection or indwelling, then of course one could just as well say that a man became God (was joined to God) as that God became a man (was joined to a man). Terms that figure as subject terms of propositions are interpreted materially, that is to say, as standing for some ontological subject; but when they figure as predicates they are interpreted formally, that is to say, as signifying some nature. So when we say *A man became God* the becoming is not attributed to the human nature but to the subject of the human nature, who was eternally God and therefore couldn't rightly become God. But when we say *God became a man* the becoming is a process terminating in a human nature. So it is right to say *God became a man* but wrong to say *A man became God*. Just as if Socrates, when already a man, turned white, then we could point to Socrates and truly say *This man today became white* but not *This white thing today became a man*. But if the subject term of the proposition is a word signifying human nature in the abstract, then we can attribute becoming to that nature as subject: for example, *The human nature became the Son of God's nature.*

8   *Careless expressions lead to heresies.* The Arians said that Christ was a creature, subordinate to the Father not only in virtue of his human nature, but also as a divine person. So nowadays, when we say that Christ is a creature or subordinate to the Father, we have to add the qualifying phrase: *in virtue of his human nature.* We can predicate of

Christ without such qualification only things that no one can suppose are being predicated in virtue of his divine person: thus we say without qualification that Christ suffered, died and was buried. Similar cases occur in ordinary life when doubt arises as to whether an attribution affects a subject as a whole or only partially. We do not say *this African is white* without qualification, but that he is *white-haired*; though we could perhaps say that he was *curly*, since that could only mean *curly-haired*. The reverse is also true: we cannot say without qualification that Christ was immaterial and not subject to suffering, lest we be taken to approve the Manichean error which denied Christ a true suffering body. We rather qualify and say that Christ, in virtue of his godhead, is immaterial and not subject to suffering.

The term *a man*, used to refer to Christ, signifies his human nature 9 which started to exist, but refers to the eternal subject whose existence had no beginning. When used as a subject term it refers to a subject, and when used in a predicate it signifies a nature; so it is false to say *A man Christ started to be*, but true to say *Christ started to be a man*. The 10 phrase *Christ as man* contains a doubling-up that could induce reference to the subject or to the nature. The latter is more proper, because a doubled-up term is a sort of predicate and should be interpreted formally: *Christ as man* means *Christ as being a man*. So it is better to admit *Christ as man is a creature* than deny it; though if we added to the doubling-up something clearly involving reference to the subject we should have to deny it, saying that *Christ, as this man, is not a creature*. In the same way, we deny rather than admit that *Christ as man is God*, 11 though it would be true to say that *Christ as man has the grace of union*. *The son of man has power on earth to forgive sins* not in virtue of his human nature but in virtue of his divine nature. The divine nature is the source of that power, the human nature its tool or minister. As Chrysostom writes, *He says pointedly: power on earth, so as to weld together in an indivisible union the divine power and the human nature. For even though he became man, he still remained the Word of God.* Note however that the proposition *Christ as this man is God* is true.

Christ's existence. Since in Christ there are two natures in one 17 2 subject, Christ must have two of whatever relates to nature and one of whatever relates to subject. Existence however relates to both: to the subject of the nature as to that which exists, and to the nature as to that which gives the subject existence. For nature we think of as a form, which exists only in the sense that something exists under that form: whiteness is what makes things white, and human nature is what makes men men. But notice that if some form or nature exists that is not related to the personal existence of its subject then that form's existence is not the person's existence in the straightforward sense of the term, but only some way in which he exists: being white is not Socrates' existence as Socrates, but only his existence-as-white. A subject or person can have many existences in this sense: the existence by which Socrates is white is not the existence by which he is musical. But the existence of the subject or person as such is one, and one thing cannot have more than one existence in that sense. So if the Son of God's human nature had supervened secondarily on him as subject, in a way unrelated to his personal existence, then Christ would have had two existences, one as God and one as man. Just as Socrates' existence-as-white differed from his existence as man, which was his personal existence as Socrates.

On the other hand, having his head or his body or life was all part of being the one person Socrates, all part of his one existence. If after Socrates had been in existence as a person he had happened to acquire more hands or feet or eyes – suppose, for example, he had been born blind – he wouldn't thereby have acquired another existence, but only a sort of relationship to these extra additions, so that now he existed with added parts as well as with those he had had before. It is because the Son of God takes up human nature not as something supervening and secondary, but as something contributing to him as person and subject, that his taking it on brings with it no new personal existence, but only a new relationship to human nature of the personal existence already enjoyed: his person exists now as a subject not only under a divine nature but also under a human one. The existence of the Son of God, which is the eternal divine nature itself, becomes the existence of a man, inasmuch as the Son of God takes this human nature into the unity of his person. Christ's soul gives existence to his body in the sense of making it into an actual living thing, completing it in nature and species. But when we conceive of the soul-body whole in abstraction from its existence in a subject, as it is signified by the phrase *human nature* – not itself a subject that exists, but that by which a subject exists – then existence belongs to the person that takes up a relationship to such a nature, the soul being a cause of that relationship inasmuch as it completes that human nature by giving life to the body.

18 1 **Christ's will.** For a variety of reasons people have maintained that Christ has only one will. Apollinarius held that the Word replaced the soul in Christ, so that he had no soul and no human will. Eutyches held

Christ had one composite nature, so one will. Nestorius thought the unity of Christ consisted precisely in a unity of affection and will. Others admitted two natures in Christ but thought he never acted on his own account but only as God moved him, and so had only one will. But the sixth ecumenical council at Constantinople resolved the matter proclaiming there were *two natures of will in Christ and two natures of activity*. This must be so because the Son of God took on human nature complete, and the integrity of human nature implies the powers that derive naturally from it, mind and will. And since the taking on of human nature involves no loss in the divine nature, which also has a will, Christ must have had two wills, one human and one divine. The whole of Christ's human nature responded at a nod to the divine will, but that doesn't deprive it of a will of its own, since that happens with other holy men too. A craftsman moves a lifeless tool like an adze by physical movement alone; a rider moves a tool like his horse, endowed with perception, by means of its appetite: a master moves his servant endowed with reason by means of the servant's own will. Christ's human nature is a tool of his divine nature in this last sense, moved by way of its own will. Some acts of will are natural and necessary – the willing of happiness, for example – and some arise from free rational decision and are neither natural nor necessary (though the reason itself is a natural faculty). So in Christ, over and above his divine will and his human power of will and its natural acts, there must be rational willing as well. Moreover, since human nature is generically an animal nature, in taking 2 it on the Son of God also took on whatever belongs to the integrity of animal nature. And that includes a sense-appetite which we can call a sensuous will, inasmuch as it shares in will by obeying it. In Christ there 3 were two kinds of act of will: willing goals and willing the means to goal. Goals (health, for example) are willed directly and absolutely as good in themselves; means to goals (for example, medicine) are willed for their connection with their goal, as good in relation to something else. These two types of willing Damascene called *thelesis* and *boulesis* – simple natural will and deliberated rational will; but they both belong to one power of will since they are concerned with one common aspect of things, goodness. So, not counting the sensuous will, we attribute to Christ one human will when we are talking of will as power, and two – natural and rational – when we are talking of will as activity.

Aristotle distinguishes willing from choosing, meaning by willing 4 natural willing, and by choosing rational free willing. Because Christ has rational will he is able to choose and choose freely. Choosing presupposes weighing things up and coming to a decision, and in us this follows on inquiry; but when a decision can be made without such preliminary doubt and inquiry it would suffice for choosing. Doubt and inquiry accompany choosing only where there is ignorance, and that 5 was not so in Christ. By special provision the Son of God during his life on earth *allowed his flesh to do and suffer according to its own proper nature*, and similarly also the powers of his soul. Clearly sensuous will has a natural abhorrence of physical pain and bodily injury, and natural will rejects intrinsically evil and unnatural things like death, even though rational will can sometimes choose them with a view to a goal. So clearly, Christ by his sensuous will and by the natural willing of his human will can will something different from God: *not as I will but as you do*, he says, willing the divine will with his rational will but admitting he wills 6 something else with some other will. But even though Christ's natural will and sensuous will may have willed something different from his divine will and his rational will, there was no opposition of wills in Christ. In the first place, neither his natural will nor his sensuous will rejected the motives for which his divine will and rational will willed his sufferings. Christ's natural will willed mankind's salvation, but it was not its function to will things as means to that end; whereas his sensuous will was incapable of stretching to that at all. And secondly, the divine and rational wills were not hampered or impeded by these movements of natural and sensuous will. Nor, in reverse, did his divine and natural wills reject or hamper the movements of his natural and sensuous wills. Rather, it pleased his divine will and his rational will that his natural and sensuous wills should act in accordance with their own natures. Christ's agony was not an agony of decision such as results from weakness of reason unable to decide which of two courses of action is best. Christ's agony was an agony of the senses, fear of the approaching calamity.

19 1 **Christ's activity.** When one thing moves another there are two activities in what is moved: the activity it has by its own nature, and the activity derived from the mover. The activity proper to an adze is cutting, but when moved by the craftsman it shapes a plank. The activity proper to the tool belongs to the craftsman only in the sense of serving his activity; but the other activity is nothing else than the craftsman's activity itself present in the tool. Whenever mover and thing moved have different natures or powers of action there will always be different activities proper to tool and tool-user, though because the tool shares in the tool-user's activity and the tool-user uses the tool's activity the

activities cooperate. In Christ the human and divine natures each have their own form and power to act, so that the human nature has an activity distinct from the divine activity and vice versa. But the divine nature uses the activity of the human nature as a tool, and the human nature shares in the activity of the divine nature as a tool shares in the activity of its user. The activity of Christ's human nature in so far as it is acting as a tool of the divine nature is not distinct from the divine activity: it is one and the same saving activity by which Christ's humanity and his divinity cooperate to save us. Still his human nature, as a nature, has its own activity distinct from that of the divine nature. Existence and activity both belong to a person by nature, but in different ways. Existence relates to the very realization of the person; the person is so to speak the end-result here and the unity of the person requires the unity of a completed personal existence. But activity is an effect of the person according to some form or nature, so that diverse activities do not prejudice someone's personal unity. What is done by Christ's divine activity differs formally from what is done by his human activity – the human activity touches and the divine activity heals the leper – but the two activities cooperate in the one effect, one nature acting with the other. Any activity in man that is not rooted in mind and will is not a human activity in the proper sense of the word, but is attributed to him in virtue of some other element in his nature. Thus he is subject to the laws of gravity as a body made of physical matter; he feeds and grows because of what he has in common with plants; and he sees, hears, imagines, remembers, desires and feels angry because of his animal nature. Though sense-activities are to some extent obedient to reason and to that extent human. In the ordinary man then the physico-chemical activities of his body are separate from the properly human activity of will. And the same is true of his sense-activities to the extent that they are not controlled by reason. In the ordinary man there is only one properly human activity, and his other activities are not properly human. In the man Jesus Christ however there was no movement of sense that was not controlled by reason; and even his natural bodily activities were in a sense voluntary, inasmuch as he willed that *his flesh should do and suffer according to its own proper nature*. So there is even greater unity of activity in Christ than there is in other men. We distinguish faculties and dispositions according to the different ways in which they relate to their objects, so that distinguishing activities according to different faculties and dispositions to activity is the same as distinguishing them by their objects. It is not such diversity of activity that we are excluding from Christ's human nature, any more than we exclude enumeration of his activities over time; what we are excluding is a diversity of primary source.

3   A person who earns something for himself possesses it in some sense by his own power; and it is more dignified to deserve what one has rather than to have it without deserving it. So, since we should attribute to Christ every dignity and perfection, he must deserve to possess whatever others do, with this proviso: the earning of the thing must add more to his dignity than the thing's previous absence would have subtracted from it. Thus, Christ did not earn his grace or knowledge or happiness of soul or divine nature, for in order to earn them he would first have had to be without them, and that would have diminished his dignity more than earning them would have increased it. Glorification of the body, however, and other things like that are less to be valued than the dignity of earning them (which derives from love of charity); so Christ earned that and all other things related to his external majesty like his ascension and the veneration we pay him.

4   Christ's grace was not just his own personal grace but the grace proper to the head of the whole church, to whom all the members are joined so as to constitute one person mystically. So what Christ earned he earned for all his members, just as what a man does with his head serves all his members. The sin of Adam, whom God had appointed to beget the whole of humanity, passed as an inheritance to others by bodily propagation; the earnings of Christ, whom God has set up as the head of all men by grace, pass on to all his members by the spiritual birth of baptism which makes us members of Christ's body: *as many of you as have been baptized in Christ have put Christ on.* That a man is granted such rebirth through Christ is a grace; and so the salvation of man [though earned by Christ] is still a grace.

20 1 **Christ's relations to his Father and to us.**   By its very constitution human nature is subject to God in level of goodness, in power and by voluntary obedience to his commands. Christ acknowledged these subjections to the Father in himself: *Why do you ask me about good? One is good: God*; and he took *the form of a servant, becoming obedient to the Father unto death.* Christ was subject to the Father with this implicit qualification: in his human nature, a qualification it is better to make explicit so as to avoid the Arian heresy that the Son is subordinate to the Father. *When everything is subject to the Son,* says St Paul, *the Son will himself be subject to the one who made things subject to him.* This means that the Son will then be subject to the Father not only in himself but in all his members, through their fully sharing in divine goodness.

At that moment too all things will be subject to him, inasmuch as his will for them shall have been finally fulfilled. But this does not mean that there are things not yet subject to him in power. The name *Christ*, 2 like the name *Son*, is the name of a person, so that what is said of Christ by reason of his eternal person can be attributed to him under that name without qualification, but what is said of Christ by reason of his human nature should rather have an explicit qualification. Christ is without qualification the Greatest, the Lord, the Ruler; but he is subject or a servant or inferior only under this qualification: in his human nature.

There are two wills in Christ, one human and one divine, and the 21 1 human will is not powerful enough to give effect to what it wills without divine help. So Christ as man and as having a human will needed to pray. Even as the person who was both God and man he willed to offer prayer to his Father, not now as lacking power in himself, but for our instruction *that they may believe that you have sent me*, and as an example of prayer for us. Prayer is a mental act, but we can say that Christ prayed 2 what he sensuously willed inasmuch as his prayers gave expression to his sense-desires as an advocate might. He wanted to show us that his human nature was a genuine one with all man's natural affections, that it was lawful for a man to will by those natural affections things God did not will, but that a man must also submit those natural affections to God's will. [So though he prayed what he sensuously willed: *May this cup pass from me*], yet because he also willed to be a just man guided by God he added *yet not as I will but as you do*. Man wills in the 4 straightforward sense of the word what he rationally wills; what he sensuously or naturally wills he wills with the qualification: as long as nothing to the contrary emerges from my reasoned deliberation. So Christ's straightforward human will was always conformed to God's will, and in consequence always heard.

We have a high priest who has entered into the heavens: Jesus, the Son 22 1 *of God*. The characteristic role of a priest is to act as go-between between God and his people, handing on to the people the things of God, offering to God the prayers of the people, and in some degree making amends to him for their sins. This is a role suited to Christ above all, for he made us *sharers in God's nature* and reconciled mankind to God. Other men possess particular graces, being legislators or priests or kings; but Christ is all of these and the fount of all graces. *Every visible sacrifice is* 2 *a sacrament or sacred sign of an invisible one*, namely, man's offering of his own *contrite spirit* to God; and everything we offer to God in order to raise our spirit to him can be called a sacrifice. We need such sacrifice for three reasons: to forgive the sin which leads us away from God (*sacrifices for sins*); to preserve us in God's grace where our peace and welfare lies (*peace-offerings*); and to unite our spirit totally to God (*burnt-offerings*). Now we have received all these things through Christ's human nature: our sins have been wiped out and we have received saving grace and laid hold of perfection of glory itself. So Christ himself as a man was not only our priest but also the most perfect of offerings: at once a sacrifice for sin, a peace-offering and a burnt-offering. The wilful slaying of the man Christ by his killers was not a sacrifice but a sin, and to that extent it resembled the impious pagan sacrifices of human beings to idols. It was the freely willed acceptance by the sufferer that made him a sacrificial victim; and in that respect there is no resemblance to pagan

3 sacrifices. The priesthood of Christ removes both our stain of guilt (giving us grace to turn our hearts back from sin to God) and our liability to punishment (making amends as man to God). It is as man that Christ is a priest, not as God, though one and the same person is both priest and God; but since his humanity worked as a tool of his godhead, his sacrifice was the most effective sacrifice for wiping out sin. The sins that go on being remembered under the New Law are either sins of people who do not wish to share in Christ's sacrifice – the unbelievers for whose conversion we pray – or sins of people who have fallen away after sharing in that sacrifice. But the daily sacrifice that goes on being offered in the churches is not another sacrifice over and above the one Christ offered, but its remembrance. *Christ is the offering and Christ the priest who offers*

4 *it; he wills the sacrifice of the church as its daily sacrament.* Christ did not need the effects of priesthood for himself but communicated them to others. He is the source of all priesthood: the priests of the Old Law prefigured him, the priests of the New Law act in his person. By the effects of priesthood I mean effects deriving from the sacrifice itself; what Christ earned for himself by his sufferings came not from the sacrifice as a work of amends, but in return for the devotion of love with

5 which he humbly bore the sufferings. Christ is *an eternal priest.* In priesthood the act of offering a sacrifice is consummated by achievement of the purpose of the sacrifice, in the case of Christ's sacrifice by the eternal gifts to come. This consummation was prefigured by the high priest of the Old Law entering the holy of holies once a year with the blood of a goat and a calf. Christ has entered the holy of holies of heaven itself, once for all, and prepared a way for us to enter in virtue of the

6 sacrifice of his blood shed for us on earth. His priesthood is *of the order of Melchizedek.* The priesthood of the Old Law inadequately foreshadowed Christ's priesthood: it did not cleanse from sin and it was not eternal. But precisely this pre-eminence of Christ's priesthood over

that of the levitical priesthood was prefigured in the priesthood of Melchizedek: when Melchizedek received tithes from Abraham the priesthood of the law, still *in his loins*, paid their tithes too. Christ's priesthood is said to be of *the order of Melchizedek* because it surpasses the priesthood of the law.

He predestined us to adoption as children of God. A man adopts a son 23 1 when in his goodness he admits someone to share his inheritance. God in his infinite goodness admits creatures to a share in his goods, especially thinking creatures whom he has made to his own image, capable of sharing the happiness in himself which has made him rich, his inheritance. When God in his goodness admits men to this inheritance he is said to adopt them. Men act in order to supply needs, God in order to communicate riches. He shares a likeness of his goodness with all creatures when he creates them, and by adopting men he shares a likeness of his natural Son with them: *those whom he foreknew to be made conformable to the image of his Son. We have received the Spirit of adoption* 2 *of sons whereby we cry: Abba! father!* The natural Son of God is *begotten not made*; adopted sons are made, though sometimes said to be begotten by a spiritual rebirth which comes not from nature but from grace. Within God begetting is the prerogative of the Father, but created effects are common to all three persons acting through their one nature. By adoption we become brothers of Christ having the same Father as he does: his Father by a natural begetting proper to himself, and ours by a voluntary action shared with his Son and Holy Spirit. So Christ was not the Son of the whole Trinity as we are. Adoptive sonship is an imitation of natural sonship, common to the whole Trinity, but appropriated to the Father as author, to the Son as model and to the Holy Spirit as imprinting in us a likeness to the model. The Son of God 3 proceeds by nature from the Father as a mental Word of one existence with the Father. All creatures resemble this Word in form, just as houses resemble their architect's mental picture; but thinking creatures resemble the Word both in its form and its mentality, as a student's knowledge resembles his teacher's idea; and by grace and charity those who are divinely adopted resemble the eternal Word of God in his union with the Father: *that they may be one in us, as we also are one.* Adoption is a privilege reserved to thinking creatures, but actually possessed only by those in whose hearts *the Spirit of adoption as sons* pours out his love of charity. Sonship is properly an attribute of a person, not a nature. 4 Christ who is in person the natural Son of God cannot be called an adopted Son; his grace-as-disposition doesn't turn someone who was not a son into an adopted son, but is rather an effect in Christ's soul derived from his natural sonship: *We saw his glory, as it were of the only-begotten of the Father, full of grace and truth.*

24 1   Predestination in the strict sense is the pre-ordaining by God in eternity of what he will do by his grace in time. That a man should be God and God a man was something God did in time by the grace of union, so Christ must have been predestined: *predestined to be Son of God in power.* It is the person Christ who was predestined, but not to be himself or be divine, but to exist in a human nature, as *he who was made of the seed of David according to the flesh.* For though being the Son of God in power was natural to the person in himself, it was not natural to him by his human nature but derived from the grace of union.

3   God predestined both Christ and us in one and the same eternal act: Christ to be the Son of God by nature, and we to share a likeness of his natural sonship in what we call adopted sonship: *Whom he foreknew he also predestined to conform to the image of his Son.* Both are effects of grace, as is clear above all in the case of Christ, whose human nature,

4   without any previous merit, was united to the Son of God. The pre-destination of Christ is the cause of our predestination in the sense that God, in one eternal act of predestination, pre-ordained that our salvation should come about through Jesus Christ. For not only what happens in time is subject to God's eternal predestination but also the way in which it happens.

25 1   Since there is in Christ only one person, divine and human, there is only one whom we reverence and honour, though we have many reasons for doing so. In the Trinity on the other hand there are three whom we

2   honour and one reason for honouring them. The veneration of Christ's flesh, if regarded as veneration of the Word whose flesh it is, is divine worship; but if it is regarded as reverence for a humanity perfected with every gift of grace, it is not worship but a sort of honour. God the Father himself receives divine worship only by reason of his divine nature, and

3   a sort of honour for the masterly way in which he rules the world. One should not reverence an image of Christ for the thing it is, carved or painted wood, since only thinking creatures deserve reverence. But one can reverence it as an image, and then the reverence paid is really reverence of Christ himself, and a form of divine worship. The true God is immaterial and cannot be represented by a material image, but in the New Covenant he has become man and can now be adored in that material image. Reverence is due to all thinking creatures as such, but paying divine worship to a thinking creature because he is made in the image of God could provoke error: the movement of worship might stop at the man himself and not be carried through to the God in whose

image he is. There is no such danger in the case of images carved or painted out of senseless material. The true cross on which Christ was 4 actually crucified, is venerated partly as representation of Christ but also because it came into contact with his body and blood; images of that cross are venerated simply as images of Christ. Unbelievers see in the cross nothing but Christ's ignominy, but we see the instrument of our salvation representing God's power triumphing over his enemy: *the word of the cross to those that perish is indeed foolishness but to those that are saved it is the power of God.* The Blessed Virgin is a thinking creature 5 who can be honoured with our service but not divinely worshipped; though as mother of God she is given higher honour and service than any other creature. Such honour of the mother honours her son, since it is because of her son that the mother is honoured. Nevertheless she is not honoured simply as an image or representation of her son, because she, unlike images, has a claim to be honoured in herself. When we hold 6 others in affection we venerate the things they leave behind when they die: not just their body but also their possessions, clothing and the like. In the same way we reverence God's saints as members of Christ, sons and friends of God and our advocates, and we honour the relics they have left behind: primarily their bodies which were temples and instruments of the Holy Spirit who dwelt and worked in them, and which are to become like Christ's body in glory at the resurrection. Admittedly, the dead body of a saint is not numerically the same body as the body that lived, since the soul which made it what it was is no longer present. But the same matter is still there and will later take on the same form again.

There is one mediator of God and men, the man Christ Jesus, who gave 26 1 *himself a redemption for all.* The function of a mediator is to bring together those between whom he mediates. Christ, having reconciled man to God through his death, is the only perfect mediator between God and man. Others can mediate between man and God in a secondary sense, cooperating by preparing the way or as ministers. The prophets and priests of the Old Law were such, announcing and prefiguring a true and perfect mediator of God and men; and the priests of the New Law are ministers of that true mediator, administering in his name the sacraments of salvation to men. A mediator stands in the middle, 2 separated from either extreme, uniting them by carrying things across from one to the other. Christ as man, set apart from God in nature and from the rest of men by the eminence of his grace and glory, communicates the commandments and gifts of God to men and made amends and intercedes for men to God. So in the truest sense of the word he is, as man, a mediator. The personal power to take away sin belongs to Christ as God, but making amends for mankind's sin belongs to him as a man; and it is in this respect that he is called the mediator between God and man.

Chapter 14

THE LIFE OF CHRIST

In this chapter we consider the things done and suffered in his human [vol 51] nature by the Son of God made flesh.

Introductory comment. In the chapter that follows Thomas considers the life of Christ as it is presented to us in the New Testament and in the Christian creed, not as a merely human biography but as a theological account of how that life was used by the one who lived it to salvage the whole of a disintegrated creation. As we have seen in the comment on chapter 13 (p 473), Thomas organizes his whole theological treatment of Christ round a concept drawn from John Damascene: Christ's human life as the tool of his divine life, contributing, as all tools do, its own cutting edge to the use it is put to by its agent. This cutting edge, in Christ's case, is the pattern his life has: the passing through death to a new and eternal life. Christ is seen as willingly accepting the responsibility for creation from his Father – he is the Word of creation made flesh – and willingly undergoing uncreation from men in order to bring creation through to recreation, so to speak: going through death to resurrection. As Mark says, the pattern of Christ's life was revealed in *the way he died*: in his *exodus* or road of departure, as Luke calls it; in his *lifting up* on the cross to glory, to use St John's word. For the act of human love with which that was done was the vehicle of God's own act of love for all creation: the act of love which God himself is. So this *passage* or *journey* of Christ makes visible and effective the true nature of God.

Thomas's study of Christ's life is the culminating study in a theological account of the whole history of salvation (or as I prefer to say, salvage) of creation. That account started with a treatment of sin at the end of chapter 8 (pp 249ff), and continued in chapter 9 with the study of Old Testament law (pp 294ff) and its need for fulfilment in a New Testament law (pp 303ff), which would be more than a law, indeed nothing less than a gracious setting of man right by God and a bursting forth of God's Spirit within men (pp 307ff). The innermost pattern of that history had already been outlined in chapter 3, when revealed history was identified as the visible and invisible embedding into time of the eternal life of the Trinity themselves (pp 79–81). Christ came as the visible Word of God made flesh, and on the cross he *breathed out* his Spirit and *handed it on* to men. By re-orienting themselves with this life and living through the decomposition that sin has brought upon creation, all mankind and the whole cosmos can *work off* sin (as St Paul puts it) and rise to a new life with God, the life that God himself lives with God.

Thomas's treatment is thus no quest for the historical Jesus, such as occupied scholars early in this century. Though he follows a chronological order – just as the gospels and the creeds do – more attention is given to the notions of Christ taking up his life and laying it down, than to the events that happened during that life. The first section is entitled **Christ's entry into the world**, and we might well ask why, if the pattern of Christ's life is to be discerned in Christ's journey out of it, does Thomas, following Matthew and Luke, make so much of his journey into it. One answer is that the section has a theological point to make: that the life of Christ was deliberately begun, so to speak: God planned it in the beginning and Christ humanly and willingly involved himself in its pattern. But a second conception also surfaces again here: the idea that Christ (and Mary too) were willingly involved in the pattern from the very moment of Christ's conception. This involves Thomas in biological difficulties, because, according to his Aristotelian biology a foetus is not even human at the moment of conception, never mind knowledgeable and self-controlled. The difficulties are a spin-off from Thomas's position that Christ had to start perfect: that his gifts and blessings are divinely instilled from above, not humanly acquired from below. We saw this argument already in the previous chapter apropos of Christ's knowledge, and saw too that Thomas had begun to feel his way to another standpoint: that to be truly man, Christ would not only be a recipient of grace from above, but also have a nature that grew from below as other men have. How Thomas would have re-thought his position on these points if he had lived in our times each reader must assess for himself. It is clear that his notions of how the virgin birth reconciled absence of inherited sin in Christ with presence of such sin in the virgin Mary (for Thomas does not hold that Mary was immaculately conceived) depend heavily on a biology which is now known to be inadequate. This point has already been mentioned elsewhere (ch 8 pp 223ff).

A short section follows on **Christ's life in the world**, starting from the Father's acknowledgement of his Son at Christ's baptism and ending with the similar acknowledgement at his transfiguration. In between there is a description of Christ's public life which, among other things, sees Christ as the first exemplar of all Dominican preachers: compare the description of Christ's way of life at p 521 below, with the account Thomas gives of his Dominican teaching and preaching ideal in chapter 12 (p 465).

Finally, we reach the weightiest section of all: **Christ's departure from the world**, which contains the theological centre of the chapter: the paragraphs headed *The meaning of Christ's sufferings*. Under that heading we are given a threefold assessment of Christ's life as consummated in his passion: Christ as God was the creative agent of that life as of everything else in creation, and used it as his tool to recreate the whole world – as God he was the effective cause of the world's salvaging; Christ as man was the willing cooperator in his own use by God – and so the earner of salvation; and what was used as the tool of salvation was Christ's bodily life and death, variously conceived as making amends for sin (mending its damage), as ransoming the world from a slavery it had itself embraced (*redemption* is simply the Latin word for ransom), or as a priestly act of sacrificial worship proclaiming and effecting a reconciliation with God. The earning aspect applies only to those parts of Christ's life which were humanly willed, up to and including the moment of his dying. But the notion of God as agent and Christ's human life as his tool does not end there; these conceptions apply to the whole divinely willed pattern of Christ's life including his burial, his resurrection, his ascension and his present and future life in heaven, sitting as judge at the right hand of his Father.

Christ's entry into the world

His virgin mother.   We can reasonably suppose that the woman who 27 1 gave birth *to the only Son of the Father, full of grace and truth*, received greater privileges of grace than anyone else: *Hail, full of grace*, said the angel. Other people have had the privilege of being sanctified in the womb: *Before you came forth from the womb,* said the Lord to Jeremiah, *I sanctified you,* and the angel said of John the Baptist: *Even from his mother's womb he will be filled with the Holy Spirit.* So one can reasonably

2 suppose that Mary too was sanctified before her birth. Only grace can cleanse from faults, and only reasoning creatures can receive grace, so Mary could not have been sanctified before she received her rational soul. Moreover, since a conceived child is not liable to fault before reception of that soul, if she had been sanctified before that moment, she would never have incurred the blemish of inherited sin, and would not have needed the ransom and salvation of Christ. If Mary's soul was never infected with inherited sin that would prejudice the dignity of Christ as the saviour of all mankind; but her purity was the greatest after Christ, who as universal saviour did not himself need salvation. He did not inherit sin in any way but was holy from his conception, whereas Mary inherited sin but was cleansed from it before she was

3 born. Even before the incarnation some people were freed spiritually from the sentence of sin, but it seems unfitting that anyone should have been freed from it bodily until after the incarnation, when immunity from the sentence first appeared. Just as immortality of the flesh had to await Christ's rising from the dead, so freedom of the flesh from inflammability to sin (which St Paul calls the law of the flesh) ought to await Christ's appearance in sinless flesh. In Mary inflammability was fettered, not by reason as it is in holy men (for Christ alone had the special privilege of using free will while still in his mother's womb), but by an abundance of grace received at her sanctification, and even more perfectly by a divine providence which kept her sensuality from all unbalanced movements. Afterwards, when she conceived Christ's flesh, the first to be immune from sin, we can suppose that complete freedom from inflammability to sin passed over from child to mother, without

4 however delivering her from death and other penalties of that sort. Since Mary would not have been a worthy mother of God if she had ever sinned, we assert without qualification that Mary never committed a sinful act, fatal or non-fatal: *You are wholly beautiful, my love, and*

5 *without blemish.* Christ is the source of grace, author of it as God and instrument of it as man, and, since Mary was closest to Christ in giving him his human nature, she rightly received from him fullness of grace: grace in such abundance as to bring her closest in grace to its author, receiving into herself the one who was full of every grace [for others], and, by giving birth to him, bringing grace to all.

28 1   *Behold a virgin shall conceive.* We assert without qualification, against the Ebionite and Cerinthian heresies, that the mother of Christ was

virgin when she conceived. This fitted the dignity of the eternal Father who sent him into the world, and the dignity of the Son, who as the Word conceived in the integrity of God's heart ought to take on flesh conceived in the integrity of his mother's womb; it fitted too the sinless humanity of Christ which would have incurred the infection of inherited sin if conceived by human intercourse in a state of nature that had lost its original rightness; and finally it provided a fitting exemplar of the goal of the incarnation, namely, that men should be reborn as sons of God *not from the will of the flesh or the will of man, but by the power of God.* That power formed the body of Christ from a virgin without using male seed, as it had formed the body of the first man *from the slime of the earth.* Nor can we doubt that Christ's mother remained a virgin 2 while giving birth, so that her integrity of body should mirror the integrity of heart which brings forth a word; and so that he who came to restore our integrity should not destroy his mother's, nor he who ordered us to honour our parents dishonour his own mother. *This gate* 3 *will be kept shut forever: no one will open it or go through it, since the Lord the God of Israel has been through it.* We abhor the error of Helvidius who dared to say that Christ's mother had intercourse with Joseph after his birth and bore other children. Christ, the only begotten of the Father, was fittingly the only begotten of his mother too, nor would it have been fitting for a womb which was the shrine of the Holy Spirit to be desecrated by a man, or for Mary herself to show ingratitude by deliberately losing what God had so miraculously preserved. So we assert without qualification that the mother of God conceived as a virgin, gave birth as a virgin and remained virgin ever after the birth. The brothers of the Lord were not natural brothers, born of the same mother, but blood-relations.

It would indeed have been appropriate for Mary to consecrate her 4 virginity to God by a vow, except that in the time before Christ was born the Law insisted rather on men and women having children to spread God's worship. So before Mary was betrothed to Joseph she would not have taken such a vow absolutely, but, desiring it, would have waited on God's will; but once she had accepted Joseph as her husband according to the custom at the time, they both took a vow of virginity. For though the keeping of the counsels of perfection is a matter of grace, which started in its perfection with Christ, it was anticipated in a manner in his virgin mother. Some miracles are objects of faith – for example, 29 1 the virgin birth, the resurrection, the sacrament of the altar – the Lord wanting these to be more hidden so that faith might be more deserving. But other miracles are worked to prove the faith and done openly.

2 Marriage consists essentially in an inseparable union of souls, husband and wife pledging unbreakable loyalty to one another for the purpose of bearing and bringing up children. The marriage of Mary, the virgin mother of God, to Joseph was altogether genuine: a consent to the marital bond though not expressly to sexual intercourse unless that should please God. As to whether that fulfilled the purpose of marriage: if that includes sexual intercourse to generate children then their marriage was not consummated, but it was fulfilled as regards the bringing

30 1 up of children. Mary was told beforehand that she was to conceive Christ, and rightly so. The Son of God thus enlightened her mind before she bodily conceived him, and gave her the chance to offer herself freely to God: *I am the handmaid of the Lord*. A kind of spiritual marriage was to take place between the Son of God and human nature, and the annunciation sought the virgin's consent to this on behalf of all humanity.

[vol 52] 31 1 **He was conceived of the Holy Spirit.** Christ's body derived from Adam in bodily substance but not through the activity of a male seed, and so he did not inherit the sin that others do when begotten from

6 Adam through a line of male generation. By saying that Christ derived from Adam in bodily substance we don't mean that Christ's bodily substance existed materially in Adam, but that the matter taken from the virgin was actively prepared for the conception of Christ by the generative power of Adam and his descendants. But it was not fashioned into Christ's body by that power, and so we say Christ originated from Adam in bodily substance but not through the power of a male seed.

32 1 The whole Trinity caused the conception of Christ, but it is attributed to the Holy Spirit for three reasons. It fits with the source of the incarnation in God – namely, love – the Holy Spirit being the love of Father and Son. It fits also the source of the incarnation in man, which was not merit but grace, attributed to the Spirit. And thirdly it fits with the end-result of the incarnation: the one who was *Holy and the Son of God*; for just as the Spirit makes other men spiritually holy and adopted sons of God, so Christ was conceived in holiness through the

33 2 Holy Spirit. If what was conceived was to be the Son of God himself, as we profess in the creed, then the body had to be taken on by the Word of God at the moment of conception; this he did through Christ's soul, and the soul through its spirituality as mind, so from the first instant of conception Christ's body [unlike other men's] must have been animated by a rational soul. What Christ and other men have in common is the breathing in to their body of a human soul just as soon as the

body was formed and disposed to receive it. The difference is that Christ's body was perfectly formed earlier in the process than ours is. Christ is a natural son of man because he has a genuine human nature, 4 even though he received it in a miraculous way. A blind person's restored sight is natural even if miraculously received.

Christ in the first instant of his conception received a fullness of grace 34 1 to sanctify both soul and body. We are to conceive of a divine fullness descending into his human nature, rather than of a pre-existent human nature growing towards God. So from the very beginning Christ enjoyed a perfect spiritual life. And since ultimate perfection doesn't consist in 2 the ability or disposition to do something but in actually doing it, Christ, from the first instant of his conception, could do whatever any soul can do in an instant: will, and consider what it knows, and so choose freely. Choosing requires previous deliberation only when there is something uncertain to be inquired into. Christ, from the first instant of his conception, had the fullness of grace and holiness and known truth. So because he had certainty about everything he could immediately and instantaneously choose. [But wouldn't his mental acts presuppose senses, and wouldn't they need organs not developed at the first instant of Christ's conception?] To begin with Christ had knowledge instilled by God which did not require use of his senses; but in any case sensation, and particularly the sense of touch, is present in embryos even before they receive rational souls, so that Christ, who at conception had a body developed and organized enough to receive a rational soul, would all the more have had from that instant the sensation of touch. Christ was holy 3 from the first instant of his conception. Adults are made holy by their own act of faith, and children by the faith of their parents and the church. The first way is the more perfect, acts being more perfect than dispositions and what one does oneself more perfect than what is done through another. So if Christ's sanctification was to be the most perfect of all, sanctifying him as the source of sanctification for all others, he must have been sanctified by his own free movement of will towards God, a deserving act. From the first instant of conception then Christ started to deserve from God. Free will moves towards good spontaneously and naturally, but towards evil unnaturally and perversely. So, provided its nature is unimpaired, free will can move to good (but not to evil) instantaneously, deserving God's rewards from the first instant of its creation. Further, from the first moment of his conception 4 the grace Christ received was without measure. Since the grace of this life measures less than the grace of the next by which men see God, clearly Christ, from the first instant of his conception, received grace equal to the grace of those in heaven and indeed surpassing it. He actually saw God from that moment with a clarity such as no other creature has.

35 1 **Born of the virgin Mary.** *What is born is a person, not his nature,* though nature is what a person receives at birth: *birth is the road to nature,* our form or species being what birth naturally aims to produce.
2 Because in Christ there are two natures, we attribute two births to Christ: one in which he is eternally born of the Father in his divine nature, and one in which he is born in time of his mother in a human nature. The eternal birth is not a process or change properly speaking,
4 though we think of it in that way. Any name which signifies a nature in the concrete can be used to refer to subjects of that nature. So both divine and human attributes can be attributed to Christ, whether he is referred to by a name signifying his divinity or a name signifying his humanity. Now to be conceived and born is something attributed to a person with reference to the nature in which he is born. Since therefore it was a divine person who took human nature to himself at the very instant of Christ's conception, we can truly say that God was conceived and born of the virgin, and hence that Mary is truly the mother of God. We could deny this only if the humanity was conceived and born before the man born became the Son of God (Photinus' opinion), or if the humanity was not taken up into the personal unity of the Word of God (Nestorius' opinion). Both opinions are mistaken, and so it is heresy to
5 deny that Mary is God's mother. Christ is a son twice over because of his two births, but since there is only one subject there, the eternal subject, the only sonship that really exists in that subject is his eternal sonship. He is called his mother's son as a reciprocal of her relationship of motherhood to him. He is really her son because of the real relationship of motherhood to Christ existing in her. The birth in time would have caused a real created sonship only if there had been in Christ a subject in which that relationship could exist.
7   By being born in Bethlehem Christ confounded those who boast of the great cities from which they come. He preferred to be born in an undistinguished place and to suffer indignity in a celebrated city. *That we might acknowledge that what he did to transform the whole earth came from God, he chose a poor mother and a still poorer birthplace. God chose what is weak in this world to shame the strong.* And to show his power all the more he set up the capital of his church in the capital city of the world as a sign of his complete victory, so that the faith might spread from there throughout the world. *The lofty city he lays low; the feet of*

the poor man – Christ – *trample it and the tread of the needy* – the apostles Peter and Paul. *When the time had fully come, God sent forth his Son,* 8 *born of woman, born under the law.* Christ, Lord and Creator of all history, chose the time of his birth, just as he chose his mother and his place of birth. *He deigned to take flesh when the newborn would have to be enrolled in Caesar's census, submitting himself to subjection to bring about our liberation.* At a time when the whole world was at peace under one ruler, he who is *our peace* came *to gather together his own into one* so that there might be *one flock and one shepherd.* He chose to be born in the rough winter that he might from the first endure affliction of the flesh on our behalf. All men were to be taught about the grace of God our saviour, 36 1 but not immediately he was born, only later on after he had *worked salvation in the midst of the earth.* Only after his sufferings and resurrection did he say to his disciples *Go and make disciples of all nations.* Judgment needs recognition of the judge's authority, and for this reason Christ, when he comes to judge, will come openly. But when he first came, it was to save men by faith, which believes what it cannot see, so his first coming was rightly hidden. But just as it would have been 2 detrimental to man's salvation if Christ's birth had been made known to all men, so too if it had been known to none. Faith would have suffered in the one case by being completely visible, and in the other by having no witnesses though *believing depends on hearing.* The first wit- 3 nesses were shepherds, the first fruits of the Jews, from close at hand; and then the wise men came from far off, the *first fruits of the Gentiles.* *At the end of eight days, when he was circumcised, he was called Jesus.* By 37 1 being circumcised, Christ showed the reality of his human flesh and his approval of circumcision as an institution of God; he gave proof of his descendance from Abraham and deprived the Jews of a pretext for rejecting him; and by circumcision Christ *commended obedience to us by example, taking up the remedy custom prescribed for cleansing the sinful flesh in whose likeness he had come,* and taking on himself the burden of law that he was to take away from others.

Christ's life in this world

He was baptized. John's baptism was not itself a sacrament but [vol 53] 38 1 rather a sort of preparation for the baptism of Christ, belonging to the law of Christ rather than to the law of Moses. John was *a prophet and more than a prophet,* the end of the law and the beginning of the gospel. He prophesied: *I baptize you with water* cleansing the body, *but he will* 2 *baptize you in the Holy Spirit* interiorly, which only God can do. So

John's baptism is named after its minister, because it could do nothing more than he could, whereas the baptism of the New Law is not. All John's work and teaching looked forward to Christ, who would confirm by way of miracles both his own and John's teaching. When the Jews asked John why he baptized he appealed to the authority of scripture to confirm his role: *I am the voice of one crying in the wilderness: make*
3 *straight the way of the Lord.* John's baptism did not confer grace but prepared for grace to be conferred on men through Christ: pointing out the way to Christ, accustoming men to the rite of baptism, and preparing them by penance to receive the effects of Christ's baptism.

39 1   *The Lord was baptized not so that the waters would cleanse him but so that he could cleanse them, purifying them by his sinless flesh to assume the*
4 *power of baptism.* When the sons of Israel passed through the river Jordan they entered the promised land. What is special about Christ's baptism is that it admits one to the kingdom of God (symbolized by the promised land): *unless one is born again of water and the Spirit, one cannot enter into the kingdom of God.* Remember that Elijah divided the waters of Jordan just before being snatched up to heaven in the fiery chariot. The crossing of the Red Sea prefigured baptism as a blotting out of sin, but the crossing of the Jordan prefigured it as opening the gates of the kingdom of heaven, its principal effect, accomplished by Christ alone.
5 Christ's passion opened heaven to men in general, but needs to be applied to those who are to enter heaven through baptism: *when we were*
8 *baptized in Christ Jesus, we were baptized in his death.* As begetter of the Word the Father was appropriately revealed at Christ's baptism through a voice, a voice bearing witness to the Sonship of the Word. At the moment when Christ came of age, and the time was opportune for him to teach and work miracles and turn people to himself, his Father witnessed publicly to his divinity so that his teaching might be believed. It was especially appropriate that this accompanied baptism, through which men are born again as God's adopted sons, made like to his natural Son: *After being washed in the waters of baptism, the Holy Spirit comes down upon us from on high, and the voice of the Father declares us to have become sons of God by adoption.*

40 1 **His public life.**   Christ journeyed about, not living in one place, for he *came into the world for this: to bear witness to the truth* by preaching publicly: *I must proclaim the good news of the kingdom of God to the other nations too, because that is what I was sent to do.* Secondly, *Christ Jesus came into the world to save sinners*: and *showed us by his example that we should go about searching for those who are perishing, like a shepherd*

searching for lost sheep. Christ chose an active life of preaching and teaching, passing on to others the fruits of his own contemplation, because it is more perfect than a life of contemplating on one's own and yet presupposes abundant contemplation. To show preachers however that they must not be always in the public eye, the Lord withdrew from the crowds at times *to rest a while, to pray,* and *to teach us to do nothing for show.* By his manner of life the Lord gave an example of perfection 2 in everything that directly relates to salvation, but abstaining from food and drink is not directly related to salvation. That Christ returned from fasting and the desert to everyday life fitted the kind of life Christ was to pursue, handing on the fruits of his own contemplation to others. Such a man first spends time in contemplation, and then comes down to the market-place and associates with others. His poverty also suited his life of preaching, for a preacher of the word of God must be entirely free from the worldly concerns that accompany possessions. The Lord when sending his apostles to preach told them to *keep neither gold nor silver,* and the apostles said *it would not be right for us to neglect the word of God in order to serve at table.* Christ willingly lived in accordance with 4 the law of Moses to show his approval of it, and by bringing it to perfection in himself he showed it was preparing for him. By so acting he also deprived the Jews of occasions to calumniate him. As to his working of miracles on the sabbath, our Lord himself pointed out that the sabbath law forbids human work but not God's work of providing for his creatures: *My Father goes on working, and so do I*; nor does it forbid works necessary to man's welfare, even physical, nor the worship of God. On all three counts Christ's miracles did not break the sabbath.

Jesus was led out by the Spirit into the wilderness to be tried by the devil, 41 1 so as to give us help in such trials, to warn us that no one however holy can think himself safe from them, and to teach us how they may be overcome. *We have not a high priest incapable of having compassion on our weaknesses, but one who has been tried in every way we are, but without sinning.* Trial from the enemy can be without sin since it is suggested from outside us, but when the flesh tempts us the trial is not without sin since it comes by way of pleasure and desire. Christ submitted 2 himself to the devil's trials willingly. To be tempting suggestions must 4 concern things towards which people are inclined; so the devil will not straightaway tempt to grave sins, but first to lighter ones, and then little by little lead to greater ones. That is the way he tempted Adam: first with eating: *Why did God command you not to eat?*, then with vainglory: *Your eyes will be opened,* and finally with the extreme of pride: *You will be like gods.* Similarly with Christ: first he was tempted with food, which all men desire, however spiritual they may be; then with the vainglory of doing something for show, and here even spiritual men are sometimes found wanting; and finally with the desire of riches, a temptation which has no appeal for spiritual men. Christ resisted not with power but by appealing to the witness of the Law. The devil tried to lead him from desire of one sin to committing a second: from desiring food to the vain working of a useless miracle, and from the desire of glory to trying out God by throwing himself down headlong.

42 1   *I was sent only to the lost sheep of Israel.* It was appropriate that Christ's preaching – his and his apostles' – started with the Jews alone, so as to show that his coming fulfilled the ancient promises made, not to the Gentile peoples, but to the Jews. By the victory of his cross Christ would win power and dominion over the Gentiles, so, although before his passion he did not wish his teaching preached to them, afterwards he told his disciples: *Go and teach all nations.* This is also why shortly before his passion, when certain Gentile disciples wished to see Jesus, he answered *Unless the grain of wheat falls on the ground and dies it remains a single grain, but if it dies it yields much fruit*: here *he calls himself a grain which is to die in the Jews' lack of faith in order to multiply in the*
2 *faith of the Gentiles.* When a few perversely endanger the welfare of many, the preacher and teacher must not be afraid to offend the few if that will provide for the many. The Scribes and Pharisees and leaders of the Jews by their malice greatly hampered the welfare of the people, opposing Christ's teaching and leading the people astray by their evil ways. So the Lord, undeterred by the offence they took, publicly taught
3 the truth they hated and denounced their vices. Teaching may be secret in three senses. The teacher may be purposely hiding his teaching because he is envious of others or because what he teaches is immoral; but in Christ's teaching there was nothing immoral, and as the Lord says: *Would you bring in a light and then hide it under a bushel?* Another sense in which teaching may be secret is by being taught only to a select few; but Christ taught everything to the crowds and his disciples. Finally, the manner of the teaching may hide it from the people: Christ spoke certain things to the crowd in parables, proclaiming spiritual truths they couldn't grasp, but the pure unveiled truth he interpreted to his disciples, so that they could hand it on to those fit to receive it.
4 Christ did not put his teaching into writing. He taught it in a more excellent way, imprinting it on his hearers' hearts, which is the final purpose of writing teaching down. Nor could Christ's teaching be comprehended in the written word: it is *the law of the spirit of life* and

has to be *written not with ink but with the spirit of the living God, not on stone tablets but on the fleshly tablets of the heart.*

God empowers men to work miracles principally in order to confirm 43 1
teaching which is beyond proof by human argument and must be proved by the argument of divine power, and secondarily in order that we may believe God is dwelling by the grace of his Holy Spirit in the men working the miracles: *the works my Father has given me to carry out, these same works witness concerning me.* God alone can change the natural order 2
of things and work miracles, but human nature can be the instrument of divine action, and human activity receive power from the divine nature. *We must believe Christ to be from the Father yet equal to him; to show both things Christ sometimes does miracles by power, and sometimes by prayer.* Moreover, Christ came to save the world not only by divine 44 3
power but also by the mystery of the incarnation itself; so in healing the sick he made use not only of his divine power, healing by way of command, but frequently added some human action to it, *laying his hands on them, spitting upon his eyes, making a paste of spittle and spreading it on the eyes of the blind man.*

His transfiguration. Our Lord foretold his passion to his disciples 45 1
and persuaded them to follow him on the road to that passion. But in order to follow a road properly one must have some knowledge of the destination; an archer can only shoot straight if he can see the target. *Lord we do not know where you are going, so how can we know the road?* This is especially necessary when the road is rough and hard and the journey wearying, yet the destination delightful. Christ underwent his passion in order to obtain glory not only for his soul (which had enjoyed it from the first moment of his conception) but also for his body: *Was it not necessary that Christ should suffer and so enter into his glory?* So it was appropriate for him to be transfigured, that is, to show his disciples the glory to which they were to be configured. *He will transform our wretched bodies into copies of his glorious body.* That the glory of his soul 2
did not overflow into his body from the first moment of Christ's conception was a divine provision made so that he might fulfil the mysteries of our redemption in a body that could suffer. But that did not deprive Christ of the power to let his soul's glory flow into his body. And so far as splendour is concerned he let this happen temporarily and miraculously in the transfiguration, though not in the permanent way it happened when his body was glorified. Men are adopted as God's sons 4
by conformity of image to the natural Son of God. In this life the conformity is imperfect, but in the life of glory it will be perfect. *We*

are already the children of God and what we shall be has not yet been revealed; but we do know that when it is revealed we shall be like him, because we shall see him as he is. Since it is by baptism that we acquire grace, and since the transfiguration foreshadowed the splendour of our future glory, it was appropriate that both at Christ's baptism and at his transfiguration Christ's natural Sonship should be revealed by witness of his Father, the only one, with Son and Spirit, who is perfectly cognizant of that perfect begetting.

Christ's departure from the world

[vol 54] 46 1 He suffered.   The word *necessary* is used in more than one sense. Sometimes it means what can't be otherwise by its nature, and in this sense it wasn't necessary for Christ to suffer, either as God or as man. But sometimes the necessity meant is extrinsic: compulsion from some external agent, or something required by some goal. No force compelled Christ to suffer: God decreed it but Christ accepted it willingly. The suffering was however required for a goal: for our sakes – *the son of man must be lifted up so that whoever believes in him may have eternal life and not perish,* for his own sake – *was it not necessary that Christ should suffer and so enter into his glory?,* and for God's sake – *all the things written about me in the law of Moses and the prophets and the psalms must be fulfilled, for it is written that Christ must suffer and rise again from the dead.* That Christ should suffer to set men free was consonant with both the mercy and the justice of God: with his justice, because Christ by suffering made amends for the sin of mankind and freed them through his own justice; with his mercy, because since man could not make amends himself God gave his Son to do it, and so showed even greater mercy than if he had forgiven the sins without any amends made.

2 Absolutely speaking God could have set man free in some other way: *nothing is impossible with God.* Because God foreknew and fore-ordained the suffering we can say that it was impossible, given God's fore-knowledge, for man to be set free in any other way; but that is a reasoning that applies to everything foreknown and forewilled by God. The justice [that required Christ to suffer] itself depended on God's will requiring the human race to make amends for sin, and if God had wanted to set men free without amends being made he would not have acted unjustly. God is accountable to no higher authority, he himself is the highest general good of the whole universe, and he can forgive sins committed

3 against himself without doing anyone else an injustice. Setting man free by the sufferings of Christ, however, brought many advantages for man's

salvation. It showed man how much God loved him and aroused return of love; the sufferings gave us an example of obedience, humility, constancy, justice and many other virtues; his passion earned for men the grace that makes them pleasing and the glory of eternal happiness; man felt more bound to stay free from sin – for *you were bought with a great price, so glorify and bear God in your body*; and a greater dignity accrued to man, since he now overcame the devil who had deceived and overcome him. For all these reasons it was better for us to be set free by Christ suffering than simply by God's will. Although man was unjustly enslaved by the devil, he was justly abandoned to that slavery by God because of his sin. So it was appropriate that man should be set free by a man's justice, Christ making amends by his sufferings.

Christ couldn't be expected to suffer every kind of suffering: many 5 are mutually exclusive like being burnt and drowning. But he suffered suffering from every side: from Gentiles and Jews, from women and men, from rulers and servants and the mob, from associates and friends; he was deserted by his friends, his good name blasphemed, his honour scorned, his possessions torn from him, his soul burdened with sorrow, weariness and fear, and his body assaulted with wounds and blows. Death by crucifixion is a most painful death. The nails pierce hands 6 and feet where the most highly sensitive nerve-endings are located. The weight of the hanging body constantly increases the pain, which lasts a long time, unlike death by the sword. Add to this the inner sorrow from all the sins for which he was making amends: the sins of the Jews and of those guilty of his death, and above all the failing of his disciples who took scandal at his sufferings. And at the end of it all the loss of bodily life which human nature naturally abhors. These pains were magnified by the sufferer's sensitivity. Christ's body, formed miraculously by the workings of the Holy Spirit, was exquisitely constituted; and his interior consciousness perceived clearly all the causes of his sorrow. There are cases where inner sadness and even external pain can be mitigated by mental activity, the higher powers overflowing and affecting the lower. But this did not happen in Christ's sufferings, for as Damascene said, *he allowed each of his powers to act according to its own nature.* And 8 although Aristotle says that vehement sorrow inhibits every delight, not only those specifically opposed to the sorrow, and vice versa, this is true only when powers are allowed to overflow naturally one into the other. In Christ's case this did not happen: the pain of his passion was at a maximum, and so simultaneously was the delight of his bliss. We 12 attribute these sufferings to the divine person, though not in virtue of his divine nature which cannot suffer, but in virtue of his human nature.

If therefore someone denies that the Word of God suffered and was crucified in the flesh, let him be anathema. By reason of the personal union *the death of Christ became as it were the death of God, and destroyed death.*

47 1   Because Christ's soul did not repel from his body the hurt inflicted on it, but was willing for his bodily nature to suffer, we say he laid down

2   his life, or died willingly. *Christ was obedient to his Father even to death; for just as by the disobedience of one man many were made sinners, so by the obedience of one many shall be made just. Obedience is better than sacrifices,* so it was appropriate that this sacrifice of Christ's sufferings and death should proceed from obedience. Christ accepted a command from his Father to suffer: *I have the power to lay down my life and the power to take it up again,* he declared, *and this command I have received from my Father.* Since the Old Law reached its consummation in Christ's death – when dying he said, *It is consummated* – we may take it that his sufferings fulfilled all the precepts of the Old Law. The moral precepts based on the commandment of charity he fulfilled by suffering out of love both for his Father – *That the world may know that I love the Father and that I do as the Father has commanded me: Arise, let us go hence –* and for his fellowmen – *He has loved me and given himself up for me.* The ritual precepts concerning sacrifices and offerings he fulfilled by his sufferings, for all the old sacrifices foreshadowed the one true sacrifice offered by Christ when he died for us: *these are a shadow of things to come, but the body is of Christ.* The judicial precepts concerned with recompensing those who suffered injustice Christ fulfilled by his sufferings, for *he restored what he did not steal,* allowing himself to be nailed to a tree in the place of the fruit that man had stolen from it against God's command. He fulfilled the commandments of charity by obedience, and he was obedient for love of the Father who gave the command.

3   God the Father pre-ordained by his eternal will that the sufferings of Christ should set mankind free, he filled Christ with love and inspired him with the will to suffer for us, and he did not shield him from that suffering but abandoned him to his persecutors. It shows both God's severity, unwilling to forgive sin without punishing it – *he did not spare even his own Son –* and God's goodness, which, when men were unable to make sufficient amends by punishment they might themselves undergo, gave to men someone who could make amends on their behalf – *he has delivered him for us all.* The Father gave Christ up and Christ gave himself up out of love, and we praise them for it; but Judas gave him up out of avarice, the Jews out of envy, Pilate out of fear of Caesar,

5   and them we blame. The leaders of the Jews knew Jesus *to be the Messiah*

promised in the Law, but did not know him to be God. Still it was a wished-for ignorance that doesn't excuse them: they saw the evidence and perverted it out of hatred and envy of Christ, refusing to believe the word in which he declared himself God's Son. But the ordinary people did not know the hidden meanings of scripture and did not fully recognize him as either Messiah or Son of God. Wished-for ignorance aggravates faults rather than excuses them, for it shows a man so intent on sinning that he doesn't want to know anything that might deter him from the sin. The Jews sinned in this way, crucifying Christ not only as man but as God. The Jewish leaders' sin was the gravest, both because 6 of what they did and because it was done with malice. More excusable was the sin of the pagans at whose hands Christ was crucified, for they had no knowledge of the Law.

The meaning of Christ's sufferings.   Christ received grace not only 48 1 as an individual but as the head of the church from whom grace would flow out to his members. So what Christ does will relate not only to him but to his members just as to himself. Now clearly anyone in grace who suffers for justice's sake deserves and earns salvation for himself – *Blessed are they who suffer persecution for justice sake.* So Christ earns salvation by his sufferings not only for himself but for all his members. Christ earned eternal salvation for us from the moment of his conception, but because there were obstacles on our part to our benefiting from his previous deserving actions, it was necessary for Christ to suffer and remove these obstacles. Christ's sufferings thus had an effect that his previous actions did not have, not because of any greater love, but because the kind of deed he did was more appropriate to that effect. Properly speaking a man makes amends for an offence when he offers 2 to the offended person something that person loves at least as much as he hated the offence. Christ by suffering in a loving and obedient spirit offered God more than was required to recompense the sin of all mankind, more because of the greatness of his love and the dignity of his life (God's life as well as man's). Christ's sufferings then were more than enough to make amends for the sins of mankind. *He is a propitiation for our sins, and not for ours only but for those of the whole world.* Head and members make up a single mystical person, as it were, and so the amends made by Christ belong to all the faithful, his members. Unity of love allows one man to make amends for another, even though one man can't confess another's sin for him or repent on his behalf. This is because making amends is an external act that can be performed through instruments, and that includes friends. *True sacrifice is anything done to* 3 unite us to God in holy fellowship, anything ordered to the goal of the goodness that will make us truly happy. But *Christ offered himself up for us through his sufferings*, and the voluntary endurance of those sufferings, because motivated by such great love, was most pleasing to God. Clearly then Christ's sufferings were a true sacrifice. Other figurative sacrifices symbolized this one, and it too is a symbol of something real that we must do: *Since Christ has suffered in his own flesh, you too must arm yourself with the same intent: he who has suffered in the flesh ceases to sin, and lives the rest of his life in the flesh for God's will and not men's desires.*

4   Sin binds a man and enslaves him: *everyone who commits a sin is a slave to sin*. And because it was the devil who conquered man and led him into sin, man is also enslaved to the devil. And since sin makes man liable to God's just punishment, there is also a kind of slavery here, inasmuch as man must now suffer what he does not wish, whereas free men are able to decide their own future. But since Christ's suffering was enough and much more than enough to make amends for both the sin and the liability to punishment of mankind, his sufferings were a kind of ransom by which we are delivered from both slaveries. Christ made amends not with money, but by the greatest gift of all, himself, given up for us. And so we call the sufferings of Christ our ransom. By sin man ceased to belong to God in the sense that he ceased to be united with him in love. So that when he was set free from sin by Christ's suffering making amends for him, we can truly say that he was bought back and ransomed. Man's fault didn't enslave him to God; rather by his sin he left God's service and became enslaved to the devil, God justly allowing it because of the offence committed against him. But as regards punishment, man is principally indebted to God as sovereign judge, and to the devil only as executioner. The devil deceived man by guile and, as far as his own actions were concerned, held man enslaved unjustly in regard both to sin and its punishment; nevertheless it was just that man should suffer, God allowing it in regard to sin, and passing sentence as regards the punishment. So it was justice to God that required men's ransom, not justice to the devil. Christ offered his blood (or the life *which is in the blood*) as a ransom-price to God and not the

5 devil; and himself paid it. So payment and ransom belong immediately to Christ as man, and then to the whole Trinity. Christ as man then is quite properly called our redeemer or ransomer, though the ultimate

6 source of redemption and ransom is the whole Trinity. For God is the principal agent of our salvation, using Christ's humanity as his tool. Every activity and suffering of Christ truly effects man's salvation, but as a tool wielded by God's power. Christ's sufferings were the normal

consequences of weakness in the flesh he had taken on; but Christ's weakness, being God's, has a power that surpasses every human power, producing its effects by spiritual contact through faith and the sacraments.

So Christ's passion considered as God's action effects our salvation; as willed by Christ's soul it earns it; and as something that took place in his flesh it makes amends (freeing us from our liability to punishment), ransoms us (freeing us from slavery to sin itself), and is a sacrifice (reconciling us to God).

The effects of Christ's sufferings.   Christ's suffering is the proper 491 cause of our deliverance from sin. First because it provokes love in us, and by love we obtain pardon for sin: *many sins shall be forgiven her because she has loved much.* Secondly, it ransoms us from sin, for Christ is our head, and his sufferings – endured in love and obedience – freed us, his members, from our sins, as though they paid our ransom. It is as though a man by performing some deserving deed with his hands ransomed himself from a sin he had committed with his feet. The body, made up of different members, is a natural unity, and the church is Christ's mystical body, reckoned as one person with Christ as its head. Thirdly, Christ's sufferings are the instrument of our deliverance, because the flesh in which Christ endured his sufferings is God's tool, so that his suffering and actions have God's power in them to drive out sin. Christ by his sufferings set up a cause of deliverance from sin, which could deliver men from sins of any age, past, present or future, rather as if a doctor were to make up a medicine by which any kind of future disease could be cured. Christ's suffering is this general remedy curing sin, but it needs to be applied to any person whose individual sins are to be wiped away. This is done by baptism and penitence and the other sacraments which derive their power from Christ's sufferings. Christ's passion is also applied to us by faith, so that we perceive its effect. But the faith that cleanses us is not lifeless faith such as co-exists with sin, but faith vivified by love. Christ's passion is thus applied not only to our minds, but to our hearts, and in this way sins are forgiven by the power of Christ's passion.

Because of his sin man deserved to be handed over to the power of 2 the devil; and since men had offended God by sin, God in justice abandoned them to the devil's power. Christ's suffering delivered us from sin and from the power of the devil and reconciled us to God. Even now God allows the devil to try men's souls and vex their bodies, but in Christ's passion man has a remedy prepared by which he can

protect himself from his enemy's assaults and avoid the ruin of eternal
3 death. Christ's passion delivered us from our liability to punishment
directly and indirectly: directly inasmuch as his suffering made more
than enough amends for the sins of all mankind, causing the liability to
punishment to cease; and indirectly inasmuch as his suffering caused
deliverance from the sin which made us liable to punishment. Christ's
passion produces its effect in those to whom it is applied by faith and
love and the sacraments of the faith. Those condemned to hell are not
joined in that way to Christ's passion so do not perceive its effect. For
that we have to be configured to Christ, and that happens sacramentally
in baptism: *we were buried with him by baptism into death.* So no penalties
are imposed on people just baptized, because they have been completely
set free by the amends Christ has made. But because *Christ dies once for
our sins* men cannot be configured to Christ's death a second time by
the sacrament of baptism. A man who sins after baptism must be
configured to the suffering Christ by some penance or suffering he bears
himself, though this can be much less than his sin deserves since Christ's
amends work with it. Christ's amends are effective in us inasmuch as
we are incorporated as members of the body of which he is the head..
But members must conform themselves to the head. Hence just as Christ
first had grace in his soul, but a body that could suffer, and through his
sufferings came through to a glorious immortality, so we who are his
members are freed by his sufferings from liability to all penalty in this
way: first we receive the spirit of adoption as sons into our soul and are
listed as heirs of immortal glory, while still having a body that can suffer
and die; and later, when we have become like Christ through suffering
and death, we shall be led into eternal glory: *if we are sons, we are heirs
also; heirs indeed of God and joint heirs with Christ, provided we share his
sufferings so that we may share his glory.*

4   Christ's passion reconciled us to God in two ways: it removed the sin
which made us God's enemies, and as a most acceptable sacrifice to God
it appeased him, just as men are led to forgive offences committed
against them by some mark of respect tendered to them. The fact that
Christ voluntarily suffered was such a great good to find in human
nature that God was appeased in regard to all the offences of mankind,
given that we join ourselves to the suffering Christ in the ways we have
mentioned. To say that Christ reconciled us to God doesn't mean that
God began to love us anew: *with an eternal love I have loved you.* But
Christ's passion removed all occasion for hatred, washing away sin and
5 substituting an agreeable good. Two kinds of sin prevent us entering
the kingdom of heaven: one, common to all humanity, is the sin of

Adam, which shut the gates of heaven to man, and the other is the individual sins of men committed by their own acts. Christ's passion not only delivered all humanity from its common sin – fault and liability to punishment – Christ paying our ransom, but also freed from their individual sins all those who share in Christ's sufferings by faith and love and the sacraments of faith. So Christ's passion has opened to us the gates of the kingdom of heaven. *By performing works of justice*, the patriarchs earned entry into the kingdom of heaven *through faith* in Christ's passion, and were cleansed from their own personal sins. But neither their faith nor their justice could remove the obstacle constituted by the liability of the whole human race; that had to be removed by the ransom of Christ's blood. Before Christ's passion no one could enter the kingdom of heaven to achieve the eternal happiness of enjoying God completely.

Deserving implies some right in justice to an equivalent return. If 6 somebody takes more than his due unjustly, it is just to deprive him even of what is his due: he is said to deserve it in punishment for his injustice. And similarly if a man of just will deprives himself of something to which he was entitled, he deserves to have something additional given him as a sort of reward for his justice. Christ in his suffering humbled himself in four ways: he suffered and died when he owed no such debt, his body was buried and his soul went down to hell, he endured shame and outrage, and he was subjected to the power of human judges. And so he deserved to be lifted up in four ways: to rise again in glory, to ascend into heaven, to sit at the right hand of God and have his godhead revealed *so that at the name of Jesus every knee should bend, of those in heaven, on earth or under the earth*, and to be given power to judge. By his previous merits Christ deserved the lifting up of his soul for its charity and virtue. But in his sufferings he earned the lifting up of his body as a sort of recompense; for it was right that the body which had been subjected to suffering out of love should receive recompense in glory.

He was dead, and was buried.   It was *expedient* that Christ should 50 1 die. First to make amends for mankind sentenced to death for sin, secondly to prove the genuineness of the human nature he had taken on, thirdly to free us from fear of death, fourthly by dying to *the likeness of sin* (that is, to its penalty) to give us an example of dying spiritually to sin itself, and fifthly by rising again from the dead to show his power over death and give us the hope of rising from the dead ourselves. Christ did not die from disease, for then his death might have seemed the necessary consequence of his nature's weakness; he suffered a death which was imposed from outside but to which he offered himself

2 interiorly, showing us that his death was voluntary. The grace of union in which God united himself to Christ's flesh is a much greater grace than that of adoption which sanctifies other men, and a grace of a more lasting nature because directed towards unity of person, not only union of love. But even the grace of adoption can only be lost through sin. So since Christ never sinned the union of God with his flesh could never be dissolved. Christ's flesh was as much united to the person of the Word of God after death as before. The Word of God is said to be united to his flesh by way of his soul inasmuch as it is the soul that makes the flesh part of the human nature the Son of God took on; not as if the soul was a medium binding together the person and his flesh. But the flesh belongs to the human nature because of the soul even after the soul has separated from the flesh, for by a disposition of God there remains in the dead flesh a certain relationship to its resurrection. And so the union of God with the flesh remained. The soul gives life to a body by being the form that makes the body alive [in the sense that whiteness makes things white], so that whenever soul is present and united to body as its form the body must be living. But God doesn't give life as a form, but as an agent of life: God can't be the form of any body. So Christ's flesh didn't have to be alive just because it was joined

3 to God: God is an agent who acts not of necessity but as he wills. Since the Word of God was not separated from Christ's body by his death, still less was he separated from Christ's soul. Just as we say of the Son of God that he was buried (something true only of his body separated from its soul), so we say in the creed that he descended into hell, because

4 his soul, separated from its body, did. When a man or animal dies it stops existing as a man or animal, for death is the departure of the soul which gave it its nature of man or animal. So to say that Christ was a man during his three days in the tomb is in the simple straightforward sense of the words false; though one can say that during those three

5 days he was a dead man. The body of Christ dead was the same body that had been alive, in the sense of belonging to the same subject, the Word of God. But not in all respects the same, since it had lost an essential attribute, that of life. Otherwise we would have to say that the body suffered no disintegration. It may not have decomposed fully into its elements, but it was no longer integrated with its soul. The dead body of any other man is not the same as his live body in any simple sense, because it retains no unity with a subject. It is the same only materially, not formally. But Christ's body remained the same body

because it retained the same subject. Wherever a subject exists with a single nature, and that nature is dissolved, the unity of the subject is also lost. But the subject of the Word of God exists with two natures. So although the body did not retain its same specific nature it remained the same body numerically.

If by death we mean the process of dying, talk of Christ's death is talk 6 of his sufferings, and what we said of his sufferings causing our salvation applies in the same way to his death. But if we mean by death, as we now do, the state of being dead, then his death cannot be an act earning our salvation, though it can still be an effective tool of God, causing our salvation: for since death did not separate God from his flesh, anything that happened in either his flesh or his separated soul by God's power was effective for salvation. But the proper effects of causes resemble them. Hence Christ's death is said to have destroyed death in us, both the death of the soul through sin, and the death of our bodies through separation from our souls.

Fittingly Christ was buried. It proved that he really died, and by 51 1 rising from his tomb he gave hope of resurrection through him to those in their graves. Christ's burial, like Christ's death, is effective in our salvation: Jerome says *we rise again by Christ's burial*. So that his death 3 would not be ascribed to natural weakness Christ chose not to let his body rot or decompose in any way; to show his divine power it remained incorrupt. Christ's body would of its nature have been subject to suffering and to decomposition, but that was not deserved by any sin. So the power of God preserved it from decomposition in the same way that he raised it from the dead.

He descended into hell. There were good reasons why Christ 52 1 descended into the underworld. First, he came to bear our punishment so that we might escape it, and for his sin man deserved not only to die but to go down to the underworld. Secondly, having vanquished the devil through his sufferings, it was right that he should go down into the underworld to release those whom the devil had imprisoned there. And thirdly, having shown his power on earth by living and dying there, he showed it in the underworld by visiting and bringing light. Christ's passion is as it were a universal cause of salvation for both living and dead, which is applied in special ways to bring about particular effects. Its power is applied to the living by the sacraments that configure us to Christ's sufferings; to the dead it was applied by Christ himself descending into the underworld. Christ's descent produced effects in every part 2 of the underworld: he confounded the unbelief and malice of the damned,

he brought hope of future glory to those in purgatory, and to the holy patriarchs there only on account of sin inherited from Adam he brought the light of eternal glory. In substance his soul descended only into that part of the underworld where the just were imprisoned, but his effects reached out to every part; just as by suffering on one spot on earth he
5 delivered the whole world. Faith in Christ had already, during their own lifetimes, delivered the holy patriarchs from all sin inherited and committed and from their liability to punishment for those committed. But they remained bound by their liability for punishment for sin inherited, which meant they were excluded from glory till the price of man's ransom had been paid. Nowadays those who believe in Christ are released by baptism from liability to punishment for sins committed, and from their inherited liability to exclusion from glory, yet remain bound to the inherited liability to die. They are renewed in spirit but
7 not yet in body. Christ's descent into the underworld freed those united by faith and love to his sufferings. Infants who had died with inherited sin were not so united, for without use of their own free will they could have no faith of their own, and they had not been cleansed of inherited sin by the faith of their parents or any sacrament of faith. So Christ's
8 descent into hell did not free such infants from the underworld. His sufferings had the same efficacy then as now: those in the same situation as souls who would now be confined to purgatory were not immediately freed by Christ descending into the underworld, but those in the same situation as souls who would now be released from purgatory were released immediately. Christ's power is at work in the sacraments healing and in a way expiating. The sacrament of the eucharist releases someone from purgatory inasmuch as it is a sacrifice making amends for sin; but the descent of Christ into hell did not of itself make amends. Its power came from the sufferings of Christ which had made such amends, and those sufferings, though they made amends in general, had to be applied to each person personally. So Christ's descent into the underworld did not necessarily release everyone from purgatory. The defects from which Christ instantaneously delivered men during his earthly life were personal defects peculiar to them, whereas exclusion from God's glory is a general defect affecting the whole of the human race. Souls in purgatory were released by Christ from their exclusion from glory, but not from their liability to penalties of purgatory due to personal defects. The opposite is true of the patriarchs, who had been delivered from their personal defects before Christ's coming, but not from the common defect.

He rose again from the dead.   Christ's resurrection was necessary. [vol 55] 53 1
Firstly, to endorse God's justice which *puts down the mighty from their
thrones, and exalts the lowly*: Christ out of love and obedience to God
humbled himself even to death on a cross, so God's justice demanded
that he be exalted to a glorious resurrection. Secondly, to confirm our
faith in Christ's divinity. Thirdly, to lift up our hopes, for when we see
Christ our head rising again we hope for our own resurrection to follow.
Fourthly, to reform our lives: *Christ having risen from the dead will never
die again, and you too must reckon yourself dead to sin and alive to God.*
Fifthly, to bring our salvation to completion: *He who was given up for
our sins rose again for our justification.* The sufferings of Christ achieved
our salvation, properly speaking, by removing evil from us; his resurrection was the beginning and pattern of the good things to come. To 2
confirm our faith that Christ was truly God he had to rise quickly, not
delay it to the end of the world; but to confirm our faith that Christ was
truly man and died, there had to be a delay between his dying and his
rising again. The delay of three days was enough. When one is brought 3
back from the event of death, one lives again as before; but when one
is brought back from the necessity, or better the possibility, of dying,
then that is true and perfect resurrection. Christ was the first to rise in
this way and to attain an altogether immortal life: *having risen from the
dead he will never die again.* Those who were raised from the dead in the
Old Testament or by Christ returned to life only to die again. By its 4
created nature Christ's body was no more powerful than his soul but by
his divine power more powerful; and the soul by unity with godhead
was more powerful than the body by its created nature. So body and
soul mutually re-united themselves by God's power within them, not
by their own created power.

   Christ appeared to his disciples *in another form*, Mark says, but not 54 1
in an appearance of glory. It was in his power for his body to be seen
or not seen, to have a glorious appearance and a non-glorious one or a
mixture of the two: even slight differences are enough to disguise a
person's appearance. Some things we know in the ordinary way of nature 55 1
and others God reveals by a special gift of grace; and the way God lays
down for these is that some privileged people receive the revelation
immediately and relay it to the less privileged. The future world of glory
surpasses anything we know ordinarily and must be revealed to us by
God, so Christ's resurrection into glory was not revealed to all the
people, but to witnesses who made it known to others. Christ suffered
on the other hand in a body of a nature that could suffer, the sort known
to all. When it comes to the state of glory women are in no position of

inferiority: if they burn with greater love then they will be strengthened with greater glory when they see God. So the women who loved the Lord most closely did not leave the tomb even when his disciples did

2 and were the first to see the Lord risen in glory. Christ rose not to return to the life everyone knew, but to a kind of immortal life conformed to God: *What he lives, he lives to God.* Fittingly then the resurrection itself was not seen by men but announced to them by angels. The disciples saw the ascension's starting-point, how he was lifted from the earth, but not its end-point, how the heavens received him. Christ's resurrection on the other hand surpassed our ordinary knowledge in its starting-points (the soul returning from the underworld, and the body exiting from a closed tomb) just as well as in its ending-point (the attainment

3 of a life of glory). So it was not seen at all by men. To show that his resurrection was genuine it was enough that Christ should appear more than once to his disciples, talking with them on friendly terms, eating and drinking, and letting them touch him. But to show that his resurrection was to glory he refused to live with them uninterruptedly in the old way, lest he give the impression that he had risen to the same

4 sort of life as before. Christ's resurrection was made known to men in the way divine things are revealed, according to the different dispositions in those who received it. The well-disposed perceived it clearly, the ill-disposed in a confused way with doubt and error. That is why the risen Christ appeared in his own form to those disposed to believe, but in a different form to others whose faith had already started to cool off, and who were saying: *We had hoped that he would be the one to ransom Israel.*

6 Christ revealed his resurrection in two ways: by the witness of angels and the scriptures, and by signs. These signs were enough to show both the genuineness and the glory of the resurrection. His body was genuine because it was solid: *touch me and see for yourselves: spirits don't have the flesh and blood you see I have*; it was human, as their eyes could see; it was Christ's own body, as was shown by his wounds; it was joined to a soul, because he ate and drank, saw and heard them, talked to them and discussed the scriptures; and it was joined to a divine nature, because of the miraculous catch of fishes and his ascension into heaven. The resurrection was glorious because he came in through closed doors, and suddenly vanished from their sight, able to be seen or not as he wished.

56 1   Christ's resurrection causes ours: *Christ is risen from the dead, the first-fruits of those who have fallen asleep. Death came through one man and through one man resurrection from the dead.* We can give reasons for this. The source of human life is the Word of God. Now causes – fire, for example – naturally affect what is nearest to them first of all, and

then through that things further away. So the Word gave immortal life first to the body naturally united to him and through that resurrection works the resurrection of everyone else. The Word acts as he wills, so what he effects doesn't have to follow immediately but at the time he decides: after we have first conformed to the suffering and dying Christ in our own suffering and mortal life we shall then come to share in the likeness of his resurrection. God's justice is the principal cause of our resurrection, but the resurrection of Christ is, so to speak, its tool. The power of an agent using a tool isn't limited to working through that tool, but when it does the tool becomes a secondary cause of the effect. God's justice as such wasn't bound to cause our resurrection by way of Christ's; he could have chosen to free us in other ways. But because he decreed that way Christ's resurrection is the cause of ours. Christ's resurrection doesn't properly speaking earn our resurrection, but it effects it and sets the pattern for it. The resurrected humanity of Christ is a tool of God's power, and just as the other things Christ did and suffered in his humanity save us in virtue of his divine power, so his resurrection effects our resurrection by virtue of the power of God to bring the dead to life. That is a power present at all places and times and such contact suffices to produce its effects. The primary cause of our resurrection is divine justice, which appoints Christ judge because he is the son of man, so that the power of Christ's resurrection extends effectively to good men and bad: good and bad alike are subject to his judgment. But Christ's resurrection also sets a pattern for our resurrection: we shall rise conformed to his glorious body. So, though Christ's resurrection effectively extends both to good and bad men, it sets a pattern only for the good, who have become conformed to the image of his Sonship. Christ's 2 resurrection acts in virtue of God's power in him: a power which extends not only to the raising of bodies but to the raising of souls. Souls are raised according to merit, by justification; bodies are raised according to reward (or penalty) by judgment. Christ doesn't justify everyone but he does judge everyone. So all rise bodily but not all according to the soul. *He was put to death for our sin, and rose to justify us.* Justification is the effect of both Christ's sufferings and his resurrection acting in virtue of God's power. But his sufferings and death set the pattern for forgiveness by which we die to sin, and his resurrection the pattern for newness of life by grace and justice. And the sufferings of Christ also earn our salvation.

57 1 **He ascended into heaven.**   After his resurrection it wasn't fitting for
Christ to remain on earth where things get born and die; it was better
for him to ascend to heaven where nothing decomposes. By ascending
to heaven he achieved no additional essential glory of body or soul but
he attained the proper place for glory. The delay in going was only to
2 show the genuineness of his resurrection. *The person who ascended is the*
same one that descended. Christ descended in two senses. As God he
descended from heaven, not a spatial movement but an emptying, which
did not so much put aside his fullness as take on our smallness: *being in*
the form of God he took on the form of a slave. In this sense of descending
he did not leave heaven behind but took up an earthly nature into the
unity of his person. But Christ also *descended right down to the lower*
regions of the earth, and that was a spatial movement belonging to Christ
4 as a man. God is enthroned in the heavens, not because he is contained
in the heavens, but because he contains them. There is no heaven above
6 him; he exists above them all. Christ's ascension is a cause of our
salvation both from his side and from ours. On our side his ascension
increased our faith, lifted our hopes, directed our love towards heaven,
and increased our reverence for him. On his side he prepared a road to
heaven for us: *I am going to prepare a place for you, so that where I am*
you may also be; he entered into heaven *to intercede for us*, just as the
high-priest in the Old Testament entered the sanctuary to represent the
people in God's presence (Christ's very presence in his human nature
in heaven is an intercession for us); and being now enthroned above the
heavens as God and Lord he showers down God's gifts on men. Our
salvation is an effect of Christ's ascension but not something earned by
it. Christ's sufferings cause our ascension into heaven by removing sin,
which is the obstacle to our entry, and by earning heaven for us. But
Christ's ascension more directly causes our ascension by beginning in
our head what we shall share in as members united to him.

58 1 **He sits at the Father's right, as judge.**   Sitting is both a state of
2 rest and the position of authority when passing judgment. To sit at the
Father's right implies sharing divine glory and happiness and judging
authority with the Father, changelessly and royally; all of which belongs
to the Son as God. But the word *at* also suggests an approach to the
right hand, a coming near, yet accompanied by distinctness. In one
sense the coming near is in nature and the distinctness in person, and
in this sense sitting at the Father's right belongs to Christ by nature as
the co-equal Son of the Father; in another sense the distinction is in
nature and the unity in person, and then the sitting belongs to Christ

as man through the grace of union; and in yet a third sense it belongs to him through grace-as-disposition, by which he shares in his Father's goods to a greater degree than any other creature, with greater happiness and with authority to judge. Because Christ is our head, what is conferred 4 on him is also conferred on us in him. And so because Christ is already risen, St Paul talks of God as having raised us *with* him, though in ourselves we are still not risen and waiting on the resurrection. And in the same way St Paul says *he has made us sit* with *him in the heavens*, namely, by the very fact of our head, Christ, sitting there.

Three qualities are needed for passing judgment: authority to enforce 59 1 the judgment, righteous zeal to motivate it with proper love of justice, and wisdom to formulate it. The first two are prerequisites but the third is what really constitutes it as judgment, as an application of the law of wisdom and truth. Now since the Son is Wisdom begotten, the Truth that proceeds from the Father and perfectly expresses him, authority to judge belongs in a special sense to the Son. Even in his human nature 2 Christ is head of the entire church, and God *has set all things under his feet*; so that in his human nature too he has authority to judge. God judges men through the man Christ that his judgments may be the sweeter for men. Authority to judge belongs to Christ as divine person, 3 and also because of his headship and his fullness of grace-as-disposition, yet he has also earned it for, in God's just disposition, the judge was to be someone who fought for God's justice and conquered, and had himself been unjustly judged. One cannot pass final judgment on what 5 is altering until it is completely finished. Thus one can't judge actions until they are over and their full effects are known, since many actions appear helpful at first but later effects prove them harmful. In the same way we can't pass final judgment on a man until his life is over: there are too many ways in which he can go from good to bad or bad to good, or from good to better or from bad to worse. *Men only die once, and after that the judgment.* But we must also remember that though a person's life in time ends with his death, it still hangs in some sense on future events: his memory lives on (sometimes with a false reputation), something of the father exists in the sons, a man's actions still have effects (Arius' errors will go on causing unbelief till the end of the world), and there are our bodies and possessions left on earth. All this is to be submitted to God's judgment too; and that must wait until the last day in which everything relating to every man will be finally and clearly brought to judgment. After death the soul enters a sort of changeless state, and the judgment of its reward need be delayed no further; but everything else still developing throughout history must await a final verdict at the end of time. There can be no further earning or losing of entitlement, but there are details of final reward and punishment still to be settled.

Chapter 15

LIVING IN CHRIST

We turn now from the mysteries of the Word made flesh to the sac- [vol 56] raments of his church, through which the Word made flesh now operates.

Introductory comment.   Thomas is turning, he says, from the *mysteries* of the Word made flesh to the *sacraments* of the church. There is a deliberate play on words here. In early Rome the word *sacrament* appears to have meant a deposit or pledge made to the gods, and hence an oath, including a soldier's oath of allegiance. But in the early church the word translates the Greek *mysterion*, a state secret, a word used by the so-called mystery religions to describe their secret rituals and teachings, and by the scriptures to refer to God's eternal secrets finally revealed in Christ. By Thomas's time *sacraments* most commonly meant those six or seven external rituals of the church thought to have been instituted by Christ as means of dispensing God's grace to man: baptism, confirmation (at one time, perhaps, part of the baptismal rite), the eucharist, penitence (a more private affair by this time than the great public penitential rites of earlier times), anointing of the sick, the ordination of men to certain holy offices in the church, and possibly, though there was still dispute, marriage. Thomas however shows himself conscious of the broader background. In chapter 11 (p 409) he mentions sacraments (alongside oaths) as religious rituals by which men externally acknowledge some gift from God; he contrasts them with sacrifices, in which men offer to God. Earlier still in chapter 9 (p 297) he had sketched out his theory by which such symbolic gestures to God are natural to men, though the particular form they take in any society is specified by the humanly enacted laws or customs of that society. In God's own chosen society of Israel, specially consecrated by God to his worship, the form sacraments took was laid down by God's own Old Testament law. For Thomas the New Testament sacraments of the church are the successors to such humanly and divinely specified rituals.

He thinks of them as actions of worship, specified by Christ, which attest the faith of a new Israel – the community of Christian believers – in a gift already given by God in the mysteries of Christ's life. They therefore replace the old Israel's rituals which attested faith in a gift yet to come.

Thomas begins then from the notion of the sacraments as **the sacraments of Christ**. By sacrament he says he means primarily a sign, but it becomes clear that the kind of sign he is thinking of is a sign which represents something in action, a ritual. In fact he thinks of the sacraments as so many re-enactments of the mystery of Christ's passion and death and resurrection, that journey through death to life which his previous chapter has identified as the tool of God's salvaging of creation (see comment on pp 511ff). The re-enactments are not meant to repeat the journey, nor merely to recall it, but they are meant, as he says, to *apply* it to the participants, to draw the participants into the journey, or (in a striking phrase that Thomas uses more than once) to pass on to them the effects of that journey *as if they themselves had been the ones who suffered and died* (p 566 below). Through such rituals we *put on* the grace of Christ so that we can die to sin and live consecrated to the new life of worship begun by Christ's sacrifice. Through the sacraments of the church the mysteries of Christ's life put their mark on ours; Christ continues his work of salvage with our cooperation in our lives. To help explain this Thomas again has recourse to the concept drawn from John Damascene by which he has explained how God can give grace through creatures: the concept of Christ's human nature as the tool of his divine person (see comment on chapter 13, p 473). Chapter 13 studied the making of this tool, chapter 14 its actual employment – Christ's life. This chapter – the last chapter Thomas was to write – begins to treat of the tool's application to us through the further tools of the sacraments.

Three aspects of his treatment merit particular attention. Sacraments are seen as events or moments in history, as bodily events, and as social events. At the time the accepted way of saying that the sacraments introduce us into eternal life was to say that they *give grace*, but grace was (and is) too often conceived in a restricted mould as a general disposition, a second nature endowing men with virtues and gifts of the Spirit. In chapter 9 Thomas had already set the concept of grace in a much larger context: the notion of grace as primarily the act of favour that God himself is (p 312), and then as any and every action of God in the world by which man is helped towards salvation and new life (pp 314–16). So now Thomas goes out of his way to stress that the grace of the sacraments is not just a general dispositional equipment for living the new life, but quite particular effects of Christ's saving actions experienced at particular moments of human life (pp 551–2). The grace of baptism (and of confirmation in a related way) is a moment-of-birth grace, the moment of first identification with the death of Christ. The grace of the eucharist is the grace of repeated actual moments of embrace and bodily union with the beloved, renewing, exercising, refreshing and expanding our actual love. Each sacrament is a moment in my human life on this earth, a moment which develops the identification of my individual life with the saving life of Christ, and so at the same time marks my individual life as a continuation of that saving life. In this connection there is an interesting but unfinished aspect to Thomas's theological account: he attributes to each sacrament separately, over and above what he calls the sacrament as such (he means the outward ritual sign) and the reality it signifies (that is to say, the interior grace of new life entered into), a third half-way element, so to speak, realizing both aspects, sacrament and reality: an interior reality that is itself a sign or mark. In baptism and confirmation this third element is identified with what is called a *character* imprinted on the recipient's life, making him a participant in the active priesthood of Christ; in the eucharist it is identified with the invisible presence of that priest himself within the symbols of bread and wine; in penitence with the interior repentance of the sacrament's recipient underlying his external ritual acts of penance. Emerging from this approach is a second account of what is achieved by the sacraments – an incorporation of men into Christ's act of sacrificial worship of his Father – which Thomas is attempting to integrate into the more usual account of the sacraments as medicines of grace to forgive our sins.

These historical moments of identification with Christ's priestly sacrifice are bodily events. That means not only that they are outwardly visible rituals accompanying and making symbolically visible some interior application of past events of Christ's life to our present lives in order to raise them to future eternal life; but also that the present outward bodily rituals are the means by which those events are being presently applied. In Thomas's words, the sacraments do not only signify, they cause; and *it is by signifying that they cause.* The rituals are tools the cutting edge of which is their symbolic representation of Christ's sacrifice, tools actually being wielded in history by Christ (through his institution of the church ministry of those sacraments) to incorporate men into his own life. The sacraments are visible historical gestures of Christ in the present world. They are the outward bodily tools of the life of unity with God, just as kisses and embraces are the outward bodily tools of love between human beings.

And finally, this is a communally shared life, bodily incorporating the whole society of human history into the history of the man Christ. Indeed, for Thomas the sacraments are all parts of one great ritual present in the eucharist, and that ritual's effect is through the evoking of love to constitute the church a community. By an analogy we might call this community a religious community (here we should remember again the treatment of religion in chapter 11 of this book, and the place that sacraments were allotted there, at p 409); but the fact is that the church is far more than a religious community. The church in Thomas's theology is a society for the recreation of the cosmos, fulfilling in itself every kind of society devoted to the good of mankind and of the world. Nowadays, people frequently complain that the church is meddling in politics; and it does, just as it has meddled in religion all these centuries. For the church is a movement of human renewal, renewing the way we relate to God and the way we relate to our fellowmen. In that sense the church falls short of itself whenever it attempts to put on a merely worldly face – be it that of a human political society or that of a human religious society in any narrow sense of the words.

After Thomas has finished his treatment of the sacraments in general he starts to treat each of the seven sacraments separately, as so many stages in the application of Christ's life to ours. In **baptism** we are born into that life, in **confirmation** we celebrate a certain maturity in it; in **the eucharist** the very source of the life – the act of love that is God become incarnate in the flesh of Christ passing through death to life on Calvary – is made incarnate in the community of taking part, the communion of partaking in the ritual; in **penitence** the external actions of *penance* expressing a sinner's *repentance* – in Thomas's Latin, the three italicized words are the one word *paenitentia* – are themselves taken up by God and used as signs and tools of that sinner's forgiveness; ...
The treatment of penitence is unfinished, and what we have is a detailed expansion of what was discussed in chapter 9 as the effects

of grace working in us, the reconciliation of sinners (pp 318–21). But at this point Thomas himself passed through death to life and into everlasting love.

One thing perhaps docs need special comment: the dominant place given in Thomas's theology of the eucharist to its miraculous aspect, or what from an Aristotelian point of view – in which accidental supervening properties of a substance cannot naturally exist outside of the relevant substance – must appear miraculous. This miracle is forced in the eucharist, according to Thomas, by the fact that the words of consecration over the bread and wine cause what he calls *transubstantiation* of those substances into the body and blood of Christ; and yet the appearances of bread and wine remain. A century or so before Thomas's time Berengarius had asserted, or been understood to assert, that the body and blood of Christ were present only in the sense that they were signified as present by the bread and wine. The eucharist was nothing more than a symbol of the body and blood of Christ sacrificed on Calvary. Thomas's opinion echoes his teaching on the sacraments as a whole: the sacraments not only signify, they cause, and it is by signifying that they cause. The eucharist not only signifies Christ's body and blood to be present, it really makes them present; but it is precisely by signifying their presence that the eucharist makes them present. All the sacraments signify (and therefore are tools of) Christ acting on us, and so of Christ in contact with us and in that sense present to us. But this sacrament signifies Christ himself, present before he acts on us, so to speak, present as able to act on us, just as food is present before we eat it as something able to be eaten. In baptism Christ is present through his activity's presence in the water's action; in the eucharist Christ is present through his existence present (in some way) in the sacrament's existence. In the shadow of Berengarius this insistence on the real presence, explicitated in the face of philosophical objections as the miraculous replacement of the substance of bread and wine by the substance of Christ's body and blood, occupies centre-stage in Thomas's treatment. The consequent discussion throws many incidental lights on Thomas's notion of substance and supervening properties, on existence and creation, on the individuality of dimensioned and extensive matter. But in the wings stands the other much more important and theologically rewarding aspect: Christ's substance is really present under the outward appearances of bread and wine only because those appearances are signifying its presence by God's creative command (and indeed will depart when those appearances depart). For what Thomas makes clear is that Christ's substance is *not* present in the way that bread's substance was: underlying the dimensions and sensible properties of bread in such a way that those properties become Christ's physical properties, or that Christ's body is in physico-chemical and spatial contact with the environment. What he does not perhaps make equally clear is the way in which Christ's substance *is* really present: as the new significance (to be grasped by faith) of what previously only signified bread. Thomas, we must remember, will not allow anything to take on multiple substantial forms. It was one of the main criticisms made of him in his lifetime by antagonists who did not share his commitment to the absolute reality of created existence. Thus, for Thomas, man's mind is man's form, that which makes man the whole man; there are not also other subsidiary animal, plant and non-living forms actually present as causes of the attributes he shares in common with those substances. Man's mind is the one form *actually* present, organizing the human body and so producing the effects of those other forms, which Thomas describes as *virtually* present in the actual presence of man's human form (ch 5 pp 115–16). Transubstantiation, it would seem, is Thomas's way of saying that in the eucharist the only *actual* substantial significance of what is apparently bread and wine is the significance God's creative command has given to those appearances; though the *virtue* of bread and wine in all other senses (including the physico-chemical, nutritive and biological senses) remains. Indeed, Thomas states explicitly that the individual existence of the particular bread used, as possessed now by its properties, remains in the consecrated sacrament: remains as the existence of those properties, though no longer as the existence of that bread (pp 578–9).

The sacraments of Christ

60 1 **What is a sacrament?**   *A sacrament*, says Augustine, *is a sacred sign.* Whatever relates to something in some way can be named after it: since organisms are called healthy when they possess health, we can call medicines healthy when they cause it, diets when they preserve it, complexions when they are symptomatic of it. Our word *sacrament* is similar: primarily it names something with hidden holiness in it – a

sacred secret, but it can also name things which cause such holiness, or symbolize it, or have some other connection with it [like oaths, for example]. We shall use the word to mean a sign of something holy. Now signs are intended for men, to lead them from the known to the 2 unknown. So sacraments are properly signs of something bringing holiness to men. Thus, certain things in the Old Testament signified Christ's holiness as something that would make men holy: the sacrifice of the Passover lamb, for example, symbolized the sacrifice of Christ that makes us holy. Such things can properly be called Old Law sacraments. A sacrament properly so-called is some sign of our being 3 made holy, and that involves the cause that makes us holy (Christ's sufferings), the nature of the holiness produced (grace and virtue), and the ultimate goal for which we are made holy (eternal life). The sacraments are signs of all three: commemorating Christ's past sufferings, demonstrating the grace those sufferings are presently producing in us, and foretelling our future glory. Because a sacrament is a sign of the sanctifying cause as sanctifying, it must be a sign of the effect produced.

Man's natural path to knowing things only his mind can grasp is 4 through what he perceives with his senses. Since the sacred realities signified by the sacraments are spiritual things that only mind can grasp, the sacraments must signify them with things our senses can perceive, just as the scriptures express them with analogies drawn from the perceptible world. All our knowledge originates in sense-perception, and signs are first and foremost perceptible things: *a sign is something which by impressing a certain form on our senses, simultaneously makes something else known to us.* Nothing that only mind can grasp can act as a sign, unless it is itself made known by signs. Sacraments are used in 5 man's worship of God and God's sanctification of men. Since human sanctification lies in God's power, man cannot decide what should be used for the purpose, that is for God to determine. So the sacraments of the New Law, which make men holy, use things God has decided on. Just as the Holy Spirit decided the symbols this or that passage of scripture would use to signify spiritual things, so God determined what things should act as signs in this or that sacrament. For whether a thing makes us holy or not depends not on its natural power, but on God's decision. In the period when men relied on the law that is in them by nature, interior instinct alone prompted them to worship God and choose what signs to use in worship. Later, men had to be given a law from above: partly because the law in their nature had become obscured by their sins, and partly to make more explicit that it was the grace of

Christ which was to make the whole race of mankind holy. So God decided what things men should use in their sacraments. This didn't restrict the road to salvation, since the things chosen were easily available.

6   For three reasons it was appropriate to include words in the sacramental signs. The cause that makes us holy is himself Word made flesh, so the sacraments fittingly unite words to the perceptible things they use. Again, what is made holy is man, made up of body and soul, so the medicine of the sacraments should contain both things our bodies can touch and words our souls can believe. Finally, the very notion of sacraments as signs requires words, since *words have pride of place in our signifying*: they can be formed in countless different ways to signify different mental ideas, and so can express much more distinctly what we are thinking about. To define the signification of sacraments more precisely, then, we need words as well as things: water by itself could be a sign of washing or cooling, but by saying *I baptize you* we show that in baptism we are using it to signify spiritual cleansing. Words and thing together make a unified sign in the sacraments, the thing providing a sort of material the meaning of which is formed and completed by words. The material thing, notice, can be an action as long as it is perceptible: something like washing or anointing. The Old Law sacraments foretold a future Christ and hadn't to be so explicit about him as the New Law sacraments, which flow from Christ himself and bear in themselves his likeness; though even in the Old Law sacraments

7 words also had a place. Determinate form is even more important to things than determinate matter; indeed determinate matter is required only to accommodate the form's determinateness. So if the material used by sacraments has been predefined, much more must the form of words be. The words are effective in the sacraments *not as spoken but as believed*, that is, not in virtue of their external sound but in virtue of the sense faith can find in them. This sense is the same whatever language it is spoken in, so the sacraments take effect in any language. If someone deliberately speaks them wrong, presumably he is not intending to do what the church wants done and the sacrament will not take effect. But if he gets the words wrong by mistake, by a slip of the tongue, then it will depend on how wrong he gets them: if the words lose all their

8 meaning then the sacrament can't take effect, but otherwise it will. This is true too of addition or subtraction of words. If the person uttering the changed words has the intention of introducing a rite different from the one accepted in the church, presumably the sacrament will not take effect; for the person apparently doesn't intend to do what the church

wants done. And the same will happen if the changes deprive the words of their due meaning. But if the additions or subtractions don't substantially alter the meaning then they won't change the nature of the sacrament either.

Do we need sacraments?   *You can't unite men in a religion unless they* 61 1 *share visible symbols or sacraments keeping them together.* Mankind's salvation requires sacraments. They suit man's nature: he comes to know the spiritual world that only mind can grasp by way of the physical world he perceives with his senses. They also suit man's state after sin: he has subjected himself to an affection for the physical, and the remedies he needs must be applied to the place where the wound is. And finally they suit man's leanings toward external activities, offering him salutary alternatives to superstitious observances and worship of idols. It is true that *purely external practices are not of much use*, but sacramental practices are not purely external: they signify and cause something spiritual. And though Christ's sufferings are enough to save man, that doesn't make sacraments unnecessary. It is Christ's sufferings that give them their efficacy, and which they apply to men: *All of us who have been baptized into Christ Jesus have been baptized into his death.*

Sacraments were not needed in the state of innocence either as 2 remedies for sin or as means of achieving knowledge and grace in the soul. Though Adam needed grace in that state, he acquired it spiritually and invisibly, not through external perceptible signs. But after Adam's sin, the highest parts of man's soul need to receive their perfection through the physical world. Marriage, it is true, was instituted in the state of innocence, but for the sake of its natural function, not as a sacrament. It symbolized the future relationship of Christ and his church, just as everything else that preceded Christ prefigured him. *The* 3 *first sacraments observed and celebrated under the Law foretold the Christ who was to come,* for no one can be made holy after Adam's sin except through Christ, *whom God has put forward as a reconciliator through faith in his blood, showing his justice: that he is just and can make just whoever believes in Jesus Christ.* So before Christ's coming there needed to be certain visible signs that a man could use to attest his faith in the future coming of the saviour. As time passed sin began to take an even greater hold on man, so darkening his mind that the injunctions of the law that is present in him by nature were no longer adequate to the task of living rightly. There had to be a written law spelling out those injunctions. And the same is true of sacraments of the faith: with the passage of time the knowledge of faith had to be made more explicit; so the Old Law

defined special sacraments of faith in a Christ to come, more specific
4 than the sacraments that existed before the Law. But now even the Old
Law sacraments *are abrogated because fulfilled, and others have been
instituted, more powerful and efficacious, easier to do and fewer in number.*
The patriarchs were saved through faith in a Christ to come; we are
saved through faith in a Christ who has already been born and suffered.
Sacraments are signs expressing the faith by which we are saved, and
it is right to have different signs for what is future, past or present. So
in the New Law our sacraments signify what has already taken place in
Christ, and differ from those of the Old Law which prefigured it as
future. The New Law stands half-way between the Old Law, which
prefigured it, and the glory to come in which every truth will be unveiled
and made perfectly clear and in which there will be no sacraments.
St Paul calls the Old Law sacraments *weak and needy elements* because
they neither contained nor caused grace, and he says that those using
such sacraments served God *under the elements of the world*, since that
is all they were. Our sacraments however contain and cause grace, and
don't merit the same judgment. The fact that God after Christ's
coming instituted different sacraments doesn't show change in God;
the earlier were suitable for prefiguring grace, the later showed grace
present.

62 1 **How the New Law sacraments cause grace.** We have to accept
that in some way the New Law sacraments cause grace. Through them
we are incorporated into Christ, become part of his body: *as many of
you as have been baptized in Christ have put on Christ*; and man is not
made a member of Christ except through grace. Some people however
say the sacraments don't cause grace by anything they do themselves,
but God, at the time the sacraments are applied to the body, himself
simultaneously produces grace in the soul. They give the example of
somebody who receives a hundred pounds by ordinance of the king
when he produces a lead penny: the large amount of money arises from
nothing in the penny, but only from the king's will. But if you think
about that properly, the role of the lead penny is just that of a symbol,
a sign of the king's ordinance that a man presenting such a penny shall
receive that amount of money. Yet we have it on the authority of many
holy men that the sacraments of the New Law not only signify grace
but cause it. So we must adopt a different approach based on the
difference between two kinds of cause: principal causes and instrumental
causes, agents and their tools. A principal cause or agent produces an
effect in virtue of its own form or nature, reproduced in some way in

the effect: fire, in virtue of its own heat, heats other things. Only God can cause grace in this way, since grace is a shared likeness in God's nature: *you are to be sharers of the divine nature.* Tools or instruments, on the other hand, don't produce effects in virtue of their own form, but in virtue of being moved by the agent wielding them. The effect doesn't reproduce the form of the tool but that of the tool-user: the bed is not like the adze but like a design in the carpenter's mind. And this is the way the New Law sacraments cause grace: they are used by God's ordinance for the sake of the grace that is caused in them. Augustine says *All these [sacramental actions] come and go, but the power [of God] working through them remains*; but what someone works *through* is precisely his tool. And so in Paul's letter to Titus we read: *He saves us through the washing of rebirth.* A principal agent isn't properly a sign of its effects, even if the effects are hidden and the agent itself manifest and perceptible. But an instrumental agent, if manifest, can be called the sign of some hidden effect it produces, since it is itself not only cause but also effect, something used by the principal agent. This is how sacraments of the New Law are both signs and causes. As the common formula has it: they effect what they symbolize. And so they are complete as sacraments, related to the sacred reality not only as signs but as causes. Tools are active at two levels: precisely as tools they act not in virtue of their own power but in virtue of the agent that wields them, but they also have a natural action of their own. An adze cuts in virtue of its own sharpness, but makes a bed only in virtue of the carpenter's craft; what it contributes to the activity of which it is a tool is its own proper activity: it makes the bed by cutting. In the same way the bodily sacraments, by means of their own action performed on the body they touch, carry out on the soul the activity of which they are God's tool. The waters of baptism, washing the body in virtue of their own power, wash that body's soul as a tool of God's power. And this is what Augustine was saying: *it touches the body and cleans the heart.*

Grace itself is a sort of share in God's existence by likeness, a 2 disposition of the soul's substance. And just as the soul's powers derive from its substance, so there derive from grace virtues and gifts which dispose those powers to act well. The sacraments however produce certain special effects that are needed in the Christian life: baptism, for example, achieves a kind of spiritual rebirth in which man dies to sins and becomes a member of Christ, and this is something special over and above the ordinary activity of the soul's powers. The same can be said of the other sacraments. Just as virtues and gifts add something to our generic notion of grace – namely, the perfect disposing of our powers to their own activities – so the grace of each sacrament adds something to the generic notion of grace and to that of the virtues and gifts – namely, a certain divine help in achieving that sacrament's goal. In this way the grace of a sacrament is something more than the grace of the virtues and gifts. The grace of the virtues and gifts disposes the substance and powers of the soul well enough in regard to the general structure of its activities, but the grace of the sacraments serves certain special effects needed in a Christian life. The virtues and gifts are enough to eliminate present and future vices and sins, inasmuch as they restrain a man from sinning. But in respect of past sins which, though finished as actions, have left a liability for punishment behind, the sacraments offer man special remedies. The relationship of the grace of the sacrament to grace in general is that of a species to its containing genus. There is no more equivocation in meaning when the word *grace* is used in this way, than there is when the word *animal* is used both as a general term and also to refer to man.

3   Hugh of St Victor talked of the sacraments as *consecrated containers of invisible grace*. Grace exists *in* the sacraments in the way things exist in signs, and also in the way things exist in instrumental causes. This is not the way effects are contained in their so-called univocal causes, by a likeness of species; nor the way they are contained in their non-univocal causes – organic life in the energy of the sun, for example – by some form which is stably proper to that cause yet bears some sort of correspondence to the form of the effect. Grace is in a sacrament in virtue of the sacrament's instrumental power, which is only transiently and incompletely present in it. Grace does not exist in the sacrament as in a graced subject; nor as in a vessel or channel spatially containing the grace, but as in an instrument or tool doing something: the sense of vessel Ezechiel uses when he says that *everyone carries a vessel of slaughter in his hand*. Supervening qualities of things, though they can't be taken out of one thing and put into another, are in a way passed from their agent through its tool into their subject, not existing in the same way in each of those things, but in the way appropriate to each. A spiritual reality that reaches completeness of existence in something contains that something rather than being contained by it; but grace doesn't exist in a sacrament completely, but flows through it. In that sense we can

4 talk of the sacrament as containing grace. Those who say the sacraments cause grace only by a certain concomitance mean to deny the existence in the sacrament of any power producing the effect of the sacrament; rather they say God's power accompanies the sacrament to produce the

sacramental effect. But in holding the sacrament to be an instrumental cause of grace we are attributing to the sacrament a sort of instrumental power for producing that effect, power of the sort appropriate to a tool. Now tools only work when moved by the tool-user who is originating the action; so whereas the power of principal agents is permanent and naturally complete, the power in the tool is something passed through from one thing to another, incomplete in the tool in the same way that change in something being changed is an incomplete actuality, deriving from some agent. The sounds a speaker makes have a certain spiritual power to excite man's mind and provoke ideas, and that is the way sacraments have spiritual power in them from God, ordaining them to their spiritual effects. Instrumental power is not properly speaking a new or independent kind of power but an incomplete derivation of the complete power producing it. Just as the power of tools comes from being moved by their user, so the sacraments derive their spiritual power from Christ's blessing and the action of the person administering the sacrament.

We use two types of tool: tools separate from our bodies, like sticks, 5 and tools connected with our bodies, like hands. Separate tools we operate by way of connected tools, sticks by way of hands. Now the primary agent of grace is God, to whom Christ's humanity is like a connected tool, and the sacraments separated ones. So the saving power passes from Christ's godhead through his humanity into his sacraments. The grace of the sacraments seems to have two functions: it removes defects left by past sins, which though finished as actions leave behind liability to penalties; and it disposes and strengthens the soul to worship God through the religion of a Christian life. Now it is already clear that Christ freed us from our sins chiefly though his sufferings, effectively [by power of his godhead], meritoriously [by his human soul's earning], but also by making amends [by his body's sacrifice]. Through his sufferings he also inaugurated the rite of the Christian religion, *making himself an offering and a sacrifice to God*. Clearly then the sacraments of the church derive their power from Christ's sufferings, the power of which is applied to us in some way through the sacraments we receive. As a sign of this there flowed from Christ's side as he hung on the cross water and blood, the water of baptism and the blood of the eucharist, the two most powerful sacraments. *The Word who was in the beginning with God* is the primary agent giving life to our souls, his flesh and the mysteries enacted in that flesh acting as his tools in giving souls life, and not only acting as tools but setting the pattern for our bodies' lives. *Christ dwells in us by faith*, so his power connects up with us through faith. And because the power of forgiving sin belongs in a special way to Christ's sufferings, men are freed from sin especially by faith in those sufferings: *God has put him forward as a reconciliator through faith in his blood.* So the power of the sacraments to remove sin chiefly derives from faith in Christ's sufferings. The resurrection of Christ causes men to be set right again, inasmuch as that leads to a new life through grace; Christ's sufferings cause it inasmuch as it starts with forgiveness of our faults.

6   The Old Law sacraments can't be said to have conferred justifying grace by their own power, for then Christ's sufferings would have been unnecessary: *if justice could come from the Law Christ died for nothing.* But neither can we say that they derived power from Christ's sufferings. Christ's sufferings connect up to us through faith and the sacraments, connection through faith being by a mental act, and connection through the sacraments by external use of things. Now something future can move us by way of a mental act as goals move agents to conceive and desire them. But something still future can't move an external thing. Agents can't come into existence after their effects, as goals can. Clearly then the New Law sacraments can derive their justifying power from the sufferings of Christ, but not the sacraments of the Old Law. Nevertheless the patriarchs were justified by Christ's sufferings, for the sacraments of the Old Law were a sort of attestation of their faith, signs of Christ's sufferings and its effects. So though the sacraments of the Old Law had no power in themselves to confer sanctifying grace, they were signs of the faith which did in fact justify men. The patriarchs had faith in the suffering of Christ to come, and that suffering justified them through their mental contact with it. But we have faith in the suffering of Christ already past, which can justify us through real use of sacramental actions. About circumcision there have been many opinions. Some say it didn't confer grace, but remitted sin. This however can't be true, for only grace justifies from sin: *we are justified freely by his grace.* So others say circumcision did confer grace but only for removal of sin and not for any positive effects. This also must be wrong, for positive effects precede negative effects in the sense that only a positive form can remove a deformity. So others say circumcision did confer grace for the positive effect of making the circumcised child worthy of eternal life, but did not repress the cravings that would lead him to sin. And that is what I once thought. But on more careful consideration this too doesn't seem right, since the slightest grace is capable both of resisting our cravings and earning eternal life. So it seems better to say that circumcision too was a sign of a faith that justified: *Abraham received the sign of circum-*

cision, a sign of the justice that comes through faith. Grace was conferred through circumcision because it was a sign of the suffering of Christ to come.

The sacramental mark or character.   *God himself has anointed us* 63 1 *and set his mark on us.* The sacraments of the New Law have two functions: remedying sin and disposing and strengthening our soul to worship God according to the rite of a Christian life. When someone is deputed to a particular task we often give him some special badge or token: in ancient times enlisted soldiers were tattooed on their bodies – their task being a bodily one – and the tattoo was called a *character*. In the same way the sacraments, which depute men to spiritual functions in the worship of God, imprint on them a spiritual tattoo or character. The seal of divine predestination deputes believers to the reward of future glory, the spiritual seal we call character deputes them for certain acts appropriate to the church in the present life. The character, though invisibly imprinted on the soul, is a sign inasmuch as it is imprinted by a sacrament we can perceive; we know a person is marked with the baptismal character because we have seen him washed with water. In any case, anything that marks out and identifies somebody can be said to imprint him with a character, even if it is not apparent to the senses. Christ, for example, is said to be *the imprint or character of the Father's own being.* The sacraments of the New Law imprint a character because 2 they depute men to worship God according to the rite of the Christian religion. Worship of God consists either in receiving something from him or in handing it on to others, and to do either a man must be given some ability or power: receptive in the first case, operative in the second. So a character must be a kind of spiritual ability to take part in the worship of God. This spiritual ability will be an instrumental power in the same way as the power in the sacraments is, characterizing the recipient as a minister or tool of God. Just as the power in the sacraments is no new or independent species of power but an incomplete and passing derivation from [God's] power, so also a character is no new genus of ability but a sort of derivation of ability. The essence of a character therefore doesn't consist in its relationship of sign. Characters are signs only inasmuch as the perceptible sacraments which imprint them are; in themselves they are abilities.

Men of faith are deputed first and foremost to the enjoyment of glory, 3 and in that respect marked with the seal of grace. But they are also deputed to receive or hand on to others things relating to God's worship, and in that respect marked with a sacramental character. Since the whole rite of the Christian religion is derived from Christ's own priesthood, the sacramental character is a special imprint of Christ's priesthood, a sharing in it derived from Christ himself. The sacramental character is a reality signified by the external sacrament, but also itself a sacramental sign of the ultimate effect of the sacrament. As sacramental sign it signifies the invisible grace conferred in the sacrament [by the whole Trinity], but as character it specially conforms us to Christ, by whose authority we are deputed to Christian worship. The mark of a Christian man is what distinguishes him from the servants of the devil, either in regard to eternal life or in regard to church worship in the present life. In the first respect he is marked by charity and grace, in the second by a sacramental character. In the same way *the mark of the beast* means either the obstinate wickedness which deputes certain people to eternal punishment, or their commitment to unlawful worship.

4   The immediate effect of a character is to enable us to act in God's worship; but since doing that well requires grace, God's generosity accompanies reception of a character with a gift of grace [disposing our very being], the character meanwhile disposing our abilities to act. Character is not an ability to act derived from human nature and belonging naturally to men, but a sort of spiritual ability men get from outside. Just as the nature by which the soul is our source of human life is perfected by grace so as to make us spiritually alive, so the soul's natural abilities are perfected by a spiritual ability, called a character. For just as dispositions to act in a certain way perfect our ability to act in that way, so whatever else has as function a certain way of acting will perfect our ability to act in that way; so because a character enables us to act to God's worship, attesting our faith by outward signs, it must perfect the abilities that enable us to have faith, namely, our cognitive

5 powers. A sacramental character is Christ sharing his priesthood with the Christian faithful; Christ enjoys the full power of spiritual priesthood, and those who believe in him are conformed to him by sharing in his spiritual power as it relates to the sacraments and the worship of God. Christ's priesthood is however an eternal priesthood: *he is a priest for ever according to the order of Melchizedek.* So every consecration made by him as priest lasts for ever, or as long as the thing consecrated lasts. The soul however is indestructible; so character is imprinted on it indelibly. Grace has a complete existence within the soul, but character exists only as an instrumental power. Now a form that exists complete in a subject puts on the conditions of that subject, and since the soul during our present life is subject to alteration according to our free will, so too is grace: it can come and go. But instrumental power depends

rather on the condition of the agent, and character exists indelibly in the soul: not because of any completeness of character as such, but because of the completeness of Christ's priesthood from which the character is derived as a sort of instrumental power. For by definition a tool is moved by something outside it, not by itself as will is. So however much will may move in the opposite direction character is not removed, because the principal agent doesn't change. After this life there will be no more external worship, but the goal of that worship will still exist, and the character too, to the glory of the good and the shame of the bad, just as the soldier's tattoo outlasts victory or defeat.

All the sacraments confer grace and provide some remedy against sin, 6 but not all are directly related to the worship of God. The sacrament of penitence for example frees man from sin, but it makes no changes in his status *vis-à-vis* God's worship. And among the sacraments that are related to worship the eucharist is constitutive of the very activity of worship, being the sacrifice of the church. So it imprints no new character on a man since it does not depute him to minister or receive any other sacrament, but rather constitutes *the goal and consummation of all the sacraments*. It contains Christ himself in whom there is not character but the fullness of priesthood itself. The sacrament of order on the other hand deputes a man to the active role of handing on sacraments to others, whilst the sacrament of baptism gives a man the ability to receive other sacraments: it is *the gateway of the sacraments* (and confirmation is similar to baptism). So these are the three sacraments which imprint a character. All the sacraments give man a share in Christ's priesthood, if that means they confer some effect of that priesthood; but not all the sacraments depute men to minister or receive things relating to the worship of Christ the priest, and this is what is needed for a sacrament to imprint a character. All the sacraments make men holy, because holiness is the cleanness from sin that grace produces. But certain sacraments imprint characters, which make men sacred in a special sense, consecrated to God's worship, just as lifeless things can be consecrated and deputed to the worship of God. Though character is both reality signified and sacrament signifying, not everything which is both reality and sacrament is a character; what has this status in the other sacraments will be explained later.

The power at work in the sacraments.   God alone is the principal 64 1 agent of a sacrament's interior effects: he alone has access to the soul, he alone is the author of grace, his alone is the power in which character shares instrumentally. But men administer the sacraments and are then

instrumental causes of the sacrament's interior effects. The sacramental effect is not something that happens in answer to the prayer of either the church or the minister, but it is something earned by Christ's sufferings, the power of which is at work in the sacraments. So the sacramental effect is no better when administered by a better minister. The minister's devotion may win some associated effect for the recipient, but even that is not something the minister himself produces, but
2 something God produces in response to the minister's prayer. A sacrament then has two agents: its institutor and the user applying it. The power of the sacrament can't derive from its minister, so must derive from its institutor; and since it is God's power, God alone must be the institutor of the sacraments. Those parts of a sacramental rite that men institute are not essential to the sacrament, but there to add solemnity. Everything essential to the sacrament is instituted by Christ himself, God and man, and handed down, if not in scripture, then from the apostles in the family of the church. Certain of the things we perceive have a natural aptitude for signifying spiritual effects, but this aptitude needs further determination to a special sign by God's institution. The apostles and their successors are God's representatives in ruling his church founded on faith and the sacraments of the faith. So they can no more hand on another faith or institute other sacraments than they can institute another church.

3   Christ produces the interior effects of the sacraments both as God (the source of their effectiveness) and as man (earning that effectiveness, and acting as a tool of his godhead). As a tool connected to his godhead in one person his humanity is prior causally to separated tools such as the ministers of the church and the sacraments themselves. Christ as God then has power of authorship in the sacraments, and as man principality of ministry: the sacraments operate by virtue and merit of his sufferings, attest to faith in him, are consecrated in his name, instituted by him, and he, if he wished, could confer their effect without using its external sacrament. His power of authorship of the sacraments God cannot share with any creature. His principality of ministry could be shared with other ministers by bestowing on them the fullness of grace needed to earn the effects of the sacraments and have sacraments consecrated in their names, to institute sacraments and confer their sacramental effects at will without use of sacramental rites. For the more powerful a connected instrument, the more power it can give its separated tools, as a hand to sticks it uses. Christ didn't share this principality of ministry with others, not from envy, but for the sake of the faithful, lest they trust in man and differences in the sacraments lead

to divisions within the church: *I am for Paul, I am for Apollo, I am for Cephas.*

A tool acts not in virtue of its own power but in virtue of its user's. It makes no difference to the tool as tool what forms or powers it has over and above what it requires as a tool. So the ministers of the church can confer sacraments even if they themselves are sinners. The effect in those receiving the sacraments is not a likeness to the ministers but conformity to Christ. For an agent can use even lifeless tools as long as there is some way he can communicate movement through them: thus the carpenter takes his adze in his hands. So also Christ in his sacraments sometimes works through evil tools lacking life, and sometimes through good tools, his own living members. However, appropriateness requires that the ministers of the sacraments should be good men, conformed to their Lord. Wicked ministers of God and the church certainly sin, and sin fatally, when they dispense the sacraments. We receive sacraments from a minister of the church as minister of the church, not in his private and personal capacity. As long as the church allows a sinner to minister, a recipient will not share the minister's sin but the life of the church. But if the church forbids a sinner to minister and excommunicates or suspends him, a recipient will sin, sharing the minister's sin.

The whole power of the sacraments derives from the sufferings of Christ and those belong to him as man. Thus it is for men, not angels, to dispense and administer the sacraments. However God does not so bind his power to the sacraments that he cannot bestow their effects in other ways; and he does not so bind his power to the ministers of the church that he can't choose to grant power to administer sacraments to angels. The actions performed in the sacraments can be done with different aims in view: we can wash with water, as in baptism, for reasons of cleanliness or health or recreation and so on. So the action must be defined to its sacramental effect by the intention of the one who does the washing, expressed in the words of the sacrament: *I baptize you in the name of the Father.* Inanimate tools don't intend effects: their movement by a user takes the place of intention. But a living tool like a minister is not only moved but self-moving, inasmuch as his will is needed to move his limbs. So the action needs his intention to submit himself to the principal agent, to do what Christ and the church want done. Some people say that intention must be mentally present, otherwise the sacrament will not take effect. But others say more truly that the minister is acting in the person of the church as a whole and expressing in his words the church's intention, and that is enough for

the efficacy of the sacrament unless some intention to the contrary is expressed on the part of either minister or recipient. Though the minister should take the utmost pains to ensure that he is actually intending, this is not always in a man's power and even when he wants
9 to be very intent on something he starts to think of something else. Just as a minister doesn't have to love with charity and sinners can administer the sacraments, so he doesn't have to believe with faith and an unbeliever can dispense a true sacrament if everything else necessary is present. Even if he doesn't himself believe the sacrament has any interior effect, he is well aware that the Catholic church intends to confer something by performance of the external action. So despite his own lack of faith he can intend to do what the church wants done, even though he thinks that is nothing. Such an intention suffices for the sacrament since the minister acts in the name of the whole church and her faith makes good his lack of it. Some heretics don't keep to the church's prescribed form when conferring the sacraments and so confer neither the sacrament nor the reality it signifies. But some do observe the church's form and so confer the sacrament but not the reality signified. Here I am talking of heretics clearly cut off from the church, so that anyone receiving the sacrament from them sins and thus prevents the sacrament from taking effect. The ability to administer the sacraments is part of the indelible spiritual character. The fact that someone is suspended or excommunicated from the church or unfrocked doesn't destroy that ability, but only his licence to exercise it. So he confers the sacrament but sins in doing so; and the same applies to the recipient, who, as a result, doesn't receive the reality signified by the sacrament unless ignorance
10 excuses him. A minister's intention to confer a sacrament might be corrupt in two ways. He might not intend to confer the sacrament at all but only to pretend to, and that would invalidate the sacrament especially if he made his intention plain. Alternatively he might use the conferring of the sacrament for ulterior purposes: baptizing this woman in order to sin with her, consecrating the body of Christ to use as a poison. Such a corruption would leave both intention and sacrament intact, but would be gravely sinful.

65 1 **The seven sacraments.**   The sacraments of the church have two functions: to dispose and strengthen men to worship God according to the religion of Christian life, and to remedy the effects of sin. From both points of view it is fitting to have seven sacraments. Our spiritual life resembles our bodily life in needing to be strengthened in us both as individuals and as members of the whole community in which we

live as naturally social animals. Individually we are born (cf *baptism*), we mature (cf *confirmation*) and we must feed (cf *the eucharist*); and since we also suffer disease and sin we need cure (cf *penitence*) and recuperation (cf *last anointing*). In the community as a whole, men share in government (cf *holy order*) and engage in propagation of the species (cf *marriage*). The sacraments perfecting the individual naturally precede 2 those which serve the whole community (so holy order, and the less spiritual *marriage*, are considered last). Among the sacraments perfecting the individual those dealing with removal of obstacles (penitence and last anointing) come after the sacraments that positively promote the spiritual life (baptism, confirmation and the eucharist). Penitence is not an essential preparation for the eucharist, but only if a recipient is in fatal sin. The sacrament of the eucharist is the greatest of all sacraments, 3 simply speaking. Firstly, it contains the substance of Christ himself whereas the others contain a sort of instrumental power deriving from him. Secondly, all the other sacraments seem to prepare for this one as their goal. Holy order prepares its consecration, baptism and confirmation prepare its reception, penitence and last anointing ensure its worthy reception, and even marriage symbolically relates to the eucharist, being a sign of the union of Christ and the church which the eucharist expresses. And this is indicated in the rituals for all these sacraments, which nearly all culminate in the eucharist. The common spiritual good of the whole church is contained in its very substance in the sacrament of the eucharist. Three of the other sacraments are necessary if we are 4 to achieve our goal at all: individuals require baptism simply speaking, and penitence if they sin fatally after baptism; and the church as a whole needs holy order. The remaining sacraments are necessary if we are to achieve our goal more easily: confirmation completes baptism, and last anointing completes penitence, whilst marriage maintains the church by way of propagation.

Baptism: sacramental rebirth

The sacramental action.   There are three things to consider in the [vol 57] 66 1 sacrament of baptism: that which is sign only, that which is both reality and sign, and that which is reality only and not sign. The sign only is the externally visible sign of the interior effect, and this visible sign we call the sacrament. Now externally we perceive not only water but its use in the action of washing. Some people thought that the sacrament is the water as such, but that is not so. Since New Law sacraments make us holy, the sacrament is to be found where the making holy is done, and that is not in the water: in the water there is a sort of instrumental power to make holy, passing through to man, the subject that is truly made holy. So the sacrament is found not in the water as such, but in the applying of the water to the man, namely in the action of washing. That is the sacramental sign. That which is reality as well as sign is the baptismal character, signified by external washing and itself a sacramental sign of an interior justification which is reality only, signified

2 but not itself a sign. Sacraments get their power of conferring grace from their institution. Baptism received this power when Christ was baptized, though the necessity of baptism was announced to men only after Christ had suffered and risen again: partly because then all the previous prefiguring sacraments came to an end, and partly because baptism conforms us to the pattern of Christ's sufferings and resurrection, making us dead to sin and starting a new life of justice. Even before Christ suffered, baptism received efficacy from his sufferings, by prefiguring them, though in a different way from the Old Law sacraments. For they were only prefigurings, whereas baptism had a power of justifying received from Christ himself, from whom came the saving power of even his own sufferings. After his suffering and rising again Christ made baptism necessary for both Jew and Gentile when he said *Go, teach all nations, baptizing them.* What the Lord told Nicodemus before his suffering: *Unless a man be born again of water and the Holy Spirit, he cannot enter into God's kingdom,* seems to refer more to the future than to the time at which it was said.

3 By God's institution water is the proper material to baptize with, and appropriately so. Firstly, baptism is by definition rebirth to spiritual life and this fits with water: all seeds are moist and connected with water. Secondly, water's properties fit baptism's effects: its wetness cleans, its coldness tempers inflammability, its transparency lets through the light. Thirdly, it symbolizes Christ's saving mysteries well: *when we submerge our heads in the water as in a tomb, the old man is buried and hidden below to rise renewed.* Fourthly, it is an abundantly common material easily obtainable anywhere and thus suited to this most necessary sacrament.

5 The words which give form to the baptismal sign should express its causes: the primary cause of its power, the Holy Trinity, and the instrumental cause externally conferring it, its minister. So *I baptize thee in the name of the Father and the Son and the Holy Spirit* is a

6 suitable form. Christ commanded this calling on the Trinity, so any incompleteness of this invocation will destroy the integrity of the

7 baptism. The washing can be done by immersion, sprinkling or pouring. What is essential is *washing*, and whether it be done this way or that is

incidental. Immersion more expressly symbolizes Christ's burial, and so is the commoner usage and more praiseworthy.

Baptism can't be repeated. Firstly it is a kind of spiritual rebirth in 9 which we die to an old life and start to live a new one; and one can only be born once. Secondly, *we are baptized in the death of Christ*; and *Christ died only once.* Thirdly, baptism imprints an indelible character. Fourthly, it is principally given to remove inherited sin. The sacraments of baptism and the eucharist both symbolize Christ's death and suffering, but in different ways. Baptism commemorates Christ's death in this man's dying in Christ to be reborn into new life. The eucharist commemorates it by offering us the Passover meal containing the very Christ who suffered: *Christ, our Passover lamb, has been sacrificed: let us therefore banquet.* A man is born once but eats frequently, so baptism is given once but the eucharist many times.

Essential to this sacrament are its verbal form signifying its primary 10 and instrumental causes, and its use of material, washing with water, signifying its primary effect. Everything else the church does in the ritual of baptism is there to give solemnity.

We consecrate priests to celebrate the sacrament of Christ's body, the 67 2 sacrament of the church's unity: *We though many are one bread and one body, all sharing in the one bread and the one cup.* But it is by baptism that we are made sharers in this unity of the church and receive the right to approach the Lord's table. So just as it is the priest's task and principal function to consecrate the eucharist, so it is properly his task to baptize: the person who produces the whole should arrange the parts. Baptism however is the most necessary of all the sacraments, being the 3 rebirth of man into a spiritual life: infants have no other way of salvation, and without baptism adults cannot receive full forgiveness of both sin and its punishment. So, lest man be lost for lack of such a necessary remedy, God decided to use water, a common material, obtainable everywhere, and let anyone administer the sacrament, ordained or not. So though it is more fitting and solemn for a priest to do the baptizing it is not necessary. Even a non-baptized person can baptize in case of 5 necessity, for though he does not belong to the church either in interior reality or by external sign, he can belong in intention and outward action, intending to do what she wants done and observing her form of baptism; and so he operates as a minister of Christ, who does not limit his power to either the baptized or the sacraments.

68 1 **The effects of baptism.**   No one can be saved except through Christ: we are given baptism so that in it we may be reborn and made members of Christ's body. Clearly then we are all obliged to receive baptism, for without it a man cannot be saved. Before Christ's coming men became members of his body through faith in his future coming: circumcision was the *sign* of this faith, but before the institution of circumcision the patriarchs attested their faith with sacrifices. After Christ's coming men are still made members of Christ's body through faith, but the sign attesting faith in what is already present differs from that used when it was still in the future. The sacrament of baptism itself was not always necessary for salvation, but the faith of which baptism is the sacrament

2 or sign was always necessary. A man can be unbaptized both in reality and in desire, neither baptized nor wanting to be. Clearly in those who have free will this shows disdain for the sacrament, and people unbaptized in this sense cannot achieve salvation: neither sacramentally nor mentally are they members of Christ's body, through whom alone salvation comes. But sometimes a man, though unbaptized in reality, is baptized in desire. If he wanted to be baptized but died before he could receive baptism, he can achieve salvation without actual baptism, because of his desire for it; a desire which arises from *faith working through love*, through which God inwardly sanctifies him, not having limited his power to the visible sacraments. No one achieves eternal life if he is not absolved from all fault and liability to punishment; and such complete absolution takes place in both baptism and martyrdom. So a catechumen desirous of baptism yet dying without it would not immediately enter eternal life, but would first suffer the penalties for his past sins: *he will be saved yet as through fire* The sacrament of baptism is said to be necessary for salvation in so far as there can be no salvation for man unless he at least has a will for it, which, with God, counts for the deed.

3   Baptism of infants should not be delayed: they can't be any better instructed and if they die have no other remedy. Adults can be saved by their desire for baptism, so their baptism should happen not immediately they are converted but after a fixed time. This will safeguard the church against baptizing people who are not really serious, allow the recipient to be fully instructed in the faith and trained in Christian living, and the sacrament to be more solemnly celebrated on some feast like Easter or Pentecost. But the delay can be dispensed with if those to be baptized seem already fully instructed and prepared, or in case of sickness and danger of death. If someone happens to die while awaiting the time set by the church *he will be saved, yet as through fire.*

5   In baptism we are incorporated into the very death of Christ. That

death made enough amends for all our sins, and *not only ours, but also those of the whole world*. So no other amends are to be demanded of persons being baptized for any sin whatsoever. Confession is part of 6 sacramental penitence and not required before baptism, though the virtue of interior repentance is. We receive justification in baptism not 7 by force but willingly. So a person must intend to receive what he is being given. True faith is also a prerequisite since grace, the ultimate 8 effect of this sacrament cannot be received without it. But the baptismal character can, and to that extent faith in the one being baptized is no more required than faith in the baptizer, as long as everything else necessary for the sacrament is present. The sacrament operates not through the righteousness of minister or recipient but through the power of God.

Infants are heirs of Adam's sin, otherwise they wouldn't die. So it 9 was necessary to baptize infants so that those on whom Adam brought damnation at birth might achieve salvation by rebirth through Christ. And it was fitting that children should be brought up from infancy in Christian living, so that they might persevere more firmly in it. Children not yet able to use their own reasons are so to speak in the womb of the church and receive salvation not by their own act but by hers. One can say they intend it not by their own act of intention (since they sometimes struggle against it and cry), but by the act of those who offer them for baptism. The children of unbelievers, if not yet able to use their own 10 free will, are by the law of our natures in their parents' care until they can look after themselves; so it would offend just as much against natural justice to baptize such children against their parents wishes, as it would to baptize someone who could use his reason against his own wishes. It would also be dangerous to baptize such children, since their natural affection for their parents would easily lead them back into unbelief. No one should break the arrangement of natural justice by which children are in the care of their parents, in order to free them from the danger of eternal death. Man is related to God through his reason, by which he is able to know God. The child before it can use its own reason is in the natural order of things related to God through its parents' reason, in whose care nature has put him; so whatever is done to him in relation to God must be decided by the reasons of his parents. The insane who 12 never had the use of their reasons are baptized with the church doing the intending and the church's ritual doing their believing and repenting for them. But those who at some time have or had the use of their reason must be baptized according to their own intentions made known at the time they were of sound mind.

69 1   In baptism a man dies to the oldness of sin and starts to live in
2 newness of grace; so every sin is taken away by baptism. In baptism a
man is incorporated into Christ's suffering and death: *If we have shared
death with Christ, we believe we shall share life with him.* Clearly every
baptized person shares in Christ's suffering for his own healing as if he
himself had suffered and died. Now the suffering of Christ makes enough
amends for all men's sins. So someone who is baptized is freed from all
liability to punishment for his sins, just as if he himself had made enough
amends for all his sins. The penalty Christ suffered is shared with the
baptized person, become a member of Christ's body, as if he himself
3 had suffered that penalty. Baptism has the power to remove even the
inherited defects of our present life, but that power takes effect not in
the present life but only when just men rise again. And for this reason.
By baptism we are joined to Christ's body as one of his members. But
Christ himself, though from the first moment of his conception filled
with grace and truth, had a body that could suffer, and which came to
its risen life of glory only through suffering and dying. Inherited sin
first infected all human nature and that nature then infects every person
who owns it. Conversely, Christ first cures the person and afterwards
will cure, at one and the same time for all, human nature. The inherited
fault together with the punishment of not seeing God, which is personal,
is removed immediately in baptism. But the defects of our present life
(like death, hunger, thirst and so on) which are natural and arise from
natural causes to which we have been abandoned by the absence of
inherited rightness, will not be taken away until all nature is healed by
the final resurrection into glory.
9   Whoever is baptized into Christ and is conformed to him through
faith and charity puts on Christ through grace. But if we receive the
sacrament of Christ [with only a pretence of faith and charity] we put
on Christ only by being configured to him by our baptismal character,
10 but not by being conformed to him by grace. The character is like the
form one receives at birth; it should be accompanied by its proper effect,
grace to forgive all sins, but sometimes this effect is impeded by pretence.
When the pretence is repented of, baptism immediately achieves its
effect.

Confirmation: sacramental maturity

72 1   The New Law sacraments are directed to certain special effects of grace,
and wherever there is such a special effect there will be a special
sacrament. Now a special level of perfection is reached in bodily life

when a man comes of age and can perform mature human acts. In confirmation man comes of age, so to speak, in the spiritual life. Christ instituted this sacrament not by conferring it but by promising it: *If I do not go the Advocate will not come to you, but if I go I will send him to you.* In this sacrament the fullness of the Holy Spirit was to be given, and that had to wait until Christ had risen and ascended: *The Spirit had not yet been given because Jesus was not yet glorified.* In this sacrament 2 the fullness of the Spirit strengthens a man for spiritual maturity, for that coming of age when he begins to cooperate with others, having previously lived as if for himself alone. And so the grace of the Holy Spirit is signified in this sacrament by oil mixed with a balsam which makes it fragrant to others. A sacramental character is a spiritual ability 5 to take part in certain sacred actions. In baptism a man is enabled to do those things which belong to his own salvation in so far as he lives for himself; in confirmation he receives the power to engage in spiritual battle against the enemies of the faith. Compare the apostles who before they received the fullness of the Spirit were *in the upper room persevering in prayer*, but afterwards came out boldly to confess the faith in public, even in front of the enemies of the Christian faith. Clearly a new character is imprinted in the sacrament of confirmation, a sign which distinguishes not believers from unbelievers, but those who are spiritually grown up from those who are *like newborn babes.* The grace of a 7 sacrament has power to produce that sacrament's own special effect over and above the grace that makes us pleasing in general. If we think of grace in general, the grace given in this sacrament is no different from that of baptism, simply increasing it. But if we consider its own special effectiveness then the grace of confirmation differs from that of baptism. The finishing touch to any piece of work is reserved to the man with 11 the highest craft or authority. The material is prepared by the lowest workman, the form imposed by a higher, and the thing applied to its purpose by the highest of all: the letter written by the secretary is signed by the boss. Now the sacrament of confirmation is a final perfecting of the sacrament of baptism. In baptism man is built up as a spiritual house, written as a spiritual letter. In the sacrament of confirmation that house is dedicated as a temple of the Holy Spirit; the letter is signed with the sign of the cross. For this reason the conferring of confirmation is reserved to bishops who hold the highest authority in the church; just as in the early church the fullness of the Holy Spirit was given through the laying on of hands by the apostles, whose place the bishops now occupy.

The eucharist: sacramental sacrifice and meal

[vol 58] 73 1 **The sacramental sign.**   The sacraments of the church are needed to support man's spiritual life: baptism is spiritual rebirth, confirmation spiritual maturing, and the sacrament of the eucharist provides spiritual food. New Law sacraments are visible signs that cause the invisible effects they signify: washing with water, for example, imprints the baptismal character it signifies (and which is itself a sign) and cleanses us spiritually (signified, but not itself a sign). Do we find this structure in the eucharist? The outward appearances of bread and wine don't seem to cause the body of Christ, whether we mean his actual body (signified-and-sign) or his mystical body (signified-and-not-sign). But even in baptism water doesn't cause its spiritual effects by its own power but by the power of the Holy Spirit within it. In the eucharist the actual body of Christ is related to the appearances of bread and wine as the power of the Holy Spirit is to the baptismal water: those appearances are a sign which causes its effects by the power of the actual body of Christ. There is however this difference between the eucharist and other sacraments that make use of visible material: the eucharist contains something sacred and holy in itself, Christ; the water of baptism and the chrism of confirmation contain only a power of making something else holy. So the eucharist consists in the very consecration of the material it uses, whereas the other sacraments consist in applying material to a man to make him holy. And another difference follows from this: in the sacrament of the eucharist what is signified-and-sign [Christ's body and blood] exists in the sacrament's own material, and what is signified-but-not-sign (namely, the conferred grace) exists in the sacrament's recipient; in baptism both the baptismal character and the grace of

2 forgiveness of sins exist in the recipient. The eucharist is one sacrament, despite having two signs [bread and wine] and two consecrations. It is indeed the sacramental sign of church unity: *We being many are one bread, one body, all that partake of one bread and one cup.* For to be one a thing does not have to be continuous and undivided; all things that are complete are one, like houses and men. A complete thing is one because it is a whole with all the parts needed to realize cooperatively one goal: man has the parts required to live his life, a house everything needed for a dwelling. In this sense the eucharist is one sacrament, in which spiritual food and spiritual drink combine to give one spiritual nourishment: *My flesh is food indeed and my blood is drink indeed.* Bread and wine may be two signs in a material sense but in the formal sense they make up one complete meal.

What this sacrament signifies and causes is the unity of Christ's 3 mystical body, the church, the one ark in the flood outside of which there is no salvation. But as we saw in the case of baptism, by desiring to receive a sacrament one can enjoy its effect before receiving it, and this is true of the eucharist though with two differences. Firstly, baptism is the *gateway to the sacraments* and the beginning of the spiritual life, whereas the eucharist is the summing-up of the spiritual life and the destination of all the sacraments, which all prepare us either to receive or consecrate the eucharist. Baptism is needed to start the spiritual life, the eucharist to bring it to fulfilment. So the spiritual life is possible without actually receiving the eucharist, but not without desiring the eucharist as a goal. The second difference is that baptism itself aims men at the eucharist as at a goal, so that baptized infants are aimed at the eucharist by the church and desire it with the church's intention just as they believe with her faith, and so they enjoy its effect already. But there is no preceding sacrament to aim them at baptism, so there is no way infants can desire baptism before receiving it (as adults can), and no way for them to enjoy its effect except by being baptized. The eucharist then is not as necessary for salvation as baptism is. As to the Lord's words: *Unless you eat the flesh of the son of man and drink his blood, you will not have life in you*, Augustine comments: *this feeding and drinking is the very communion of his body with its members, the church, predestined, called, made holy and believing in him.* And elsewhere he writes: *be in no doubt that a believer starts to share in the body and blood of Christ the moment he is made a member of Christ's body at baptism; and once part of the unity of that body he does not lose his place in the fellowship of bread and cup even if he leaves this world before actually eating and drinking it.* Notice that bodily food nourishes by being changed into the eater's own substance, and what is needed to preserve our life is its physical consumption. But our spiritual food changes us into itself: *you will not change me into yourself as you do the food of your flesh, but you will be changed into me.* Now a man can be changed into Christ and become part of his body by spiritual desire, even without receiving the sacrament. Baptism is a sign of Christ's suffering and death bringing men to new birth in Christ; whereas the eucharist is a sign of Christ's suffering bringing men into finished unity with the Christ who suffered. Baptism is *the sacrament of a faith* which lays the spiritual life's foundation; the eucharist is *the sacrament of a love* which is *the bond of perfection*.

The eucharist commemorates the past suffering of our Lord, and as 4 such is called a sacrifice. It also expresses the present unity of the church into which it gathers men together, and as such it is called *communion with Christ in flesh and godhead, communion and unity with one another*. It also prefigures the future enjoyment of God in heaven, and as such

5 it is called *viaticum* [food for the road] and *eucharist* (good grace). Most appropriately the sacrament was instituted at the last supper Christ spent with his disciples. Firstly, it contains Christ himself as in a sacramental sign, so at the moment of departing from them in his own appearance, he left himself among them in a sacramental appearance. Secondly, men are saved only by faith in the suffering Christ, so every age needed some representation of his sufferings. The Old Law prefigured them in the Passover lamb, but this was replaced in the New Law by the eucharist commemorating them. So just as his sufferings were about to begin, and just after celebrating the old sacrament, was the most appropriate moment to institute this new one. Thirdly, things last said, especially by departing friends, are best remembered: so that was the time to institute a sacrament whose excellence our Saviour

6 wished most strongly to recommend to us. In the Old Testament Melchizedek's offering best prefigured the sign of this sacrament (the bread and wine); the Old Law sacrifices and especially the sacrifice of expiation best prefigured the suffering Christ contained in the sacrament; and manna best prefigured the refreshment of soul which is this sacrament's grace. But the Passover lamb prefigured this sacrament in all three of these respects: it was eaten with unleavened bread, it was sacrificed before all the people in a figure of Christ's passion, and through its blood it protected the children of Israel from the destroying angel and led them out from their slavery in Egypt.

74 1   Christ instituted this sacrament using bread and wine, so those are its appropriate materials. They are the most common food of mankind; by separately signifying Christ's body and blood they commemorate Christ's passion in which his blood was separated from his body; they contain *Christ's flesh offered for our body's welfare and his blood for our soul's* (since as Leviticus says *the soul is in the blood*); and since *bread is compacted of grains and wine flows from grapes* they signify the whole church being gathered together from believers. Wheat and wine are not native to every country, but the amounts needed are easily transported.

2 Baptism consists in actual application of its material, and by the form of words used only the amount of water applied is sanctified; but the eucharist consists in consecration of its material, so all the material

4 present is consecrated. The bread must be wheaten bread, else there is no sacrament; but it does not matter whether it is leavened or not: on that point the proper thing is to observe the rite of one's own church.

The wine must be wine of the grape, for that is the way Christ instituted 5
it. The mixing of water with the wine represents the people united to 7
Christ. But since it is the consecration of the material which constitutes
this sacrament, and the reception by the faithful is not essential but
secondary, the mixing with water is itself inessential.

Christ in the sacrament – transubstantiation. That this sac- 75 1
rament contains the actual body and blood of Christ cannot be perceived
with our senses but only by faith in God's authority: *This is my body
which is to be given up for you.* But we can see that it is appropriate.
Firstly, appropriate to the perfection of the New Law. The Old Law
sacrifices prefigured the true sacrifice of Christ's sufferings; the New
Law sacrifice instituted by Christ should be something more, containing
not only in figure but in very truth the Christ who suffered for us.
Secondly, this fits with Christ's love since *living together is what friendship
is all about.* While we await his bodily presence in heaven he does not
deprive us of his bodily companionship in our pilgrimage, joining us to
his very body and blood in this sacrament: *He who eats my flesh and
drinks my blood dwells in me and I in him.* It joins Christ to us in such
friendly unity that it is our greatest sign of his love, and the raising of
our hope. And thirdly, his bodily presence perfects our faith in the
unseen: he offers his godhead to us invisibly in his human nature, and
now his very flesh invisibly in this sacrament. The body of Christ is
present in this sacrament not in the way a body is present in a place
with its dimensions matching those of the place, but in a way altogether
special to this sacrament. We talk of the body of Christ being on different
altars not as if it simultaneously filled different places, but *in sacrament.*
By that however we don't only mean *in sign* (though a sacrament is a
sign), but we mean that the body of Christ is really there but in a way
proper to this sacrament. All this means that after the consecration the 2
bread and wine are no longer there. To begin with it is clear that the
body of Christ doesn't start to exist in this sacrament by coming there
through space. It would have to stop being where it is locally in heaven,
move through all the intervening space, and end up in more than one
place at once. The only other alternative is that [what is in that place,]
the substance of bread, should be converted into Christ's body. But in
that case, after the conversion, the substance of the bread is no longer
there. Add to this the words used in the sacrament: *This is my body;* that
would not be true if the substance of bread remained (for certainly the
substance of bread is not Christ's body) and one would rather have to
say *Here is my body.* The sacrament, in order to signify, needs only the

appearances of bread and wine to remain, our usual means of knowing what substance is there.

3   Some theologians, accepting that the bread and wine are no longer present after their consecration, but thinking it impossible for the substance of bread and wine to be converted into the body and blood of Christ, say rather that the consecration breaks the bread and wine down into their underlying matter or annihilates them. But where would the underlying matter go to? If it moved away in space we would see it go. Moreover, the substance of bread and wine won't go away until the words of consecration are complete, and at that very moment the substance of Christ's body and blood is there. So there is no moment at which the underlying matter could be there. It is no use saying that the substance of the bread and wine breaks down gradually and takes time to depart from its apparent place. If such a process started at the moment the words of consecration were complete then in some part of the host we would have the body of Christ and the substance of bread present together, which we have already ruled out; and if it started before the consecration then in some part of the host there would be neither the substance of bread nor the body of Christ, which is difficult to conceive. Nor does annihilation help. For there is no other way for the actual body of Christ to start to exist in this sacrament except by the substance of bread being converted into it; and annihilation or break-up of the bread both exclude such conversion. Anyway what could cause them to happen? The effects of a sacrament are brought about by the words said: and the words *This is my body* say nothing about either annihilation or breaking up bread into its underlying constituents. It is like air changing into flame in a fire: though no longer there, nor anywhere else either, it hasn't been annihilated. After the consecration it is no longer true to say *The substance of bread exists in some way*, but since that into which it has been converted exists, the substance of the bread has not been annihilated. But this conversion is not like any

4   natural change, and only God has the power to bring it about. The activity of created agents is always directed at actualizing some defined thing, and since what defines actual things is their forms, no natural or created agent can do anything else but give a new form to something; so that all changes in accordance with the laws of nature can be called transformations. God however is unlimited in his actuality. So he can act on the whole substance of existing things. He can not only bring about conversions of form, in which one form replaces another in a subject, but conversions of the whole existent thing, in which the whole substance of one thing converts into the whole substance of another.

And this is what he does with his divine power in this sacrament. He converts the whole substance of bread into the whole substance of Christ's blood. This is not exchange of form but exchange of substance, and it is not a natural type of change but needs a name to itself: transubstantiation. In this conversion there is no single subject which is first potentially and then actually something. Rather, since this conversion of whole substances implies an order of the substances, one being converted into the other, the conversion has both substances as its subject, like order and number do. No limited agent has power to convert form into form or matter into matter; but the power of an unlimited agent, acting on the whole existent thing, can make such conversions: for both forms and both matters have existence in common, and the author of existence can change that which is existent in one into that which is existent in the other, taking away whatever distinguished it from the other.

What our senses tell us remain after the consecration are properties 5 of bread and wine. By the power of God, the first of all causes, something secondary is left existing when what is primary has been removed. There is no deception: the senses tell us the properties are there and they are; and our mind which might tell us the substance was there is kept from that mistake by our faith. Our faith doesn't contradict our senses; it just penetrates further than they do. Though strictly speaking there is no subject of this conversion, the properties behave like a subject inasmuch as they last through the conversion. They remain so that the 6 body of Christ can appear under those properties and not under its own. The soul is the form that gives the body every level of its existence: that it exists at all, that it is a dimensioned body, that it is alive, and so on. The form that gives the bread existence is converted into the form of Christ's body in its role as source of dimensioned existence, but not in its role as source of the kind of life Christ has. The effects of bread that depend on its properties (its effects on our eyes, for example) accompany those properties when they remain after the consecration; the effects that depend on it having matter (being able to change into some other substance) or specific to the form of bread as such (*strengthening the heart of man*) remain miraculously in the properties in the absence of the bread's matter and form.

There are three reasons why a change may occur instantaneously. 7 Firstly, the form the change introduces may not admit of degrees (health, for example, does but forms constituting substances do not); secondly, the subject may be completely ready to receive the form and require no preparation; thirdly, the agent may be infinitely powerful, able to prepare the subject instantaneously. On all three counts transubstantiation is instantaneous: the substance of Christ's body doesn't admit of degrees, there is no subject to prepare, and God is infinitely powerful. Nevertheless there is a difficulty. The substance of the bread and the substance of Christ's body can't exist at the same instant, so it seems they must exist at two different instants. But two instants can only be separated by time. So between the last instant when the bread is there and the first instant when the body of Christ is there, there must occur a change occupying time. Some people deny that instants must be separated by time. They say that two instants of one and the same change must, but not instants belonging to successive changes: the instant in which rest ends and the instant in which movement begins are not separated by time. But this is a mistake. The unity or distinctness of times and instants doesn't depend on this or that particular change but on the fundamental underlying process of change in the physical universe, by which all other changes and states of rest are measured. So other people say that though two instants must be separated by time if they are measured by this universal underlying physical process, still certain changes are not physical in this sense. But this isn't relevant. For though the eucharistic conversion is not subject to the physical universe, it follows on an uttering of words which is so subject; so that any two instants in it must be separated by time. Some people say two instants are only two in relation to what is measured by time, not in relation to the time doing the measuring; as for example when two lines meet the ends of the lines are separate points in the lines themselves, but not on the surface containing them. But this analogy is misleading: lines and points are intrinsic to bodies, whereas times and instants are extrinsic measures of changes like the extrinsic places of bodies. So yet other people say there is really only one instant which is mentally treated as two: but then we really would have two things that exclude each other present at the same time; treating them as two won't change the real situation. So what we ought to say is that this conversion is caused by the words of Christ spoken by the priest: the instant when these words are complete is the first instant at which the body of Christ is present; during the whole of the preceding time the substance of bread is there. There is no such thing as an instant immediately preceding that last one, because time is not composed of a succession of instants as Aristotle proved. You can point to an instant when the body of Christ exists there, but there is no last instant in which the substance of bread is there, only a last time. And this is no different from the situation Aristotle showed to be true of all natural changes. The conversion takes place at the moment the words have been completed, because then their meaning is complete and that is what is causative in the sacraments.

This conversion of the bread into the body of Christ is similar in 8 some ways both to creation and to natural change yet different in others. Common to all three is a certain order: after this, that. In creation after non-existence existence, in this sacrament after the substance of bread the body of Christ, in natural change after black white, or after air fire. The two extremes never co-exist. The eucharistic conversion is similar to creation but differs from natural change in having no common subject of both extremes. It is similar (with provisos) to natural change but different from creation in two respects: one extreme passes into the other, and something remains the same. In transubstantiation it is the whole substance of the bread that passes into the whole body of Christ, whereas in natural change matter takes on a new form, laying aside the form it previously had; in creation non-existence is not converted into existence at all. Again in natural change it is the matter or subject that remains the same, in transubstantiation the properties, and in creation nothing. All this helps us decide what words best express the three cases. In none of them can we predicate one extreme of the other in the present tense, saying *non-existence is existence* or *bread is the body of Christ* or *white is black*. But because the extremes are ordered we can use the word *after*: *after non-existence existence* and so on. We cannot call creation a conversion as we can the other two. Natural change is a transformation, but the eucharistic conversion is transubstantiation, a change of one whole substance into another whole substance. Whatever is true of natural change because of the shared subject must be denied of transubstantiation: we can say that *what is white could be black* but we can't say that *what is non-existent could be existent* or that *what is bread could be the body of Christ*. Nor can we properly say that *existence is made out of non-existence* or *the body of Christ out of bread*, nor that *the bread will be the body* or *becomes the body*, though because the properties do remain we use some of these ways of speaking in a sort of analogous way, not meaning by *bread* the substance of bread, but using it as a general term for *what underlies the properties of bread*, though that is at first the substance of bread and later the body of Christ. We deny that *the bread could be the body of Christ* because the possibility of its conversion is not founded on some potentiality to become in the bread, but on a power to convert in the Creator.

76 1 Christ in the sacrament – the real presence.   The Catholic faith requires us to say that every part of Christ is contained in this sacrament, but not always in the same way: some parts may be present by power of the sacramental sign, and others as naturally accompanying them. What is present by the power of the sacramental sign is whatever the words uttered say is present and so cause to be present: *This is my body* said of the bread, and *This is my blood* said of the wine. Naturally accompanying the sacramentally present body or blood there is also present whatever is joined to Christ's real body or blood. Because the bread and wine are not converted into the godhead or soul of Christ these are present not by the power of the sacramental sign but as natural accompaniments. The godhead has never laid aside the body it took up and wherever the body of Christ is there also must his godhead be. Christ's soul was really separated from his body for a time, and if during those three days this sacrament had been celebrated his soul would not have been present, either by the power of the sacramental sign or as a real accompaniment. But because *Christ being raised will never die again* his soul is now always united to his body in reality, and in this sacrament, because his body is present by the power of the sacramental sign, his soul is present as a real accompaniment. It is not only Christ's flesh which is present by the power of the sacramental sign under the appearances of bread, but his whole body: bones, nerves and everything else. After the bread and wine have been converted into Christ's body and blood, their properties, including their dimensions, remain. The dimensions of the bread are not converted into the dimensions of Christ's body, only the substance of the bread into his body's substance. It is the substance of Christ's body and blood that is present by the power of the sacramental sign, not his dimensions. So Christ's dimensioned body is present, but by way of its substance, not by way of its dimensions. Now the wholeness of a substance as such is as truly present in small quantities of it as in large: the whole of what air is is as present in a little air as it is in much air. So the whole substance of Christ's body and blood is contained in this sacrament after the consecration, just as the substance of bread and wine was before.

2   The whole Christ is present under both appearances: under the appearance of bread his body is present by power of the sacramental sign with his blood as a real accompaniment, and under the appearance of wine his blood is present by power of the sign with his body accompanying. For his body and blood are no longer really separate as they were during the period of his death. If the sacrament had been celebrated during that period Christ's body, without blood, would have

been present under the appearances of bread, and his blood, without his body, under the appearances of wine. Having the whole Christ present under two appearances is not superfluous: it represents the suffering of Christ when his body and blood were separated, enables the faithful to eat and to drink of Christ, profiting both their bodies and their souls.

Since the substance of Christ's body is present by the power of 3 the sacramental sign, whereas his dimensions are present as a real accompaniment, the body of Christ exists in the sacrament in the way substance exists under its dimensions, not in the way the dimensions of a body exist within the dimensions of the place containing it. Clearly the whole nature of any substance exists under every smallest part of its dimensions, whether these dimensions are broken into fragments or not. The measurable distance between the parts of an organic body is a consequence of its dimensions, but the nature of its substance precedes these dimensions. That measurable distance between the parts is there in the actual body of Christ, but it doesn't determine the way in which that body is present in the sacrament, which is rather according to its substance. The dimensions of Christ's body are present in the sacrament 4 not in the way peculiar to dimensions – the whole only in the whole, and each part in its part – but in the way natural to substance – the whole nature not only in the whole but also in each part; but the dimensions of the bread are present in the way normal to dimensions. Localized bodies are in their places in the way peculiar to dimensions, 5 their dimensions matching the dimensions of the places they are in. So Christ's body is not in this sacrament as in a place, but in the way substance is contained under its dimensions. But the substance of Christ's body is not subject to the dimensions of the bread as was the bread's substance. The bread was localized there by way of its own dimensions relating it to that place, but the substance of Christ's body is related to that place by way of dimensions not its own, whereas its own dimensions are related to the place by way of its substance. Since that is not the way bodies are localized in places, Christ's body is not localized in this sacrament. In other words, Christ's body is not confined to the place of this sacrament; if it were, it couldn't be anywhere else, yet it exists in heaven in its own proper appearance, and in many other altars in its sacramental appearances. The place where Christ's body is is not however empty: it is not properly speaking filled with the substance of Christ's body, which is not localized there, but it is filled with the sacramental appearances which have dimensions able to fill place naturally, or at least miraculously in virtue of the miraculous fact that they subsist as though they were substance.

6   The body of Christ remains present in this sacrament as long as the sacramental appearances last. When they cease to exist, the body of Christ ceases to be present under them, not because its existence depends on them, but because the relationship of those appearances to his body has ceased to exist. That is the way God ceases to be Lord of any creature that ceases to exist.

7   No bodily eye can see the body of Christ as contained in this sacrament. The properties of Christ's body exist in the sacrament by way of his substance, so do not immediately relate to either the sacramental sign or its environment, and cannot affect the surrounding medium so as to become bodily visible. Substance as such can only be perceived by mind: and since the way Christ exists in this sacrament totally transcends nature, his body can be seen only by God's own mind and the blessed in heaven with whom he shares the vision. Men can know it in this life only by faith.

77 1 **The properties of bread and wine.**   The properties of bread and wine which our senses tell us remain in this sacrament after the consecration do not have the substance of bread and wine as their subject. That substance is no longer present. Neither clearly do they have Christ's body as their subject, because the human body can't have such properties. Some theologians say they have the surrounding air as their subject; but a property that changes subject is no longer the same property numerically, and where have the air's own properties gone to? In any case the words of consecration effect only what they express, and no such thing is expressed in those words. So we are left to conclude that the properties have no subject. God, who is the first cause of every substance and property, can preserve a property in existence by his infinite power even though the substance which is normally the immediate cause preserving that property in existence has been removed. But, you may ask, don't properties exist in subjects by definition? How can a thing be deprived of what belongs to it by definition, even by a miracle? Now *something existing* isn't a genus which substances and their properties have in common. Substance is not defined as *something existing by itself without subject*, and property as *something existing in a subject*; substances have natures suited to existing without a subject, and properties natures suited to existing in a subject. In this sacrament we have properties actually existing without a subject, but in virtue of God's power holding them in existence, not in virtue of their own nature. They don't stop being properties; they are not deprived of what belongs to properties by definition, nor do they put on the definition of a

substance. These properties are individually existing properties, having that individual existence they acquired in the substance of bread and wine, and which, now that substance has been converted into Christ's body and blood, they retain by the power of God. They are particular properties which we can sense. As long as the substance of bread and wine remains those properties don't themselves possess existence, but the substance possesses existence of this or that sort by reason of those properties. (This is generally true of properties: snow is white by reason of its whiteness.) But after the consecration the properties themselves possess their existence: one can distinguish in them existence and what possesses that existence. And they themselves possess their dimensions.

We must also conclude that all other properties remaining in this 2 sacrament exist in the dimensions of the bread and wine as if in their subject. Firstly, our senses tell us there is something extended there which is coloured and affected by other properties, and in such matters our senses don't make mistakes. Secondly, the primary subject of a thing's properties is normally its matter, and all other properties pre-suppose dimensions in this matter: colour, for example, must be colour of a surface. When the subject is taken away the properties remain with the existence they had when the subject was there, so they must still be subjected in the same dimensions. Thirdly, distinct instances of a property derive that distinctness from existing in individually distinct subjects. So whatever is said to be the subject of those properties must be able to generate individual distinctness. Now individual distinctness is an inability to exist in more than one thing. This may derive from inability to exist in anything at all: immaterial spirits are like this, forms that exist by themselves and are therefore individual of themselves. Forms that are forms of subjects derive their individual distinctness from the matter that takes them on; as forms they can exist in subjects, but as taken on by matter (which can't itself exist in anything else) they can't exist in anything else either. But even as form, such a form may be individually distinct if it is able to exist in only one subject (for example, the particular whiteness of this particular white body). Dimensions are the source of individual distinctness in this sense. Now the reason why something can exist in only one thing is because it gets divided off from everything else while remaining undivided in itself, and such division depends on dimensions. Dimensions introduce individual distinctness into a form, enabling individually distinct instances of it to exist in different parts of matter. Dimensions have individual distinctness built into them: we can imagine many similar lines differing only in spatial position (something that belongs to dimensions by definition, since dimension is quantity set out in space). This is why dimensions can be the subject of other properties but not vice versa. Property *a* is said to be the subject of property *b* if having *b* presupposes having *a*: colour presupposes surface. If by a miracle *a* exists without a subject, it itself acts as subject to property *b*.

3   Only things that actually exist act. Since the sacramental appearances miraculously continue in the existence they had when the substance of bread and wine existed, they continue to be active. Properties are active in virtue of their substance's activity just as they exist in virtue of their substance's existence. So just as the sacramental appearances exist without a substance by God's power, so they are active without a substance by God's power, the power on which the activity of all substances and properties depend. New substances form as a result of interactions of the active and passive qualities of things, all acting as tools of agent substances. By divine power this instrumental or tool activity is still present in the sacramental appearances just as before. So those properties contribute instrumentally to the formation of new substances, in that sense acting outside their nature in the power of a

4   more fundamental agency. The properties of bread and wine also change and disappear in the absence of the substance just as they would have done when the substance was there: either directly by alteration, expansion, contraction and so on, or indirectly by disintegration of the underlying subject. For although after the consecration there is no subject, the properties still exist with the existence they had in that subject, an existence fitted to that subject. That existence can be destroyed by any agent opposed to it, just as the original substance of bread and wine would have been; indeed destruction of the substance of bread and wine would have needed prior alteration of just those properties. If after consecration a change of properties occurs that would not have sufficed to destroy the bread and wine, then the change will not be enough to affect the presence of Christ's body and blood in the sacrament; but if the change would have been great enough to have destroyed the substance of bread and wine, then Christ's body and blood will no longer remain present, whether the change be qualitative – in colour, taste or the like – or quantitative – atomizing the bread or wine.

5 Since *one thing's decomposition is another thing's formation* something will always be formed when the sacramental appearances decay. But from what? Not from Christ's body and blood, which are immune to decay. Some people say: from the substance of bread and wine that returns when the sacramental appearances decompose, and then turns to ashes or worms or whatever. But this doesn't seem possible. Clearly while the

appearances last Christ's body and blood remain, and they can't co-exist in the sacrament with the substance of bread and wine. So the substance of bread and wine can't return as long as the sacramental appearances last. But neither can they later, because then they would have to exist without their natural properties, and that is impossible. Unless perhaps we say that at the moment the appearances are completely decomposed what returns is not the substance of bread and wine (since this is the very moment at which the substance newly generated from the appearances starts to exist), but the matter which was bread and wine (though properly speaking this will not so much be a return of the matter as a new creation of it). Since it isn't reasonable to call for miracles in this sacrament over and above those demanded by the consecration itself (and that doesn't demand either the creation or the return of matter), it is better to say that since at the consecration the dimensions of the bread and wine were miraculously given the role of subject of all subsequent forms, the role proper to matter, whatever could have been generated out of the matter of the bread can now be generated out of those dimensions, not by a new miracle but in virtue of the original one. The dimensions of bread and wine retain their own nature, but miraculously receive the power and role proper to substance, and so they change into both the substance and the dimensions of whatever is newly generated. And for the same reason that sacramental 6 appearances can turn to worms and ashes, they can also be assimilated into the human body and nourish it when eaten. A man could live quite a long time on a quantity of consecrated hosts and wine.

The words of consecration.   This sacrament differs from the others 78 1 in two respects. Firstly, it consists in consecration of its material whereas the others consist in use of material already consecrated. Secondly, consecrating in the other sacraments consists only in a blessing by which the material, an inanimate tool, receives instrumental spiritual power passed on to it by a minister, acting as a sort of animate tool; but in the eucharist consecrating consists in a miraculous conversion of substance such as only God can perform, and the minister's only contribution to the action of the sacrament is uttering the words which consecrate. The sacramental form of words must reflect these points, so in this sacrament it expresses only consecration of the material by transubstantiation (*This is my body* and *This is the cup of my blood*); whereas in the other sacraments it expresses some action of using the material: baptizing or signing a person. Secondly, in the forms of other sacraments the minister speaks the words in his own person (saying *I baptize* or *I confirm* or

Receive the power or *By this anointing and our intercession*), but in the eucharist the minister speaks in Christ's person, so that we can understand that the minister does nothing in the action of this sacrament but utter Christ's words. The words *Take and eat* which precede the consecration proper refer to subsequent use of the consecrated material, which is not of the essence of this sacrament, so these words are not an essential part of the form. But the use of the consecrated material is nevertheless a fulfilment of the sacrament, just as anything's activity fulfils its nature; so these words are there to express the sacrament fully.

2   The form of words of a sacrament should signify what the sacrament does. So the form of consecration of bread signifies the conversion of bread into Christ's body. The conversion is not gradual but instantaneous, and must be signified not as a process but as an accomplished fact; the starting-point and end-point of the conversion must therefore be expressed from the standpoint of the accomplished conversion, when the substance with which we started is already gone, though the appearances which present themselves to our senses remain and are suitably expressed by a demonstrative pronoun: *This*. The end-point is however present in substance and can be so referred to: *my body*. *This is my body* is therefore the most appropriate form. God's word acts here sacramentally: that is to say, it does what it does by virtue of what it signifies. So it appropriately uses the present indicative. At the creation God's word was purely effective, working as a command of God's

3   wisdom, and so appropriately used the imperative. Some people have thought the only essential part of the form over the wine is *This is the cup of my blood*, and that all that follows is inessential. This is awkward, since the words that follow expand the predicate and are part of one complete sentence. It is better to say that the words from *As often as you do these things* onwards which are concerned with the using of the sacrament are inessential to the form, but that everything up to that point is essential: *This is the cup of my blood* signifying the actual conversion of the wine into Christ's blood, and the rest signifying the power of the blood shed in Christ's sufferings and at work in this sacrament. The separate consecration of the blood explicitly represents the actual sufferings of Christ; so the mention of the effects of that suffering occur there rather than in the consecration of the body, the

4   subject that suffered. The words of consecration have created instrumental power to bring about the conversion in this sacrament. Since they are uttered in the person of Christ, they gain this power from Christ by his command, in the same way that everything else he said and did has an instrumental power to save. The words work sacra-

mentally, that is to say, as a sign. So their power to convert follows on their meaning, which is complete only when the last word is uttered. That is the moment at which they receive their power, a power as single as their meaning, even if the actual words uttered are many.

One might object that if transsubstantiation only occurs when the words of consecration have been completely uttered, then when the minister utters the word *This* the substance of bread is still present. But in that case *This is my body* means *This bread is my body*, and that is a false statement. There are many opinions on this matter. Some theologians say the word *This* is being quoted rather than used at the moment of consecration. But that can't be true, because if it isn't being applied to the material physically present at the time, then there is no sacrament: *the word enters into the matter and constitutes the sacrament.* In any case, the real difficulty isn't fully faced by this answer, because we can still raise it in connection with Christ's original utterance of these words. So others say that the word *This* does point at something here and now, but to something present to our minds, not our senses: *This is my body* means *What is signified by this is my body*. But this will not do, since sacraments bring to pass what they signify, and on this view Christ's body would be made present only in sign, and not in reality, which is a heresy. So yet others say that the word *this* points to something present to our senses, but not to what is present at the moment it is uttered, but to what is present when the whole sentence is complete; rather as the word *now* in the sentence *now I keep quiet* refers to the moment immediately after the utterance of the sentence. But this also won't do: for then the words simply mean *My body is my body*, and that is certainly not something the words bring about (it was true before they were spoken) so not what they mean either. Rather we must say that just as utterances of our mind when planning action don't presuppose the truth of what they say but make it come true, so this formula doesn't presuppose the truth of what it expresses but makes it come true. So we understand it at the last moment of its uttering, but not presupposing as its subject what is present at the end-point of the conversion (the body of Christ), nor what preceded it (the substance of the bread), but what they have in common, the fact of being contained in general under these appearances. That is why a pronoun is used, to refer to what is referred to without determining what it is.

The sacrament of love.   *The bread which I shall give is my flesh for* [vol 59] 79 1 *the life of the world.* To define the effect of this sacrament consider first and foremost that the sacrament contains Christ: coming visibly into this world he brought with him the life of grace, and now coming sacramentally into men he applies that life of grace to them: *He who eats me shall also live by me.* Or consider that the sacrament represents the suffering of Christ: the effect of that suffering on the world this sacrament applies to man: *This is my blood which will be shed for you to forgive sins.* Or consider that the sacrament is given to us as food and drink: everything that physical food and drink does for our bodily life – sustaining, building up, restoring and gladdening the heart – this sacrament does for our life in the spirit. Or finally consider that it is given under the appearances of bread and wine: *our Lord entrusted his body and blood to materials in which many elements are fused into one, O sacrament of love, O sign of unity, O bond of charity.* Since Christ and his passion cause grace, and spiritual nourishment and love depend on grace, all the considerations show that this sacrament confers grace on us. This sacrament contains within itself the power that confers grace, and no one can receive grace except by receiving this sacrament or desiring to receive it: desiring it himself if he is an adult, the church desiring it for him if he is a child. It is a measure of the effectiveness of the sacrament's power that even desiring it brings a person grace and makes him alive spiritually; really receiving the sacrament increases and perfects the grace and spiritual life that are already there, though in a different way from the sacrament of confirmation. Confirmation strengthens and increases grace so that we can remain firm against external attack by Christ's enemies; but in this sacrament grace is increased and our spiritual life perfected in such a way that we are perfected in ourselves and made more one with God. For this sacrament confers grace together with the love of charity: it is *a living coal of fire* in which *God's love is never idle but powerfully at work.* So this sacrament by its own power not only bestows dispositions of grace and virtue but arouses them to activity: *The love of Christ presses us forward.* And that is how it nourishes us in the spirit, gladdening and as it were inebriating the soul with the sweetness of God's goodness: *Eat, friends, and lovers, drink until you are drunk.* Because sacraments operate through representations of their effects we can talk of the body as offered for the health of our bodies and the blood for the health of our souls, although both work for both since they both contain the whole of Christ. In any case, our body, even if it isn't the immediate recipient of grace, receives the effects of grace flowing over from the soul: in the present life when we *yield our members to God as instruments of his righteousness,* and in the life to come when we receive in our body a share of the soul's immortality and glory.

2   *If any man eat of this bread he shall live for ever.* As we saw above this

sacrament contains the source of its effect (Christ present and his suffering represented in it) as well as the means by which that effect is brought about (the use of the sacrament and the sacramental appearances). On both counts the sacrament is the appropriate cause of our entry into eternal life. For Christ himself by his sufferings opened for us the gate to eternal life, and nourishment by spiritual food and the unity expressed in the appearances of bread and wine are both imperfect realizations in the present life of what we shall possess eternally in the state of glory, *where in the companionship of the saints, there will be peace and full and perfect unity.* The suffering of Christ, the power at work in this sacrament, is quite powerful enough to win glory for us. It does not immediately introduce us into heaven only because *we must first suffer with him if we are to be glorified with him.* So this sacrament gives not immediate glory but the strength to get there, and that is why we call it *viaticum.* Because the suffering of Christ does not produce its effect in people who do not relate to it as they should, those who receive this sacrament unworthily do not come to glory.

He who eats and drinks unworthily, eats and drinks a judgment on 3 *himself.* Because of what it contains within itself – Christ's suffering, the fount and cause of forgiveness of sin – this sacrament has the power to forgive all sins. But consciousness of fatal sin hinders the sinner from experiencing the effect of this sacrament: unless one is spiritually alive one is unable to profit from nourishment for the spiritual life, and being in love with fatal sin prevents the unity with Christ that this sacrament causes. So the sacrament does not forgive sin in anyone who receives it while conscious of fatal sin. Nevertheless this sacrament can forgive such sin: firstly when received by desire at the moment one is first made right from sin; and secondly when actually received by someone who though actually in fatal sin is neither conscious of it nor attached to it (perhaps though not sufficiently contrite to begin with, he approaches this sacrament with reverence and devotion and receives in it a grace of love which completes his contrition and forgives his sin). Baptism is spiritual birth, a change from spiritual death to spiritual life, represented as a washing: on both counts it is appropriate for someone conscious of fatal sin to approach baptism. But in this sacrament man takes into himself Christ, represented as spiritual nourishment, and this is not appropriate for one dead in sin. The body needs nourishing by food in 4 order to restore the energy it consumes daily. In the spiritual life too, we daily lose our energy of love, weakening it by non-fatal sins; so an appropriate effect of this sacrament is the forgiving of non-fatal sin. The reality behind the sign of this sacrament is love, not merely the dis-

position but the activity of love, which this sacrament so arouses that
5 non-fatal sin is dissolved away. The eucharist is at one and the same
time offered as sacrifice and received as a sacrament. It takes effect as a
sacrament in those who receive it, as a sacrifice in those who offer it or
for whom it is offered. By its direct sacramental power the sacrament
does what it was instituted to do: which is not to make amends for sin,
but to nourish spiritually the members of Christ on Christ himself,
uniting them to him as food. This unity is one of love, the fervour of
which leads to forgiveness not only of faults but of penalties incurred,
so that as an accompaniment of the direct sacramental effect a recipient
can have his sins forgiven: not indeed all, but in proportion to his
measure of devotion and fervour. Considered as a sacrifice however, the
sacrament has power to make amends: indeed its offering is enough in
itself to make amends for all penalties, and that takes effect within those
who offer it or for whom it is offered in proportion to their devotion.
Baptism is directly intended to forgive fault and penalty, since it gives
us the gift of dying in Christ's company; but the eucharist is not directly
intended for that, but for nourishing and making us perfect in Christ.

6   *This is the bread which comes down from heaven, that men may eat of it
and not die.* Sin is a sort of spiritual death of soul, and we are preserved
against future sin as we are against future death of our body: by
nourishment and medicine against decay, and by armour against external attack. This sacrament preserves us from sin in both these ways. By
joining us to Christ through grace it strengthens our spiritual life like
spiritual food and medicine; and by representing the suffering whereby
Christ conquered the devil it repels all the devil's attacks. While we are
still on the road to heaven our free will can turn either to good or to
bad. So although this sacrament contains in itself power to guard us
against sin, it doesn't remove the possibility of our sinning. Charity too,
of itself, preserves man from sin, since *love does no wrong to our fellows.*
But because we have freedom to change our minds and wills, we can sin
after having loved, and in the same way we can sin after having received
7 this sacrament. Because the eucharist represents the suffering of Christ,
through which Christ *offered himself as a victim to God,* it is a sacrifice;
and because it bestows invisible grace under a visible appearance it is a
sacrament. It benefits its recipients both as a sacrament and as a sacrifice
offered for them: *As we receive from this altar the sacred body and blood
of your son, let us be filled with every grace and blessing.* It also benefits
those who do not receive it as a sacrifice offered for their salvation:
*Remember, Lord, your servants and handmaidens for whom we offer or who
offer to you this sacrifice of praise, for them and theirs, for the ransom of*

their souls, for the hope of their safety and salvation. Our Lord spoke of both benefits when he spoke of his blood *which shall be shed for you*, the recipients, *and for many*, the others, *unto remission of sins.* Just as Christ's suffering is enough to benefit everyone, forgiving their sin and bringing them to grace and glory, yet benefits only those who are united to that suffering through faith and love, so this sacrifice, the commemoration of the Lord's sufferings, benefits only those united to the sacrament through faith and love. Baptism is not intended to produce actual fervour 8 of love as the eucharist is. It is a spiritual rebirth which establishes in us an initial perfection of form or disposition; whereas this sacrament is a spiritual meal, providing actual enjoyment.

Taking communion.   In the eucharist we distinguish *eating in sign* 80 1 *only*, when we receive the sacrament without its effect, from *eating in spirit*, when we experience the sacrament's effect and are joined to Christ in spirit by faith and love. We can make a similar distinction in baptism and the other sacraments, for some people receive them only in sign, others in sign and reality. But there is a difference in the eucharist. The other sacraments consist in applying their material to men and are achieved by receiving the sacrament, but the eucharist consists in consecrating its material, and receiving it, either in sign or reality, is something that follows on the sacrament. Moreover, since baptism and the other sacraments imprint a character, all who receive those sacraments in sign also receive a spiritual reality (namely, the character); but not in this sacrament. So in the eucharist this distinction of receiving only in sign or also in spiritual reality is stressed more than it is in baptism. Some have eaten this sacrament in spirit before ever they receive it in sign, since they have received it by desire. Nevertheless eating in sign is not superfluous because actually receiving the sacrament produces its effect more fully than simply desiring it, as we said before about baptism.

There are two realities signified by this sacrament: one is contained 4 in the sacrament, namely Christ himself, and the other signified but not contained, namely the mystical body of Christ, the companionship of the saints. By receiving this sacrament we signify that we are united to Christ and joined in one body with his members, and that is true of a man with living faith but not of a man in fatal sin. Clearly then to receive this sacrament while in fatal sin is to act out a falsehood, and indeed to commit a sacrilege by violating the sacrament's truth: which is itself a fatal sin. Baptism and the sacrament of penitence are like purgatives given to take away sin's fever, whereas this sacrament is more like a

tonic only to be given to those recovered from their sin. We don't receive the body of Christ simply by seeing this sacrament, since sight doesn't penetrate to the substance of Christ's body: we see only the sacramental appearances. But we eat not only those appearances but Christ himself present under them. So nobody baptized is forbidden to behold the body of Christ, but only those really one with Christ, not just sac-
5 ramentally, are allowed to eat it. Since Christ's divine nature is something greater than his human nature, and that in turn is greater than its sacramental signs, the greatest sins are those committed against God's nature (disbelief and blasphemy), then those against Christ's humanity, then those against the sacraments, and finally those committed against
10 mere creatures. We are conformed by the sacrament of baptism to Christ's death, receiving his character; and just as Christ dies once we should be baptized only once. But in this sacrament we don't receive a character from Christ but Christ himself, whose power lasts for ever: *by a single offering he has perfected for all times those who are sanctified*; and since we need this saving power of Christ every day, it is a good thing for us to receive this sacrament daily. Again, baptism is a spiritual rebirth, so just as we are born bodily only once, so we should be born spiritually only once; but the eucharist is our spiritual food, so just as we eat bodily food every day so it is good for us to eat this sacrament daily. But since our Lord said *Give us this day our daily bread*, we should not communicate more than once a day, the once representing the fact
11 that Christ suffered once for all. A man cannot be saved without the desire to receive this sacrament, and desire is pointless if it is not implemented when the opportunity offers. Clearly then a person is bound to go on receiving this sacrament not only by church law but by the Lord's own command to *do this in memory of me*. This sacrament is not so necessary as baptism where children are concerned, for they can be saved without the eucharist but not without baptism; but both are
12 necessary for adults. The sacrament is fittingly received under both appearances, body and blood, since both go to make up the full sac-ramental sign. So the priest, whose role it is to consecrate and so fulfil this sacrament, ought never to receive Christ's body without also receiving his blood. The sacrament is complete when it is consecrated, even if the faithful do not receive it at all. So if the people receive only the body and not the blood this doesn't detract from the completeness of the sacrament, as long as the consecrating priest receives both.
82 1	Such is the dignity of this sacrament that it is only consecrated in the person of Christ. But when we perform something in another's name we must have his authority to do so. Christ grants authority to receive

this sacrament in baptism, but authority to consecrate it in his person is granted only to priests at their ordination. The power to consecrate lies in the words of consecration plus the authority given to the priest at his consecration: *Receive the power of offering sacrifice in the church for the living and the dead.* For instrumental power can reside in a combination of instruments through which the one primary agent acts. Bishops receive authority in Christ's person over his mystical body, the church, an authority not given to priests at their consecration, though it may be committed to them by a bishop; but powers not related to organizing the mystical body, such as consecrating this sacrament, are not reserved to bishops. Since priests consecrate in the name of Christ, 2 and many are one in Christ, it is irrelevant whether the sacrament is consecrated by one priest or many, as long as the church's rites are observed. The eucharist is not only a sacrament, but a sacrifice. But 4 those who offer a sacrifice must also partake of it, to show that the outward sacrifice is a sign of their own inward sacrifice of themselves to God; and that is why the priest, every time he consecrates, must receive the sacrament in its integrity. The sacrament of baptism consists in the action of applying its material; so no one can baptize himself and be active and passive in the sacrament at the same time. In this sacrament too the priest doesn't consecrate himself: he consecrates the bread and wine, and that is what the sacrament consists in; that he then uses the sacrament is something that follows on from the sacrament itself. The 5 priest consecrates the sacrament not by his own power but as a minister acting in the person of Christ. But wickedness doesn't stop one being a minister nor, since consecration of the eucharist is an act enabled by the 7 reception of holy order, are priests separated from the church by heresy, schism or excommunication unable to consecrate the eucharist; and if they do the sacrament will contain the true body and blood of Christ. But such priests don't act rightly; they commit a sin and do not gather the fruit of their sacrifice. The celebration of this sacrament is said to 83 1 sacrifice Christ for two reasons. First because the celebration of this sacrament is an image and representation of the sufferings in which Christ was truly sacrificed. Secondly, because by this sacrament we come to share in the fruits of the Lord's suffering: *Whenever the commemoration of this sacrifice is celebrated the work of our redemption is carried on.* In the first sense Christ could be said to have been sacrificed in the Old Testament prefigurings of his sufferings. In the second sense it is peculiar to this sacrament that in its celebration Christ is sacrificed.

Sacramental penitence

[vol 60] 84 1 **The sacrament of penitence.** *A sacrament is a ritual so performed that it is a sign of something we should holily receive.* In the sacrament of penitence actions are performed by both the penitent sinner and the absolving priest that signify something holy. For the deeds and words of the penitent sinner signify that his heart has turned away from sin, and the deeds and words of the priest in regard to that penitent signify that God is forgiving his sin. So clearly penitence as celebrated in the church is a sacrament. Notice that in those sacraments which confer grace so excellent that it surpasses entirely man's capacity to act, we use external bodily materials to represent it: in baptism where sins are totally forgiven both as to fault and to penalty; in confirmation, where the Holy Spirit is given in fullness; and in the last anointing, in which perfect health of spirit comes from Christ's power as from an external source. What human activity there is in such sacraments is not part of their essential material but disposes us to receive them. In sacraments like penitence and marriage, however, which produce effects proportionate in some way to human activity, externally perceptible human actions take the place of material. In bodily medicine too we sometimes apply external materials like ointments and plasters, but sometimes the patient himself performs certain exercises. In sacraments which employ physical materials, those materials must be applied by a minister of the church playing the part of Christ, as a sign that the excellence of power at work in the sacrament comes from Christ. But in the sacrament of penitence interiorly prompted human activity serves as the material, material not supplied by a minister but by God himself working interiorly, and the minister completes the sacramental sign by absolving the penitent. Even in the sacrament of penitence we can distinguish that which is only sign (the actions performed by the penitent sinner and by the absolving priest), that which is sign but also a reality signified (the sinner's interior repentance), and that which is a reality signified but no sign (the forgiveness of the sin). The actions performed taken all together cause the interior repentance, and that in some sense causes the sin's forgiveness.

2   As immediate material of this sacrament then we have the penitent's own actions, which in turn take sins as material to grieve over, confess and make amends for. In that sense, the chief and proper material of penitence is fatally sinful action; non-fatally sinful action is proper material for penitence since it is willed, but it is not what the sacrament was chiefly instituted to combat; inherited sin is neither the chief thing combatted by this sacrament (that is rather baptism's task), nor proper

material for penitence since it is not something we have willed. Unless perhaps we think of Adam's will as ours, and say with St Paul that *in him all sinned*. Only by extending our concept of penitence to include any and every detestation of things past could we talk of repenting inherited sin.

This sacrament is completed by actions of the priest: what the penitent 3 says and does is a sort of material for the sacrament, and what the priest says gives it form. And since New Law sacraments bring about what they signify, their forms signify what is being done with the material of the sacrament. The forms of baptism and confirmation say *I baptize you* and *I sign you with the sign of the cross and I confirm you with the chrism of salvation*, since these sacraments apply their material in these ways. In the eucharist, which consists in the very consecration of its material, the form expresses the truth of that consecration: *This is my body*. But this sacrament of penitence consists neither in consecrating material nor in applying it once consecrated, but rather in removing certain material (in the sense that sins can be called the material of our repentance). So the priest signifies this by saying *I absolve you*, for sins are like bonds that must be loosened or dissolved. The form derives from Christ's own words to Peter: *Whatsoever you shall loose upon earth ...* , and is the form used in sacramental absolution. There are other forms of liturgical absolution which are not sacramental but rather prayers for the forgiveness of non-fatal sin: *May almighty God have mercy on you, May God grant you absolution and forgiveness*: these formulae don't signify that absolution is being granted, but rather ask that it may be. Only God can be the original source of absolution and forgiveness, but the priest can minister both, his words acting as instruments of the divine power at work within all sacramental signs, be they things or words.

Laying on of hands is used in the sacraments of the church to indicate 4 some abundance of grace which unites those on whom hands are laid with ministers in whom that grace abounds. It occurs in the sacrament of confirmation when the fullness of the Spirit is bestowed, and in the sacrament of order when a certain excellence of power to minister to God is conferred. But the sacrament of penitence is not designed to bring about any such abundance of grace, but simply to remove sin, and so it does not include any laying on of hands; nor does baptism. In the eucharist the priest completes the sacrament simply by uttering words over the material; he completes the sacrament of penitence in the same way, simply saying words of absolution over the penitent.

The sacrament of penitence is necessary not for all, but for those in 5 sin. *Sin when full-grown begets death*, and so, for the sinner's salvation, sin must be removed; and this can only be done by the sacrament of penitence in which the power of Christ's suffering, working through a priest's absolution and the actions of a penitent cooperating with grace, destroys sin: *he who has created you without your help will not make you just without it.* Clearly then the sacrament of penitence is as necessary for salvation after sin, as bodily medicine for a man who has fallen

6 dangerously ill. Penitence is a secondary requisite for a man's salvation as it were, on the presupposition that the man has sinned. Unless he has actually sinned he doesn't need penitence, though he needs baptism and confirmation and the eucharist; men need birth, growth and nourishment as such, but medicine only if they fall ill. Jerome calls it metaphorically *a second plank after shipwreck*, meaning that in the sea of this life it is better not to suffer damage in the first place, but if you do then a secondary remedy can repair it through penitence.

7   In this sacrament a penitent's actions provide material, and a priest's actions as minister of Christ gives them form and completes the sacramental sign. The material of other sacraments pre-exists either by nature, like water, or by artifice, like bread; but the institution of the sacrament decides how the material will be used. So the forms of these sacraments and their power derive entirely from Christ's institution and his suffering. The same is true of the sacrament of penitence. Its material pre-exists by nature, for man's natural reason prompts him to repent the evils he does; but how he should repent is determined by God. When the Lord began his preaching he commanded men not only to repent but *to do penance*, indicating that this sacrament would require definite ways of acting; when he said to Peter *I will give you the keys of the kingdom of heaven* ... he defined the role of the ministers in the sacrament; and when after his resurrection he spoke of it and said *it was necessary to preach penance and forgiveness of sins in his name to all people*, he showed that sacramental penitence has power and efficacy to forgive sin in the name of Jesus Christ suffered and risen. The law that is in us by nature prescribes that men repent the evils they do by grieving over them, seeking remedies for the evil and displaying the grief. But just as in other cases how we are to do what is prescribed by natural law is determined by institution of the law of God, imperfectly in the Old Law but more perfectly in the New. In the Old Law it is prescribed that the grief should be interior: *Rend your hearts, not your garments*; and the remedy is to be found in confessing one's sin to God's ministers at least in the general sense that making an offering for sin is tantamount to confessing it to the offering priest. But, because the power of the keys deriving from Christ's sufferings had not yet been instituted, the Old

Law did not require, as the New Law does, that grief for sin should take the form of intending submission to the keys of the church through confession and making amends, hoping for pardon by virtue of Christ's sufferings.

Penitence is twofold: inner repentance and outward penance. Inner 8 repentance is grief for sin committed and ought to last one's life long. But outward penance shows external signs of grief and verbally confesses sins to the absolving priest, making amends according to his judgment. Such penance doesn't need to be lifelong, but lasts for a fixed period measured by the sin. To be actively penitent all the time is impossible: 9 sleep and other bodily needs interfere with both the inner and outward activity. But we must have a continuous disposition to penitence, doing nothing incompatible with it and being resolved that our past sins will always displease us.

Some people mistakenly say that one cannot be pardoned for sin more 10 than once. Either they think that love once possessed cannot be lost (though it is subject to our free will, and even after true repentance one is still able to commit fatal sin again), or they think that sin committed after one has been pardoned is so grave that it can never be pardoned. But this is a mistake not only about sin (which after pardon is able to be more or less grave just as before), but even more seriously about God's unlimited mercy, which is greater than any multitude or magnitude of sins. A man who repeats or intends to repeat a sin at the moment he is doing penance for it is clearly making a mockery of penitence; but sinning by act or intention later on doesn't of itself make previous repentance insincere. The truth of earlier actions is not excluded by later incompatible ones, otherwise a man wouldn't truly have been running if afterwards he sits down.

The virtue of repentance.   A virtue is *a disposition to make choices* 85 1 *according to right reason.* Now the penitence we have been speaking about grieves where there is good reason to grieve, in proportion to past sins and with the intention of getting rid of them. So clearly it is a virtue or a virtuous act, not just an emotion. Human actions make up the material of the sacrament of penitence, but not of baptism or confirmation; so since virtues dispose to actions it is more possible for this sacrament to be a virtue or an act of virtue than for baptism or confirmation. To grieve over something done in the hope of turning it into something not done is foolish; but that's not what penitence is about. The penitent disapproves a past deed with the intention of getting rid of its consequences, the offence to God and the penalty incurred.

2 Penitence has its own special kind of praiseworthy action belonging to no other virtue, namely, action to wipe out past sin as offensive to God. So penitence is a special virtue. Displeasure at past sin, like rejoicing in past good, is an act of love of charity; but intending to work at blotting out past sin needs a special virtue that serves that love. The matter repented of is not in itself specific: it can include any type of sin. But the respect under which we repent of it is specific: namely, as remediable

3 with the help of God's justifying grace. Penitence's specific role is to grieve over sin committed because it offends God and to purpose amendment. Amendment means not simply ceasing to offend, but recompensing the one we have offended. Recompense is like retribution except that it comes not from the one offended but from the offender. Both are matters of just exchange, so the virtue of penitence is allied to justice. But notice that justice can be strict or relative. Strict justice obtains between equals and is called by Aristotle political or civil justice, since the state is a community of equals. But a relative justice governs the relations of people one of whom is subordinate in some way to the other: servants and master, children and parents, wife and husband. It is this sort of justice that is involved in penitence. The penitent returns to God with an intention of amendment as a servant to his master, a child to his father, a wife to her husband. Just as one can exchange kindnesses so one can exchange offences, either involuntarily by punishment as in retributive justice imposed by a judge, or voluntarily by making amends as in penitence displayed by the sinner himself. Penitence then is directly a type of justice, but it includes things to do with every virtue. Because it relates in some way to God it shares some things with the theological virtues defined by our ways of relating to God: so penitence is associated with faith in Christ's sufferings justifying us, with hope of pardon, with the hate of vice which characterizes charity. God however is not the matter of repentance: that is the human action which has offended God, and God enters in as the one to whom justice is due. Like all moral virtues penitence shares in the virtue of prudence, which directs all moral virtue; and as a sort of justice it shares not only the characteristics of justice, but also those of courage and moderation since matters involved in just exchanges cause pleasure or arouse fear. The just man must courageously sustain hardship and moderately abstain from pleasure.

5   The beginning of the actions by which a penitent cooperates with God working in him is God's own turning of our heart to himself: *Turn us, o Lord, and we shall be turned*. The second act is a movement of faith, then of slavish fear withdrawing from sin for fear of punishment, then

a movement of hope purposing amendment in the hope of pardon, then love in which the penitent hates his sin in itself and not merely from fear of punishment, and so finally a movement of filial fear in which the penitent seeks to make amends to God out of reverence for him as a father.

I will remember none of the iniquities he has done. If there were any sin 86 1 impossible for penitence to blot out this would be either because the sinner hadn't the ability to repent it, or the sacrament hadn't the power to blot it out. The first is the case with devils and damned whose wills are so fixed in evil that they cannot be displeased with sin as fault but only regret the punishment suffered for it. Such regret is unfruitful and despairing, not a hope of pardon. But it is a mistake to think one cannot repent sin in this life where our wills are still flexible to good and evil; such a view denies free will and detracts from the power of grace. And it is also a mistake to say penitence hasn't power to forgive sins: that denies God's mercy and detracts from the power of Christ's suffering which is at work in penitence as it is in the other sacraments. So we must unequivocally assert the power of penitence to blot out all sins in this life. *The word against the Holy Spirit* [that Christ says is unpardonable] is either final impenitence, unforgivable because after this life there is no further forgiveness for sin; or it is sin done with a bad will, and what Christ means is that within such sin there is nothing to excuse it.

Fatally sinful actions cannot be forgiven without the virtue of repent- 2 ance. For sins are offences against God and are forgiven in the way God forgives offences. Offences are the direct opposite of graces, for to be offended with someone is to exclude him from one's good graces. Now there is this difference between the graces of man and the graces of God: the graces of man presuppose rather than cause the goodness, true or fancied, of the person in his favour, but the graces of God and his goodwill create goodness in the person God favours. As a result man can cease to be offended with someone without any change occurring in that person's will; but when God ceases to be offended with someone, the person's will is changed. Now the offence caused by fatal sin is due to man having turned his will away from God towards some transitory good. So pardon for the offence involves a change in the direction of man's will towards God with a renunciation of its previous direction and an intention of making amends; and all these are acts of the virtue of repentance. So without the virtue of repentance sin cannot be forgiven. The sacrament of penitence also needs the action of a priest binding and loosing to complete it; God can pardon sin without that, but not without the virtue of repentance. The only sin in a child is inherited sin, involving no actual disorder of the child's will but only a certain disordered disposition in its nature, so that forgiving it involves no actual re-ordering of will, but only the change of disposition caused by instilling grace and virtue. Adult sins however involve actual disorder of will and cannot, even in baptism, be forgiven without actual change of that will, repentance.

3   Penitence cannot forgive one sin and leave another unforgiven. All fatal sin excludes grace, so all must be forgiven together. Moreover, true repentance turns against sin because sin is against God, and this is true of all fatal sins. So one cannot truly repent of one sin without repenting every one. External debts are not incompatible with friend-ship, and friendship can remit one without remitting another. But the debts offences cause are incompatible with friendship and one can't forgive one unless one forgives all. It seems absurd to beg someone's pardon for one offence but not for another. Still, we think, perhaps God could love a man in one respect and not in another, much as he loves the sinner as man though not as sinning? The love of God for a man's nature does not as such bring him to heavenly glory, and is not hindered by the man's fatal sins. The gracious love which forgives those fatal sins is the love which brings man to eternal life, and a different matter entirely.

4   There are two sides to fatal sin: it turns away from our eternal good and fixes in a disordered way on a transitory good. Because it turns away from the eternal good it incurs an eternal punishment; because it turns to a transitory good in a disordered way it incurs such punishment as is needed to repair the balance of justice upset by the fault. For justice demands that someone who has indulged his will more than he ought, should suffer something against his will to restore the balance. Since however the turning is finite the punishment in this respect is not eternal. Non-fatal sin, where there is disordered turning towards a transitory good but no turning away from God, incurs no eternal punishment but only the temporary penalty. And when grace forgives faults it joins the soul again to God, removing both the turning away from God and the eternal punishment it incurred, but not the liability to a transitory penalty. The turning away from God is the formal element that makes a fatal sin fatal, whereas the turning towards the created good provides what we might call the matter of the sin. Remove the formal element in anything and it is no longer the same sort of thing: take away a man's reason and he is no longer human. Fatal faults are removed in that way: grace removes the spirit's turning away from God

and the eternal punishment it incurs, but the material of the sin remains: the disordered turn to a created good, and it is this which incurs the temporal penalty. Grace works *in* man to justify him from sin, and *with* man to help him live rightly. Pardon for sin and release from eternal punishment are the results of grace working *in* man; release from transitory punishment is the result of grace working *with* man, helping him bear his punishment patiently and so obtain release from it. And just as what grace does by working in a man comes before what it does by working with him, so the forgiveness of sin and eternal punishment precedes his full release from transitory punishment. Each is a result of grace, but the first of grace alone and the second of grace and free will together. Christ's suffering is sufficient of itself to remove all liability to punishment, eternal and temporary, but how a particular man receives absolution from such punishment depends on his way of sharing the power of those sufferings. In baptism he shares it totally, dying to sin with Christ through water and the Spirit, so that he might be born again to a new life; so in baptism man is totally forgiven all punishment for sin. In penitence however a man benefits from the power of Christ's sufferings in proportion to his own actions, which constitute the matter for the sacrament as water does for baptism. So the liability to all punishment is not taken away in one go with the first act of repentance forgiving the fault, but only when all the acts of penance are completed.

Even when sin is forgiven certain after-effects of sin remain, dis- 5 positions caused in us by the acts we have done. But these dispositions are now less powerful since they no longer have man in their grip. Indeed they are transitory conditions rather than habitual dispositions, like the inflammability remaining after baptism.

The virtue of repentance is a source of those human actions provided 6 by the sinner as material for the sacrament of penitence. Now all sacraments produce their effect not only in virtue of their form but also of their matter, the two making up one sacrament. Thus baptism forgives sin principally in virtue of its form, but also in virtue of its material, water, which receives power to do so from the form. In the same way the sacrament of penitence forgives sin principally in virtue of the power of the keys which its ministers possess and which serves as the formal element of the sacrament; but secondarily by the power that the acts of the penitent, acts of the virtue of repentance, have when referred to the keys of the church. Forgiveness of sin is an effect of repentance the virtue, but principally of penitence the sacrament. The effect of God's grace working in us is the justification of the sinner, in which not only is grace instilled and sin removed, but also man's free will responds to

God with an act of living faith, and reacts against sin with an act of repentance. These human actions are an effect of grace working in us and brought into being at the same time as sin is removed. So although forgiveness of sin is an effect of grace working in us, it cannot exist without an act of the virtue of repentance. The *justification of the unrighteous* not only involves an act of repentance but also an act of faith. So we don't talk of the forgiveness of sin as an effect of the virtue of repentance only, but as even more an effect of faith and love. An act of the virtue of repentance is related to Christ's sufferings both through faith and through submission to the keys of the church. So in both these ways it causes forgiveness of sin in virtue of Christ's sufferings. The reason why forgiveness of sin cannot occur without an act of the virtue of repentance is that it is an inseparable effect of grace, the primary source of sin's forgiveness at work in every sacrament. Grace is the first cause of the forgiveness of sin, even prior to the sacrament of penitence. Though even in the Old Law and the law written into us by nature there existed a sort of sacramental penance.

87 1   Through fatal sin, action incompatible with the love of charity, man turns away from God altogether. Through non-fatal sin man's readiness to turn to God is slowed down. Both are disorders in man's will due to unbalanced turning towards created goods, and both are forgiven by way of repentance. But more perfect repentance is required for forgiveness of fatal sin, namely that a person actually detest each fatal sin he has committed as much as he can, striving to remember them and reject them individually. This is not required for the forgiveness of non-fatal sin, though even here it is not enough simply to have the disposition to reject such sins that the virtues of repentance and love give one. If that were so the disposition to love would be incompatible with non-fatal sin and that is clearly false. So what is needed is a kind of virtual rejection, in which a person's will is so drawn to God and the things of God that anything that would hold him back would displease him and cause him grief, even if he is in fact not thinking about that thing. Such an attitude however won't suffice to forgive a fatal sin, unless even the most diligent examination of conscience has failed to bring it to mind. A man in grace can avoid all and every single fatal sin; he is also able to avoid each non-fatal sin considered singly, but not all. Repenting fatal sins requires a man to resolve to abstain from all and every fatal sin; but repenting of non-fatal sin requires him to resolve to abstain from each sin considered singly, but not from all, because the weakness of the present life doesn't allow that. He ought to intend to try and reduce their number: otherwise he would be in danger of going backwards; he would lose his desire to

progress and rid himself of the obstacles to progress which non-fatal sins are.

To pardon non-fatal sin doesn't need a special disposition of grace, 2 but some act of grace or love. In people with free will there can be no instilling of grace that is not accompanied by an act of free will directed to God and away from sin, and so any new instilling of grace will forgive non-fatal sin, and be accompanied by an act of the virtue of repentance, explicit or implicit. This can happen without the sacrament of penitence, which needs the absolution of the priest to complete it. So non-fatal sin doesn't need a special instilling of grace such as happens in every sacrament but not in every act of a virtue. The forgiveness of non-fatal 4 sin needs no new instilling of grace-as-disposition, but it does require some activity of grace. So it can't happen to somebody in fatal sin.

Penitence restores us to virtue in the same way that it causes grace, 89 1 that is to say as a sacrament, for as a virtue it is rather an effect of grace. So there is no implication that the virtue of repentance can cause all the other virtues, but that the virtue of repentance is caused by the sacrament at the same time as all the other virtues are. The power of the keys causes grace and the virtues in an instrumental sense. The first act of a repentant man – contrition – is the last disposition required for grace, whereas all the other acts of repentance have grace and virtue as their source. Sometimes after the first act of penitence – contrition – after-effects of sin remain, conditions caused in us by previous acts of sin which make it difficult for us to perform acts of virtue, even though the dispositions to love and the other virtues make such acts easy and pleasing to perform. We are like virtuous men experiencing difficulty in performing virtuous acts because of sleepiness or some similar physical condition. The grace a penitent receives will vary in proportion to the 2 intensity of his free response and repentance. A penitent sometimes achieves greater grace and virtue than before, sometimes the same, sometimes less. By sinning man loses dignity before God, principally 3 his dignity as a son of God by grace which he can recover by repentance, but also a dignity of innocence which he can never recover (though he may gain something greater). The sinner may also make himself unworthy to exercise a church dignity, and this he may sometimes not recover because he does not repent or is negligent in performing his penance or has incurred an irregularity or has caused scandal. Deserving 5 works earn us eternal life not only while they are being performed but also afterwards, because they are still alive in God's acceptance of them. And they still exist in this way even if they have been killed off in the sinner himself, in the sense that the obstacle presented by his sin has lost these works their power to bring the sinner to eternal life. But repentance forgives the sin and revives that power, and that is what is meant by saying that repentance revives works which have been dead. Sinful acts are wiped out in themselves by repentance, so that by God's mercy no stain or liability can ever more be revived. But works of love are never wiped out by God and remain always accepted by him. On man's side an obstacle may arise, but when the obstacle on man's side is removed again God will fulfil on his side what those works deserve.

90 1   In the sacrament of penitence human action serves as the material of the sacrament and is differentiated into contrition, confession and making amends: what we call the parts of the sacrament. Repentance as a virtue doesn't have parts: the human acts differentiated in the sacrament are effects of the virtue rather than parts of it. It is as parts of 2 the matter of the sacrament that they are differentiated. Redress for an offence in retributive justice follows on the decision of a judge, rather than the will of either offender or offended. In penitence however redress follows on the will of the sinner and the judgment of God against whom he sinned, because what is sought here is not just restoration of the balance of justice (as in retributive justice) but reconciliation between friends. This takes place when the offender offers the one he offended some recompense he would like to have. So on the part of the penitent is required a will to compensate (which we call contrition), a subjection of himself to the judgment of a priest standing in the place of God (which we call confession), and recompense made according to the judgment of God's minister (which we call making amends). This is why contrition, confession and satisfaction are named as parts of penitence. In itself contrition is the inner repentance of the heart, but it carries the power of external penance in it, including the resolve to confess and 3 make amends. One constituent part can contain others not in what it is but in what it has the power to do. The foundation of a building carries the whole building, and in the same way contrition contains the virtue of the whole of penitence. Constituent parts are ordered among themselves, sometimes only in position (following after, touching, joined, continuous); sometimes adding to that a position of power, like the heart among the parts of the body; sometimes also an order in time. The parts of penitence, because they are actions, have these last two relationships of power and order in time, but no order of position ...

At this point, on the morning of 6 December, the feast of St Nicholas, 1273, Thomas Aquinas suddenly fell into a trance, or a coma, while celebrating mass. From that moment, and without explanation, he stopped writing and spoke little. According to his secretary, persistent questioning drew the reply that in comparison with what God had now revealed to him, all he had written seemed chaff. An alternative modern opinion – if it is an alternative – suggests that Thomas suffered a severe stroke and could not go on. Less than three months later, riding a mule to the Council of Lyon, he ran into the branch of a tree and was injured. Within two weeks, at the age of forty-nine, he was dead.

INDEX OF QUOTATIONS

This index of quotations is in three parts, of which the third is the index proper, identifying the quotations made in Thomas's text by citing their original sources in scripture or in other works. Those citations of original sources, are, however, abbreviated. The first part of this index, entitled *Scripture references* (p 605 below), lists all the abbreviations used in the index proper to refer to the books of the bible. The second part, entitled *Philosophical and theological references* (p 606 below), lists the abbreviations used to refer to works other than the books of the bible.

In the index proper (p 610 below), numbers in the left-hand margin indicate places where a quotation is to be found in Thomas's text; the numbers are not page-numbers but reproduce the marginal references accompanying Thomas's text in this edition. (These marginal references are references to Thomas's own division of his text, and are explained in the editor's note on p xiv above.) The quotation then follows. More-or-less literal quotations – the kind printed in italics in the *Summa* text itself – are represented by their first few words; citations of an author without literal quotation are represented by the author's name followed by a colon and an identifying word or two. Notice, however, that the difference between such a citation and a literal quotation is not as marked in medieval texts as it would be in a modern scholarly work. Medieval authors used no typographical devices such as quotation marks or italics to indicate where they meant quotations to start and end, and in any case often quoted from memory or at second hand or in some summary way. Consequently, I have often allowed myself to translate quotations differently in different contexts: for example, the same passage from book 3, chapter 3 of Aristotle's *Physics* is cited in chapter 3 at question 28, article 3 as *the same change is both active doing and passive undergoing*, in chapter 7 at q17 a4 as *what is done to a patient* is *the agent's doing*, and in chapter 8 at q74 a1 as *the agent of a change does what he does in what he acts on*. The same passage appears as a quotation in chapter 9 at q110 a2 as *the act of a mover is the movement of what it moves*. All these translations are tailored to fit the language of their context. And anyone who looks up the original in some translation of Aristotle will find that Aristotle's treatment stretches to a page or two.

The bracketed reference that ends a quotation in the index proper is an abbreviated reference to its original source: the work (and the author of the work if that work is not scriptural) to the left of the comma, the location within the work to the right of the comma. If the reference is entirely in roman type then the work is scriptural, the abbreviations used are explained in the first part of the index below, and the location in the work is indicated by the usual chapter and verse references. If the reference is partly in italic type the work is philosophical or theological, and the abbreviations used are explained in the second part of this index. In that case, the first word (in roman type) usually abbreviates the author's name, and the second (in italic type) abbreviates the name of the work being quoted. After the comma, the location in the work is given: first in italic (a reference to the internal divisions of the work in question) and then in roman (the usual reference to the Bekker edition in the case of Aristotle's works, or a reference to the column in the appropriate volume of Migne's *Patrologia* in the case of patristic references). Thus the first quotation below in the index proper is a scriptural one from the prophet Isaiah, chapter 44, verse 4, referenced as [Is, 44 4]; the passage from Aristotle already mentioned above is referenced as [Ar *Phys, 33* 202a13 & 202b8–13]; and the third quotation in the index proper is referenced as [Greg *Morals, 20 1 1* 76/135], indicating, as the list of abbreviations explains, that the quotation comes from the first division of the first chapter of book 20 of the *Magna Moralia* of St Gregory the Great, and can be found in Migne's *Patrologia Latina*, volume 76, column 135.

Scripture references

Ac	*Acts*	Lam	*Lamentations*
		Lk	*Luke*
1 C	*1 Corinthians*	Lv	*Leviticus*
2 C	*2 Corinthians*		
Col	*Colossians*	Mi	*Micah*
		Mk	*Mark*
Da	*Daniel*	Mt	*Matthew*
Dt	*Deuteronomy*		
		Nu	*Numbers*
Eph	*Ephesians*		
Ex	*Exodus*	1 P	*1 Peter*
Ez	*Ezechiel*	2 P	*2 Peter*
		Ph	*Philippians*
Gal	*Galatians*	Ps	*Psalms*
Gn	*Genesis*	Pv	*Proverbs*
Hb	*Hebrews*	Qo	*Ecclesiastes/Qoheleth*
Hos	*Hosea*		
		R	*Romans*
Is	*Isaiah*	Rev	*Revelation*
1 J	*1 John*	1 S	*1 Samuel*
2 J	*2 John*	2 S	*2 Samuel*
Jer	*Jeremiah*	Sir	*Sirach/Ecclesiasticus*
Jl	*Joel*	Ss	*Song of songs*
Jm	*James*		
Jn	*John*	Tit	*Titus*
Job	*Job*	1 Tm	*1 Timothy*
Jon	*Jonah*	2 Tm	*2 Timothy*
Jos	*Joshua*		
Ju	*Judges*	Wis	*Wisdom*
1 K	*1 Kings*	Zc	*Zechariah*
2 K	*2 Kings*		

Philosophical and theological references

The left-hand column below lists in alphabetical order the abbreviations for authors and their works to be used in the quotation index that follows. The right-hand column expands these abbreviations. In the case of works to be found in J.P. Migne's *Patrologia Graeca* (MG) or *Patrologia Latina* (ML), the expansion also gives the volume or volumes of that collection containing the work, and the quotation references in the index proper then contain a reference to the column in the volume. Since most later editions of these works reproduce the Migne references this should enable the reader to locate the quotation in any edition he is using. In a similar way, the quotation references to Aristotle's works in the index proper give references to the Bekker edition of Aristotle's works: references reproduced in all modern editions of those works. That leaves a few other authors and works (Plato, Cicero, Ibn Roschd and others) to which reference is made not by quoting any particular edition, but by the accepted internal references of the works concerned.

Amb *Duties*	Ambrose of Milan *de officiis ministrorum* ML16
Amb *Holy Spirit*	— *de spiritu sancto* ML16
Amb *Luke*	— *expositio evangelii secundum Lucam* ML15
Amb *Paradise*	— *de paradiso* ML14
Amb *Sermons*	— *sermones* ML17
Ambr	Ambrosiaster ML17
Ambr *Questions*	— *quaestiones veteris et novi testamenti* ML35
Anath	*dissertatio ad contradictionem xii anathematismi* ML48
Ans *Proslog*	Anselm of Canterbury *Proslogion* ML158
Aphro *Soul*	Alexander of Aphrodisias *de anima*
Ar *Categ*	Aristotle *Categories*
Ar *Ethics*	— *Nicomachean Ethics*
Ar *Eud Ethics*	— *Eudemian Ethics*
Ar *Gen et Corr*	— *de generatione et corruptione*
Ar *Gen Animals*	— *de generatione animalium*
Ar *Heavens*	— *de caelo et mundo*
Ar *Metaphysics*	— *Metaphysics*
Ar *Meteor*	— *Meteorology*
Ar *Motu*	— *de motu animalium*
Ar *Peri*	— *peri hermeneias (On Interpretation)*
Ar *Phys*	— *Physics*
Ar *Pol*	— *Politics*
Ar *Post*	— *Posterior Analytics*
Ar *Prior*	— *Prior Analytics*
Ar *Prob*	(pseudo-) Aristotle *Problems*
Ar *Rhet*	Aristotle *Rhetoric*

truth reveals ... [Aug *Religion, 36* 151] [Hil *Trinity, 5* 131]
each thing's truth ... [Avic *Metaphysics*, 8 6]
truth is a correspondence ... [Avic *Metaphysics*, 1 9]
17 3 Augustine: we can't understand falsehood [Aug *83 Quest, 32* 22]
19 6 our God is in the heavens ... [Ps, 113 11]
God desires all men ... [1 Tm, 2 4]
John Damascene: an initial will of God ... [Dam *Faith*, 2 29 968–9]
7 God is not a son of man ... [Nu, 23 19]
20 1 God is love ... [1 J, 4 16]
2 you love everything that exists ... [Wis, 11 25]
21 1 the Lord is just and loves justice [Ps, 108]
Aristotle: commutative justice [Ar *Ethics, 5 4* 1131b24]
who has given him a gift ... [R, 11 35]
3 the Lord is gracious and merciful ... [Ps, 110 4]
22 1 it is your providence, O Father ... [Wis, 14 3]
Aristotle: the proper function of prudence [Ar *Ethics, 6 5* 1140a28]
2 God made man in the beginning ... [Sir, 15 14]
God is concerned for oxen [1 C, 9 9]
23 2 those he predestined he also called ... [R, 8 30]
5 he saved us, not because of any good deeds ... [Tit, 3 5]
before they were born ... [R, 9 11–13]
we are not sufficient ... [2 C, 3 5]
turn us back to yourself, Lord ... [Lam, 5 21]
Paul: why God chooses some ... [R, 9 22–3]
take what belongs to you and go ... [Mt, 20 14–15]
8 for we are fellow workers ... [1 C, 3 9]
26 4 Boethius: earthly happiness [Boet *Consolation, 3 pr 2* 724]

3 Father, Son and Holy Spirit

27 1 I came forth from God [Jn, 8 42]
3 the Spirit of truth ... [Jn, 15 26]
28 3 Aristotle: the same change ... [Ar *Phys, 3 3* 202b8–13]
4 the same road ... [Ar *ibid*]
20 1 an individual substance ... [Boet *Natures, 3* 1343]
2 Aristotle: two meanings of *substance* [Ar *Metaphysics*, △ 8 1017b23]
31 2 Jerome heresies ... Quoted in [Lomb *Sentences, 4 13 2*]
32 1 Augustine: explanation of the Trinity [Aug *Trinity, 9 4ff* 963]
33 2 I bend my knee to the Father of my Lord ... [Eph, 3 14–15]
3 father of the rain [Job, 38 28]
the Spirit bears witness to our spirit ... [R, 8 16–17]
we hope for the glory of God's sons [R, 5 2]
predestined to be made conformable ... [R, 8 29]

34 1   whoever can grasp the nature ... [Aug *Trinity, 15 10* 1071]
  3   he spoke and they were made [Ps, 32 9]
35 2   the Image of the invisible God ... [Col, 1 15]
       to God's image [Gn, 1 27]
38 2   through the Gift that is the Holy Spirit ... [Aug *Trinity, 15 19* 1084]
       God so loved the world ... [Jn, 3 16]
41 2   if anyone say that the Son was made ... [Hil *Synods, canon 24* 512]
43 1   he was in the world [Jn, 1 10 cf 10 36]
  3   the love of God is poured forth ... [R, 5 5]
  5   we will come to him and make our abode ... [Jn, 14 23]
  7   to each is given ... [1 C, 12 7]

4 Creation

44 2   inclined circle [Ar *Gen et Corr, 2 10* 336a32]
45 6   creator ... things were made ... Lord and lifegiver [*Nicea Creed*]
46 3   God created heaven and earth ... [Gn, 1 1]
47 2   Origen: God created [Orig *Beginnings, 1 6–8* 166–78 cf *2 1–2*
       181–7 & *9* 229]
       God saw all the things that he had made ... [Gn, 1 31]
       forms are like numbers ... [Ar *Metaphysics,* H *3* 1043b34]
48 1   the basic contrariety ... [Ar *Metaphysics,* I *4* 1055a33]
  2   pseudo-Denys: providence fulfils nature [Dion *Names, 4 33* 733]
       Augustine: God brings good from bad [Aug *Enchir, 11* 236]
50 5   all things would come to nothing ... [Greg *Morals, 16 37* 75/1143]
55 1   Aristotle: the activity of sensing ... [Ar *Soul, 3 2* 425b30 cf *3 7*
       431a1]
56 3   the invisible things of God ... [R, 1 20]
       in a mirror [1 C, 13 12]
61 3   work is perfect [Dt, 32 4]
62 1   Aristotle: happiness as divine contemplation [Ar *Ethics, 10 7–8*
       1177a12–b23]
  2   turn us back to yourself, Lord ... [Lam, 5 21]
67 1   and God said Let there be light [Gn, 1 3]
69 1   darkness ... the deep ... without form [Gn, 1 2]
  2   without form and void [Gn, *ibid*]
73 1   grace and truth came through Jesus Christ [Jn, 1 17]
  3   good ... blessing [Gn, 1 *passim*]

5 Man's place in creation

76 1   Aristotle: proof ... [Ar *Soul, 2, 2* 414a12]
       with intrinsic appropriateness ... [Ar *Phys, 5, 1* 224a21]
       Ibn Roschd: mind and body ... [Aver *Soul, 3 5 5*]
       Aristotle: to explain mind ... [Ar *Soul, 3 5* 430a10 cf *3 7* 431a14]

Aristotle: understanding uses no bodily organ [Ar *Soul, 3 4* 429a27–b5]

separate, yet in matter … [Ar *Phys, 2 2* 194b12]

2   Plato: man is his mind [Plato *Alcibiades, 125*]

Aristotle: soul is man's form [Ar *Soul, 2 2* 414a13 cf *2 3* 414a32]

Ibn Roschd: all men have one mind [Aver *Soul, 3 5 5*]

Aristotle: the stone is not in our mind … [Ar *Soul, 3 8* 431b29ff]

Aristotle: we sense particularity [Ar *ibid*]

3   Plato: souls act on bodies [Plato *Timaeus, 31*]

Aristotle: grades of life [Ar *Soul, 2 3* 414b28]

4   that which actuates … [Ar *Soul, 2 1* 412a27 & 412b25]

Ibn Sina: elements in compounds [Avic *Soul, 4 5*] cf [Avic *Sufficientia, 1 6*]

Ibn Roschd: elements in compounds [Aver *Heavens, 3 67*]

Aristotle: elements in compounds [Ar *Gen et Corr, 1 10* 427b22]

5   tender flesh … [Ar *Soul, 2 9* 421a26]

Augustine: the way things are in nature [Aug *Genesis, 2 1* 263]

78 1   anything with sense-power … [Ar *Soul, 2 3* 414b1]

79 1   mind is a sort of susceptibility [Ar *Soul, 3 4* 429b24]

a blank page … [Ar, *ibid*]

3   in the mind, just as in the rest of nature … [Ar *Soul, 3 5* 430a10]

Plato: forms as Ideas [Plato *Timaeus, 18*]

Aristotle: forms exist only in matter … [Ar *Metaphysics,* α *4* 999a24–b20 cf H *3* 1043b19]

10   Some philosophers: [Aphro *Soul,* Them *Soul,* Aver *Soul*]

11   practical understanding … [Ar *Soul, 3 10* 433a14]

80 1   in whom everything pre-exists … [Dion *Names, 5 5* 820]

2   we can hate the whole genus … [Ar *Rhet, 2 4* 1382a5]

81 3   our soul rules our physical body … [Ar *Pol, 1 2* 1254b2]

82 4   Aristotle: our planning and understanding … [Ar *Eud Ethics, 7 14* 1248a24]

83 1   God made man in the beginning … [Sir, 15 14]

man's course is not in his control [Jer, 10 23]

the goals we pursue … [Ar *Ethics, 3 5* 1114a32]

2   lost by sin [Aug *Enchir, 30* 246]

84 1   you can't step … Quoted in [Ar *Metaphysics,* Γ *5* 1010a14]

like knows like … Quoted in [Ar *Soul, 1 2* 404b16 cf *1 5* 409b24]

3   as a clean slate [Ar *Soul, 3 4* 430a1]

Plato: the mind … [Plato *Phaedo, 18*] [Plato *Memo, 15*] [Plato *Phaedrus, 30*]

6   Democritus: [Aug *Letters, 118 4* 446] & [Ar *Somn, 2* 464a2]

Augustine: objects don't act on our senses [Aug *Genesis, 12 24* 475]

Aristotle: sensation [Ar *Soul, 2 5* 416b32] cf [Ar *Somn, 1* 454a7]

agent mind … [Ar *Soul, 3 5* 430a18]

PART TWO Journeying to God

7 Human life as a journey to God

8 Living well and living badly

6   we are born to virtue [Ar *Ethics, 2 1* 1103a25]
     if you are led by the Spirit of God ... [Gal, 5 18]
     where the Spirit of the Lord is, there is freedom [2 C, 3 17]

94 2   nature teaches all animals [*Digest, 1 1 1*]
   4   all peoples agree ... [Isid *Etymologies, 5 4* 199]
   5   Scriptural examples: Isaac [Gn, 22 2] Hosea [Hos, 1 2] the Egyptians
        [Ex, 12 35]
        common ownership ... [Isid *Etymologies, 5 4* 199]

95 1   man when perfectly virtuous ... [Ar *Pol, 1 1* 1253a31]
        better to regulate issues by law ... [Ar *Rhet, 1 1* 1354a31]
        living justice [Ar *Ethics, 5 4* 1132a22]
   2   legal rights ... [Ar *Ethics, 5 7* 1134b20]
        not so much on reasoned proof ... [Ar *Ethics, 6 11* 1143b11]
   3   worthy, fair, possible ... [Isid *Etymologies, 5 21* 203]
   4   sanctioned both by men of birth ... [Isid *Etymologies, 5 10* 200 & *2
        10* 130]

96 1   you mustn't want ... [Ar *Ethics, 1 3* 1094b13]
   2   possible according to nature ... [Isid *Etymologies, 2 10* 131 & *5 21*
        203]
        blow your nose too hard and it bleeds [Pv, 30 33]
        pour new wine into old wineskins ... [Mt, 9 17]
        civil laws let many things pass unpunished ... [Aug *Free will, 1 5*
        1228]
   4   we must obey God rather than men [Ac, 5 29]
   5   law heavy loads on other men's shoulders ... [Mt, 23 3]

97 1   Augustine: a once well-ordered republic ... [Aug *Free will, 1 6* 1229]

98 1   the Law itself is holy ... [R, 7 12]
        the Law was given through Moses ... [Jn, 1 17]
        for the Law of Moses ... [Hb, 7 19]
        sin found its chance ... [R, 7 11]
        law was introduced ... [R, 5 20]
        a yoke which neither we nor our fathers ... [Ac, 15 10]
   2   Moses wrote of me [Jn, 5 46]
        before faith came ... [Gal, 3 23]
        and if Satan casts out Satan ... [Mt, 12 26]
        the Law was our tutor in Christ [Gal, 3 24]
        now that faith has come ... [Gal, 3 25]
   3   St Paul: the Law was given by angels [Gal, 3 19]
        God spoke to us in his Son [Hb, 1 2 & 2 2]
   4   why he attracts this one ... [Aug *John, 26 (on 6 44)* 1607]
   6   slaves are excluded ... [Ar *Pol, 3 5* 1280a32 cf *4 4* 1291a9]

99 1   the goal of the Law ... [1 Tm, 1 5]
        you shall love your fellowman ... [R, 13 9]
        to which all the law and the prophets reduce [Mt, 22 40]

3	since you can't do good to everybody ... [Aug *Doctr, 1 28* 30]
32 5	let us not love in words and talk ... [1 J, 3 18]
	it is the bread of the hungry ... [Basil *Homilies, 6 (on Luke 12 18)* 275]
	Ambrose: the same [Amb *Sermons, 81* 613]
	take thought of the morrow [Mt, 6 34]
6	if you want to be perfect ... [Mt, 19 21]
33 2	as though by chance [Aug *Doctr, 1 28* 30]
4	pseudo–Denys: reproved Demophilus [Dion *Letters, 8 1* 1088]
34 2	God tells us to bear punishment ... [Aug *Confess, 10 28* 795]
3	whoever hates his brother ... [1 J, 2 9]
35 1	a sort of depression [Dam *Faith, 2 14* 932]
	torpor of spirit ... [Rab *Church, 3* 1251]
36 1	discontent with another's good [Dam *Faith, 2 14* 932]
2	Aristotle: just indignation ... [Ar *Rhet, 2 9* 1386b12–1387a8]
3	we know we have passed from death to life ... [1 J, 3 14]
37 1	I came not to bring peace ... [Mt, 10 34]
40 1	I say to you, offer the wicked man no resistance [Mt, 5 39]
3	Ambrose: rights must be observed ... [Amb *Duties, 1 29* 68]
43 1	any not so right word or deed ... [*Glossa Interlin, on Mt 18 8*] = [Jer *Matthew, 2 (on 15 12)* 111]
44 1	the goal of the commandment is charity ... [1 Tm, 1 5]
	the greatest of all [Mt, 22 38]
	where the spirit of the Lord is ... [2 C, 3 17]
2	this is the command we have from God ... [1 J, 4 21]
3	on these two commandments ... [Mt, 22 40]
	rejoice in the Lord always [Ph, 4 4]
	keep peace with everyone [Hb, 12 14]
	while you have the chance do good to all [Gal, 6 10]
	do not hate your brother in your heart [Lv, 19 17]
	do not lie down in your bonds [Sir, 6 26]
	stop being envious [Gal, 5 26]
4	love the Lord your God ... [Dt, 6 5]
5	with all your heart ... [Dt, *ibid*] cf [Mt, 22 37]
7	love your fellowman as yourself [Mt, 22 39]
8	with one's whole heart [Dt, 6 5]
	him as ourselves [Mt, 22 39]
	lay down our life for our friends [1 J, 3 16]
	our brethren in the faith [Gal, 6 10]
	our own relations [1 Tm, 5 8]
45 1	who reaches into the depths of everything ... [1 C, 2 10]
5	distributes as he wills [1 C, 12 8]

12 Special walks of life

I appointed you as a prophet ... [Jer, 1 5]

5   a mysterious inner stimulus ... [Aug *Genesis, 2 17* 278]
   Abraham [Gn, 22 2]

6   yet forty days and Nineveh will be destroyed [Jon, 3 4]

173 2   Pharaoh [Gn, 41 15] Nebuchadnezzar [Da, 2 1] Belshazzar [Da, 5
   5] Joseph [Gn, 41 16] Daniel [Da, 5 17]
   saw a pot boiling over from the north [Jer, 1 13]
   Solomon [1 K, 3] the apostles [Ac, 2]

4   David [2 S, 23 2] Caiphas [Jn, 11 51] Jeremiah [Jer, 13 5–9] the
   soldiers [Jn, 19 24]

174 2   Samson [Ju, 15 14] Solomon [2 K, 4 32]

4   he saw God clearly ... [Nu, 12 8]
   the Lord spoke to him face to face ... [Ex, 33 11]
   never has there arisen in Israel ... [Dt, 34 10]

175 1   the Spirit lifted me up ... [Ez, 8 3]

3   Peter [Ac, 10 10] David [Ps, 115 2] Moses [Nu, 12 8] Paul [2 C, 12
   2]

176 1   Christ: chose disciples [Mt, 28 19]
   scattered their languages [Gn, 11 7]

177 1   St Paul: gift of utterance [1 C, 12 8]

2   St Paul: women and public utterance [1 C, 13 34] & [1 Tm, 2 12]
   Genesis: female sex submissive ... [Gn, 3 16]
   St Paul: male and female ... [Col, 3 10]

178 1   confirming the message ... [Mk, 16 20]

179 1   to share with his friends [Ar *Ethics, 9 12* 1172a5]

2   the life of pleasure [Ar *Ethics, 1 5* 1095b20]

180 1   Gregory: contemplative life [Greg *Ezechiel, 2 2* 953]

2   Aristotle: considering truth ... [Ar *Ethics, 2 4* 1105b2]

5   Paul's ecstasy [2 C, 12 2]

181 2   Aristotle: knowing ... [Ar *Ethics, 2 4* 1105b2 cf *10 8* 1178a9]

182 1   it is better to pursue wisdom ... [Ar *Topics, 3 2* 118a10]

183 2   some he established as apostles ... [Eph, 4 11]
   as our one body has many organs ... [R, 12 4]
   from him the whole body is compact ... [Eph, 4 16]
   God so orders things ... [1 C, 12 24]

4   slaves to sin, slaves to justice [R, 6 20]

184 2   offend in many ways ... [Jm, 3 2]

3   you shall love the Lord your God ... [Dt, 6 5]
   wholeness is perfection [Ar *Phys, 3 6* 207a13]
   and your fellowman ... [Lv, 19 18]
   charity is the goal of law [1 Tm, 1 5]

6   no one putting his hand to the plough ... [Lk, 9 62]
   pseudo-Denys: priests and bishops [Dion *Church, 5* 500]
   Augustine: priests and bishops [Aug *Heresies, 53* 40]

PART THREE The road to God
13 Jesus Christ – God and man

4   the light came into the world . . . [Jn, 3 19]
     the good of a whole people . . . [Ar *Ethics, 1 2* 1094b8]
5   when the fullness of time had come [Gal, 4 4]
     God first left us to our free will . . . [*Glossa Ordin, (on Gal 3 19)* 128]
     the physical first and then the spiritual . . . [1 C, 15 46]
     the greater the coming judge . . . [*Glossa Ordin,* 135] = [Aug *John, 31 (on 7 30)* 1638]
6   of his fullness have we all received [Jn, 1 16]
2 1 the union of natures . . . [*Chalcedon, 2 5*]
     nature is the inner essential source . . . [Ar *Phys, 2 1* 192b21]
     nature is what specifies a thing . . . [Boet *Natures, 1* 1342]
  2 not divided or separated . . . [*Chalcedon, 2 5*]
     an individual existing . . . [Boet *Natures, 3* 1343]
  3 an individual substance with a rational nature [Boet *ibid*]
  6 Eutychus, Dioscoros, Nestorius, Theodore of Mopsuestia [Dam *Faith, 3 3* 993] [*Chalcedon, 2 5*] [*2 Const,* 8 4–5]
     Damascene: Christ's human nature . . . [Dam *Faith, 3 15* 1060]
10   the fullness of godhead . . . [Col, 2 9]
3 8 those whom he foreknew he predestined . . . [R, 8 29]
4 6 he was to be like his brothers . . . [Hb, 2 17]
5 3 Augustine: Arius and later Apollinarius . . . [Aug *Heresies, 49* 39 & *55* 40]
     the Word was made flesh [Jn, 1 14]
     all flesh shall see God's salvation [Is, 40 5]
     and we have seen his glory [Jn, 1 14]
6 1 the justice of God comes to all . . . [R, 3 22]
     by God's gracious decision [R, 4 5]
     filled with grace and truth [Jn, 1 14]
  6 we have seen his glory . . . [Jn *ibid*]
7 1 the Lord gives grace and glory [Ps, 83 12]
     mediator between God and man [1 Tm, 2 5]
     from his fullness we have all received . . . [Jn, 1 16]
  6 fear of the Lord [Is, 11 3]
     perfect love casts out the fear [1 J, 4 18]
  7 to teach all nations [Mt, 28 19]
     I was sent only to the lost sheep . . . [Mt, 15 24]
11   he has graced us in his beloved Son [Eph, 1 6]
12   grew in wisdom and grace . . . [Lk, 2 52]
8 1 for those whom he foreknew he also predestined . . . [R, 8 29]
  2 yield the members of our body to God . . . [R, 6 13]
     he who raised Christ Jesus from the dead . . . [R, 8 11]
     in splendour, without spot or wrinkle [Eph, 5 27]
     if we say that we have no sin . . . [1 J, 1 8]
     faith without works is dead [Jm, 2 20]

contrite spirit ... [Ps, 50 19]
sacrifices for sins [Hb, 5 1] peace-offerings [Lv, 3] burnt-offerings
[Lv, 1]
3   Christ is the offering ... [Aug *City, 10 20* 298]
5   an eternal priest [Ps, 109 4]
with the blood of a goat [Lv, 16 11]
once for all [Hb, 10 14]
5   of the order of Melchizedek [Ps, 109 4]
in his loins [Hb, 7 10]
23 1   he predestined us to adoption ... [Eph, 1 5]
those whom he foreknew ... [R, 8 29]
2   we have received the Spirit of adoption of sons ... [R, 8 15]
begotten not made [*Nicea Creed*]
3   that they may be one in us ... [Jn, 17 21]
the Spirit of adoption as sons [R, 8 15 cf 5 5]
4   we saw his glory ... [Jn, 1 14]
24 1   he was predestined to be Son of God ... [R, 1 4]
he who was made of the seed of David ... [R, 1 3]
3   whom he foreknew he also predestined ... [R, 8 29]
25 4   the word of the cross to those that perish ... [1 C, 1 18]
26 1   there is one mediator of God and men ... [1 Tm, 2 5]

14 The life of Christ

27 1   to the only Son of the Father ... [Jn, 1 14]
hail, full of grace [Lk, 1 28]
before you came forth from the womb ... [Jer, 1 5]
even from his mother's womb ... [Lk, 1 15]
3   St Paul: the law of the flesh [R, 7 23–5]
4   you are wholly beautiful, my love ... [Ss, 4 7]
28 1   behold a virgin shall conceive [Is, 7, 14]
not from the will of the flesh ... [Jn, 1 13]
from the slime of the earth [Gn, 2 7]
3   this gate will be kept shut forever ... [Ez, 44 2]
30 1   I am the handmaid of the Lord [Lk, 1 38]
32 1   holy and the Son of God [Lk, 1 35]
35 1   what is born is a person ... [Dam *Faith, 4 7* 1113]
birth is the road to nature [Ar *Phys, 2 1* 193b13]
7   that we might acknowledge ... [Theod *Homilies, 1 in Nat Salv*
1360]
God chose what is weak ... [1 C, 1 27]
the lofty city he lays low ... [Is, 26 5]
8   when the time had fully come ... [Gal, 4 4]
he deigned to take flesh ... [Bede *Luke, 1 (on Luke 2 4)* 330]
our peace [Eph, 2 14]

to gather together his own into one [Jn, 11 52]
one flock and one shepherd [Jn, 10 16]

36 1   worked salvation in the midst of the earth [Ps, 73, 12]
go and make disciples of all nations [Mt, 28 19]

2   believing depends on hearing [R, 10 17]

3   first fruits of the Gentiles [Aug *Sermons*, *200 1 & 202 1* 38/1028 &
1033]

37 1   at the end of eight days ... [Lk, 2 21]
commended obedience ... [Bede *Homilies*, *1 10* 54]

38 1   a prophet and more than a prophet [Mt, 11 9]

2   I baptize you with water ... [Mt, 3 11]
I am the voice of one crying in the wilderness ... [Jn, 1 19]

39 1   the Lord was baptized ... [Amb *Luke*, *2 (on Luke 3 2)* 1665]
unless one is born again ... [Jn, 3 5]
Elijah [2 K, 2 7] the Red Sea [Ex, 14] the Jordan [Jos, 3]

5   when we were baptized in Christ Jesus ... [R, 6 3]

8   after being washed ... [Hil *Matthew*, *2* 927]

40 1   came into the world for this ... [Jn, 18 37]
I must proclaim the good news ... [Lk, 4 42]
Christ Jesus came into the world ... [1 Tm, 1 15]
showed us by his example ... [untraced]
to rest a while [Mk, 6 31]
to pay [Lk, 6 12]
to teach us to do nothing for show [Chrys *Matthew*, *15* 57/223]

2   keep neither gold nor silver [Mt, 10 9]
it would not be right for us to neglect the word of God ... [Ac, 6 2]

4   my Father goes on working, and so do I [Jn, 5 17]

41 1   Jesus was led out by the Spirit ... [Mt, 4 1]
we have not a high priest incapable of having compassion ... [Hb,
4 15]

4   why did God command you not to eat? [Gn, 3 1]

42 1   I was sent only to the lost sheep of Israel [Mt, 15 24]
go and teach all nations [Mt, 28 19]
unless the grain of wheat falls on the ground ... [Jn, 12 20]
he calls himself a grain ... [Aug *John*, *51 (on 12 20)* 1766]

3   would you bring in a light ... [Mk, 4 21]

4   the law of the spirit of life [R, 8 2]
written not with ink ... [2 C, 3 3]

43 1   the works my Father has given me ... [Jn, 5 36]

2   we must believe Christ ... [Chrys *Matthew*, *49 (on Mt 14 19)*
58/497]

44 1   laying his hands on them [Lk, 4 40]
spitting upon his eyes [Mk, 8 23]
making a paste of spittle ... [Jn, 9 6]

the likeness of sin [R, 8 3]
51 1   we rose again by Christ's burial [Jer *Mark, (on Mark 14 63)* 659]
53 1   puts down the mighty ... [Lk, 1 52]
       Christ having risen from the dead ... [R, 6 9–11]
       he who was given up for our sins ... [R, 4 25]
  3   having risen from the dead ... [R, 6 9]
54 1   in another form [Mk, 16 12]
55 2   what he lives, he lives to God [R, 6 10]
  4   we had hoped that he would be the one to ransom Israel [Lk, 24 21]
  6   touch me and see for yourselves ... [Lk, 24 39]
56 1   Christ is risen from the dead ... [1 C, 15 20]
  2   he was put to death for our sin ... [R, 4 25]
57 2   the person who ascended ... [Eph, 4 9]
       being in the form of God ... [Ph, 2 6–7]
       descended right down to the lower regions ... [Eph, 4 9]
  6   I am going to prepare a place for you ... [Jn, 14 23]
       to intercede for us [Hb, 7 25]
58 4   he has made us sit *with* him [Eph, 2 6]
59 2   has set all things under his feet [Eph, 1 22–3]
  5   men only die once ... [Hb, 9 27]

15 Living in Christ
60 1   a sacrament is a sacred sign [Aug *City, 10 5* 282]
  4   a sign is something ... [Aug *Doctr, 2 1* 35]
  6   words have pride of place ... [Aug *Doctr, 2 3* 37]
  7   not as spoken but as believed [Aug *John, 80 (on 15 3)* 1840]
61 1   you can't unite men in a religion ... [Aug *Faustus, 19 11* 355]
       purely external practices ... [1 Tm, 4 8]
       all of us who have been baptized into Christ Jesus ... [R, 6 3]
       marriage [Eph, 5 32]
  3   the first sacraments observed ... [Aug *Faustus, 19 13* 355]
       whom God has put forward as a reconciliator ... [R, 3 25–6]
  4   are abrogated because fulfilled ... [Aug *Faustus, 19 13* 355]
       weak and needy elements [Gal, 4 9]
       under the elements of the world [Gal, 4 3–7]
62 1   as many of you as have been baptized in Christ ... [Gal, 3 27]
       you are to be sharers of the divine nature [2 P, 1 4]
       all these [sacramental actions] ... [Aug *Faustus, 19 16* 357]
       he saves us through the washing of rebirth [Tit, 3 5]
       it touches the body and cleans the heart [Aug *John, 80 (on 15 3)* 1840]
  3   consecrated containers of invisible grace [Hugh *Sacraments, 1 9 2* 317]
       everyone carries a vessel of slaughter in his hand [Ez, 9 1]

6   Melchizedek [Gn, 14 18] expiation [Hb, 9 13–15] manna [Wis, 16 20] passover lamb [Ex, 12 8] cf [1 C, 5 7]

74 1   Christ's flesh offered ... [Ambr?, (on 1 Cor 11 20) 256]
the soul is in the blood [Lv, 17 14]
bread is compacted of grains ... [Glossa Ordin, 191/1624] = [Aug John, 26 (on 6 56) 1614] cf [Cypr Letters, 63 & 76 3/1189 & 4/396 & 427]

75 1   this is my body ... [Lk, 22 19]
living together ... [Ar Ethics, 9 12 1171b32]
he who eats my flesh ... [Jn, 6 57]

6   strengthening the heart of man ... [Ps, 103 15]

76 1   Christ being raised will never die again [R, 6 9]

77 5   one thing's decomposition ... [Ar Gen et Corr, 1 3 318a23]

78 5   the word enters into the matter ... [Aug John, 80 (on 15 3) 1840]

79 1   the bread which I shall give ... [Jn, 6 52]
he who eats me shall also live by me [Jn, 6 58]
this is my blood ... [Mt, 26 28]
our Lord entrusted his body ... [Aug John, 26 (on 6 56) 1614]
O sacrament of love ... [Aug John, 26 (on 6 41) 1613]
a living coal of fire [Is, 6 6]
God's love is never idle ... [Greg Gospels, 2 30 1221]
the love of Christ presses us forward [2 C, 5 14]
eat, friends, and lovers, drink ... [Ss, 5 1]
yield our members to God ... [R, 6 13]

2   if any man eat of this bread ... [Jn, 6 52]
where in the companionship of the saints ... [Aug John, 26 (on 6 56) 1614]
we must first suffer with him ... [R, 8 17]

3   he who eats and drinks unworthily ... [1 C, 11 29]

6   this is the bread which comes down from heaven ... [Jn, 6 50]
love does no wrong to our fellows [R, 3 10]

7   offered himself as a victim to God [Eph, 5 2]
as we receive from this altar ... [Roman Missal, canon of the mass]
remember, Lord, your servants ... [Roman Missal, canon of the mass]
which shall be shed for you and for many ... [Mt, 26 28]

80 1   eating in sign only ... [Glossa Ordin, 1647]

10   by a single offering he has perfected for all times ... [Hb, 10 14]
give us this day our daily bread [Lk, 11 3]

11   do this in memory of me ... [Lk, 22 19]

82 1   receive the power of offering sacrifice ... [Roman rite of priestly ordination]

83 1   whenever the commemoration ... [Roman Missal, canon of the mass]

SELECT BIBLIOGRAPHY

The following list contains only a very few of the many books on Thomas published in English this century. But they can all be highly recommended to anyone wanting to know Thomas better. Most of them have been published and reprinted many times on both sides of the Atlantic, so the date given is usually that of the book's first appearance. A much fuller bibliography can be found in Mary T. Clark's *An Aquinas Reader*, New York, 1972.

- **Life**
  G. K. Chesterton, *St Thomas Aquinas*, 1933
  James A. Weisheipl, *Friar Thomas d'Aquino: His Life, Thought and Work*, 1974

- **Thought and Work**
  M.-D. Chenu, *Toward Understanding Saint Thomas*, 1964: a translation of *Introduction à l'étude de saint Thomas d'Aquin*, 2nd edn, 1954
  E. Gilson, *The Christian Philosophy of St Thomas Aquinas*, 1971: a translation of *Le Thomisme*, 6th edn, 1965
  J. Pieper, *A Guide to Thomas Aquinas*, 1962: a translation of *Einführung zu Thomas von Aquin*
  ———, *The Silence of St Thomas*, 1965: a translation of *Ueber Thomas von Aquin: Negativa Theologia*

- **Contemporary discussion**
  G. E. M. Anscombe and P. T. Geach, *Three Philosophers*, 1961
  A. Kenny, ed., *Aquinas: a collection of critical essays*, 1969

- **Full translation of the *Summa***
  St Thomas Aquinas: Summa Theologiæ in 60 vols, London: Eyre and Spottiswoode; New York: McGraw Hill

INDEX

Notes:
(1) Only the translated text of Thomas is indexed, not the preface or added editorial matter.
(2) I have appended to the indexed English word the Latin word(s) most often translated by it, unless the English derives from the Latin.
(3) Cross-references are introduced with the word *see*; translation equivalences with the sign =. But these last usually also serve as cross-references.
(4) Many references are indexed by their first page only, and the reader should also consult succeeding pages. An explicit multiple-page reference indicates an extended discussion of the topic.

abilities (*potentiae*) = powers, 96–101, 118–29, 208, 225, 232, 481, 555
Abraham, 295, 302, 329, 446, 449
absolution, sacramental, 591–2, 597, 599
abstinence: from food, 427; sexual, *see* continence
abstract and concrete terms, 15, 30, 34, 76, 497
abstraction, 27, 29, 40, 46, 114, 122, 130, 132–9, 141, 490, 492
abstractness, 19, 84, 88, 94
acceptance (*consentire*) = consent, 185, 191
accident (*accidens*) = supervening = concomitant property, 119, 500
accidie, *see* apathy
acquired: dispositions, 229; knowledge, 491; virtues, 232, 241, 243, 313
acts (*actus*), action (*actio*), activity (*operatio*), 14, 49, 67, 77, 92, 111, 113, 116, 141, 176, 182, 211, 249, 426, 481, 503; chemical and physical, 112, 159, 503; Christ's, 502; consequences, 200; external and interior, 33, 36, 38, 65, 96, 112, 176, 194, 255, 315, 549; goal-directed, 13, 49, 84, 152, 172; God's, 60, 118, 156; goodness and badness of, 193–200; human = moral, 157, 171, 173, 194, 503; identity of action with passion, 67, 78, 85, 192; of senses, 503; of tools, 86, 112, 159, 580; voluntary, 182–200, 255; *see* agency
active life, 61, 176, 180, 442, 451–2, 464 *see* contemplative life
actual sin, 264
Adam, 117, 142–9, 266, 332, 516; grace, 146; immortality, 147; integrated state (*integritas, rectitudo, innocentia*), 145–6, 265, 270, 275, 307, 311, 318, 438, 494; knowledge, 145; sin, 158, 193, 212, 263–7, 269, 270, 296, 303, 307, 339, 438–9, 476, 493, 494, 504, 549, 591

adoration, 405
adultery, 103, 253, 431
affirmations, 35
age of discretion, 275, 466, 565
agency, agents, 77, 90, 118, 154, 156, 172, 185, 320, 502, 554: defective, 93; and goals, 18, 49, 56; resemblance to effects, 17; and tools, 113, 192, 550
agent mind (*intellectus agens*), 97, 110, 122, 131, 134, 139, 161, 230, 233, 445, 447, 490, 492 *see* receptive mind
agreeableness (*affabilitas*), 419, 440
allegiance, 292, 343
allegory, 4
allied virtues *see* virtues, parts of
alms (*eleemosyna*), 362
ambition, 239, 365, 424
amends, making (*satisfactio*), 476, 493, 510, 524, 526, 529, 565, 586, 593, 600
analogy, 17, 32, 71, 132, 273: example of health, 32, 46, 547
angels, 21, 27, 90, 94–103, 111, 117, 122, 131, 140, 157–8, 161, 227, 295, 410, 489, 559
anger (*ira*), 55, 202, 208, 211, 217–19, 268, 434
animal, 38, 90, 99, 113, 125, 146, 188, 226, 389: desire, 50, 53, 99, 124, 140; intelligence, 188–9; love of, 354; subordination to man, 146; wildness, 146
annihilation, 155
apathy (*acedia*), 268, 365
Apollinarius, 483, 500
apostasy, 340, 343
apostles, 330, 337, 449, 558, 567
appetite = inclination = tendency = desire, 120, 124, 128, 160, 201, 227, 501
appropriation, 76